W9-BMA-542

¡Ven conmigo!

Adelante

¡Ven conmigo!

En camino

Your
passport to
proficiency

*Pasaporte
al mundo*

Plan your itinerary for success

What's your **Destination?**

Communication!

Adelante and *En camino*

take your classroom there.

It's even possible that

"What's next?"

becomes your

students' favorite

question!

Communication
and culture in context

The clear structure of each chapter makes it easy to present, practice, and apply language skills—all in the context of the location where the chapter takes place!

Grammar support and practice in every lesson

Adelante and *En camino* build a proven communicative approach on a solid foundation of grammar and vocabulary so students become proficient readers, writers, and speakers of Spanish. With the Grammar and Vocabulary Workbook, Grammar Tutor, and the CD-ROM Tutor, students can practice the way they learn best.

Technology that takes you there

Bring the world into your classroom with integrated audio, video, CD-ROM, and Internet resources that immerse students in authentic language and culture.

Assessment for state and national standards

To help you incorporate standardized test practice, the Standardized Assessment Tutor provides reading, writing, and math tests in Spanish that target the skills students need. The ¡Lee conmigo! Reader and Reading Strategies and Skills Handbook offer additional reading practice and reading skills development.

Easy lesson planning for all learning styles

Planning lessons has never been easier with a Lesson Planner with Substitute Teacher Lesson Plans and a One-Stop Planner® with all resources on CD-ROM.

Travel a balanced program that's easy to navigate.

¡El mundo a su alcance!

The ¡Ven conmigo!® family

Program components
Adelante and *En camino*

Texts
- Pupil's Edition
- Teacher's Edition

Planning and Presenting
- One-Stop Planner CD-ROM with Test Generator
- Exploratory Guide
- Lesson Planner with Substitute Teacher Lesson Plans
- Teaching Transparencies

Native Speakers
- Cuaderno para hispanohablantes

Grammar
- Grammar and Vocabulary Workbook
- Grammar Tutor for Students of Spanish

Reading and Writing
- Reading Strategies and Skills Handbook
- ¡Lee conmigo! Reader
- Practice and Activity Book

Listening and Speaking
- Audio CD Program
- Listening Activities
- Activities for Communication
- TPR Storytelling Book

Assessment
- Testing Program
- Grammar and Vocabulary Quizzes
- Alternative Assessment Guide
- Standardized Assessment Tutor

Technology
- One-Stop Planner CD-ROM with Test Generator
- Audio CD Program
- Interactive CD-ROM Tutor
- Video Program
- Video Guide

Internet
- go.hrw.com
- www.hrw.com
- www.hrw.com/passport

ANNOTATED TEACHER'S EDITION

¡Ven conmigo!

En camino

HOLT SPANISH

LEVEL 1B

HOLT, RINEHART AND WINSTON

A Harcourt Education Company

Austin • New York • Orlando • Atlanta • San Francisco • Boston • Dallas • Toronto • London

Copyright © 2003 by Holt, Rinehart and Winston

All rights reserved. No part of this publication may be reproduced or transmitted in any form or by any means, electronic or mechanical, including photocopy, recording, or any information storage and retrieval system, without permission in writing from the publisher.

Requests for permission to make copies of any part of the work should be mailed to the following address: Permissions Department, Holt, Rinehart and Winston, 10801 N. MoPac Expressway, Building 3, Austin, Texas 78759.

Copyright © 2000 **CNN** and **CNNfyi.com** are trademarks of Cable News Network LP, LLLP, a Time Warner Company. All rights reserved. Copyright © 2000 Turner Learning logos are trademarks of Turner Learning, Inc., a Time Warner Company. All rights reserved.

¡VEN CONMIGO! is a trademark licensed to Holt, Rinehart and Winston, registered in the United States of America and/or other jurisdictions.

Printed in the United States of America

ISBN 0-03-065957-4

1 2 3 4 5 6   048   05 04 03 02 01

In the *Annotated Teacher's Edition:*

Photography Credits
Abbreviations used: (t) top, (b) bottom, (c) center, (l) left, (r) right.
All pre-Columbian symbols by EclectiCollections/HRW.
All other photos by Marty Granger/Edge Video Productions/HRW except:
Front Cover: bkgd, Suzanne Murphy-Larronde; teens, Steve Ewert/HRW Photo. **Back Cover:** Robert Frerck/Tony Stone Images; frame, ©1998 Image Farm Inc. **Front Matter:** Page T13 (cr), Lawrence Migdale; T14 (tl), John Langford/HRW Photo; T14 (br), Miriam Austerman/Animals Animals; T15 (tl), Sam Dudgeon/ HRW Photo; T15 (br), Christine Galida/HRW Photo; T16 (tl), Michelle Bridwell/Frontera Fotos; T16 (tc), Sam Dudgeon/HRW Photo; T17 (tl), Christine Galida/HRW Photo; T17 (tr), Bob Daemmrich/Tony Stone Images; T17 (br), Sam Dudgeon/HRW Photo; T18 (tl), John Langford/HRW Photo; T21 (tl), /Image Copyright © 1996 Photodisc, Inc./HRW; T22 (tc), Stuart Cohen/Comstock; T23 (tl), Christine Galida/HRW Photo; T23 (bc), Peter Van Steen/HRW Photo; T24 (cl), Richard Hutchings/HRW Photo; T32 (br), T43 (br), T51 (b), T55 (bc), Michelle Bridwell/Frontera Fotos; T61 (b), Sam Dudgeon/HRW Photo. **Location Opener—Ecuador:** 37D (c), Sylvia Stevens/Zephyr Pictures. **Chapter 7:** 41J (all), Sam Dudgeon/HRW Photo. **Chapter 8:** 79E (bl), Sam Dudgeon/HRW Photo; 79I (bl), Michelle Bridwell/HRW Photo; 79I (br), Sam Dudgeon/HRW Photo. **Location Opener—Texas:** 119C (bl), Courtesy *Texas Highways* Magazine. **Chapter 9:** 123F (all), 123J (all), Sam Dudgeon/HRW Photo. **Chapter 10:** 161H (all), Christine Galida/HRW Photo. **Location Opener—Puerto Rico:** 201D, Ron Watts/Westlight.

Illustration Credits
All art, unless otherwise noted, by Holt, Rinehart & Winston.
Bridge Chapter: Page T71, Edson Campos, T73, Edson Campos **Location Opener—Ecuador:** Page 37B, Eva Vagretti Cockrille; 37C, MapQuest.com. **Chapter Seven:** Page 41F, Bob McMahon; 41K, Lori Osiecki. **Chapter Eight:** Page 79K, Brian White. **Location Opener—Texas:** Page 119B, Lori Osiecki; 119C, MapQuest.com, 119D, Eva Vagretti Cockrille. **Chapter Nine:** Page 123F, Elizabeth Brandt, 123H, Elizabeth Brandt; 123K, Brian White. **Chapter Ten:** Page 161E, Holly Cooper; 161F (l), Ignacio Gomez/Carol Chislovsky Design, Inc.; 161F (r), Edson Campos. **Location Opener—Puerto Rico:** Page 201C, MapQuest.com. **Chapter Eleven:** Page 205F, Edson Campos, 205H, Edson Campos.

In the *Pupil's Edition:*

Acknowledgments
For permission to reprint copyrighted material, grateful acknowledgment is made to the following sources:

Banco Central de Cuenca: Excerpts and illustrations from "Calendario de Eventos" from *60 Aniversario de la Fundación del Banco Central de Cuenca, Antiguo Hospital San Vicente de Paul,* June–July 1988.

Bayard Revistas-Súper Júnior: Excerpts and illustrations from "¡Anímate a escribir!" from *Súper Júnior,* no. 22–23, July–August, 1996. Copyright © 1996 by Súper Júnior Bayard Revistas, Hispano Francesa de Ediciones, S.A.

Cines Lumiere: Advertisement for "Cines Lumiere" from *Guía El País,* no. 57, December 27, 1990.

Club de Tenis Las Lomas: Advertisement for "Club de Tenis Las Lomas" from *Guía El País,* no. 57, December 27, 1990.

Editorial Atlántida, S.A.: Videocassette cover from *Billiken presenta: Mundo Marino.* Jacket cover from *La isla del terror* by Tony Koltz, illustrations by Ron Wing. Photograph from "Empezar con todo" from *Billiken: Diccionario Escolar,* primera entrega, no. 3765, March 9, 1992. Copyright © 1992 by Editorial Atlántida, S.A. Illustration on page 34 from *Billiken de Regalo: Almanaque 1997,* no. 4016, December 30, 1996. From "Deportes en el agua" by Alejandra Becco from *Billiken,* February 17, 1992. Copyright © 1992 by Editorial Atlántida, S.A.

Editorial Eres: Illustration "Regresa a clases" from *Eres,* December 16, 1993. Copyright © 1993 by Editorial Eres.

Editorial Everest, S.A.: Front cover and text from *Everest enciclopedia ilustrada de los animales, Tomo I: Mamíferos* by Dr. Philip Whitfield. Copyright © by Editorial Everest, S.A.

Editorial Televisa, S.A.: Adapted from *Tele*Guía,* año 42, no. 2159, December 25–31, 1993. Copyright ©1993 by Editorial Television, S.A. From "La Chica Sándwich" from *Tú internacional,* año 14, no. 1, January 1993. Copyright ©1993 by Editorial América, S.A. Header and adapted excerpts from "línea directa" from *Tú internacional,* año 14, no. 6, June 1993. Copyright ©1993 by Editorial América, S.A.

Emecé Editores España, S.A.: Illustration and text from jacket cover for *50 cosas que los niños pueden hacer para salvar la tierra* by The Earth Works Group.

Gativideo S.A.: Videocassette cover from *Las nuevas aventuras de Mofli* by Gativideo.

Hotel Agua Escondida: Advertisement for Hotel Agua Escondida.

Instituto Municipal de Deportes, Ayuntamiento de Madrid: Advertisement for "Piscina Municipal Aluche" from the "En Forma" section from *Guía El País,* no. 57, December 27, 1990.

Metro Vídeo Española, S.L.: Videocassette cover from *Los dinosaurios. Su descubrimiento.*

The Quintus Communications Group: Excerpts from "Diez cosas curiosas para hacer en la Pequeña Habana" from *Miami Mensual,* año 13, no. 3, March 1993. Copyright © 1993 by The Quintus Communications Group.

ANNOTATED TEACHER'S EDITION CREDITS

Contributing Writers

Dr. Marjorie E. Artzer
Northern Kentucky University
Highland Heights, KY

Jackie Moase-Burke
Language Arts Oakland Schools
Clinton Township, MI

Elizabeth Coscio
Houston, TX

Pablo Muirhead Montesinos
Shorewood Intermediate School
Milwaukee, WI

Jacqueline Hall-Muirhead
Pius XI High School
Milwaukee, WI

Lois Seijo
Churchville Middle School
Elmhurst, IL

Paula Camardella Twomey
Ithaca High School
Ithaca, NY

The following people researched and wrote culture features:

Mildred Cancel-García
Austin, TX

Mary Nichols
Austin, TX

Mariángeles LaPointe
Austin, TX

Amy Propps
Austin, TX

Field Test Participants

Bill Braden
South Junior High School
Boise, ID

Paula Critchlow
Indian Hills Middle School
Sandy, UT

Frances Cutter
Convent of the Visitation School
St. Paul, MN

Carlos Fernández
Sandy Creek High School
Tyrone, GA

Maureen Fischer
Marian Catholic High School
Chicago Heights, IL

Jan Holland
Lovejoy High School
Lovejoy, GA

Nancy Holmes
Marian Catholic High School
Chicago Heights, IL

Gloria Holmstrom
Emerson Junior High School
Yonkers, NY

K. A. Lagana
Ponus Ridge Middle School
Norwalk, CT

Michelle Mistric
Iowa High School
Iowa, LA

Rubén Moreno
Aycock Middle School
Greensboro, NC

Fred Pratt
San Marcos High School
San Marcos, TX

Regina Salvi
Museum Junior High School
Yonkers, NY

Lorraine Walsh
Lincoln Southeast High School
Lincoln, NE

Reviewers

Dr. Edward D. Allen
Ohio State University
Columbus, OH

Daniel J. Bender
Adlai Stevenson High School
Lincolnshire, IL

Marie Carrera Lambert
Iona College
New Rochelle, NY

Dr. June Carter
The University of Texas
Austin, TX

Myrtress G. Eddleman
Carver High School
Birmingham, AL

Rubén Garza
James Bowie High School
Austin, TX

Joseph N. Harris
Poudre School District
Fort Collins, CO

Stephen L. Levy
Roslyn Public Schools
Roslyn, NY

Laura Olson
Austin Waldorf School
Austin, TX

Carmen Reyes
Jonesboro High School
Jonesboro, GA

Dr. Yolanda Russinovich Solé
The University of Texas
Austin, TX

Brian A. Souza
Plymouth South High School
Plymouth, MA

Elena Steele
Clark County School District
Las Vegas, NV

Dora Villani
John F. Kennedy High School
Bronx, NY

Jo Anne S. Wilson
J. Wilson Associates
Glen Arbor, MI

Professional Essays

Technology in the Foreign Language Classroom
Cindy A. Kendall
Williamston High School
Williamston, MI

Standards for Foreign Language Learning
Paul Sandrock
Foreign Language Consultant
Wisconsin Department of Public Education

Teaching Culture
Nancy A. Humbach
Miami University
Oxford, OH

Dorothea Bruschke
Parkway School District
Chesterfield, MO

Using Portfolios in the Foreign Language Classroom
Jo Anne S. Wilson
J. Wilson Associates
Glen Arbor, MI

Learning Styles and Multi-Modality Teaching
Mary B. McGehee
Louisiana State University
Baton Rouge, LA

New Perspectives for Native Speakers
Cecilia Rodríguez-Pino
New Mexico State University
Las Cruces, NM

AUTHORS

Nancy A. Humbach
Miami University
Ms. Humbach collaborated in the development of the scope and sequence and video material, and created activities and culture features.

Dr. Oscar Ozete
University of Southern Indiana
Dr. Ozete collaborated in the development of the scope and sequence, reviewed all Pupil's Edition material, and wrote grammar explanations.

CONTRIBUTING WRITERS

Dr. Pennie Nichols-Alem
Baton Rouge, LA
Dr. Nichols-Alem wrote the **Enlaces.**

Susan Peterson
The Ohio State University
Columbus, OH
Mrs. Peterson selected realia for readings and developed reading activities.

CONSULTANTS

John DeMado
John DeMado Language Seminars
Washington, CT

Dr. Ingeborg R. McCoy
Southwest Texas State University
San Marcos, TX

Jo Anne S. Wilson
J. Wilson Associates
Glen Arbor, MI

REVIEWERS

Susan Campbell
Lisha Kill Middle School
Albany, New York

Rocco Fuschetto
Northside Middle School
Muncie, Indiana

Gabriela Gándara
Austin, TX

Ester García
Coral Gables Senior High
Coral Gables, FL

Francisco González-Soldevilla
Mast Academy
Miami, FL

Gretchen Hatcher
Foley Senior High School
Foley, AL

Sheila D. Landre
Turlock Junior High School
Turlock, CA

Steve Lucero
Arrowview Middle School
San Bernardino, CA

Mary Luzzi
Lisha Kill Middle School
Albany, NY

Marta Meacham
Bethlehem Central High School
Delmar, NY

Joanne Micale
Lisha Kill Middle School
Albany, NY

Linda Nass
Farnsworth Middle School
Guilderland, NY

Francisco Perea
Austin, TX

Gail Saucedo
Coronado Middle School
Coronado, CA

Barbara Sawhill
The Noble and Greenough School
Dedham, MA

Lois Seijo
Churchville Middle School
Elmhurst, IL

Teresa Shu
Austin, TX

Paula Twomey
Ithaca High School
Ithaca, NY

Cristina Villarreal
Houston, TX

FIELD TEST PARTICIPANTS

We express our appreciation to the teachers and students who participated in the field test. Their comments were instrumental in the development of this program.

Bill Braden
South Junior High School
Boise, ID

Paula Critchlow
Indian Hills Middle School
Sandy, UT

Gloria Holmstrom
Emerson Junior High School
Yonkers, NY

K.A. Lagana
Ponus Ridge Middle School
Norwalk, CT

Rubén Moreno
Aycock Middle School
Greensboro, NC

Regina Salvi
Museum Junior High School
Yonkers, NY

TO THE STUDENT

Some people have the opportunity to learn a new language by living in another country. Most of us, however, begin learning another language and getting acquainted with another culture in a classroom with the help of a teacher, classmates, and a book. To use your book effectively, you need to know how it works.

En camino *(Let's get started)* is the first book in a series called *¡Ven conmigo!* It's organized to help you learn about the Spanish language and about the cultures of people who speak Spanish. A Preliminary Chapter presents some basic concepts in Spanish and offers some strategies for learning a new language. This is followed by six chapters and three Location Openers. Each of these six chapters and each Location Opener follow the same pattern.

En camino takes you to three different Spanish-speaking locations. Each location you visit is introduced with photos and information on four special pages called the Location Openers. You can also see these locations on video and on CD-ROM.

The two Chapter Opener pages at the beginning of each chapter tell you about the chapter theme and goals. These goals outline what you learn to do in each section of the chapter.

De antemano *(Getting started)* This part of the chapter is an illustrated story that shows you Spanish-speaking people in real-life situations, using the language you'll learn in the chapter. You also might watch this story on video.

Primer, Segundo, and **Tercer paso** *(First, Second, Third Part)* After **De antemano,** the chapter is divided into three sections called **pasos.** At the beginning of each **paso,** there is a reminder of the goals you'll aim for in this part. Within the **paso,** you will find boxes called **Así se dice** *(Here's how to say it)* that give the Spanish expressions you'll need to communicate. You'll also find boxes called **Vocabulario** that list new vocabulary you'll need to know and that you'll be responsible for on the Chapter Test. Along with the new expressions and vocabulary words, you'll need to learn certain structures. These structures are provided in the **Gramática** and **Nota gramatical** boxes. To learn all the new expressions, vocabulary, and grammar,

there are several fun activities to practice what you're learning. These activities help you develop your listening, speaking, reading, and writing skills. By the end of each **paso,** you'll have met your goal.

Panorama cultural *(Cultural Panorama)* On this page of the chapter, you'll read interviews with Spanish-speaking people around the world. They'll talk about themselves and their lives, and you can compare their culture to yours. You can watch these interviews on video or listen to them on CD. You can also watch them on a computer using the CD-ROM program, then check to see if you've understood by answering some questions.

Nota cultural *(Culture Note)* Within each chapter, there are culture notes to give you more information about the culture of Spanish-speaking people. These notes might tell you interesting facts, describe common customs, or offer other information that will help you understand what's expected of you if you visit a Spanish-speaking area.

Encuentro cultural *(Cultural Encounter)* This culture section is found in every even-numbered chapter. A native Spanish-speaker will host a first-hand encounter with some aspect of Spanish-speaking culture. You can also watch this section on the video.

Enlaces *(Links)* These pages link the study of Spanish-speaking culture with other subjects you might be studying at school, such as social studies, science, or math.

Vamos a leer *(Let's read)* You'll find the reading section after the three **pasos**. The readings, which are related to the chapter theme, will help you develop your reading skills in Spanish. The **Estrategia** in each chapter will give you helpful strategies to improve your reading comprehension.

Repaso *(Review)* These review pages give you the chance to practice what you've learned in the chapter. You'll improve your listening and reading skills and practice communicating with others. You'll also practice what you've learned about culture.

A ver si puedo *(Let's see if I can . . .)* This page will help you check what you've learned without your teacher's help. A series of questions, followed by short activities, will help you decide how well you can do on your own. Page numbers beside each section will tell you where to go for help if you need it.

Throughout each chapter, certain special features provide extra tips and reminders. **Sugerencia** *(Suggestion)* offers helpful study hints to help you succeed in a foreign language class. **¿Te acuerdas?** *(Do you remember?)* reminds you of grammar and vocabulary you may have forgotten. **Vocabulario extra** *(Extra Vocabulary)* gives you some extra words to use when talking about yourself and your own special interests.

Vocabulario *(Vocabulary)* You'll find a Spanish-English vocabulary list on the last page of the chapter. The words are grouped by the **paso** they're in. These are the words that will be required on the quizzes and tests.

You'll also find Spanish-English and English-Spanish vocabulary lists at the end of the book. The words you'll need to know for the quizzes and tests will be in bold face type.

Also, at the end of your book, you'll find more helpful material, such as:

- a summary of the expressions you'll learn in the **Así se dice** boxes
- a summary of the grammar you'll study
- additional vocabulary words you might want to use
- a grammar index to help you find where grammar structures are introduced

En camino You're on your way to an exciting trip to new cultures and a new language!

¡Buen viaje!

EXPLANATION OF ICONS IN EN CAMINO

Throughout *En camino* you'll see these symbols, or icons, next to activities. They'll tell you what you'll probably do with that activity. Here's a key to help you understand the icons.

Listening Activities
This icon means that this is a listening activity. You'll need to listen to the CD or your teacher in order to complete the activity.

CD-ROM Activities
Whenever this icon appears, it lets you know that there's a related activity on the *Interactive CD-ROM Program.*

Internet Activities
This icon will remind you to check the *¡Ven conmigo!* Internet site for additional activities and games to practice what you are learning. Enter the keyword under the icon and click on "Go."

Writing Activities
When you see this icon, it means that the activity is a writing activity. The directions may ask you to write words, sentences, paragraphs, or a whole composition.

Pair Work Activities
Activities with this icon are designed to be completed with a partner. Both you and your partner are responsible for completing the activity.

Group Work Activities
If an activity has this icon next to it, you can expect to complete it with two or three of your classmates. Each person in the group is responsible for a share of the work.

PARA MEJOR APRENDER EL ESPAÑOL

How best to learn Spanish

LISTEN

It's important to listen carefully in class. Take notes and ask questions if you don't understand, even if you think your question seems a little silly. Other people are probably wondering the same thing you are. You won't be able to understand everything you hear at first, but don't feel frustrated. You're actually absorbing a lot even when you don't realize it.

ORGANIZE

Your memory is going to get a workout, so it's important to get organized. Throughout the textbook you'll see learning tips (**Sugerencias**) that can improve your study skills. For starters, here's a hint: see things with your mind. Associate each new word, sentence, or phrase with an exaggerated or unusual mental picture. For example, if you're learning the word **regla** *(ruler)*, visualize an enormous ruler on an enormous desk as you practice saying a sentence with the word.

EXPAND

Increase your contact with Spanish outside of class in every way you can. You may be able to find someone living near you who speaks Spanish. It's easy to find Spanish-language programs on TV, on the radio, or at the video store. Many magazines and newspapers in Spanish are published or sold in the United States. Don't be afraid to read, watch, or listen. You won't understand every word, but that's okay. You can get a lot out of a story or an article by concentrating on the words you do recognize and doing a little intelligent guesswork.

SPEAK

Practice speaking Spanish aloud every day. Talking with your teachers and classmates is an easy and fun way to learn. Don't be afraid to experiment. Your mistakes will help identify problems, and they'll show you important differences in the way English and Spanish "work" as languages.

PRACTICE

Learning a foreign language is like learning to ride a bicycle or play an instrument. You can't spend one night cramming and then expect instantly to be able to ride or play the next morning. You didn't learn English that way either! Short, daily practice sessions are more effective than long, once-a-week sessions. Also, try to practice with a friend or a classmate. After all, language is about communication, and it takes two to communicate.

CONNECT

Some English and Spanish words have common roots in Latin, and the two languages have influenced each other, so your knowledge of English can give you clues about the meaning of many Spanish words. Look for an English connection when you need to guess at unfamiliar words. You may also find that learning Spanish will help you in English class!

HAVE FUN!

Above all, remember to have fun! The more you try, the more you'll learn. Besides, having fun will help you relax, and relaxed people learn better and faster. **¡Buena suerte!** *(Good luck!)*

ANNOTATED TEACHER'S EDITION

Contents

En camino *Contents*

Come along—to a world of new experiences!

En camino offers you the opportunity to learn the language spoken by millions of people in the many Spanish-speaking countries around the world. Let's find out about the countries, the people, and the Spanish language.

CAPÍTULO PUENTE

¡En camino!

ASÍ SE DICE
- Greeting others
- Saying what you have

VOCABULARIO
- Pastimes

GRAMÁTICA
- The verb **estar**
- The verb **tener** and **ser**

ASÍ SE DICE
- Talking about what you do and when
- Describing people and places

GRAMÁTICA
- Regular -**ar** verbs
- The verb **ir**
- Adjective agreement

¿Qué haces los fines de semana?

ASÍ SE DICE
- Talking about how often you do things
- Talking about your family

VOCABULARIO
- Weather expressions
- Household chores

GRAMÁTICA
- Regular -**er** and -**ir** verbs

Vamos a escribir: Using adjectives
(Writing about two places where you like to go)

¡Ven conmigo a Ecuador!

VISIT THE ENCHANTING CITIES OF QUITO AND OTAVALO
WITH FIVE ECUADOREAN TEENAGERS AND—

Make plans • CAPÍTULO 7

Talk about meals and food • CAPÍTULO 8

CAPÍTULO 7

¿Qué te gustaría hacer? 42

Capítulo 8

¡A comer! 80

ix

T15

¡Ven conmigo a Texas!

CAPÍTULO 9

¡Vamos a compras! 124

CAPÍTULO 10

Celebraciones *162*

xi

T17

¡Ven conmigo a Puerto Rico!

VISIT THE COLORFUL CITY OF SAN JUAN, PUERTO RICO
WITH SOME HISPANIC TEENAGERS AND—

Make suggestions and express feelings
• CAPÍTULO 11

Say where you went and what you did on vacation
• CAPÍTULO 12

CAPÍTULO 11

Para vivir bien *206*

CAPÍTULO 12

Las vacaciones ideales 244

CULTURAL REFERENCES

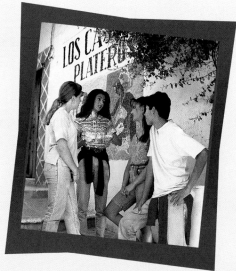

Money

People

Points of Interest

Telephone

Transportation

Vacation

Variations in the Spanish Language

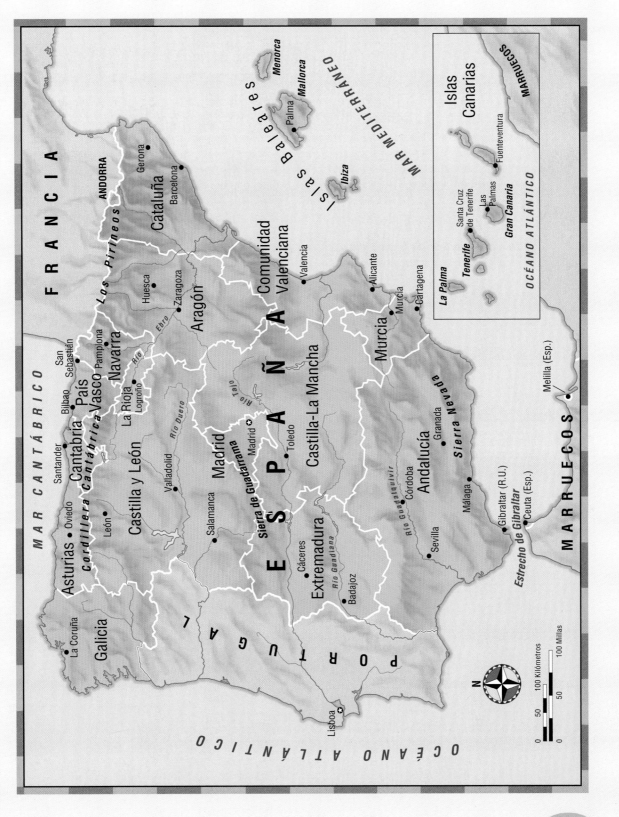

FRANCIA

MAR CANTÁBRICO

Los Pirineos

ANDORRA

Menorca

Mallorca
Palma

Islas Baleares

MAR MEDITERRÁNEO

Gerona

Cataluña

Barcelona

Ibiza

Huesca

Zaragoza

Aragón

Comunidad
Valenciana

Valencia

Alicante

Islas Canarias

MARRUECOS

La Palma

Tenerife
Santa Cruz
de Tenerife

Fuenteventura

Gran Canaria
Las
Palmas

OCÉANO ATLÁNTICO

San
Sebastián

Pamplona

Navarra

País
Vasco

La Rioja
Logroño

Río Ebro

Río Tajo

Murcia
Murcia

Cartagena

Santander

Bilbao

Cantabria

Cordillera Cantábrica

Castilla y León

Valladolid

Río Duero

Madrid
Madrid

Sierra de Guadarrama

Toledo

Castilla-La Mancha

ESPAÑA

Granada

Sierra Nevada

Melilla (Esp.)

Oviedo

Asturias

León

Salamanca

Extremadura

Cáceres

Río Guadiana

Badajoz

Córdoba

Río Guadalquivir

Andalucía

Málaga

Gibraltar (R.U.)

Ceuta (Esp.)

Estrecho de Gibraltar

MARRUECOS

La Coruña

Galicia

PORTUGAL

Sevilla

OCÉANO ATLÁNTICO

Lisboa

N

100 Millas

100 Kilómetros

50

50

0

0

T25

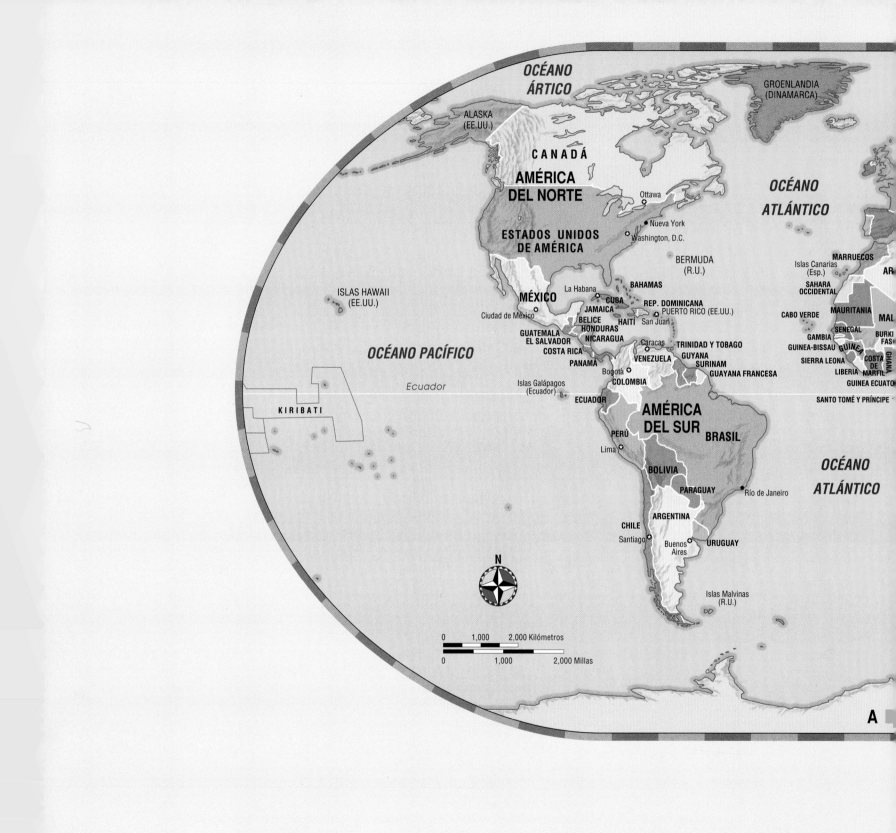

OCÉANO
ÁRTICO

GROENLANDIA
(DINAMARCA)

ALASKA
(EE.UU.)

CANADÁ

AMÉRICA
DEL NORTE

Ottawa

OCÉANO
ATLÁNTICO

ESTADOS UNIDOS
DE AMÉRICA

Nueva York

Washington, D.C.

BERMUDA
(R.U.)

MARRUECOS

Islas Canarias
(Esp.)

AR

ISLAS HAWAII
(EE.UU.)

La Habana

BAHAMAS

SAHARA
OCCIDENTAL

MÉXICO

CUBA

REP. DOMINICANA

CABO VERDE

MAURITANIA

MAL

Ciudad de México

JAMAICA

PUERTO RICO (EE.UU.)

BELICE

HAITÍ

San Juan

GAMBIA

SENEGAL

BURKI

HONDURAS

GUINEA-BISSAU

GUINEA

FAS

GUATEMALA

NICARAGUA

Caracas

TRINIDAD Y TOBAGO

SIERRA LEONA

COSTA

GHAN

EL SALVADOR

DE

COSTA RICA

VENEZUELA

GUYANA

LIBERIA

MARFIL

PANAMÁ

SURINAM

GUINEA ECUATO

OCÉANO PACÍFICO

Bogotá

GUAYANA FRANCESA

SANTO TOMÉ Y PRÍNCIPE

COLOMBIA

Ecuador

Islas Galápagos
(Ecuador)

ECUADOR

KIRIBATI

AMÉRICA
DEL SUR

PERÚ

BRASIL

Lima

OCÉANO

BOLIVIA

ATLÁNTICO

PARAGUAY

Río de Janeiro

ARGENTINA

CHILE

Santiago

Buenos
Aires

URUGUAY

N

Islas Malvinas
(R.U.)

0   1,000   2,000 Kilómetros

0   1,000   2,000 Millas

A

xviii

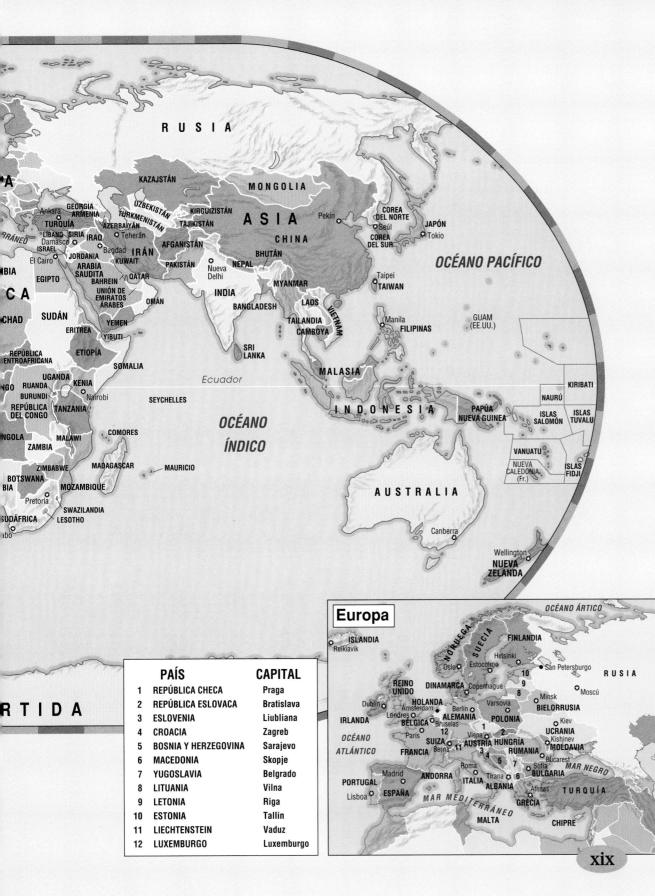

PAÍS		CAPITAL
1	REPÚBLICA CHECA	Praga
2	REPÚBLICA ESLOVACA	Bratislava
3	ESLOVENIA	Liubliana
4	CROACIA	Zagreb
5	BOSNIA Y HERZEGOVINA	Sarajevo
6	MACEDONIA	Skopje
7	YUGOSLAVIA	Belgrado
8	LITUANIA	Vilna
9	LETONIA	Riga
10	ESTONIA	Tallin
11	LIECHTENSTEIN	Vaduz
12	LUXEMBURGO	Luxemburgo

xix

América del Sur

MAR DE LAS ANTILLAS

OCÉANO ATLÁNTICO

América Central

Cartagena
Maracaibo
Caracas
VENEZUELA
Río Orinoco
GUYANA
SURINAM
Medellín
Ciudad Bolívar
Georgetown
Cayena
COLOMBIA
Paramaribo
GUYANA FRANCESA
Bogotá

Islas Galápagos (Ecuador)
Quito
Río Putumayo
ECUADOR
Guayaquil
Cuenca
Río Amazonas
Manaus
Ecuador
Belén

BRASIL

PERÚ
Lima
Andes
Cuzco
Recife

Lago Titicaca
La Paz
BOLIVIA
Sucre
Brasilia
Salvador

OCÉANO
Cordillera de los Andes
PARAGUAY
Río Paraná
Río de Janeiro
Asunción
San Pablo

Trópico de Capricornio
CHILE
Tucumán
ARGENTINA
Río

PACÍFICO
Córdoba
URUGUAY
Valparaíso
Mendoza
Santiago
Buenos Aires
Montevideo
Río de la Plata

N

Bariloche
OCÉANO ATLÁNTICO

0   500   1.000 Kilómetros
0   500   1.000 Millas

Cordillera de los Andes
Estrecho de Magallanes
Islas Malvinas (R.U.)
Punta Arenas
Tierra del Fuego
Cabo de Hornos

OCÉANO

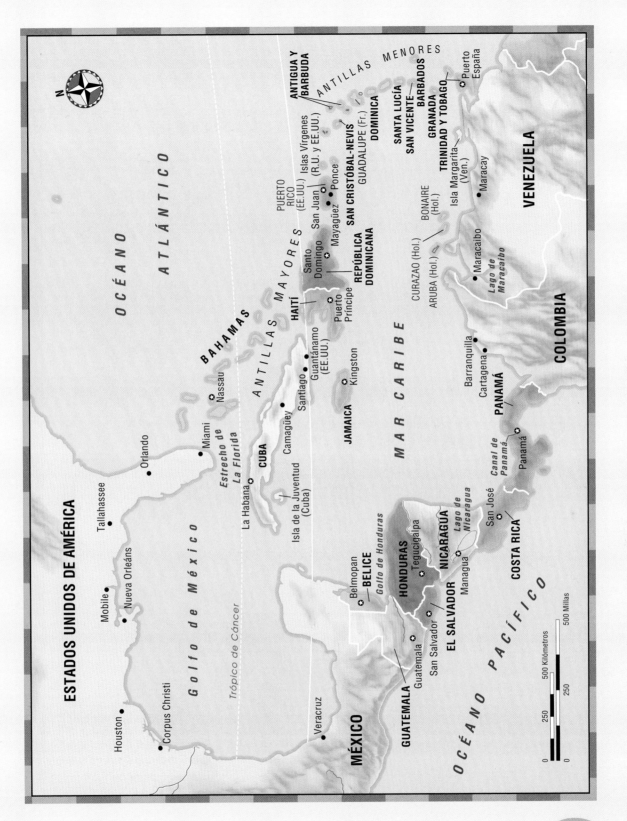

AMÉRICA CENTRAL Y LAS ANTILLAS

N

ESTADOS UNIDOS DE AMÉRICA

OCÉANO

ATLÁNTICO

Houston

Corpus Christi

Mobile

Nueva Orleáns

Tallahassee

Orlando

Miami

Golfo de México

Trópico de Cáncer

Estrecho de La Florida

Nassau

B A H A M A S

MÉXICO

Veracruz

GUATEMALA

Guatemala

BELICE

Belmopan

Golfo de Honduras

La Habana

Isla de la Juventud (Cuba)

CUBA

Camagüey

Santiago

A N T I L L A S

Kingston

JAMAICA

Guantánamo (EE.UU.)

A N T I L L A S   M A Y O R E S

HAITÍ

Puerto Príncipe

Santo Domingo

REPÚBLICA DOMINICANA

PUERTO RICO (EE.UU.)

San Juan

Mayagüez

Ponce

Islas Vírgenes (R.U. y EE.UU.)

ANTIGUA Y BARBUDA

A N T I L L A S   M E N O R E S

SAN CRISTÓBAL-NEVIS

GUADALUPE (Fr.)

DOMINICA

SANTA LUCÍA

SAN VICENTE

BARBADOS

GRANADA

TRINIDAD Y TOBAGO

Puerto España

Isla Margarita (Ven.)

Maracay

VENEZUELA

CURAZAO (Hol.)

BONAIRE (Hol.)

ARUBA (Hol.)

Maracaibo

Lago de Maracaibo

COLOMBIA

Barranquilla

Cartagena

M A R   C A R I B E

HONDURAS

Tegucigalpa

NICARAGUA

Managua

Lago de Nicaragua

EL SALVADOR

San Salvador

COSTA RICA

San José

PANAMÁ

Panamá

Canal de Panamá

OCÉANO   PACÍFICO

0   250   500 Kilómetros

0   250   500 Millas

250

250

xxi

T29

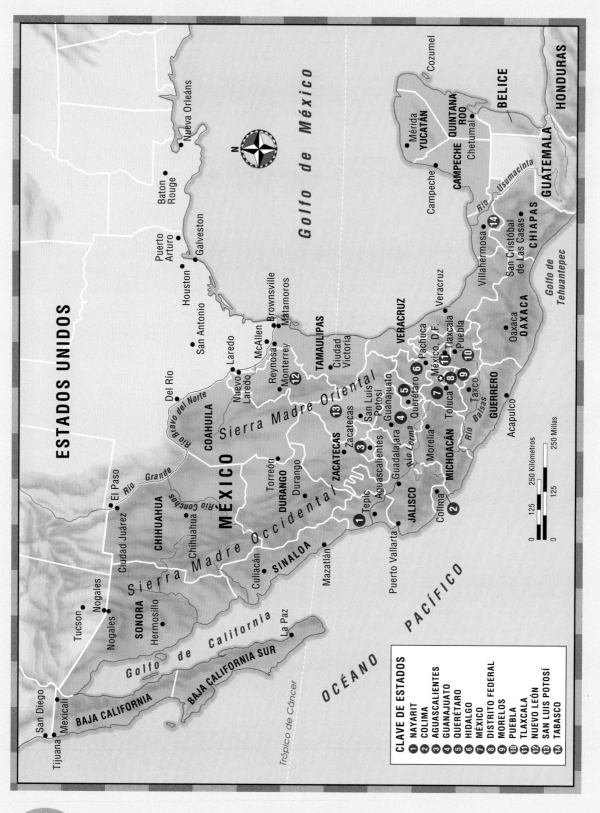

ESTADOS UNIDOS

San Diego
Tijuana
Mexicali
Tucson
Nogales
Nogales
El Paso
Ciudad Juárez

BAJA CALIFORNIA
BAJA CALIFORNIA SUR

La Paz

SONORA
Hermosillo

CHIHUAHUA
Chihuahua

Río Grande
Río Bravo del Norte
Río Conchos

COAHUILA

Del Río
Nuevo Laredo
Laredo
San Antonio

MÉXICO

Sierra Madre Occidental
Sierra Madre Oriental

Torreón
DURANGO
Durango

SINALOA
Culiacán
Mazatlán

Puerto Vallarta

ZACATECAS
Zacatecas

Aguascalientes
San Luis Potosí
JALISCO
Guadalajara
3

Río Lerma
Río Balsas

1
Tepic

Colima
2
Morelia
MICHOACÁN

4 **5**
Guanajuato
6 Querétaro
7 **8** México, D.F.
Toluca **9**
Taxco
GUERRERO
Acapulco

Pachuca
Tlaxcala
11
Puebla **10**

VERACRUZ
Veracruz

Oaxaca
OAXACA

Golfo de Tehuantepec

San Cristóbal
de Las Casas
CHIAPAS
14
Villahermosa

GUATEMALA
HONDURAS

Río Usumacinta

Chetumal
QUINTANA ROO
CAMPECHE
Campeche
Mérida
YUCATÁN
Cozumel

BELICE

Golfo de México

N

Nueva Orleáns
Baton Rouge
Galveston
Puerto Arturo
Houston
Brownsville
Matamoros
TAMAULIPAS
Ciudad Victoria
12
Reynosa
McAllen
Monterrey
13

Sierra Madre Occidental

OCÉANO PACÍFICO

Golfo de California

Trópico de Cáncer

0   125   250 Kilómetros
0   125   250 Millas

CLAVE DE ESTADOS
1 NAYARIT
2 COLIMA
3 AGUASCALIENTES
4 GUANAJUATO
5 QUERÉTARO
6 HIDALGO
7 MÉXICO
8 DISTRITO FEDERAL
9 MORELOS
10 PUEBLA
11 TLAXCALA
12 NUEVO LEÓN
13 SAN LUIS POTOSÍ
14 TABASCO

xxii

T30

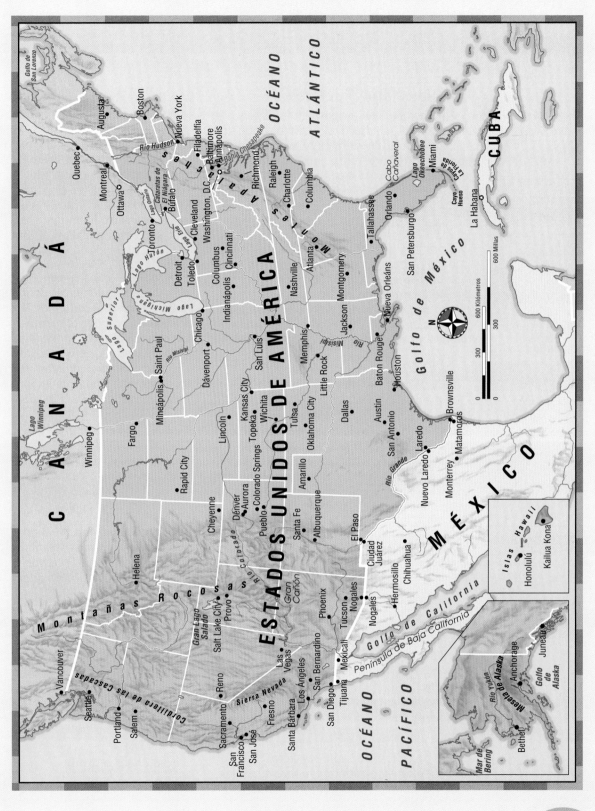

TO THE TEACHER

In recent years, we have seen significant advances in modern foreign language curriculum practices:

1. *a redefinition of the objectives of foreign language study involving a commitment to the development of proficiency in the four skills and in cultural awareness;*

2. *a recognition of the need for longer sequences of study;*

3. *a new student-centered approach that redefines the role of the teacher as facilitator and encourages students to take a more active role in their learning;*

4. *the inclusion of students of all learning abilities.*

The new Holt, Rinehart and Winston foreign language programs take into account not only these advances in the field of foreign language education, but also the input of teachers and students from around the country. ◆

Principles and Practices

As nations become increasingly interdependent, the need for effective communication and sensitivity to other cultures becomes more important. Today's youth must be culturally and linguistically prepared to participate in a global society. At Holt, Rinehart and Winston, we believe that proficiency in more than one language is essential to meeting this need.

The primary goal of the Holt, Rinehart and Winston foreign language programs is to help students develop linguistic proficiency and cultural sensitivity. By interweaving language and culture, our programs seek to broaden students' communication skills while deepening their appreciation of other cultures.

◆◆◆

We believe that all students can benefit from foreign language instruction. We recognize that not everyone learns at the same rate or in the same way; nevertheless, we believe that all students should have the opportunity to acquire language proficiency to a degree commensurate with their individual abilities.

Holt, Rinehart and Winston's foreign language programs are designed to accommodate all students by appealing to a variety of learning styles.

◆◆◆

We believe that effective language programs should motivate students. Students deserve an answer to a question they often ask: "Why are we doing this?" They need to have goals that are interesting, practical, clearly stated, and attainable.

Holt, Rinehart and Winston's foreign language programs promote success. They present interesting content in manageable increments that encourage students to achieve the functional objectives.

We believe that proficiency in a foreign language is best nurtured by programs that encourage students to think critically and to take risks when expressing themselves in the language. We also recognize that students should strive for accuracy in communication. While it is imperative that students have a knowledge of the basic structures of the language, it is also important that they go beyond the simple manipulation of forms.

Holt, Rinehart and Winston's foreign language program reflects a careful progression of activities that guides students from comprehensible input of authentic language through structured practice to creative, personalized expression. This progression, accompanied by consistent re-entry and spiraling of functions, vocabulary, and structures, provides students with the tools and the confidence to express themselves in their new language.

◆◆◆

Finally, we believe that a complete program of language instruction should take into account the needs of teachers in today's increasingly demanding classrooms.

At Holt, Rinehart and Winston, we have designed programs that offer practical teacher support and provide resources to meet individual learning and teaching styles.

USING THE PUPIL'S EDITION

En camino *offers an integrated approach to language learning. Presentation and practice of functional expressions, vocabulary, and grammar structures are interwoven with cultural information, language-learning tips, and realia to facilitate both learning and teaching. The technology, audiovisual materials, and additional print resources integrated into each chapter allow instruction to be adapted to a variety of teaching and learning styles.* ◆

¡Ven conmigo! En camino Level 1B

En camino consists of a preliminary chapter that introduces students to Spanish and the Spanish-speaking world, followed by six instructional chapters. Below is a description of the various features in *En camino* and suggestions on how to use them in the classroom. While it is not crucial for students to cover all material and do all activities to achieve the goals listed at the beginning of each chapter, the material within each chapter has been carefully sequenced to enable students to progress steadily at a realistic pace to the ultimate goal of linguistic and cultural proficiency. As presenter, facilitator, and guide, you will determine the precise depth of coverage, taking into account the individual needs of each class and the amount and type of alternative instructional material to be used from the *En camino* program.

Setting the Scene . . .

In *En camino* chapters are arranged in groups of two, with each pair of chapters set in a different Spanish-speaking location. Each new location is introduced by a **Location Opener**, four pages of colorful photos and background information that can be used to introduce the region and help motivate students.

The two-page **Chapter Opener** is intended to pique students' interest and focus their attention on the task at hand. It is a visual introduction to the theme of the chapter and includes a list of objectives they will be expected to achieve.

Starting Out . . .

Language instruction begins with **De antemano**, comprehensible input that models language in a culturally authentic setting. Whether presented on video or as a reading accompanied by the compact disc recording, the highly visual presentation—in **fotonovela** format—ensures success as students practice their receptive skills and begin to recognize some of the new functions and vocabulary they will encounter in the chapter. Following **De antemano** is a series of activities that can be used to help guide students through the story and to check comprehension.

Building Proficiency Step by Step . . .

Primer, Segundo, and **Tercer paso** are the three core instructional sections where the greater part of language acquisition will take place. The communicative goals in each chapter center on the functional expressions presented in **Así se dice** boxes. These expressions are supported and expanded by material in the **Vocabulario, Gramática,** and **Nota gramatical** sections. Activities immediately following these features are designed to practice recognition or to provide closed-ended practice with the new material. Activities then progress from controlled to open-ended practice where students are able to express themselves in meaningful communication. Depending on class size, general ability level, and class dynamics, you may wish to proceed sequentially through all activities in a chapter, supplementing presentation or practice at various points with additional materials from *En camino,* or you may proceed more quickly to open-ended pair and group work.

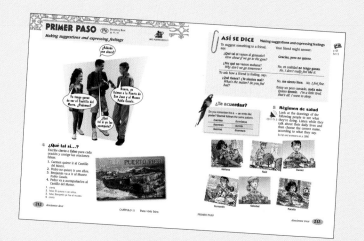

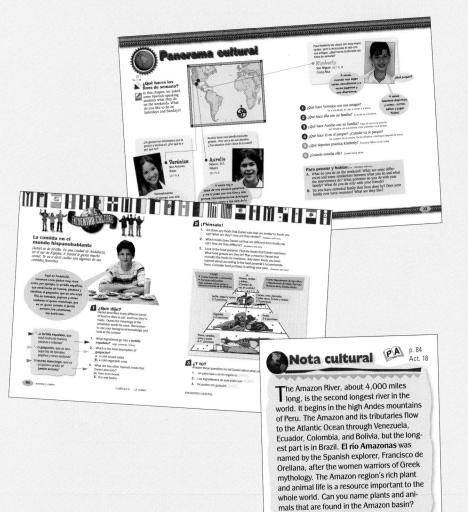

Discovering the Culture . . .

Cultural information has been incorporated throughout the chapter wherever possible. There are also three types of culture features to help students develop an appreciation and understanding of the cultures of Spanish-speaking countries.

Panorama cultural presents spontaneous interviews conducted in various countries in the Spanish-speaking world on a topic related to the chapter theme. The interviews may be presented on video or done as a reading supplemented by the compact disc recording. Culminating activities on this page may be used to verify comprehension and encourage students to think critically about the target culture as well as their own.

Encuentro cultural introduces students to people, places, and customs throughout the Spanish-speaking world and invites them to compare and contrast the target culture with their own. The presentation may be done through the use of video or as a reading.

Nota cultural provides short presentations of both "big C" and "little c" culture that can be used to enrich and enliven activities and presentations at various places throughout each chapter.

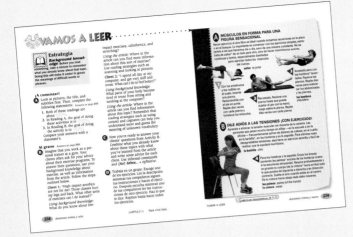

Understanding Authentic Documents . . .

Vamos a leer presents reading strategies that help students understand authentic Spanish-language documents and literature. The reading selections vary from advertisements to letters to short stories or poems in order to accommodate different interests and familiarize the students with different styles and formats. The accompanying activities progress from prereading to reading and postreading tasks and are designed to develop students' overall reading skills and challenge their critical thinking abilities.

Targeting Students' Needs . . .

In each **paso** special features may be used to enhance language learning and cultural appreciation.

Vocabulario extra presents optional vocabulary related to the chapter theme. These words are provided to help students personalize activities; students will not be required to produce this vocabulary on the Chapter Quizzes and Test.

VOCABULARIO EXTRA

el abrigo	coat
la bolsa	purse
la gorra	cap
los guantes	gloves
el impermeable	raincoat
las medias	stockings
el paraguas	umbrella
el sombrero	hat

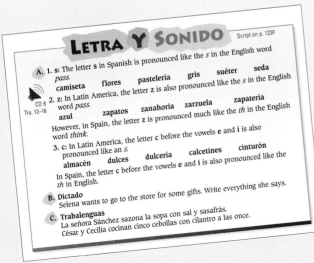

Letra y sonido

At the end of each **Tercer paso** is **Letra y sonido**, a recorded pronunciation feature that explains sounds and spelling rules. Pronunciation is practiced using vocabulary words that contain the targeted sounds. In a dictation exercise that follows, students hear and write sentences using the targeted sounds and letters. The last part of this feature, the **trabalenguas**, gives students an additional opportunity to practice the targeted sounds in amusing and challenging tongue twisters.

Interdisciplinary Connections

Enlaces is an interdisciplinary feature that links the learning of Spanish to other subjects students might be studying. Each **Enlaces** presents further aspects of Spanish-speaking culture and relates them to an academic subject. It encourages students to apply what they learn in other classes to the acquisition of a second language and culture.

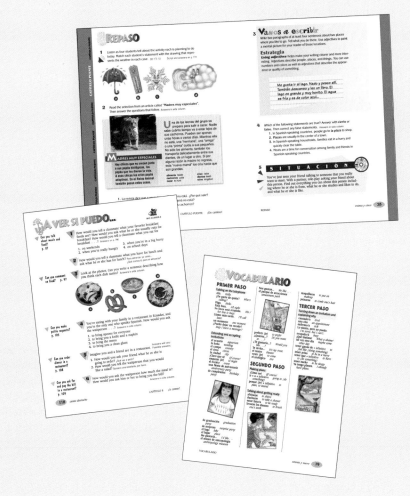

Wrapping it All Up . . .

Repaso, at the end of each chapter, gives students the opportunity to review what they have learned and to apply their skills in new communicative contexts. Beginning in Chapter 3, **Repaso** contains **Vamos a escribir**, a process-writing feature that provides students with guided writing activities as well as strategies to further develop their writing skills. Focusing on all four language skills as well as cultural awareness, **Repaso** can help you determine whether students are ready for the Chapter Test.

A ver si puedo... follows **Repaso** and is a checklist that students can use on their own to see if they have achieved the goals stated in the Chapter Opener. Each communicative function is paired with one or more activities for students to use as a self-check. Page references are given for students who need to return to the chapter for review.

Vocabulario presents the chapter vocabulary grouped by **paso** and arranged according to communicative function or theme. This list represents the active words and expressions that students will be expected to know for the **Paso** Quizzes and Chapter Test.

ANCILLARIES

¡Ven conmigo! En camino

The **En camino** *Spanish program offers a state-of-the-art ancillary package that addresses the concerns of today's teachers. Because foreign language teachers work with all types of students, the activities in our ancillaries accommodate all learning styles. The variety of activities provided in the ¡Ven conmigo! ancillary materials are both innovative and relevant to students' experiences. ◆*

Technology Resources

Adelante and *En camino* are the first Spanish programs to offer technology resources specifically designed for students in the middle grades. Interviews with young adolescent native speakers and an **Encuentro cultural** feature enhance a highly effective video program. The cultural interviews are incorporated in the middle school *Interactive CD-ROM Tutor* with appropriate activities and with vocabulary support in the online reference section. For a detailed description of all the technology resources available with *En camino*, see pages T40–T41.

Grammar and Vocabulary Workbook

The *Grammar and Vocabulary Workbook* re-presents all major grammar points and offers additional focused practice with the structures, words, and phrases targeted in each **paso**. Instruction lines and exercise items have been revised to ensure that students in Grades 6–9 will be able to follow directions and succeed at these important practice activities whether they are done in class or at home. Suggestions for using these activities as homework can be found in the Chapter Interleaf pages of the *Annotated Teacher's Edition*. The *Grammar and Vocabulary Workbook Teacher's Edition* contains the same pages as the workbook with overprinted answers.

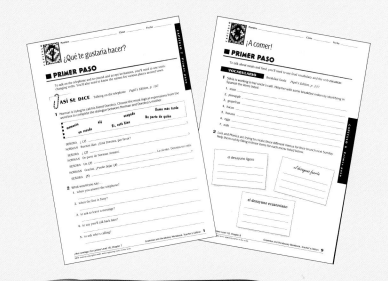

Practice and Activity Book

The *Practice and Activity Book* is filled with a variety of activities that provide further practice with the functions, grammar, and vocabulary presented in each **paso**. Additional reading, culture, and journal activities for each chapter give students the opportunity to apply the reading and writing strategies they've learned in relevant, personalized contexts. The Practice and Activity Book reinforces many of the same concepts practiced in the Grammar and Vocabulary Workbook and provides opportunities to use them in more open-ended, creative contexts. *The Practice and Activity Book Teacher's Edition* contains the same pages as the student edition plus overprinted answers for convenient use.

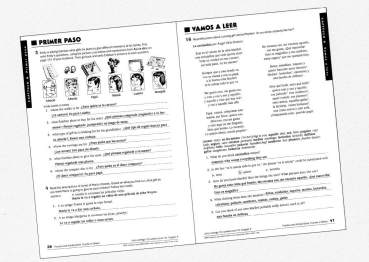

Listening Activities

This component contains all print material associated with the *Audio Program*. Student Response Forms for Textbook Listening Activities and scripts and answers appear here for convenient use.

Additional Listening Activities provide students with a unique opportunity to actively develop their listening skills in a variety of authentic contexts. They appear here as activity masters with scripts and answers.

Each chapter contains a song culturally or thematically related to the chapter or location. The lyrics for each of these songs are provided with each chapter's listening material.

Audio Assessment Items are integrated into the **Paso** Quizzes and Chapter Tests, and the scripts and answers for these items complete the *Listening Activities* component.

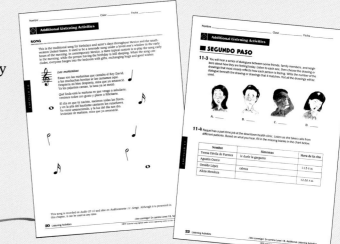

Activities for Communication

Oral communication is the most challenging language skill to develop and test. The *En camino Activities for Communication* book is designed to help facilitate students' development of listening and speaking skills through pair activities in which students communicate in a variety of life-like situations and contexts. The Communicative Activities offer information-gap tasks in which students rely on a partner to fill in the gaps, and the Situation Cards offer opportunities for interviews and role-playing.

This component also contains **Realia** pages, which reproduce real documents to provide students with additional reading and language practice. Included with the **Realia** are teacher suggestions and student activities.

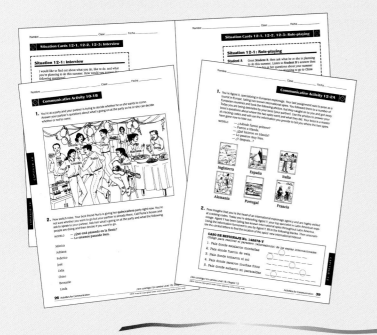

Testing Program

The *Testing Program* encourages students to work toward realistic, communicative goals.

• Three **Quizzes** per chapter (one per **paso**); each **Quiz** includes a listening, reading, and writing section, and very often a culture section

• Each **Chapter Test** includes listening, reading, writing, and culture sections and a score sheet for easy grading. Selected sections of each Chapter Test can be corrected on ScanTron®

• One **Speaking Test** per chapter

• One **Midterm** and one **Final Exam**

Also included in the *Testing Program* are scripts and answers to the **Paso Quizzes, Chapter Tests, Midterm,** and **Final Exam**.

Additional quizzes targeting specific grammar points and vocabulary are available in the *Grammar and Vocabulary Quizzes*.

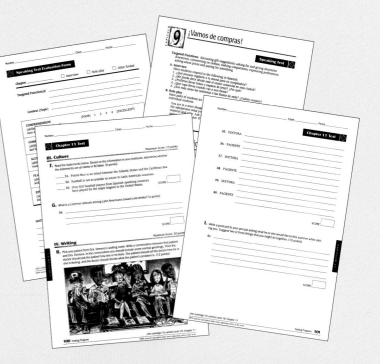

Alternative Assessment Guide

The *Alternative Assessment Guide* describes various testing and scoring methods. This guide also includes **Portfolio Assessment** suggestions and rubrics as well as suggestions for **Performance Assessment**.

Exploratory Guide

The *Exploratory Guide* provides suggestions and techniques for teaching an exploratory class using *Adelante* and *En camino's* wealth of materials, such as the *Video* and *Audio Programs,* the *Interactive CD-ROM Tutor,* the *Teaching Transparencies,* and a host of workbook materials.

Teaching Transparencies

Colorful teaching transparencies benefit all students, and the visual learner in particular, by adding variety and focus to your daily lesson plans. Situations, Vocabulary, and Maps allow you to present and practice vocabulary, culture, and a variety of communicative functions. Each transparency in the *Teaching Transparencies* package comes with a copying master as well as suggestions to practice four skills and culture. In addition to the teaching suggestions that accompany the transparencies, numerous other activities, projects, and games using the maps can be found throughout the *Annotated Teacher's Edition.* Answer transparencies for the *Grammar and Vocabulary Workbook* are also found in the *Teaching Transparencies.*

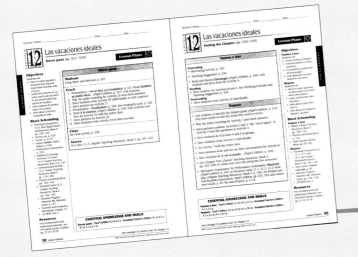

Lesson Planner

The *Lesson Planner* contains chapter-by-chapter suggestions on how to structure the daily lesson for optimal pacing and effectiveness. Each chapter's Lesson Plan guides the teacher through the program's cycle of presentation, practice, and assessment. Specific suggestions for block scheduling give the teacher the option of expanding the material as needed. In addition, all lesson material is correlated to the Standards for Foreign Language Learning and can readily be adapted to document weekly or monthly progress.

¡Ven conmigo!
LEVEL 1

Cuaderno para hispanohablantes

The *¡Ven conmigo!* Level 1 *Cuaderno para hispanohablantes* includes suggestions and activities designed to address the needs of the native speakers in your Spanish class. It includes reading, writing, and speaking tasks for native speakers to complete, rounding out their Spanish language learning.
The Teacher's Edition contains an answer key at the back.

En camino Video and Audio Programs bring the textbook to life and introduce your students to people they will encounter in every chapter of the Pupil's Edition. *The video and audio programs feature native speakers of Spanish in realistic, interesting situations.* ◆

VIDEO TECHNOLOGY

En camino *Video Program*

Video is an ideal medium for providing authentic input needed to increase proficiency in Spanish. Both informative and entertaining, the episodes of the *Video Program* provide rich visual clues to aid comprehension and motivate students to learn more.

The *Video Program* is fully integrated and correlates directly with the *En camino Pupil's Edition:*

Location Opener A narrated collage of images from regions of the Spanish-speaking world expands students' acquaintance with the geography and people presented in each Location Opener.

De antemano The introductory dialogue or story in each chapter is a videotaped dramatic episode based on the chapter theme. It introduces the targeted functions, vocabulary, and grammar of the chapter, in addition to re-entering material from previous chapters in new contexts. Since this video episode corresponds directly with the **De antemano** and the chapter, it can be used as a general introduction to the chapter, as a chapter review, and as a visual support for presenting the elements of the lesson.

A continuación These continuations of the dramatic episodes provide high-interest input that helps motivate students and offers additional opportunities to expand on what they have learned. **A continuación** continues the story and resolves the dramatic conflict that was created in **De antemano**. Designed to facilitate proficiency by providing additional comprehensible input, this episode offers an extended presentation of the chapter material and re-enters functions, vocabulary, and structures from previous chapters.

Panorama cultural Authentic interviews with native speakers of Spanish bring the Spanish-speaking world to life as real people talk about themselves, their country, and their way of life. Each interview topic is thematically related to the chapter.

Encuentro cultural A tour guide from one of the many Spanish-speaking locations of *En camino* introduces students to people, places, and customs.

Videoclips Students will enjoy the authentic footage from Spanish and Latin American television: music videos, commercials, and more. These short segments of video give students confidence as they realize that they can understand and enjoy material that was produced for native speakers of Spanish!

En camino *Video Guide*

En camino Video Guide provides background information together with suggestions for presentation and pre- and postviewing activities for all portions of the *Video Program.* In addition, the *Video Guide* contains reproducible student activity sheets as well as a transcript and synopsis of each episode and supplementary vocabulary lists.

AUDIO TECHNOLOGY

En camino *Audio Program*

Audio is another ideal medium for providing authentic input needed to increase language proficiency. The activities in the **Audio Program** allow students to focus their attention on the sound of the language while at the same time accomplishing authentic real-life linguistic tasks.

The *Audio Program,* available in compact disc format, is fully integrated and correlates directly with the following sections of *En camino Pupil's Edition:*

De antemano The **De antemano** as it appears in the *Pupil's Edition* is an abridged version of the video episode. The *Audio Program* contains the soundtrack of the video episode edited to match **De antemano** to bring the page to life and to give students an opportunity to practice pronunciation.

DVD/VIDEO

The *¡Ven conmigo! DVD Tutor* may also be used with *En camino.* It contains all the **De antemano/ A continuación** dramatic videos, the **Location Openers,** and the *¡Ven conmigo!* **Panorama cultural** interviews with interactive comprehension questions. It also contains all the **Videoclips** as well as the *¡Ven conmigo!* CD-ROM Tutor in DVD-ROM format.

Textbook Listening Activities Each chapter contains various listening activities that give students aural practice with the chapter's linguistic functions and communicative goals. These listening activities integrate previous chapter material with new structures being taught in the chapter.

Panorama cultural Audio recordings of these authentic interviews are contained in the *Audio Program.* The interviews are on separate tracks on the Audio CDs for convenient random access.

En camino *Listening Activities*

En camino Listening Activities contains all print material related the *Audio Program* including Student Response Forms, scripts and answers for the Textbook Listening Activities, copying masters for the Additional Listening Activities, and song lyrics.

CD-ROM TECHNOLOGY

Adelante *and* En camino *Interactive CD-ROM Tutor*

CD-ROM technology offers students an opportunity to interact with the target language and culture in new and exciting ways. This medium brings together print, graphics, video, and audio to provide a language-learning experience that is both enjoyable and challenging. Simulated real-life tasks provide a realistic context for language learning and will appeal to students with a variety of learning styles.

The **Interactive CD-ROM Tutor** is correlated to both *Adelante* and *En camino* to offer students a complete interactive language-learning experience.

Location Opener

The ¡**Ven conmigo a... !** presentations include a travelogue movie about specific locations around the Spanish-speaking world. The map on the right-hand side of the screen contains a map of the featured country and buttons that control the

different portions of the travelogue. After students have watched the travelogue presentation, they use what they have learned to complete a related activity.

En contexto

Students complete a lifelike conversation with a video character that targets the chapter functions, vocabulary, and grammar in meaningful, realistic contexts. Students choose the best response based on a series of audio and visual prompts. When students choose the correct response, the conversation continues. If students answer incorrectly, feedback will then help guide them.

¡**A escoger!** This multiple-choice activity practices vocabulary, grammar concepts, functional expressions, or culture. Students respond to each item based on what they see or hear.

¿**Cuál es?** In this game students organize words and phrases according to two or more categories.

Imagen y sonido In the presentation mode of this activity, students identify and pronounce vocabulary and/or functional expressions by exploring an image. The test mode evaluates students' aural recognition of vocabulary words and expressions.

Patas arriba In this activity, students will sequence words into sentences or sentences into paragraphs or dialogues.

¿**Qué falta?** This activity makes use of a familiar game, Tic Tac Toe, to practice vocabulary or grammar. Students can play with each other or against the computer.

¡**Super memoria!** This activity gives students an opportunity to practice vocabulary, grammar concepts, functional expressions, or culture by matching sound or text with images.

Panorama cultural

Each **Panorama cultural** screen includes six QuickTime™ movies with interviews of students from around the Spanish-

speaking world as well as multiple-choice comprehension questions.

Speaking and Writing

¡**A hablar!** and ¡**A escribir!** provide both guided and open-ended speaking and writing tasks that combine the functions, vocabulary, grammar, and culture of each chapter. These sections can be used for self evaluation, for peer evaluation, or assessment by the teacher.

En voz alta and ¡**Exprésate!** features allow students to record and write original assignments.

Reference Sections

Vocabulary The vocabulary reference section provides a glossary of Spanish-English and English-Spanish words and expressions. Students can access this online reference at any time.

Grammar The grammar reference section provides a summary of the grammar concepts presented in ¡*Ven conmigo!* Students can access this online reference at any time.

Help This section guides users through the mechanics of the program. Students may access this online reference at any time to find information about navigation, control panels, directions for activities, and file storage and retrieval.

INTERACTIVE CD-ROM TUTOR

The *Interactive CD-ROM Tutor* offers a Teacher Management System that allows teachers to view and assess students' work, manage passwords and records, track students' progress as they complete the activities, and activate English translations if desired.

The **En camino** *Annotated Teacher's Edition is designed to help you meet the increasingly varied needs of today's students by providing an abundance of suggestions and strategies. The* **Annotated Teacher's Edition** *includes the pages of the* **Pupil's Edition** *with teacher annotation, side column teacher text with video references, notes, suggestions, answers, and additional activities, as well as icon annotations that correlate each presentation to a corresponding ancillary. The* **Annotated Teacher's Edition** *also includes interleafed pages with scripts, suggestions for use of technology, projects, games, and homework suggestions before each chapter.* ◆

Using the Location Opener and Location Opener Interleaf

In the interleaf and side column extension of each student page you will find background information about the photographs and settings. In addition, teaching suggestions help you motivate students to learn more about the history, geography, and culture of Spanish-speaking countries.

Using the Chapter Interleaf

The chapter interleaf includes a chapter overview correlation chart for teaching resources, *Pupil's Edition* listening scripts, and suggestions for homework, the use of technology, projects, and games.

The **Chapter Overview** chart outlines at a glance the functions, grammar, vocabulary, culture, and re-entry items featured in each **paso.** A list of corresponding print and audiovisual resource materials for each section of the chapter is provided to help integrate media and print ancillaries into your lessons. The pronunciation, reading, interdisciplinary, and review features for each chapter are also referenced,

as are a variety of assessment and portfolio options.

The **Technology** pages provide a variety of suggestions on how to effectively implement the various technology components that accompany *En camino.*

Textbook Listening Activities Scripts provide the scripts of the chapter listening activities for reference or for use in class. The answers to each activity are provided below each script for easy reference.

Projects propose extended four-skills activities based on the chapter theme and content. **Projects** suggestions are provided to give students the opportunity to personalize the information they've learned in the chapter. Individual projects offer students the chance to explore topics related to the chapter theme that are of interest to them. Group and cooperative learning projects encourage students to work together to apply what they've learned in the chapter by creating a poster, brochure, or report, often accompanied by an oral presentation.

Games provide students with informal, entertaining activities in which they can apply and reinforce the functions, structures, vocabulary, and culture of the chapter. Games appeal to a variety of learners and encourage teamwork and cooperation among students of different levels and learning styles.

Answers to Chapter Activities contains answers to selected activities from the chapter.

Homework Suggestions provide a list of assignments from the *Pupil's Edition, Grammar and Vocabulary Workbook, Practice and Activity Book,* and *Interactive CD-ROM Tutor* that would be appropriate for students to do as homework. Each suggestion is correlated to a specific presentation from the chapter.

Using the Side-Column Teacher Text

Side-column teacher text gives point-of-use suggestions and information to help you make the most of class time. The side-column style of the *Annotated Teacher's Edition* also conveniently presents video references and activity answers together on the same page with the *Pupil's Edition* page.

Teaching Cycle

For each **paso,** a logical instructional sequence includes the following steps:

- **Bell Work** gives your students an individual writing activity that focuses their attention on previously learned material while they wait for class to begin.

- **Motivate** introduces students to the topic in a personalized and contextualized way.

- **Teach** provides suggestions for presenting and practicing the functions, vocabulary, structures, and culture.

- **Close** suggests activities that review and practice the goals of each **paso.**

- **Assess** indicates materials that allow you to evaluate students' progress. **Performance Assessment** suggestions provide an alternative to pen and paper tests and give you the option of evaluating students' progress by having them perform communicative, competency-based tasks. These may include teacher-student interviews, conversations, dialogues, or skits that students perform for the entire class. These tasks can also be recorded or videotaped for evaluation at a later time.

Portfolio icons signal activities that are appropriate for students' oral or written portfolios. They may include lists, posters, letters, journal entries, or taped conversations or skits. A variety of suggestions are provided within each chapter so that you can work with your students to select the activities that would best document their strengths and progress in the language. Portfolio information, including checklists and suggestions for evaluation, are provided in the *Alternative Assessment Guide,* which also contains suggestions for the expansion of the designated portfolio activities from the *Pupil's Edition.* For a discussion of portfolio creation and use, see *Using Portfolios in the Foreign Language Classroom,* pages T52–T53.

For Individual Needs

Suggestions under the following categories provide alternative approaches to help you address students' diverse learning styles.

- **Visual, Auditory, Tactile, and Kinesthetic Learners** benefit from activities that accommodate their unique learning styles.
- **Slower Pace** provides ideas for presenting material in smaller steps to facilitate comprehension.
- **Challenge** extends activities into more challenging tasks that encourage students to expand their communicative skills.

Native Speakers

Native speakers benefit from the various projects and activities that validate their individual culture and language. They are encouraged to share their knowledge of Spanish regionalisms and culture with non-native Spanish-speaking students. Native-speaker activities are designed to highlight the skills and culture of native speakers and channel their input to the advantage of the entire class. The in-class activities and out-of-class assignments for native speakers often integrate family and community into the students' learning experience. Native speaker work lends authenticity to Spanish-language instruction and guides students toward a comprehensive understanding of the Spanish-speaking world. For more information on native speakers, see the essay *New Perspectives for Native Speakers* by Cecilia Rodríguez-Pino on pages T56–T57.

Making Connections

To help students appreciate their membership in a global society, suggestions for linking Spanish with other disciplines, their community, and other cultures appear under several categories:

- **Math... Geography... Health... Science... History... Language** and **Arts Links** relate the chapter topic to other subject areas, and make Spanish relevant to the students' overall academic experience.
- **Multicultural Links** provide students the opportunity to compare and contrast their language and culture with those of Spanish-speaking countries and other parts of the world.
- **Community... Family Links** encourage students to seek opportunities for learning

outside of the classroom by interacting with neighbors and family members. These suggestions also call on students to share their learning with their family and community.

Developing Thinking Skills

Critical Thinking helps students develop their higher-order thinking skills with suggestions to extend activities beyond an informational level. It increases comprehension of language and cultures and helps students exercise and develop higher-order thinking skills.

Establishing Collaborative Learning

Cooperative Learning allows students to work together in small groups to attain common goals by sharing responsibilities. Students are accountable for setting group objectives, completing the assignment, and ensuring that all group members master the material. Working together in cooperative groups allows students to take an active role in the classroom, to develop more confidence as they contribute to the success of the group, and to experience less anxiety by working in small groups. Cooperative learning enables students to improve interpersonal communication skills by encouraging them to listen to and respect other opinions.

Total Physical Response (TPR) techniques reinforce structures and vocabulary visually and kinesthetically. They are active-learning exercises that encourage students to focus on class interaction while learning Spanish.

Teaching Vamos a leer

Teacher's notes and suggestions in **Vamos a leer** offer prereading, reading, and postreading skills. Background information and useful terms related to the reading are provided as well.

ADELANTE AND EN CAMINO IN THE MIDDLE GRADES

Middle-grade teachers can readily describe the excitement they feel when students are able to make complex connections for the first time, and are so fired up about what they are learning that sparks fly. Teachers at these grade levels delight in their students' wonderful curiosity about and openness to others. They can also describe the challenges of teaching students who can't seem to sit still, who want to hang out with friends all the time, and who are painfully self-conscious.

Increased understanding of this exciting age group, a well-designed curriculum and textbook, and appropriate classroom management approaches can maximize teaching fun and effectiveness, greatly decrease teacher frustration, and enhance the students' experiences in a multitude of ways.

Characteristics of the Middle-Grades Learner

Young adolescents undergo tremendous physical and mental growth. This is a time when they undertake the important tasks of forming a personal identity, acquiring social skills, establishing personal autonomy, and developing discipline.

This is also a time of rapid cognitive growth. Around the age of twelve, most students begin a gradual transition from concrete operations (the ability to think logically about real experiences) to formal operations (the ability to think reflectively, to reason, and to consider complex issues). For the majority of students, this highly unique and individual process may continue until age 15. An integrated curriculum that involves students in global thinking and interdisciplinary learning furthers the higher-order thinking skills that the students are beginning to develop. A task-focused curriculum that organizes content around themes or issues increases student engagement in learning and leads to increased skill and understanding. It recognizes effort and progress, utilizing portfolios and other authentic assessment tools.

As formal thinking skills develop, the middle-grades student is able to consider the thoughts of others and to perceive him or herself as the object of others' attention. While this means the student now lives in a broader and more interesting world, the student can also feel alone, unsure, and self-conscious. These feelings can manifest themselves as intense egocentrism and self-consciousness, qualities that the teacher needs to understand and work with creatively. It is generally more effective with young adolescent learners to provide cooperative group learning opportunities while avoiding singling out students. This helps maintain an atmosphere of emotional safety and high motivation while facilitating the development of autonomy and self-confidence.

The middle-grades teacher needs to assist students in increasing their concentration span, improving self discipline, and beginning to think about long-term goals. Because young adolescents have a relatively short attention span, an ideal curriculum should provide for diversity in both presentation and practice. It should also provide opportunities for students to move around in non-disruptive ways and work in a variety of groups.

Increased understanding of this exciting age group, a well-designed curriculum and textbook, and appropriate classroom management approaches can maximize teaching fun and effectiveness and enhance students' learning experiences.

Curriculum Materials in the Middle-Grades

A well-constructed set of curriculum materials should take advantage of students' thirst for peer interactions and their willingness to learn. The ideal program builds on students' strengths with concrete, contextualized learning activities, gradually offering more opportunities to challenge students and stretch their skills into new areas of development. This can be accomplished in a variety of ways: by strategically introducing abstract topics that require creativity and flexibility, by making connections with other disciplines, and by providing as many opportunities as possible to apply new learning in authentic, life-like settings. The well-designed curriculum should also address the special characteristics of the middle-grade learner and allow the teacher to turn students' preoccupations into assets.

Using En camino in the Middle Grades

Levels 1A and 1B of the Holt Spanish program have been designed to accomplish two major goals. First, *Adelante* and *En camino* were specifically created to address the unique needs and interests of young adolescents with a rich and highly diverse program that engages students' interest and promotes enthusiasm for learning at various stages of development. Second, *Adelante* and *En camino* teach the full scope and sequence of *¡Ven conmigo!* Level 1, allowing students who have completed Levels 1A and 1B to continue successfully with *¡Ven conmigo!* Level 2.

Adelante and *En camino* capitalize on young adolescents' interest in peer interaction and physical activity by building in a wide selection of projects, games, and pair and group activities. A variety of TPR (Total Physical Response) suggestions are included in the *Annotated Teacher's Edition.*

High-interest themes (such as sports, food, shopping, and friendships) and geographic locations integrate the audio, video, and text, and workbook content. Short learning units called **pasos** allow for frequent assessment. The testing program, oriented to the specific needs of the middle grades learner, includes **paso** quizzes, chapter tests, speaking tests, and authentic assessment tools such as portfolios and performance-based activities. A structured approach to peer assessment is included to further profit from students' interest in peer interaction.

Each proficiency-oriented learning unit flows from concrete, closed-ended activities to more abstract, open-ended activities. These offer opportunities for students to interact with a variety of realia and other multisensory input. This progression solidifies the active use of language and generates opportunities to employ newly emerging cognitive skills.

Global thinking is inspired through a variety of program features. **Enlaces** tie the theme or location of the chapter to other disciplines, encouraging students to draw together thoughts and ideas from different sources and to use their background knowledge. **Encuentro cultural** and **Panorama cultural** furnish an opportunity for students to relate to the interests, thoughts, and priorities of young adolescents in the Spanish-speaking world. Students are encouraged to think reflectively about their own lives and interests in comparison to their counterparts in other parts of the world. **Notas culturales** present high-interest cultural information and again invite students to make connections and comparisons.

References

Irvin, Judith L. *Cognitive Growth During Early Adolescence: The Regulator of Developmental Tasks.* Middle School Journal. September 1995.

Irvin, Judith, L. *Developmental Tasks of Early Adolescence: How Adult Awareness Can Reduce At-Risk Behavior.* The Clearing House Vol. 69 (4). March/April 1996.

Raven, Patrick T. and Wilson, Jo Anne S. *Focus on Teaching Foreign Languages in the Middle Grades: A Summary Statement from the Central States Conference.* Central States Conference on the Teaching of Foreign Languages. April, 1997.

EN CAMINO

En camino *supports the middle-grades teacher in the following ways:*

- Engages students with Spanish-speaking adolescents through new video, audio, and CD-ROM programs.
- Promotes skill development with both print and technology resources.
- Provides appealing, age-appropriate reading selections.
- Instructs students on the process of writing.
- Relates language learning to other disciplines.

En camino *also builds on young adolescents' growing social skills by*

- Providing diverse pair, group, and cooperative learning experiences.
- Offering a wide variety of games, projects, and activities.
- Including peer assessment of writing.
- Building connections with the lives of young adolescents in Spanish-speaking countries.

En camino *supports appropriate classroom management strategies in the following ways:*

- Provides suggestions for how to modify activities for different types of learners.
- Includes portfolio management.
- Offers lesson-planning suggestion for traditional or block-scheduling.
- Provides materials and suggestions for building an exploratory Spanish course.

TECHNOLOGY IN THE FOREIGN LANGUAGE CLASSROOM

BY *CINDY A. KENDALL*

Many remember when overhead projectors and audiocassettes were on the cutting edge. Today's foreign language teachers and their students are discovering new technological applications that make teaching and learning more exciting and effective. Teachers are integrating these technologies into their classes and fundamentally changing the way students learn languages.

The wealth of technological possibilities available to foreign language teachers, such as multimedia computer software, and the Internet, is more sophisticated than ever. This wider range of technological possibilities offers new challenges. In order to use technology effectively, teachers must become familiar with the resources available and understand how the use of technology can enhance language learning.

What role does technology play in the foreign language classroom?

Technology is a powerful tool in the foreign language classroom because it combines visual, auditory, and cultural input and allows for the simultaneous practice of listening, speaking, reading, and writing skills. It can help the instructor reach the five goals of the Standards for Foreign Language Learning: Communication, Culture, Connections, Comparisons, and Community.

The versatility, immediacy, and interactive nature of technology make studying a foreign language more relevant and meaningful to students. Through technology, students can "visit" countries where the target language is spoken and listen to and interact with native speakers. On the Internet, students can perform tasks in the target language at World Wide Web sites created in target-language countries. Technology makes the notion of the global village a reality for today's foreign language students.

In addition, technology helps the teacher work with students of differing skills and learning styles. Technology-based instruction offers teachers and students the flexibility of working as a class, in small groups, or as individuals.

What technological resources are available?

Overhead Projection

The overhead projector, a long-time companion in the classroom, provides a way to effectively combine visual and auditory practice. Transparencies can be an alternative to writing on the chalkboard, and have the added advantage of permitting the teacher to write presentations in advance that can be used over and over.

Audio

Foreign language instructors are familiar with the use of audiocassettes as part of students' listening comprehension practice, and know all too well some common problems with this format: the loss of time in cueing the appropriate segment and wear and tear on the audiocassette. Audio compact discs enable the teacher to cue the desired track quickly and deliver the same content with much greater ease. Other benefits of compact discs include higher-quality recordings and longer product shelf life.

Video

Video technology offers multiple benefits to teachers and is increasingly becoming a standard part of the curriculum system. Videos that are shot on location and feature native speakers in real settings can supply linguistically and culturally authentic input and facilitate comprehension with richer contexts, while at the same time reinforcing new language and structures. The use of video has progressed beyond simply watching. Videos and the print-matter guides that often accompany them give teachers ideas to motivate students, to provide comprehensible input, and to review material. By watching videoclips of interviews, ads, music performances, and other authentic target-language programming, students get a taste of the "real" foreign language.

Multimedia Software

Interactive CD-ROM programs are easy-to-use computer software programs that deliver large amounts of sound and images along with text. In the most effective CD-ROM programs, students not only hear and see language in action, but interact with it as well. This powerful learning tool weaves listening, reading, speaking, writing, and culture into a tapestry of realistic situations that motivates students to practice and communicate in the foreign language. As an added benefit for busy teachers, CD-ROM technology requires little or no training and is virtually foolproof. No matter how many students use the disk, it is impossible to erase the program or write over it.

CD-ROM technology gives teachers flexibility in several areas. They can work with students as a whole class, in small groups, or individually; they can use the program at any phase of the lesson cycle; and they can easily help students with varied learning strengths and styles.

Internet

The Internet is an electronic resource that offers unmatched potential for connecting the foreign language classroom to the outside world. The World Wide Web (WWW) is a treasure trove of authentic materials that can bring target-language cultures into the classroom on a daily basis. By connecting to the Internet and using WWW resources, teachers can overcome the difficulties inherent in teaching a foreign language in an English-speaking country and provide students with experiences they would otherwise not have. Students can find out what is playing at the movies in Buenos Aires or what the hours of operation are at the Prado Museum; they might read the latest headlines in Santiago de Chile or get information about the Spanish royal family; or they can scan weather reports in Puerto Rico or soccer scores in Mexico. They can also download audio; thanks to this new resource, accessing international music and broadcasts is easier than ever.

What implications does increased use of technology have for teachers and students?

Both teachers and students benefit in many ways from the growing variety of technological tools available for use in and out of the classroom. Students are more motivated to learn, and motivated students are easier to teach. The variety of formats the teacher can now offer makes it much easier to address individual learning styles

in classrooms that have grown increasingly diverse.

New technologies also facilitate classroom management in many ways. Software programs can help the teacher build more effective presentations using less time and energy. Multimedia programs can often give students immediate feedback, track their progress through different types of assignments, and make accurate records management much easier for the teacher.

Along with their many benefits, teachers will find that new technologies also bring new responsibilities. Teachers who have used magazine articles and books understand the need to review such materials to be sure content is appropriate and will naturally apply similar standards to CD-ROM programs and to Internet activities. In addition, activities that put students in contact with the public on the Internet make it imperative that teachers set standards and communicate clearly with both parents and students about what is acceptable and safe.

As students move into working more independently with creative technologies both as individuals and in groups, teachers may also need to modify their strategies for monitoring students' work to maintain accountability and to make sure students are getting the most out of their time with each medium. Teachers may want to re-examine how they assess students; performance assessment and portfolio assessment offer opportunities for students to demonstrate their increasing skill in the language and can help prepare them for the kinds of proficiency tests that are becoming more common at checkpoints or as exit requirements.

Properly used, new technology tools can bring the language to life for students and make teachers' work easier and more effective. Teachers are learning new skills and adapting their approaches to classroom management and assessment. Students are also learning "how to learn" with these new resources, and the rewards can be great.

EN CAMINO

En camino's *technology package facilitates presentation, practice, review, and assessment in the following ways:*

Video
◆ Provides high-interest stories, interviews, and travelogues shot on location.
◆ Is fully integrated into each corresponding section of the *Pupil's Edition*.

Audio Program
◆ Allows students ample practice in every chapter listening to native speakers.
◆ Is available on audio CDs for ease of use.

Interactive CD-ROM Tutor
◆ Provides interactive, authentic, multi-sensory practice with corrective feedback.
◆ Practices each chapter's functions, grammar, vocabulary, and culture.
◆ Offers an online teacher management system to insure student accountability.

Teaching Transparencies
◆ Present situations, vocabulary, and maps that practice key concepts and skills.

Test Generator
◆ Allows teachers to create and print alternate tests and make short practice tests.

En camino's *planning tools facilitate the integration of technology in the following ways:*

Pupil's Edition
◆ Indicates for both teacher and student when CD-ROM activities are available.

Annotated Teacher's Edition
◆ Includes a quick guide to technology resources for each chapter.

Ancillaries
◆ Include a *Lesson Planner* that suggests appropriate places to integrate technology.

STANDARDS FOR FOREIGN LANGUAGE LEARNING

BY PAUL SANDROCK, FOREIGN LANGUAGE CONSULTANT, WISCONSIN DEPARTMENT OF PUBLIC EDUCATION

Bringing Standards into the Classroom

The core question that guided the development of the National Standards and their accompanying goals was simply: what matters in instruction?

Each proposed standard was evaluated. Did the standard target material that will have application beyond the classroom? Was the standard too specific or not specific enough? Teachers should be able to teach the standard and assess it in multiple ways. A standard needs to provide a target for instruction and learning throughout a student's K–12 education.

In the development of standards, foreign languages faced other unique challenges. The writers could not assume a K–12 sequence available to all students. In fact, unlike other disciplines, they could not guarantee that all students would experience even any common sequence.

From this context, the National Standards in Foreign Language Education Project's task force generated the five C's, five goals for learning languages: communication, cultures, connections,

comparisons, and communities. First presented in 1995, the standards quickly became familiar to foreign language educators across the US, representing our professional consensus and capturing a broad view of the purposes for learning another language.

To implement the standards, however, requires a shift from emphasizing the means to focusing on the ends. It isn't a matter of grammar versus communication, but rather how much grammar is needed to communicate. Instead of teaching to a grammatical sequence, teaching decisions become based on what students need to know to achieve the communicative goal.

The Focus on Communication

The first standard redefined communication, making its purpose **interpersonal, interpretive,** and **presentational** communication. Teaching to the purpose of interpersonal communication takes us away from memorized dialogues to spontaneous, interactive conversation, where the message is most important and where meaning needs to be negotiated between the speakers. Interpretive communication is not an exercise in translation, but asks beginners to tell the gist of an authentic selection that is heard, read, or viewed, while increasingly advanced learners tell deeper and

STANDARDS FOR FOREIGN LANGUAGE LEARNING

Communication Communicate in Languages Other than English	**Standard 1.1**	Students engage in conversations, provide and obtain information, express feelings and emotions, and exchange opinions.
	Standard 1.2	Students understand and interpret written and spoken language on a variety of topics.
	Standard 1.3	Students present information, concepts, and ideas to an audience of listeners or readers on a variety of topics.
Cultures Gain knowledge and understanding of Other Cultures	**Standard 2.1**	Students demonstrate an understanding of the relationship between the practices and perspectives of the culture studied.
	Standard 2.2	Students demonstrate an understanding of the relationship between the products and perspectives of the culture studied.
Connections Connect with other disciplines and Acquire Information	**Standard 3.1**	Students reinforce and further their knowledge of other disciplines through the foreign language.
	Standard 3.2	Students acquire information and recognize the distinctive viewpoints that are only available through the foreign language and its cultures.
Comparisons Develop Insight into the Nature of Language and Culture	**Standard 4.1**	Students demonstrate understanding of the nature of language through comparisons of the language studied and their own.
	Standard 4.2	Students demonstrate understanding of the concept of culture through comparisons of the cultures studied and their own.
Communities Participate in Multilingual Communities at Home and Around the World	**Standard 5.1**	Students use the language both within and beyond the school setting.
	Standard 5.2	Students show evidence of becoming life-long learners by using the language for personal enjoyment and enrichment.

deeper levels of detail and can interpret based on their knowledge of the target culture. In the presentational mode of communication, the emphasis is on the audience, requiring the speaker or writer to adapt language to fit the situation and to allow for comprehension without any interactive negotiation of the meaning.

Standards challenge us to refocus many of the things we've been doing all along. The requirements of speaking and our expectation of how well students need to speak change when speaking is for a different purpose. This focus on the purpose of the communication changes the way we teach and test the skills of listening, speaking, reading, and writing.

Standards help us think about how to help students put the pieces of language to work in meaningful ways. Our standards answer *why* we are teaching various components of language, and we select *what* we teach in order to achieve those very standards.

The 5 C's

Originally the five C's were presented as five equal circles. During the years since the national standards were printed, teachers implementing and using the standards to write curriculum, texts, and lesson plans have come to see that communication is at the core, surrounded by four C's that influence the context for teaching and assessing.

The four C's surrounding our core goal of **Communication** change our classrooms by bringing in real-life applications for the language learned:

- **Cultures:** Beyond art and literature, learning occurs in the context of the way of life, patterns of behavior, and contributions of the people speaking the language being taught.
- **Connections:** Beyond content limited to the culture of the people speaking the target language, teachers go out to other disciplines to find topics and ideas to form the context for language learning.
- **Comparisons:** Foreign language study is a great way for students to learn more about native language and universal principles of language and culture by comparing and contrasting their own to the target language and culture.

- **Communities:** This goal of the standards adds a broader motivation to the context for language learning. The teacher makes sure students use their new language beyond the class hour, seeking ways to experience the target culture.

Implementation at the Classroom Level: Assessment and Instruction

Standards provide the organizing principle for teaching and assessing. Textbook writers and materials providers are responding to this shift. Standards provide our goals; the useful textbooks and materials give us an organization and a context.

To really know that standards are the focus of teaching materials, look at the assessment. If standards are the target, assessment won't consist only of evaluation of the means (grammatical structures and vocabulary) in isolation. If standards are the focus, teachers will assess students' use of the second language in context. The summative assessment of our target needs to go beyond the specific and include open-ended, personalized tasks. Regardless of how the students show what they can do, the teacher will be able to gauge each student's progress toward the goal.

Assessment is like a jigsaw puzzle. If we test students only on the means, we just keep collecting random puzzle pieces. We have to test, and students have to practice, putting the pieces together in meaningful and purposeful ways. In order to learn vocabulary that will help students "describe themselves," for example, students may have a quiz on Friday with an expectation of close to 100% accuracy. But if that is all we ever do with those ten words, they will quickly be gone from students' memory, and we will only have collected a puzzle piece from each student. It is absolutely essential to have students use those puzzle pieces to complete the puzzle to provide evidence of what they "can do" with the language.

During this period of implementing our standards, we've learned that the standards provide a global picture, the essence of our goals. But they are not curriculum, nor are they lesson plans. The standards influence how we teach, but do not dictate one content nor one methodology. How can we

implement the standards in our classrooms? Think about the targets; think about how students will show achievement of those targets through our evaluation measures; then think about what we need to teach and how that will occur in our classrooms. Make it happen in your classroom to get the results we've always wanted: students who can communicate in a language other than English.

EN CAMINO

En camino *supports the Foreign Language Goals and Standards in the following ways:*

The Pupil's Edition

◆ Encourages students to take responsibility for their learning by providing clearly defined chapter objectives.

◆ Provides pair- and group-work activities in which students use the target language in a wide range of settings and contexts.

◆ Offers culture activities and questions that develop students' insight and encourage observational and analytic skills.

The Annotated Teacher's Edition

◆ Provides a broad framework for developing a foreign language program and offers specific classroom suggestions for reaching students with various learning styles.

◆ Offers ideas for multicultural and multidisciplinary projects as well as community and family links that encourage students to gain access to information both at school and in the community.

The Ancillary Program

◆ Provides students with on-location video footage of native speakers interacting in their own cultural and geographic context.

◆ Includes multiple options for practicing new skills and assessing performance, including situation cards, portfolio suggestions, speaking tests, and other alternatives.

◆ Familiarizes students with tasks they will be expected to perform on exit exams.

TEACHING CULTURE

BY NANCY A. HUMBACH AND
DOROTHEA BRUSCHKE

Ask students what they like best about studying a foreign language. Chances are that learning about culture, the way people live, is one of their favorite aspects. Years after language study has ended, adults remember with fondness the customs of the target culture, even pictures in their language texts. It is this interest in the people and their way of life that is the great motivator and helps us sustain students' interest in language study.

We must integrate culture and language in a way that encourages curiosity, stimulates analysis, and teaches students to hypothesize and seek answers to questions about the people whose language they are studying. Teaching isolated facts about how people in other cultures live is not enough. This information is soon dated and quickly forgotten. We must go a step beyond and teach students that all behavior, values, and traditions exist because of certain aspects of history, geography, and socio-economic conditions.

There are many ways to help students become culturally knowledgeable and to assist them in developing an awareness of differences and similarities between the target culture and their own. Two of these approaches involve critical thinking, that is, trying to find reasons for a certain behavior through observation and analysis, and putting individual observations into larger cultural patterns. ◆

First Approach: Questioning

The first approach involves questioning as the key strategy. At the earliest stages of language learning, students begin to learn ways to greet peers, elders, and strangers, as well as the use of **tú** and **usted.** Students need to consider questions such as: "How do Spanish-speaking people greet each other? Are there different levels of formality? Who initiates a handshake? What's considered a good handshake?" Each of these questions leads students to think about the values that are expressed through word and gesture. They start to "feel" the other culture and, at the same time, understand how much of their own behavior is rooted in their cultural background.

Magazines, newspapers, advertisements, and television commercials are all excellent sources of cultural material. For example, browsing through a Spanish magazine, one finds an extraordinary number of advertisements for health-related products. Could this indicate a great interest in staying healthy? Reading advertisements can be followed up with viewing videos and films, or with interviewing native speakers or people who have lived in Spanish-speaking countries to learn about customs involving health. Students might want to find answers to questions such as: "How do Spanish speakers treat a cold? What is their attitude toward fresh air? toward exercise?" This type of questioning might lead students to discover that we view health matters and the curative properties of food and exercise differently. As in this country, many of the concepts have their roots in the traditions of the past.

An advertisement for a refrigerator or a picture of a Spanish or Latin American kitchen can provide an insight into practices of shopping for food. Students first need to think about the refrigerator at home, take an inventory of what is kept in it, and consider when and where their family shops. Next, students should look closely at a Spanish or Latin American refrigerator. Is it smaller? What could that mean? (Shopping takes place more often, stores are within walking distance, and people eat more fresh foods.)

Food wrappers and containers also provide good clues to cultural insight. For example, laundry detergent is packaged in small plastic bags in many Spanish-speaking countries. Further, instead of "blue-white" cleaning properties, a "red-white" is preferred and considered the epitome of clean. Because of the lack of paper board for boxes, the humidity in many areas, the use for hand laundry, and shopping habits, plastic bags are a more practical form of packaging.

> We must integrate culture and language in a way that encourages curiosity, stimulates analysis, and teaches students to hypothesize.

Second Approach: Associating Words with Images

The second approach for developing cultural understanding involves forming associations of words with the cultural images they suggest. Language and culture are so closely related that one might actually say that language is culture. Most words, especially nouns, carry a cultural connotation. Knowing the literal equivalent of a word in another language is of little use to students in understanding this connotation. For example, **relación** cannot be translated simply as relationship, **comida** as food, or **paseo** as walk. The Spanish phrase **dar un paseo,** for instance, carries with it such social images as people out walking with friends or family, sitting in a sidewalk café, seeing people and being seen by others. In Spanish-speaking countries, "to go for a walk" often means something entirely different than it does for North Americans.

When students have acquired some sense of the cultural connotation of words—not only through teachers' explanations but, more importantly, through observation of visual images—they start to discover the larger underlying cultural themes, or what is often called "deep culture."

These larger cultural themes serve as organizing categories into which individual cultural phenomena fit to form a pattern. Students might discover, for example, that Spanish speakers, because they live in much more crowded conditions, have a great need for privacy (cultural theme), as reflected in such phenomena as fences or walls around property, and curtains on windows. Students might also discover that love of nature and the outdoors is an important cultural theme, as indicated by

such phenomena as flower boxes and planters in public places—even on small traffic islands—well-kept public parks in every town, and people going for a walk or going hiking.

As we teach culture, students learn to recognize elements not only of the target culture but also of their American cultural heritage. They see how elements of culture reflect larger themes or patterns. Learning what constitutes American culture and how that information relates to other people throughout the world can be an exciting journey for a young person.

As language teachers, we are able to facilitate that journey into another culture and into our own, to find our similarities as well as our differences from others. We do not encourage value judgments about others and their culture, nor do we recommend adopting other ways. We simply say to students, "Other ways exist. They exist for many reasons, just as our ways exist due to what our ancestors have bequeathed us through history, traditions, values, and geography."

EN CAMINO

En camino *develops cultural understanding and awareness in the following ways:*

The Pupil's Edition

◆ Informs students about Spanish-speaking countries through photo essays, maps, almanac boxes, and **Notas culturales** that invite comparison with the students' own cultural experiences.

◆ Engages students in analysis and comparison of live, personal interviews with native speakers in the **Panorama cultural** section.

◆ Uses the **Encuentro cultural** section to expose students to cross-cultural situations.

◆ Helps students integrate the language with its cultural connotations through a wealth of authentic art, documents, and literature.

The Annotated Teacher's Edition

◆ Provides the teacher with additional culture, history, and language notes, background information on photos and almanac boxes, and multicultural links.

◆ Suggests problem-solving activities and critical thinking questions that allow students to hypothesize, analyze, and discover larger underlying cultural themes.

◆ Suggests opportunities for native Spanish speakers to share information about the customs and beliefs of their countries of origin.

The Ancillary Program

◆ Includes additional realia to develop cultural insight by serving as a catalyst for questioning and direct discovery.

◆ Offers activities that require students to compare and contrast cultures.

◆ Provides songs, short readings, and poems as well as many opportunities for students to experience regional variation and idioms in the video and audio programs.

¡Ven conmigo!
En camino

USING PORTFOLIOS IN THE FOREIGN LANGUAGE CLASSROOM

BY JO ANNE S. WILSON

The communicative, whole-language approach of today's foreign language instruction requires assessment methods that parallel the teaching and learning strategies in the proficiency-oriented classroom. We know that language acquisition is a process. Portfolios are designed to assess the steps in that process. ◆

What Is a Portfolio?

A portfolio is a purposeful, systematic collection of a student's work. A useful tool in developing a student profile, the portfolio shows the student's efforts, progress, and achievements for a given period of time. It may be used for periodic evaluation, as the basis for overall evaluation, or for placement. It may also be used to enhance or provide alternatives to traditional assessment measures, such as formal tests, quizzes, class participation, and homework.

Why Use Portfolios?

Portfolios benefit both students and teachers because they

- **Are ongoing and systematic.** A portfolio reflects the real-world process of production, assessment, revision, and reassessment. It parallels the natural rhythm of learning.

- **Offer an incentive to learn.** Students have a vested interest in creating the portfolios, through which they can showcase their ongoing efforts and tangible achievements. Students select the works to be included and have a chance to revise, improve, evaluate, and explain the contents.

- **Are sensitive to individual needs.** Language learners bring varied abilities to the classroom and do not acquire skills in a uniformly neat and orderly fashion. The personalized, individualized assessment offered by portfolios responds to this diversity.

- **Provide documentation of language development.** The material in a portfolio is evidence of student progress in the language learning process. The contents of the portfolio make it easier to discuss their progress with the students as well as with parents and others.

- **Offer multiple sources of information.** A portfolio presents a way to collect and analyze information from multiple sources that reflects a student's efforts, progress, and achievements in the language.

Portfolio Components

The foreign language portfolio should include both oral and written work, student self-evaluation, and teacher observation, usually in the form of brief, non-evaluative comments about various aspects of the student's performance.

Portfolios offer a more realistic and accurate way to assess the process of language teaching and learning.

The Oral Component

The oral component of a portfolio might be an audio- or videocassette. It may contain both rehearsed and extemporaneous monologues and conversations. For a rehearsed speaking activity, give a specific communicative task that students can personalize according to their individual interests (for example, ordering a favorite meal in a restaurant). If the speaking activity is extemporaneous, first acquaint students with possible topics for discussion or even the specific task they will be expected to perform. (For example, tell them they will be asked to discuss a picture showing a sports activity or a restaurant scene.)

The Written Component

Portfolios are excellent tools for incorporating process writing strategies into the foreign language classroom. Documentation of various stages of the writing process—brainstorming, multiple drafts, and peer comments—may be included with the finished product.

Involve students in selecting writing tasks for the portfolio. At the beginning levels, the tasks might include some structured writing, such as labeling or listing. As students become more proficient, journals, letters, and other more complicated writing tasks are valuable ways for them to monitor their progress in using the written language.

Student Self-Evaluation

Students should be actively involved in critiquing and evaluating their portfolios and monitoring their own progress. The process and procedure for student self-evaluation should be considered in planning the contents of the portfolio. Students should work with you and their peers to design the exact format. Self-evaluation encourages them to think about what they are learning (content), how they learn (process), why they are learning (purpose), and where they are going in their learning (goals).

Teacher Observation

Systematic, regular, and ongoing observations should be placed in the portfolio after they have been discussed with the student. These observations provide feedback on the student's progress in the language learning process.

Teacher observations should be based on an established set of criteria that has been developed earlier with input from the student. Observation techniques may include the following:
- Jotting notes in a journal to be discussed with the student and then placed in the portfolio
- Using a checklist of observable behaviors, such as the willingness to take risks when using the target language or staying on task during the lesson
- Making observations on adhesive notes that can be placed in folders
- Recording anecdotal comments, during or after class, using a cassette recorder.

Knowledge of the criteria you use in your observations gives students a framework for their performance.

How Are Portfolios Evaluated?

The portfolio should reflect the process of student learning over a specific period of time. At the beginning of that time period, determine the criteria by which you will assess the final product and convey them to the students. Make this evaluation a collaborative effort by seeking students' input as you formulate these criteria and your instructional goals.

Students need to understand that evaluation based on a predetermined standard is but one phase of the assessment process; demonstrated effort and growth are just as important. As you consider correctness and accuracy in both oral and written work, also consider the organization, creativity, and improvement revealed by the student's portfolio over the time period. The portfolio provides a way to monitor the growth of a student's knowledge, skills, and attitudes and shows the student's efforts, progress, and achievements.

How to Implement Portfolios

Teacher-teacher collaboration is as important to the implementation of portfolios as teacher-student collaboration. Confer with your colleagues to determine, for example, what kinds of information you want to see in the student portfolio, how the information will be presented, the purpose of the portfolio, the intended purposes (grading, placement, or a combination of the two), and criteria for evaluating the portfolio. Conferring among colleagues helps foster a departmental cohesiveness and consistency that will ultimately benefit the students.

The Promise of Portfolios

The high degree of student involvement in developing portfolios and deciding how they will be used generally results in renewed student enthusiasm for learning and improved achievement. As students

compare portfolio pieces done early in the year with work produced later, they can take pride in their progress as well as reassess their motivation and work habits.

Portfolios also provide a framework for periodic assessment of teaching strategies, programs, and instruction. They offer schools a tool to help solve the problem of vertical articulation and accurate student placement. The more realistic and accurate assessment of the language learning process that is provided by portfolios is congruent with the strategies that should be used in the proficiency-oriented classroom.

EN CAMINO

En camino supports the use of portfolios in the following ways:

The Pupil's Edition
◆ Includes numerous oral and written activities that can be easily adapted for student portfolios, such as **En mi cuaderno** and the more global review activities in Repaso.

◆ Includes a process writing strategy in Chapters 3–6 that progressively develops students' skills at drafting, revising, and evaluating assignments suitable for their portfolios.

The Interactive CD-ROM Program
◆ Includes word-processing and sound-recording capabilities that allow students to create original or guided work for their portfolios.

The Annotated Teacher's Edition
◆ Suggests activities in the Portfolio and Performance Assessment features that may serve as portfolio items.

The Ancillary Program
◆ Includes criteria in the *Alternative Assessment Guide* for evaluating portfolios, as well as Speaking Tests in the *Testing Program* for each chapter that can be adapted for use as portfolio assessment items.

LEARNING STYLES AND MULTI-MODALITY TEACHING

By Mary B. McGehee

The larger and broader population of students who are enrolling in foreign language classes brings a new challenge to foreign language educators, calling forth an evolution in teaching methods to enhance learning for all our students. Educational experts now recognize that every student has a preferred sense for learning and retrieving information: visual, auditory, or kinesthetic. Incorporating a greater variety of activities to accommodate the learning styles of all students can make the difference between struggle and pleasure in the foreign language classroom. ◆

Accommodating Different Learning Styles

A modified arrangement of the classroom is one way to provide more effective and enjoyable learning for all students. Rows of chairs and desks must give way at times to circles, semicircles, or small clusters. Students may be grouped in fours or in pairs for cooperative work or peer teaching. It is important to find a balance of arrangements, thereby providing the most comfort in varied situations.

Since visual, auditory, and kinesthetic learners will be in the class, and because every student's learning will be enhanced by a multisensory approach, lessons must be directed toward all three learning styles. Any language lesson content may be presented visually, aurally, or kinesthetically.

Visual presentations and practice may include the chalkboard, charts, posters, television, overhead projectors, books, magazines, picture diagrams, flash cards, bulletin boards, films, slides, or videos. Visual learners need to see what they are to learn. Lest the teacher think he or she will never have the time to prepare all those visuals, Dickel and Slak (1983) found that visual aids generated by students are more effective than ready-made ones.

Auditory presentations and practice may include stating aloud the requirements of the lesson, oral questions and answers, paired or group work on a progression of oral exercises from repetition to communication, CDs, computer sound recordings, dialogues, and role-playing. Jingles, catchy stories, and memory devices using songs and rhymes are good learning aids. Having students record themselves and then listen as they play back the recording allows them to practice in the auditory mode.

Kinesthetic presentations entail the students' use of manipulatives, chart materials, gestures, signals, typing, songs, games, and role-playing. These lead the students to associate sentence constructions with meaningful movements.

A Sample Lesson Using Multi-Modality Teaching

A multi-sensory presentation on greetings might proceed as follows.

For Visual Learners
As the teacher begins oral presentation of greetings and introductions, he or she simultaneously shows the written forms on transparencies, with the formal expressions marked with an adult's hat, and the informal expressions marked with a baseball cap.

The teacher then distributes cards with the hat and cap symbols representing the formal and informal expressions. As the students hear taped mini-dialogues, they hold up the appropriate card to indicate whether the dialogues are formal or informal. On the next listening, the students repeat the sentences they hear.

Incorporating a greater variety of activities to accommodate the learning styles of all students can make the difference between struggle and pleasure in the foreign language classroom.

For Auditory Learners
A longer recorded dialogue follows, allowing the students to hear the new expressions a number of times. They write from dictation several sentences containing the new expressions. They may work in pairs, correcting each other's work as they "test" their own understanding of the lesson at hand. Finally, students respond to simple questions using the appropriate formal and informal responses cued by the cards they hold.

For Kinesthetic Learners

For additional kinesthetic input, members of the class come to the front of the room, each holding a hat or cap symbol. As the teacher calls out situations, the students play the roles, using gestures and props appropriate to the age group they are portraying. Non-cued, communicative role-playing with props further enables the students to "feel" the differences between formal and informal expressions.

Helping Students Learn How to Use Their Preferred Mode

Since we require all students to perform in all language skills, part of the assistance we must render is to help them develop strategies within their preferred learning modes to carry out an assignment in another mode. For example, visual students hear the teacher assign an oral exercise and visualize what they must do. They must see themselves carrying out the assignment, in effect watching themselves as if there were a movie going on in their heads. Only then can they also hear themselves saying the right things. Thus, this assignment will be much easier for the visual learners who have been taught this process, if they have not already figured it out for themselves. Likewise, true auditory students, confronted with a reading/ writing assignment, must talk themselves through it, converting the entire process into sound as they plan and prepare their work. Kinesthetic students presented with a visual or auditory task must first break the assignment into tasks and then work their way through them.

Students who experience difficulty because of a strong preference for one mode of learning are often unaware of the degree of preference. In working with these students, I prefer the simple and direct assessment of learning styles offered by Richard Bandler and John Grinder in their book *Frogs into Princes,* which allows the teacher and student to quickly determine how the student learns. In an interview with the student, I follow the assessment with certain specific recommendations of techniques to make the student's study time more effective.

It is important to note here that teaching students to maximize their study does not require that the teacher give each student an individualized assignment. It does require that each student who needs it be taught how to prepare the assignment using his or her own talents and strengths. This communication between teacher and student, combined with teaching techniques that reinforce learning in all modes,

can only maximize pleasure and success in learning a foreign language.

References

Dickel, M.J. and S. Slak. "Imaging Vividness and Memory for Verbal Material." *Journal of Mental Imagery* 7, i (1983):121–126.

Bandler, Richard, and John Grinder. *Frogs into Princes.* Real People Press, Moab, UT. 1978.

EN CAMINO

En camino *accommodates different learning styles in the following ways:*

The Pupil's Edition

◆ Presents basic material in audio, video, and print formats.

◆ Includes role-playing activities and a variety of multi-modal activities, including an extensive listening strand and many art-based activities.

The Annotated Teacher's Edition

◆ Provides suggested activities for visual, auditory, and kinesthetic learners as well as suggestions for slower-paced learning and challenge activities.

◆ Includes Total Physical Response activities.

The Ancillary Program

◆ Provides additional reinforcement activities for a variety of learning styles.

◆ Presents a rich blend of audiovisual input through the video, audio, and CD-ROM programs, and through transparencies and copying masters.

NEW PERSPECTIVES FOR NATIVE SPEAKERS

By Cecilia Rodríguez-Pino

Spanish teachers often simultaneously teach two groups of students whose learning needs are markedly different. The first group, the majority, for whom most curricula are developed, are English-proficient but at a beginner's level in Spanish. The second group consists of students whose proficiency in English varies but who already speak Spanish, often quite proficiently. From their own experience they already understand a great deal about the Spanish language and the cultures of Spanish speakers. Many schools have not yet set up Spanish for Native Speakers (SNS) sections with specialized curricula that would build on these students' linguistic and cultural strengths. As a result, in some schools native speakers who want to study Spanish are enrolled in courses where Spanish is taught as a foreign language. Addressing their learning needs thus becomes the particular challenge of the teacher, who must create and implement supplemental classroom materials. ◆

Types of Native Spanish Speakers

The greatest number of native Spanish speakers in the classroom are Spanish-speaking immigrants and American students of Hispanic descent. Many immigrants have been uprooted from their native countries and find themselves in a new and foreign environment without the skills to communicate. Often they must struggle to adapt to mainstream sociocultural norms and values. Psychological adjustment, cultural integration, and the acquisition of new communicative skills are daily concerns for them. Building teacher-student and peer-peer learning relationships may be harder for such students.

American students of Hispanic descent are often bilingual. Some are highly proficient in both written and oral Spanish, but many are proficient to varying degrees, depending on the circumstances, topics, tasks, and informal situations. These students reflect the various socio-economic classes of society and speak a wide range of Spanish dialects. Research indicates that the dialect they speak affects how they are viewed at school. When they speak a "standard" variety of Spanish or are from an educated class, as are many Cuban Americans in Florida, reactions to them are usually positive. But when Spanish speakers are from a rural background, speak a "non-standard" dialect, or come from a non-literate background, reactions in school are often negative. Attempting to modify their dialect can be detrimental to their linguistic and social development.

Linguistic Needs

Native Spanish speakers need to retrieve any Spanish they may have lost, maintain the competency they already have, and expand their knowledge and skills in Spanish.

The problem of native language loss is receiving much attention in the profession. Children appear to lose production skills more quickly than they lose comprehension ability. Thus retrieval efforts should focus on production. Rapid changes in society and in the patterns by which Spanish is transmitted from one generation to the next account for much of students' language loss. Word borrowing and code switching to English may also account for language loss. These practices are not unique to bilingual students in the United States; they are common linguistic phenomena, observed wherever languages are in contact. A native speaker may switch from Spanish to English when referring to activities generally associated with the dominant culture—even when the speaker is perfectly familiar with the relevant Spanish vocabulary. Efforts to eradicate code switching may harm students' linguistic and social development.

Affective Needs

Native Spanish-speaking students bring to class much valuable cultural and linguistic experience. Cultural opportunities need to be provided for them through which they can express their knowledge of their own particular Spanish-speaking culture and gain a greater overview of other Spanish-speaking communities and countries. They need to understand that their heritage, language, culture, dialect, and individual abilities are valuable to society. As teachers we must respect and value the different languages and dialects our students speak, and we must create an instructional context in which students will develop positive attitudes toward their own ethnic group and their own ethnic identity.

An SNS Program Approach

A task-based, whole-language approach is recommended. Receptive and productive skills can be developed through culturally meaningful activities whose contexts are community, school, home, and self. These activities can be carried out in conjunction with textbook thematic units. Such an approach creates a student-centered classroom in which the teacher acts as a facilitator connecting students to the bilingual community.

Expanding Receptive Skills

Students should perform activities in which they listen to their native language in a broad range of formal and informal contexts, from simple topics to complex ones. Audio- or videotaped versions of stories, songs, documentaries, speeches, or debates can be adapted for class assignments. Guest speakers from the community are extremely valuable resources for presentations or interviews on the chapter topic.

Students should have access to diverse, authentic reading materials from the popular culture as well as from more formal subject areas. Chicano, Cuban, Dominican, Colombian, Nicaraguan, Honduran, Panamanian, and Puerto Rican writings—which are underrepresented in the mainstream literary canon—can play an important role in instilling in students a sense of pride and awareness of their cultural heritage. Students relate well to literature written by contemporary Hispanic authors who have had experiences similar to the students' in the United States. For example, they might read the short story "Desde que se fue," from the collection *Madreselvas en flor* by literary prize-winning Chicano author Ricardo Aguilar-Melantzón, about growing up in a bilingual setting.

Developing Productive Skills

Oral history projects, ethnographic interviews, sociolinguistic surveys, dialogue journals, letter writing, and other purposeful authentic activities are effective techniques that focus on interactions among students, teacher, and community. These kinds of activities give students the opportunity to develop individual strengths and to explore their language and culture in a community context.

Classroom Environment

We can change the classroom space itself to create an environment that recognizes the prestige of the students' language and cultural heritage. Using a brief questionnaire, the teacher can find out the students' backgrounds and then display relevant posters, travel brochures, art, literature, or historical information. Students can contribute captioned photographs depicting cultural events and family traditions, so that the bulletin board reflects their personal view of the Spanish-speaking world rather than just the teacher's perspective.

Individual Assessment and Evaluation

Individual assessment at the beginning of the year should be based primarily on content so that students' errors are not the main focus. Use content, organization, and language as criteria for evaluating speaking and writing. In evaluating students' work for the year, take into account how students have broadened their functional range. This requires students to be responsible for the concepts that are essential to comprehension and production. A writing portfolio is a valuable component of the evaluation process. Oral presentations of ethnographic and sociolinguistic projects are contextualized activities for evaluating speaking.

EN CAMINO

En camino *supports native speakers' continued development of Spanish in the following ways:*

The Pupil's Edition

◆ Promotes pride and awareness of cultural heritage through Location Openers on U.S. Spanish-speaking areas, as well as cultural features, interviews with native speakers, and literary selections by U.S. and non-U.S. native speakers.

◆ Fosters the student's self-concept by encouraging individual expression in journal entries and other authentic tasks, such as letter writing.

The Annotated Teacher's Edition

◆ Includes specific suggestions for activities to be performed by native speakers, both independently and with other students.

◆ Provides the teacher with additional vocabulary suggestions and language notes that validate regional variants.

◆ Suggests family and community links that strengthen students' ties to the wider bilingual community via family and community interviews and reports.

¡VEN CONMIGO! LEVEL 1

Offers a **Cuaderno para hispanohablantes** with a diagnostic instrument and, chapter by chapter, additional reading practice based on authentic literature on topics of interest to native speakers. This book, which can be adapted for Grades 6–9, addresses issues of formal usage and pronunciation and provides additional writing and speaking practice.

This section provides information about resources that can enrich your Spanish class. Included are addresses of Spanish and Latin American government offices, pen pal organizations, subscription agencies, and many others. Since addresses change frequently, you may want to verify them before you send your requests. ◆

Pen pal organizations

For the names of pen pal groups other than those listed below, contact your local chapter of AATSP. There are fees involved, so be sure to write for information.

**Student Letter Exchange
(League of Friendship)**
211 Broadway, Suite 201
Lynbrook, NY 11563
(516) 887-8628

World Pen Pals
1694 Como Avenue
St. Paul, MN 55108
(612) 647-0191

Embassies and consulates

Addresses and phone numbers of embassies and consulates for Spanish-speaking countries are available in most U.S. city telephone directories. All are available in the directory for Washington, D.C.

Periodicals

Subscriptions to the following cultural materials are available through jobbers or directly from the publishers. See also the section on Subscription Services.

- **Blanco y negro,** a general interest weekly magazine in Spain
- **Eres,** a Mexican magazine for teens
- **El País,** a major daily newspaper in Spain

- **Hispanic,** an English-language magazine about Hispanics in the U.S.
- **La Prensa,** a major daily paper in Argentina
- **Tú internacional,** a magazine for teens published in several Spanish-speaking countries
- **México desconocido,** a cultural and environmental magazine about Mexico

Cultural agencies

For historical and tourist information about Spanish-speaking countries, contact:

Tourist Office of Spain
666 Fifth Avenue
New York, NY 10022
(212) 265-8822

Intercultural exchange

CIEE Student Travel Services
205 East 42nd St.
New York, NY 10017
(888) 268-6245

American Field Service
198 Madison, 8th Floor
New York, NY 10016
(212) 299-9000

Professional organizations

The American Council on the Teaching of Foreign Languages (ACTFL)
6 Executive Plaza
Yonkers, NY 10701
(914) 963-8830

American Association of Teachers of Spanish and Portuguese (AATSP)
Butter-Hancock Hall #210
University of Northern Colorado
Greeley, CO 80639
(970) 351-1090

Subscription services

Spanish-language magazines can be obtained through subscription agencies in the United States. The following companies are among the many which can provide your school with subscriptions:

EBSCO Subscription Services
P.O. Box 1943
Birmingham, AL 35201-1943
(205) 991-6600

Continental Book Company
8000 Cooper Ave., Bldg. 29
Glendale, NY 11385
(718) 326-0560

Miscellaneous

Educational Resources Information Center (ERIC)
2277 Research Blvd.
Rockville, MD 20852
(800) 538-3742
- Foreign language periodicals

The International Film Bureau
332 South Michigan Ave.
Chicago, IL 60604-4382
(312) 427-4545
- Foreign language videos for sale and/or rent

Américas
Organization of American States
17th and Constitution Ave. NW
Room #307
Washington, D.C. 20006
(202) 458–3000
- Magazine available in English or Spanish text

This bibliography is a compilation of resources available for professional enrichment. ◆

Selected and annotated list of readings

I. Methods and Approaches

Cohen, Andrew D. *Assessing Language Ability in the Classroom, 2/e.* Boston, MA: Heinle, 1994.

- Assessment processes, oral interviews, role-playing situations, dictation, and portfolio assessment.

Hadley, Alice Omaggio. *Teaching Language in Context, 2/e.* Boston, MA: Heinle, 1993.

- Language acquisition theories and models and adult second language proficiency.

Krashen, Stephen, and Tracy D. Terrell. *The Natural Approach: Language Acquisition in the Classroom.* New York: Pergamon, 1983.

- Optimal Input Theory: listening, oral communication development, and testing.

Oller, John W., Jr. *Methods That Work: Ideas for Language Teachers, 2/e.* Boston, MA: Heinle, 1993.

- Literacy in multicultural settings, co-operative learning, peer teaching, and computer-assisted instruction.

Shrum, Judith L., and Eileen W. Glisan. *Teacher's Handbook: Contextualized Language Instruction.* Boston, MA: Heinle, 1993.

- Grammar, testing, using video texts, microteaching, case studies and daily plans.

II. Second-Language Theory

Krashen, Stephen. *The Power of Reading.* New York: McGraw-Hill, 1994.

- Updates Optimal Input Theory by incorporating the reading of authentic texts.

Liskin-Gasparro, Judith. *A Guide to Testing and Teaching for Oral Proficiency.* Boston, MA: Heinle, 1990.

- Oral proficiency through interview techniques and speech samples.

Rubin, Joan, and Irene Thompson. *How To Be a More Successful Language Learner, 2/e.* Boston, MA: Heinle, 1993.

- Psychological, linguistic, and practical matters of second-language learning.

III. Video and computer-assisted instruction

Altmann, Rick. *The Video Connection: Integrating Video into Language Teaching.* Boston, MA: Houghton Mifflin, 1989.

- Diverse strategies for using video texts to support second- language learning.

Dunkel, Patricia A. *Computer-Assisted Language Learning and Testing.* Boston, MA: Heinle, 1992.

- CAI and computer-assisted language learning (CALL) in the foreign language classroom.

Kenning, M. J., and M. M. Kenning. *Computers and Language Learning: Current Theory and Practice.* New York, NY: E. Horwood, 1990.

- Theoretical discussions and practical suggestions for CAI in second-language development.

IV. Teaching Native Speakers

Aguilar-Melantzón, Ricardo. "Desde que se fue."

- Produced for Teaching Spanish to Southwest Hispanic Students, National Endowment for the Humanities Summer Conference, Cecilia Rodríguez-Pino, project director. Las Cruces: New Mexico State University, 1993. Available through Spanish for Native Speakers Program, New Mexico State University. Audiotape of short story narrated by author.

Merino, Barbara J., Henry T. Trueba, and Fabián A. Samaniego. *Language and Culture in Learning: Teaching Spanish to Native Speakers of Spanish.* London, England: Falmer Press, 1993.

Rodríguez-Pino, Cecilia, and Daniel Villa. "A Student-Centered Spanish for Native Speakers Program: Theory, Curriculum Design and Outcome Assessment." *In Faces in a Crowd: The Individual Learner in Multisection Courses.* Edited by Carol A. Klee. American Association of University Supervisors Series. Boston, MA: Heinle, 1994.

Valdés, Guadalupe. "The Role of the Foreign Language Teaching Profession in Maintaining Non-English Languages in the United States." In *Northeast Conference Reports: Languages for a Multicultural World in Transition.* Edited by Heidi Byrnes. Lincolnwood, IL: National Textbook, 1992.

SCOPE AND SEQUENCE: SPANISH LEVEL 1A

FUNCTIONS	GRAMMAR	VOCABULARY	CULTURE	RE-ENTRY

CAPÍTULO PRELIMINAR ¡Adelante!

FUNCTIONS	GRAMMAR	VOCABULARY	CULTURE	RE-ENTRY
• Map of the Spanish-speaking world	• ¿Cómo te llamas?, Los acentos • El alfabeto, Los cognados • Frases útiles	• Los colores • El calendario	• El español—¿Por qué? • ¿Sabías? • ¿Los conoces?	• Los números

España

CAPÍTULO 1 ¡Mucho gusto!

FUNCTIONS	GRAMMAR	VOCABULARY	CULTURE	RE-ENTRY
• Saying hello and goodbye • Introducing people and responding to an introduction • Asking how someone is and saying how you are • Asking and saying how old someone is • Asking where someone is from and saying where you're from • Talking about likes and dislikes	• Punctuation marks • Pronouns tú and yo • Soy, eres and es • Asking questions • Nouns and definite articles	• Numbers 0–30, p. 36 • Sports, p. 44 • Classes at school, p. 44 • Musical genres, p. 45 • Foods, p. 45	• First and last names in Spanish • First names and Catholicism • Saint's Days • Greetings • Handwriting in Spanish-speaking countries • Snack foods in Spain • ¿De dónde eres?	• Accents (from Capítulo preliminar) • Numbers 0–30 (from Capítulo preliminar)

España

CAPÍTULO 2 ¡Organízate!

FUNCTIONS	GRAMMAR	VOCABULARY	CULTURE	RE-ENTRY
• Talking about what you want or need • Telling what's in your room • Talking about what you need and want to do	• Indefinite articles un and una • Noun plurals • Plural indefinite articles • Subject pronouns él and ella • Plurals of ¿cuánto? and mucho • Identifying infinitives	• School supplies, p. 65 • The contents of your room, p. 75 • Things you do, p. 86 • Numbers 31–199, p. 88	• Extended family • School uniforms • Apartment in Spain/Sharing TV set • Exclamations • Los saludos • ¿Qué necesitas para el colegio?	• Subject pronouns: tú and yo (from Capítulo 1) • Definite articles: el and la (from Capítulo 1) • Numbers 0–30 (from Capítulo preliminar) • Using cognates (from Capítulo preliminar)

México

CAPÍTULO 3 Nuevas clases, nuevos amigos

FUNCTIONS	GRAMMAR	VOCABULARY	CULTURE	RE-ENTRY
• Talking about classes and sequencing events • Telling time • Telling at what time something happens • Talking about being late or in a hurry • Describing people and things • Talking about things you like and explaining why	• Plural definite articles los and las • Telling time with ser • The preposition de • The verb ser for descriptions • Adjective agreement • Tag questions	• School subjects, p. 109 • Time expressions, p. 119 • Words that describe people and things, p. 125 • Free-time activities and things you like, p. 130	• Class schedules in Spanish-speaking countries • Grades in Spanish-speaking countries • The siesta • Titles of respect • ¿Cómo es un día escolar típico?	• Present tense of tener • Numbers 0–99 • School supplies • Forming questions • Present tense of tener • Noun-adjective agreement • necesitar and querer • Talking about likes and dislikes • Question formation

FUNCTIONS	GRAMMAR	VOCABULARY	CULTURE	RE-ENTRY

México

CAPÍTULO 4 ¿Qué haces esta tarde?

FUNCTIONS	GRAMMAR	VOCABULARY	CULTURE	RE-ENTRY
• Talking about what you and others like to do • Talking about what you and others do during free time • Telling where people and things are • Talking about where you and others go during free time	• Present tense of regular -ar verbs • **con, conmigo, contigo** • Relative pronoun **que** • The verb **estar** • Subject pronouns • The verb **ir** • Days of the week	• Things you like to do, p. 154 • Places in town and their location, p. 163 • The days of the week, p. 174	• Hispanic athletes • Referring to or greeting friends • Sights and activities in Cuernavaca • **tú** and **usted** • **Un recorrido de la Plaza de las Armas** • **¿Te gusta pasear con tus amigos?**	• Present tense of **tener** • Present tense of **gustar** • Subject pronouns **yo, tú, él, ella** • Describing with **ser** • Telling time • Days of the week

Florida

CAPÍTULO 5 El ritmo de la vida

FUNCTIONS	GRAMMAR	VOCABULARY	CULTURE	RE-ENTRY
• Discussing how often you do things • Talking about what you do and your friends like to do together • Talking about what you do during a typical week • Giving today's date • Talking about the weather	• Negation • The question words **¿quién?** and **¿quiénes?** • The pronoun **les** • -er and -ir verbs • The formula for giving today's date	• Weekend activities, p. 204 • Frequency terms, p. 208 • The seasons and the months, p. 214 • Weather expressions, p. 216	• Leisure time activities • Meeting places • The seasons of the year in South America • **¿Cómo es una semana típica?**	• Present tense of regular -ar verbs • Negation with **no** • **¿quién?** • **gustar** • Subject pronouns • Days of the week

Florida

CAPÍTULO 6 Entre familia

FUNCTIONS	GRAMMAR	VOCABULARY	CULTURE	RE-ENTRY
• Describing a family • Describing people • Discussing things a family does together • Discussing problems and giving advice	• Possessive adjectives • the verbs **hacer** and **salir** • The personal **a** • The verb **deber** • The verb **poner** • Present tense of **decir: dice**	• Members of the family, p. 235 • Pets and the words to describe them, p. 241 • Words that describe people, pp. 245, 248 • Household chores, p. 256	• Diminutive names • El Compadrazgo • **La importancia de la familia hispana** • **¿Cuántos son en tu familia?**	• **hay** • Possessive adjectives • Demonstrative adjectives • Use of **de** • Colors • Descriptions of people • Pastimes/hobbies • **¿con qué frecuencia?** • Adjective agreement • Forming questions with **¿cómo?** and **¿cuántos?**

SCOPE AND SEQUENCE: SPANISH LEVEL 1B

FUNCTIONS	GRAMMAR	VOCABULARY	CULTURE	RE-ENTRY
CAPÍTULO PUENTE En camino *Pages xxiv–37*			***Bridge Chapter***	
• Greeting others; saying what you have • Talking about what you do and when; describing people and places • Talking about how often you do things; talking about your family	• The verbs **estar, ser,** and **tener** • Indirect object pronouns • Using **hay** • Possessive adjectives • Telling time • Present tense of regular -**ar**, -**er**, and -**ir** verbs • Adjective agreement • The verbs **hacer, salir, poner, deber,** and **ir**	• Pastimes • Family members • Weather expressions • Place names • Time expressions	• The **Capítulo puente** reviews material presented in chapters 1–6 of ***Adelante***.	
Ecuador — **CAPÍTULO 7 ¿Qué te gustaría hacer? *Pages 42–79***				
• Talking on the telephone • Extending and accepting invitations • Making plans • Talking about getting ready • Turning down an invitation and explaining why	• **e** to **ie** stem-changing verbs • **pensar** + infinitive and **ir** + **a** + infinitive • Reflexive verbs (infinitives only) • Expressions with **tener**	• Places and events • Transportation • Personal items • Expression of apology	• Telephone greetings • Modes of transportation • **¿Qué haces para conocer a un nuevo estudiante?**	• Invitations: **gustar** • Days of the week • Future expressions: **hoy, mañana,** etc. • Expressions of frequency • The verb **tener**
Ecuador — **CAPÍTULO 8 ¡A comer! *Pages 80–119***				
• Talking about meals and food • Commenting on food • Making polite requests • Ordering dinner in a restaurant • Asking for and paying the bill in a restaurant	• The verb **encantar** and indirect object pronouns • **o** to **ue** stem-changing verbs • **Ser** and **estar** with food • Expressions with **tener** • **Así se dice:** Indirect object pronouns **nos** and **me** • **otro** • **Así se dice:** Indirect object pronoun **le; quisiera**	• Breakfast foods • Lunch foods • Foods • Tableware • Dinner foods • Numbers 200–100,000	• Names of fruits and vegetables • Main meal of the day • Eating out in Ecuador • Table manners • Dinner and snacks • Types of foods • **La comida en el mundo hispanohablante** • **¿Cuál es un plato típico de tu país o región?**	• Expressing likes and dislikes • Present tense of regular and **e** to **ie** stem-changing verbs • Times of day • **estar** versus **ser** • Expressions with **tener** • Numbers 200–100,000 • Question words **¿qué?** and **¿cuánto?**

FUNCTIONS	GRAMMAR	VOCABULARY	CULTURE	RE-ENTRY

Texas

CAPÍTULO 9 ¡Vamos de compras! *Pages 124–161*

FUNCTIONS	GRAMMAR	VOCABULARY	CULTURE	RE-ENTRY
• Talking about giving gifts • Asking for and giving directions downtown • Commenting on clothes • Making comparisons • Expressing preferences • Asking about prices and paying	• Indirect object pronouns **le** and **les** • Use of **ser** to tell what something is made of • Making comparisons: **más... que, menos... que, tan... como** • Using the demonstrative adjectives **este** and **ese**	• Gift items • Store names • Clothing • Expressions related to cost	• Specialty stores in Spain • Personal care and dress in Spanish-speaking countries • Currencies in Spanish-speaking countries • **¿Estás a la moda?**	• **ir** + **a** + infinitive for planning • Describing family • Talking about locations • Talking about where things are • Present tense of **ser** for description • Numbers 0–100,000

Texas

CAPÍTULO 10 Celebraciones *Pages 162–201*

FUNCTIONS	GRAMMAR	VOCABULARY	CULTURE	RE-ENTRY
• Talking about what you're doing right now • Asking for and giving an opinion • Asking for help and responding to requests • Telling a friend what to do • Talking about past events	• Present progressive • Informal commands • Preterite tense of regular **-ar** verbs • Direct object pronouns **lo** and **la**	• Holidays • Party expressions • Time expressions	• **Día del santo** • **La quinceañera** • Traditional holiday foods • **El Paseo del Río** • **¿Qué hacen ustedes para celebrar?**	• **estar** • Dates, months, seasons • Extending, accepting, turning down invitations • **tú** versus **usted** • Household chores • Days of the week • Question words **¿quién?** and **¿quiénes?** • Free-time activities

Puerto Rico

CAPÍTULO 11 Para vivir bien *Pages 206–243*

FUNCTIONS	GRAMMAR	VOCABULARY	CULTURE	RE-ENTRY
• Making suggestions and expressing feelings • Talking about moods and physical condition • Saying what you did • Talking about where you went and when	• **¿Te acuerdas?**: the verb **dormir** • Present tense of **sentirse** • The verb **doler** with **me, te, le** • The verb **jugar** in the preterite • The verb **ir** in the preterite	• Keeping fit • Physical conditions • Parts of the body • Different sports fields	• Body parts in common expressions • Baseball in Spanish-speaking countries • Sports in Spanish-speaking countries • **¿Qué deporte practicas?**	• **e** to **ie** stem-changing verbs • Food vocabulary • Expressions of frequency • Definite articles • **estar** + condition • **o** to **ue** stem-changing verbs • Use of preterite tense to discuss past events

Puerto Rico

CAPÍTULO 12 Las vacaciones ideales *Pages 244–281*   *Review Chapter*

FUNCTIONS	GRAMMAR	VOCABULARY	CULTURE	RE-ENTRY
• Talking about what you do and like to do every day; making future plans • Discussing what you would like to do on vacation • Saying where you went and what you did on vacation	• **e** to **ie** and **o** to **ue** stem-changing verbs • Verbs followed by an infinitive • Uses of **ser** and **estar** • Uses of the preterite	• Vacation items • Vacation activities • Countries	• **¿Adónde vas y qué haces en las vacaciones?**	• Chapter 12 reviews material presented in chapters 7–12 of *En camino*.

¡Ven conmigo! Spanish 2

	FUNCTIONS	GRAMMAR	VOCABULARY	CULTURE	RE-ENTRY

Andalucía — CAPÍTULO 1 Mis amigos y yo, *Pages 4–33* — *Review Chapter*

FUNCTIONS	GRAMMAR	VOCABULARY	CULTURE	RE-ENTRY
• Introducing yourself and others • Describing people • Talking about what you and others do • Saying what you like and don't like	• Present tense of **tener** • Adjective agreement • Present tense of regular verbs • Indirect object pronouns with verbs like **gustar**	• Nationalities • Numbers • Colors • Family members	• Description of appearance of Hispanics • **¿Qué es americano?** • Planning evening activities in Spain • **¿Qué es un buen amigo?** • **cafeterías**	• Chapter 1 reviews Spanish taught in *Adelante, Level 1A* and *En camino, Level 1B*.

Andalucía — CAPÍTULO 2 Un viaje al estranjero, *Pages 34–61* — *Review Chapter*

FUNCTIONS	GRAMMAR	VOCABULARY	CULTURE	RE-ENTRY
• Talking about how you're feeling • Making suggestions and responding to them • Saying if something has already been done • Asking for and offering help • Describing your city or town	• The verb **estar** • Preterite of **-ar** verbs • Present tense of **querer** and **poder**	• Calendar expressions • Places around town • Weather expressions • Clothing	• Extended family living together • **¿En dónde te gustaría vivir?** • Celsius vs. Fahrenheit	• Chapter 2 reviews Spanish taught in *Adelante, Level 1A* and *En camino, Level 1B*.

Valle de México — CAPÍTULO 3 La vida cotidiana, *Pages 66–93*

FUNCTIONS	GRAMMAR	VOCABULARY	CULTURE	RE-ENTRY
• Talking about your daily routine • Talking about responsibilities • Complaining • Talking about hobbies and pastimes • Saying how long something has been going on	• Reflexive verbs and pronouns • **e** to **i** stem change in **vestirse** • Adverbs ending in **-mente** • Direct object pronouns **lo, la, los, las** • **hace** + quantity of time + **que** + present tense	• Daily activities • Chores • Hobbies and pastimes	• **¿Cuál es tu profesión?** • Household chores • Expressions of agreement • Popular free-time activities among teenagers	• Verbs of personal grooming • Adverbs of time and place • Vocabulary of hobbies and pastimes • making excuses • Question formation

FUNCTIONS	GRAMMAR	VOCABULARY	CULTURE	RE-ENTRY

Valle de México

CAPÍTULO 4 ¡Adelante con los estudios *Pages 94–123*

FUNCTIONS	GRAMMAR	VOCABULARY	CULTURE	RE-ENTRY
• Asking for and giving opinions • Giving advice • Talking about things and people you know • Making comparisons • Making plans	• **deberías** vs. **debes** • **ser** + adjective to describe people • **estar** + adjective to describe location • Present tense of the verb **conocer** • Direct object pronouns	• Classroom activities • School and computer terms • Describing people • Activities around town	• School levels in Mexico • Cost of university education in Latin America • **¿Qué haces después del colegio?** • **¿Cuándo asistes a clases?**	• School subjects • **para** (in order to) + infinitive • **ser** vs. **estar** • Comparisons: **más... que** • **ir** + **a** + infinitive

Texas

CAPÍTULO 5 ¡Ponte en forma!, *Pages 128–157*

FUNCTIONS	GRAMMAR	VOCABULARY	CULTURE	RE-ENTRY
• Talking about staying fit and healthy • Telling someone what to do and not to do • Making excuses	• Preterite of the verb **dormir** • Preterite of regular **-er** and **-ir** verbs • Informal commands • Irregular informal commands • Preterite of **poder** • Reflexives with verbs of emotion	• Sports • Fitness activities • Health and fitness terms • Body parts • Injuries and explanations	• Student responses about health habits in Spanish-speaking countries • Vending machines in high schools • Snack foods in Spanish-speaking countries • **Garnachas, antojitos y bocadillos** • **Qué haces para mantenerte en forma?**	• Preterite of regular **-ar** verbs • Informal commands • Spelling changes in verbs that end in **-car, -gar, -zar** • Reflexive verbs

Texas

CAPÍTULO 6 De visita en la ciudad, *Pages 158–185*

FUNCTIONS	GRAMMAR	VOCABULARY	CULTURE	RE-ENTRY
• Asking for and giving information • Relating a series of events • Ordering in a restaurant	• Present tense of **saber** • **saber** vs. **conocer** • Preterite forms of **pedir, servir, traer**	• In the city • Places in the city • In the train station • In a restaurant	• San Antonio • **¿Cómo llegas al colegio?** • Birthday celebrations	• Direct object pronouns • **poder** • The preterite for listing events • Food vocabulary

FUNCTIONS	GRAMMAR	VOCABULARY	CULTURE	RE-ENTRY

El Caribe

CAPÍTULO 7 ¿Conoces bien tu pasado?, *Pages 190–219*

FUNCTIONS	GRAMMAR	VOCABULARY	CULTURE	RE-ENTRY
• Talking about what you used to do • Saying what you used to like and dislike • Describing what people and things were like • Using comparisons to describe people	• The imperfect tense of **-ar, -er, -ir** verbs • The imperfect tense of **ir** and **ver** • Spelling change of **o** to **u** and **y** to **e** to avoid vowel repetition • Imperfect of **ser** to describe people and things • The imperfect of **hay** • **tan** + adjective/ adverb + **como**	• Childhood activities • Describing peole • Describing places • Conveniences	• **Lo mejor de lo antiguo** • Public services in Latin American cities • **dichos** • **¿De quién es esta estatua?**	• The preterite • Talking about likes and dislikes using the preterite • Comparisons: **más/menos** + adjective + **que** • Complaining • Descriptive adjectives

El Caribe

CAPÍTULO 8 Diversiones, *Pages 220–247*

FUNCTIONS	GRAMMAR	VOCABULARY	CULTURE	RE-ENTRY
• Describing a past event • Saying why you couldn't do something • Reporting what someone said	• Adjectives with **-ísimo/a** • Superlatives • Verbs with prepositions • Using **mientras** in the past • Preterite of **decir**	• In the zoo, the amusement park, and movie theater • Running errands • At a festival	• **El Yunque** and **el coquí** • **¿Cuáles son las fiestas más importantes de tu ciudad o país?** • Holidays and festivals in Spanish-speaking countries	• Describing things • Describing what you did • The imperfect tense • The preterite

Los Andes

CAPÍTULO 9 ¡Día de mercado!, *Pages 252–281*

FUNCTIONS	GRAMMAR	VOCABULARY	CULTURE	RE-ENTRY
• Asking for and giving directions • Asking for help in a store • Talking about how clothes look and fit • Bargaining in a market	• Formal commands with **usted, ustedes**	• Giving directions • In a clothing store • In a market	• **En la ventanilla tres, por favor** • Clothing and shoe sizes • **¿Dónde compras tu comida?** • Expressions for shopping • Mural art	• Numbers • **ser** + **de** + material • Comparisons • Clothing material and pattern • Direct and indirect objects

FUNCTIONS	GRAMMAR	VOCABULARY	CULTURE	RE-ENTRY

Los Andes

CAPÍTULO 10 ¡Cuéntame!, *Pages 282–311*

FUNCTIONS	GRAMMAR	VOCABULARY	CULTURE	RE-ENTRY
• Setting the scene for a story • Continuing and ending a story • Talking about the latest news • Reacting to news	• The preterite vs. the imperfect • Preterite of **oír, creer, leer, caerse** • The preterite and the imperfect to tell a story	• Weather • Accidents, mishaps, and daily events • Science fiction and fairy tales • The latest news	• **¿Te sabes algún cuento?** • A Chilean folk tale • An Ecuadorean legend • **Mafalda** comic strip • **La Llorona**	• Reflexive verbs • Preterite of **ser** • Weather expressions

California

CAPÍTULO 11 Nuestro medio ambiente, *Pages 316–345*

FUNCTIONS	GRAMMAR	VOCABULARY	CULTURE	RE-ENTRY
• Describing a problem • Talking about consequences • Expressing agreement and disagreement • Talking about obligations and solutions	• Negative words • **si** clauses in present tense • **nosotros** commands	• Environmental problems • Animals • Protecting the environment • Materials and resources	• The rain forest • **¿Qué haces para el medio ambiente?** • Environmental programs • **el medio ambiente** • San Diego and Tijuana	• Affirmative and negative words • Giving an opinion • Cognates • Informal commands

California

CAPÍTULO 12 Veranos pasados, veranos por venir, *Pages 346–371*   *Review Chapter*

FUNCTIONS	GRAMMAR	VOCABULARY	CULTURE	RE-ENTRY
• Exchanging the latest news • Talking about where you went and what you did • Telling when something happened • Saying how you feel about people • Describing places • Saying when you're going to do something	• The subjunctive mood	• Writing a letter • Vacation activities • Describing places	• Baja California • **¿Cómo celebran el fin de cursos?** • **viaje de curso**	• Chapter 12 is a global review of Chapters 1–11, *Level 2.*

CAPÍTULO
Puente

¡En camino!
CHAPTER OVERVIEW

	FUNCTIONS	GRAMMAR	VOCABULARY
¿Te acuerdas? España, pp. 2–3			
Primer paso pp. 4–11	• Greeting others, p. 4 • Saying what you have, p. 9	• **Gramática:** The verb **estar,** p. 5 • **Gramática:** The verbs **tener** and **ser,** p. 6 • **¿Te acuerdas?:** Indirect object pronouns, p. 7 • **Nota gramatical:** Using **hay,** p. 9 • **¿Te acuerdas?:** Possessive adjectives, p. 10	• Pastimes and hobbies, p. 8
¿Te acuerdas? México, pp. 12–13			
Segundo paso pp. 14–21	• Talking about what you do and when, p. 14 • Describing people and places, p. 19	• **¿Te acuerdas?:** Telling time, p. 14 • **Nota gramatical:** Regular -ar verbs, p. 16 • **Nota gramatical:** The verb **ir,** p. 18 • **Gramática:** Adjective agreement, p. 19	• Leisure activities, p. 17
¿Te acuerdas? La Florida, pp. 24–25			
Tercer paso pp. 26–33	• Talking about how often you do things, p. 26 • Talking about your family, p. 29	• **Nota gramatical:** Regular -er and -ir verbs, p. 26 • **¿Te acuerdas?:** The verbs **hacer, salir,** and **poner,** p. 27 • **¿Te acuerdas?:** The verb **deber,** p. 31	• Chores, p. 31
Review pp. 34–37	**Repaso,** pp. 34–35	**A ver si puedo...,** p. 36	**Vocabulario,** p. 37

Culture
- **Nota cultural: Plazas** in Spanish-speaking countries, p. 21
- **Panorama cultural: ¿Qué haces los fines de semana?,** pp. 22–23
- **Nota cultural:** The **sobremesa,** p. 27

PRINT

Lesson Planning

One-Stop Planner
Lesson Planner with Substitute Teacher
Lesson Plans, pp. 1–5

Listening and Speaking

Listening Activities
- Student Response Forms for Listening Activities, pp. 52–54

Video Guide
- Teaching Suggestions, pp. 1–2
- Activity Masters, pp. 3–5
- Scripts and Answers, pp. 51–52, 61

Activities for Communication
- Communicative Activities, pp. 1–6

Reading and Writing

Practice and Activity Book, pp. 1–12

Assessment

Testing Program
- Paso Quizzes and Chapter Test, pp. 1–12
- Score Sheet, Scripts and Answers, pp. 13–18

Alternative Assessment Guide
- Portfolio Assessment, p. 10
- Performance Assessment, p. 18

MEDIA

Online Activities
- Juegos interactivos
- Actividades internet

Video Program
- Videocassette 1
- Videocassette 3 *(captioned version)*

Audio Compact Discs
- Textbook Listening Activities, CD 7, Tracks 1–24
- Assessment Items, CD 7, Tracks 14–18

Interactive CD-ROM Tutor, Discs 1–2, Chapters 1–6

Teaching Transparencies
- Vocabulary **¡En camino!** Transparencies A to C

One-Stop Planner CD-ROM

Use the **One-Stop Planner CD-ROM with Test Generator** to aid in lesson planning and pacing.

For each chapter, the **One-Stop Planner** includes:

- Editable lesson plans with direct links to teaching resources
- Printable worksheets from resource books
- Direct launches to the HRW Internet activities
- Video and audio segments
- Test Generator
- Clip Art for vocabulary items

For Student Response Forms, see Listening Activities pp. 52–54.

PRIMER PASO   pp. 4–11

3 ¿Vienen o se van?   p. 4

1. — Bueno, Martín, tengo que irme. Adiós.
   — Hasta luego, David.
2. — Hola, Samuel.
   — Ah, buenas tardes, señorita Ríos.
3. — Buenos días, Lupe. ¿Cómo estás?
   — Regular. ¿Y tú, Miguel? ¿Qué tal?
   — Yo, estupendo.
4. — Uf, ya son las once. Tengo clase. Chao.
   — ¡Date prisa, Ana! Hasta luego.
5. — Bueno, tengo que irme. Buenas noches, señor Irigoyen.
   — Hasta mañana, Juan Pablo.
6. — Buenas noches, doña Carolina.
   — Buenas noches, Marisa. ¿Cómo estás?
   — Muy bien, gracias. ¿Y usted?
   — Bastante bien, gracias.

Answers to Activity 3

1. goodbye	**4.** goodbye
2. hello	**5.** goodbye
3. hello	**6.** hello

7 El comité de bienvenida   p. 6

1. ¿Qué tal? Me llamo Federico López Garza. Tengo quince años y soy de San Luis Potosí, México.
2. Hola. Soy María Luisa Fuentes Hernández. Tengo doce años y soy de Buenos Aires, Argentina.
3. Buenos días. Soy Marta García Betancourt y soy de Bogotá, Colombia. Tengo catorce años.
4. Me llamo Alfredo Montañer y soy de la República Dominicana. Tengo trece años.

Answers to Activity 7

a. México	**c.** Marta
b. doce años	**d.** trece años

SEGUNDO PASO   pp. 14–21

21 ¿Día escolar o tiempo libre?   p. 14

1. Tengo que organizar mi cuarto primero y luego quiero jugar al tenis.
2. Me gusta mucho dibujar y pintar. Tengo arte los martes y los jueves por la mañana.
3. Jorge, ¿qué quieres hacer mañana? ¿Quieres ir al partido de voleibol o ir al cine?
4. Mi amiga practica el piano y después lee una revista.
5. ¡Estoy atrasado! Tengo computación a las nueve y cuarto y ya son las nueve y veinte.
6. ¡Uf, ya son las ocho! ¡Date prisa! El señor Vicario es un profesor muy estricto.
7. Tengo el almuerzo después de historia.
8. ¿A qué hora es tu programa de televisión favorito?

Answers to Activity 21

1. el tiempo libre	**5.** el colegio
2. el colegio	**6.** el colegio
3. el tiempo libre	**7.** el colegio
4. el tiempo libre	**8.** el tiempo libre

30 El sábado   p. 18

SRA. CALDERA	Querido, ¿adónde vas hoy?
SR. CALDERA	Voy al gimansio esta mañana. Mi clase de ejercicios aeróbicos es a las once y media. Antes de la clase voy a nadar.
SRA. CALDERA	Pepe, tú y tu hermana van a salir juntos, ¿no?
PEPE	Juana y yo vamos al parque a las diez. Vamos a jugar al voleibol con unos amigos.
SRA. CALDERA	Y, ¿adónde va Érica?
PEPE	Ella va a la biblioteca para estudiar geografía. Tiene un examen el lunes.
SRA. CALDERA	Pues, yo voy a descansar aquí en casa y luego voy a preparar una buena cena para todos.

Answers to Activity 30

1. Sr. Caldera—el gimnasio
2. Juana y Pepe—el parque
3. Érica—la biblioteca
4. Sra. Caldera—la casa

TERCER PASO   pp. 26–33

41 ¿Con qué frecuencia?   p. 26

SUSANA   Oye, ¿quieren ir al cine esta tarde?

ADRIANA   Sí, vamos a ver en el periódico qué películas hay.

ESTEBAN   Mira esta película nueva. Es de terror.

ADRIANA   Nunca voy a las películas de terror. A veces me gusta ir a ver películas cómicas o de romance.

ESTEBAN   Tengo una idea. Muchas veces hay conciertos en el parque. Sí, mira, hay un concierto de jazz esta noche.

ADRIANA   A nadie le gusta el jazz.

ESTEBAN   No, Adriana, no es cierto. Yo escucho el jazz a veces y me gusta bastante.

SUSANA   Mis padres escuchan el jazz muchas veces por la noche. A mí me gusta un poco.

ESTEBAN   Pues, ¿qué hacemos?

ADRIANA   Vamos a mirar la televisión. ¿Quieren?

Answers to Activity 41

1. falso   **2.** cierto   **3.** cierto   **4.** falso

REPASO   pp. 34–35

1 p. 34

1. Hoy mi mamá, mi hermano, mi amigo Juan y yo vamos a esquiar. La montaña donde esquiamos está lejos de casa. Salimos de casa a las seis de la mañana. Por supuesto, todos necesitamos mucha ropa.

2. Hoy no quiero salir de la casa para nada. Está lloviendo demasiado. Quiero leer mi revista nueva primero y después voy a hablar con mis amigos por teléfono.

3. Voy a ir a la playa con la familia de mi amiga hoy. ¡Qué bueno! Emilia y yo vamos a nadar todo el día.

4. Quiero ir al parque. Fernando y yo siempre corremos cuando hace fresco, y especialmente nos gusta correr cuando hace viento y no hace sol.

Answers to Repaso Activity 1

1. c   **2.** a   **3.** b   **4.** d

¡En camino!
PROJECTS

PASAPORTE AL ECUADOR

Introduction

Ask students what document one shows upon entering a foreign country. Do any students have a passport? What information is included in a United States passport? In this project they design a passport as if they were citizens of Spain.

Materials students may need

- Colored construction paper
- Recent photos
- Glue sticks
- Markers
- Stapler
- Stamp pad, stickers

Sequence

1. Give students construction paper folded into a booklet and have them label the front **Pasaporte de España.** They may draw Spain's flag and official seal.
2. Have students prepare the inside pages of their passport including their photo and personal information. Ask students to use **me llamo..., tengo ... años,** and **soy de...,** instead of language usually found on passports.
3. Have students prepare about 10 general questions and full-sentence answers in their passport. They also leave blank pages for stamps and for visas from various Spanish-speaking countries. The class as a whole may design the stamps and visas.
4. Have students make a rough draft for peer review before turning in a final version.
5. Have students design **La Aduana,** a mock checkpoint to pass through by correctly answering their general questions. The **aduanero/a** may wear a sign and a hat designed by the class.

Grading the project

Suggested point distribution (total = 100 points):

Appearance/Creativity	**40**
Originality	**25**
Peer-editing	**15**
Accurate use of vocabulary	**20**

¡A CONOCERTE MEJOR!

Introduction

Ask students what the role of the TV host is. What kinds of questions does the host ask? What do students want to learn about each other? Explain that students will put on a TV talk show to get to know each other.

Materials you may need

- Markers
- Name tags

Sequence

1. Divide students into groups of four: Host(ess) and three Guests. The group brainstorms appropriate personal questions for the Host(ess) to ask the Guests.
2. Students practice answering the questions, talking about their likes, dislikes, their schedules, and so on.
3. Teams stage mock TV presentations of their talk shows.
4. Members of the class, who are the audience, take notes during the TV show. After all teams have presented their shows, the class discusses what they have learned.

Grading the project

Suggested point distribution (total = 100 points):

Group questions	**25**
Oral presentation	**25**
Delivery of information	**25**
Group effort	**25**

🗼 LAS MATEMÁTICAS

This game provides students with a review of numbers 1–100. It is interdisciplinary and helpful for students with strong Logical/Mathematical intelligence.

Materials students may need

- ◆ Index cards
- ◆ Fine-tip markers

Procedure

1 Divide students into groups of three. Have groups make flash cards to practice their numbers in Spanish. They may look them up in the Review Vocabulary on pages 291–293.

2 Then introduce the phrases for addition, subtraction and multiplication. (**Uno y uno son dos; cinco menos tres son dos; cuatro por cuatro son dieciséis.**)

3 Each group makes five addition, five subtraction, and five multiplication problems. They are to be simple math problems. Have students write numerals on the cards for the equations and the answers.

4 The groups use the number and simple math problem flashcards to review the numbers.

5 Groups can interchange cards. You may wish to have a play-off between the winners from each group. This game can be played as a class by combining all cards and playing on teams.

🗼 EL RITMO

Use this game to review a variety of vocabulary and vocabulary categories. See Review Vocabulary on pages 291–293.

Preparation

1 Write categories on the board. (**la familia, las descripciones, los quehaceres**)

2 Demonstrate the following four-beat rhythm: On beat 1, slap your hands on your thighs. On beat 2, clap your hands. On beat 3, snap with the fingers of your left hand. On beat 4, snap with the fingers of your right hand.

3 Have students copy the four-beat rhythm.

Procedure

1 One person calls out a category such as **la familia** on beats three and four.

2 The next student adds a vocabulary item such as **el hijo** on the next beats three and four. Another student continues, adds **el tío,** and so on.

3 If the rhythm breaks down, stop and start again with a new category.

¡En camino!
TECHNOLOGY APPLICATIONS IN THE CLASSROOM

For a complete list of the media resources and their accompanying print matter guides, see page T69.

¿TE ACUERDAS?   pp. 2–3

Video
- Show *¿Te acuerdas?* See *Video Guide* pp. 1–4 for synopsis, teaching suggestions, and activity masters.

Audio
- As you play the **fotonovela,** have students read along.

PRIMER PASO   pp. 4–11

Video
- Show the **paso** opener to model greeting others and saying what you have. Have students read along.

Audio
- In Textbook Listening Activity 3, students listen to excerpts from conversations and decide whether the person is saying hello or goodbye.
- In Textbook Listening Activity 7, students practice saying where people are from.

Transparencies
- Use **¡En camino!** Teaching Transparency A to practice and review vocabulary for free-time activities.

¿TE ACUERDAS?   pp. 12–13

Video
- Show *¿Te acuerdas?* See *Video Guide* pp. 1–4.

Audio
- As you play the **fotonovela,** have students read along.

SEGUNDO PASO   pp. 14–21

Video
- Show the **paso** opener to model talking about what you do and when and describing people and places.

Audio
- In Textbook Listening Activity 21, students listen to students' comments and then decide whether the activities would be done at school or during the person's free time.
- In Textbook Listening Activity 30, students listen to people describing where they're going and then match the statements with the places.

PANORAMA CULTURAL   pp. 22–23

Audio
- Play the **Panorama cultural** as students read along.

Video
- Show the interviews to students. See *Video Guide* pp. 1–2, 5 for transcripts, teaching suggestions, and activity masters.

¿TE ACUERDAS?   pp. 24–25

Video
- Show *¿Te acuerdas?* See *Video Guide* pp. 1–4 for synopsis, teaching suggestions, and activity masters.

Audio
- As you play the **fotonovela,** have students read along.

TERCER PASO   pp. 26–33

Video
- Show the **paso** opener to model talking about how often people do things and talking about family.

Audio
- In Textbook Listening Activity 41, students listen to various statements and then answer questions about them.

Transparencies
- Use **¡En camino!** Teaching Transparency B to practice and review weather expressions.
- Use **¡En camino!** Teaching Transparency C to practice and review expressions for household chores.

REPASO   pp. 34–35

Video
- Replay *¿Te acuerdas?* and ask students to point out exchanges in which the characters perform the linguistic functions targeted in this chapter.

Test Generator
- Use the Test Generator to make a short practice test to help students prepare for the regular Chapter Test.

¡En camino!

🏠 HOMEWORK SUGGESTIONS

CAPÍTULO
Puente

Chapter Section	Presentation	Homework Options
Primer paso	**Así se dice,** p. 4	*CD-ROM Tutor,* Disc 1, Chapter 1, Activities 1–2
	Gramática, p. 5	*Pupil's Edition,* p. 5, Activities 4–5 *CD-ROM Tutor,* Disc 1, Chapter 4, Activity 4
	Gramática, p. 6	*Practice and Activity Book,* pp. 1, 2, Activities 1, 4
	¿Te acuerdas?, p. 7	*Pupil's Edition,* p. 7, Activity 9 *Practice and Activity Book,* p. 2, Activity 3
	Así se dice/ Nota gramatical, p. 9	*Pupil's Edition,* p. 9, Activity 13 *Practice and Activity Book,* pp. 3–4, Activities 5–7
	¿Te acuerdas?, p. 10	*Pupil's Edition,* p. 10, Activity 15 *CD-ROM Tutor,* Disc 1, Chapter 6, Activity 2
Segundo paso	**Así se dice,** p. 14	*Practice and Activity Book,* p. 5, Activity 8 *CD-ROM Tutor,* Disc 1, Chapter 3, Activity 1
	Nota gramatical, p. 16	*Pupil's Edition,* p. 17, Activity 28 *CD-ROM Tutor,* Disc 1, Chapter 4, Activity 2
	Nota gramatical, p. 18	*Pupil's Edition,* p. 18, Activity 29 *Practice and Activity Book,* p. 5, Activity 9
	Así se dice, p. 19	*Pupil's Edition,* p. 19, Activity 32
	Gramática, p. 19	*Pupil's Edition,* p. 20, Activity 33 *Practice and Activity Book,* p. 6, Activity 10
Tercer paso	**Nota gramatical,** p. 26	*Pupil's Edition,* p. 26, Activity 42 *Practice and Activity Book,* p. 8, Activity 14 *CD-ROM Tutor,* Disc 1, Chapter 5, Activity 4
	¿Te acuerdas?, p. 27	*Pupil's Edition,* pp. 27–28, Activities 43, 45
	Vocabulario, p. 28	*Pupil's Edition,* p. 28, Activity 46 *Practice and Activity Book,* p. 9, Activities 15–16
	Así se dice, p. 29	*Pupil's Edition,* p. 29, Activity 47 *Practice and Activity Book,* p. 10, Activities 17–18 *CD-ROM Tutor,* Disc 1, Chapter 6, Activity 2

¡En camino!

REVIEW

Students will need to refresh their memories after summer break. To make activities go more smoothly, begin each **paso** with a thorough vocabulary review. **Dibújalo** (students draw the noun, adjective, or action) and word-chain vocabulary games such as **¿Y qué más?** (**Tengo un perro divertido. ¿Y que más? gordo ...**) are fun ways to review.

MOTIVATING ACTIVITIES

• Ask students **¿Qué tiempo hace?** What other weather expressions do they remember? Ask a volunteer to draw pictures of each on the board.

• Ask students to talk in Spanish about what school supplies they need this year. List supplies on the board as students mention them.

PHOTO FLASH!

① The photo of Paco and his grandmother is from *Adelante* Level 1A Chapter 2. They check his room to find out which school supplies he already has and which ones he needs.

CAPÍTULO

Puente

¡En camino!

① Ya tienes una calculadora y muchos bolígrafos, ¿no?

xxiv

In this chapter you will review

PRIMER PASO

- greeting others
- saying what you have

SEGUNDO PASO

- talking about what you do and when
- describing people and places

TERCER PASO

- talking about how often you do things
- talking about your family

2 Éste es mi amigo. Trabaja conmigo después del colegio.

3 Debes cortar el césped con más frecuencia, hija.

FOCUSING ON OUTCOMES
Have students read the list of objectives for this chapter, then have them match each of the first three learner outcomes to a photo. (Photo 1: talking about what you have; Photo 2: talking about what you do and when; and Photo 3: discussing how often you do things.) Ask students to think of items they want at the beginning of a school year and several things they really need.

NATIVE SPEAKERS
Explain that a syllable is a group of letters (sounds) pronounced as a unit. (**ma-no, ca-ra, o-jo**) In Spanish all syllables have at least one vowel. Have students count the syllables in the sentences under the Chapter Opener photos as they say them aloud. Have students focus on the number of syllables (**golpes de voz**), not where the word breaks. Ask them to identify the stressed syllable (**sílaba tónica**) in each word.
1. Ya tie-nes u-na cal-cu-la-do-ra y mu-chos bo-lí-gra-fos. (17)
2. És-te es mi a-mi-go. Tra-ba-ja con-mi-go des-pués del co-le-gio. (19)
3. De-bes cor-tar el cés-ped con más fre-cuen-cia, hi-ja. (14)

Have them practice counting syllables in other words and phrases they know.

VIDEO INTEGRATION

En camino LEVEL 1B
Video Program
Videocassette 1, 1:32–3:18 OR
Videocassette 3, 00:00–00:00
(captioned version)

¡Ven conmigo! LEVEL 1
DVD Tutor, Disc 1

TEACHER NOTE

The **fotonovela** contains clips of video episodes from *Adelante* Level 1A *Video Program*.

VIDEO SYNOPSIS

Paco writes a letter to his pen pal Mercedes with the help of his friend Felipe. In the letter Paco describes himself and asks Mercedes to meet him at **pizzería Nápoli** on Saturday.

NATIVE SPEAKERS

Explain to native speakers from Latin America that while it may sound like Spaniards speak with a lisp, it's actually an additional sound in the language, similar to the *th* in the English word *think*. Model how Spaniards would distinguish between pairs of words. For example: **casa** *(ka sa)*, **caza** *(ka tha)*, **siento** *(syen to)*, **ciento** *(thyen to)*, **coser** *(ko ser)*, **cocer** *(ko ther)*. Examples from the video are **excelente** *(eks the len te)*, **sincero** *(sin the ro)*, and **organizado** *(or ga ni tha do)*.

¿TE ACUERDAS? PRIMER PASO

CD 7 Tr. 1

You met Paco and his friend Felipe in Chapters 1 and 2 of *Adelante, Level 1A.* Here, Paco has just gotten a letter in the mail from Mercedes, and Felipe is helping him write a reply. Look at the **fotonovela** to find out what kinds of things he talks about in his letter.

Paco　　**Felipe**

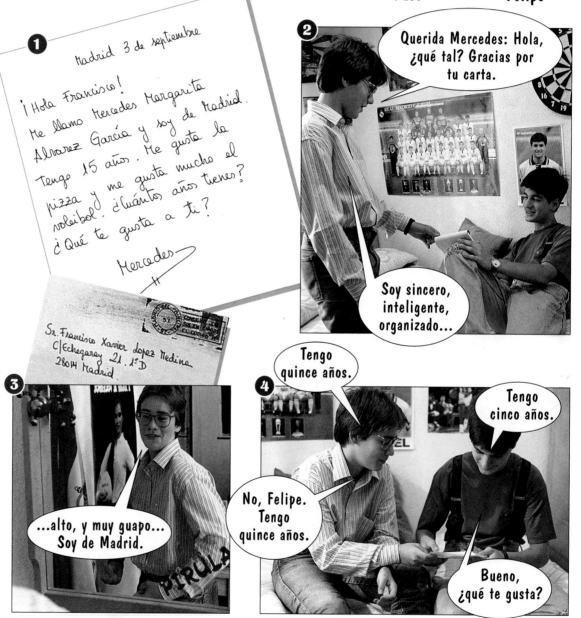

1 Madrid 3 de septiembre

¡Hola Francisco!
Me llamo Mercedes Margarita Álvarez García y soy de Madrid. Tengo 15 años. Me gusta la pizza y me gusta mucho el voleibol. ¿Cuántos años tienes? ¿Qué te gusta a ti?

Mercedes

Sr. Francisco Xavier López Medina
C/Echegaray 21, 1º D
28014 Madrid.

2 Querida Mercedes: Hola, ¿qué tal? Gracias por tu carta.

Soy sincero, inteligente, organizado...

3 ...alto, y muy guapo... Soy de Madrid.

4 Tengo quince años.

Tengo cinco años.

No, Felipe. Tengo quince años.

Bueno, ¿qué te gusta?

Pues... me gusta el fútbol... la biología... ¡ah! y me gusta mucho la pizza también. Mercedes, ¿conoces la pizzería Nápoli? ¿Qué tal si tú y yo comemos una pizza el sábado en la pizzería Nápoli?

1 ¿Comprendes?

Did you understand the **fotonovela**? Answer the questions. If you don't know the answer, use clues you see on the page. Answers in side column

1. Look at Mercedes's letter. What does she ask Paco?
2. How does Paco describe himself to Mercedes?
3. Where is Paco from? And Mercedes?
4. Why does Paco correct Felipe?
5. What does Paco say that he likes? What do both of them have in common?

2 Cierto o falso

Look at the **fotonovela** and respond to the following statements with **cierto** or **falso**. Change the false statements to make them true.

1. En su carta, Mercedes dice que tiene catorce años.
2. Paco dice que no es muy alto.
3. Felipe es bastante cómico.
4. A Paco y a Mercedes no les gustan los deportes.
5. Paco invita a Mercedes a comer pizza.

1. falso; Dice que tiene quince años.
2. falso; Paco dice que es alto.
3. cierto
4. falso; A Paco y a Mercedes les gustan los deportes.
5. cierto

¿TE ACUERDAS?   PRIMER PASO

tres **3**

CAPÍTULO PUENTE

PRESENTATION

Before showing the video ask students what they recall about Paco and Felipe from Chapters 1 and 2. Why did Paco get a letter from Mercedes? How did Mercedes get his address?

SUGGESTION

Have students correspond with pen pals. See the list of pen pal organizations on page T58 for names and addresses.

NATIVE SPEAKERS

Have native speakers begin an accent notebook. Have them title the first two pages **palabras llanas** and **palabras llanas con acento**. Explain these are words with the main stress on the next-to-the-last syllable (**la penúltima sílaba**). They often end in a vowel (**pluma**, *n*, or *s*). They are written with an accent mark (**con acento**) when they end in a consonant other than *n* or *s*. (**fútbol, césped**) Have them scan the **fotonovela** for **palabras llanas** with or without accents. Have them think of others that end in a consonant other than *n* or *s* (**árbol, lápiz, azúcar**) to include in their notebooks.

Answers to Activity 1

1. his age, what he likes to do.
2. as tall, good-looking, intelligent, sincere, and organized
3. Both are from Madrid.
4. Paco is not five years old.
5. He likes soccer, biology, and pizza. Both like pizza.

STANDARDS: 4.1   **3**

Bell work

Draw four or five weather symbols on the board. Have students write sentences saying what they like to do in each kind of weather.

☀ MOTIVATE

Ask students how they would greet a teacher after summer vacation. What would they say? How would they greet their friends? new classmates? Are they more formal or informal with their friends?

☀ TEACH

PRESENTATION
ASÍ SE DICE

Review formal and informal greetings as shown. Have students pick names from a jar (a teen's first name or the last name of an adult preceded by **señor, señorita,** or **señora**) Students come to the front of the room with a partner and introduce themselves using the names they drew. They greet one other appropriately, using gestures, then say goodbye in an appropriate manner.

KINESTHETIC LEARNERS

3 Have students raise their right hand for *hello* and left for *goodbye* in response to the taped conversations. Have them repeat the word or words used.

Greeting others; saying what you have

All grammar and vocabulary presented in the Bridge Chapter are review material.

ASÍ SE DICE   Greeting others

If you wanted to greet a friend, you might say:

> ¡Hola! ¿Qué tal?
> ¿Cómo estás?

Your friend might answer:

> Más o menos.
> Estupendo/a. ¿Y tú?

If you wanted to greet a teacher, you might say:

> ¡Buenos días, profesor/a! ¿Cómo está usted?

> Estoy bastante bien, gracias. ¿Y tú?

If you wanted to say goodbye, you might say:

> Chao.
> Adiós.

> Hasta luego.

---

3 ¿Vienen o se van?   Script and answers on p. T70

CD 7 Tr. 2

You overhear bits of many conversations throughout the day. Listen to the conversations and decide if people are saying hello or goodbye.

1. Martín
2. la señorita Ríos
3. Miguel
4. Ana
5. Juan Pablo
6. Marisa

GRAMÁTICA   The verb estar

PA
p. 1
Act. 2

You learned to use the verb **estar** to talk about how someone is doing and to say where someone or something is.

(yo)	est**oy**	(nosotros) (nosotras)	est**amos**
(tú)	est**ás**	(vosotros) (vosotras)	est**áis**
(usted) (él) (ella)	est**á**	(ustedes) (ellos) (ellas)	est**án**

4 En el pasillo

It's the first day of school, and Mauricio and Laura haven't seen each other in a while. Choose the correct form of **estar, tener,** or **ser** to complete each sentence.

1. LAURA ¡Hola, Mauricio! Hombre, ¿cómo (está/estás)? estás

2. MAURICIO ¡Buenos días, Laura! Yo (estamos/estoy) muy bien. ¿Y tú? estoy

3. LAURA Yo también (estoy/está) estupenda. estoy

4. MAURICIO Ésta es mi amiga Sara. Ella (soy/es) de Honduras. es

5. LAURA Hola, Sara. Yo (es/soy) de Iowa. Oye, ¿cuántos años (tienes/tengo)? soy tienes

6. SARA (Tiene/Tengo) quince años. Bueno, tengo que irme. Mucho gusto, Laura. Hasta luego. Tengo

Esta tortuga tiene ciento veintitrés años. Es de México.

5 Los chicos

Read the questions in column one. Then find the correct answer for each question in column two. Remember to pay attention to the verb forms.

1. ¿De dónde eres, Manuel? d
2. ¿Cuántos años tienes? c
3. Oye, ¿quién es la chica? e
4. ¿Cuántos años tiene tu amiga? a
5. ¿De dónde son ustedes? f
6. ¿Cuántos años tienen Marcos y Felipe? b

a. Tiene doce años. Y yo tengo trece años.
b. Tienen catorce años.
c. Tengo catorce años. Y tú, ¿cuántos años tienes?
d. Soy de Guadalajara, México.
e. Se llama Marta. Es de Chile.
f. Somos de aquí. Y tú, ¿de dónde eres?

PRESENTATION
GRAMÁTICA
Review and explain that verb forms in the book are presented with the corresponding subject pronouns. Have students explain why for **Paco, mi amiga, la mesa** the verb conjugation is **está**; while for **Ana y yo, tus hermanos y yo** it is **estamos**; and for **los chicos, las sillas** it is **están**. Have individual students name other subjects that are not pronouns. The class responds with the correct verb form.

SUGGESTION
4 Emphasize the importance of translating the meaning of a sentence, not just the words. Depending on context students will use **ser, estar,** or **tener**.

ADDITIONAL PRACTICE
5 Make two sets of flashcards of verb forms and corresponding pronouns. One set is phrased as questions and the other as answers. Pass out each set to a different side of the room. Students with question verbs take turns standing and saying their form. Students with the corresponding answer stand and form a pair with them: **¿Eres?** pairs with **Soy,** and so on.

LANGUAGE NOTE
5 Remind students that **quién** takes the third-person verb forms.

STANDARDS: 1.2, 4.1, 5.1   5

PRESENTATION
GRAMÁTICA
Brainstorm with students to generate two lists, one of classroom objects and the other of personal traits. (**cuaderno, lápiz, libro; cómico, inteligente, bajo**) Use the list of objects to have students practice the forms of (**no**) **tener** and the list of personal traits to practice the forms of **ser**.

ADDITIONAL PRACTICE
6 Have students work in pairs to copy the six phrases on strips of paper. Together they respond to each one. They turn the strips face down and take turns drawing slips and responding.

🏰 GAME
Pass out cards with 0–9 written on them. Call out a two- or three-digit number in Spanish. Those holding one of the digits used to form the number come forward and stand in order.

ADDITIONAL PRACTICE
Have pairs describe the people in the pictures as if they had just met them. Each partner talks about the people in two of the photos. (**Se llama Federico, tiene 15 años...**)

STANDARDS: 1.1, 1.2, 4.1

PA
pp. 1–2
Acts. 1, 4

GRAMÁTICA The verbs **tener** and **ser**

You learned to use the verb **tener** to talk about how old someone is or to say what they have. The verb **ser** is used to describe someone or something or to talk about where someone is from.

ten**go**	ten**emos**		**soy**	**somos**
t**ienes**	ten**éis**		**eres**	**sois**
t**iene**	t**ienen**		**es**	**son**

6 ¡Mucho gusto!

How would you respond to each of these statements or questions? Act out each short conversation with a partner. Then switch roles. Answers will vary.

1. ¡Buenos días!
2. Adiós.
3. ¿Cómo está usted?
4. ¿Cuántos años tienes?
5. ¿De dónde eres?
6. Estoy bien, gracias, ¿y tú?

¿Se te ha olvidado?
numbers 0–199
Consulta las páginas 291–293

7 El comité de bienvenida Script and answers on p. T70

You're making a photo directory for your summer camp, but you need more information. First look at each photo and figure out what information is missing. Then listen as each student tells you about him- or herself. Write the needed information on a separate sheet of paper.

CD 7 Tr. 3

	a	b	c	d
NOMBRE	Federico	María Luisa		Alfredo
EDAD	quince años		catorce años	
ORIGEN		Argentina	Colombia	República Dominicana

8 ¡Vamos a conocernos!

Imagine that you're a new student at your school. Introduce yourself to two students sitting near you. Tell them your name, how old you are, and where you're from. Then introduce your new friends to another student.

MODELO

KIM ¡Hola! Me llamo Kim. Tengo trece años y soy de Kentucky.

EFRAÍN Mucho gusto, Kim. Soy Efraín.

KIM Mucho gusto, Efraín. Ésta es mi amiga, Alicia. Tiene doce años.

Nos gusta mucho bailar.

¿Te acuerdas? p. 2 Act. 3

To talk about what you and others like, use the indirect object pronouns with the verb **gustar**.

me	nos
te	os
le	les

—¿Te gusta la música pop?

—Sí, me gusta. A Ana le gusta también.

To talk about liking more than one thing, use **gustan**.

—Te gustan los libros cómicos, ¿no?

9 La fiesta del club de español

It's up to Chuy to plan the next Spanish Club party. He needs to find out what the members like. Fill in the blanks with the correct pronouns to complete conversations he had with some members.

1. —Inés, ¿__1__ gusta el voleibol?
   —Bueno, Chuy, no __2__ gustan mucho los deportes, pero el voleibol está bien.

2. —Amado, ¿a ti y a Ana __3__ gusta la música de Maná?
   —Sí, claro. Es estupenda. __4__ gusta muchísimo.

3. —David, ¿a ustedes __5__ gusta comer comida mexicana?
   —A mí __6__ gusta mucho la comida mexicana, pero a Tere no __7__ gustan los jalapeños *(hot chile peppers)*.

1. te
2. me
3. les
4. Nos
5. les
6. me
7. le

COOPERATIVE LEARNING

8 Divide the class into groups of four. Have each group write a script for the scene in Activity 8. They decide together what each person says. (name, age, and where he or she is from) Students rehearse and perform for the class.

PRESENTATION

¿Te acuerdas?
Talk to students about your likes and dislikes. Ask volunteers what sports, music, or food they like. Then pass out two copies of each vocabulary flashcard with phrases like **jugar al fútbol, comer tacos, escuchar música rock.** Students search for their twin, asking **¿Qué te gusta hacer?** When students finish, ask pairs **¿Qué les gusta hacer? Nos gusta...**

PAIR WORK

9 Have the class come up with a list of 10 things they like or don't like. (both singular and plural things) List them on the board. Have students work in pairs, each numbering 1 through 10 on a piece of paper. Pairs take turns going down the list, saying whether they like each thing. (**Me gusta(n)...** or **No me gusta(n)...**) Have students report their partners' likes and dislikes.

PRESENTATION

VOCABULARIO

Display **¡En camino!** Teaching Transparency A to review these activities. Have students identify the action in each scene using the infinitive. Have students work in pairs to find out which activities their partners like to do.

LANGUAGE NOTE

10 Remind students that all answers in this activity will use the form **gusta**, not **gustan**. Point out that **gusta** agrees with the verb in the infinitive, and not with the infinitive's plural object. (**leer revistas, practicar deportes, jugar a los videojuegos**)

COOPERATIVE LEARNING

11 Divide students into groups of three or four. Pass out sheets listing the 13 activities reviewed in the vocabulary. One member of the group fills in the chart as students take turns asking each other whether or not they like each activity. Another student serves as spokesperson to report the results of the survey to the class.

¡En camino! A

VOCABULARIO

mirar la televisión

hacer la tarea

practicar deportes

organizar el cuarto

escuchar música

dibujar

cuidar a tu hermano/a

correr por el parque

leer revistas

ir al centro comercial	*to go to the mall*
comer comida mexicana	*to eat Mexican food*
hablar por teléfono	*to talk on the phone*
jugar a los videojuegos	*to play videogames*

10 ¿Qué les gusta hacer?

Choose four of the activities shown above. Use each of the people listed in the word box and say if that person likes or doesn't like the activity.   Answers will vary.

MODELO   A mi amigo Julio le gusta dibujar.

yo
nosotros/as
mi amigo/a
mis amigos/as

11 Y a nosotros, ¿qué nos gusta?

How much do you have in common with the members of your group? Take turns asking each other whether you like each of the activities shown in the **Vocabulario**. Record everyone's responses in a chart. Then choose a spokesperson to report to the class. Use **(no) nos gusta, (no) les gusta, (no) le gusta,** or **(no) me gusta** in your report.

ASÍ SE DICE   Saying what you have

To find out what a friend has, ask:

¿Qué hay en tu cuarto?

¿Qué tienes en tu cuarto?

¿Cuántos bolígrafos y cuántas calculadoras hay en tu mochila?

Your friend might answer:

En mi cuarto hay una silla, pero necesito dos.

Tengo un escritorio, pero no tengo carteles. Quiero un cartel.

Hay tres bolígrafos y una calculadora.

p. 3
Acts. 5–6

12 ¿Cuántos tienes?

Work with a partner. Take turns asking each other the following questions. For more words for things you have, look on pages 291–293. Answers will vary.

1. ¿Qué tienes en tu escritorio?
2. ¿Cuántos lápices tienes?
3. ¿Qué quieres para tu cuarto?

NOTA GRAMATICAL

To say *there is* or *there are* in Spanish, use **hay.**

En mi cuarto **hay** una cama.
También **hay** dos sillas y un escritorio.

13 ¿Qué hay en tu cuarto?

Imagine that the photo is of your room. Write sentences telling four things that are in your room. Then write two sentences about what you want or need for your imaginary room. Use **Necesito...** and **Quiero...**
Answers will vary.

PRESENTATION
ASÍ SE DICE
Say what you have in your classroom and reintroduce **necesitar** and **querer.** Talk about what you want and need. Remind students of the stem change in **querer.**

NOTA GRAMATICAL
To review the uses of **hay, está,** and **es,** display **Adelante** Level 1A Teaching Transparency 2-B to talk about what is in the room (**hay**), 4-2 to say where things are in the city (**estar**), and 3-B to talk about what people or things are like (**ser**).

PAIR WORK
12 Have the class create a vocabulary pool to use in their answers. Write the vocabulary on the board. Then have students do the activity in pairs.

PREWRITING
13 Before students do individual writing, ask them to name objects in the room. Then, as a class, create "a wish list" on the board for the imaginary room. Then have them work individually.

PAIR WORK

14 In pairs, students make the two lists. They may use the dictionary in the back of the textbook. Have volunteers write their lists on the board. Which items appear most frequently? Which are the most creative? Have the class check for correct usage of **un** and **una** in the lists on the board and correct any errors.

LANGUAGE NOTE

Explain the article is dropped after a negated **hay**. (**hay una cama; no hay cama**)

PRESENTATION

¿Te acuerdas?
List up to eight classroom or bedroom items on the board. Make half of the items singular and half plural. Write a subject pronoun next to the list and have students read it with the corresponding possessive pronoun. For example, write **yo** next to the list and students read it with **mi** before each item.

SUGGESTION

15 Read this dialogue aloud. Explain that the characters have forgotten things, but they end up helping each other. In pairs, have students read through the dialogue to find out who helps whom. Then go through the dialogue as a class.

14 En la sala de clase

Look at the photo of the room for Activity 13 on page 9. Which things are also found in your classroom and which are not? Make two lists, one showing how many there are of each thing (**hay**) and another showing what isn't there (**no hay**).

Hay:	No hay:
	una cama

¿Te gustan mis anteojos nuevos?

¿Te acuerdas?

To show possession in Spanish, use the possessive adjectives **mi, tu, su,** and **nuestro/a**. They agree in number with the item possessed.

Aquí están **mis** libros y **tu** cuaderno.

Los libros de **nuestra** profesora de español están encima de **su** escritorio.

15 En el colegio

Read and complete the following dialogue with the correct possessive adjectives. Make sure they match the items they describe.

1. —Antonio, ¿dónde están (tus/tu) lápices de colores? tus
2. —¿(Tus/Mis) lápices de colores? Están en casa. Mis
3. —Ay, yo no tengo (mis/sus) lápices aquí tampoco. Necesitamos unos lápices para hacer la tarea de geografía. ¿Y Silvio? mis
4. —Silvio tiene (su/sus) lápices de colores hoy, pero no tiene el libro de geografía. sus
5. —Tengo una idea... Silvio usa (su/tu) libro de geografía y tú y yo usamos los lápices de colores de Silvio. ¿Está bien? tu
6. —Sí. Así *(that way)* todos hacemos (nuestro/nuestra) tarea. Perfecto. Vamos a hablar con Silvio. nuestra

16 ¿Qué tienes?

First make a list of six things that you would have in your ideal room. Then ask your partner if he or she has each of those items in his or her ideal room.

MODELO —¿Tienes un televisor en tu cuarto?
—Sí, tengo un televisor grande.

17 El chico travieso

Read the cartoon. Remember to use the reading strategies of looking at pictures, looking for familiar words, and looking for cognates. After you read the cartoon, answer the questions. Answers will vary. Possible answers:

pan tostado *toast*   te vas *you're going*

©Watterson, Dist. by Universal Press Syndicate. Reprinted with permission. All rights reserved.

1. Why do you think Calvin is eating in bed? Because he's sick.
2. Why does Calvin shout? He shouts to get his mom to bring him more toast.
3. Where does his mother say he is going tomorrow? Why? He's going to school. Because if he's well enough to shout, he's well enough to go to school.

18 Una carta a Melitza

First read the letter from your new pen pal, Melitza. Then answer her letter. Greet her and tell her how old you are and where you're from. Tell your pen pal four things you like or like to do and two things you don't like or don't like to do. Remember to start your letter with **Querida Melitza,** or **Hola, Melitza.**

el 24 de septiembre

Hola,

¿Qué tal? Yo me llamo Melitza Bello. Tengo catorce años y soy de La Paz, Bolivia. Me gusta estudiar el inglés. Quiero estudiar el francés también. No me gusta practicar los deportes. Me gusta más leer y escuchar música. No me gusta la música de jazz, pero me gusta mucho la música pop. Y tú, ¿estudias el español? ¿Qué te gusta hacer? ¿Cuántos años tienes? Escribe pronto, por favor.

Saludos,
Melitza Bello

SUGGESTION

17 Have students work through the assignment in pairs. Then answer the questions with the whole class. Have students identify familiar words and cognates.

RE-ENTRY

18 Remind students to use **me gusta** or **no me gusta** with activities (verbs) or when talking about one thing that is liked and to use **(no) me gustan** with plural things that are liked.

☀ CLOSE

Divide the class into groups of three. Each group writes three sentences on the board: one stating something they all like, another stating two things they don't like, and a third stating what they all like to do. (**Nos gusta cantar.**)

☀ ASSESS

▶ Testing Program, pp. 1–2
Quiz 1
Audio CD 7, Tr. 14

▶ Grammar and Vocabulary Quizzes
Quiz 1A or
Alternative Quiz 1A

▶ Alternative Assessment Guide, p. 18

PERFORMANCE ASSESSMENT

Have pairs of students role-play a situation in which an interviewer asks a famous sports figure questions related to the star's likes and dislikes.

VIDEO INTEGRATION

En camino LEVEL 1B
Video Program
Videocassette 1, 3:17–5:05

¡Ven conmigo! LEVEL 1
DVD Tutor, Disc 1

TEACHER NOTE
The **fotonovela** contains clips of video episodes from **Adelante** Level 1A *Video Program*.

VIDEO SYNOPSIS
Claudia is starting the year at a new school. She meets the school principal, who introduces her to the students in her first class. While they wait for their teacher, Claudia talks with her new classmates. They ask her where she is from. She shows them some pictures of places in Mexico City, and they talk about some likes and dislikes. (parks and museums)

PRESENTATION
Before showing the video ask if students remember what Claudia does with her friends in Chapters 3 and 4. What do they remember about her? (she is a new student at the school in Cuernavaca, she is from Mexico City, she likes to go to parks and museums with friends, she and her friends go to Taxco)

¿TE ACUERDAS? SEGUNDO PASO

CD 7 Tr. 4

In Chapters 3 and 4 you met Claudia and her friends from Mexico. Here, you'll see her and her new friends describing what they like to do and where they like to go. Do you like to do any of the same things that Claudia does?

María Inés, Fernando y Claudia

> Mira... me gusta ir al parque con mi familia y también me gusta visitar los museos. Son buenos. Éste es el Museo Antropológico. Y ella es una amiga. A ella le gusta ir a los museos también.

> A mí no me gustan los museos. Son aburridos. ¡Pero me gusta ir a los parques!

19 ¿Cierto o falso?

Responde a las oraciones con **cierto** o **falso**.

1. A Claudia le gusta ir al Museo Antropológico en la capital. cierto
2. Fernando dice que la amiga de Claudia en la foto es bonita. cierto
3. Al amigo de Fernando no le gusta jugar al basquetbol. falso
4. Hay mucha tarea en la clase. cierto
5. Los exámenes en la clase son fáciles. falso

20 ¿Quién lo diría?

Which of the characters in the **fotonovela** would be most likely to say the following? Look at the photo on page 12 to help you remember the characters' names.

1. ¿Quieres ir al museo conmigo?
2. Quiero conocer a la amiga de Claudia.
3. No me gustan los exámenes difíciles.
4. Es más divertido el parque que el museo.

1. Claudia
2. Fernando
3. Fernando
4. María Inés

¿TE ACUERDAS?   SEGUNDO PASO

trece 13

CAPÍTULO PUENTE

CULTURE NOTE
The National Museum of Anthropology in Mexico City contains sculpture, jewelry, ceramics, and other artifacts from many civilizations, including the Olmec, Toltec, Mayan, and Aztec. It contains exhibits that explain the region's civilizations, architecture, and art.

LANGUAGE NOTE
Asks students what they think **buena onda** and **híjole** mean from context. *(nice, wow)*

SUGGESTIONS
19 Ask volunteers to talk about their experiences being a student at a new school. What did people ask to get to know them? How was the new school different?

NATIVE SPEAKERS
Have native speakers add two pages to their accent notebooks and title them **palabras agudas** and **palabras agudas con acento.** Explain that these have the main stress on the last syllable (**la última sílaba**) and that they are written with an accent mark when they end in a vowel or the consonants *n* or *s.* (**sartén, maní**) Explain that they often end in the consonants *d, l, r,* and *z.* (**director**) When they end in these consonants, no accent is needed. Have students scan the **fotonovela** for **palabras agudas.** (**también, está**) Have them think of other examples. (**café, jamás, avión**)

STANDARDS: 1.2, 5.1   **13**

Bell work

Write the names of two adults and two children on the board. Have students copy them and write an appropriate greeting and goodbye for each.

☀ MOTIVATE

Write class times on the board and ask students what classes they have. Why would they ask a friend about a class schedule? (to see if they have a class or lunch together)

☀ TEACH

PRESENTATION
ASÍ SE DICE

Create a list of school-subject vocabulary with students. Then have partners ask each other which subjects they like and **¿Quién es el profesor de…?** Then list the words in **Así se dice** on the board that tell "when" and review their meanings.

KINESTHETIC LEARNERS

21 Have students make a letter *c* or *t* with their hands to indicate if the activity is during **el colegio** or **el tiempo libre**.

Answers to Activity 22

a. Son las cinco de la tarde.
b. Son las doce menos veinte de la mañana.
c. Son las seis y cinco de la tarde.
d. Es la una y diez de la tarde.
e. Son las deiz y cuarto de la mañana.

SEGUNDO PASO

Talking about what you do and when; describing people and places

PA
p. 5
Act. 8

ASÍ SE DICE   Talking about what you do and when

If someone asked you:

¿Qué clases tienes por la mañana?

¿A qué hora tienes la clase de arte?

¿Qué haces después de clases?

¿Qué te gusta hacer los sábados?

You might answer:

Primero tengo francés, después historia y luego computación.

A las dos de la tarde.

Voy a casa. Primero estudio y luego mis amigos y yo nadamos.

Los sábados me gusta descansar. Mis hermanas y yo vamos al cine.

¿Se te ha olvidado?
school subjects
Consulta las páginas 291–293

¿Te acuerdas?

To find out what time it is, ask **¿Qué hora es?** To tell time say **son las (ocho), son las (nueve) y cuarto, son las (diez) y media, son las (once) menos cuarto.** For times including 1:00 say **es la una (y media).**

de la mañana	A.M.
de la tarde	P.M.
de la noche	P.M.

21 ¿Día escolar o tiempo libre?
Script and answers on p. T70

CD 7 Tr. 5

Listen to each student's comment. Then decide if they're talking about something they do during **el colegio** or **el tiempo libre**.

22 ¿Qué hora es?

Say what time it is according to the watches. Answers in side column

a
P.M.

b
A.M.

c
P.M.

d
P.M.

e
A.M.

23 El horario Answers in side column

Imagine that you're in a new school. First use the times and classes in the boxes to write your own schedule. Then, with a partner, take turns asking each other the questions that follow. Answer by using the schedule you wrote.

| 8:30 – 9:15 |
| 9:20 – 10:05 |
| 10:10 – 10:55 |
| 11:50 – 12:30 |
| 12:55 – 1:20 |
| 1:25 – 2:10 |
| 2:15 – 3:00 |

el español
el inglés
las matemáticas
la geografía
las ciencias
la educación física
el arte

1. ¿Qué clases tienes por la mañana?
2. ¿A qué hora tienes la clase de arte?
3. ¿A qué hora tienes la clase de inglés?
4. ¿Qué clases tienes por la tarde?
5. ¿A qué hora tienes la clase de ciencias?

24 Adivina

A Imagine that you're visiting the Dominican Republic. Look at the schedule of upcoming events. Pick the event you want to see and decide what time you'll go.

Guía de Actividades Culturales - III

PALACIO DE BELLAS ARTES

Dirección: Ave. Máximo Gómez Esq. Ave. Independencia Teléfono: 682-1325 Boletería: 687-3300

"Conejitos Navideños"
Domingo 1ero / Hora: 5:30 p.m.
Entrada: $60.00 p/p

"Ricitos de Oro"
Miércoles 4, Jueves 5 y Viernes 6
Hora: 9:00 y 11:00 a.m. / 4:00 p.m.
Sábado 7 y Domingo 8
Hora: 4:00 y 6:00 p.m. Entrada: $75.00 p/p

"La Niña y el Universo"
Función de Ballet Infantil
Martes 10 y Miércoles 11
Hora: 5:30 p.m. / Entrada: $50.00 p/p

"Los Miserables"
Universidad Autónoma de
Santo Domingo (UASD)
Viernes 13, Sábado 14 y Domingo 15
Hora: 8:30 p.m.
Entrada: $50.00 p/p

"Fiesta Mágica de Navidad"
Miércoles 18 y Jueves 19
Hora: 10:00 y 11:00 a.m. - 12:00 m
4:00, 6:00 y 8:30 p.m.
Entrada: $50.00 p/p

B Based on the schedule, take turns asking each member of your group what time his or her favorite event is. Then guess which one they're planning to attend. Be prepared to report to the class about which event most people liked.

MODELO —¿A qué hora es tu evento?
—Es a las cuatro de la tarde.
—Tú vas a "Ricitos de Oro", ¿verdad?

RE-ENTRY

23 Review the difference between **son las ocho** and **a las ocho.** Using a transparency of an imaginary student's schedule and a paper-plate clock, alternate asking **¿Qué hora es?** and **¿A qué hora es...?** Change the position of the hands on the paper clock every other question.

CULTURE NOTE

Explain that people say **Son las siete y media de la tarde** for 7:30 PM in some Spanish-speaking countries. Ask students what times they think are afternoon and evening. Is 7:30 PM afternoon or evening for them?

ADDITIONAL PRACTICE

24 After students have completed the activity in small groups, list the events at the **Palacio de Bellas Artes** on the board. Have each student report on a classmate's favorite activity by saying **Mary va a _____.** Tally the totals for each event. Have students report them. (**Seis estudiantes van a _____.**)

Answers to Activity 23

Answers will vary. Possible answers:
1. Por la mañana tengo...
2. Tengo la clase de arte a la/las...
3. Tengo la clase de inglés a la/las...
4. Por la tarde tengo...
5. Tengo la clase de ciencias a la/las...

KINESTHETIC LEARNERS
25 Have small groups of students review the vocabulary by miming an activity. Other students guess the verb they are acting out.

PREWRITING
26 As a prewriting activity, have students write **primero, antes, Palacio de Bellas Artes** and **después** on their paper with several spaces between each. Then have them choose two activities listed next to the writing activity and decide which they would like to do before the event and which they would like to do after. They write their choices under **antes** and **después**. Then have students look at the events calendar to decide which event to attend with their friend. They list the activity under **Palacio de Bellas Artes** on their paper.

PRESENTATION
NOTA GRAMATICAL
Have students practice verb conjugation in a dialogue format. Students choose a verb according to what they would like to talk about. For example, —**¿Qué compras para las clases? —Compro bolígrafos, carpetas y papel. ¿Qué compran tú y tus hermanos? —Compramos...**

25 ¿Qué te gusta hacer?

Rosa is getting to know her new classmates. Complete her questions or comments by choosing the correct verb.

1. Olga, ¿te gusta más (practicar/montar) en bicicleta o (nadar/pasear) en la piscina? montar, nadar
2. Silvia y Diego, a ustedes les gusta (mirar/escuchar) música y (mirar/practicar) la televisión, ¿verdad? escuchar, mirar
3. A mí me gusta pasear con mi amiga los sábados, pero necesito (mirar/cuidar) a mi hermano. cuidar
4. José, a ti te gusta (comprar/practicar) deportes los sábados, ¿verdad? practicar
5. Julio y Zoraida, a ustedes les gusta (caminar/hablar) por teléfono todos los días, ¿no? hablar
6. Y Diana, ¿te gusta más (tocar/cantar) el piano o la guitarra? tocar

26 ¿Quieres ir?

Write a note to a friend. Ask if he or she wants to go with you to one of the events that you read about in Activity 24. Say what time the event is. Then say what you want to do before and after the event. Use **antes de, primero,** and **después de.** Look on pages 291–293 for more activities.

MODELO Hola, Carmela. ¿Quieres ir a...? Y antes de...

tomar un refresco

caminar en el parque

comer un helado

montar en bicicleta

mirar la televisión

NOTA GRAMATICAL
To conjugate **comprar** or any other regular -**ar** verb, take the part of the verb called the stem (**compr**-) and add these endings:

compr**o**	compr**amos**
compr**as**	compr**áis**
compr**a**	compr**an**

Ella siempre compra flores después del trabajo. Cuando caminan por la calle, todos miran las flores bonitas.

27 Después de clases

Take turns asking if your partner and others do the activities shown in the drawings. Your partner will answer when they do the activity. Use phrases like **después de clases, en el tiempo libre, siempre, a veces,** and **todos los días.** Answers in side column

MODELO —¿Estudias el francés?
—Sí, estudio el francés todos los días.

tú y tu amiga/
practicar el basquetbol

ellos/preparar la cena

la señora Cedeño/
tocar el piano

ellas/bailar

tú/cuidar a tu hermano

Manuel/hablar por teléfono

28 Hacemos de todo

Create six sentences by combining elements from each of the three boxes. Remember to use the correct form of each word. Then go back and add a fourth element to your sentences telling when or how often. Use the time phrases given in Activity 27.

MODELO Nosotras hablamos por teléfono todos los días. Answers will vary.

tú	practicar	un refresco
él, ella	tomar	en la piscina
yo	hablar	la guitarra
nosotros/as	montar	en bicicleta
ellos, ellas	nadar	la ropa
	preparar	por teléfono
	lavar	el fútbol
	escuchar	la cena
	tocar	la música

SEGUNDO PASO

diecisiete **17**

SLOWER PACE
27 Before students do this activity, write the five adverbial phrases on the board. Tell students that for each drawing you will give them a clue as to which phrase to use in their responses by paraphrasing the idea. For example, you say **los lunes, los martes, los miércoles,** and so on. Students say **todos los días** or **siempre.** You say **a las cuatro de la tarde.** They say **después de clases** as part of their answer. Leave the five phrases on the board for Activities 27 and 28.

ADDITIONAL PRACTICE
28 After students complete this exercise, have them work with a partner. One chooses words from the first two columns. The partner says an original sentence using the words and one of the adverbial phrases on the board. Be sure students use appropriate prepositions. (**en, a,** and **por**)

Answers to Activity 27

Answers will vary. Possible answers:
1. Nosotras practicamos el basquetbol después de clases.
2. Ellos preparan la cena todos los días.
3. La señora Cedeño toca el piano en su tiempo libre.
4. Ellas bailan después de clases.
5. Yo cuido a mi hermano a veces por la tarde.
6. Manuel habla por teléfono a veces.

PRESENTATION

NOTA GRAMATICAL
¿Te acuerdas?
Talk about where you go during your day. (**Voy al colegio a las siete de la mañana. Después de clases voy a la piscina para nadar...**) Ask students **¿Adónde vas después de clases?** Students answer using the places listed in **¿Te acuerdas?** Then ask them **¿Qué haces allí?**

SUGGESTIONS
30 Before playing the tape, have students copy the four names on a piece of paper. As they listen, they write the correct place from the list in **¿Te acuerdas?** next to each name. Review answers as a class.

31 To review **¿dónde?** and **¿adónde?** give several examples of questions using **¿dónde?** with **estar** and **¿adónde?** with **ir.** Show how **tú y tu mamá** is **ustedes** and **mi mamá y yo** is **nosotros/as.**

Answers to Activity 31
Van al colegio a las siete y media de la mañana.
Voy a la biblioteca para hacer la tarea a las cuatro de la tarde.
Van a la tienda para comprar ropa a las cuatro y media de la tarde.
Va al cine para ver la película a las cinco y cuarto de la tarde.

PA p. 5 Act. 9

NOTA GRAMATICAL
You learned to use the verb **ir** to talk about where someone is going.

voy *I*		**vamos** *we*	
vas *you*		**vais** *you*	
va *he, she*		**van** *they*	

¿Te acuerdas?

Do you remember the names for places?

la piscina	*pool*	**el correo**	*post office*
el parque	*park*	**el supermercado**	
la tienda	*store*		*supermarket*
el cine	*movie theater*	**la casa**	*house*
la biblioteca	*library*	**el gimnasio**	*gym*

30 El sábado Script and answers on p. T70

CD 7 Tr. 6 It's Saturday morning. Listen as Mrs. Caldera asks her family where they're going. On a separate sheet of paper, write where each person is going using the names of places in **¿Te acuerdas?**

1. el señor Caldera   2. Juana y Pepe   3. Érica   4. la señora Caldera

31 ¿A qué hora? Answers in side column

Take turns asking each other where the people are going. Then ask what time they'll be going.

MODELO —¿Adónde van tú y tu mamá esta tarde?
—Vamos a la casa para preparar la cena.
—¿A qué hora van?
—Vamos a las siete.

7:00 P.M./tú y tu mamá

7:30 A.M./tus amigos

4:00 P.M./tú

4:30 P.M./tus amigos

5:15 P.M./tu hermano

29 ¿Adónde vamos?
Complete the following sentences with the correct form of the verb **ir.**

1. Esteban y Cristina _____ al colegio a las ocho en la mañana. van
2. Rubén siempre _____ a la cafetería para comer su almuerzo. va
3. Yo _____ a clase primero y luego _____ a la biblioteca. voy, voy
4. Y tú, ¿_____ a la biblioteca también? vas
5. Nosotros _____ a casa después de clase. vamos

ASÍ SE DICE

Describing people and places

PA
p. 6
Act. 11

If someone asked you:	You might respond:
¿Cómo es tu profesora de inglés?	Es muy estricta, pero no es aburrida.
¿Cómo son tus amigos?	Mis amigos son muy simpáticos y divertidos.
¿Cómo es tu colegio?	Es grande y bonito.
¿Dónde está tu colegio?	No está lejos de mi casa. Está al lado del parque.

32 Los adjetivos

Complete the sentences with the best descriptive word from the word box.

> feas
> grande
> cómica
> inteligente
> fácil

1. La tarea es muy ======. fácil
2. Mi amigo es ====== porque lee muchos libros. inteligente
3. La Casa Blanca es muy ======. grande
4. Las cucarachas *(cockroaches)* son ======. feas
5. Esta novela es muy buena y ======. cómica

La biblioteca es grande y tiene libros cómicos y divertidos.

GRAMÁTICA — Adjective agreement

PA
p. 6
Act. 10

Remember that adjectives such as **divertido** change to match the nouns they describe.

un libro **divertido** → unos libros **divertidos**
una clase **divertida** → unas clases **divertidas**

1. To describe both males and females, use a masculine plural adjective.
   Ana y Luis son **simpáticos.**
2. To make adjectives ending in a vowel plural, add **-s.**
   Los libros son **interesantes.**
3. For adjectives ending with a consonant, add **-es** to form the plurals.
   Las clases son **difíciles.**

SEGUNDO PASO

diecinueve **19**

PRESENTATION

ASÍ SE DICE
Use Teaching Transparencies 2-B (**El cuarto de Débora**), 3-B (descriptions), 4-2 (city), and 1-2 (people) from **Adelante** Level 1A, if available; or use pictures from magazines to review describing nouns. Model descriptive vocabulary. Then ask students to describe the people and things in the pictures. Next have students work in pairs to describe friends or family members.

GRAMÁTICA
On the board list the feminine singular of all adjectives reviewed (except **fácil** and **difícil**). Ask students to name some females that these adjectives describe. (**Mi madre es cómica.**) Then ask them to name some males these adjectives describe. (**Mi tío Lalo es cómico.**) Repeat this with plural nouns. (**sus hermanos, mis amigas**)

SUGGESTION
32 Before students do this activity, remind them that they are looking for two things: a word that makes sense and that also agrees with the other words in the sentence.

KINESTHETIC LEARNERS

33 Review the vocabulary first by having a boy and a girl act out an agreed-upon adjective. The class responds with both the masculine and feminine forms of the word.

ADDITIONAL PRACTICE

33 When students have finished individual work, have volunteers read a sentence about each family member.

 RE-ENTRY

34 Review prepositions by putting objects on top of and under a table, by pointing to something near and far (**aquí, allí**), and by describing where students in the class are sitting. (**Susan está al lado de Mike.**) Remind students that **estar** is used to talk about location; **ser** is used in the previous activity to describe qualities of things.

VISUAL LEARNERS

When students are familiar with the vocabulary, have them describe people in magazine pictures in small groups. Group members guess which picture is being described.

33 El domingo en el parque

The Velázquez family is having a picnic in the park. Look at the drawing. Write at least five sentences describing members of the family. For more descriptive adjectives see pages 291–293.

MODELO   La señora Velázquez es muy simpática y...   Answers will vary.

alto
guapo
pequeño
cómico
travieso
inteligente
malo
antipático
bonito

La señora Velázquez

Evelina

Adriana y Alfonso

María

Sancho

34 ¿Dónde está?

Look at the drawing of the Velázquez family and use words from the box to complete the sentences telling where each person or thing is. You will not use all of the words.

1. La comida está ═══ la mesa.
2. El basquetbol está ═══ la mesa.
3. Sancho está ═══ la mesa.
4. Evelina está ═══ la mesa.
5. Adriana está ═══ Alfonso.
6. María está ═══ la mesa.

al lado de   cerca de
debajo de   aquí   allí
lejos de   encima de

1. encima de
2. debajo de
3. cerca de, al lado de, encima de

4. encima de
5. al lado de, cerca de
6. lejos de

35 La sala de clase

Take turns having your partner guess which thing in your classroom you're thinking of. Without naming the thing, say what it's near, on top of, underneath, or far from. Each of you should guess four items. Answers will vary.

MODELO   —Está cerca de la puerta, pero lejos de mi escritorio.
         —¿Es la ventana?

36 Después del colegio

Work with a partner. Take turns asking each other if the following people do the activities listed in the word box. If they do an activity, ask where. Ask your partner about three activities. Answers will vary.

MODELO   —Tú y tu amigo escuchan música, ¿verdad?
         —Sí, escuchamos música tejana y música rock.
         —¿Dónde escuchan música?
         —En la casa de mi amigo.

¿Quiénes?
tú
tú y tu amigo/a
tus amigos
tu hermano/a

Actividades
nadar
estudiar
escuchar música
comprar
pasar el rato con amigos
mirar la televisión

37 En mi cuaderno

In your journal, write two paragraphs about your friends and what you like to do together. Describe at least three of your friends in the first paragraph. Then, in the second paragraph, write about the activities that you like to do together.

MODELO   Mi amiga Claudia es muy simpática y guapa. Le gusta la música clásica y también le gusta dibujar...

Nos gusta nadar en la piscina...

Nota cultural

In towns in Spanish-speaking countries, it is common for people of all ages to spend time together in the **plaza.** A **plaza** is the heart of a town, surrounded by **la iglesia** *(church)*, police station, and local government offices. **Plazas** are great places to roller skate, visit with friends, or to hold **un baile.** There are often ice cream vendors and people playing music. Is there a town square or common where you live? Is there some other place in your neighborhood where people go to have fun?

PAIR WORK

36 Have pairs write down one of their dialogues and include with whom and when they do the activities. Then have them practice their pronunciation and perform.

☀ CLOSE

In groups of three, have students write on poster board their classes and when the classes meet, as well as what they do on school nights and at what time.

MULTICULTURAL LINK

Ask students where people in your town get together to walk, talk, and socialize. How are the places different from **plazas**? (parks, shopping centers: people go to exercise or buy things) How are they similar?

☀ ASSESS

▸ Testing Program, pp. 3–4
  Quiz 2
  Audio CD 7, Tr. 16

▸ Grammar and Vocabulary Quizzes
  Quiz 2A or
  Alternative Quiz 2A

▸ Alternative Assessment Guide, p. 18

PERFORMANCE ASSESSMENT

Have pairs talk as if they were friends comparing schedules the first day of class. They talk about classes using **primero, despues, luego,** and **por fin.**

VIDEO INTEGRATION

En camino LEVEL 1B
Video Program
Videocassette 1, 7:54–10:07

¡Ven conmigo! LEVEL 1
DVD Tutor, Disc 1

TEACHER NOTES

• Each **Panorama cultural** section consists of authentic video interviews shot on location in different parts of the Spanish-speaking world. See *Video Guide* for activity masters and teaching suggestions. The Level 1 *DVD Tutor* includes numerous interviews in addition to those featured in the *En camino* video program.

• Remind students that cultural material may be included in the Quizzes and Chapter Test.

• The language of the people interviewed represents informal, unrehearsed speech. Occasionally, text has been edited for clarity.

CRITICAL THINKING

Ask students what they think **paterno** means. *(paternal)* (hint: it begins with *pa*). Whose parents would **abuelos paternos** be? *(father's)* How would they say *maternal grandparents*? (**abuelos maternos**) (hint: it begins with *ma*)

LANGUAGE NOTES

• Be sure students make the connection between **perrita** and **perro**.

• The personal **a** is sometimes used with pets.

Panorama cultural

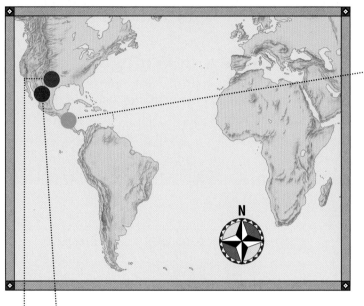

CD 7
Trs. 7–10

¿Qué haces los fines de semana?

In this chapter, we asked some Spanish-speaking students what they do on the weekends. What do you like to do on Saturdays and Sundays?

¿Te gustan las actividades que le gustan a Verónica? ¿Por qué sí o por qué no?

● **Verónica**
San Antonio, Texas
CD 7 Tr. 8

Normalmente paso el tiempo con mis amigos. Vamos a una fiesta, al cine, a comer y a bailar. A veces voy a la playa con mi familia también.

Aurelio tiene una familia bastante grande. Vive cerca de sus abuelos. ¿Tus abuelos viven cerca de tu casa?

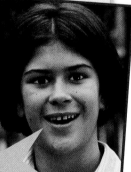

● **Aurelio**
México, D.F., México
CD 7 Tr. 9

A veces voy a casa de mis abuelos paternos y me lo paso con mis tíos y mis primos. Normalmente los domingos o sábados, como a las seis de la tarde, vamos a un parque y paseamos mi perrita.

Para Kimberly las clases son muy importantes, pero a veces pasa el rato con sus amigos. ¿Qué haces tú durante los fines de semana?

● Kimberly

San Miguel, CD 7 Tr. 10
Costa Rica

A veces, cuando nos dejan tarea, estudiamos y a veces jugamos y nos divertimos.

¿Qué juegan?

A veces hacemos deportes, y como... correr, saltar y jugar fútbol.

1 ¿Qué hace Verónica con sus amigos?

Va a una fiesta, al cine, a comer o a bailar.

2 ¿Qué hace ella con su familia? A veces va a la playa.

3 ¿Qué hace Aurelio con su familia? Pasa el rato en la casa de sus abuelos con sus primos y tíos y también va al parque.

4 ¿Qué hace él en el parque? ¿Cuándo va al parque?

Va a pasear (a) su perrita. Va los sábados y domingos después de cenar.

5 ¿Qué deportes practica Kimberly? Practica fútbol, corre y salta.

6 ¿Cuándo estudia ella? Cuando tiene tarea.

Para pensar y hablar... Answers will vary.

A. What do you do on the weekend? What are some differences and some similarities between what you do and what the interviewees do? What activities do you do with your family? What do you do only with your friends?

B. Do you have extended family that lives close by? Does your family ever have reunions? What are they like?

PRESENTATION
Have students draw four family members or friends on one side of a piece of paper. They draw each person doing something different. On the back, students describe them, telling what they look like, and something about their personality.

LANGUAGE NOTE
• Explain that the **nos** in **nos divertimos** is an example of a reflexive object. *(we amuse ourselves)* Tell students they will learn more about reflexive verbs in Chapter 7.

• Point out that when listing activities, it's possible to use just the infinitive, as Kimberly does.

PAIR/GROUP WORK
Have students interview classmates about weekend activities. What sports do they like to play? Do they go to parks? What do they do with friends or family?

23

**VIDEO
INTEGRATION**

En camino LEVEL 1B
Video Program
Videocassette 1, 5:06–7:31

¡Ven conmigo! LEVEL 1
DVD Tutor, Disc 1

TEACHER NOTE
The **fotonovela** contains clips of video episodes from **Adelante** Level 1A *Video Program*.

 Bell work
Have students list as many words or phrases as possible to name times for when they might see their friends. (**mañana, el martes, a veces, nunca, ...**)

PRESENTATION
What do students remember about Raquel from Chapters 5 and 6? (she lives in Miami, her parents are from Cuba, she has a photo album and a dog) Do students have photo albums at home? What photos do they include? If someone asked about their family, how would they answer? Ask students to identify the communicative functions modeled in the **fotonovela**. (talking about your family)

¿TE ACUERDAS? TERCER PASO

CD 7 Tr. 11 Chapters 5 and 6 took place in Miami, Florida, where you'll met Raquel. Here, you'll see Raquel talk about how often she does things. She'll also talk about her family and what they like to do together. Is Raquel's family similar to a family you know?

Raquel

Armando

1

A ver, Raquel... ¿cómo es tu familia?

Bueno, es bastante grande. Tengo tres hermanos, una hermana y muchísimos primos.

¿Y cuántos viven aquí?

Somos ocho en casa: mis padres, todos mis hermanos menos uno, una abuela y una tía.

2

¿Y cómo son tus padres? ¿Son simpáticos?

Sí, son muy simpáticos. ¿Por qué no miramos mi álbum de fotos? Así puedes conocer a toda la familia.

Pues, vamos.

3

Éstos son mis padres. Ellos son de Cuba. Les gusta mucho trabajar en el jardín. Mi mamá es muy buena cocinera. Alguna vez debes probar la barbacoa que ella prepara. ¡Es fenomenal!

4

5

Nosotros hacemos muchas cosas juntos, especialmente los domingos. Primero, vamos a la iglesia. Después, comemos juntos y salimos a alguna parte. En esta foto, salimos al parque.

¿TE ACUERDAS?   TERCER PASO

38 ¿Comprendes?

Check your understanding of the **fotonovela** by answering these questions. Don't be afraid to guess.

1. Where are Armando and Raquel? at Raquel's house
2. What does Armando want to know about Raquel? about her family
3. How many people live at Raquel's house? eight
4. What do Raquel's parents like to do? to garden
5. What does Raquel's family do together on Sundays? go to church, eat together, go out

39 ¿Cómo se dice?

Look at the **fotonovela** and find the phrases you would use . . . Answers in side column

1. to say you have three brothers and one sister
2. to ask someone what his or her family is like
3. to ask someone how many people live here
4. to point out a photo of an outing to a park
5. to tell a friend that he or she should try your mother's barbecue

40 ¿Quiénes son?

Who is Raquel talking about when she makes the following statements?

1. Es bastante grande.
2. Son muy simpáticos.
3. Son de Cuba.
4. Vamos a la iglesia.

1. su familia
2. sus padres
3. sus padres
4. su familia

veinticinco **25**

CULTURE NOTE
It is common in Spanish-speaking countries for several generations to live together. A single aunt or grandmother takes over child care and household duties while the parents work.

ADDITIONAL PRACTICE
39 Once students have located each phrase, ask them to express a slight variation. After they find **¿Cómo es tu familia?** ask them to express *What's your brother like?*

NATIVE SPEAKERS
Have native speakers add another page to their accent notebooks and title it **palabras esdrújulas.** Explain that these are words with the main stress two syllables from the last (**la sílaba antepenúltima**). Have them scan the **fotonovela** for examples. These words always need a written accent. (**simpáticos**) Have them think of other examples. (**sábado, lámpara**)

Answers to Activity 39

1. Tengo tres hermanos y una hermana.
2. ¿Cómo es tu familia?
3. ¿Cuántos viven aquí?
4. En esta foto, salimos al parque.
5. Debes probar la barbacoa que ella prepara.

STANDARDS: 1.2, 2.1, 5.1   **25**

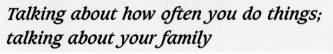

TERCER PASO

Talking about how often you do things;
talking about your family

Bell work
Write the words **casa**, **colegio**, and **parque** on the board. Have students list activities they might do in each place.

☀ MOTIVATE

Ask volunteers to say how many people live at home, what they are like, and what they do together.

☀ TEACH

PRESENTATION
ASÍ SE DICE
Model the exchanges by asking several questions and having students answer them. Then have students ask and answer them with a partner.

NOTA GRAMATICAL
Ask the class questions using **comer** and **escribir**. (**¿Ustedes comen fruta por la tarde? Sí, comemos...**) Have students ask you questions to practice the **usted** form. (**¿Con qué frecuencia come usted fruta?**)

PRELISTENING
41 First have students listen for the activities. The second time, ask them to raise their hands when they hear the information that shows if the sentence is true or false.

p. 8
Act. 13

ASÍ SE DICE   Talking about how often you do things

If someone asked you:

¿Con qué frecuencia escribes cartas?

¿Siempre lees el periódico?

¿Qué hacen tú y tus amigos típicamente por la tarde?

¿Qué comen ustedes después de clases?

You might answer:

Escribo cartas a veces.

No, nunca leo el periódico.

Muchas veces corremos en el parque.

No comemos nada después de clases.

NOTA GRAMATICAL
Look at the conjugations of **comer** and **escribir** to review how **-er** and **-ir** verbs work.

com**o**	com**emos**
com**es**	com**éis**
com**e**	com**en**
escrib**o**	escrib**imos**
escrib**es**	escrib**ís**
escrib**e**	escrib**en**

41 **¿Con qué frecuencia?**

CD 7 Tr. 12

Listen as Susana, Adriana, and Esteban try to figure out what to do this evening. Then read each sentence and respond with **cierto** or **falso**.

1. Adriana va a ver películas de terror a veces.
2. Muchas veces hay conciertos en el parque.
3. Esteban escucha el jazz a veces.
4. Los padres de Susana nunca escuchan el jazz.

Script and answers on p. T70

42 **¿Qué hacen?**

Read each sentence and complete the blank with the correct form of one of the verbs in the word box.

1. En nuestra clase, todos nosotros ——— cartas a unos chicos en otros países. escribimos
2. Yo siempre ——— en la clase de educación física. corro
3. Tú ——— revistas todos los días, ¿verdad? lees
4. Mi hermana no ——— comida mexicana nunca. come
5. Gustavo ——— jugo de naranja todas las mañanas. bebe
6. Señora Gómez, usted ——— a los conciertos de orquesta a veces, ¿no? asiste

beber
escribir
correr
asistir
leer
comer

¿Te acuerdas?

Hacer, salir, and poner are regular in the present tense except in the yo form, which has an irregular -go ending.

Yo **hago** la tarea después de clases.

Siempre **salgo** al parque con mi familia los domingos.

Pongo la mesa para la cena todas las noches.

Nota cultural

p. 12
Act. 21

In many Spanish-speaking households, it is common for people to stay at the table even after they're done eating. **La sobremesa** is a custom of lingering at the table for conversation, coffee, and continued snacking for several hours after the meal is finished. How long do you stay at the table after eating? Does your family clear the table immediately?

43 Preguntas y respuestas

Match the question with the best answer.

1. ¿Hacen ustedes algo durante el verano? f
2. ¿Sales a correr o a caminar? c
3. Bebo más agua que *(than)* tú, ¿no? e
4. ¿Beben agua o jugo con la cena? b
5. ¿Haces algo después de clases? d
6. ¿Pones la mesa todos los días? a

a. No, a veces mis hermanos ponen la mesa.
b. Bebemos agua.
c. Casi siempre salgo a correr.
d. Hago ejercicios y descanso.
e. Sí, bebes más agua que yo.
f. Siempre hacemos un viaje.

44 Todos los días

Look at the photos below. Ask your partner how often the people do each activity. Then answer your partner's questions.   Answers will vary.

MODELO   —¿Con qué frecuencia haces la tarea?
—Hago la tarea todos los días de lunes a viernes.

tú y tu amigo/a   tus amigos   Mariana   tú

PRESENTATION

¿Te acuerdas?
Remind students that **hacer** can mean *to make* or *to do*. (**Hago la cama. Hago mi tarea.**) **Poner** can mean *to put* or *to set.* (**Pongo mi cuaderno en la mochila. Pongo la mesa.**) **Salir** can mean *to leave* or *to go out.* (**Salgo a las seis. Salgo con mis amigas.**)

RE-ENTRY

43 Remind students that questions directed to **ustedes** are answered with **nosotros**. Questions directed to **tú** or **usted** are answered with **yo**.

CULTURE NOTE

Ask students if families in the United States practice the custom of **la sobremesa?** Why or why not? Is there anything about the way we live that makes it difficult? (fast-paced families not always together at meal times)

SUGGESTION

44 As a class, look at the photos and come up with words to answer the questions (**jugo de naranja, parque, periódico**) and frequency words. List them on the board. Make sure students are familiar with this vocabulary by asking questions similar to the model. Then have them work in pairs to ask and answer questions about the photos.

SUGGESTION
45 Have students check each other's work. Ask volunteers to read sentences that contain a particular word from the lists. (**Mis amigos corren juntos.**) Ask students to restate what their classmate said. (**Sus amigos...**)

PRESENTATION

VOCABULARIO

Display ¡**En camino!** Teaching Transparency B as you model weather expressions from **Vocabulario**. Then ask true-false questions about the scenes on the transparencies. Point out that **hace** is used with most weather expressions. Ask ¿**Qué tiempo hace en...?** for students to practice weather expressions using a weather map.

NATIVE SPEAKERS
Have native speakers add a page to their accent notebooks and title it **palabras interrogativas**. Explain that they introduce a direct question. (¿**qué?** ¿**cómo?** ¿**quién?**) Have them scan the **fotonovelas** from this chapter for examples. Explain that these words are written with an accent on the stressed vowel to distinguish them from the relative pronoun or conjunction spelled the same way. Ask them to think of others. (¿**cuánto?** ¿**dónde?** ¿**por qué?**)

45 ¿Qué haces?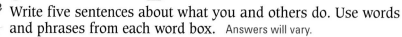

Write five sentences about what you and others do. Use words and phrases from each word box.   Answers will vary.

MODELO   Raquel y yo nadamos todos los días durante el verano.

yo mi amigo/a y yo mis amigos mi familia tú	correr nadar pescar salir beber comer asistir escribir	durante las vacaciones por la mañana juntos/as por la tarde los fines de semana después de clases

P A p. 9
Acts. 15–16

VOCABULARIO

¡En camino! B

¿Qué tiempo hace hoy?

Está lloviendo.

Hace sol.

Está nevando.

Hace frío.

Hace calor.

Hace viento.

46 El tiempo

The weather is different in the following four places today. Find the activity that best matches the weather in each place.

1. Hace buen tiempo hoy y hace fresco. b
2. Está nevando. a
3. Está lloviendo a cántaros y hace mucho frío. d
4. Hace mucho calor y sol. c

a. Eduardo quiere esquiar.
b. Quiero jugar al fútbol americano.
c. ¿Quieres ir a la piscina?
d. Anabel y Gustavo quieren mirar la televisión.

ASÍ SE DICE   Talking about your family

p. 10
Acts. 17–18

To ask about a friend's family:

¿Cuántas personas hay en tu familia?

¿Cómo es tu familia?

¿Qué hacen ustedes los fines de semana?

Your friend might answer:

Somos seis personas en mi familia.

Nuestra familia es grande. Somos muy unidos.

Casi siempre salimos a comer los domingos con nuestros abuelos.

47 La familia

Look at the following family photos. Complete the captions with words from the word box. Remember to use the correct form of the word. Answers in side column

¿Se te ha olvidado?
the family
Consulta las páginas 291–293

hermano   madrastra   padrastro

menor   esposo   abuelo   hijo   mayor

Somos seis en casa. Tengo dos ___1___. Mi ___2___ mayor tiene 18 años y mi hermano ___3___ tiene doce años. Mi ___4___ es el padre de mi mamá. Él es muy cariñoso.

Mi papá no vive en casa. En esta foto están mi mamá y su ___5___. Él es mi ___6___. Elena es la ___7___ de mi padrastro. Vive con nosotros los fines de semana. Mi ___8___ menor juega mucho con Elena.

TERCER PASO

veintinueve   **29**

CAPÍTULO PUENTE

PRESENTATION
ASÍ SE DICE
Draw your family tree as you describe your family. (**Hay seis personas en mi familia—mi padre, mi madrastra, mi hermana...**)

Have students create variations of the sentences. Ask them to tell you how they would ask what someone does on Saturdays or talk about how many people there are in their family.

RE-ENTRY
Play **Memoria** for vocabulary review. Make pairs of cards with the vocabulary words related to family. (**madre/padre; mayor/ menor; esposo/esposa**). Shuffle and arrange face down. Divide the class into two teams. Taking turns, each student picks two cards. If the cards match, the team keeps playing. If the cards don't match, the player turns them face down again, and the other team gets a turn. The team with more matches wins.

Answers to Activity 47
1. hermanos
2. hermano
3. menor
4. abuelo
5. esposo
6. padrastro
7. hija
8. hermano

STANDARDS: 1.2, 5.1   29

REVIEW
48 Review the meaning of the possessive adjectives, stressing that **su** can mean *his, her, your,* or *their.* Also remind students that these words must agree in number with the word to which they refer.

SLOWER PACE
48 List all words that appear after the blank spaces on the board. Have students practice saying *my grandparents, your grandparents, his grandparents,* and so on for each word in Spanish. Then have students read the paragraph for meaning with a partner to determine the words needed.

ADDITIONAL PRACTICE
49 Have students describe two members of their own family to a partner. Partners make stick-figure drawings of what they hear so that the student can see if his or her description was clear.

LANGUAGE NOTE
50 Remind students that, just like physical characteristics, personality traits are described by using the verb **ser. (inteligente, cómica, responsable...)**

Answers to Activity 48

1. Nuestros, Mis
2. Su
3. su
4. Sus
5. sus
6. Nuestros, Mis
7. nuestra, mi
8. tus, sus

48 Una familia simpática

Read the paragraph Rosalinda Llanes wrote to her friend. Fill in the blanks with the correct possessive adjectives.

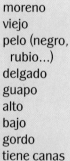

tu(s) *mi(s)* *nuestro(s)* *nuestra(s)* *su(s)*

Mi familia es grande y simpática. ___1___ abuelos pintan, corren y hacen ejercicios aeróbicos. ___2___ hijo, mi tío Felipe, y ___3___ esposa, mi tía Benita, tienen cuatro hijos. Tío Felipe escribe libros para niños. ___4___ hijos son muy inteligentes. También cuidan bien a ___5___ mascotas. Aquí en casa también tenemos mascotas. ___6___ perros son simpáticos y ___7___ gata es muy gorda y cómica. Y ___8___ mascotas, ¿cómo son? Answers in side column

49 ¿Cómo son?

Write six sentences describing the Romero family. Use the descriptive words in the word box.

MODELO La abuela es un poco gorda y tiene... Answers will vary.

moreno
viejo
pelo (negro, rubio...)
delgado
guapo
alto
bajo
gordo
tiene canas

50 ¿Cómo es...?

 Get together with a partner. Take turns asking each other about the family members in the drawing. Imagine what each one is like and answer with the best description you can. Use words from the box to get you started.

travieso
inteligente
aburrido
cómico
bueno
cariñoso
simpático
antipático
divertido

VOCABULARIO

¿Qué debes hacer?

cortar el césped	*to cut the grass*
trabajar en el jardín	*to work in the garden*
hacer la cama	*to make the bed*
limpiar la cocina	*to clean the kitchen*
pasar la aspiradora	*to vacuum*
poner la mesa	*to set the table*
cuidar al gato	*to take care of the cat*
planchar	*to iron*

¿Te acuerdas?

p. 11
Act. 20

The verb **deber** *(should, ought to)* is a regular **-er** verb. Use it to ask for and give advice.

debo	debemos
debes	debéis
debe	deben

Mi hermana y yo debemos hacer nuestras camas antes del desayuno.

¡En camino! C

PRESENTATION

VOCABULARIO

Use **¡En camino!** Teaching Transparency C to review household chore vocabulary. Then have volunteers perform the activities on the list while the class guesses which activity it is. Use eight images from the transparency or from magazines to quiz students.

PAIR WORK

51 Assign one problem to each pair of students. Together, they decide on the correct advice, find props, and dramatize the complaint and solution, while being as creative and as expressive as possible.

ADDITIONAL PRACTICE

52 Repeat the activity, having students change the statements that are **un chiste** to ones that are more **en serio**, and vice-versa.

51 ¡Qué problema!

Imagine that everyone in your family is asking for advice about their problems. Choose the best advice for each person's problem.

1. Estoy muy delgado. c
2. Voy a recibir una F en la clase de inglés. f
3. Quiero tener más amigos. e
4. No encuentro *(I can't find)* mi lápiz ni mi bolígrafo. a
5. Dibujo muy mal. d
6. Hago mi tarea muy tarde y no descanso. b

a. Debes organizar tu mochila.
b. Debes hacer tu tarea después de clase y descansar más.
c. Debes comer más.
d. Debes practicar más.
e. Debes hablar con los compañeros durante el almuerzo.
f. Debes estudiar más y leer unos libros.

52 Los quehaceres

Antonio and his sister María Eugenia have a great sense of humor. Read their list of chores and decide which ones are **un chiste** *(a joke)* and which are **en serio** *(serious)*.

1. Durante el invierno debo cortar el césped todos los días.
2. Siempre hago la cama a las diez de la noche.
3. Ponemos la mesa antes de la cena.
4. Paso la aspiradora en el césped.
5. Trabajo en el jardín sólo cuando llueve.
6. Lavamos los platos todas las noches.

1. un chiste
2. un chiste
3. en serio
4. un chiste
5. un chiste
6. en serio

SUGGESTION
53 Have students read through the interviews individually. Then volunteers read the interviewer's part and the answers of María de los Ángeles or José Alberto. Read the part of one of the people being interviewed and add intonation and facial expressions to help convey meaning. Discuss the interviews as a class, then have students work through the questions.

NATIVE SPEAKERS
Have native speakers scan the reading for three **palabras esdrújulas** to add to their accent notebooks. (**Ángeles, Cárdenas, único**)

 PORTFOLIO
53 **Oral** Have students work in pairs to interview each other using the questions asked in the interviews. The interviewers use the questions María answered if their partner has brothers and sister, or the questions José Alberto answered if their partner is an only child. Then the partners switch roles. Students may wish to add these interviews to their oral portfolios.

Answers to Activity 53
1. early; room; lazy; annoys
2. ideal son; only son; disaster
3. Possible answer: María de los Ángeles has a big family and José Alberto is an only child.
4. Answers will vary.

53 La vida familiar

Read these interviews with two students. Remember to use the reading strategies of using context, cognates, and background knowledge. Then answer the questions below.

María de los Ángeles Lares Rosado, 15 años
Montevideo, Uruguay

María de los Ángeles, ¿tienes hermanos?
Sí, tengo un hermano y tres hermanas.

¿Eres la mayor?
No, tengo una hermana y un hermano mayor. Tienen 17 y 19. Mis hermanas menores tienen 13 y 9 años.

¿Te llevas bien con tus hermanos?
Sí, bastante bien. Pero a veces mi hermano me fastidia.

¿Por qué?
Es muy perezoso y no ayuda en casa.

¿Cómo son tus padres?
Son estrictos, pero cariñosos.

¿Tienes hermanos, José Alberto?
No, no tengo hermanos. Soy hijo único.

¿Ayudas con las tareas de la casa?
Sí, todos los días porque mi mamá trabaja.

¿Eres el hijo ideal?
No. Creo que a veces los vuelvo locos°.

¿Por qué?
Porque soy bastante desordenado y a veces mi habitación es un desastre. Hay ropa y libros por todos lados.

¿De qué más se preocupan tus padres?
De que no estudio bastante.

¿Crees que tienen razón?
Sí, a veces.

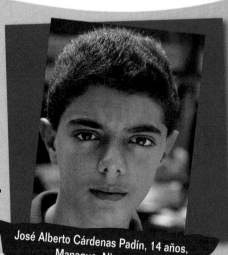

José Alberto Cárdenas Padín, 14 años,
Managua, Nicaragua

| **los vuelvo locos** | *I drive them crazy* |

1. Use context to figure out what the following words mean: Answers in side column
   temprano   perezoso
   habitación   fastidia
2. Use cognates to figure out what the following phrases mean:
   hijo ideal   hijo único   desastre
3. What is different about the two students' families?
4. Which of the families is most like your own? In what ways?

54 Mucho trabajo

Interview your partner. Find out what chores he or she does and how often they're done. Ask if your partner likes any of these chores. Find out if anyone else helps with them. Then answer your partner's interview questions. Use the word **nadie** to say that nobody helps you with a chore.

MODELO —¿Qué quehaceres haces en tu casa?
—¿Con qué frecuencia...?
—¿Te gusta...?
—¿Quién limpia la cocina contigo?

55 Dos días diferentes

Look at the two drawings. Work with a partner and make a list of six things to describe in each drawing. You can describe the weather, the place, the activity, and the family members. Then write three sentences for each drawing. Answers will vary.

Mauricio y el señor Vela

Amara y los señores Alcalá

56 En mi cuaderno

Choose a character from a movie or TV show. In your journal, write a description of this character that tells about appearance and personality. Tell the character's age and where he or she lives, and describe his or her family members. Describe any activities that the character and his or her family like to do together. Write at least ten sentences.

SLOWER PACE

56 Choose one TV character. Write the sentences on the board or on a transparency. Then erase all but the introductory words in each sentence. Have students use the outline to start working individually.

☀ CLOSE

To review material from this **paso,** have student pairs interview each other about what they do with friends and family members during various weather conditions. —**¿Qué haces con tu familia cuando hace sol? —Mis padres y yo vamos a la playa.** Have them report their findings to the class.

☀ ASSESS

▸ Testing Program, pp. 19–20
Quiz 1
Audio CD 7, Tr. 36

▸ Grammar and Vocabulary Quizzes
Quiz 3A or
Alternative Quiz 3A

▸ Alternative Assessment Guide, p. 19

PERFORMANCE ASSESSMENT

Have pairs of students pretend to be new acquaintances who want to know about each other's families. They ask who their family members are, what their names are, what they like to do together, when, and how often.

STANDARDS: 1.1, 1.3   **33**

PRELISTENING

1 As a prelistening activity, have students describe the weather in the drawings.

MOTIVATING ACTIVITY

2 Young teens are often interested in the subject of adoption. Who do they know who is adopted? What famous people have been adopted? (Former President Gerald Ford, Dave Thomas of Wendy's Hamburgers) What famous people have adopted children? (Tom Cruise and Nicole Kidman, Rosie O'Donnell)

CRITICAL THINKING

2 In item 3, have students figure out why **los cachorros** and not **una madre** must be the subject of the verb **necesitan**. (because the verb is plural)

Answers to Activity 2

1. La mamá sale a cazar.
2. Una amiga, hermana o prima de la mamá cuida a los cachorros.
3. Si la mamá nunca regresa, otra leona cuida a los cachorros hasta que son grandes.

REPASO

1 Listen as four students tell about the activity each is planning to do today. Match each student's statement with the drawing that represents the weather in each case. CD 7 Tr. 13   Script and answers on p. T71

a   **b**   **c**   **d**

2 Read the selection from an article called "**Madres muy especiales**". Then answer the questions that follow. Answers in side column

MADRES MUY ESPECIALES

Hay chicos que no crecen junto a sus papás biológicos, los papás que les dieron la vida. A esos chicos los crían papás adoptivos. En el Reino Animal también pasan estas cosas.

Una de las leonas del grupo se prepara para salir a cazar. Nadie sabe cuánto tiempo va a estar lejos de sus cachorros. Pueden ser apenas unas horas o varios días. Mientras ella no está, una "hermana", una "amiga" o una "prima" cuida a sus pequeños. No sólo los alimenta, también los transporta delicadamente entre sus dientes, de un lugar a otro. Si por alguna razón la madre no regresa, esta "nueva mamá" los cría hasta que son grandes.

alimenta *feeds*   **crían** *raise*
cachorros *cubs*   **dientes** *teeth*
cazar *to hunt*   **reino** *kingdom*

1. La revista dice que a veces la mamá leona no está. ¿Por qué sale?
2. ¿Quién cuida a los cachorros cuando la mamá no está?
3. ¿Por qué necesitan una madre adoptiva los cachorros?

3 Vamos a escribir

Write two paragraphs of at least four sentences about two places where you like to go. Tell what you do there. Use adjectives to paint a mental picture for your reader of those locations.

Estrategia

Using adjectives helps make your writing clearer and more interesting. Adjectives describe people, places, and things. You can use numbers and colors as well as adjectives that describe the appearance or quality of something.

> Me gusta ir al lago. Nado y pesco allí.
> También descanso y leo un libro. El
> lago es grande y muy bonito. El agua
> es fría y es de color azul...

4 Which of the following statements are true? Answer with **cierto** or **falso.** Then correct any false statements. Answers in side column

1. In Spanish-speaking countries, people go to **la plaza** to shop.
2. **Plazas** are usually in the center of a town.
3. In Spanish-speaking households, families eat in a hurry and quickly clear the table.
4. Meals are a time for conversation among family and friends in Spanish-speaking countries.

5 **S I T U A C I Ó N**

You've just seen your friend talking to someone that you really want to meet. With a partner, role-play asking your friend about this person. Find out everything you can about this person including where he or she is from, what he or she studies and likes to do, and what he or she is like.

CAPÍTULO PUENTE

📁 PORTFOLIO
3 Written This activity is a potential written portfolio entry. For portfolio suggestions, see *Alternative Assessment Guide,* p. 10.

LANGUAGE NOTE
Explain that feminine words that begin with a stressed **a-** take **el** as a definite article. (**el agua fría**)

PREWRITING
3 Have students make a cluster diagram of places. Then have them add adjectives to describe the places and make sure they agree in gender with the noun. Point out words in the example to make students aware of agreement. Have the students check their partner's paragraphs for agreement and clarity.

SUGGESTION
5 Have students list questions to review the ones they will need. Write the questions on a transparency or on the board. Be sure to have students formulate a question for each detail they want to know. Turn off the overhead projector and have students ask each other questions.

Answers to Activity 4

1. falso. They go to the plaza to talk and see friends.
2. cierto
3. falso. Spanish-speaking households enjoy their meal slowly and talk with each other.
4. cierto

STANDARDS: 1.1, 1.3, 4.1   35

 **A VER SI PUEDO...**

This page is intended to help students prepare independently for the Chapter Test. It is a brief checklist of the major points covered in the chapter. The students should be reminded that it is a checklist only and does not necessarily include everything that will appear on the Chapter Test.

Answers to Activity 3

1. Tengo la clase de matemáticas a las diez y cuarto.
2. ¿Qué haces después de clases?
3. Los domingos salimos a comer en un restaurante y después caminamos en el parque.
4. Voy al colegio a las siete y media de la mañana.

Answers to Activity 4

1. Answers will vary.
2. La biblioteca está cerca de la tienda.
3. La piscina está al lado del parque.
4. Answers will vary.

Answers to Activity 5

1. ¿Con qué frecuencia lees el periódico?
2. Nunca preparo la cena.
3. Answers will vary. Possible answer:
   Típicamente paso el rato con mis amigos y escucho música.

▼ **Can you greet others?** p. 4

1 How would you . . .

1. respond when the principal says good morning and asks you how you are? Buenos días. Estoy bien, gracias.
2. say goodbye to a friend after school? Hasta mañana; Adiós; Chao.
3. ask a new student what her name is and where she is from? ¿Cómo te llamas? ¿De dónde eres?
4. introduce yourself to the new student and say how old you are? Me llamo... Tengo... años.

▼ **Can you say what you have?** p. 9

2 For each of the following items, write how you would tell a friend how many of that item you have. Then write another sentence saying you don't have this item but you want one.

Answers will vary.

▼ **Can you talk about what you do and when?** p. 14

3 Can you . . .? Answers in side column

1. tell a friend that your math class is at 10:15
2. ask a friend what he or she does after school
3. tell a friend what you do on Sundays
4. say what time you go to school

▼ **Can you describe people and places?** p. 19

4 Can you . . .? Answers in side column

1. describe your friends
2. say that the library is near the store
3. say that the pool is next to the park
4. describe your room

▼ **Can you talk about how often you do things?** p. 26

5 How would you . . .? Answers in side column

1. ask how often your friend reads the newspaper
2. say you never cook dinner
3. say what you usually do in the afternoon

▼ **Can you talk about your family?** p. 29

6 Can you tell your new friend . . .? Answers will vary.

1. how many people there are in your family
2. the names of your family members
3. what they like to do in their free time

VOCABULARIO

PRIMER PASO

Greeting others

Adiós. *Goodbye.*
Buenos días. *Good morning.*
Chao. *Bye.*
¿Cómo está usted? *How are you? (formal)*
¿Cómo estás? *How are you? (informal)*
¿Cuántos años tienes? *How old are you?*
¿De dónde eres? *Where are you from?*
Estoy bien. *I'm well.*
Estupendo/a. *Great.*
gustar *to like*
Hasta luego. *See you later.*
¡Hola! *Hello!*
Más o menos. *So-so.*
¿Qué tal? *How's it going? What's up?*
Soy de... *I'm from . . .*
Tengo... años. *I'm . . . years old.*

Saying what you have

comer *to eat*
correr *to run*
cuidar a tu hermano/a *to take care of your brother/sister*
¿Cuántos/as... hay? *How many... are there?*
dibujar *to draw*
escuchar música *to listen to music*
hablar *to talk*
hacer la tarea *to do homework*
ir *to go*
jugar a los videojuegos *to play videogames*
leer revistas *to read magazines*
mirar la televisión *to watch television*
necesitar *to need*
pero *but*
organizar el cuarto *to clean the room*

practicar deportes *to play sports*
Quiero... *I want . . .*
tener *to have*

Activities

Numbers 0–199
Things you have

See pp. 291–293

SEGUNDO PASO

Talking about what you do and when

¿A qué hora...? *At what time . . .?*
antes de *before*
la biblioteca *library*
la casa *house*
el cine *movie theater*
el correo *post office*
después de *after*
durante *during*
Es la una. *It's one o'clock.*
el fin de semana *weekend*
el gimnasio *gym*
luego *later*
la mañana *morning*
la noche *night*
el parque *park*
la piscina *pool*
primero *first*
¿Qué haces...? *What do you do . . .?*
¿Qué hora es? *What time is it?*
el restaurante *restaurant*
Son las... *It's . . . o'clock.*
el supermercado *supermarket*
la tarde *afternoon*
la tienda *store*
las vacaciones *vacations*
y cuarto *quarter past*
y media *half past*

Describing people and places

School subjects
Where things are

See pp. 291–293

TERCER PASO

Talking about how often you do things

a veces *sometimes*
¿Con qué frecuencia...? *How often . . .?*
Está lloviendo. *It's raining.*
Está nevando. *It's snowing.*
Hace calor. *It's hot.*
Hace frío. *It's cold.*
Hace sol. *It's sunny.*
Hace viento. *It's windy.*
muchas veces *often*
nada *nothing*
nunca *never, not ever*
¿Qué tiempo hace? *What's the weather like?*
siempre *always*
sólo cuando *only when*

Seasons and weather

See pp. 291–293

Talking about your family

¿Cómo es tu familia? *What's your family like?*
cortar el césped *to cut the grass*
¿Cuántas personas hay? *How many people are there?*
cuidar al gato *to take care of the cat*
demasiado *too much*
los fines de semana *weekends*
hacer la cama *to make the bed*
limpiar la cocina *to clean the kitchen*
No es cierto. *It isn't true.*
pasar la aspiradora *to vacuum*
planchar *to iron*
poner la mesa *to set the table*
los quehaceres domésticos *household chores*
trabajar en el jardín *to work in the garden*

The family

See pp. 291–293

GAME
Use games from page T73 to review Bridge Chapter vocabulary.

BRIDGE CHAPTER ASSESSMENT

▶ **Testing Program**
Chapter Test, pp. 7–12
Audio Compact Discs, CD 7, Trs. 17–18
Speaking Test, p. 129

▶ **Alternative Assessment Guide**
Performance Assessment, p. 18
Portfolio Assessment, p. 10

▶ **One-Stop Planner, Disc 1–2**
Test Generator
Chapter 1–6

¡Ven conmigo a Ecuador!

LOCATION OPENER CHAPTERS 7, 8

PRINT

Video Guide Level 1B
• Activity Masters and Suggestions, pp. 6–7

MEDIA

Video Program Level 1B
Videocassette 1

Interactive CD-ROM Tutor
Disc 2

go.hrw.com
WV3 ECUADOR

¡Ven conmigo! Level 1
DVD Tutor, Disc 2

You may wish to point out the following images as students view the Ecuador Location Opener. These images will be seen on both the Video Program and the DVD Program. If you are using the DVD Program they may be freeze-framed for presentation and discussion purposes.

Quito, the second-highest major city in Latin America, is situated on a plateau 9,350 feet above sea level. Because Quito is almost directly on the equator, there is a fairly consistent amount of sunlight each day and little variation in temperature.

Many consider the outdoor market at **Otavalo** to be one of the best open-air markets in South America. The textile work of local residents is sold throughout South America and as far away as Europe. Shoppers arrive early to find the best selection of such things as **ponchos**, shawls, sweaters, and wall hangings. The Saturday morning market starts before dawn and is over by noon.

Otavaleños have a very distinctive style of dress. Women wear wrap skirts called **anakus** and embroidered blouses with wool or cotton shoulder wraps called **fachalinas.** The men wear white pants, dark-colored **ponchos** and **alpargatas,** sandal-like shoes. Both men and women often wear dark hats and keep their hair in a long braid down their backs.

Ingapirca (**Cañari** for "Inca wall") is one of Ecuador's major reminders of the Inca empire. The engraved stones are fitted together in a circular shape without mortar. Ingapirca served many purposes. Scholars believe this Inca site contained storehouses, baths, an inn, barracks, and a temple.

Cuenca, founded in 1557, is Ecuador's third-largest city. It is considered by many Ecuadoreans to be the country's most picturesque city. The three blue domes of the **Catedral Nueva** dominate the colonial city's skyline. Four rivers—Tarqui, Yanucay, Tomebamba, and Machangara—surround Cuenca and intersect in the **Parque del Paraíso,** the city's largest park.

PROJECT

VISITEMOS ECUADOR

This project will give an overview of Ecuador. Students will learn the country's location in South America, information about its culture, as well as discover interesting things to do and places to see.

Introduction

Ask your students if they can find Ecuador on the world map on pages xviii–xix. Have them also look for the center line of the equator and the name **Ecuador** *(equator)*. What are the most interesting places in the country to visit? Have students imagine they work for the Ministry of Tourism in Ecuador and they have been asked to make a travel brochure. Which places, activities, and information would they include?

Materials students may need

- ◆ Travel brochures about Ecuador from a local travel agency
- ◆ Information on Ecuador from an encyclopedia or the Internet
- ◆ Colored construction paper
- ◆ Poster board
- ◆ Glue sticks
- ◆ Tape
- ◆ Markers, colored pencils

Sequence

1 Have students work in pairs to create a travel brochure, collage, or poster about Ecuador.

2 Have them find out about the following categories for their destination:
- People and culture (music, dance, language)
- Restaurants
- Special foods
- Sports
- National parks
- Unique wildlife

3 The pairs cut pictures from magazines or draw their own illustrations of the people, places, and cultural activities that make Ecuador an interesting place to visit. Have students label the pictures in Spanish when possible.

4 In pairs, students present their brochures for an oral participation grade.

5 Students prepare a classroom bulletin board to be used for Chapters 7 and 8.

Grading the project

Suggested point distribution (total = 100 points):

Creativity	20
Neatness	20
Accuracy of information	20
Oral Presentation	20
Cooperative Effort	20

¡Ven conmigo a Ecuador!

LOCATION OPENER CHAPTERS 7, 8 (cont.)

Using the Map

• Ask students to identify the two countries that border Ecuador. (Peru and Colombia)
• Have students name the ocean that forms the western border of continental Ecuador.
• Ask students to point out the equator. Do they know what climate equatorial countries generally have? (Most equatorial lowlands have heavy rains and average temperatures over 68°F.) However, since Quito and Cuenca are both more than 9,000 feet above sea level, their climates are very cool year-round.
• Have students locate the Andes (**la Cordillera de los Andes**). You may want to point out that it is the world's longest mountain chain. They stretch over 4,500 miles from Cape Horn at the tip of South America to Panama. Only the Himalayas of northern India and Tibet have higher peaks than the Andes.

Geography Link

The Andes are formed by three parallel chains, or **cordilleras:** the eastern, central, and western ranges that divide the country into the coastal region, the mountain region (**la Sierra**), and the east. Andean people live in a rugged environment. The land is rarely flat, so Andean people must use creativity and horticultural knowledge handed down by their ancestors to terrace and cultivate the steep mountain slopes.

History Link

Quito was the ancient seat of the kingdom of Quitu, named after the people who lived there before the Spaniards arrived in 1534. Between about 1000 and 1487, Quitu was united with the Incan empire. Quito remained the center of regional political, social, and economic affairs from the 16th century until the early 20th century, when Guayaquil became the economic center.

Culture Note

Continental Ecuador is divided into three regions with distinct cultures. The Coastal Lowlands (**la Costa**) is made up primarily of descendants of African slaves. The Andes Highlands (**la Sierra**) is populated by many indigenous groups including Otavalos, Salasacas, and descendants of the Puruhá. The Eastern Lowlands (**el Oriente**), which covers almost half the country, is composed primarily of indigenous Jívaro. All three areas also have people of European descent. The Galapagos Islands in the Pacific Ocean make up the fourth region.

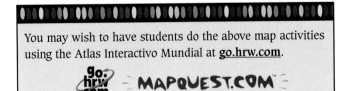

You may wish to have students do the above map activities using the Atlas Interactivo Mundial at **go.hrw.com**.

go.hrw.com — MAPQUEST.COM

Geography Link

Placed precisely at 0° latitude, the monument known as **la Mitad del Mundo** *(Middle of the World)* is 15 miles north of Quito. It marks where a French expedition made the first scientific measurements of the equator, a 24,000-mile-long imaginary line encircling the globe and dividing the Northern and Southern Hemispheres, in the 18th century. A strip of white pebbles marks where the equator crosses the monument site. Many tourists have photographs taken with one leg in each hemisphere. Have students find other countries located on the equator on the map on pages xviii–xix. (For example, Colombia, Brazil, Uganda, Kenya, and Indonesia)

Culture Notes

• Women of Otavalo wear wrap skirts called **anakus** and shoulder wraps called **fachalinas** made of handspun wool or cotton. The clothing of Otavalo closely resembles that of the Inca.

• There are many native ethnic groups in Ecuador. Each considers itself a distinct nationality and has its own culture. The most numerous are the Quechuas, who live mainly in the mountains. Among most groups are many **mestizos** (of mixed European and indigenous ancestry) and **sambos** (a mix of African and indigenous races).

¡Ven conmigo a Ecuador!

VIDEO INTEGRATION

En camino LEVEL 1B
Video Program
Videocassette 1, 10:16–12:42

¡Ven conmigo! LEVEL 1
DVD Tutor, Disc 2

MOTIVATING ACTIVITY

Ask students if they've ever heard of the global equator. What do they know about it? Explain that it's an imaginary border dividing the Northern and Southern Hemispheres.

BACKGROUND

Quito is the capital and the second-largest city in Ecuador. Set in the Quito Basin at the foot of the Pichincha volcano at an altitude of 9,350 feet, Quito is the second-highest major city in Latin America. Founded in 1534, it is also the oldest capital city in South America.

CULTURE NOTE

Indigenous people make up nearly one third of Ecuador's population. There are ten native ethnic groups, each with its own language or dialect. Spanish is widely spoken by all Ecuadoreans, and Quechua is spoken by over 10 million indigenous people.

CAPÍTULOS 7 Y 8

¡Ven conmigo a Ecuador!

HRW ATLAS INTERACTIVO MUNDIAL

MAPQUEST.COM

Have students go to the interactive atlas at **go.hrw.com** to find out more about the geography of Ecuador.

USING THE ALMANAC

- **Gobierno:** Ecuador has been an independent republic since 1822. The people elect a president to one four-year term, and the president appoints a 16-member cabinet. A 72-member Chamber of Representatives is the country's lawmaking body.

- **Productos principales: productos de madera** *wood products*, **aceite** *oil*, **plata** *silver*, **cobre** *copper*, **hierro** *iron*

- **Idiomas: Quechua** is the language of the former Incan empire. It is written and pronounced **quichua** in Ecuador. It is now widely spoken throughout the Andes highlands from southern Colombia to Chile.

CNNenEspañol.com

Have students check the CNN en español Web site for news on Ecuador or any of the neighboring countries. The CNN en español site is also a good source of timely, high interest readings for Spanish students.

Ecuador

Población: 12.920.000 (aproximadamente)

Área: 104.505 millas cuadradas (270.668 km²), similar en área al estado de Colorado

Ubicación: En el noroeste de Sudamérica, fronteras con Colombia, Perú y el océano Pacífico

Capital: Quito, con una población de 1.500.000 (aproximadamente)

Gobierno: república federal

Productos principales: productos de madera, plátanos, café, aceite, plata, cobre, hierro, petróleo

Unidad monetaria: el dólar

Idiomas: español (lengua oficial), quechua y otros idiomas indígenas

internet

MARCAR: go.hrw.com
PALABRA CLAVE:
WV3 ECUADOR

MOTIVATING ACTIVITY
Ask students if they have ever seen a 500-pound tortoise or a 4-foot iguana. Have them describe the strangest animal that they have ever seen.

USING THE PHOTO ESSAY

❶ Many Ecuadoreans consider Cuenca to be the country's most beautiful city. Its colonial architecture stands beside new construction that usually follows a neocolonial style. There are no skyscrapers to obscure the view of the surrounding mountains. Instead, the three domes of the **Catedral Nueva** dominate the skyline.

❷ Otavalo is a town in the Andean highlands in north-central Ecuador originally settled by the Otavalo Indians. The Otavalo were later conquered by the Incas. In the 16th century the Spanish began settling there.

❸ Traditional highland instruments include the following: flutes (**flautas**), panpipes (**rondadores**), conch shells (**conchas**), and various percussion instruments (**instrumentos de percusión**). Flute-like instruments used today include the **quena,** a notched bamboo recorder, and a smaller flute called a **pingullu,** which has three or four holes. Probably the most characteristic Andean instrument is the **charango,** a five-string guitar that is about two feet long. Its body is sometimes made of wood, but is more often made from an armadillo shell.

☀ECUADOR

*Ecuador is a country with an extremely diverse geography and culture. The Andes mountains divide continental Ecuador into three distinct regions— the coastal plain (**la Costa**), the mountainous region (**la Sierra**), and the Amazon jungle region (**el Oriente**). Different native ethnic groups inhabit the country. The modern capital city of Quito is in the **Sierra** region and the famous Galapagos Islands are 570 miles off the coast in the Pacific Ocean.*

▲ **Las casas colgadas**
Cuenca is a Spanish colonial city built over the ruins of the Inca city of Tomebamba. The *casas colgadas (hanging houses)* overlook the Tomebamba River.

El mercado de Otavalo ▲
Traditionally dressed *otavaleñas* sell fine rugs and tapestries at the market. The majority of *otavaleños* are weavers and spinners of textiles. The ancestors of the *otavaleños* have occupied the area for thousands of years.

▼ **La música andina**
The traditional music of the Andean mountain people reflects the rich cultural heritage of Ecuador. These musicians are playing stringed instruments introduced by the Spaniards. The flute-like *quena* and the drums were in use long before Europeans arrived.

In Chapters 7 and 8 you'll meet Carlos, Tomás, and Maria, three friends living in Quito, Ecuador. It's called "Ecuador" because the global equator runs through the country. Quito, its capital, is a beautiful city with hundreds of years of history.

④

▲ La selva del Amazonas

The rainforests of the Amazon basin are inhabited by six indigenous tribes and 550 species of birds, and many animals including howler monkeys, pumas, jaguars, sloths, and caymans.

La llama ▶

Llamas are South American members of the camel family. They are widely used as pack animals as they can carry 120 pounds and can travel 15 miles a day through the steep Andes terrain.

⑤

⑥

◀ Quito, la capital

Although Quito is only 25 miles south of the equator, its location in the Andes mountains ensures that it has a pleasant spring-like climate all year. It's located at 9,350 feet above sea level.

cuarenta y uno 41

④ La selva del amazonas
The howler monkey is found in many tropical forests, including the Amazon. Howlers are the largest monkeys in the Americas. They are also unique in that their loud cries are similar to a lion's roar.

⑤ Llamas have wool fleece similar to a sheep's that is used to make sweaters, rugs, rope, and blankets.

⑥ The full name of the city is **Villa de San Francisco de Quito.** Founded in 1534, it is the oldest of all South American capitals.

MUSIC LINK

If possible, play a recording of Andean music. You may want to use the recording of **El Cóndor Pasa** provided on Audio CD 7 Track 47. Have students guess what instruments they are listening to. Consider presenting the musical instrument vocabulary below before playing the recording.

ADDITIONAL VOCABULARY

arpa criolla *Andean harp*
mandolina *mandolin*
campana *bell*
bombo *drum*
maraca *gourd rattle*

CAPÍTULO 7

¿Qué te gustaría hacer?
CHAPTER OVERVIEW

De antemano pp. 44–47	¿Qué hacemos?			

	FUNCTIONS	**GRAMMAR**	**VOCABULARY**	**RE-ENTRY**
Primer paso pp. 48–55	• Talking on the telephone, p. 49 • Extending and accepting invitations, p. 51	• **Gramática: e → ie** stem-changing verbs, p. 52 • **Así se dice: me, te gustaría** + infinitive, p. 51	• Places and events, p. 54	• Invitations: **gustar** • Days of the week
Segundo paso pp. 58–65	• Making plans, p. 59 • Talking about getting ready, p. 63	• **Gramática: pensar** and **ir + a +** infinitive, p. 60 • **Nota gramatical:** Reflexive verbs (infinitives only), p. 64	• Transportation, p. 55 • Personal items, p. 62	• Future expressions: **hoy, mañana,** etc. • Expressions of frequency: **todos los días, a veces,** etc.
Tercer paso pp. 66–71	• Turning down an invitation and explaining why, p. 67	• **Nota gramatical:** Expressions with **tener,** p. 68	• Expressions of apology, p. 63	The verb **tener**

Letra y sonido	**p. 71**	The letters *ll* and *y*	**Dictado:** Textbook Audiocassette 1A/Audio CD 7	
Enlaces	**pp. 72–73**	**Las islas Galápagos**		
Vamos a leer	**pp. 74–75**	**Guía turística**	**Reading Strategy:** Skim for main idea	
Review	**pp. 76–79**	**Repaso,** pp. 76–77	**A ver si puedo...,** p. 78	**Vocabulario,** p. 79

Culture	• **Nota cultural:** Telephone greetings, p. 48 • **Panorama cultural: ¿Qué haces para conocer a un nuevo estudiante?,** pp. 56–57	• **Nota cultural:** Modes of transportation, p. 62

PRINT

Lesson Planning

One-Stop Planner
Lesson Planner with Substitute Teacher
Lesson Plans, pp. 6–10

Listening and Speaking

Listening Activities
- Student Response Forms for Listening Activities, pp. 55–57
- Additional Listening Activities 7-1 to 7-6, pp. 5–7
- Additional Listening Activities (song), p. 8
- Scripts and Answers, pp. 33–36

Video Guide
- Teaching Suggestions, pp. 9–10
- Activity Masters, pp. 11–13
- Scripts and Answers, pp. 52–54, 66

Activities for Communication
- Communicative Activities, pp. 7–12
- Realia and Teaching Suggestions, pp. 44–48
- Situation Cards, pp. 76–77

¡Ven conmigo! Level 1
TPR Storytelling Book, pp. 25–28

Reading and Writing

Reading Strategies and Skills, Chapter 7
¡Lee conmigo! 1, Chapter 7
Practice and Activity Book, pp. 13–24

Grammar

Grammar and Vocabulary Workbook, pp. 1–8

¡Ven conmigo! Level 1
Grammar Tutor for Students of Spanish
Chapter 7

Assessment

Testing Program
- Paso Quizzes and Chapter Test, pp. 19–30
- Score Sheet, Scripts and Answers, pp. 31–36

Grammar and Vocabulary Quizzes
- Quizzes 7-1A, 7-2A, 7-3A
- Alternative Quizzes 7-1A, 7-2A, 7-3A

Alternative Assessment Guide
- Portfolio Assessment, p. 11
- Performance Assessment, p. 19
- CD-ROM Assessment, p. 26

¡Ven conmigo! Level 1
Standardized Assessment Tutor
- Reading, pp. 27–29
- Writing, p. 30

Native Speakers

¡Ven conmigo! Level 1
Cuaderno para hispanohablantes, pp. 31–35

MEDIA

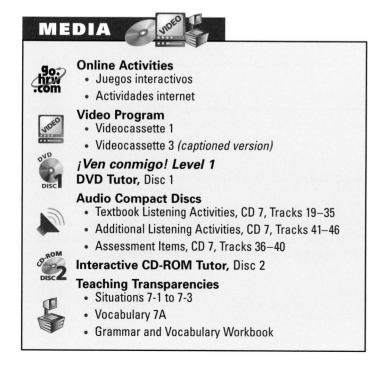

Online Activities
- Juegos interactivos
- Actividades internet

Video Program
- Videocassette 1
- Videocassette 3 *(captioned version)*

¡Ven conmigo! Level 1
DVD Tutor, Disc 1

Audio Compact Discs
- Textbook Listening Activities, CD 7, Tracks 19–35
- Additional Listening Activities, CD 7, Tracks 41–46
- Assessment Items, CD 7, Tracks 36–40

Interactive CD-ROM Tutor, Disc 2

Teaching Transparencies
- Situations 7-1 to 7-3
- Vocabulary 7A
- Grammar and Vocabulary Workbook

One-Stop Planner CD-ROM

Use the **One-Stop Planner CD-ROM with Test Generator** to aid in lesson planning and pacing.

For each chapter, the **One-Stop Planner** includes:
- Editable lesson plans with direct links to teaching resources
- Printable worksheets from resource books
- Direct launches to the HRW Internet activities
- Video and audio segments
- Test Generator
- Clip Art for vocabulary items

CAPÍTULO 7

¿Qué te gustaría hacer?
TECHNOLOGY

DVD/VIDEO

CAPÍTULO 7 — ¿Qué te gustaría hacer?
TECHNOLOGY

DVD/VIDEO

One-Stop Planner CD-ROM

To preview all resources available for this chapter, use the **One-Stop Planner CD-ROM**, Disc 2.

internet

go.hrw.com	**MARCAR:** go.hrw.com
	PALABRA CLAVE:
	WV3 ECUADOR-7

INTERNET CONNECTION

*Have students explore the **go.hrw.com** Web site for many online resources covering all chapters. All Chapter 7 resources are available under the keyword **WV3 ECUADOR-7**. Interactive games help students practice the material and provide them with immediate feedback. You will also find a printable worksheet that provides Internet activities that lead to a comprehensive online research project.*

JUEGOS INTERACTIVO

You can use the interactive activities in this chapter

- to practice grammar, vocabulary, and chapter functions
- as homework
- as an assessment option
- as a self-test
- to prepare for the Chapter Test

ACTIVIDADES INTERNET

Students describe things they would like to do and see in a Latin American country. They describe activities they might do with different companions.

- To prepare students for the Hoja de actividades, have them review the chapter functions by viewing the dramatic episode on Videocassette 3.
- After students have completed the activity sheet, have them share the "rainy day" activities with a partner. Were any the same? Could students do any of those activities in their own city? Where?

Proyecto

Working in small groups, have students plan a group vacation to a city in the **Hoja de actividades**. They should find three or four activities that everyone in the group would like to do there. They then describe their group's vacation, including places they plan to visit. You might have them post the vacation itinerary, along with images from the city, on a personal Web site.

For Student Response Forms, see Listening Activities pp. 55–57.

PRIMER PASO   pp. 48–55

5 Por teléfono   p. 49

1. — Aló.
   — Buenas tardes, señorita. ¿Está Miguel, por favor?
   — Sí, un momento. ¿De parte de quién, por favor?
   — De parte de Roberto.

2. — Bueno, Silvia. Ya es tarde y necesito estudiar para el examen.
   — Está bien. Hasta mañana, ¿eh?
   — Sí, hasta mañana, Silvia. Chao.

3. — ¿Bueno? Casa García a sus órdenes.
   — Buenos días. ¿Está el señor Alejandro García, por favor?
   — Lo siento mucho, pero el señor no está. ¿Quién habla?
   — Soy Pedro Castillo.

4. — ¿Bueno?
   — Buenas noches, señora. ¿Está María en casa?
   — ¿Eres tú, Alicia?
   — Sí, señora. ¿Cómo está usted?
   — Bien, gracias, pero María no está en casa.
   — Bueno, señora, llamo más tarde.
   — Adiós.

Answers to Activity 5

Answers will vary. Possible answers:

1. a   **2.** b   **3.** c   **4.** a and c

8 En el tiempo libre   p. 51

1. ¿Quieres jugar al tenis esta tarde?
2. ¿Quieres ir a cenar esta noche?
3. ¿Te gustaría ir al centro conmigo?
4. ¿Te gustaría estudiar con nosotros?
5. ¿Prefieres la comida mexicana o la comida china?
6. ¿Te gustaría ir al cine conmigo esta tarde?

Answers to Activity 8

1. ilógico	**3.** lógico	**5.** ilógico
2. ilógico	**4.** lógico	**6.** lógico

15 Las vacaciones   p. 54

MÓNICA   Bueno, Carlos, ¿qué hacemos mañana?

CARLOS   Quiero ir al museo de antropología.

MÓNICA   Ay, Carlos, a mamá y a mí no nos gustan los museos. Tengo otra idea. Si hace buen tiempo mañana, ¿quieres ir al lago o al campo?

CARLOS   Prefiero el lago porque me gusta nadar. Y a papá también le gustaría pescar.

MÓNICA   ¡Excelente! Vamos más o menos a las diez de la mañana.

Answers to Activity 15

1. They decide to go to the lake.
2. The weather is nice. Carlos likes to swim and his dad likes to fish.
3. They're going at about ten in the morning.

26 **¿Todos listos?   p. 63**

1. MAMÁ   Manuel, aquí viene el autobús.
   MANUEL   ¡Ay, no! Mamá, todavía necesito lavarme los dientes.
   MAMÁ   Pues, ¡apúrate, hijo!

2. MAMÁ   Gabi, ya son las ocho. Vas con tu novio a la fiesta de cumpleaños de Miguel a las ocho y media, ¿no? ¿Estás lista?
   GABI   No, mamá. Estoy un poco atrasada. Necesito maquillarme.

3. MAMÁ   Armando, ¿estás listo para ir al circo con tus primos?
   ARMANDO   Sí...
   MAMÁ   Pero hijo, tu pelo es un desastre.
   ARMANDO   Ah, tienes razón, Mamá. Necesito peinarme.

4. MAMÁ   ¿Estás listo, querido? Tenemos que estar en el teatro en media hora.
   PAPÁ   Lo siento, mi amor. Todavía necesito afeitarme.
   MAMÁ   Está bien, pero apúrate, por favor.

5. MAMÁ   Berta, hoy es la boda de tu amiga Verónica, ¿verdad?
   BERTA   Sí, mamá. A las tres. Hombre, son las dos y todavía necesito ducharme.

Answers to Activity 26

1. d   **2.** e   **3.** a   **4.** c   **5.** b

32 **¿Te gustaría...?   p. 67**

1. — Hola, Miguel. ¿Te gustaría ir con nosotros al partido de fútbol esta noche?
   — Lo siento, pero tengo que estudiar.

2. — Hola, Gabriela. Este fin de semana vamos al lago. ¿Te gustaría ir con nosotros?
   — ¡Qué lástima! Ya tengo planes para este fin de semana.

3. — Oye, Roberto, ¿te gustaría cenar con nosotros esta noche?
   — ¿Esta noche? Ay, tengo una cita esta noche.

4. — Mariana, ¿te gustaría tomar un refresco esta tarde?
   — Estoy un poco cansada. Tal vez otro día, ¿eh?

Answers to Activity 32

1. c   **2.** d   **3.** a   **4.** b

LETRA Y SONIDO   p. 71

For the scripts for Parts A and C, see page 71. The script for Part B is below.

B. Dictado

¡Qué lástima! Lupita y Yolanda quieren ir al lago el lunes, pero ya tengo planes con Lorena. Yo no voy allí con ellas.

REPASO   pp. 76–77

1 **p. 76**

1. — ¿Te gustaría ir al cine esta noche?
   — Lo siento, pero estoy un poco enferma. Tengo que descansar.

2. — ¿Te gustaría ir al museo el sábado?
   — Me gustaría, pero ya tengo planes. Pienso ir al parque de atracciones.

3. — ¿Quieres ir a caminar por la plaza?
   — Me gustaría, pero necesito ducharme. Tal vez en dos horas.

4. — ¿Quieres ir al partido de fútbol el domingo?
   — Sí, me gustaría. ¿A qué hora es?

Answers to Repaso Activity 1

1. b   **2.** b   **3.** a   **4.** a

CAPÍTULO 7

¿Qué te gustaría hacer?

PROJECTS

LA INVITACIÓN

*This is an individual project. Students use the vocabulary from this chapter to make written formal or informal invitations, which may be used as part of the **En mi cuaderno** activity on page 71. Encourage students to include information about the host, the occasion, the time, and the place. Encourage them to describe the event or activities.*

Introduction

Lead a discussion with students about why people send invitations. Have students give examples of some events for which they might receive written invitations. What are some formal invitations they might receive? (a formal dance, a party given by an organization, or a special holiday celebration) When do they receive informal written invitations? (birthday parties, a lunch invitation from a friend)

Materials students may need

- ◆ Poster board or cardboard
- ◆ Colored paper
- ◆ Markers
- ◆ Index cards
- ◆ Old magazines

Sequence

1. Have students write a formal or an informal invitation. Remind them to be creative, humorous, and imaginative.

2. If students choose to write an informal invitation to a friend for a party or get-together, they may use the informal vocabulary from the chapter and the friend's first name.

3. If students choose to write a formal invitation, they use the person's last name preceded by one of the following titles or abbreviations: **Sr. (señor)**, **Srta. (señorita)**, or **Sra. (señora)**, followed by their last name. The following is an example of a formal invitation: **El señor Fernández le invita a una fiesta en su casa el martes próximo, a las nueve de la noche, México D.F., 17 de diciembre.** The underlined words may be replaced with the student's information.

4. Once students have decided whether to make formal or informal invitations, they should decide what specific occasions they are designing the invitations for.

5. Have students decorate the invitation by drawing borders, attaching pictures from old magazines, and gluing on cut out colored paper.

Grading the project

Suggested point distribution (total = 100 points):

Vocabulary use	**20**
Appearance	**20**
Creativity	**20**
Grammar usage	**20**
Comprehensibility	**20**

ME ARREGLO

In this project, students prepare a box of materials representing the vocabulary for personal care. Students identify and label the products in Spanish, and present them orally with a partner. This is an excellent exercise for visual and kinesthetic learners.

Introduction

Ask students about their morning routines. What do they do to get ready for school? To review some vocabulary, you may act out part of your morning routine and have students guess in Spanish what you are doing. Or you may ask volunteers to act out their morning routines as the other students guess in Spanish.

Materials students may need

- ◆ Empty containers (shampoo, toothpaste, etc.)
- ◆ Toothbrush
- ◆ Comb or hairbrush
- ◆ Cardboard box/shopping bag
- ◆ Index cards
- ◆ Markers
- ◆ Tape

Sequence

1. Students work in pairs to brainstorm a list of items they use to get ready every day. Have them draw pictures of the items as they think of them and then write a list in Spanish. Then have pairs collect some or all of the personal care items on their list as homework.

2. Have each pair bring in empty containers of personal care items and put them in a box or bag. Empty toothpaste cartons, soap boxes, and shampoo containers are good examples. Students label the items in Spanish.

3. In pairs, students practice the item vocabulary orally and practice the verb that demonstrates the action using the item. For example, one partner holds a comb and says **¿Qué es esto?** After vocabulary is familiar, students remove the labels and quiz each other. For example, one partner holds up toothpaste and asks **¿Qué voy a hacer?** and the other answers **Vas a lavarte los dientes.**

4. Students practice saying the reflexive verb and the item. (**Voy a lavarme los dientes con el cepillo de dientes.**)

5. Partners can share their vocabulary items with other pairs and quiz each other with the new items. Have students present their items to the class with their partner.

Grading the project

Suggested point distribution (total = 100 points):

Appropriate number of items included. **20**

Correct labels for items **20**

Spanish pronunciation. **20**

Correctness of verb & noun form **20**

Cooperative effort. **20**

✂ 🪮 HAGAMOS UNA FIESTA

In this project students are responsible for planning an imaginary party. It reinforces vocabulary for extending an invitation, planning activities for a party, and making a guest list. This activity utilizes and reinforces interpersonal intelligence.

Introduction

Ask students what kind of celebrations they like. Have they ever helped plan a party? What are the steps involved in planning a guest list, sending invitations and planning activities?

Materials students may need

◆ Large poster board   ◆ Colored pens or markers
◆ Glue sticks   ◆ Colored paper

Sequence

1. Tell students to imagine they have their own party-planning business. They have been hired to plan a surprise party for a client. They are responsible for designing an invitation, writing a guest list, planning the party activities, and making a party preparation checklist. They have one week to pull the surprise party together.

2. Divide students into groups of four. Each group of party planners has one person in charge of each of the following: invitations, the guest list, activities, and the preparation checklist. Their jobs are as follows:

   • To create an invitation that has the time, date, location, host name, and other important information.

   • To make a list of family members to invite, identifying them by relationship (**madre, padre, abuelo, hermana**) and name. (Refer students to the family vocabulary on pages 291–292 for a review.)

   • To make a list of activities (verbs) that the guests can do and to suggest possible locations for the party.

   • To make a checklist of personal preparations (**ducharse, peinarse, lavarse los dientes.**)

3. Each team arranges the lists and invitation in an attractive way for a presentation to the client. Each member of the group presents his or her own part of the plan to the class for evaluation. The class can vote for the party planners they would hire to plan their party.

Grading the project

Suggested point distribution (total = 100 points):

Information sheets complete (10 each) **40**

Neatness, overall presentation. **10**

Pronunciation and clarity of presentation (10 each). **40**

Cooperative effort. **10**

CAPÍTULO 7

¿Qué te gustaría hacer?

GAMES

LA LLAMADA

This game gives students an opportunity to practice telephone numbers and some telephone vocabulary.

Materials students may need

◆ Index cards
◆ Pens or markers

Preparation

1 Make two master lists of twenty different telephone numbers, an A list and a B list.

2 Copy the numbers from the master lists onto index cards for students to use during the game. Write a different phone number on each. (Use numerals; don't spell the numbers.)

Procedure

1 Hand out the A cards to Team A and the B cards to Team B. Each student should receive at least one card.

2 Assume the role of the **operador/a**. In Spanish, call out a telephone number from either list.

3 The student who has the card with the matching number raises his or her hand and says **Aló**.

4 Play until all students have answered their phone numbers.

A CONTINUACIÓN

*This game allows students to learn many vocabulary words at a time. It can be played with a large number of students or as few as six or eight. **A continuación** is helpful for auditory learners.*

Preparation

Choose a category from chapter vocabulary and assign one word from that category to each player, including yourself. (food, family members, outdoor activities) In the example below, the theme is "morning routine" and the teacher's word is **desayunar**.

Procedure

1 Have students stand. This game works best if students can see each other. Start the game by saying a sentence with your verb along with someone else's: **Voy a desayunar y ducharme**.

2 The person who has the word **ducharse** must make up a sentence quickly, using his or her verb followed by someone else's: **Voy a ducharme y lavarme los dientes**. The student sits down if he or she says the sentence correctly. The person who has the phrase **lavarse los dientes** continues.

3 Students may not choose previously used words. The game is meant to be fast-paced.

4 When a person fails to respond with his or her sentence or responds incorrectly, he or she should remain standing. Continue until everyone is seated.

5 You will need to change the repeated sentence according to the theme you choose. For example, **Voy a visitar a** (family vocabulary).

ADIVINA

This game allows students to apply the expressions and vocabulary that they learned in this chapter. It can be played with the whole class or with as few as two students.

Materials students may need

◆ Empty containers (shampoo, toothpaste, etc.)
◆ A towel or washcloth
◆ A bar of soap
◆ A brush or comb

Procedure

1 The first player leaves the room and the others choose an object for him or her to guess.

2 When the student returns, he or she asks the group a question about the use of the object with **¿cuándo? ¿por qué?** or **¿dónde?** For example, if the guesser asks **¿Cuándo uso esto?**, any student may raise his or her hand to answer, **por la mañana**.

3 The player guessing continues asking questions until he or she guesses the object. When the player guesses correctly, he or she sits down.

4 A second player leaves the room, and the procedure is repeated.

5 This game may be played for five minutes or until all the related chapter vocabulary has been practiced.

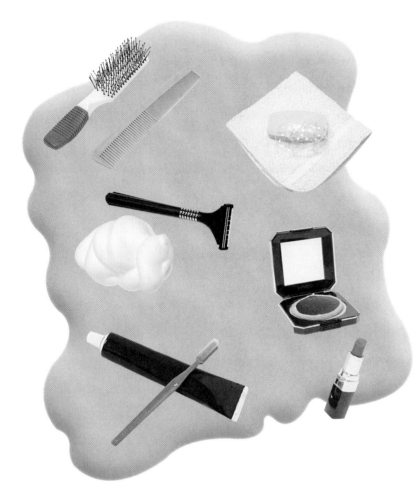

CONTRA EL RELOJ

Students make their own game using containers, boxes, and packages from personal care products. The game reinforces noun and verb vocabulary from this chapter. This game is excellent for visual and kinesthetic learners.

Materials students may need

◆ Empty containers (shampoo, toothpaste, etc.)

◆ Index cards

◆ Pens or markers

◆ Removable memo notes or removable tape

Preparation

1 If students have brought in empty containers for the **Me arreglo** project on pages 41G–41H, pool the class resources into one large box. If not, ask students to bring in two or three boxes or containers from personal care products.

2 Each student will label his or her items on index cards. Students should make two sets of cards: one for the item (**jabón**) and one for the verb that goes with it (**lavarse**). Tape these cards to the item for practice only. Later, for the game, they should remove the label.

Sequence

1 Choose approximately 15–20 items with their corresponding cards.

2 Lay out the containers on a long table and give the packet of cards to a student.

3 The object of the game is to place the correct cards next to each product on the table while being timed. The student must say the Spanish word for the product and the corresponding infinitive as he or she puts down the cards.

4 This game can also be played with teams. Divide the products into two boxes and the class into two teams to compete against each other for the better time.

ANSWERS TO CHAPTER 7 ACTIVITIES

Listening activity answers appear on Scripts pages 41E–41F. Answers to all other activities appear on corresponding pupil pages.

DE ANTEMANO   pp. 44–47

1
1. They're talking about María's party.
2. Tomás is in a bad mood because María hasn't invited him to her party.
3. He suggests they do something on Saturday.
4. María calls to invite Carlos to her party. Carlos says he can't go because he has plans.
5. Answers will vary. Possible answer: Tomás will not get María's message because it got lost under the notebooks.

PRIMER PASO   pp. 48–55

11 Answers will vary. Possible answers:
1. (Ellos) quieren un perro.
2. Sandra prefiere las frutas.
3. (Él) tiene dos cuadernos.
4. ¿Prefieres una pizza o un sándwich?
5. La película empieza a las siete de la noche.
6. (Nosotros) queremos un helado.
7. Siempre vengo a la casa después de las clases.

SEGUNDO PASO   pp. 58–65

27
1. afeitarse/ducharse
2. ducharse
3. lavarse los dientes
4. peinarte
5. maquillarme

TERCER PASO   pp. 66–71

34 Answers will vary. Possible answers:
1. Tienen prisa.
2. Tienen ganas de comer pizza.
3. Tengo que estudiar.
4. Tenemos que practicar el fútbol.
5. Tiene que lavarse los dientes todos los días.
6. Tienen que peinarse.
7. Tiene que ir a la biblioteca.
8. Tengo ganas de escuchar música jazz.

VAMOS A LEER   pp. 74–75

B
1. You can camp or stay in a floating hotel.
2. Llamas, vicuñas, condors; you can take pictures and hike to the peak.

3. Walk or swim among animals and explore the islands on a yacht.
4. El Chimborazo is the closest to Quito. You can get to the Galápagos by boat.

C
1. El Chimborazo
2. el Parque Nacional Cuyabena
3. el Parque Nacional Galápagos
4. el Parque Nacional Cuyabena and el Parque Nacional Galápagos
5. el Parque Nacional Cuyabena, el Parque Nacional Galápagos, and El Chimborazo

REPASO   pp. 76–77

3
1. Piensa escuchar música, leer una novela y ver unas películas.
2. No puede ir porque está enferma.

¡Ay! ¡Los abuelos van a estar aquí mañana! ¡Voy a limpiar la casa!

Chapter Section	Presentation	Homework Options
Primer paso	**Así se dice,** p. 49	*Grammar and Vocabulary,* p. 1, Activities 1–2 *Practice and Activity Book,* pp.14–15, Activities 3–4
	Así se dice, p. 51	*Pupil's Edition,* p. 51, Activity 9 *Practice and Activity Book,* p. 15, Activity 5
	Gramática, p. 52	*Pupil's Edition,* pp. 52–53, Activities 11–12 *Grammar and Vocabulary,* p. 2, Activities 3–4 *CD-ROM,* Disc 2, Chapter 7, Activity 2
	Vocabulario, p. 54	*Grammar and Vocabulary,* p. 3, Activities 5–7 *Practice and Activity Book,* p. 16, Activities 6–7 *CD-ROM,* Disc 2, Chapter 7, Activity 1
Segundo paso	**Así se dice,** p. 59	*Pupil's Edition,* p. 59, Activities 20–21 *Practice and Activity Book,* p. 17, Activity 8
	Gramática, p. 60	*Pupil's Edition,* pp. 60–61, Activities 22–24 *Grammar and Vocabulary,* pp. 4–5, Activities 8–11 *Practice and Activity Book,* pp. 18–19, Activities 10–11 *CD-ROM,* Disc 2, Chapter 7, Activity 3
	Así se dice, p. 63	*Practice and Activity Book,* p. 19, Activity 12 *CD-ROM,* Disc 2, Chapter 7, Activity 4
	Nota gramatical, p. 64	*Pupil's Edition,* pp. 64–65, Activities 27, 29 *Grammar and Vocabulary,* p. 6, Activities 12–13
Tercer paso	**Así se dice,** p. 67	*Grammar and Vocabulary,* p. 7, Activities 14–15 *Practice and Activity Book,* p. 20, Activities 13–14 *CD-ROM,* Disc 2, Chapter 7, Activity 5
	Nota gramatical, p. 68	*Pupil's Edition,* pp. 68–71, Activities 34, 37, 39, 41 *Grammar and Vocabulary,* p. 8, Activities 16–17 *Practice and Activity Book,* pp. 21–22, Activities 15–18 *CD-ROM,* Disc 2, Chapter 7, Activity 6

¿Qué te gustaría hacer?

MOTIVATING ACTIVITY
Discuss with your students when and how they use the telephone. Who are the people they call most often? What do they usually talk about? Are there rules at their house about the use of the telephone?

RE-ENTRY
Write the following questions on the board: **¿Con quién hablas más por teléfono? ¿De qué hablan ustedes?** Ask students to identify the verbs. (**hablas, hablan**) Then have them determine the form that the verb in the answer will take (**hablo, hablamos**) and how they might answer the question. Write the minidialogues on the board or transparency. Once they are comfortable with the dialogue format, have them ask and answer these questions with a partner.

 CULTURE NOTE
During certain times of the year in Spain, Mexico, Ecuador, and other Spanish-speaking countries, it is common to spend a weekend afternoon at a bullfight (**una corrida de toros**). Families and friends go to the large bullrings (**plazas de toros**) to watch the bullfight and equestrian events, to socialize, and to eat.

CAPÍTULO

7

¿Qué te gustaría hacer?

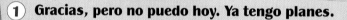

1 Gracias, pero no puedo hoy. Ya tengo planes.

In this chapter you will learn to

PRIMER PASO

- talk on the telephone
- extend and accept invitations

SEGUNDO PASO

- make plans
- talk about getting ready

TERCER PASO

- turn down an invitation and explain why

🖅 internet

MARCAR: go.hrw.com
PALABRA CLAVE:
WV3 ECUADOR-7

② **Buenos días. ¿Está Pablo, por favor?**

③ **Necesito peinarme y lavarme los dientes.**

Invitación para Ana Macías Gómez

Vamos a celebrar mi cumpleaños con una fiesta en mi ...

cuarenta y tres **43**

FOCUSING ON OUTCOMES

Have students describe the people in these photos (see questions below) and match them with the learner outcomes. (Photo 1: turning down an invitation and explaining why; Photo 2: talking on the telephone; Photo 3: getting ready) Ask students to list in Spanish at least five things they do for fun with friends. Encourage them to use vocabulary from past chapters, such as **ir a un partido de fútbol, salir, ir al cine, caminar, comer,** and **bailar.** Tell students that in this chapter they will learn how to invite people to do things, to accept or turn down an invitation, and to talk about what they need to do to get ready.

PREGUNTAS

Have your students describe the people in these photos by asking them the following questions: **¿Cómo es el chico en la foto número uno? ¿Con quién habla? ¿Qué dice? ¿Cómo es el chico en la foto número dos? ¿Es rubio? ¿Qué dice él? En la foto número tres, ¿cuántas personas hay? ¿Qué hace? ¿Qué necesita hacer?**

VIDEO INTEGRATION

En camino LEVEL 1B
Video Program
Videocassette 1, 12:43–18:07 OR
Videocassette 3, 1:06:18–1:11:41
(captioned version)

¡Ven conmigo! LEVEL 1
DVD Tutor, Disc 2

TEACHER NOTE
The **fotonovela** is an abridged version of the video episode.

VIDEO SYNOPSIS
Tomás tells his friend Carlos that he is in a bad mood because María is having a party on Saturday and didn't invite him. The two decide to go to a concert on Saturday, as Carlos doesn't have plans either. While they are at Carlos's house watching a video, María calls to invite Carlos to the party. Carlos tells her that he is sorry but he has other plans for Saturday. While Tomás is at Carlos's house, María calls Tomás's house and leaves a message with Tomás's father about the party. The message gets buried under a stack of papers near the telephone. Will Tomás find it?

DE ANTEMANO

 ¿Qué hacemos?

CD 7 Trs. 19–20

Look at the photos. What kind of mood is Tomás in? How is Carlos trying to help Tomás? Who is Maria and how is she involved? Read the story and see what happens.

p. 13
Acts. 1–2

Carlos   **María**

Tomás   **Sr. Ortiz**

44 *cuarenta y cuatro*   CAPÍTULO 7   ¿Qué te gustaría hacer?

44   STANDARDS: 1.2

MOTIVATING ACTIVITY
Ask students to imagine that they're planning a celebration. (a birthday party, a holiday party) How would they invite people? Would they mail out invitations? Would they call to invite guests? How would they respond if they received an invitation? How would they accept or turn down the invitation? Explain that in this chapter they will learn how to make plans, extend invitations, and accept them or turn them down.

NATIVE SPEAKERS
Point out that these characters speak with a typical Ecuadorean accent and inflection. Ask students if they find this regional accent easy to understand. How is it similar or different from the way they speak?

Have native speakers scan the **fotonovela** for two **palabras esdrújulas,** words accented two syllables from the last and always written with an accent. (**sábado, lástima**) Have them add these to their spelling notebooks.

GROUP WORK
Divide students into groups of four. Assign each student the role of one of the characters in the **fotonovela.** Ask students to role-play the **fotonovela** with their group members.

45

PRESENTATION

First, have students look at the photos and scan the captions. Have them scan for familiar words and cognates. Ask them to guess what happens in the story frame by frame. Then play the video. As a follow-up, ask students if their predictions were correct.

LANGUAGE NOTES

• Other common words for eyeglasses are **los anteojos, los espejuelos,** and **las gafas.**

• **Chao,** an informal and popular way to say *good-bye,* is from the Italian word *ciao.*

A continuación

You may choose to continue with *¿Qué hacemos? (a continuación)* at this time or wait until later in the chapter. At this point, Tomás and Carlos change their weekend plans when they discover that they are both invited to María's party. They arrive for the party, but it has been rescheduled because the guest of honor will not arrive until Monday. You may wish to have students predict what will happen in the second part of the video.

Cuaderno para hispanohablantes, pp. 31–35

1 ¿Comprendes? Answers on p. 41K

What's happening in the **fotonovela**? Answer the questions. If you don't know the answer, guess!

These activities check for global comprehension only. Students should not yet be expected to produce language modeled in **De antemano**.

1. What are Tomás and Carlos talking about?
2. How does Tomás feel? Why does he feel that way?
3. What suggestion does Carlos make?
4. Why does María call Carlos? How does he react?
5. Do you think Tomás will get María's message? Why or why not?

2 ¿Cierto o falso?

Indica si las oraciones son ciertas o falsas.

1. Tomás está de mal humor. cierto
2. Carlos y Tomás deciden ir a un concierto el sábado. cierto
3. María invita a Carlos, pero no a Tomás. falso; María invita a los dos chicos.
4. Carlos no acepta la invitación de María. cierto
5. Tomás recibe el recado de María. falso; Tomás no recibe el recado de María.

3 ¿Cómo se dice?

Find and copy the words and phrases that . . .

1. Tomás uses to say what he'd rather do Prefiero salir.
2. Carlos uses to ask if Tomás has to do something ¿Tienes que hacer algo?
3. María uses to invite Carlos to her party ¿Quieres ir a una fiesta este sábado?
4. Carlos uses to turn down María's invitation Lo siento pero no puedo. Ya tengo planes.
5. Mr. Ortiz uses to ask who's calling ¿De parte de quién?

SLOWER PACE

1 Have students work in small groups to discuss these comprehension questions. They should record how many different ideas and opinions they have about what happens in the **fotonovela**.

CHALLENGE

1 Ask students to close their books while you ask these questions in Spanish: **¿De qué hablan Tomás y Carlos?** (de la fiesta de María) **¿Por qué llama María a Carlos?** (para invitarlo a su fiesta)

Encourage students to take risks and use as much Spanish as possible when answering. You might consider having students write their answers in Spanish first and then say them aloud.

SUGGESTION

2 Have students correct the sentences that are false.

CHALLENGE

3 Once students have identified the Spanish expressions, have them practice those expressions with a partner. If students have difficulty finding them, play the segment of the videocassette or DVD where these expressions are used.

VIDEO INTEGRATION

En camino LEVEL 1B
Video Program
Videocassette 1, 14:53–15:17 OR
Videocassette 3, 1:08:20–1:08:44
(captioned version)

¡Ven conmigo! LEVEL 1
DVD Tutor, Disc 2

Bell work

Write the following telephone numbers on the board or on a transparency: 15-41-21, 78.52.18, 53-69-10, 28.36.17, and 442-2230. Explain that some countries in Latin America use dashes and others use periods to separate the numbers. Have students write out the numerals as words as they would be spoken in Spanish. Tell students that phone numbers in Spanish-speaking countries are usually read two digits at a time. (15-41-21 = **quince, cuarenta y uno, veintiuno**) If the phone number has seven digits, the first digit is spoken alone, then the other six in pairs. (555-4321 = **cinco, cincuenta y cinco, cuarenta y tres, veintiuno**)

PRIMER PASO (TPR) Storytelling Book pp. 25, 28

WV3 ECUADOR-7

Talking on the telephone; extending and accepting invitations

¿Aló?

Ah...hola, María

Hola, Carlos. Habla María.

Carlos, ¿quieres venir a una fiesta este sábado? Es para un estudiante de intercambio de Estados Unidos.

4 Los planes

Answer the questions about María and Carlos's conversation.

1. What does Carlos say as a greeting when he answers the phone?
2. What does María say to identify herself as the caller?
3. What event or activity does María invite Carlos to?
4. Who is the party for?

1. ¿Aló?
2. Habla María.
3. María invites Carlos to a party.
4. an exchange student from the United States

Nota cultural

In Spanish-speaking countries, people answer the phones in a variety of ways. Businesses generally use a more formal greeting such as **Buenos días** or **Buenas tardes.** A common telephone greeting in Mexico is **¿Bueno?** In other countries, you might hear **Hola, Diga,** or **Pronto.** How do you answer the phone? How is the phone answered in your school's office?

p. 24
Act. 20

ASÍ SE DICE Talking on the telephone

If you called a friend who wasn't home, your conversation with your friend's mother might go like this:

SEÑORA **Diga.**
Hello.

PABLO Buenos días, señora. ¿Está Cristina, por favor?

SEÑORA ¿Quién habla?

PABLO Soy yo, Pablo.

SEÑORA Ah, Pablo. ¿Cómo estás hoy?

PABLO Muy bien, ¿y usted?

SEÑORA Muy bien, gracias. Pero Cristina no está.

PABLO Bueno, **llamo más tarde.**
Well, I'll call later.

SEÑORA Adiós, Pablo.

If you needed to leave a message for someone, your conversation might go like this:

SECRETARIA **Aló,** oficina de la señorita Álvarez.
Hello, Miss Álvarez's office.

DIEGO ¿Está la señorita Álvarez, por favor?

SECRETARIA **¿De parte de quién?**
Who's calling?

DIEGO De parte de Diego Vásquez.

SECRETARIA **Un momento...** lo siento pero **su linea está ocupada.**
One moment . . . I'm sorry but her line is busy.

DIEGO Gracias. **¿Puedo dejar un recado?**
May I leave a message?

SECRETARIA **Está bien.**
All right.

rin-rin

5 Por teléfono

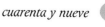

CD 7 Tr. 21

Listen to the four telephone calls. Decide if the caller is: Script and answers on p. 41E

a. greeting someone
b. saying goodbye
c. unable to reach the person

There may be more than one correct answer.

PRIMER PASO

cuarenta y nueve 49

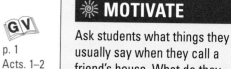
☀ **MOTIVATE**

Ask students what things they usually say when they call a friend's house. What do they say if the friend isn't home? Do they leave a message if they get an answering machine?

☀ **TEACH**

PRESENTATION
ASÍ SE DICE
Use puppets or other props to role-play the conversation for students. If possible, use phones as props. Have students practice the conversations with a partner, then reverse roles. After the class has practiced, walk around the room and take the role of one of the participants. Pick a student to take the other role. Repeat with different students.

LANGUAGE NOTE
In Mexico, a common telephone greeting is **¿Bueno?**

PA
p. 14
Act. 3

GV
p. 1
Acts. 1–2

7-1

COOPERATIVE LEARNING

Divide the class into groups of three. One member of the group asks the other group members **¿Cuántos minutos hablas por teléfono cada día?** The second member adds up the totals of the three group members for each question. The third member reports the totals to the class: **En total, hablamos por teléfono dos horas todos los días.**

RE-ENTRY

On a transparency or on the board, write several names with phone numbers by them. **(Miguel: 42-58-74, Sara: 27-64-31)** Ask students the number for each name. **(¿Cuál es el teléfono de Miguel?)** Students should answer by saying the numbers two digits at a time.

TEACHER NOTE

7 Explain to students that the phones shown here indicate that they should imagine that they're talking on the phone and should use appropriate telephone expressions.

6 ¡Hola!

Choose a phrase from column B that is an appropriate telephone response to the phrase in column A.

MODELO   —¿Está Amalia, por favor?
　　　　　　　—Un momento, por favor.

A

1. ¿Quién habla, por favor? d
2. El señor Chávez no está. a
3. ¿Está Omar, por favor? b
4. ¿Aló? f
5. Bueno, señora, llamo más tarde. e
6. ¿Cómo está? c

B

a. ¿Puedo dejar un recado?
b. Un momento, por favor.
c. Bien, gracias, ¿y usted?
d. Gustavo Muñoz.
e. Adiós.
f. ¿Está la doctora Pérez?

7 ¡Diga!

Working with a partner, read the speech bubbles below. Take turns pretending to be person **a** and person **b**. Say what should go in the empty speech bubbles and role-play the telephone conversations. Then switch roles.   Answers will vary.

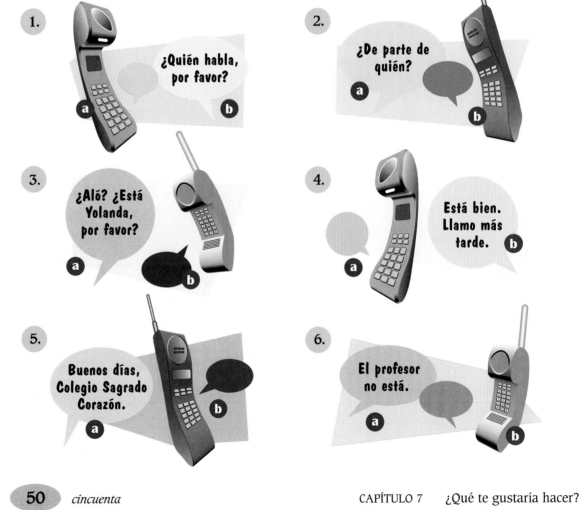

50   STANDARDS: 1.1, 5.1

ASÍ SE DICE
Extending and accepting invitations

To invite a friend to do something, say:

¿Te gustaría ir al cine con nosotros?
Would you like to go to the movies with us?

Nos gustan las películas de aventura y hay una a las nueve.
We like adventure movies and there's one at 9 o'clock.

¿Quieres ir a comer el sábado?
Te invito. *It's my treat.*

Your friend might answer:

Sí, **me gustaría** ir con ustedes.
Yes, I'd like to go with you.

¡Claro que sí! Gracias.
Of course!

p. 15
Act. 5

7-1

8 En el tiempo libre
Script and answers on p. 41E

CD 7 Tr. 22

First read each sentence. Then listen to the questions. If the sentence is a logical response to the question, on a separate sheet of paper write **lógico**. If it's not an appropriate response, write **ilógico**.

1. Sí, me gustaría ir a comer.
2. No, me gustan los deportes.
3. ¡Claro que sí!
4. ¡Cómo no! La clase es muy difícil.
5. Prefiero las películas de aventura.
6. No, no me gustan las películas.

9 Te invito

Write five questions inviting friends to go somewhere. Use words from the box to help you. Answers will vary.

MODELO ¿Te gustaría ir a la playa con mi familia el domingo?

el centro comercial
el cine
el concierto de rock
el baile

el parque
la casa de...
el restaurante
la fiesta

la piscina
el gimnasio
la biblioteca

10 ¿Quieres ir?

Now get together with a partner. Take turns reading the questions you wrote for Activity 9. Accept your partner's invitations. Answers will vary.

MODELO —¿Quieres ir a la playa con mi familia este fin de semana?
—¡Claro que sí! Me gusta mucho nadar.

¿Te acuerdas?

Remember that **al** is a contraction of **a** and **el**. **Voy al parque.**

PRESENTATION
ASÍ SE DICE

Ask for two volunteers to come to the front of the class and help you role-play the dialogues. With one student at your side, ask the other student to read the role of "your friend" in the book. Use hand gestures as you invite the student to be sure the class understands the invitation is from both you and the person at your side. (**¿Te gustaría ir al cine con nosotros?**) Then have students break into groups of three and practice the dialogues. Ask students to take turns inviting each other to other events such as **un partido de fútbol, una fiesta, el cine,** or **el centro comercial.**

LANGUAGE NOTE

Point out that Spanish, just like English, has many different ways to express an idea. Ask the students if they can think of an equivalent in Spanish for **te gustaría** and **me gustaría.** (**quieres, quiero**) Native speakers may be used to using the more polite **quisiera.** (*I would like...*) Tell students that as they continue their study of Spanish, they will learn many different ways to express themselves.

PRESENTATION
GRAMÁTICA
Write the conjugation of **querer** in two columns on the board. Have one volunteer underline all forms with the stem change and another draw a line around them. Ask students what shape the line looks like. (a capital *L* or a boot) Then have another student draw the shape on the board. Then volunteers write the pronouns in the shape, except **nosotros**, which they write above the toe of the boot. Have students conjugate the verb **empezar** in the "boot," writing the **nosotros** form outside the box.

RE-ENTRY
Remind students what an infinitive is and how to conjugate a regular **-er** verb. Then ask students if they remember two verbs they have already learned that have the irregular **-go** in the **yo** form. (**poner** and **salir**)

NATIVE SPEAKERS
11 In casual speech, native speakers may not hear the stem change in the verb **querer**. Remind them that no matter how they pronounce the forms of **querer**, they should always spell all forms except **nosotros** and **vosotros** with an **ie**.

The **vos** form of the verb does not have a stem change: **vos querés.**

GRAMÁTICA e → ie stem-changing verbs

1. In **e → ie** stem-changing verbs, the letter **e** in the stem changes to **ie** in all forms except the **nosotros** and **vosotros** forms.

   You've been working with an **e → ie** verb: **querer.**

   GV
   p. 2
   Acts. 3–4

(yo)	qu**ie**ro	(nosotros)(nosotras)	quer**emos**
(tú)	qu**ie**res	(vosotros)(vosotras)	quer**éis**
(usted)(él)(ella)	qu**ie**re	(ustedes)(ellos)(ellas)	qu**ie**ren

   Preferir *(to prefer)* and **empezar** *(to begin)* follow the same pattern.

2. Another **e → ie** stem-changer is the irregular verb **venir** *(to come)*. It follows the same pattern as **tener.**

t**e**ngo	ten**emos**	v**e**ngo	ven**imos**
t**ie**nes	ten**éis**	v**ie**nes	ven**ís**
t**ie**ne	t**ie**nen	v**ie**ne	v**ie**nen

11 ¿Qué puedes decir?

Based on the cues, write a sentence or question for each photo. Remember to use the correct form of the verb.   Answers on p. 41K

MODELO   ellas / tener
Ellas tienen dos novelas de romance.

MODELO ellas/tener   **1** ellos/querer   **2** Sandra/preferir   **3** él/tener

4 tú/preferir   **5** la película/empezar   **6** nosotros/querer   **7** yo/venir

12 Una conversación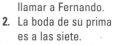

Read Fernando's and David's conversation about their Saturday plans. Then answer the questions.

FERNANDO   Mañana tengo que practicar fútbol a las ocho y media. Después, ¿quieres ir a pescar?

DAVID   Sí, me gustaría ir, pero quiero estar en mi casa a las cuatro de la tarde.

FERNANDO   ¿Por qué? ¿Adónde vas?

DAVID   Vamos a la boda de mi prima Raquel. Es a las siete de la noche.

FERNANDO   Bueno, no hay problema. Venimos temprano *(early)*. ¿Quieres llamarme más tarde? Tengo que hablar con mi mamá.

DAVID   Está bien. Te llamo esta noche a las nueve, después de hacer la tarea.

1. Hacer la tarea y llamar a Fernando.
2. La boda de su prima es a las siete.
3. Tiene que practicar fútbol a las ocho y media.
4. Van a pescar.

1. ¿Qué va a hacer David el viernes por la noche? Menciona dos actividades.
2. ¿Qué va a hacer David el sábado? ¿A qué hora?

3. ¿Qué va a hacer Fernando el sábado? ¿A qué hora?
4. ¿Qué van a hacer juntos?

13 ¿Prefieres...?

Work with a partner to write a questionnaire for your classmates about personal preferences. Write at least five questions about topics such as food, sports, and pets. Answers will vary.

MODELO   ¿Prefieres un gato o un perro como mascota?

14 Una encuesta

Get together with five classmates. Use your questionnaire from Activity 13 to ask them about some personal preferences. Choose a spokesperson for the group to report your results to the class. Answers will vary.

MODELO   Una persona prefiere...
Tres personas prefieren...

VOCABULARIO EXTRA

un pez de colores   *goldfish*
una lagartija   *lizard*
una culebra   *snake*
un canario   *canary*

SLOWER PACE
12 Before answering the questions, students should read each line of the conversation and determine which language function is being used. For example, in Fernando's first line, he's extending an invitation, and so on.

SUGGESTIONS
12 Review days of the week before beginning this activity.
13 Refer students to the Additional Vocabulary on pages 294–296.

ADDITIONAL PRACTICE
Write the subject pronouns on the board or a transparency and ask sudents to secretly choose one and write it on scratch paper. Write a few familiar phrases on the board (**querer un refresco, tener una bicicleta, ir al colegio**). Then call out one of the phrases (**querer un refresco**). Walk around the room and point to a student. He or she holds up the pronoun he or she wrote and gives the sentence that corresponds to that subject pronoun. (A student who had chosen **yo** would say **¡Quiero un refresco!**)

PRESENTATION

VOCABULARIO

Display Teaching Transparency 7-A. As you point to the places depicted in the transparency, use the functional phrases from **Así se dice** on page 51 to invite individual students or groups of students to go there. (**Juan, ¿quieres ir al acuario? Raimundo y Claudia, ¿les gustaría ir al campo?**)

TPR Tape pictures of several places mentioned in **Vocabulario** around the classroom. If you have a copying machine that can enlarge, use Copying Master 7-A to generate the images. Ask students questions (**Juan, ¿dónde está el lago? Paula, ¿dónde está el circo?**) and have students walk or point to the pictures.

SLOWER PACE

15 Pause the tape or CD between each exchange to ask students these questions:
1. What is Mónica asking?
2. What word tells you that Mónica is giving Carlos a choice? (**prefieres**)
3. What does Mónica say that tells you she doesn't want to go to the museum? (**No me gustan los museos.**)
4. Where would Carlos rather go? (**al lago**)
5. What phrase explains why? (**...porque me gusta nadar.**)

PA p. 16 Acts. 6–7

GV p. 3 Acts. 5–7

7-A

VOCABULARIO

CD-ROM DISC 2

Lugares *Places*

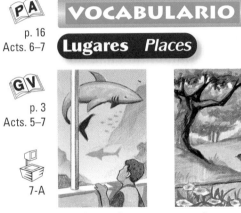

el acuario

el campo

el circo

la ciudad

el lago

el museo de antropología

el parque de atracciones

el teatro

el zoológico

Eventos *Events*

la fiesta de cumpleaños
de aniversario
de graduación
de sorpresa

la boda

---

15 Las vacaciones Script and answers on p. 41E

Mónica and Carlos are on vacation. Their family has asked them to make plans for the whole family for tomorrow. Listen to their CD 7 Tr. 23 conversation and answer these three questions.

1. Where do they decide the family should go?
2. Why do they decide to go there?
3. When are they going?

16 Invitación

Work with a partner. Look at the new vocabulary on page 54. Make a list of three places where you both want to go. Then take turns inviting each other to each place and accepting each other's invitations. *Answers will vary.*

17 ¡Conversación!

Work with a partner. Choose one of the two situations and create a conversation. *Answers will vary.*

1. **a.** Call your friend on the phone and greet the person who answers.
   b. The person asks who's calling.
   c. Say who you are and ask to speak to your friend.
   d. You find out your friend's not there, so leave a message.
   e. Say goodbye to each other.
2. **a.** Call and greet your friend, who answers.
   b. Invite your friend to go someplace with you.
   c. Your friend accepts your invitation.
   d. Say goodbye to each other.

18 Un fin de semana en Quito

There are a lot of fun things to do in Quito. Look at María's schedule for the weekend. Write your weekend schedule modeled after hers. Include the times for each day.

AGENDA

19	jueves	11:00 el museo 6:00 la fiesta de cumpleaños de Pablo
20	viernes	9:00 el zoológico 7:30 el teatro
21	sábado	10:00 el acuario 3:00 el parque de atracciones
22	domingo	12:00 el circo 4:00 el lago con Diego

SLOWER PACE

17 Have students write some expressions they will need for the situation they choose.

18 Allow students time to prepare their schedules. Then have partners peer-edit each other's work.

☀ CLOSE

To review material and verify completion of objectives, use Teaching Transparency 7-3. You might point to different scenes and have students orally describe them in Spanish, or have students invite each other to some of the locations pictured.

☀ ASSESS

▶ Testing Program, pp. 19–20
   Quiz 7-1
   Audio CD 7, Tr. 36

▶ Grammar and Vocabulary Quizzes
   Quiz 7-1A or
   Alternative Quiz 7-1A

▶ Alternative Assessment Guide, p. 19

PERFORMANCE ASSESSMENT

Have students role-play Activity 17, part 2 in pairs. Students use at least three verbs and three new vocabulary words. Have students role-play the conversation for the class. You may record this for an oral Portfolio entry or have students perform it for a grade. Some students can also write the dialogue instead of acting it out.

VIDEO INTEGRATION

En camino LEVEL 1B
Video Program
Videocassette 1, 23:45–25:17

¡Ven conmigo! LEVEL 1
DVD Tutor, Disc 2

TEACHER NOTES
• See *Video Guide* for activities related to the **Panorama cultural.**

• Remind students that cultural information may be included in the Chapter Quizzes and Test.

• The language of the people interviewed represents informal, unrehearsed speech. Occasionally, text has been edited for clarity.

MOTIVATING ACTIVITY
Ask students what they do to get to know new people. Do they invite them to join their friends or do they wait for the person to approach them first?

LANGUAGE NOTE
Mariano does not use the personal **a** after **conocer** in this context because he is referring to unknown people.

Panorama cultural

CD 7
Trs. 24–27

¿Qué haces para conocer a un nuevo estudiante?

How would you get to know someone new in a Spanish-speaking country? We asked some students to tell us how they make friends with someone new.

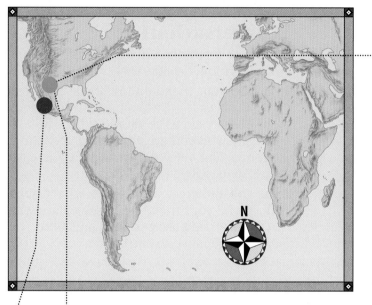

Mariano tries to get to know people in his class. Is it easy for you to get to know new people at school?

Mariano
México, D.F., México
CD 7 Tr. 25

Trato de conocer personas que estén en mi salón y en el recreo. Si estoy jugando algún deporte lo invito a jugar.

Would you ask someone to have a soft drink with you, like Valeria does?

Valeria
San Antonio, Texas
CD 7 Tr. 26

Me acerco a la persona y me presento. Yo le digo: ¿quieres tomar un refresco conmigo?

Alan has a strategy for getting to know someone. How many Spanish phrases have you learned that you might use in this same situation?

CD 7 Tr. 27

●**Alan**

San Antonio, Texas

Yo me presento y luego le pregunto su nombre. Le pregunto si le gustaría venir a mi casa a jugar videojuegos o no más ver la tele.

1 Where does Mariano make new friends?

In class and at recess.

2 Name one way Mariano makes a new friend feel welcome.

He invites them to play a sport with him.

3 How does Valeria first get to know someone new?

She introduces herself.

4 What does Valeria like to invite new friends to do?

She invites them to have a soft drink with her.

5 What does Alan do before asking someone their name?

He introduces himself.

6 What does Alan like to invite friends to do when he asks them over to his house? He likes to watch TV and play video games.

Para pensar y hablar Answers will vary.

A. With a partner, role-play meeting a new person at school. What do you both say? What do you invite the new student to do?

B. Alan likes to invite new friends to his house. Where do you like to get together with your friends?

Cuaderno para hispanohablantes, pp. 34–35

PRESENTATION
Before showing the video or playing the audio recording, have students scan the interview for cognates and known vocabulary. Have students use the lead-in text above each interview to guess the meaning of new words.

NATIVE SPEAKERS
Ask native speakers to compare and constrast the accents of the people interviewed. Which one(s) do they find easiest to understand? Why?

Have native speakers find two examples of **palabras agudas con acento** and add them to their spelling notebooks. **(algún, salón)** Remind them that words accented on the last syllable and ending in a vowel, *n*, or *s* have an accent mark and are called **palabras agudas.**

VIDEO INTEGRATION

En camino LEVEL 1B
Video Program
Videocassette 1, 14:06–14:52 OR
Videocassette 3, 1:07:41–1:08:27
(captioned version)

¡Ven conmigo! LEVEL 1
DVD Tutor, Disc 2

Bell work
On a transparency or the board write the question **¿...es durante la estación de...?** and the following dates: **28 de diciembre, 5 de abril, 15 de julio, 3 de octubre,** and **16 de junio.** Students who need to review the names of the seasons may turn to pages 291–293.

PREVIEWING
19 Have students read these questions as advance organizers before showing the video.

SEGUNDO PASO

(TPR) Storytelling Book pp. 26, 28

WV3 ECUADOR-7

Making plans; talking about getting ready

19 ¿Qué te gustaría hacer?

Use Carlos and Tomás's conversation in the photo to help you answer the questions.

1. ¿Cuándo quiere hacer algo Carlos?
2. ¿Qué prefiere Tomás: salir o hacer algo en casa?
3. ¿Qué hay en el Coliseo Mayor?
4. ¿A Tomás le gustaría ir?

1. el sábado
2. salir
3. un concierto de guitarra
4. sí

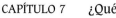

ASÍ SE DICE   Making plans

To make plans with a friend, say:

Pienso ir al zoológico hoy. **Voy a
ver** muchos animales interesantes.
¿Te gustaría ir conmigo?
*I'm planning on going to the zoo
today. I'm going to see a lot of
interesting animals.*

Your friend might answer:

¡Cómo no! ¡Me gustan
mucho los animales!
Of course!

p. 17
Act. 8

7-2

20   Pienso ir... ⬛

Your friends like to do a lot of different things. Match what they
tell you they're planning to do with their interests.

1. Pienso ir al correo esta tarde. b
2. Hoy pienso ir al centro comercial. e
3. Después de las clases, pienso ir al parque. f
4. Pienso ir a la piscina con mi hermano. d
5. Pienso ir al concierto en el coliseo. c
6. Pienso ir a la biblioteca por la mañana. a

a. Melanie (leer, estudiar)
b. Trey (escribir cartas)
c. Alicia (escuchar música)
d. David (nadar)
e. Nicole (comprar ropa)
f. Michael (correr)

21   El fin de semana ⬛

Rogelio and Samuel live in a small town. Read the conversation
they have on Friday afternoon. Then answer the questions with
cierto or **falso**.

SAMUEL   ¡Por fin! Es el fin de semana. ¿Qué piensan hacer
ustedes, Rogelio? ¿Tienes planes?

ROGELIO   Pensamos ir a la ciudad mañana. Primero vamos a ver
el acuario nuevo. Quiero ver los tiburones *(sharks)*.
Después mi hermana piensa ir al centro comercial para
comprar ropa. Mi papá y yo vamos a ir al parque de
atracciones.

SAMUEL   ¡Qué suerte tienes! Yo no tengo planes. Sólo voy a
limpiar mi cuarto y cortar el césped.   Answers below

1. Samuel piensa ir al teatro.
2. La familia de Rogelio piensa
   ir al acuario el sábado.

3. La hermana de Rogelio
   piensa ir al museo.
4. Samuel va a trabajar
   en su casa.

1. falso   2. cierto

3. falso   4. cierto

※ MOTIVATE

Ask students to discuss what
they plan to do today, tomorrow, or this weekend. Ask them
what they will have to do to get
ready for these plans. How do
they usually respond to unexpected changes in plans?

※ TEACH

PRESENTATION
ASÍ SE DICE
Have students read the text
aloud. Then have them role-
play the conversation with
a partner. When they are
comfortable with the ex-
pressions, give them a new
plan, such as **ir al parque,**
and have them change the
rest of the conversation as
necessary. In this case they
could change **ver muchos
animales** to **jugar al fútbol.**
**¡Me gustan mucho los ani-
males!** could become **¡Me
gustan mucho los deportes!**

KINESTHETIC LEARNERS
21 Have students role-play
this conversation before
answering the questions.

cincuenta y nueve   **59**

CAPÍTULO 7

PRESENTATION
GRAMÁTICA

Write the conjugation of **pensar** on the board or on a transparency in the traditional two-column format. Remind students that the "shoe" or "boot" forms (the first, second, third person singular and third person plural) all have the stem change, while the **nosotros** and **vosotros** forms do not. Pronounce the forms and have students repeat them after you.

Write the conjugation of **ir** on the board. Point out that, with the exception of the **yo** form (**voy**), its conjugation follows the same pattern as regular -ar verbs.

ADDITIONAL PRACTICE

22 Have students do this exercise again, this time filling in the blanks with the correct form of the verb **querer.**

1. quieres
2. queremos
3. quiero
4. quieren
5. quiere

GRAMÁTICA Pensar and ir + a + infinitive

1. **Pensar** *(to think)* is another **e → ie** stem-changing verb.

(yo)	p**ienso**	(nosotros) (nosotras)	pens**amos**
(tú)	p**iensas**	(vosotros) (vosotras)	pens**áis**
(usted) (él) (ella)	p**iensa**	(ustedes) (ellos) (ellas)	p**iensan**

PA p. 17 Act. 9 p. 19 Act. 11

GV p. 4 Acts. 8–9

When followed by an infinitive, **pensar** means *to plan,* or *to intend* to do something.

¿Piensas jugar al tenis? *Are you planning to play tennis?*

2. You already know the verb **ir.** This verb can also be used to talk about the future, using the formula **ir + a +** infinitive.

¿Cuándo vas a practicar el piano?
When are you going to practice the piano?

Voy a practicar mañana. *I'm going to practice tomorrow.*

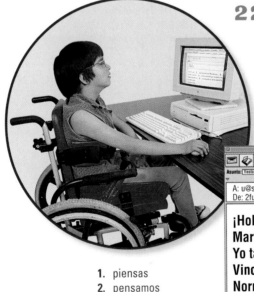

22 ¿Piensas hacer algo?

You're helping Mónica plan a surprise party for another friend. She sent you an e-mail about what she and other people are doing for the party, but your printer didn't print every word. Fill in the blanks with the correct form of **pensar.**

1. piensas
2. pensamos
3. pienso
4. piensan
5. piensa

> **Mensaje**
>
> Asunto: fiesta
>
> A: u@school.edu
> De: 2fun@school.edu
>
> ¡Hola! Tú, ¿qué __1__ hacer para la fiesta?
> Mariela y yo __2__ comprar la comida.
> Yo también __3__ invitar a unos amigos.
> Vincent y Theo __4__ limpiar la sala.
> Norma __5__ tocar la guitarra. ¡No te
> olvides! La fiesta es a las siete en punto.
> Escríbeme pronto :-)

23 ¿Qué van a hacer?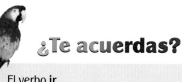

You and your family are going to be very busy this weekend. Use the forms of **ir** to complete your weekend calendar. Answers in side column

¿Te acuerdas?

El verbo **ir**

voy	vamos
vas	vais
va	van

sábado 4 de enero

Mami y Papi __1__ a ir al lago.
Leona __2__ a ir a la boda de su amiga.
Luis y yo __3__ a ir al museo.
Tío Carlos __4__ a jugar al tenis conmigo.

domingo 5 de enero

Abuelita __5__ a visitar a los primos.
¡Nosotros __6__ a limpiar la casa!

24 ¿Qué piensan hacer?

¿Qué van a hacer estas personas? Escribe una frase para cada situación.

MODELO Necesitas más cuadernos.
Voy a ir a la librería.

1. Los estudiantes de la clase de francés tienen un examen muy difícil.
2. Yo tengo una invitación para la fiesta de cumpleaños.
3. Tu hermano quiere jugar al basquetbol pero no tiene zapatos de tenis.
4. Los abuelos vienen a visitar y el cuarto de María Eugenia está completamente desorganizado.
5. Mamá y yo queremos comer pero no hay comida en la casa.

Answers in side column

¡Ay! ¡Los abuelos van a estar aquí mañana! ¡Voy a limpiar la casa!

GAME
Write either **pensar** or **ir** on the board. Have all students stand. Call out a subject pronoun and toss a foam ball to a student. The catcher then calls out the correct form of the verb, calls out another pronoun, tosses the ball to a classmate, and sits down. Continue until all students are seated. If the student calls out an incorrect form, he or she should remain standing and wait for another turn. If a student is unsure of the correct form, he or she may call out **paso** and await another turn. Repeat the activity with another verb.

Answers to Activity 23

1. van
2. va
3. vamos
4. va
5. va
6. vamos

Answers to Activity 24

Answers will vary. Possible answers:
1. Van a estudiar.
2. Voy a ir a la fiesta.
3. Va a comprar unos zapatos.
4. Va a limpiar su cuarto.
5. Vamos a ir al supermercado.

SLOWER PACE
25 If students have trouble recalling vocabulary, write some familiar activities on the board. (**esquiar, hacer ejercicios, leer, pescar, hacer un viaje, salir, visitar**)

ADDITIONAL PRACTICE
25 After students have completed this activity, ask them to tell a partner how they plan to get to each of the activities they are planning.

CRITICAL THINKING
Ask students to use what they already know about teens in Spanish-speaking countries to compare and contrast how the plans of Hispanic teens might be different from those of teenagers in the United States. Ask about playing sports, using public transportation, and so on.

ADDITIONAL PRACTICE
Ask students to pick a destination in a Spanish-speaking country that interests them and write a short paragraph in Spanish telling where they plan to go and what they would like to do there.

🌎 CULTURE NOTE
While London's subway is called the "Underground," it is the "Metro" in Madrid, Paris, Caracas, and Mexico City. What's the name of the public transportation system where you live?

25 ¿Adónde van a ir?

First, work with a partner and take turns asking each other what you plan to do during the days or times listed. Include where you're going to go or what you're going to do. Then get together with another pair of students and report your findings to each other. Use the words in the word box for suggestions. Answers will vary.

MODELO —¿Qué piensas hacer hoy?
—Pienso ir al acuario con mi primo.

el próximo (next) verano   el sábado por la noche
el miércoles
el próximo domingo   mañana
el viernes por la mañana
hoy
este fin de semana

📖 p. 24 Act. 21

🌎 Nota cultural

If you and your family lived in Spain and Latin America you would have many ways of getting around without using a car. Public transportation is inexpensive and convenient in most cities. In big cities, many people use the subway, taxis, buses, or **motos** *(mopeds)*. Sometimes people just walk! Is there public transportation where you live?

VOCABULARIO EXTRA

el metro   *subway*
el autobús   *bus*
el coche, el carro   *car*
la moto   *moped, motorcycle*
la bicicleta, la bici   *bicycle, bike*

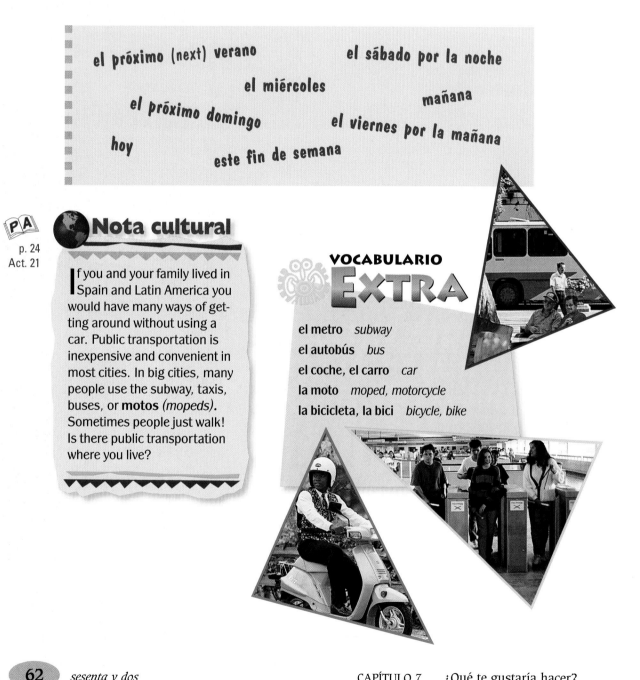

ASÍ SE DICE Talking about getting ready

To ask if a friend is ready, say:

¿Estás listo/a?
Are you ready?

Your friend might answer:

No, **todavía necesito ducharme y afeitarme.**
No, I still need to shower and to shave.

No, porque **necesito lavarme los dientes, peinarme** y **maquillarme.**
No, because I need to brush my teeth, comb my hair, and put on makeup.

p. 19
Act. 12

7-2

26 ¿Todos listos? Script and answers on p. 41F

Listen to some members of the Garza family as they talk about getting ready at different times of day. Based on what you hear, write the letter of the item each person would need in order to get ready.

CD 7 Tr. 28

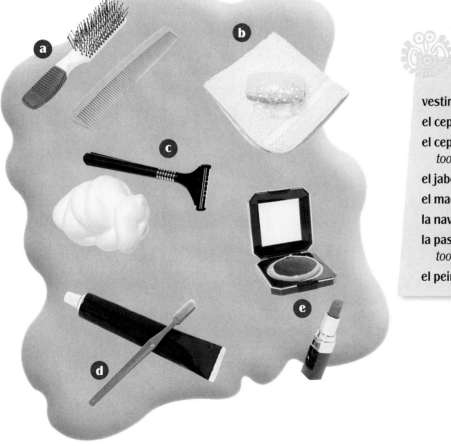

VOCABULARIO EXTRA

vestirse   *to get dressed*

el cepillo   *brush*

el cepillo de dientes
   toothbrush

el jabón   *soap*

el maquillaje   *makeup*

la navaja de afeitar   *razor*

la pasta de dientes
   toothpaste

el peine   *comb*

PRESENTATION
ASÍ SE DICE

Bring in some props. (a washcloth, toothbrush, comb, and makeup) In Spanish, tell the class some plans that you and someone else have for the evening and what you need to do to get ready. **Esta noche, pienso ir al cine con mi esposo/a. Pero no estoy lista/o. Primero, necesito...** (pantomime different grooming verbs as you say them in Spanish). **Mi esposa/o (amiga/o) también necesita ducharse, afeitarse...** (Use the props as you tell about the other person as well.) Then hand the props to different volunteers in the class and call upon them individually to pantomime as you ask the class to respond in unison to your question, **¿Qué necesita hacer (Juan)?** The class responds with you, **Necesita peinarse.**

LANGUAGE NOTE
Another word for **afeitarse** is **rasurarse.**

SLOWER PACE
26 As a prelistening activity have students identify the items pictured and write them on the board.

PRESENTATION

NOTA GRAMATICAL

Use the props that you used to present **Así se dice.** Hold the comb, muss your hair, and say **YO necesito peinarME.** Ask for a volunteer to come forward, hand him or her the comb, and have the class say **ÉL (ELLA) necesita peinarSE.** Explain that a verb is called reflexive when the person doing the action, does that action to him or herself. Write the matching subject and reflexive pronouns on the board in pairs: **yo, me; tú, te; él (ella), se.** Point out that both pronouns occur together in these examples. Ask students if they can remember a similar verb phrase. (**me llamo,** etc.)

LANGUAGE NOTE

Point out to students that the phrase **lavarte el coco** in the shampoo advertisement is a humorous reference to *brainwash,* as in to control someone's thoughts.

ADDITIONAL PRACTICE

28 Ask students to tell their partner how their routine changes on Saturday and Sunday. (**Los sábados no tengo que ir al colegio.**)

G V
p. 6
Acts. 12–13

NOTA GRAMATICAL

A *reflexive verb* is a verb in which the subject of the sentence does something to himself or herself: *I bathe myself.* In Spanish, the infinitives of reflexive verbs have **-se** attached to them (**afeitarse, ponerse**). The **-se** changes according to the subject of the verb:

(Yo) necesito **ducharme.**

(Tú) necesitas **peinarte.**

Mi papá necesita **afeitarse.**

Con Champú Sedoso vas a querer lavarte el coco día y noche.

Al peinarte vas a notar el fresco aroma de Flor de Naranja en tu cabello suave y saludable.

Champú Sedoso.
Para toda la familia.

27 ¿Están listos por fin?

Ernestina is telling her brothers and sisters what to do in order to get ready for their mom's surprise party. Complete what she says, using the words in the word box. Check the reflexive word endings to help you pick the correct word! Answers on p. 41K

Nachita, apúrate en el baño porque Papi necesita ___1___.
Después de Papi, Rosa necesita ___2___. ¿Qué come José? ¿No ve que necesita ___3___ ahora mismo? Y tú, con tu pelo que es un desastre, ¿piensas ___4___? ¡Ay! ¡Ya es tarde y todavía necesito ___5___.

ducharse   **peinarte**   **maquillarme**

lavarse los dientes   **afeitarse**

28 Mi rutina

Work with a partner. Each of you write five sentences about your daily routine, using **necesito** and reflexive verbs. Then ask each other questions about your routines. Include such phrases as **todos los días, ¿a qué hora?, a veces, nunca, por la mañana, por la noche,** and the days of the week. Answers will vary.

MODELO   TÚ   Por la mañana, necesito ducharme.

              TU COMPAÑERO   ¿A qué hora?

64   *sesenta y cuatro*   CAPÍTULO 7   ¿Qué te gustaría hacer?

64   STANDARDS: 1.1, 1.2, 4.1, 5.1

29 ¡Escribamos!

Write a sentence telling what each person in the López family
needs to do or is going to do. Answers will vary. Possible answers in side column

| el señor López | Ernesto | la señora López | Adela |

30 ¡Vamos a celebrar!

Tonight is your cousin's wedding and your whole family
is invited! With a partner, read the invitation and answer
the following questions. Then tell each other whether
you would like to go. Explain why or why not.

1. ¿De quién es la boda?
2. ¿Dónde es la boda? ¿la recepción?
3. ¿Cuál es la fecha de la boda?
4. ¿A qué hora empieza la boda?
   ¿la recepción?
5. Son las cuatro de la tarde. ¿Qué
   vas a hacer antes de la
   fiesta? (ducharte, etc.)
6. ¿Qué tiene que hacer cada
   miembro de tu familia para
   estar listo?

1. De Rubén Alberto Gómez Morro
   y Maribel del Carmen Quijada Castro.
2. Es en la Iglesia Catedral Nuestra
   Señora del Rosario. Es en Campo
   Junín en Cabimas.
3. Es el 17 de diciembre.
4. Es a las siete de la noche. Es a las
   ocho y media.
5. Answers will vary.
6. Answers will vary.

Con la bendición de Dios y de nuestros padres.
Nosotros:

Rubén Alberto Gómez Morro
y
Maribel del Carmen Quijada Castro

hemos decidido iniciar una nueva vida juntos
el día 17 de diciembre de 2001,
en la Iglesia Catedral Nuestra Señora del Rosario
a las 7:00 p.m.

Recepción: Campo Junín 18-09 - Cabimas
Hora: 8:30 p.m.

SEGUNDO PASO

☀ CLOSE

Ask students to close their
books and write at least three
things they need to do to get
ready for a party they have
been invited to. Check answers
by asking several students
¿Estás listo/a? and having
them tell what they need to do.

☀ ASSESS

▶ Testing Program, pp. 21–22
  Quiz 7-2
  Audio CD 7, Tr. 37

▶ Grammar and Vocabulary
  Quizzes
  Quiz 7-2A or
  Alternative Quiz 7-2A

▶ Alternative Assessment
  Guide, p. 19

PERFORMANCE ASSESSMENT

Ask students to work with a
partner. Each pair is to create
a party invitation that contains
all the usual information: host,
guest of honor, occasion, time,
and place. Encourage them to
embellish the invitation with
activities planned, to indicate if
it's a surprise party, and to suggest what to bring. Have them
decorate the invitations and
post them on a class bulletin
board.

Answers to Activity 29

1. El señor López necesita
   afeitarse.
2. Ernesto necesita ducharse.
3. La señora López va a lavarse
   los dientes.
4. Adela va a maquillarse.

VIDEO INTEGRATION

En camino LEVEL 1B
Video Program
Videocassette 1, 15:18–15:48 OR
Videocassette 3, 1:08:53–1:09:23
(captioned version)

¡Ven conmigo! LEVEL 1
DVD Tutor, Disc 2

 Bell work
Write the following
times on the board or on a
transparency: **a las 7:00 de la
mañana, 1:30 de la tarde, 9:15
de la noche, 10:00 de la mañana,
4:30 de la tarde.** Have students
write a sentence in Spanish
for each, telling where they
usually are or what they are
usually doing at that time.

TERCER PASO TPR

Storytelling Book
pp. 27, 28

go.
hrw
.com
WV3 ECUADOR-7

Turning down an invitation and explaining why

¿Una fiesta? ¿El sábado? Eh... lo siento, María, pero no puedo. Ya tengo planes.

Ay...qué lástima. Bueno, tal vez otro día. Chao.

31 ¿Qué dicen?

Match the phrases that Carlos and María say to the corresponding phrases in English. Two phrases will not be used.

1. Ya tengo planes. d
2. Lo siento. f
3. Tal vez otro día. c
4. No puedo. b

a. See you later.
b. I can't.
c. Maybe some other day.
d. I already have plans.
e. I don't want to.
f. I'm sorry.

ASÍ SE DICE

Turning down an invitation and explaining why

To find out if your friend would like to do something with you, say:

¿Te gustaría ir al museo de arte conmigo hoy?

¿Te gustaría jugar al fútbol?

No puedo. Estoy enfermo.

Your friend might say:

¡Qué lástima! Ya tengo planes. Tal vez otro día.
What a shame! I already have plans. Maybe some other day.

¿Hoy? **Lo siento, pero no puedo.** Estoy **ocupado.** Tengo **una cita con el dentista.**
Today? I'm sorry, but I can't. I'm busy. I have an appointment with the dentist.

Lo siento, pero **tengo prisa. Tengo que** trabajar.
I'm sorry, but I'm in a hurry. I have to work.

Me gustaría, pero no puedo. Estoy **cansado** y un poco **enfermo.**
I'd like to, but I can't. I'm tired and kind of sick.

PA
p. 20
Acts. 13–14

GV
p. 7
Acts. 14–15

7-3

32 ¿Te gustaría...?
Script and answers on p. 41F

Listen as Margarita invites several friends to go with her to do some things. Match the name with that person's explanation for not being able to go.

CD 7 Tr. 29

1. Miguel
2. Gabriela
3. Roberto
4. Mariana

a. Tiene cita.
b. Necesita descansar.
c. Necesita estudiar.
d. Ya tiene planes.

¡Hola, Sabiondy! ¿Te apetece ir esta tarde al Parque de Atracciones?

¡No puedo! ¡Estoy molida!

Nicole Claveloux

33 ¡No puedo!

Sabiondy says **estoy molida.** This is a saying that literally means "I'm ground up."

1. What do you think this means?
2. What other phrases do you know that mean the same thing?

1. It means she's exhausted.
2. Estoy cansado/a. Necesito descansar.

TERCER PASO

sesenta y siete **67**

CAPÍTULO 7

☀ MOTIVATE

Ask students to think of explanations they have used in the past to turn down an invitation. Have volunteers share the expressions in Spanish. You might list these on the board or on a transparency and ask the students to tell you which ones they find in **Así se dice.**

☀ TEACH

PRESENTATION
ASÍ SE DICE

Have volunteers role-play a situation in which someone invites them to an event they can't attend. Have them use the new phrases from **Así se dice** to act out the parts.
—**Ramona, ¿te gustaría ir al museo de arte conmigo hoy? —¡Qué lástima! Ya tengo planes. Tal vez otro día.** Have other volunteers repeat the demonstration with different examples to model the other explanations taught. Then invite other students to different events and have them respond with an explanation from **Así se dice.**

LANGUAGE NOTE

Explain to students that **cita** means *appointment* or *date,* while **fecha** is *calendar date.*

STANDARDS: 1.2, 4.1, 5.1

PRESENTATION

NOTA GRAMATICAL

Go over the explanation in the book. Then practice by asking students to turn down invitations that you extend to them. They should use the expressions in the **Nota gramatical** on this page to explain why they are turning down the invitation. Ask other students to listen carefully to everyone's explanation so that they can remind you why your invitations were turned down:

—**María, ¿te gustaría ir al museo conmigo?**

—**Gracias, pero tengo que estudiar.**

—**Juan, ¿por qué no puede ir María al museo conmigo?**

—**Tiene que estudiar.**

ADDITIONAL PRACTICE

34 Give students additional sentences in Spanish and have them summarize:

1. Claudia llega tarde a su clase de alemán.
2. Raimundo tiene un examen muy importante mañana.
3. María Elena está en la cama.
4. A Chelita y a Nena les gusta mucho el cine.

NOTA GRAMATICAL

As you already know, **tener** means *to have.* But when used in certain phrases, it means *to be.* Do you remember **Tengo... años** *(I'm . . . years old)* from Chapter 1? Here are some expressions with **tener** you can use to explain why you can't do something.

tener ganas de + infinitive
to feel like (doing something)

tener prisa
to be in a hurry

tener que + infinitive
to have to (do something)

tener sueño
to be sleepy

CD-ROM DISC 2

PA p. 22 Act. 17

GV p. 8 Acts. 16–17

34 **Actividades** **H** Answers on p. 41K

Read the sentences. Then write a sentence in Spanish that summarizes the sentence. Use the correct form of **tener.**

MODELO You slept three hours last night.
—**Tengo sueño.**

1. Eva and Paloma are late for class again.
2. We'd love to eat something for dinner.
3. You have a big test tomorrow.
4. You and Felipe have a big game on Saturday.
5. Edgardo has a cavity.
6. Miriam's and Veronica's hair is a mess.
7. Amalia needs some information for a science report.
8. You feel like listening to some jazz.

¿Te acuerdas?

Tener is an **e→ie** stem-changing verb.

ten**go**	ten**emos**
t**ie**nes	ten**éis**
t**ie**ne	t**ie**nen

Estoy muy cansado. Tengo sueño.

¡Qué horror! Tengo que estudiar más.

35 Lo siento

In pairs, take turns inviting one another to do four different activities. Turn down your partner's invitation and give an explanation. Use the word box and the drawings for some ideas. Remember, your explanations should be believable and polite. Answers will vary.

MODELO —¿Te gustaría ir a patinar en línea esta tarde?
—Lo siento, pero ya tengo planes. Voy al cine con mi hermano.

Estoy ocupado/a   Tengo planes   Tengo que...

Lo siento   Estoy enfermo/a   No puedo   Estoy cansado/a

36 ¿Quieres ir?

Loida llama a su amiga Sandra un sábado por la mañana. Lee la conversación y después contesta *(answer)* las preguntas.

—Hola, Sandra. ¿Cómo estás? Oye, ¿quieres ir al cine esta tarde? Quiero ver la nueva película de acción.

—Ay, Loida, lo siento pero esta tarde es la fiesta de cumpleaños de mi hermanito, Juan. Tal vez otro día. La verdad es que quiero ver esa película también.

—¡Qué lástima!

—Loida, ¿te gustaría ir mañana?

—Me gustaría pero no puedo. Después de ir a la iglesia, tengo que ir de paseo con mi familia. Vamos a pasar el día en el campo.

—Bueno, te llamo durante la semana. Tal vez vamos el próximo *(next)* fin de semana.

—Chao, Sandra.

1. ¿Por qué no puede ir Sandra al cine el sábado?
2. ¿Cuándo quiere ir al cine Sandra?
3. ¿Por qué no puede ir Loida ese día?
4. ¿Cuándo piensan ir al cine?

1. Tiene que ir a la fiesta de cumpleaños de su hermanito.
2. Sandra quiere ir el domingo.
3. Tiene que ir a la iglesia y a pasear con su familia.
4. Tal vez el próximo fin de semana.

CHALLENGE
35 Have pairs of students choose one of these scenes and write the complete script of a dialogue. Their script should include greetings, a brief discussion about what they like and don't like, a brief discussion about plans for the weekend, and an invitation to do something. One speaker should turn down the invitation and explain why. The script should end with a brief discussion on the possibility of getting together some other time and friendly goodbyes. Ask volunteers to act out their script for the class.

KINESTHETIC LEARNERS
36 Have students work in pairs and personalize this conversation. Then have them role-play their version for the class.

📁 **PORTFOLIO**

38 Oral or **Written** Have students choose three of the activities and come up with outrageous reasons for not doing them. Ask them to be creative (...**voy a la luna, tengo que jugar con los Lakers de Los Ángeles...**). Have them enter these in their Oral or Written Portfolio.

ADDITIONAL PRACTICE

38 Have students use the additional vocabulary on pages 294–296 and continue the activity.

CHALLENGE

39 Ask students to form pairs and create a brief but complete dialogue for one of the three scenes illustrated. Then ask them to present the dialogue to the class.

37 Mucho que hacer 🏠

Lee las conversaciones. Completa las oraciones con la forma correcta de **querer** o **tener**.

1. —Hola, Paco. ¿ __1__ ir al zoológico con nosotros? Quieres
   —Lo siento, Felipe. __2__ planes con Daniel. Vamos al centro comercial. Tengo

2. —Hola, chicas. ¿ __3__ venir a mi casa a escuchar música? Quieren
   Mi hermano __4__ unos discos compactos nuevos. tiene
   —Nos gustaría, pero __5__ que estudiar. __6__ un examen de ciencias mañana. tenemos Tenemos

3. —Isabel, ¿cómo estás? Nosotras __7__ jugar al voleibol esta tarde. ¿Quieres ir? queremos
   —Hace buen tiempo. Me gustaría, pero __8__ que limpiar mi cuarto primero. tengo

38 ¡Qué problema!

Imagine that you've been invited to do the following activities, but you don't want to do any of them. Take turns with your partner inviting and turning down the invitations. Use expressions with **tener**. Answers will vary.

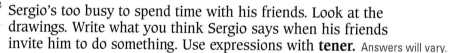

1. ir al museo de arte
2. estudiar para el examen de matemáticas
3. comer en la casa del profesor
4. ir a un partido de fútbol
5. estudiar en la biblioteca
6. ir a un concierto de violín

39 Gracias, pero... 🏠

Sergio's too busy to spend time with his friends. Look at the drawings. Write what you think Sergio says when his friends invite him to do something. Use expressions with **tener**. Answers will vary. Possible answers below

a Tengo prisa.

b No tengo ganas de nadar.

c Tengo que estudiar ahora.

40 Un drama

Work with two classmates. Choose one of the following situations to role-play. Practice your conversation and be prepared to present it to the class.

a. You and your family are visiting tía Emilia, who has a very old video collection. Tía Emilia tries to talk you into watching two movies. Turn down her invitation politely.

b. You and two friends are visiting your tío Celestino, who always likes going to Western movies (**películas vaqueras**). He invites you and your friends to go with him. Turn down his invitation and give an explanation.

41 En mi cuaderno

You've just received an invitation from a friend to do something on Saturday night. Write a reply in which you turn down the invitation, give an explanation, and tell your friend what you plan to do instead. Use the **modelo** to get you started.

MODELO

Querido Julio,
Gracias por la invitación, pero...

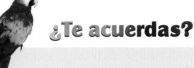

¿Te acuerdas?

Remember to use **Querida...** if you're writing to a girl. You can also use **Hola** as a greeting. Some closings for your letter might be **Saludos**, **Hasta luego**, and **Abrazos** (hugs).

LETRA Y SONIDO

Script on p. 41F

CD 7
Trs. 30–34

A. 1. The letters **ll** and **y** are usually pronounced alike. Their pronunciation in many Spanish-speaking countries is similar to the *y* in the English word *yes.*

yo	yate	yema	yugo	yerno
llamo	lleva	llora	maquillaje	toalla

2. The single **l** in Spanish is pronounced like the *l* in the English word *live.* Keep the tip of the tongue behind the upper teeth when pronouncing **l**.

zoológico	lavarse	levantarse	¡Qué lástima!
lo siento	el lago	Aló.	línea

B. **Dictado**
Lalo is trying to make plans with his friends. Write what he says.

C. **Trabalenguas**
La nublada neblina lava las lomas de un lugar lejano.

📖 EN MI CUADERNO

40 Have students decline the invitation, give a reason, and tell their friend what they plan to do instead. See *Practice and Activity Book,* p. 86.

LANGUAGE NOTE
Speakers from parts of South America may pronounce *y* and *ll* like the *g* in the word *genre.* Some speakers in Argentina say them like the *sh* sound. In northern Mexico and southern Texas, it is pronounced with a soft *y* sound.

☀ CLOSE

Invite students to do things they would like to avoid. Have them turn down your invitation and explain why: ¿**Te gustaría lavar mi coche esta semana?**

☀ ASSESS

▶ Testing Program, pp. 23–24 Quiz 7-3 Audio CD 7, Tr. 38

▶ Grammar and Vocabulary Quizzes Quiz 7-3A or Alternative Quiz 7-3A

▶ Alternative Assessment Guide, p. 19

PERFORMANCE ASSESSMENT
Divide the class into "families" of four or five. Have family members ask each other to do household chores. Each one declines, refuses, or accepts what they are asked to do.

PRESENTATION

Ask students if they have ever heard of the Galapagos Islands. Then go over with them some of the interesting facts from the History Link below before doing the math problems.

HISTORY LINK

To protect the giant turtles and other wildlife and plants, the Galapagos Islands were declared a World Heritage Site in 1959. Today the islands are known as the Galapagos National Park and Marine Reserve. Tourism is strictly controlled. Just over 36,000 people a year are allowed to visit (100 per day maximum). Visitors to the islands are carefully guided by naturalists along the shores in small boats and down designated paths on the islands. The islands are home to 58 bird species, various types of iguanas and lizards, several species of giant tortoises, sea lions, dolphins, penguins, and many other forms of wildlife. Ask students what they think might happen if tourism were not strictly controlled on the islands. Do they think the animals would continue to be unafraid of humans? Would there be more pollution and graffiti?

Énlaces

LAS MATEMÁTICAS

Las islas Galápagos Volcanoes rising out of the Pacific Ocean formed the **Archipiélago de Colón,** a cluster of islands lying about 600 miles west of the shores of Ecuador. The ocean currents and winds brought animals and plants to these lava formations, which are known today as the Galapagos Islands. The name **galápago** is the Spanish word for *tortoise.* Many of the animals and plants found there don't exist anywhere else in the world.

1 Los animales

Use the information in the charts to answer the following questions.

1. If a Galapagos tortoise celebrated its 198th birthday today, what year was it born? Answers will vary according to year.

2. If a Galapagos tortoise walks .5 miles per hour, how long will it take to travel two miles to its nesting site? 4 hours

3. If a marine iguana drank sea water and sneezed out the salt three times a day, how many times would it sneeze in a year? 1095 times

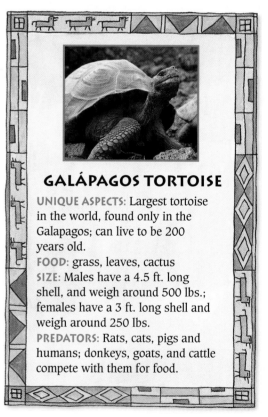

GALÁPAGOS TORTOISE

UNIQUE ASPECTS: Largest tortoise in the world, found only in the Galapagos; can live to be 200 years old.
FOOD: grass, leaves, cactus
SIZE: Males have a 4.5 ft. long shell, and weigh around 500 lbs.; females have a 3 ft. long shell and weigh around 250 lbs.
PREDATORS: Rats, cats, pigs and humans; donkeys, goats, and cattle compete with them for food.

LAS CIENCIAS NATURALES

MARINE IGUANA

UNIQUE ASPECTS: The only lizard in the world that swims in the sea; it drinks salt water and later sneezes out the salt.
FOOD: sea lettuce, a type of algae
SIZE: 10 inches to 2 feet long
PREDATORS: hawks, herons, snakes, humans

2 Conserva la naturaleza   Answers will vary.

In a small group, follow the steps below to preserve the unique wildlife of the Galapagos Islands. Each team should do the following to protect the Galapagos National Park animals:

1. Focus on one of the animals described in this section.

2. Brainstorm about what the species needs to survive. How might pollution affect it?

3. Think of rules to ensure that the Galapagos animals will survive and remain healthy. What rules could you make to:
   - protect food sources?
   - protect the species from pollution?
   - prevent vandalism of the islands?
   - discourage hunters?

4. Think about how to enforce the rules. Would you post signs? have small tour groups so the guide can keep track of everyone? How else would you enforce them?

5. Present your conservation rules and ideas to the class.

GALÁPAGOS PENGUIN

UNIQUE ASPECTS: The only penguin that lives on the ecuator; it can live 15–20 years.
FOOD: small fish
SIZE: 1 ft. high and 4.5 lbs.
PREDATORS: Sea lions, killer whales, sharks, hawks; rats eat their eggs.

PRESENTATION
Before students begin this project, read them the History Link on page 72. It will give them some ideas to start brainstorming what rules they would suggest.

CRITICAL THINKING
- Have students brainstorm what kind of unique or endangered animals live in your area. How are the animals protected? Are they unafraid of humans, like the Galapagos animals? Why or why not?

- Have students compare and contrast a visit to the zoo with a visit to the Galapagos Islands. What are three ways it would be different for visitors? What are three ways it would be different for the animals?

SUGGESTION
2 As part of their conservation project, you may assign students to draw posters of the Galapagos animals listing suggestions about how to preserve them. Some additional Galapagos animals that students may draw are lava herons, finches, pelicans, flamingos, hawks, geckos, and seals.

STANDARDS: 1.3, 3.1, 5.1   **73**

VAMOS A LEER

READING STRATEGY
Skimming for the main idea

MOTIVATING ACTIVITY
Bring in a guidebook about Ecuador. What information would students want to find in a guidebook if they were going to Ecuador?

☀ PREREADING

SUGGESTION
A Have students preview the readings. Then ask them to tell you what they think the readings are about. How did they figure it out? What clues did they get from pre-reading?

☀ READING

SUGGESTION
C Have students pretend the class has won a free trip to Ecuador. According to what they know about their class members, which one of these three parks should they visit? Assign small groups and have students write down the names and preferences of each group member as in Activity C.

NATIVE SPEAKERS
Ask native speakers to scan the readings for words with *h*, *ll*, and *y*. Then ask them to form a group to read these **Vamos a leer** passages aloud. The designated reader stops after saying a word with *ll* or *y*, and the others indicate with *ll* or *y*. The reader says what letter it was and then continues reading.

 Estrategia

Skimming
The quickest way to figure out what a reading passage is about is to skim it. When you skim, you should look at the titles and pictures. Look at the first sentence in the paragraph, since it often states the main idea. Identify familiar words in the paragraph in order to get a general idea of what the paragraph is about. This will allow you to guess the meaning of unfamiliar words more easily.

¡A comenzar!

If you were planning a family vacation to Ecuador, you'd want to find out what there is to do and what the different regions are like.

A Skim the **Guía turística**. Based on what you see, what do you think it's about?

1. interesting places in Quito
2. national parks in Ecuador
3. a history of Ecuador

 **¿Te acuerdas?**

Remember to scan for specific information by looking for one thing at a time.

Al grano
B You're helping to plan your family's summer trip. Scan the **Guía turística** sections to answer these questions. Answers on p. 41K

1. According to the description of the **Parque Nacional Cuyabena,** where can you stay while in this park?
2. Read the description of **Chimborazo.** What animals does it say you can see there? What activities can you do there?
3. What activities can you do at the **Parque Nacional Galápagos**?
4. Which of these national parks is closest to Quito? Which one could you get to by boat?

C Everybody in your family has set different goals for this summer trip. It's going to be hard to narrow down where the family should go! List which park or parks would accomplish each goal. Answers on p. 41K

1. Mom is in great shape and wants a challenge.
2. Dad would like to see monkeys.
3. Beatrice wants to swim a lot.
4. Ralph wants to go in a boat.
5. Ann wants to hike.

D Invita a tus compañeros a uno de los parques. Di qué actividades vas a hacer. Ellos pueden decir si aceptan la invitación o no. Luego tus compañeros te van a invitar a ti y vas a responder.

Localizado a 198 millas de Quito, el Parque Nacional Cuyabena le da la oportunidad de explorar las riquezas naturales de las selvas del Amazonas. Explore los lagos y ríos en canoa o haga una excursión a pie. Vea la variedad y el colorido de los pájaros, los caimanes, monos y jaguares. Hay oportunidad de acampar en tienda de campaña o en hamaca, o se puede dormir en un lindísimo hotel flotante.

Una visita al Parque Nacional Galápagos, a 622 millas del continente ecuatoriano, es una de las experiencias más extraordinarias de toda la tierra. Aquí se puede caminar o nadar con algunos de los animales más raros, como los pingüinos y las iguanas marinas. Visite estas islas preciosas en un yate, sobre el cual puede dormir, probar comidas exquisitas y explorar el parque. La mayoría de las excursiones varían de tres a cinco días.

El Chimborazo, a 109 millas de Quito, con su cono nevado, alcanza una altura de más de 20.000 pies. Este volcán es el pico más elevado del país. Aquí hay oportunidades de hacer grandes excursiones, ver llamas, vicuñas, cóndores y muchos otros animales. Hay oportunidades sin iguales para sacar fotos espectaculares. Hay que estar en muy buena condición física para realizar una excursión hasta el pico.

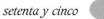

Cuaderno para hispanohablantes, pp. 31–33

☼ POSTREADING

SUGGESTION
D Ask your students to prepare interview questions about the three parks in Ecuador. Which would interest class members the most: the Amazon jungle, the Chimborazo volcano, or the Galapagos islands? Students should conduct a survey of the class to find out which park is interesting to the most people and why.

📁 PORTFOLIO
Oral Have students work with a partner to role-play a telephone conversation with a relative about visiting a national park together. Each student picks his or her favorite park that is described on this page and explains why. The two partners talk about the benefits of the different parks and try to decide upon one park during the conversation. Have them record the conversation and use it as a Portfolio entry.

TEACHER NOTE
For additional readings, see *Native Speaker Activity Book,* pp. 31–32; and *Practice and Activity Book,* p. 23.

STANDARDS: 1.1, 1.2, 5.1   **75**

The **Repaso** reviews and integrates all four skills and culture in preparation for the Chapter Test.

PORTFOLIO

1 Oral This telephone conversation would be an appropriate Portfolio entry for students. For Portfolio suggestions, see *Alternative Assessment Guide,* p. 11.

CHALLENGE

2 Have students suggest alternatives to the invitations they decline. They may offer alternate times or activities.

REPASO

internet
MARCAR: go.hrw.com
PALABRA CLAVE:
WV3 ECUADOR-7

1 Listen to the conversations. Choose the sentence that best describes the response to each invitation. Script and answers on p. 41F

 CD 7 Tr. 35

1. **a.** No puede ir porque tiene que practicar el piano.
   b. No puede ir porque está enferma.
2. **a.** No puede ir al campo porque tiene otros planes.
   b. No puede ir al museo porque tiene otros planes.
3. **a.** Quiere ir a caminar más tarde.
   b. No quiere ir porque está cansado.
4. **a.** Tiene ganas de ir al partido de fútbol.
   b. No puede ir porque tiene una cita.

2 Get together with a partner. Look at the drawing and invite your partner to go to five of the places shown in the drawing. Either accept or turn down your partner's invitation. If you turn down the invitation, explain why or tell what you prefer to do.

3 Read the paragraph that Amara wrote in her diary about her weekend plans. Then answer the questions.

1. Escribe las tres actividades que Amara piensa hacer este fin de semana.
2. ¿Por qué no va a ir con sus amigas el sábado? Answers on p. 41K

Este fin de semana pienso descansar. Estoy un poco enferma. Lo siento mucho, porque mis amigas piensan ir al parque de atracciones el sábado.
Voy a escuchar música y ver unas películas. También pienso leer una novela de misterio. Si estoy bien el domingo, voy a ir a la casa de Maribel.
La verdad es que no voy a hacer mucho este fin de semana.

4 Name two ways in which transportation differs in Spanish-speaking countries from what you're used to.

Many people travel on buses, subways, taxis, on motorcycles. Many people walk.

5 # Vamos a escribir

What are your plans for the weekend? First choose five activities. Then write a paragraph about your plans. Include when, where and with whom you will do each activity. Use **quiero ir a...**, **tengo que...**, **me gustaría...**, and **pienso...**

Estrategia

Topic sentences are often at the beginning of a paragraph. They tell you the general subject of the paragraph. Paragraphs often end with a summarizing sentence that restates what you've read.

Este fin de semana tengo muchos planes con mis amigos Quiero ir al ... ir a la playa Voy a estar muy ocupada este fin de semana

6 ## SITUACIÓN

Imagine that your **tía Hortensia** has two tickets to an accordion concert (**concierto de acordeón**) this Saturday and wants you to go with her. You already have plans to go out with your friends. With a classmate, take turns role-playing a conversation between you and **tía Hortensia**. Politely turn down her invitation and explain that you have plans, but remember to thank her for inviting you.

Cuaderno para hispanohablantes, pp. 34–35

REPASO

setenta y siete **77**

PORTFOLIO
5 **Written** You may wish to point this activity out to your students as a potential written Portfolio entry. For Portfolio suggestions, see *Alternative Assessment Guide*, p. 11.

ADDITIONAL PRACTICE
5 Have students write a paragraph describing what people in their area do in their free time. Ask them to include as much detail as possible, such as what they like and dislike doing, where people go, and how the weather affects people's plans. For movies and plays they can include show times and the cost of tickets.

TEACHER NOTE
To reduce students' fear of speaking Spanish, show that there are many ways to say the same thing. Write an English word on the board and draw a sun around it. Draw several rays coming from the sun. At the ends of the rays, write Spanish synonyms for the English word. For example, if the word you write in the center is TRUE, the Spanish words could include **verdad, cierto, precisamente, correcto, exactamente.** You might have a contest between groups to see who can come up with the most synonyms or antonyms for a vocabulary word.

This page is intended to help students prepare independently for the Chapter Test. It is a brief checklist of the major points covered in the chapter. The students should be reminded that it is a checklist only and does not necessarily include everything that will appear on the Chapter Test.

Answers to Question 1

Answers will vary. Possible answers:
—Aló.
—¿De parte de quién?
—Lo siento, está ocupada.
—Está bien.

Answers to Question 2

Answers will vary. Possible answers:
1. —¿Te gustaría ir conmigo al cine?
   —Sí, me gustaría ir contigo.
2. —¿Quieres jugar al voleibol esta tarde?
   —¡Claro que sí!
3. —¿Te gustaría cenar con mi familia mañana?
   —¡Claro que sí!
4. —¿Le gustaría caminar en el parque conmigo hoy?
   —Sí, me gustaría caminar contigo.

Answers to Question 4

Answers will vary. Possible answers:
1. Para ir al colegio, necesito ducharme y lavarme los dientes.
2. Para salir con amigos, mi hermana necesita ducharse y maquillarse.
3. Para ir a una boda, mi papá tiene que ducharse, afeitarse y peinarse.
4. Para ir al trabajo, mi mamá necesita ducharse, lavarse los dientes y maquillarse.

▼ **Can you talk on the telephone?** p. 49

1 You're answering phones at the office at your school. What would you say in the following situation? Answers in side column

El teléfono suena. (The telephone rings.)

TÚ ＿＿＿＿＿
SR. GARCÍA Buenas tardes. ¿Está la profesora Margarita García, por favor?
TÚ ＿＿＿＿＿
SR. GARCÍA De parte de su esposo.
TÚ ＿＿＿＿＿
SR. GARCÍA ¿Puedo dejar un recado?
TÚ ＿＿＿＿＿

▼ **Can you extend and accept invitations?** p. 51

2 How would you invite the following people to do something with you? How might they accept your invitation? Answers in side column
1. tu mejor amigo/a (ir al cine)
2. tu hermano/a (jugar al...)
3. tu primo/a (cenar...)
4. tu abuelo/a (caminar...)

▼ **Can you make plans?** p. 59

3 What do you plan to do this weekend? Give specific days, times, and places you plan to go, people you plan to see, and things you plan to do. Answers will vary.

▼ **Can you talk about getting ready?** p. 63

4 What would each person need to do to get ready in these situations? Answers in side column
1. tú / para ir al colegio
2. tu hermana / para salir con amigos
3. tu papá / para ir a una boda
4. tu mamá / para ir al trabajo

▼ **Can you turn down an invitation and explain why?** p. 67

5 How would you turn down the following invitations?
1. your friend invites you to a surprise birthday party for his four-year-old brother
2. your parents invite you to go to the theater with them
3. your teacher invites you and your parents to go to the amusement park with him and his family

Answers will vary. Possible answers:
1. Me gustaría ir a la fiesta, pero no puedo. Estoy cansada.
2. Hoy no puedo ir al teatro. Tengo que hacer mi tarea.
3. ¡Qué lástima! Ya tenemos otros planes. Tal vez otro día.

¡SHHHHHHHH!

¡Es una fiesta de sorpresa!

VOCABULARIO

PRIMER PASO

Talking on the telephone

Aló. *Hello.*
¿De parte de quién? *Who's calling?*
Diga. *Hello.*
Está bien. *All right.*
Su línea está ocupada. *His / her line is busy.*
Llamo más tarde. *I'll call later.*
un momento *one moment*
¿Puedo dejar un recado? *May I leave a message?*

Extending and accepting invitations

el acuario *aquarium*
la boda *wedding*
el campo *country*
el circo *circus*
la ciudad *city*
¡Claro que sí! *Of course!*
empezar (ie) *to begin*
el evento *event*
una fiesta de aniversario *anniversary party*
de cumpleaños *birthday party*

de graduación *graduation party*
de sorpresa *surprise party*
el lago *lake*
el lugar *place*
Me gustaría... *I'd like . . .*
el museo de antropología *anthropology museum*

Nos gustan... *We like . . .*
el parque de atracciones *amusement park*

preferir (ie) *to prefer*
¿Quieres...? *Do you want to . . .?*
¿Te gustaría...? *Would you like . . .?*
Te invito... *It's my treat.*
el teatro *theater*
venir (ie) *to come*
el zoológico *zoo*

SEGUNDO PASO

Making plans

¡Cómo no! *Of course!*
ir + a + infinitive *going to (do something)*
pensar (ie) + infinitive *to plan, to intend*

Talking about getting ready

afeitarse *to shave*
ducharse *to take a shower*
estar listo/a *to be ready*
lavarse los dientes *to brush one's teeth*

maquillarse *to put on makeup*
peinarse *to comb one's hair*

TERCER PASO

Turning down an invitation and explaining why

cansado/a *tired*
una cita *an appointment*
enfermo/a *sick*
Lo siento, pero no puedo. *I'm sorry, but I can't.*
ocupado/a *busy*
¡Qué lástima! *What a shame!*
tal vez otro día *maybe some other day*
tener ganas de + infinitive *to feel like (doing something)*
tener prisa *to be in a hurry*
tener que + infinitive *to have to (do something)*
tener sueño *to be sleepy*
Ya tengo planes. *I already have plans.*

TEACHER NOTE

Remind students of the Additional Vocabulary feature starting on page 294.

TPR In two teams, play **Mímica**. On slips of paper, write some of the sports, activities, and places of interest from this chapter. Alternating teams, players act out the word or words on their paper for their team to guess.

CHAPTER 7 ASSESSMENT

▸ **Testing Program**
Chapter Test, pp. 25–30
Audio Compact Discs, CD 7, Trs. 39–40
Speaking Test, p. 130

▸ **Alternative Assessment Guide**
Performance Assessment, p. 19
Portfolio Assessment, p. 11
CD-ROM Assessment, p. 26

▸ **Interactive CD-ROM Tutor, Disc 2**
¡A hablar!
¡A escribir!

▸ **Standardized Assessment Tutor**
Chapter 7

▸ **One-Stop Planner, Disc 2**
Test Generator
Chapter 7

STANDARDS: 1.2, 5.1   **79**

CAPÍTULO 8

¡A comer!

CHAPTER OVERVIEW

De antemano pp. 82–85	¿Qué vas a pedir?			
	FUNCTIONS	**GRAMMAR**	**VOCABULARY**	**RE-ENTRY**
Primer paso pp. 86–93	• Talking about meals and food, p. 87	• **Gramática:** The verb **encantar** and indirect object pronouns, p. 89 • **Gramática: o** to **ue** stem-changing verbs, p. 92	• Breakfast foods, p. 88 • Lunch foods, p. 90	• Expressing likes and dislikes • Present tense of regular and **e** to **ie** stem-changing verbs • Times of day
Segundo paso pp. 96–101	• Commenting on food, p. 97	• **Nota gramatical:** **Ser** and **estar** with food, p. 98 • **Nota gramatical:** Expressions with **tener,** p. 100	• Foods, p. 100	• **estar** versus **ser** • Expressions with **tener**
Tercer paso pp. 104–111	• Making polite requests, p. 105 • Ordering dinner in a restaurant, p. 108 • Asking for and paying the bill in a restaurant, p. 109	• **Así se dice:** Indirect object pronouns **nos** and **me,** p. 105 • **Nota gramatical: otro,** p. 106 • **Así se dice:** Indirect object pronoun **le; quisiera,** p. 108	• Tableware, p. 105 • Dinner foods, p. 107 • Numbers 200—100,000, p. 110	• Numbers 0–199 • Question words **¿qué?** and **¿cuánto?**
Letra y sonido	p. 111 The letter *c*		**Dictado:** Textbook Audiocassette / Audio CD 8	
Enlaces	pp. 112–113 **La historia de la comida y las artes culinarias**			
Vamos a leer	pp. 114–115 **Batidos**		**Reading Strategy:** Using outlines	
Review	pp. 116–119 **Repaso,** pp. 116–117		**A ver si puedo...,** p. 118	**Vocabulario,** p. 119

Culture
- **Notas culturales:** Fruits and vegetables, p. 86; Main meals, p. 92
- **Encuentro cultural: La comida en el mundo hispanohablante,** pp. 94–95
- **Notas culturales:** Types of foods, p. 96; Andean foods, p. 101
- **Panorama cultural: ¿Cuál es un plato típico de tu país o región?,** pp. 102–103
- **Notas culturales:** Eating out in Ecuador, p. 104; Table manners, p. 106; Dinner and snacks, p. 107

PRINT

Lesson Planning

One-Stop Planner
Lesson Planner with Substitute Teacher
Lesson Plans, pp. 11–15

Listening and Speaking

Listening Activities
- Student Response Forms for Listening Activities, pp. 58–60
- Additional Listening Activities 8-1 to 8-6, pp. 9–11
- Additional Listening Activities (song), p. 12
- Scripts and Answers, pp. 36–38

Video Guide
- Teaching Suggestions, pp. 15–16
- Activity Masters, pp. 17–20
- Scripts and Answers, pp. 54–56, 66–67

Activities for Communication
- Communicative Activities, pp. 13–18
- Realia and Teaching Suggestions, pp. 49–53
- Situation Cards, pp. 78–79

¡Ven conmigo! Level 1
TPR Storytelling Book, pp. 29–32

Reading and Writing

Reading Strategies and Skills, Chapter 8
¡Lee conmigo! 1, Chapter 8
Practice and Activity Book, pp. 25–36

Grammar

Grammar and Vocabulary Workbook, pp. 9–17

¡Ven conmigo! Level 1
Grammar Tutor for Students of Spanish
Chapter 8

Assessment

Testing Program
- Paso Quizzes and Chapter Test, pp. 37–48
- Score Sheet, Scripts and Answers, pp. 49–54

Grammar and Vocabulary Quizzes
- Quizzes 8-1A, 8-2A, 8-3A
- Alternative Quizzes 8-1A, 8-2A, 8-3A

Alternative Assessment Guide
- Portfolio Assessment, p. 12
- Performance Assessment, p. 20
- CD-ROM Assessment, p. 27

¡Ven conmigo! Level 1
Standardized Assessment Tutor
- Reading, pp. 31–33
- Writing, p. 34

Native Speakers

¡Ven conmigo! Level 1
Cuaderno para hispanohablantes, pp. 36–40

MEDIA

Online Activities
- Juegos interactivos
- Actividades internet

Video Program
- Videocassette 1
- Videocassette 3 *(captioned version)*

¡Ven conmigo! Level 1
DVD Tutor, Disc 2

Audio Compact Discs
- Textbook Listening Activities, CD 8, Tracks 1–18
- Additional Listening Activities, CD 8, Tracks 24–29
- Assessment Items, CD 8, Tracks 19–23

Interactive CD-ROM Tutor, Disc 2

Teaching Transparencies
- Situations 8-1 to 8-3
- Vocabulary 8-A to 8-D
- Grammar and Vocabulary Workbook

One-Stop Planner CD-ROM

Use the **One-Stop Planner CD-ROM with Test Generator** to aid in lesson planning and pacing.

For each chapter, the **One-Stop Planner** includes:

- Editable lesson plans with direct links to teaching resources
- Printable worksheets from resource books
- Direct launches to the HRW Internet activities
- Video and audio segments
- Test Generator
- Clip Art for vocabulary items

DVD/VIDEO

Videocassette 1, Videocassette 3 (captioned version)
DVD Tutor, Disc 2 See Video Guide, pages 14–20.

De antemano • ¿Qué vas a pedir?
María, her brother Roberto, and Tomás take Hiroshi to a restaurant that serves typical Ecuadorean dishes. They describe the food to Hiroshi, who decides to order **locro.** After eating, they set off for **La Mitad del Mundo.** On their way, they suddenly have car trouble.

A continuación
A passerby helps the characters, and they are soon on their way. While at an open-air market, Hiroshi and María bargain with vendors and buy traditional tapestries, sweaters, and gifts for Hiroshi and his family. They return to the car and recount their experiences.

¿Cuál es un plato típico de tu país?
Three teenagers from Florida, Venezuela, and Ecuador tell about typical dishes from the regions where they live. In additional interviews, people from various Spanish-speaking countries tell us about dishes typical to their regions.

La comida en el mundo hispano-hablante

Videoclips
- **Leche Ram®:** advertisement for milk
- **Néctares Dos Pinos®:** advertisement for juice
- **La Casera®:** advertisement for bottled water

INTERACTIVE CD-ROM TUTOR

Activity	Activity Type	Pupil's Edition Page
En contexto	*Interactive conversation*	
1. Gramática	¿Qué falta?	p. 92
2. Vocabulario	¿Cuál es?	pp. 88, 90
3. Así se dice	Imagen y sonido ¡Exploremos! ¡Identifiquemos!	p. 97
4. Vocabulario	¡Super memoria!	p. 107
5. Vocabulario	¡A escoger!	p. 110
6. Así se dice	Patas arriba	pp. 105, 108, 109
Panorama cultural	¿Cuál es un plata típico de tu país o región? ¡A escoger!	pp. 102–103
¡A hablar!	*Guided recording*	pp. 116–117
¡A escribir!	*Guided writing*	pp. 116–117

Teacher Management System
Launch the program, type "admin" in the password area and press RETURN. Log on to **www.hrw.com/CDROMTUTOR** for a detailed explanation of the Teacher Management System.

DVD-ROM TUTOR ¡VEN CONMIGO! LEVEL 1

The *DVD Tutor* contains all material from the Level 1 *Video Program.* Spanish captions are available for use at your discretion for all sections of the video. The *DVD Tutor* also provides a variety of video-based activities that assess students' understanding of the **De antemano, A continuación,** and **Panorama cultural.**

This part of the *DVD Tutor* may be used on any DVD video player connected to a television or video monitor.

In addition to the video material and the video-based comprehension activities, the *DVD Tutor* also contains the entire Level 1 *Interactive CD-ROM Tutor* in DVD-ROM format. Each DVD disc contains the activities from all 12 chapters of the *Interactive CD-ROM Tutor.*

This part of the *DVD Tutor* may be used on a Macintosh® or Windows® computer with a DVD-ROM drive.

One-Stop Planner CD-ROM

To preview all resources available for this chapter, use the **One-Stop Planner CD-ROM**, Disc 2.

MARCAR: go.hrw.com
PALABRA CLAVE:
WV3 ECUADOR-8

INTERNET CONNECTION

*Have students explore the **go.hrw.com** Web site for many online resources covering all chapters. All Chapter 8 resources are available under the keyword **WV3 ECUADOR-8**. Interactive games help students practice the material and provide them with immediate feedback. You will also find a printable worksheet that provides Internet activities that lead to a comprehensive online research project.*

JUEGOS INTERACTIVO

You can use the interactive activities in this chapter

- to practice grammar, vocabulary, and chapter functions
- as homework
- as an assessment option
- as a self-test
- to prepare for the Chapter Test

ACTIVIDADES INTERNET

Students act as restaurant critics for a magazine. They evaluate restaurants they find on the Internet based on menu, price, and atmosphere.

- In preparation for the **Hoja de actividades,** have students complete the Practice and Activity Book activities from the **Segundo** and **Tercer pasos.**

- After students have completed the activity sheet, encourage them to record their restaurant critique. You might also have them share their critique as well as the restaurant's Web site with the class.

Proyecto

Have students create a Web site for restaurant critiques. Once they post the critique they wrote for the **Hoja de actividades** on their site, they should then post a "real" critique as well: the next time they eat at a local restaurant or the school cafeteria, ask students to take note of and critique the food, the service, and the atmosphere on their Web site.

¡A comer!
TEXTBOOK LISTENING ACTIVITIES SCRIPTS

For Student Response Forms, see Listening Activities pp. 58–60

PRIMER PASO   pp. 86–93

8 El desayuno   p. 88

MARCELA	¿Te gustan los huevos?
ROBERTO	Sí, me encantan los huevos revueltos con tocino.
MARCELA	A mí me encanta el pan dulce. ¿Y a ti?
ROBERTO	No, no me gusta para nada.
MARCELA	Bueno... a ver... ¿tomas café?
ROBERTO	Uy, no me gusta el café para nada. Es horrible.
MARCELA	Entonces, ¿qué prefieres tomar, jugo de naranja o leche?
ROBERTO	Prefiero tomar leche.
MARCELA	A mí me gusta más el jugo de naranja. Me encantan las frutas.
ROBERTO	A mí también. Especialmente los plátanos.

Answers to Activity 8

Marcela—**f.** el pan dulce, **g.** el jugo de naranja, **a.** las frutas

Roberto—**d.** los huevos revueltos con tocino, **b.** la leche, **a.** las frutas, **c.** los plátanos

16 ¿Cómo es la comida de aquí?   p. 92

ADELA	Pablo, quiero saber cómo son las comidas en los Estados Unidos. En general, ¿a qué hora desayunas?
PABLO	Bueno, en general desayunamos a las siete de la mañana.
ADELA	¿Y qué hay para el desayuno?
PABLO	Hay de todo. Muchas veces hay huevos, pan tostado, jugo de frutas y café.
ADELA	¿Y a qué hora almuerzan ustedes?
PABLO	Durante la semana, almorzamos a las doce.
ADELA	¿Y qué hay para el almuerzo?
PABLO	A veces hay sopa, sándwiches y leche.

Answers to Activity 16

1. cierto   **2.** falso   **3.** falso   **4.** cierto

SEGUNDO PASO   pp. 96–101

22 Comentarios   p. 97

1. Este pescado está muy rico. ¡Me encanta!
2. Esta sopa no me gusta. Está fría.
3. ¿Qué tal la ensalada? Está deliciosa, ¿no?
4. Este pollo está muy picante. ¡Necesito agua!
5. La sopa está muy salada. ¡Qué horrible!
6. La ensalada de frutas no está muy buena hoy.

Answers to Activity 22

1. pescado—está muy rico
2. sopa—está fría
3. ensalada—está deliciosa
4. pollo—está muy picante
5. sopa—está muy salada
6. ensalada de frutas—no está buena

28 Cuatro amigos   p. 100

DIEGO   ¿Tienes hambre, Isabel?

ISABEL   No, Diego, no tengo mucha hambre pero tengo sed.

DIEGO   ¿Por qué no tomas una limonada?

ISABEL   Buena idea. Me encanta la limonada.

DIEGO   Estela, ¿qué quieres almorzar? ¿Tienes hambre?

ESTELA   Sí, sí, pero me gustaría desayunar. ¿Qué hay para el desayuno?

DIEGO   Sólo hay jugo de manzana y pan tostado. Yo voy a comer la sopa de legumbres. ¡Me encanta la sopa de aquí! Y Rafael, ¿qué vas a almorzar tú?

RAFAEL   Nada. No tengo mucha hambre.

Answers to Activity 28

1. cierto   **2.** cierto   **3.** falso   **4.** falso   **5.** falso

TERCER PASO   pp. 104–111

36 Me trae...   p. 107

1. — Voy a pedir una sopa de pollo, pescado, verduras y una ensalada, por favor.
— Muy bien, señorita.

2. — ¿Me trae fruta, café y pan tostado, por favor?
— Sí, con mucho gusto.

3. — ¿Nos trae café y un pastel, por favor?
— Claro que sí, señora.

4. — No tengo mucha hambre. Voy a pedir una sopa de pollo, pan y un refresco, nada más.
— Gracias, señor.

5. — Um, son las dos y media. Tengo mucha hambre. ¿Me trae la sopa de tomate, el bistec, papas fritas, zanahorias, una ensalada, pan y el postre, por favor? Y café más tarde. Gracias.
— Muy bien, señor.

6. — ¿Nos trae huevos revueltos con jamón, pan tostado, jugo de naranja y café, por favor?
— Claro que sí.

Answers to Activity 36

1. almuerzo o cena   **4.** almuerzo o cena
2. desayuno   **5.** almuerzo
3. postre   **6.** desayuno

41 ¿Cuánto es?   p. 110

1. catorce mil sucres
2. diecisiete mil quinientos sucres
3. ocho mil sucres
4. once mil quinientos sucres
5. ocho mil ochocientos sucres
6. diecisiete mil setecientos cincuenta sucres

Answers to Activity 41

1. sancocho
2. ceviche de camarón
3. helado de naranjilla
4. ensalada mixta
5. canoa de frutas
6. pollo al ajillo

LETRA Y SONIDO   p. 111

For the scripts for Parts A and C, see page 111. The script for Part B is below.

B. Dictado

Para este pastel de chocolate, necesito harina, azúcar y huevos. También quiero poner coco y dos cucharadas de cacao.

REPASO   pp. 116–117

1 p. 116

No me gusta para nada el pescado, pero la sopa de pollo sí, me gusta mucho. Los frijoles no me gustan porque son salados. Me encanta la ensalada, pero la carne de res no me gusta mucho. Para el desayuno los huevos con pan tostado son muy ricos.

Answers to Repaso Activity 1

Le gusta: la sopa de pollo, la ensalada, los huevos con pan tostado

No le gusta: el pescado, los frijoles, la carne de res

¡A comer!
PROJECTS

LA PIRÁMIDE DE LA NUTRICIÓN

This project reviews the food vocabulary in this chapter and links it to the importance of good nutrition via the food pyramid. Students work in cooperative groups of three.

Introduction

Ask students if they are familiar with the food pyramid categories and which are the most nutritious foods. Once students have identified the categories, discuss the types of foods in each. List the categories and different foods in Spanish.

Materials students may need

- Large colored posterboard
- Metersticks, rulers
- Pencils, markers (wide and narrow tip)
- Magazines and food circulars from newspapers
- Glue sticks, scissors

Sequence

1. Refer students to the model of the food pyramid on page 95. Identify the categories in English, and then translate these categories into Spanish with the class: **pan y cereal, frutas y vegetales, leche y carne, grasa y dulces.**

2. Divide the class into groups of three: Architect, Artist, and Presenter. The Architect designs and constructs the pyramid; the Artist draws or finds pictures of the foods on the list; the Presenter gives an oral presentation of the pyramid to the class.

3. The group cooperatively writes a list of foods to include in each category of the food pyramid.

4. The Architect constructs the pyramid outline on the poster board and labels the categories in Spanish.

5. The Artist draws or cuts out the pictures of food and pastes them on the pyramid. The Architect and Artist label the foods in Spanish.

6. The Presenter shares the group's food pyramid with the class and is responsible for the Oral Presentation.

Grading the project

Suggested point distribution (total = 100 points):

Pyramid	**30**
Accuracy of information	**15**
Selection of foods	**15**
Oral presentation	**30**
Group effort	**10**

EL RESTAURANTE

Students work cooperatively to design nutritious meals for a hotel restaurant. They use chapter vocabulary to identify the three daily meals and the foods offered at each meal.

Introduction

Ask students to imagine that they work for a large hotel. This hotel is offering a special two-day vacation package that includes three meals a day: breakfast, lunch and dinner.

Materials students may need

- Blank menu outlines for 6 meals
- Colored markers/colored pencils
- Poster board (large size)

Sequence

1. Divide class into cooperative learning groups of four: Breakfast Chef, Lunch Chef, Dinner Chef, and Manager. Groups select a name for their restaurant.

2. Distribute two blank menu sheets to each chef. The group decides on three menus for each. Each meal should have at least five items to offer. They may repeat some.

3. Each chef prepares a menu using colored markers. Additional art work can be added to enhance the presentation of the menu.

4 The Manager compiles the menus and designs a poster that represents each day at the Restaurant.

5 The Manager presents the "Vacation Package" menus to the class. The class can then vote on which "package" they would prefer.

Grading the project

Suggested point distribution (total = 100 points):

Selection of foods **15**
Nutritional value, variety of foods **15**
Creativity **30**
Oral presentation **30**
Group effort **10**

UNA FIESTA

In this project students plan a tasting party of desserts. They write invitations, accept the invitations through acted-out phone calls, bring desserts, sample them while conversing in Spanish with classmates at the fiesta, and write thank-you notes. The project may require one or more class periods.

Materials students may need

◆ Paper ◆ Paper glasses
◆ Markers ◆ Plastic utensils
◆ Paper plates ◆ Paper napkins

Sequence

1 Set a date for the **fiesta**.

2 Students work in groups of four. Each group selects a dessert to bring to the class.

3 Students divide the responsibilities for the food preparation. Desserts are to be prepared outside of class. Students only need to prepare enough for everyone to have a taste.

4 Each student designs and writes an invitation in Spanish. Students exchange invitations with classmates from another group.

5 At the **fiesta,** groups present their desserts. Then students sample them and use Spanish to converse and comment on them.

6 On the following day, students write and hand-deliver a thank-you note in Spanish to the person from whom they received their invitation. The thank-you notes become a part of the assessment.

Grading the project

Suggested point distribution (total = 100 points):

Written invitation **20**
Dessert **10**
Presentation of the dish **15**
Using Spanish at the **fiesta** **35**
Thank-you note **20**

COMMUNITY LINK

If students know people who are from or have lived in Spanish-speaking countries, they might contact them to obtain recipes to prepare. You may want to invite native speakers to attend the **fiesta** and converse in Spanish with students.

Ingredientes
TORONJAS CON CAMARONES
6 toronjas   2 tomates
1 lechuga americana
1/2 kg de camarones pelados
3 huevos duros   1 taza de mayonesa
Partir las toronjas en dos. Sacar la pulpa, extrayendo las semillas y fibras. Mezclar la pulpa de toronja con los camarones. Hacer una cama de hojas de lechuga en las toronjas vaciadas. Rellenar con la mezcla de toronja y camarones. Pelar los huevos duros y cortar en cuartos. Colocar los huevos cuarteados decorativamente. Verter la mayonesa por encima de cada toronja antes de servir.

¡A comer!

GAMES

EL GRAN CAMPEONATO DE LA COMIDA

Students use boxes or cans for this "Name That Food" Game. In this game students compete to see who knows the food vocabulary the most accurately and quickly.

Materials you may need

- ◆ Index cards
- ◆ Posterboard
- ◆ Colored markers or crayons
- ◆ Magazines with pictures of food

Preparation

Students write the Spanish words for the foods they brought on index cards. For example: **leche, café, mantequilla, huevos, jugo de naranja, cereal,** and **galletas.**

Sequence

1. Select approximately 20 food containers with the corresponding cards.
2. The object of the game is for the student to put a card by each product on the table and say the word in Spanish for each.
3. Put the containers on a long table, give the packet of cards to a student, and tell the Timekeeper to start timing.
4. Have students take turns labelling the products as the Timekeeper records the time for each.
5. The student with the lowest time and the most food labeled wins.

UN CRUCIGRAMA PARA TODOS

*Students use chapter vocabulary to create a large crossword puzzle on the board. Play it after the **Primer paso.***

Procedure

1. Write a vocabulary word on the board in large, separated, capital letters (**P L Á T A N O**).
2. Have a student write a second word vertically using one of the letters of the first. For example:

```
              M

    P L Á T A N O

              N

              G

              O
```

3. Now ask another student to write a word horizontally through the second word, and so on. This may also be played by two teams on two different boards simultaneously.
4. The team that adds the most words to their puzzle in a set time period wins.
5. You may change the difficulty level of this game by limiting words to a narrow category like **frutas,** or a broader category like **comida,** or opening it up to all Spanish words.

MUCHOS NÚMEROS

*This game helps students practice numbers from 1 to 100,000. It should be played after **Tercer paso**.*

Procedure

1 Divide the class into two teams. Write any number from 1 to 100,000 on the board.

2 The first player on Team A reads the number aloud in Spanish. If it is correct, Team A gets a point.

3 If it is not correct, Team B gets one chance to read it correctly for a point.

4 Then change the number by adding, removing or changing one digit. (205 could become 105 or 215, for example, or 2,056, or 20.)

5 The next team starts this round by having their second player read the new number. Continue alternating after each team's turn.

A LA CARTA

This game helps review Chapter 8 vocabulary and grammar. Students role-play being wait staff and diners to practice food and phrases for ordering food.

Materials students may need

- ◆ Pictures of food from magazines
- ◆ Construction paper
- ◆ Markers

Preparation

Have students draw or cut out pictures from magazines to make a picture menu to match their written one from the **Repaso.**

Procedure

1 Use a sample menu to play the game the first time, playing the part of the waiter or waitress.

2 The waiter or waitress asks each individual student **¿Qué desea usted?**, offering the picture menu.

3 The student chooses an item on the menu and answers **¿Me puede traer _____?**

4 They choose a picture of one of the food items. Their team receives five points for correctly identifying the Spanish word for the item in the picture. The group with the most points wins. To repeat the game, groups may exchange menus and choose a different student to be the **camarero/a.**

MIS AMIGOS

*This game may be adapted to your particular class situation personalizing the descriptions and vocabulary needs. It provides a review of **tener, gustar**, and other regular verbs.*

Materials you may need

- ◆ Paper
- ◆ Ruler

Preparation

1 Make a Bingo® sheet to reproduce for the class. You may include a *free space* for the student's name.

2 On the other spaces include personal descriptions that students have written such as: **Tengo un perro. Tengo 13 años. Tengo mucha sed. Mi hermana toca el piano. Mi amigo juega tenis. Mi padre es moreno.**

Procedure

1 The object of the game is to find the person who matches the description for a square by asking them a question. For example, **¿Tienes un perro?** Make it clear that those using English to ask the question are disqualified.

2 Then, if that person answers **Sí, tengo un perro,** he or she signs the card on that square. If the person answers no, the person asking the questions may ask one more. But, each classmate can only sign an individual's sheet once.

3 The winners may be decided as in Bingo®. For example, the individual who gets signatures across, vertically or diagonally wins, or you may play "black out" where they must fill the entire sheet. When the winner is declared, he or she must read off their winning categories in Spanish, for example, **Marisa tiene un perro.**

¡A comer!

ANSWERS TO CHAPTER 8 ACTIVITIES

Listening activity answers appear on Scripts pages 79E–79F. Answers to all other activities appear on corresponding pupil pages.

PRIMER PASO   pp. 86–93

19 Answers will vary. Possible answers:
1. La señora Vélez come el desayuno a las ocho de la mañana. Le encanta comer cereal, jugo de naranja y café.
2. A Yoshi y a Daniel les gusta comer sándwiches de atún, manzanas y leche para el almuerzo. Por lo general almuerzan a la una de la tarde.
3. Ángela y yo almorzamos a las doce en punto. Nos gusta comer perros calientes con papas fritas y tomar limonada.

SEGUNDO PASO   pp. 96–101

23 Answers will vary. Possible answers:
— Cristóbal, ¿cómo está la manzana?
— Está dulce y deliciosa.

— Leticia, ¿cómo está la sopa?
— ¡Está muy caliente!

— Mariano, ¿cómo está la comida?
— ¡Está muy picante!

— Gloria, ¿cómo están los huevos?
— No están muy buenos. Están fríos.

TERCER PASO   pp. 104–111

34 Answers will vary. Possible answers:
1. Necesito una cuchara y un tazón/plato hondo.
2. Necesito un tenedor y un plato.
3. Necesito una cuchara y un tazón/plato hondo.
4. Necesito un vaso.
5. Necesito una cuchara y un tazón/plato hondo.
6. Necesito un tenedor y un plato.

VAMOS A LEER   pp. 114–115

B [Title:] Los batidos
[Author:] **Bárbara Benavides**
II. Tres recetas
  B. Batido de plátano con fresas
  C. Batido de moras
C 1. Las frutas tropicales, como el plátano, la piña y el mango.
2. one

A VER SI PUEDO...   pp. 118

1 Answers will vary. Possible answers:
1. Los fines de semana como cereal con leche y plátanos para el desayuno.
2. Cuando tengo mucha hambre me encanta comer huevos revueltos con pan tostado y jugo de naranja.
3. Cuando tengo prisa, me gusta comer el cereal con leche y un vaso de jugo.
4. Por lo general tomo cereal con frutas y leche cuando tengo que ir al colegio.

Chapter Section	Presentation	Homework Options
Primer paso	**Así se dice,** p. 87	*Pupil's Edition,* p. 87, Activity 6
	Vocabulario, p. 88	*Pupil's Edition,* p. 88, Activity 9 *Grammar and Vocabulary,* p. 9, Activities 1–2 *Practice and Activity Book,* p. 86, Activities 3–4
	Gramática, p. 89	*Pupil's Edition,* p. 89, Activity 11 *Grammar and Vocabulary,* p. 10, Activities 3–4
	Vocabulario, p. 90	*Pupil's Edition,* pp. 90–91, Activities 13–15 *Practice and Activity Book,* p. 88, Activity 7 *CD-ROM,* Disc 2, Chapter 8, Activity 2
	Gramática, p. 92	*Pupil's Edition,* p. 93, Activity 17 *Grammar and Vocabulary,* p. 12, Activities 7–8 *CD-ROM,* Disc 2, Chapter 8, Activity 1
Segundo paso	**Así se dice,** p. 97	*Pupil's Edition,* p. 97, Activity 23 *Practice and Activity Book,* p. 29, Activities 9–10
	Nota gramatical, p. 98	*Pupil's Edition,* p. 98, Activity 24 *Grammar and Vocabulary,* p. 13, Activities 9–10
	Nota gramatical, p. 100	*Pupil's Edition,* p. 100, Activity 29 *Grammar and Vocabulary,* p. 14, Activities 11–12
Tercer paso	**Así se dice,** p. 105	*Pupil's Edition,* p. 106, Activity 34
	Vocabulario, p. 105	*Grammar and Vocabulary,* p. 15, Activities 13–15 *Practice and Activity Book,* p. 32, Activity 14
	Vocabulario, p. 107	*Grammar and Vocabulary,* p. 17, Activities 18–19 *Practice and Activity Book,* p. 93, Activity 16
	Así se dice, p. 108	*Pupil's Edition,* p. 109, Activity 38 *Practice and Activity Book,* p. 34, Activity 17
	Así se dice/Vocabulario, pp. 109, 110	*Grammar and Vocabulary,* p. 17, Activities 20–21 *Practice and Activity Book,* p. 94, Activity 18 *CD-ROM,* Disc 2, Chapter 8, Activities 5–6

¡A comer!

MOTIVATING ACTIVITY

Ask students what they usually eat at a meal. How often do they eat meals as a family? How long are meals? Where do they buy their food? Have they ever seen a market like the one on this page?

TEACHER NOTE

Have students collect used magazines from which to clip pictures of food and bring in non-perishable food items to use as realia for this chapter.

PHOTO FLASH!

① Ask students to name the fruits they recognize in the photo. They might mention **plátano** *(banana)*, **piña** *(pineapple)*, **fresa** *(strawberry)*, and **coco** *(coconut)*. Ecuador also has many fruits students may not have tried, such as **maracuyás** *(passion fruit)*, **papayas, mangos,** and **naranjillas,** a fruit that tastes like a bitter orange.

SOCIAL STUDIES LINK

Have students choose a Spanish-speaking country and do research to prepare a report on what types of foods are popular there. Their report should include information on what foods are grown there.

CAPÍTULO 8

¡A comer!

Ingredientes

EMPANADAS DE QUESO
Tiempo: la hora
500 g de masa de maíz
de queso blanco

Ingredientes

ENSALADA MIXTA
Tiempo: 15
Raciones
la

① ¡Me encantan las frutas!

80

In this chapter you will learn to

PRIMER PASO

- talk about meals and food

SEGUNDO PASO

- comment on food

TERCER PASO

- make polite requests
- order dinner in a restaurant
- ask for and pay the bill in a restaurant

internet

go.
hrw
.com

MARCAR: go.hrw.com
PALABRA CLAVE:
WV3 ECUADOR-8

② **¡La sopa está muy rica!**

③ **¿Qué vamos a pedir?**

FOCUSING ON OUTCOMES

Have students match the learner outcomes to the photos on these pages. (Photo 1: talking about meals and food; Photo 2: commenting on food; and Photo 3: making polite requests and ordering dinner in a restaurant.) Point out that talking about food is an important use of a language. This includes being able to order and pay for meals and to express what they want. By the end of the chapter, students will be able to participate in this important aspect of Spanish-speaking culture.

PHOTO FLASH!

Photos 1 and 2 were taken in Ecuador.

① People are shopping at an outdoor market, a popular place to shop in many Spanish-speaking countries.

② The man is eating **sancocho,** a typical Ecuadorean dish. Point out that the corn is still on the cob and the meat is still left on the bone. In Latin American countries stew-like soups are often served this way.

CULTURE NOTES

• Soups and stews are very popular dishes in Ecuador. **Caldo de pollo** (chicken soup) is among the most popular.

• A popular soup in Chile is one made with **porotos** (beans).

81

VIDEO INTEGRATION

En camino LEVEL 1B
Video Program
Videocassette 1, 26:18–32:33 OR
Videocassette 3, 1:17:25–1:23:40
(captioned version)

¡Ven conmigo! LEVEL 1
DVD Tutor, Disc 2

TEACHER NOTE
The **fotonovela** is an abridged version of the video episode.

VIDEO SYNOPSIS
Roberto, Tomás, and María take Hiroshi to a restaurant that serves typical Ecuadorean dishes. Tomás orders **sancocho,** María orders **empanadas,** and Roberto orders **carne colorada.** They describe the food to Hiroshi, who decides to order **sancocho.** After eating and paying the bill, they leave the restaurant. They are driving along a mountain road when they suddenly have car trouble.

MOTIVATING ACTIVITY
Ask students if they like trying new foods. If they were to visit a foreign country, would they like to try regional dishes? What foods from other countries are popular in their area? Which ethnic foods are their favorites?

DE ANTEMANO

¿Qué vas a pedir?

CD 8 Trs. 1–2 María, her brother Roberto, and their friend Tomás take Hiroshi to the town of Otavalo, famous for its market. On the way, they get hungry and stop to eat. Why won't they get to Otavalo on time?

p. 25
Acts. 1–2

Maria **Tomás** **Hiroshi** **Roberto**

En camino…

Tengo mucha hambre. Ya es la una y media y por lo general almuerzo a las doce.

No te preocupes. Vas a comer bien en el restaurante. Para el almuerzo hay platos especiales típicos de la región andina.

Eh….No sé...¿qué van a pedir ustedes?

Qué vas a pedir?

Mm...creo que voy a pedir sanchoco. Pero, el locro es delicioso aquí también.

¿Qué son ésos? ¿son sopas?

Platos del Día

Carne colorada	$/7.65
Sancocho	$/5.00
Yahuarlocro	$/4.00
Lomo al carbón	$/8.50
Empanadas de morocho	$/2.50
Llapingachos	$/4.50

Postres

Helado de naranjilla	$/3.00
Tomatillos en almíbar	$/2.50

82 *ochenta y dos*

CAPÍTULO 8

PRESENTATION
First, have students scan the **fotonovela**. Then, play the video. Have students repeat the dialogue lines after you. Periodically stop and ask comprehension questions. (**¿Quiénes van al restaurante? En el restaurante, ¿qué come Tomás? ¿María? ¿Roberto? ¿Hiroshi?**) Play the video again, then have students play the parts of the characters in groups of four.

LANGUAGE NOTES
- **Carne colorada** is meat cooked with **achiote**, a spice that gives the cooked meat a reddish color and a special flavor. **Achiote** is made from the seeds of a shrub that is grown in home gardens.
- **Empanadas** (also called **pasteles** or **hojaldías**) are small pies or turnovers, filled with seasoned meat, fish, vegetables, or sweets. They are popular in almost all Spanish-speaking countries. Small **empanadas** are served as hors d'oeuvres.

DE ANTEMANO

ochenta y tres 83

STANDARDS: 1.2, 2.2

LANGUAGE NOTES

- In Spanish, fast-food restaurants are called **restaurantes de comida rápida o comida para llevar.** Meals *to go* are **para llevar.** Meals to eat in are called **para tomar.**

- In addition to **sopa,** *soup* is also called **caldo** (or **locro,** if corn is used). Stew is called **guiso de pollo o carne,** or at times, **seco,** which means *dry.* (By comparison with soups, it is less liquid and "drier.")

A continuación

You may choose to continue with *¿Qué vas a pedir? (a continuación)* at this time or wait until later in the chapter. At this point, the characters are helped with their car trouble by a passerby. They continue to **el Monumento de la Mitad del Mundo** where they buy traditional handicrafts from vendors in an open-air market. You may wish to have students write alternative versions of the second part of the video.

CAPÍTULO 8   ¡A comer!

Cuaderno para
hispanohablantes,
pp. 36–40

1 ¿Comprendes?

Answer these questions about the **fotonovela.** If you aren't sure, guess! Answers in side column

These activities check for global comprehension only. Students should not yet be expected to produce language modeled in **De antemano.**

1. Where do Hiroshi, María, Tomás, and Roberto go at the beginning of the **fotonovela?**
2. Is Hiroshi familiar with the food of Ecuador? How do you know?
3. What happens when Hiroshi tastes the **ají?**
4. Does Hiroshi like the food he orders?
5. What happens after the group leaves the restaurant?

2 ¿Cómo se dice?

Match the Spanish phrase with its description. What phrases from the **fotonovela** can you use . . .?

1. to ask what someone will order c
2. to explain what **sancocho** is f
3. to say that you love **empanadas** b
4. to ask a waiter to bring you **carne colorada** e
5. to say that something is really good a
6. to ask how much the bill is d

a. Está muy rico.
b. Me encantan las empanadas.
c. ¿Qué vas a pedir?
d. ¿Cuánto es?
e. ¿Me puede traer carne colorada?
f. Es una sopa de pollo, carne, plátanos, maíz y otras verduras.

3 ¿Quién lo diría?

According to the **fotonovela,** who would be most likely to say each of the following things? Answers in side column

1. Me encanta la comida de Ecuador.
2. ¿Empanadas? ¡Qué horrible!
3. ¿Y para usted?
4. ¿Empanadas? ¡Qué rico!

4 ¡Qué lío!

Con base en la fotonovela, pon las oraciones en el orden correcto.

a. Para Hiroshi, ¡el ají está muy picante! 4
b. Hay un problema con el carro. 6
c. Los amigos van a un restaurante que tiene comida típica de Ecuador. 2
d. A Hiroshi le encanta el sancocho. ¡Está muy rico! 5
e. Tomás quiere comer sancocho. 3
f. Hiroshi tiene mucha hambre. 1

Felipe y su madre preparan empanadas de carne.

SLOWER PACE

1 Have students first identify the frame or frames in the **fotonovela** where the answer for each question may be found. Then have them work in pairs comparing the frames they chose and checking the answers.

VISUAL/AUDITORY LEARNERS

2 Play the video again and have students raise their hands to pause the videotape when they hear the phrase or see a visual clue to one of the answers. Then have them identify which question was being answered when they asked you to pause the recording.

SUGGESTION

Have students work in groups of four to read and act out the restaurant scene. Ask one or two groups to perform it for the class.

Answers to Activity 1

1. They go to a restaurant.
2. No, he isn't. His friends tell him about the food.
3. He thinks it's very spicy.
4. Yes
5. Their car breaks down.

Answers to Activity 3

1. Hiroshi
2. Tomás
3. the waiter
4. María

VIDEO INTEGRATION

En camino LEVEL 1B
Video Program
Videocassette 1, 28:30–28:57 OR
Videocassette 3, 1:19:37–1:20:04
(captioned version)

¡Ven conmigo! LEVEL 1
DVD Tutor, Disc 2

Bell work
On the board or a transparency write the following: **¿Cuál es la fecha?** and **¿Cuál es el pronóstico del tiempo para hoy?** Have students respond in writing.

PREVIEWING
5 Use the questions in Activity 5 as a previewing activity to focus students' attention on the phrases when the **fotonovela** characters talk about what they like and don't like.

NATIVE SPEAKERS
Have native speakers compare the following words, which are common in Andean countries, with the words they use.
el choclo   corn
el zapallo   squash
la palta   avocado
los porotos   beans

PRIMER PASO (TPR) Storytelling Book pp. 29, 32

WV3 ECUADOR-8

Talking about meals and food

Sí, mira allí. El locro es una sopa de papa, aguacate y queso.

Para mí, el sancocho, por favor.

El sanchoco está bien, pero a mí me encantan las empanadas. Empanadas, por favor.

No, no me gustan para nada las empanadas.

5 El restaurante
Mira la foto y contesta las preguntas.
1. ¿María prefiere el sancocho o las empanadas?
2. ¿A quién no le gustan las empanadas?
3. ¿Qué come la gente en la otra mesa?
4. ¿A María le gusta la comida que comen las personas en la otra mesa?

1. María prefiere las empanadas.
2. A Tomás no le gustan las empanadas.
3. Come locro.
4. Sí, le gusta, pero le gustan más las empanadas.

Nota cultural

Throughout Spanish-speaking countries, a fruit or vegetable may have a variety of names. Many of these names derive from words used by the indigenous, or native, people in each area. In addition to **maíz,** corn is also called **choclo** and **elote.** In different regions, bananas may be called **guineos, cambures, plátanos, bananos,** and **bananas.** Can you think of any foods that have different names in English?

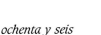

ASÍ SE DICE   Talking about meals and food

p. 26
Acts. 3–4

8-1

To ask your friend about meals and food, say:

¿Qué tomas para el desayuno?
What do you have for breakfast?

¿Qué comes para el almuerzo?
What do you eat for lunch?

Tengo sed. ¿Qué hay para tomar?
I'm thirsty. What's there to drink?

Your friend might answer:

A veces tomo un vaso de jugo y un poco de pan. **¡No me gusta** el cereal **para nada!**
. . . I don't like cereal at all!

Por lo general, como un sándwich, una manzana y tomo un vaso de leche. *Usually I have a sandwich, an apple, and a glass of milk.*

Hay jugo, refrescos y agua. **¿Qué prefieres?** *What do you prefer?*

6 Las comidas

Use the following words to complete the conversations.

1. —Es hora para el almuerzo. ¿Quieres un __1__? sándwich
   —No, gracias. No me __2__ para nada. gusta
2. —¿Qué comes para el desayuno?
   —A veces tomo __3__ con __4__ y un vaso de jugo. cereal, leche
3. —¿Qué comes para el __5__? almuerzo
   —Por lo general, como una hamburguesa o un sándwich.
4. —Mamá, ¿qué hay para tomar?
   —No hay más refrescos. Hay __6__ de manzana y __7__. ¿Cuál prefieres?
   jugo, agua

cereal · gusta · jugo · agua · almuerzo · leche · sándwich

7 ¿Qué prefieres?

Work with a group. Take turns asking each other if you prefer juice, soda, milk, or water for lunch. Take notes. Choose a spokesperson to report your results to the class.

MODELO   ¿Qué prefieres tomar para el almuerzo?

¿Te acuerdas?

Remember that the verb **preferir** is an **e→ie** stem-changing verb.

prefiero	preferimos
prefieres	preferís
prefiere	prefieren

☀ MOTIVATE

Ask students to compare the breakfasts they eat on school days with those they eat on weekends. What are the similarities and differences?

☀ TEACH

PRESENTATION
ASÍ SE DICE
Display and go over images (drawings or cutouts from magazines) of the foods and drinks presented in **Así se dice.** Model the vocabulary by describing what you have for breakfast and lunch. Then ask students the questions from **Así se dice** and have them answer referring to the images.

ADDITIONAL PRACTICE
6 Have students practice the conversations with a partner, alternating roles.

CHALLENGE
7 To model first, second, and third person, count off students in groups of three. Have them do this activity according to the following model:

JUAN   María, ¿qué prefiere Pablo?
MARIA   No sé. Pablo, ¿qué prefieres?
PABLO   Prefiero un refresco.
MARIA   Juan, Pablo prefiere un refresco.

PRESENTATION

VOCABULARIO

Display Teaching Transparency 8-A and have students role-play the conversation about breakfast from **Así se dice** on page 87 replacing the foods and drinks presented there with ones of their choice from the **Vocabulario** overhead.

SUGGESTIONS

Have students make vocabulary flashcards. Ask them to label the back of the cards with the Spanish definitions. They can use magazine pictures, newspaper grocery ads, or their own drawings on the front. For additional food-related vocabulary, refer them to pages 119, 294–296.

8 As a postviewing activity students can use *CD-ROM* Activity 2 to practice classifying foods by meal.

LANGUAGE NOTES

Some speakers from Mexico prefer the word **blanquillos** for **huevos**. The word **panceta** is common in Argentina and Uruguay for **tocino**.

Answers to Activity 9

Answers will vary. Possible answers:
1. cereal o pan dulce con frutas
2. huevos con tocino y pan tostado
3. pan dulce o fruta
4. cereal
5. pan dulce o huevos y tocino

GV p. 9 Acts. 1–2

VOCABULARIO

8-A

¡Me encanta el desayuno! *I love breakfast!*

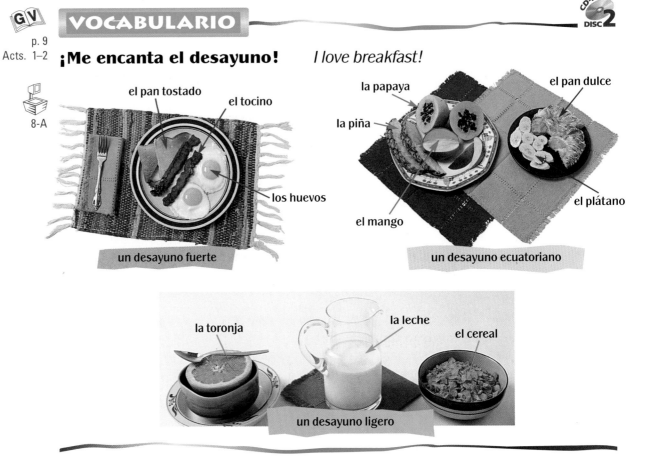

el pan tostado
el tocino
los huevos
un desayuno fuerte

la papaya
la piña
el mango
el pan dulce
el plátano
un desayuno ecuatoriano

la toronja
la leche
el cereal
un desayuno ligero

8 El desayuno Script and answers on p. 79E

CD 8 Tr. 3

Listen to Marcela and Roberto as they talk about the foods they like for breakfast. Which foods does Marcela like and which does Roberto like?

a. las frutas
b. la leche
c. los plátanos
d. los huevos revueltos con tocino
e. el café
f. el pan dulce
g. el jugo de naranja

9 ¿Qué quiere para el desayuno? Ⓗ

Di lo que la señorita Román probablemente come para el desayuno en diferentes situaciones. Answers in side column

1. ¿Qué come cuando está en casa pero no tiene mucho tiempo?
2. ¿Qué come cuando tiene ganas de cocinar *(to cook)*?
3. ¿Qué come para el desayuno cuando quiere comer algo frío y fácil en el trabajo?
4. ¿Qué come cuando no hay fruta y no quiere cocinar?
5. ¿Qué come cuando no hay leche en su casa?

10 Te gusta

Interview your partner. Find out about his or her preferred breakfast foods. Ask **¿Te gusta...?** and **¿Prefieres... o...?** Make sure you remember what your partner likes best. Then switch roles. Be prepared to present your partner's breakfast preferences to the class.

GRAMÁTICA The verb **encantar** and indirect object pronouns

1. The verb **encantar** *(to really like; to love)* works just like the verb **gustar**.

   Me gusta la leche, pero **me encanta** el jugo de naranja. A Juan **le gusta** la piña, pero **le encanta** el mango. **Nos encantan** los plátanos.

2. The pronouns **me, te, le, nos,** and **les** are called *indirect object pronouns.* They generally tell *to whom* or *for whom* something is done.

   Te gusta la leche, ¿verdad?   *Milk is pleasing to you, right?*

3. Remember to use the definite article with **encantar** or **gustar** when you're saying what you like.

   Me encanta **el** jugo de naranja.   *I love orange juice.*

PA p. 27 Act. 5

GV p.10 Acts. 3–4

11 ¿A quién le gusta?

Fill in the blank with the correct indirect object pronoun.

1. A mi abuela _____ gustan la piña, las manzanas y los mangos. le
2. A mis padres _____ encanta el chocolate. les
3. A mí _____ encantan las uvas verdes. me
4. A mis primos _____ gustan los perros calientes con papitas. les
5. A ti _____ encanta la sopa de pollo con legumbres, ¿no? te
6. A mi amiga y a mí _____ gusta tomar agua con el almuerzo. nos

instantáneo
con vitaminas y minerales
CHOCO LISTO
300g
Compañía Nacional de Chocolates S.A

Me gusta la leche pero me encanta el chocolate caliente.

PRESENTATION

GRAMÁTICA

List ten breakfast foods on the board in Spanish. Model pronunciation and structure by saying what you or others like to eat. Point out that the pattern for **encantar** is the same as **gustar**. Then have students ask their partners **¿Qué piensas de...?** The partner responds with **No me gusta, me gusta,** or **me encanta.** Then ask students **¿A quién le gusta...?** Stress the need for the preposition **a** in students' answers. (**A Roberta le gusta.**)

SUGGESTION

11 After students have completed this activity, ask them to write what they and their families like for breakfast. Is there a difference between weekdays and weekends? Do they eat at home or in restaurants? Are their favorite breakfast foods different from their siblings'?

GEOGRAPHY LINK

Ecuador lies on the Earth's equator. Ask students what this means regarding Ecuador's climate and crops. (Ecuador has little change of climate throughout the year. For this reason, some fruits and vegetables are always in season and may be bought all year long.)

VOCABULARIO

GV p. 11
Acts. 5–6

Para almorzar...

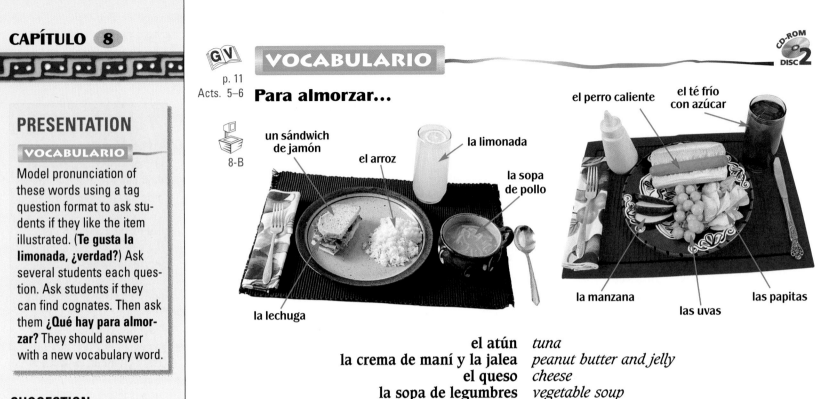

8-B

el perro caliente

el té frío con azúcar

un sándwich de jamón

el arroz

la limonada

la sopa de pollo

la lechuga

la manzana

las uvas

las papitas

el atún	*tuna*
la crema de maní y la jalea	*peanut butter and jelly*
el queso	*cheese*
la sopa de legumbres	*vegetable soup*

12 El almuerzo

A Imagine that it's up to you to decide what will be served in the cafeteria today. Write a menu of foods and beverages that you would like to have for your lunch.   Answers will vary.

B Then ask three classmates if they like the foods on your menu.

> MODELO   ¿Te gusta el sándwich de crema de maní y jalea para el almuerzo?

13 Mis preferencias

 Make a list of foods that you love, that you like, and that you don't like. Write at least 15 foods. You can include breakfast and lunch foods. Then choose six of the foods and write a sentence about each one. Say how you feel about each food.   Answers will vary.

MODELO   Siempre tomo leche porque me gusta.

	la leche
me encanta	
me gusta	✓
no me gusta para nada	

PRESENTATION

VOCABULARIO

Model pronunciation of these words using a tag question format to ask students if they like the item illustrated. (**Te gusta la limonada, ¿verdad?**) Ask several students each question. Ask students if they can find cognates. Then ask them **¿Qué hay para almorzar?** They should answer with a new vocabulary word.

SUGGESTION

Have students add pictures of the lunch items to their flash-card set.

ADDITIONAL VOCABULARY

un sándwich de queso fundido
grilled cheese sandwich
la sopa de tomate
tomato soup
una ensalada de frutas
fruit salad

TEACHER NOTE

13 The additional vocabulary on pages 294–296 will allow students to personalize answers to any open-ended activities.

14 El cumpleaños

The twins Rodrigo and Ricardo are arguing about what to have for their special birthday lunch. Read their conversation. Then read each sentence that follows. Answer **cierto** or **falso**. If the sentence is false, correct it.

RICARDO —Oye, Rodrigo, tenemos que hablar. ¿Qué vamos a comer el día de nuestro cumpleaños? Mamá nos va a preparar un almuerzo especial.

RODRIGO —Bueno, a mí me encantan las hamburguesas, la pizza, los perros calientes, las papas fritas, los refrescos y el helado de chocolate.

RICARDO —Y a mí me gusta la pizza con queso y legumbres, pero no me gustan las hamburguesas ni los perros calientes para nada. Me encanta la ensalada de frutas, especialmente si tiene mango, y la leche para tomar.

RODRIGO —Bueno, ¿qué hacemos entonces?

RICARDO —Vamos a ver lo que le gusta a mamá.

1. A los hermanos les encanta la leche. Answers in side column
2. Ricardo prefiere la ensalada de frutas.
3. A Rodrigo le gustan comidas saludables *(healthy)*.
4. A Ricardo le encantan los perros calientes.

15 ¿A quién le gusta...?

 Mira las fotos de las comidas y bebidas. Escribe una oración por cada una de las fotos diciendo *(telling)* a quién o a quiénes les gusta. Usa algunas de las personas en la lista.

MODELO A mi padrastro, Julián, le encanta...

Answers will vary.

tu padre / madre
el / la profesor(a) de español
tu familia
tu hermano
tu amigo(a)
tu gato(a)

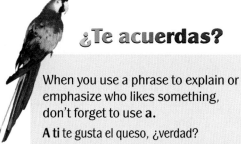

¿Te acuerdas?

When you use a phrase to explain or emphasize who likes something, don't forget to use **a.**

A ti te gusta el queso, ¿verdad?

Sí, y también les gusta **a mis amigos.**

SUGGESTION

14 Remind students of some of the reading strategies they've learned: to look for cognates and to use context to understand unfamiliar words.

CULTURE NOTE
At some restaurants in Spanish-speaking countries, an inexpensive lunch menu consists only of two or three complete meals for which substitutions cannot be made. These **comidas corridas** often include **el primer plato** such as **una sopa** or **una ensalada, el segundo plato,** and **el postre.** These restaurants are popular, as American-style cafeterias are rare.

Answers to Activity 14

1. falso; A Ricardo le encanta la leche.
2. cierto
3. falso; A Ricardo le gustan las comidas saludables.
4. falso; A Ricardo no le gustan los perros calientes para nada.

PRESENTATION
GRAMÁTICA

Say **Yo almuerzo a las...,
Mis amigos Paco y Diana
almuerzan a las...** Then ask
students around the room
**¿A qué hora almuerzas tú?
¿A qué hora almuerzan tú
y tu familia? ¿A qué hora
almorzamos nosotros?** Students respond using the
appropriately conjugated
verbs. Continue with
desayunar and **cenar.**

ADDITIONAL PRACTICE
16 Have students work with
a partner to role-play a conversation between a student from
the United States and a student from Ecuador. They talk
about what they like to eat for
breakfast, lunch, and dinner
and when they eat their meals.

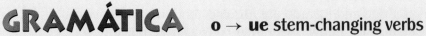

GRAMÁTICA o → ue stem-changing verbs

1. You've already learned about **e → ie** stem-changing verbs such as **querer** and **preferir.**

PA
p. 28
Act. 8

GV
p. 12
Act. 7–8

2. Another type of stem change is **o → ue.** **Almorzar** *(to eat lunch)* is an example; all forms have a stem change except the **nosotros** and **vosotros** forms.

(yo)	alm**uerzo**	(nosotros) (nosotras)	almorz**amos**
(tú)	alm**uerzas**	(vosotros) (vosotras)	almorz**áis**
(usted) (él) (ella)	alm**uerza**	(ustedes) (ellos) (ellas)	alm**uerzan**

3. Another **o → ue** stem-changing verb is **poder** *(can; to be able to).* It's usually followed by an infinitive.

p**uedo**	pod**emos**
p**uedes**	pod**éis**
p**uede**	p**ueden**

No puedo estudiar contigo esta noche porque tengo que trabajar.

¿**Almuerzas** en el colegio o en casa?

16 ¿Cómo es la comida de aquí?

CD 8 Tr. 4

Listen as Adela, an Ecuadorean student, asks Pablo about the typical meals in the United States. Write **cierto** or **falso** for each sentence, according to what Pablo says.

Script and answers on p. 79E

1. Por lo general, Pablo desayuna a las siete de la mañana.

2. Para el desayuno, Pablo sólo come pan tostado.

3. Durante la semana, Pablo almuerza a las dos de la tarde.

4. A veces toma leche en el almuerzo.

Nota cultural

In many Spanish-speaking countries, the main meal is often called simply **la comida.** It's typically a heavier meal than lunch in the U.S. It consists of soup, meat, or fish with rice and vegetables, followed by a dessert and often coffee. What time does your family eat its big meal of the day? What advantages do you see to eating the main meal earlier in the day?

17 ¿Puedes almorzar conmigo?

Completa las oraciones usando las formas correctas de **almorzar** o **poder**.

1. Mi hermana Casandra y yo _____ en la casa de nuestra amiga. almorzamos
2. Yo siempre _____ a la misma hora. almuerzo
3. Y tú, ¿_____ en el colegio o en tu casa? almuerzas
4. Lo siento Héctor, no _____ almorzar en tu casa. puedo
5. ¿Tú _____ jugar al voleibol conmigo después de las clases? puedes
6. ¿En Ecuador, ellos _____ con un plato fuerte? almuerzan

18 ¿Dónde almuerzan?

Trabaja con un/a compañero/a. Pregúntale dónde generalmente almuerzan las personas en la lista los días indicados. Después, contesta las mismas preguntas que te hace tu compañero/a.

MODELO   tu tía / los viernes   Answers will vary.
Los viernes mi tía generalmente almuerza en un restaurante con sus compañeros de trabajo.

1. tú / los domingos
2. tus padres / de lunes a viernes
3. los estudiantes / los lunes
4. tú y tu amigo(a) / los miércoles
5. yo / de lunes a viernes
6. tu amigo / los sábados

19 Tienen hambre

Write two sentences about each drawing. Identify the meal the people are eating, the time, and what they like to eat. Answers on p. 79K

la señora Vélez **8:00**

Yoshi y Daniel **1:00**

Ángela y tú **12:00**

20 Y ustedes, ¿qué almuerzan?

Work with a group. Take turns asking each other what time you have breakfast and lunch. Ask each other what you usually eat for those meals. Write what each person says. Then report to the class on those that eat meals at the same time or have similar foods for breakfast or lunch.   Answers will vary.

ADDITIONAL PRACTICE

19 Have students write their sentences on the board. The class then identifies which caption the sentence describes.

☀ CLOSE

Divide the class into groups of four or five. Each group develops a five-question survey (**encuesta**) of their classmates' eating habits. (¿**Tomas un vaso de jugo para el desayuno?**) All students should respond to every survey's questions. Students write their answers for each **encuesta** on a piece of paper and return it to the correct group.

☀ ASSESS

▸ Testing Program, pp. 37–38
  Quiz 8-1
  Audio CD 8, Tr. 19

▸ Grammar and Vocabulary
  Quizzes
  Quiz 8-1A or
  Alternative Quiz 8-1A

▸ Alternative Assessment
  Guide, p. 20

PERFORMANCE ASSESSMENT

Have students make a shopping list of foods to buy for a week of breakfasts and lunches. They then make a meal calendar for the week and describe to the class what they plan to eat at each meal.

VIDEO INTEGRATION

En camino LEVEL 1B

Video Program

Videocassette 1, 39:12–41:29

PRESENTATION

Have students watch the video or read the speech bubbles and identify as many of the ingredients in **gazpacho** and **tortilla española** as they can. Then, based on those ingredients, have them determine which dishes sound appetizing to them. Have them answer with **Me gustaría comer...** or **No me gustaría comer...**

CRITICAL THINKING

Have students think about some of the reasons why certain foods and types of foods might be popular in some parts of the world and not in others. (Regional diet is often based on the local climate, which plants do well, what types of plants and animals are native to the area)

ENCUENTRO CULTURAL

La comida en el mundo hispanohablante

Daniel es de Sevilla. Es una ciudad de Andalucía, en el sur de España. A Daniel le gusta mucho comer. Te va a decir cuáles son algunas de sus comidas favoritas.

> Aquí en Andalucía, tenemos unos platos muy ricos como, por ejemplo, la tortilla española, que está hecha de huevos, patatas y cebollas; el gazpacho, que es una sopa fría de tomates, pepinos y otras verduras; el queso manchego, que es un queso curado; el jamón serrano; los calamares; las aceitunas.

1 ¿Qué dijo?

Daniel describes many different kinds of food he likes to eat, and how they're made. Guess the meanings of the unfamiliar words he uses. Remember to use your background knowledge and look at the context.

> "...la **tortilla española**, que está hecha de huevos, patatas y cebollas" ·········▶

> "...el **gazpacho**, que es una sopa fría de tomates, pepinos y otras verduras" ·········▶

> "el **queso manchego**, que es un queso curado; **el jamón serrano**" ·········▶

1. What ingredients go into a **tortilla española?** eggs, potatoes, onions

2. Which is the best description of **gazpacho?**
   a. a cold tossed salad
   (b.) a cold vegetable soup

3. What are two other Spanish foods that Daniel also eats?
   (a.) ham and cheese
   b. rice and beans

2 ¡Piénsalo!

1. Are there any foods that Daniel eats that are similar to foods you eat? What are they? How are they similar? Answers will vary.

2. Which foods does Daniel eat that are different from foods you eat? How are they different? Answers will vary.

3. Look at the food pyramid. Find the foods that Daniel mentions. What food groups are they in? Plan a meal for Daniel that includes the foods he mentions. Add other foods you have learned about according to the food pyramid's recommendations. Consider food portions in writing your plan. Answers will vary.

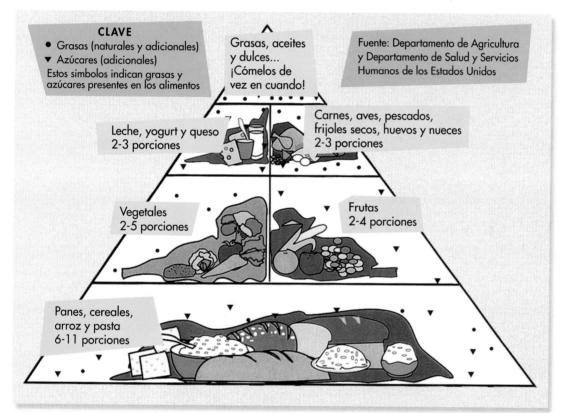

CLAVE
- Grasas (naturales y adicionales)
- Azúcares (adicionales)

Estos símbolos indican grasas y azúcares presentes en los alimentos

Grasas, aceites y dulces... ¡Cómelos de vez en cuando!

Fuente: Departamento de Agricultura y Departamento de Salud y Servicios Humanos de los Estados Unidos

Leche, yogurt y queso 2-3 porciones

Carnes, aves, pescados, frijoles secos, huevos y nueces 2-3 porciones

Vegetales 2-5 porciones

Frutas 2-4 porciones

Panes, cereales, arroz y pasta 6-11 porciones

3 ¿Y tú?

Answer these questions to tell Daniel about what you eat. Answers will vary.

1. Un plato típico de mi región es ———.

2. Los ingredientes de este plato son ———.

3. De postre me gusta(n) ———.

ENCUENTRO CULTURAL

noventa y cinco **95**

STANDARDS: 1.2, 2.2, 3.1, 3.2 **95**

SUGGESTION

2 Have students do **La pirámide de la nutrición** project suggested on page 79G. Students work in groups of three to create a food pyramid model with categories in Spanish to present to the class.

MULTICULTURAL LINK

Have students talk about the types of foods they eat at home and what the traditions of those foods are. Consider having a party in which all students agree to bring a special dish from home and share it with the class.

HEALTH LINK

Have students do research to find out how the prescribed diet in the United States has changed over the last 50 years. Have them learn about the four food group outline from the 1950's and compare it to the food pyramid used today.

VIDEO INTEGRATION
En camino LEVEL 1B
Video Program
Videocassette 1, 29:18–30:04 OR
Videocassette 3, 1:20:25–1:21:11
(captioned version)

¡**Ven conmigo!** LEVEL 1
DVD Tutor, Disc 2

Bell work

Ask students to look at the photos on page 88 and decide what they would like to order for breakfast. Ask them to list each item they would like. Are their choices closest to a **desayuno fuerte, ligero,** or **ecuatoriano?**

☀ MOTIVATE

Ask students to consider polite ways to comment on food. At a friend's or relative's, what do they do if they don't like something they are served? If they are served something they don't like and are asked to comment on it, what should they say? to whom? Explain that in Latin America, etiquette requires that you eat it and act as if you like it.

Commenting on food

21 ¡Está picante!

1. **Está picante** means
   a. it's sweet
   b. it's salty
   c. it's spicy

2. What does one of Hiroshi's friends say that gives you a clue about the meaning of **está picante?**
   a. esto es ají
   b. ¡Cuidado Hiroshi...!
   c. te va a gustar

3. **Ají** is a condiment. Tomás suggests that Hiroshi eat it with some bread. What other food(s) would **ají** taste good with?
   a. la toronja
   b. el pollo
   c. el pan dulce

Nota cultural

Many people in the U.S. are familiar with popular Mexican foods, and therefore believe that all Spanish-speaking people eat hot and spicy food. Spicy foods are more likely to be eaten in Mexico and the Caribbean countries. In general, foods in Spanish-speaking countries are not spicy, but are highly seasoned with **ajo** *(garlic),* **cebolla** *(onion),* **azafrán** *(saffron),* and herbs like **cilantro, orégano,** and **albahaca** *(basil).* It is common for **el picante** *(the hot sauce)* to be placed on the table for people to add to their food if they wish. Are there any hot and spicy foods that you like?

ASÍ SE DICE Commenting on food

To find out how something tastes, ask:

¿Cómo está la sopa?
How is the soup?

Your friend might answer:

Está **deliciosa**.
It's delicious.

Está **fría** y **salada**.
It's cold and salty.

¡Está **caliente**!
It's hot.

¿Cómo están los frijoles?
How are the beans?

Están muy **picantes** pero están **ricos**.
They're very spicy, but they're delicious.

¿Y cómo está el postre?
And how's the dessert?

¡Está muy **dulce**!
It's very sweet!

p. 29 Acts. 9–10

8-2

---

22 Comentarios Script and answers on p. 79E

CD 8 Tr. 5

Listen as customers comment on the food at El Rincón, a restaurant. Then, on a separate paper, match each food with the customer's opinion.

el pescado	la sopa
la sopa	la ensalada
la ensalada	de frutas
el pollo	

está muy picante	está frío/a
está muy rico/a	no está bueno/a
está delicioso/a	está muy salado/a

---

23 ¿Cómo está la comida?

Write a caption for each drawing. First ask how the food tastes. Then write how the person would answer. Answers on p. 79K

Cristóbal

Leticia

Mariano

Gloria

☀ TEACH

PRESENTATION
ASÍ SE DICE
Review the descriptive uses of **estar.** (locations, people's moods and conditions) Explain that **estar** is also used to describe food. Ask students **En la cafetería de aquí, ¿cómo está la comida? ¿el pollo? ¿la fruta?** Use Teaching Transparency 8-2 for more presentation ideas. Have students use *CD-ROM* Activity 3 for more practice.

SUGGESTION
Have students make **Así se dice** vocabulary picture flashcards.

NATIVE SPEAKERS
Have native speakers add the present-tense forms of **estar** to their accent-mark notebooks under **palabras agudas con acento.**

ADDITIONAL PRACTICE
22 Have students use the word boxes to create sentences about what their opinions of the various foods would be. Have them compare sentences with a partner's and say **es cierto** if they agree, or **no es cierto** if they disagree.

LANGUAGE NOTE
Point out that Spanish expresses two kinds of hot: **picante,** hot in the spicy or peppery sense, and **caliente,** hot in temperature.

PRESENTATION

NOTA GRAMATICAL

Have students read the explanation. Point out that this use of **estar** focuses on the speaker's present reaction. Bring in pictures of poorly prepared foods. (burnt French fries, strawberries with lots of sugar, chips drenched in hot sauce) If possible, tape or glue them to paper plates. Students make statements expressing their opinions about the food in general using **ser.** They then imagine they are eating and comment about the way it tastes: **Las papas fritas son buenas, pero estas papas fritas están malas.**

AUDITORY LEARNERS

Read the following sentences aloud and have students indicate whether you're commenting about a food you're eating right now or talking about a food in general.

1. Las fresas están dulces.
2. Los frijoles están salados.
3. El postre es dulce.
4. El ají es picante.
5. Las uvas son deliciosas.
6. El helado es muy, muy frío.
7. La sopa está fría.

ADDITIONAL PRACTICE

24 Have students indicate which foods Gustavo and Eneida are eating right now and which they eat in general.

NOTA GRAMATICAL

PA p. 30 Act. 11

GV p. 13 Acts. 9–10

The verb **estar** often says how things taste, look, or feel. **Ser,** which also means *to be,* tells how things normally are. Look at the two sentences below. Which would you use to talk about the dish in the photo to the right? Which would you use to say that you like shrimp in general?

Los camarones son ricos.
Shrimp are delicious. in general

¡Qué ricos están los camarones!
The shrimp taste delicious! with photo

coctel de camarones con salsa picante

24 ¡Son ricos!

Gustavo y Eneida are having lunch in the school cafeteria. They're talking about their food while they eat. Read their conversation and answer the questions. Answers below

GUSTAVO En el verano, siempre como ensaladas de frutas. ¡Son deliciosas! Me encantan las comidas frías cuando hace calor.

ENEIDA Yo prefiero las comidas calientes. Las sopas son muy deliciosas, especialmente las de pescado. Yo les pongo mucha salsa picante. ¡Qué rico!

GUSTAVO A mí también me gusta el pescado. Lo prefiero frito *(fried),* pero como lo prepara mi mamá. Este pescado frito está muy salado. ¿Y cómo están las papas fritas?

ENEIDA Están un poco frías, pero me gustan.

GUSTAVO Las papas fritas que hace mi abuela son las más ricas del mundo. ¿Te gustaría venir a almorzar en mi casa algún día?

ENEIDA Me encanta la idea. Mira, ¡termina de comer! ¡Ya es hora de ir a clase!

1. ¿A Gustavo le gustan las ensaladas de frutas? ¿Por qué?
2. ¿Qué tipo de comida le gusta a Eneida?
3. ¿Qué come Gustavo para su almuerzo?
4. ¿Cómo está su comida?

1. Sí, porque le gustan las comidas frías.
2. Le gustan las comidas calientes.
3. pescado
4. Está muy salada.

25 El buffet

 You and a friend are having lunch at a restaurant that has a buffet. Take turns asking your partner how the foods in the drawing taste. Answer with different comments about the foods.

26 Comidas extrañas

 Work with two partners to come up with some peculiar foods for a contest. Think up four foods for each category. Choose a spokesperson to present your creative food ideas to the class! *Answers will vary.*

MODELO   comidas frías: helado de frijoles con uvas

1. comidas frías
2. comidas picantes
3. comidas dulces
4. comidas saladas
5. comidas calientes
6. comidas malas

27 Vegetariano no es mala palabra

Read the cartoon about mealtime at Calvin's house. Write a paragraph with at least three sentences about the cartoon. Explain Calvin's attitude about the vegetarian food. What do you think Calvin means by the word **guácala**? What would he rather have? *Answers in side column*

asqueroso *gross*   **salud** *health*

© Watterson. Dist. by Universal Press Syndicate. Reprinted with Permission. All rights reserved.

KINESTHETIC LEARNERS
Have students make hand and face gestures as they comment on how the foods taste.

SUGGESTION
25 Have volunteers share their conversations about the buffet with the class.

ADDITIONAL PRACTICE
26 Have students pretend they have been served the peculiar foods and comment on them using the phrases from **Así se dice** on page 97.

27 Have students create comic strips about food in small groups.

ENGLISH LINK
Point out that **postretariano** is not an actual word; it's a word Calvin makes up to describe his food preferences. Ask students what word they would make up in English to express the same thing. (dessertatarian)

Answer to Activity 27

Answers will vary. Possible answer:

A Calvin no le gusta la comida vegetariana. Dice "guácala" porque no le gusta la comida. Le gustan los postres. Prefiere comer postres todos los días.

STANDARDS: 1.1, 1.3, 5.1

99

PRESENTATION

NOTA GRAMATICAL

Present students with situations to respond to. For example, **Son las doce. Tengo hambre. Me gustaría _____. Tengo sed. Me gustaría _____.** Ask students to complete the sentences with a vocabulary word or words from this chapter.

SUGGESTION

29 After students have completed this activity in class or at home, have them talk with a partner about what they prefer to eat and drink.

✦ CLOSE

📁 PORTFOLIO

Oral Have students review ways of commenting on food and discussing preferences. Then have students role-play a restaurant scene in groups of four or five. One student is the waitperson and the others are a group of friends who order lunch. They should discuss how the food tastes, what they would like to order, what they don't like, and what activities they will do after eating. For Portfolio information, see *Alternative Assessment Guide,* p. 12.

PA pp. 30–31 Act. 12

GV p. 14 Acts. 11–12

NOTA GRAMATICAL

Do you remember the **tener** expressions in Chapter 7? Two other **tener** phrases are **tener hambre** *(to be hungry)* and **tener sed** *(to be thirsty)*. Use the feminine form **mucha** with these expressions to mean *very*.

> Tengo **mucha sed** pero no tengo **mucha hambre.**

28 Cuatro amigos   Script and answers on p. 79F

CD 8 Tr. 6

Cuatro amigos están en un café popular. Escucha mientras hablan de lo que van a comer. Luego, lee cada oración y escribe **cierto** o **falso.** Corrige las oraciones falsas.

1. Isabel no tiene hambre.
2. Estela no quiere almorzar.
3. Para el desayuno, hay huevos y tocino.
4. Diego va a comer una hamburguesa y una ensalada.
5. Rafael tiene sed y quiere un vaso de leche.

29 Mis preferencias 🏠

Completa las siguientes oraciones con tus preferencias personales.   Answers will vary.

1. Cuando tengo hambre, prefiero comer...
2. Cuando tengo sed, prefiero tomar...
3. En el verano, cuando hace mucho calor me gusta comer...
4. En el invierno cuando hace frío me gusta comer... y tomar...
5. No me gusta(n) para nada...
6. Los fines de semana me encanta comer...

VOCABULARIO EXTRA

el tomate   *tomato*

la pasta   *spaghetti / pasta*

la salsa   *sauce*

la chuleta de cerdo   *pork chop*

el puré de papas   *mashed potatoes*

el pavo   *turkey*

los macarrones con queso   *macaroni and cheese*

30 La sed *Answers will vary.*

Work with a partner. For each of the given situations, ask your partner five questions about what he or she would like to eat or drink in that situation. Switch roles halfway through and answer your partner's qustions.

MODELO
1. Tienes mucha sed pero no tienes hambre.
—¿Quieres una galleta?
—No, gracias. Pero tengo mucha sed. Me gustaría un refresco.
—No hay refrescos. ¿Quieres agua?
—Sí, gracias.

SITUACIONES

1. Tienes mucha sed pero no tienes hambre.
2. Es hora de almorzar pero no tienes hambre.
3. Tienes mucha hambre antes de ir al colegio.
4. Tienes hambre a las diez de la noche.
5. Tienes mucha hambre y estás en el centro comercial.
6. Es tarde y tienes que ir al colegio.
7. Tienes hambre después de las clases.

31 Un almuerzo en casa

Create a phone conversation in which you invite your partner to come over to your house for lunch. Tell your partner what you're having for lunch and what time you eat lunch at your house. If your partner turns down the invitation, ask why he or she can't come. Make sure he or she explains why.

🌐 Nota cultural

Two common dishes in the Andes are **sancocho** (a thick stew-like soup made of green plantains and corn) and **carne colorada** (beef prepared with **achiote,** or ground annatto, a red coloring). These dishes, like most Ecuadorean cuisine, are not spicy. **Ají,** a spicy condiment made of tomatoes, onion, and hot, red chili peppers is placed on most tables for those who want added flavor. Do you add anything to your food to make it spicier?

el ají

el sancocho

☀ ASSESS

▶ Testing Program, pp. 39–40
Quiz 8-2
Audio CD 8, Tr. 20

▶ Grammar and Vocabulary Quizzes
Quiz 8-2A or
Alternative Quiz 8-2A

▶ Alternative Assessment Guide, p. 20

🎋 RE-ENTRY

31 Have students review extending, accepting, and turning down invitations from Chapter 7 by working in pairs and inviting each other to lunch. Remind them that to invite they should use phrases like **¿Quieres...?** and **¿Te gustaría...?** To accept they should use phrases like **¡Cómo no!** or **Sí, me gustaría.** To turn down, they can use **Gracias, pero no puedo.** Have volunteers present their conversations to the class.

PERFORMANCE ASSESSMENT

Have students review a restaurant. They should include a description of the restaurant and what it serves (breakfast foods, lunch specials).

📖 EN MI CUADERNO

For an additional Chapter 8 journal entry suggestion, see *Practice and Activity Book,* page 87.

VIDEO INTEGRATION

En camino LEVEL 1B
Video Program
Videocassette 1, 41:30–43:15

¡Ven conmigo! LEVEL 1
DVD Tutor, Disc 2

TEACHER NOTES

- See *Video Guide* for activities related to the **Panorama cultural.**
- Remind students that cultural information may be included in the Quizzes and the Chapter Test.
- The interviewees' language represents informal, unrehearsed speech. Occasionally, text has been edited for clarity.

MOTIVATING ACTIVITY

Ask students what is the most exotic food they have ever eaten and where they tried it. Did they like it? Have they had it since? Have they ever introduced a friend to a new food?

PRESENTATION

Have students read the captions, then show the video. Have students identify as many ingredients as they can. Then have them decide which foods sound appetizing to them. Ask them if any of the foods described sound like anything they usually eat.

Panorama cultural

CD 8
Trs. 7–10

¿Cuál es un plato típico de tu país o región?

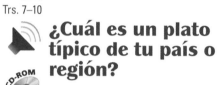

There are as many different "typical" dishes in the Spanish-speaking world as there are countries and regions. In this chapter we asked people to tell us about the dishes typical of their areas.

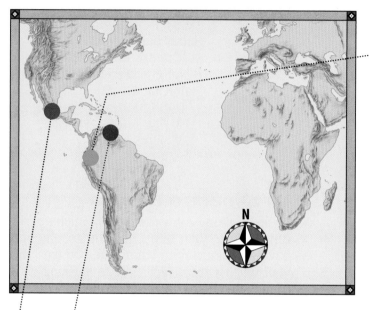

Renata describe una sopa típica de su país. ¿Cuál es un plato típico donde vives tú?

● **Renata**
México, D.F., México
CD 8 Tr. 8

El pozole, que es una especie de sopa que tiene granos de maíz o de elote, con pollo.

Claudia habla de las arepas de Venezuela. Son como sándwiches, pero el pan es de maíz.

● **Claudia**
Caracas, Venezuela
CD 8 Tr. 9

Arepa es una comida de aquí que se hace con masa. [La] rellena con lo que quiera: con queso, con carne, con cazón, que es un pescado.

¿Conoces un plato como el ceviche que describe Marcela?

Marcela CD 8 Tr. 10
Quito, Ecuador

El *ceviche*
de camarón. Tiene
camarón, tiene limón,
tiene tomates, cebolla.
Es poquito, pero es
muy bueno.

1 **Pozole** is
a. a soup
b. a dessert

2 What does Renata say goes in **pozole?** maíz or elote

3 Name two things Claudia says you can stuff
arepas with. Possible answers: cheese and meat

4 Given what you know about **arepas,** why do you
think people take them for lunch at work or school?
Possible answers: They are like a sandwich and are easy to wrap up and carry with you.

5 What are two ingredients of **ceviche?** Possible answers: shrimp, lemons

6 Do you think Marcela is describing a main dish or a
snack? Why? a snack; She says it's small.

Para pensar y hablar... Answers will vary.

A. Which of the foods sounds the most appetizing to you?
Why?

B. What is a typical dish in your region or in your family?
Form a small group and talk about the dish. How do
you make it? Where does it comes from?

Cuaderno para
hispanohablantes,
pp. 39–40

103

NATIVE SPEAKERS
Have native speakers describe a typical food they eat home and compare it to some of the foods the interviewees describe.

PREGUNTAS
1. ¿Cuál es el plato típico de México, según Renata? (el pozole)
2. Según lo que dice Claudia, ¿qué plato es típico de Venezuela? (las arepas)
3. Según Claudia, ¿qué es una arepa? (masa rellenada con queso, carne y pescado)
4. Según Marcela, ¿cuál es un plato típico de Ecuador? (el ceviche)

SUGGESTION
Have students think about some typical dishes in the United States. Ask volunteers to share their answers with the class. Could they pick just one? Explain that there are many typical dishes in other countries, not just one, just like in the United States.

DVD

VIDEO INTEGRATION

En camino LEVEL 1B
Video Program
Videocassette 1, 30:45–31:04 OR
Videocassette 3, 1:20:05–1:20:24
(captioned version)

¡Ven conmigo! LEVEL 1
DVD Tutor, Disc 2

Bell work
On the board or a transparency write **¿Qué hay en tu comida ideal?** Have students list five things. Tell them the meal can be outrageous and should include their favorite foods. When would they eat it? where? with whom?

☀ MOTIVATE

Discuss the ideal meals from **Bell work.** Have students say in Spanish what they love to eat. See how many unusual combinations students have come up with.

Answers to Activity 32

1. Hiroshi: ...quisiera locro, por favor.
   Roberto: ¿Me puede traer carne colorada con papas, por favor?
2. **usted;** to be polite to people he doesn't know
3. cuatro aguas

TERCER PASO (TPR)

Storytelling Book pp. 31, 32

WV3 ECUADOR-8

*Making polite requests; ordering dinner in a restaurant;
asking for and paying the bill in a restaurant*

Nota cultural

Eating out with family or friends is much less common in Ecuador than in the United States. Friends might go out to a neighborhood ice cream store or snack stand together on a regular basis, but a restaurant meal is reserved for special occasions, such as a visit by out-of-town guests or a birthday or anniversary. Does your family sometimes go out to eat for special occasions? If so, for what occasions?

32 ¿Qué comen?

Look at the photo and answer the following questions.

1. Can you find at least two ways in which the customers politely ask the waiter to bring them things?
2. Does the waiter use **tú** or **usted** with his customers? Why?
3. Have they ordered anything besides food?

Answers in side column

 104 *ciento cuatro*

CAPÍTULO 8   ¡A comer!

ASÍ SE DICE   Making polite requests

To ask the waitperson to bring you something, you might say:

Camarera, ¿nos puede traer el menú y unas servilletas, por favor?
Waitress, can you bring us the menu and some napkins, please?

Camarero, este plato está sucio. ¿Me puede traer un plato limpio?
Waiter, this plate is dirty. Can you bring me a clean plate?

¿Me trae un vaso de agua, por favor?
Will you bring me a glass of water, please?

p. 33
Act. 16

8-3

VOCABULARIO

p. 32
Act. 14

p. 15
Acts. 13–15

8-C

la servilleta
la cuchara
el cuchillo
el tenedor
el vaso
el tazón/ el plato hondo
el plato

33 ¡Camarero!

Look at the drawings and match each one with what the people in it are probably saying.

a. ¿Nos puede traer unas servilletas, por favor? 2
b. ¿Nos puede traer el menú, por favor? 3
c. ¿Me puede traer un plato limpio, por favor? 4
d. ¿Me trae un vaso de agua, por favor? 1

Salsa

❶   ❷   ❸   ❹

TERCER PASO

ciento cinco   **105**

CAPÍTULO 8

☀ TEACH

PRESENTATION
ASÍ SE DICE

Bring in the following items or pictures of them: a clean and a dirty napkin, a clean and a dirty plate, a clean and a dirty glass. Tell students what the items are using the expressions from **Así se dice.** Give items one by one to students and ask them to make appropriate requests from **Así se dice.** (When you give a student a dirty glass, he or she says **Este vaso está sucio. ¿Me trae otro, por favor?**)

VOCABULARIO

Hold up real items and model the pronunciation of each as you arrange a table setting at the front of the room. Have a student come forward and "sit at the table." Ask the student to close his or her eyes while you remove one of the utensils from the setting. The student then opens his or her eyes, and asks you, the waitperson, to bring what is missing. Repeat this with several students, removing a different utensil each time.

 **CULTURE NOTE**
Spanish speakers feel it's more polite to leave their left hand resting on the table when they're using only a fork.

PRESENTATION

NOTA GRAMATICAL

Bring in dirty or bent silverware and dirty napkins. Place them on a mock table setting and have volunteers come forward and ask for *other* items: **¿Nos trae otros vasos, otras servilletas y otro tenedor?**

KINESTHETIC LEARNERS

34 Have students hold up the utensil as they give the answers. Add several items from the menu to continue the activity.

TPR Have a student set a table (**poner la mesa**) according to your instructions for when, where, and who the student will be dining with. Using **Pon** and **No pongas** and the prepositions of place, tell the student what utensils to put on the table and where to put them. After students are comfortable with the vocabulary, ask one of them to give instructions while another sets the table. You might also do this activity with all of the students while they sit at their own desks and use plastic utensils.

Answers to Activity 35

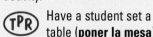

1. otro
2. otros
3. otra
4. otras
5. otra

Nota cultural

In Spain and Latin America, people tend to use utensils more than people in the United States do when they eat. Spaniards usually cut chicken or fruit with a knife and a fork. When Spaniards and Latin Americans cut their food, they don't switch hands as many people in the United States do. The knife stays in the right hand and the fork in the left. Do you do this? What foods do you eat without utensils?

GV
p. 16
Acts. 16–17

NOTA GRAMATICAL

Otro means *other* or *another*. It agrees in gender and number with the noun it modifies.

> ot**ro** cuchill**o**
> ot**ros** plat**os**
> ot**ra** servillet**a**
> ot**ras** cuchar**as**

Camarero, necesitamos ot**ra** cuchar**a**, por favor.

---

35 Pepito, el travieso

You're eating out with your family in Quito. Your baby brother Pepito keeps throwing things on the floor. Refer to the **Nota gramatical** to help you use the forms of **otro** correctly so that you can ask for what you need. Answers in side column

¡Ay, Pepito! Camarera, ¿nos puede traer ___1___ vaso de leche, por favor? ¡Ay, no! Y también ___2___ tenedores y ___3___ cuchara. Y ahora, ¿qué? Camarera, ¿nos puede traer ___4___ servilletas y ___5___ ensalada?

---

34 ¿Con qué vas a comer? 🏠

Your Spanish class is having a potluck supper. The food is great, but you can't eat anything until you have a plate, a glass, and some utensils. Write how you would tell your Spanish teacher what you need in order to eat and drink.

MODELO Voy a tomar una limonada. → Necesito un vaso.

1. Voy a comer sopa. Answers will vary. Possible
2. Voy a comer arroz. answers on p. 79K
3. Voy a comer un helado.
4. Voy a beber leche.
5. Voy a comer sancocho.
6. Voy a comer una ensalada.

> Debo poner otro tenedor, otro cuchillo y otra cuchara. Después voy a poner los vasos.

CD-ROM DISC **2** GV
p. 17
Acts. 18–19

8-D

el bistec

los camarones

las zanahorias

las cebollas

el pescado

el tomate

el maíz

el batido de fresa
y las fresas

el agua
mineral

la galleta

el pastel

el flan

la bebida *drink, beverage*
la carne *meat*
la carne de res *beef*

36 Me trae...

CD 8 Tr. 11

Imagine that you're eating with your family at Restaurante El Molino, a busy restaurant in Quito. Listen to these orders that you overhear from other tables and decide if each order is a **desayuno, almuerzo, cena,** or **postre.**
Scripts and answers on p. 79F

🌐 Nota cultural

In Spanish-speaking countries, **la cena** is a light meal, usually eaten around 8:00 P.M., sometimes as late as 10:00 P.M. (or even later) in Spain. People generally eat a snack (**una merienda**) around 5:00 P.M. In Ecuador, **la merienda** usually consists of tea or coffee with bread or perhaps a bowl of soup. Would you like this kind of schedule for eating meals? What time do you usually eat the evening meal?

PRESENTATION

VOCABULARIO

To model pronunciation, tell students you are very hungry and say which items on the menu you would like to eat. Then ask students, **¿Qué te gusta para cenar?** and **¿Qué hay para cenar?** Have them answer using the new vocabulary. Then have students practice ordering from the menu, with you playing the role of the **camarero/a.**

▢ MULTICULTURAL LINK

Ask students from other backgrounds to describe their eating customs. Have them describe any other utensils they might use. They can also talk about the types of foods they eat and what their mealtimes are.

SUGGESTION

If possible, plan a trip to a Spanish or Latin American restaurant. You might prearrange with the restaurant manager that Spanish-speaking employees speak only Spanish with the students. Students should order their food in Spanish.

CHALLENGE
37 Have students write statements like those in Activity 37 about their families and themselves. Then have them share the statements with a partner.

PRESENTATION
ASÍ SE DICE
Use the menu on p. 107 as you model the expressions, asking several students **¿Tienes hambre? ¿Qué vas a pedir?** Then ask a student, **¿Qué le puedo traer?** The students responds with **Me puede traer...** Have the student turn to a classmate and ask the question as the **camarero/a.** The next student responds and then becomes the server, asking a pupil who will respond as a customer.

37 ¿Me puede traer un postre?

Imagine that your family is visiting María's family in Quito. Write the letter of the item that María would serve based on what you tell her.

1. A mi papi le gustan los desayunos fuertes. ¡Él tiene mucha hambre por la mañana! b
2. A mi mamá le gustan las bebidas calientes. Nunca toma refrescos. c
3. ¡Tengo mucha sed! ¿Me puedes traer una bebida fría, por favor? d
4. No queremos comer mucho para la cena. e
5. Sí, quiero postre. ¡Gracias! a

PA
p. 34
Act. 17

ASÍ SE DICE   Ordering dinner in a restaurant

To find out what a friend is going to order, ask:	Your friend might say:
¿Qué vas a pedir?	**Voy a pedir** los camarones.
What are you going to order?	*I'm going to order shrimp.*
The waitperson might ask:	You might answer:
¿Qué le puedo traer?	Yo **quisiera** el bistec.
What can I bring you?	*I would like steak.*

CD-ROM DISC 2

38 ¿Qué vas a pedir?

You're in a restaurant and the waiter is taking your order. Complete the dialogue using the following words.

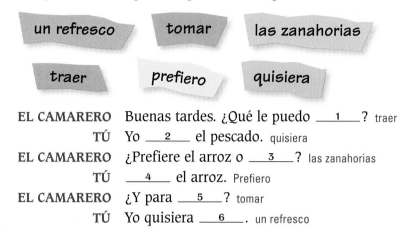

un refresco   tomar   las zanahorias

traer   prefiero   quisiera

EL CAMARERO	Buenas tardes. ¿Qué le puedo ___1___? traer
TÚ	Yo ___2___ el pescado. quisiera
EL CAMARERO	¿Prefiere el arroz o ___3___? las zanahorias
TÚ	___4___ el arroz. Prefiero
EL CAMARERO	¿Y para ___5___? tomar
TÚ	Yo quisiera ___6___. un refresco

39 ¿Qué van a pedir ustedes?

Imagine that a popular restaurant is offering your class a free lunch. Make a list of what you're going to order. Then ask two classmates what they're going to order. Find out who has tastes similar to yours. Be prepared to share your results with the class.

ASÍ SE DICE — Asking for and paying the bill in a restaurant

To ask the waitperson for the bill, say:

¿Nos puede traer la cuenta?

La cuenta, por favor.

The waitperson might say:

¿Desean algo más?
Do you want anything else?

To ask about the amount of the bill and the tip, say:

¿Cuánto es?

Son veinte dólares.
It's 20 dollars.

¿Está incluida la propina?
Is the tip included?

No, no está incluida. **Es aparte.**
No, it's not included. It's separate.

8-3

40 La cuenta

Work with a partner. Role-play being a waitperson and a customer. The customer wants to pay the bill and to find out if the tip is included. The waitperson asks if the customer wants anything else and brings the bill.

AUDITORY LEARNERS
38 Have students do this activity orally in pairs before writing the answers.

VISUAL LEARNERS
39 Have students refer to their flashcard set for help with this activity. Encourage them to compile their lists without looking at the Spanish definitions on the back of the cards.

PRESENTATION
ASÍ SE DICE
Replay the restaurant scene from the **paso** opener. Tell students to listen carefully to the phrases used by the server and the customers. Then have the class ask for the bill and about the tip, with you responding as the server. Then switch roles, so they practice both sides of the dialogue.

CULTURE NOTE
In Ecuador and other Spanish-speaking countries, servers in restaurants are generally male. Being a waiter is considered a profession. In many places, the bill is still hand-written.

PORTFOLIO
40 **Oral** Tell your students that a recording of their role-play would be an appropriate oral activity to include in their Portfolio. For Portfolio suggestions, see *Alternative Assessment Guide*, p. 12.

p. 17
Acts.
20–21

VOCABULARIO

Los números del 200 al 100.000

200	doscientos/as	**700**	setecientos/as	**10.000**	diez mil
300	trescientos/as	**800**	ochocientos/as	**45.000**	cuarenta y cinco mil
400	cuatrocientos/as	**900**	novecientos/as	**80.000**	ochenta mil
500	quinientos/as	**1.000**	mil	**100.000**	cien mil
600	seiscientos/as				

1. When numbers from 200 to 900 modify a noun, they agree with the gender of the noun.

    seiscient**os** libr**os**
    seiscient**as** cas**as**

2. Notice that in Spanish a period is sometimes used instead of a comma when writing large numbers (one thousand or greater).

    15.216   23.006   1.800
    47.811   9.433

41 ¿Cuánto es?

CD 8 Tr. 12

Look at the menu and listen to the following prices in pesos. Match the price mentioned with the correct item on the menu. Scripts and answers on p. 79F

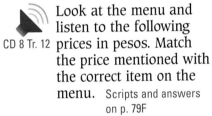

Platos del día
Ensalada mixta $2.000
Ceviche de camarón $4.250
Sancocho $3.500
Arroz con pollo $4.750
Plato Vegetariano $3.800

Bebidas
Gaseosas $850
Té helado $550

Postres
Helado de naranjilla $1.260
Canoa de frutas $2.230

42 ¿Cómo se dice?

Take turns saying these numbers with a partner. Write the words in Spanish for each number your partner says. Check each other's work.

1. 27.750	**6.** 615
2. 3.609	**7.** 45.370
3. 534	**8.** 8.112
4. 94.800	**9.** 19.400
5. 2.710	**10.** 100.000

1. veintisiete mil setecientos cincuenta
2. tres mil seiscientos nueve
3. quinientos treinta y cuatro
4. noventa y cuatro mil ochocientos
5. dos mil setecientos diez
6. seiscientos quince
7. cuarenta y cinco mil trescientos setenta
8. ocho mil ciento doce
9. diecinueve mil cuatrocientos
10. cien mil

PRESENTATION

VOCABULARIO

Make up large-print flashcards of the numbers in the box as well as some numbers in between. Begin by modeling the pronunciation. Have students read the explanation of gender agreement in the book. Then have students practice the masculine and feminine forms. For example, hold up 800, say **ochocientos dólares, ochocientas pesetas,** then ask students **¿Cuántos dólares? ¿Cuántas pesetas?**

ADDITIONAL PRACTICE

Have students practice the new numbers, counting by hundreds. You say **cien.** A student continues with **doscientos.** The next student adds 100, and so on.

MATH LINK

Have students look up exchange rates for several currencies and convert prices of things they buy (music, fast food, clothes) from dollars into **pesos, pesetas,** etc.

CULTURE NOTES

In many Spanish-speaking countries, travelers need to know how to express large numbers. Sometimes local currency units are hundreds or even thousands to the U.S. dollar.

Esta ensalada de tomate está deliciosa.

43 Te invito

Role-play a restaurant scene with two classmates in which one of you is the waitperson and the other two are customers. One of you has 12,000 pesos and wants to treat the other to dinner. Using the menu from Activity 41, decide on and order a meal. Comment on the food. Then, ask the waitperson for the bill and pay for the meal.

44 En mi cuaderno

Where do you go when you go out to eat? Write five sentences about your favorite restaurant. Be sure to mention why you like it, what the food is like, and what your favorite meal is when you eat out there.

LETRA Y SONIDO

Script on p. 79F

A. The letter **c** before the vowels **e** and **i** is pronounced like *s*, as in **centro, cielo.** Before the vowels **a, o,** and **u** the letter **c** is pronounced like the **k** in the English word *kitchen*.

CD 8
Trs. 13–17

| carne | rico | cuchara | delicioso | cebolla | dulce | camarero |

To spell the *k* sound (as in *kitchen*) before the vowels **e** and **i**, use the letters **qu**

| que | química | saque | quien | quinientos | queso |

Do you notice the pattern similar to the one you learned with the letters **g** and **j**?

B. Dictado
Anita needs help with a cake recipe. Write what she says.

C. Trabalenguas
¿Quién quiere pastel de chocolate?
¿Cuánto queso cabe en la caja?
¿Cómo quiere que Queta conduzca el carro?

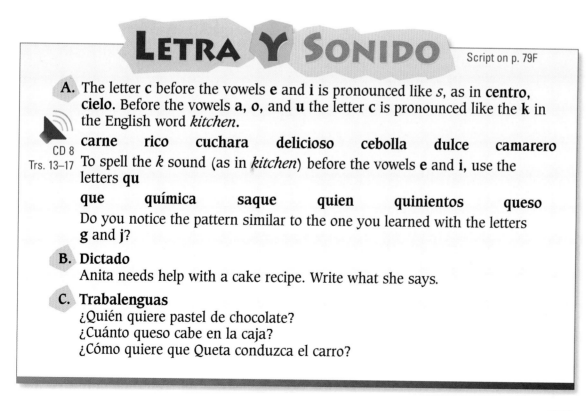

KINESTHETIC LEARNERS
43 Provide two or three sets of props for students to use during this activity. Other groups may practice or work on written assignments while "waiting to be seated" in the "dining area."

☀ CLOSE

Use Teaching Transparencies 8-1, 8-2, and 8-3 to review vocabulary and target phrases. Hold up the number flashcards from **Vocabulario** on p. 110, asking ¿**Cuánto es la cuenta?** To practice agreement, prompt student responses with **pesetas** for feminine forms and **pesos** for masculine forms.

☀ ASSESS

▸ Testing Program, pp. 41–42
Quiz 8-3
Audio CD 8, Tr. 21

▸ Grammar and Vocabulary Quizzes
Quiz 8-3A or
Alternative Quiz 8-3A

▸ Alternative Assessment Guide, p. 20

PERFORMANCE ASSESSMENT
Modify Activity 43 for performance assessment. Every time the customer asks for something, the server says they do not have it. The customer orders five times, and the server comes up with five different alternatives. Students present their conversations to the class.

PRESENTATION

Ask students what their favorite foods are. Are the foods or ingredients originally from the Americas or Europe? Have them guess which of the foods on this page the Spanish explorers found in the New World and which they brought with them from the Old World. Ask them if they realize that the all-American meal (cheeseburger, fries, and apple pie) is actually a mix of European and American foods.

HISTORY LINKS

• Christopher Columbus brought cacao beans, from which we make chocolate, back to Europe. Twenty seven years later Montezuma, the ruler of the Aztecs, shared his chocolate drink recipe—**chocolatl**—with Cortez, who took it to the Spanish king and queen. The Spanish did not share the chocolate recipe with other Europeans for about one hundred years, when Queen María Teresa decided to divulge the secret to her husband, King Louis XIV of France.

• The Mayans were the first to make chewing gum, taking chicle sap from the chicozapote tree found in the Yucatan Peninsula.

LA HISTORIA

Bienvenido al nuevo mundo de comida   Some believe that the New World's most important gift to Europe was not gold, silver, or jewels, but food. In the 1400's, Europeans were used to a bland diet with little fresh food. After the Spaniards brought back fruits and vegetables from the Americas, the eating habits of Europeans changed forever. The Spaniards, in turn, brought the first cattle, sheep, pigs, and chickens to the Americas.

NUEVO MUNDO	VIEJO MUNDO
blueberries	apples
chili peppers	chickens
cacao	cattle
corn	grapes
cranberries	lemons
pecans	lettuce
pinto beans	limes
potatoes	mangoes
pumpkins	oranges
squash	pigs
string beans	sheep
sunflowers	wheat
tomatoes	
turkeys	

1 El día de acción de gracias

Below are some foods you might find at a typical Thanksgiving meal. Based on the maps and information on page 112, which of these foods in boldface come from the "Old World" and which from the Americas?

Answers in side column

roast **turkey**   **pecan** pie   **cranberry** sauce

orange ambrosia   **apple** pie   **string beans**   **ham**

bread   **pumpkin** pie   **corn**   mashed **potatoes**

LA ECONOMÍA DOMÉSTICA

Tostadas   El origen del maíz
Corn was developed by the Maya in what is now Mexico. Corn tortillas, made from ground corn flour, were central to the daily diet of the Maya.

Conversions
1 kilogram (kg) = 2.2 pounds (lbs.)

2 ¿De dónde son?
¿Cuáles de los ingredientes para las tostadas son originalmente de Europa y cuáles son de las Américas?   Answers in side column

3 ¿Cuánto necesito?
Convert the kilogram measurements for refried beans, cheese, and chicken to pounds using the conversion formula below. For example, if a recipe called for 3 kilograms (kg) of flour, then you would multiply 2.2 × 3 to find out you need 6.6 lbs. of flour.
1.1 lbs. refried beans, 2.2 lbs. cheese, 4.4 lbs. chicken

Tostadas

24 tostadas
1/2 kg de frijoles refritos
1 kg de queso
8 chiles

2 kg de pollo cocido
2 cabezas de lechuga
4 tomates

Procedimiento. Pon los frijoles, el queso, los chiles y el pollo encima de las tostadas. Entonces, pon las tostadas en el horno a 400° F por tres minutos. Ponles la lechuga y los tomates.

CULTURE NOTE
The Mayans also grew many other crops and hunted turkey, duck, pheasant, and deer for meat.

CRITICAL THINKING
Ask students what is on the school menu today. Which foods are American and which are European in origin? Do any of the dishes combine ingredients from both the Americas and Europe? For example: spaghetti with meat balls: beef (Europe), wheat noodles (Europe), tomatoes (Americas). What parts of their lunches come from the "Old World" and what parts from the Americas?

SUGGESTION
Before checking the correct answers, have students compare answers with those of other classmates. Were they surprised to learn that some foods associated with tropical countries and islands were actually brought to the Americas by Europeans?

Answers to Activity 1

Americas: roast turkey, string beans, corn, cranberry sauce, potatoes, pumpkin, pecan; **Old World:** ham, apple pie, bread, oranges

Answers to Activity 2

Europa: queso, pollo, lechuga
Las Américas: maíz, frijoles, chiles, tomates

READING STRATEGY
Recognizing text organization.

☀ PREREADING

SUGGESTION
A Have students paraphrase the title and subtitle of this essay in Spanish.

COGNATES
Working in pairs, ask students to make a list of all the cognates in one of the recipes.

CRITICAL THINKING
Ask students why they think these drinks are popular in many Spanish-speaking countries (warm climates, fruit is plentiful and healthy, drinks are inexpensive).

☀ READING

SUGGESTION
Al grano Have students read the passage and describe how it is organized. Once they recognize a rough outline, ask if they have other ideas about how the author could have organized the essay. (recipes with orange first, recipes with other fruit second; discussion of tropical fruits first, recipes second)

ADDITIONAL PRACTICE
B After students finish adding the missing information to the outline, have them reorganize a previous chapter's reading.

C Ask students to make up additional questions using more of the text.

Estrategia

Using outlines
Many things you read are organized in a clear way. To do this, the author probably followed an outline. If you can find the organization of something you read, you can understand the main ideas. Look for the boldfaced print and the larger print to help you see this article's organization.

¡A comenzar!
Before you read the article, read the title and subtitle to find out what this article is about.

A Which of the following best expresses the meaning of the <u>title</u> and <u>subtitle</u>?

   1. milkshakes
     a cold fruit drink
   2. milkshakes
     a combination that refreshes
   ③ milkshakes
     a refreshing combination of fruit, milk, and ice

Al grano
B The article **Batidos** is organized and easy to outline. Outlining is a great way to understand a reading, whether it be in your social studies chapter or an article in Spanish like this one. On a piece of paper, create an outline like the one at the top of the next column and fill in the missing information. Answers on p. 79K

Title: ═══
Author: ═══
  I. Introduction
    A. How milkshakes are made
    B. Tropical fruits are ideal for these drinks

 II. ═══
    A. Batido de papaya
    B. ═══
    C. ═══

¿Te acuerdas?

Skim to figure out what a reading is about. Look at titles, pictures, and the first sentences of paragraphs.

C You'd like your school cafeteria to offer some of these delicious milkshakes. Your cafeteria director agrees, but has a few questions. Answers on p. 79K
  1. What kinds of fruits are recommended (according to the third paragraph)?
  2. How many servings does the "Batido de papaya" make?

D ¡Ahora te toca a ti! Inventa una receta nueva para un batido. Si usas palabras y frases de estas recetas, puedes hacer tu receta en español.

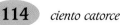

Los batidos por Bárbara Benavides

Son una combinación refrescante de frutas, leche y hielo.

Una de las mejores maneras de disfrutar del verano es experimentar la increíble sensación de un buen refresco. Muchas veces tenemos ganas de tomar limonada o té helado o sólo agua fría. Pero, a veces, es más divertido preparar batidos.

Los batidos se hacen con frutas combinadas con leche y hielo. Para darles una consistencia espesa, se necesita batir los ingredientes en una licuadora.

Las frutas tropicales, como el plátano, la piña y el mango, añaden un sabor exótico y son ideales para la creación de los batidos. También, tienen vitaminas y minerales importantes para la nutrición diaria.

Tres recetas

Batido de papaya (Sirve uno)

2 tazas de pulpa de papaya
1-1/2 taza de leche o agua
1/2 taza de azúcar
jugo de limón si se usa agua
hielo picado

Mezcle todos los ingredientes en la licuadora.

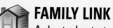

Batido de plátano con fresas

1/2 taza de plátanos
1/2 taza de fresas
1 vaso de leche
1/3 taza de hielo picado
azúcar al gusto

Mezcle en la licuadora.
Sírvalo bien frío.

Batido de moras

1 vaso de leche
1 taza de moras
   (fresas, frambuesas)
2 cucharadas de azúcar
hielo picado

Mezcle los ingredientes en la licuadora. Sírvalo bien frío.

Cuaderno para hispanohablantes, pp. 36–38

POSTREADING

CHALLENGE
D Have students create a **batido** recipe using unlikely ingredients. Ask volunteers to read their recipes aloud and have the class vote on the ones they think would taste the best and the worst.

FAMILY LINK
Ask students to prepare one of the recipes at home. Then have them report to the class what their family thinks of it.

TEACHER NOTES
Helpful cooking vocabulary:
un tercio de taza, la tercera parte de una taza   a third of a cup
media taza   a half cup
una taza y media   a cup and a half

MULTICULTURAL LINK
Tropical fruits popular in Latin America that are also popular in Africa include oranges, tangerines, bananas, mangoes, pineapples, papayas, soursop (**guanábana**), and sweetsop (also called sugar apple). Have students research what fruits are native to other parts of the world (Southeast Asia, East Africa, Australia). Ask them to report using as much Spanish as possible.

The **Repaso** reviews all four skills and culture in preparation for the Chapter Test.

SUGGESTION

1 Have students compare the foods that Ángel likes and doesn't like with their own preferences (**A Ángel le gusta el pollo, pero a mí no me gusta. A Ángel no le gusta el pescado y a mí no me gusta tampoco.**)

ADDITIONAL PRACTICE

2 Have students alter these recipes to include ingredients that they especially like. What would they add or delete from the **ensalada?**

REPASO

internet

CD-ROM DISC 2

MARCAR: go.hrw.com
PALABRA CLAVE:
WV3 ECUADOR-8

Script and answers on p. 79F

1 Listen as Ángel talks about some foods he likes and doesn't like. On a piece of paper make two columns, one for foods he likes, and the other for foods he doesn't like. Write the foods Ángel mentions in the correct columns.

CD 8
Tr. 18

le gusta	no le gusta

2 Your school is having an international food festival and you've agreed to make a salad. Read the two recipes and answer the questions.

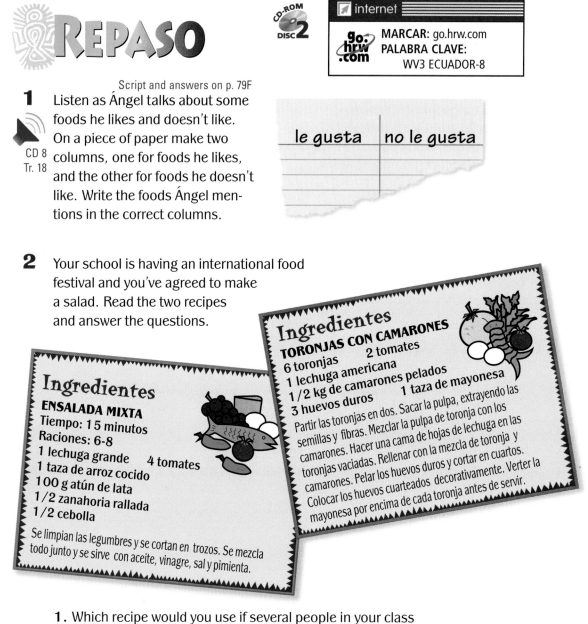

Ingredientes

ENSALADA MIXTA
Tiempo: 15 minutos
Raciones: 6-8
1 lechuga grande   4 tomates
1 taza de arroz cocido
100 g atún de lata
1/2 zanahoria rallada
1/2 cebolla

Se limpian las legumbres y se cortan en trozos. Se mezcla todo junto y se sirve con aceite, vinagre, sal y pimienta.

Ingredientes

TORONJAS CON CAMARONES
6 toronjas   2 tomates
1 lechuga americana
1/2 kg de camarones pelados
3 huevos duros   1 taza de mayonesa

Partir las toronjas en dos. Sacar la pulpa, extrayendo las semillas y fibras. Mezclar la pulpa de toronja con los camarones. Hacer una cama de hojas de lechuga en las toronjas vaciadas. Rellenar con la mezcla de toronja y camarones. Pelar los huevos duros y cortar en cuartos. Colocar los huevos cuarteados decorativamente. Verter la mayonesa por encima de cada toronja antes de servir.

1. Which recipe would you use if several people in your class didn't like tuna?   toronja con camarones
2. Which recipe would you use if you had some leftover cooked rice?   ensalada mixta
3. Which recipe calls for fruit?   toronja con camarones
4. Which ingredient do both recipes call for?   lettuce
5. Which recipe would you like better? Why?   Answers will vary.

3 Responde a las oraciones con **cierto** o **falso** y corrige las oraciones falsas. Basa tus respuestas en las **Notas culturales**, el **Panorama cultural** y el **Encuentro cultural**.

1. El gazpacho es una sopa caliente. falso; es una sopa fría
2. La tortilla española es un plato típico de Andalucía. cierto
3. En Ecuador es muy común comer en restaurantes. falso; comer en casa
4. Las arepas son un plato típico de Ecuador. falso; de Venezuela
5. El pozole es una sopa típica de México. cierto

4 **Vamos a escribir**

Imagine that your parents want to reward you for all the good work you've been doing in Spanish class lately. As a treat you'll be allowed to plan your family's meals for a day. Write out the menu, including for each meal the foods you like the best from those you've learned in this chapter.

Estrategia

Proofreading First, organize your ideas by writing a list of what you'd like to eat for the day. Then write a first draft of your menu. Now you're ready for the next important step in the writing process: proofreading, or checking for errors. The best way is to have someone else proofread for you. Exchange papers with a classmate and correct your classmate's paper using a pen or pencil of a different color. Check spelling, punctuation, and accents. Write your name on the paper you proofread, so that the author can come to you with questions.

5 **SITUACIÓN**

Get together with two classmates and create an original scene for one of the following situations. Role-play your scene for the class.

a. You and a classmate are eating breakfast at a restaurant. Another classmate is the waitperson. You're really hungry, but your friend isn't. Order two appropriate breakfasts, talk about how the food tastes, then ask for and pay the bill.

b. You and your family are out for a nice dinner, but everything is going wrong! The waitperson forgets to give you the menu, the silverware is dirty, and when the food comes, it's cold and doesn't taste good. Politely point out the problems and request the things that you need.

Cuaderno para hispanohablantes, pp. 39–40

CHALLENGE

3 Have students correct any of the false statements.

📁 PORTFOLIO
4 Written

Your students may want to consider including their finished menus in their Portfolio. For Portfolio suggestions, see *Alternative Assessment Guide*, page 12.

MULTICULTURAL LINK

Oranges have been cultivated in China since ancient times; they have been grown in Europe only since the 13th century. In southern China, people bring a small mandarin tree into their home for good luck during the Chinese New Year. Have students choose one country and research one custom from that country that includes food. Have them report what they find.

This page is intended to help students prepare independently for the Chapter Test. It is a brief checklist of the major points covered in the chapter. The students should be reminded that it is only a checklist and does not necessarily include everything that will appear on the Chapter Test.

SUGGESTION

Have students make a list of foods that people in Spanish-speaking countries eat, according to what they have learned. Then have them compare their new list with the one they made at the beginning of Chapter 8. Have their ideas changed? If so, how and why?

Answers to Activity 3

Answers will vary. Possible answers:
a. Está muy fría y deliciosa.
b. Está salada.
c. Está muy caliente.
d. Está muy picante.

Answers to Activity 4

1. Por favor, ¿nos puede traer unas cucharas?
2. ¿Me puede traer un cuchillo y una servilleta, por favor?
3. ¿Nos trae los menús, por favor?
4. Este vaso está sucio. ¿Me puede traer otro vaso limpio?

Answers to Activity 6

Answers will vary. Possible answers:
¿Cuánto es?
La cuenta, por favor.

¡A VER SI PUEDO...

Can you talk about meals and food? p. 87

1 How would you tell a classmate what your favorite breakfast foods are? How would you ask what he or she usually eats for breakfast? How would you tell a classmate what you eat for breakfast . . .? Answers on p. 79K

1. on weekends
2. when you're really hungry
3. when you're in a big hurry
4. on school days

2 How would you tell a classmate what you have for lunch and ask what he or she has for lunch? Para almorzar yo como...
¿Qué comes tú para el almuerzo?

Can you comment on food? p. 97

3 Look at the photos. Can you write a sentence describing how you think each dish tastes? Answers in side column

Can you make polite requests? p. 105

4 You're eating with your family in a restaurant in Ecuador, and you're the only one who speaks Spanish. How would you ask the waitperson . . .? Answers in side column

1. to bring spoons for everyone
2. to bring you a knife and a napkin
3. to bring the menu
4. to bring you a clean glass

5 Imagine you and a friend are in a restaurant. Answers will vary. Possible answers:

1. How would you ask your friend what he or she is going to order? ¿Qué vas a pedir?
2. How would you tell the waitperson that you would like a salad? Quisiera una ensalada, por favor.

Can you order dinner in a restaurant? p. 108

Can you ask for and pay the bill in a restaurant? p. 109

6 How would you ask the waitperson how much the meal is? How would you ask him or her to bring you the bill? Answers in side column

CAPÍTULO 8   ¡A comer!

VOCABULARIO

PRIMER PASO

Talking about meals and food

almorzar (ue)   *to eat lunch*
el almuerzo   *lunch*
el arroz   *rice*
el atún   *tuna*
el azúcar   *sugar*
el cereal   *cereal*
la crema de maní   *peanut butter*
el desayuno   *breakfast*
encantar   *to really like, to love*
fuerte   *strong, heavy*
los huevos   *eggs*
la jalea   *jelly*
el jamón   *ham*
el jugo de naranja   *orange juice*

la leche   *milk*
la lechuga   *lettuce*
las legumbres   *vegetables*
ligero   *light*
la limonada   *lemonade*
el mango   *mango*
la manzana   *apple*
el pan dulce   *sweet roll*
el pan tostado   *toast*
la papaya   *papaya*
las papitas   *potato chips*
para nada   *at all*
el perro caliente   *hot dog*
la piña   *pineapple*
el plátano   *banana*
poder (ue)   *to be able; can*
el pollo   *chicken*
por lo general   *usually*
¿Qué hay para tomar?   *What's there to drink?*
¿Qué prefieres?   *What do you prefer?*

el queso   *cheese*
el sándwich   *sandwich*
la sopa   *soup*
el té frío   *iced tea*
Tengo hambre.   *I'm hungry.*
Tengo sed.   *I'm thirsty.*
el tocino   *bacon*
la toronja   *grapefruit*
las uvas   *grapes*
un vaso de leche   *a glass of milk*

SEGUNDO PASO

Commenting on food

caliente   *hot*
delicioso/a   *delicious*
dulce   *sweet*
los frijoles   *beans*

frío/a   *cold*
picante   *spicy*
el postre   *dessert*
rico/a   *rich, delicious*
salado/a   *salty*
tener (mucha) hambre   *to be (really) hungry*
tener (mucha) sed   *to be (really) thirsty*

TERCER PASO

Making polite requests

la camarera   *waitress*
el camarero   *waiter*
la cuchara   *spoon*
el cuchillo   *knife*
limpio/a   *clean*
¿Me puede traer...?   *Can you bring me . . .?*
el menú   *menu*
otro/a   *other, another*
el plato   *plate*
el plato hondo   *bowl*
por favor   *please*
la servilleta   *napkin*
sucio/a   *dirty*
el tazón   *bowl*
el tenedor   *fork*
traer   *to bring*

Ordering dinner in a restaurant

el agua mineral   *mineral water*
el batido   *milkshake*
la bebida   *beverage*
el bistec   *steak*
los camarones   *shrimp*
la carne   *meat*
la carne de res   *beef*
la cebolla   *onion*
el flan   *custard*
la fresa   *strawberry*
la galleta   *cookie*
el maíz   *corn*
el pastel   *cake*
pedir (i)   *to order, to ask for*
el pescado   *fish*
quisiera   *I would like*
el tomate   *tomato*
la zanahoria   *carrot*

Asking for and paying the bill in a restaurant

¿Cuánto es?   *How much is it?*
la cuenta   *bill*
¿Desean algo más?   *Do you want anything else?*
Es aparte.   *It's separate.*
¿Está incluida?   *Is it included?*
¿Nos puede traer la cuenta?   *Can you bring us the bill?*
la propina   *the tip*

Numbers 200–100,000

See p. 110

GROUP WORK

Divide the class into small groups. Each student lists five situations in which he or she is hungry. Students take turns telling each other they're hungry and asking what they should eat. The other group members then suggest what to eat. (— **Son las siete de la mañana y tengo hambre. ¿Qué debo comer? — Debes comer el desayuno. — Sí, debes comer el cereal con plátano.**)

CHAPTER **8** ASSESSMENT

▶ **Testing Program**
Chapter Test, pp. 43–48
Audio Compact Discs, CD 8, Trs. 22–23
Speaking Test, p. 130

▶ **Alternative Assessment Guide**
Performance Assessment, p. 20
Portfolio Assessment, p. 12
CD-ROM Assessment, p. 27

▶ **Interactive CD-ROM Tutor, Disc 2**
¡A hablar!
¡A escribir!

▶ **Standardized Assessment Tutor**
Chapter 8

▶ **One-Stop Planner, Disc 2**
Test Generator
Chapter 8

¡Ven conmigo a Texas!
LOCATION OPENER CHAPTERS 9, 10

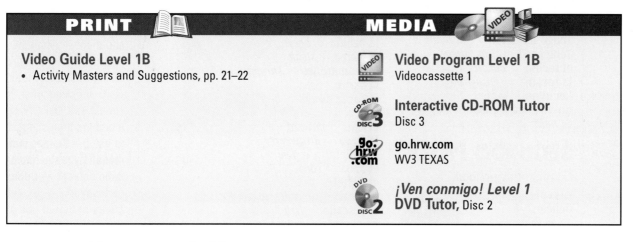

PRINT

Video Guide Level 1B
• Activity Masters and Suggestions, pp. 21–22

MEDIA

Video Program Level 1B
Videocassette 1

Interactive CD-ROM Tutor
Disc 3

go.hrw.com
WV3 TEXAS

¡Ven conmigo! Level 1
DVD Tutor, Disc 2

You may wish to point out the following images as students view the Texas Location Opener. These images will be seen on both the Video Program and the DVD Program. If you are using the DVD Program they may be freeze-framed for presentation and discussion purposes.

At 750 feet tall from the base to the antenna, the **Tower of the Americas** is one of the tallest freestanding structures in the Western Hemisphere. The restaurant at the top of the tower offers panoramic views of the city of San Antonio. The tower was built for the HemisFair '68, a world's fair celebrating the city's 250th anniversary.

Spanish missionaries founded more than thirty missions in Texas. **Misión San José**, often referred to as the Queen of Missions, was established in 1720. The most famous feature of this mission is the stone surrounding the window known as Rosa's Window in the sculpted sacristy, which was carved from locally-quarried limestone.

The **Paseo del Río** is a tree-lined promenade running along the San Antonio River. Visitors can enjoy shops, sidewalk cafés, restaurants, theaters, and galleries without ever having to leave the walkway. Taxi boats provide shuttle service for the entire length of the **Paseo.**

El Mercado, or Market Square, is the largest traditional, Mexican-style market in the United States. It has restaurants and more than 50 shops selling farm produce, local handicrafts, and Mexican imports. Many of San Antonio's festivals take place at the **Plaza del Mercado.**

The Alamo, officially **Misión San Antonio de Valero,** is the oldest of San Antonio's missions. It was established in 1718, but the church and fort were not built until 1744. During Texas' war for independence from Mexico in 1836, the mission was almost completely destroyed. The church is all that remains of the original fort. The Alamo is now a museum housing artifacts from the period of the Republic of Texas.

PROJECT

¿QUÉ SABES DE TEXAS?

In this project students learn about the cultural and linguistic heritage of Texas.

Introduction

Ask students what they know about Texas. What do they know about the indigenous people of the Southwest? What holidays and customs are of Native American heritage? What languages were spoken before the 1500s? What influence did the Spanish have in Texas?

Materials students may need

- ◆ Resource books on Texas
- ◆ Brochures on Texas
- ◆ Poster board
- ◆ Shoe boxes for dioramas
- ◆ Multicolored markers

Sequence

1 Divide the class into groups of three students.

2 Groups choose their research topic from a list like the example that follows. Students' final presentation style will depend on their topic.

- **Indigenous People of Texas:** Create a map of Texas with the location of indigenous groups such as the Nacogdoches, Nasoni, Neche, Arkokisa, Attacapa, Darankawa, Comanche, Tonkawa, or Coahuiltec.
- **Festivals and Holidays Celebrated in Texas:** Research special holidays, for example, **El Diez y Seis de Septiembre, El Cinco de Mayo, El 21 de Abril, Las Posadas,** (at Christmas) and **El Año Nuevo.** Prepare a poster, chart or diorama of the festival.
- **Geographic Names of Hispanic Origin in Texas:** Prepare a map of Texas cities, roads, rivers, and mountains that have names of Spanish origin. Present the map and explain what the names mean.

3 Each group prepares a visual presentation. For example, they make a poster or diorama to use in their oral presentation.

Teacher Note

You may want to write to the Texas Chamber of Commerce for brochures or call 1-800-8888-TEX. Also, check the Internet for on-line information. See the addresses listed on page 119A.

Grading the project

Suggested point distribution (total = 100 points):

Neatness	**25**
Accuracy of information	**25**
Presentation, clarity	**30**
Cooperative effort	**20**

¡Ven conmigo a Texas!
LOCATION OPENER CHAPTERS 9, 10 (cont.)

Using the Map
- Have students name the states that border Texas. (Louisiana, Arkansas, Oklahoma, New Mexico)
- Tell students to locate Houston, Dallas-Fort Worth, San Antonio, Austin, and El Paso. Which city is the capital of Texas? (Austin) Ask students who have been to any of these cities to describe them to the class.

Critical Thinking
Divide the class into groups of four or five, and have them research NAFTA, the North American Free Trade Agreement (**el Tratado de Libre Comercio de América del Norte** or **TLC**). Have each group choose a pro or con position on the treaty and write a brief political TV or radio commercial promoting their point of view. Have groups present their commercials to the class.

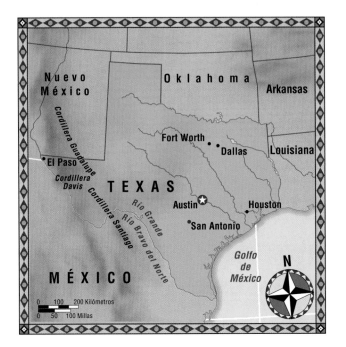

Language Note
The name *Texas* is thought to come from the Spanish pronunciation of the Caddo word for *friend* or *ally*.

Social Studies Link
At least 30,000 indigenous people lived in what is today Texas when the first European settlers arrived. These indigenous groups, which varied widely in culture, technology, and language, included the Nacogdoches, Nasoni, Neche, Arkokisa, Attacapa, Darankawa, Comanche, Tonkawa, and Coahuiltec. Divide the class into nine groups and assign each of them one of these indigenous groups to research. Students should give a short oral presentation including information about where and how the indigenous group lived. The students might also look on a map of Texas for place names derived from the name of that indigenous group.

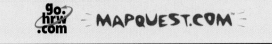

You may wish to have students do the above map activities using the Atlas Interactivo Mundial at **go.hrw.com**.

STANDARDS: 2.1, 3.1, 3.2, 5.2

Literature Link

Texas has produced more contemporary Mexican American writers than any other state. Often Tejano writers are closely linked to the South Texas communities in which they spent their youth, and the subject of their work is linked to Tejano culture. One prominent Tejano writer is Tomás Rivera, from Crystal City, Texas. His work **...y no se lo tragó la tierra** *(. . . and the earth did not swallow him)* is the story of the struggles and triumphs of a family of migrant farmworkers following crops through the Midwest and spending winters in Texas. It has been made into a film that won an award at the 1994 Santa Barbara International Film Festival. Can students think of any other Mexican American writers, actors, or musicians? (Sandra Cisneros, Carmen Lomas Garza, Tish Hinojosa)

Culture Note

San Antonio is a city with strong Spanish and Mexican influences on its history, culture, food, and art. There are an abundance of hand-crafted gifts from Mexico in the shops of **El Mercado**. Galleries and museums throughout the city are well known for their folk art and fine art inspired by the traditions of the Southwest.

Language and History Note

Bluejeans are a worldwide fashion that originated in the United States. Ask students to guess when people first started wearing bluejeans. Tell them that the first bluejeans were made in 1850 by Levi Strauss, a Bavarian Jewish immigrant living in San Francisco, California. Strauss made his overalls and pants from a durable cotton fabric he imported from France. The French name for this material was *serge de Nîmes*. In the United States the name was shorted to *denim*. In Spanish, *denim* is **mezclilla,** and in Mexico one hears **mezclillas** for *bluejeans*.

Music Link

The border region between Texas and Mexico has given rise to a unique culture, neither completely Texan nor Mexican, but a fusion of both. By the early 20th century, **música norteña,** or **conjunto** music, had grown deep roots along the border. The accordion, the heart of **conjunto** music, was introduced by German, Czech, and Polish settlers. In the last two decades **conjunto** music has spread throughout the United States and beyond. Have students research the music of a famous **conjunto** artist (Narciso Martínez, Paulino Bernal, Ramón Ayala, José "Flaco" Jiménez) Ask them to give a short oral presentation about the artist and, if possible, to play a recording of the music.

History Link

While the Alamo has been used for many different purposes, including living quarters, a hospital, and a Civil War Confederate post, it began in 1718 as a religious mission, **la Misión San Antonio de Valero**. It was the first of five missions founded in what is now San Antonio.

The first three missions in Texas were founded along the Rio Grande in 1682 near present-day El Paso. In 1689 and 1716, the Spanish established missions in East Texas. The 400-mile route between the missions in East Texas and those on the Rio Grande was called **El Camino Real** *(The King's Road)*. In 1718 the Spanish founded **Misión San Antonio de Valero** (the Alamo) and **Presidio San Antonio de Béxar** (a military fort) as a halfway station between the East Texas missions and the Rio Grande missions. San Antonio is not exactly halfway: it is about one-third of the way from Nacogdoches to Laredo.

Art Link

The painter, Fidencio Durán, says the following about his painting, *Summer Nights,* on page 123: "The front porch and yard became our domain where we staged our fantasies and dreams. With any available materials, we maintained our amusement. Common dish soap produced crystal balls of all sizes to feed our hungry minds. Their girth and longevity depended on our imaginations. A simple onion stalk served as our magic wand of dreams. Music from a portable record player brought the world to our small corner of dirt blanketed by the heavens."

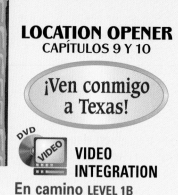

LOCATION OPENER
CAPÍTULOS 9 Y 10

¡Ven conmigo a Texas!

VIDEO INTEGRATION

En camino LEVEL 1B
Video Program
Videocassette 1, 45:23–47:24

¡Ven conmigo! LEVEL 1
DVD Tutor, Disc 2

MOTIVATING ACTIVITY
Ask students to brainstorm about what they think Texas is like. Have them describe the topography of the state. Have them list any adjectives that come to mind.

BACKGROUND
Texas is the second largest state in the United States. It is larger than Wisconsin, Michigan, Iowa, Indiana, and Illinois combined. Only Alaska is larger than Texas, but about 30 times as many people live in Texas as in Alaska. Six different flags have flown over Texas—those of Spain, France, Mexico, the Republic of Texas, the Confederacy, and the United States. The Republic of Texas lasted from 1836 to 1845. Because of the single star on its flag (adopted in 1839 by the Republic), Texas is often called the Lone Star State. Austin has been the state capital since 1845, when Texas joined the United States.

CAPÍTULOS 9 Y 10

¡Ven conmigo a Texas!

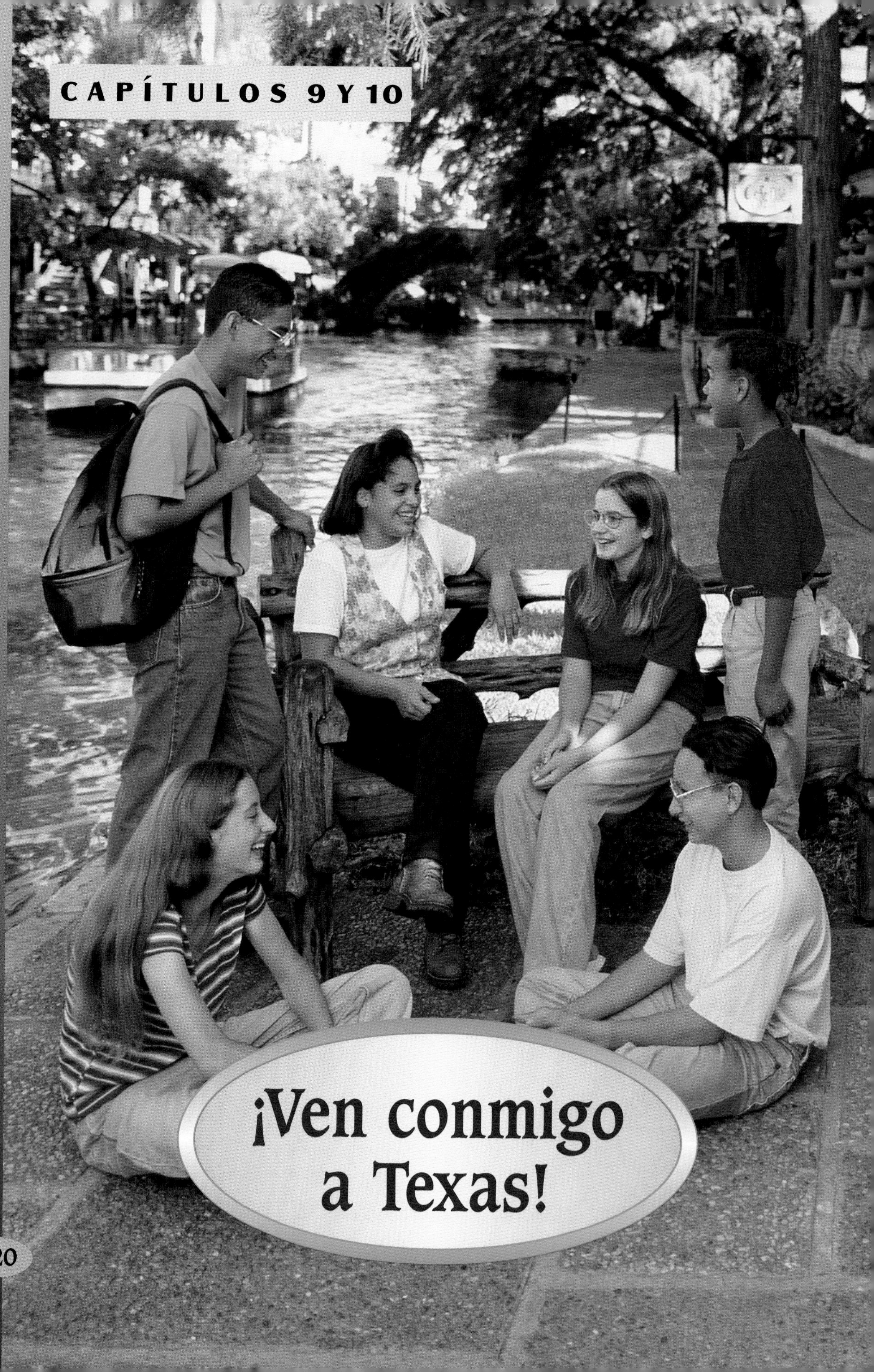

HRW ATLAS INTERACTIVO MUNDIAL

MAPQUEST.COM

Have students go to the interactive atlas at **go.hrw.com** to find out more about the geography of Texas.

USING THE ALMANAC

- **Población:** Texas is the second most populous state after California. Houston, the largest city in Texas, is the fourth-largest city in the United States.

- **Historia:** Before the arrival of the Spanish explorer Alonso Álvarez de Piñeda in 1519, Texas was populated by the Caddos and other indigenous groups. The first Spanish missions were established in 1682. Texas gained independence from Spain in 1821 and from Mexico in 1836. The Republic of Texas became a part of the United States in 1845.

CNNenEspañol.com

Have students check the CNN en español Web site for news on Texas. The CNN en español site is also a good source for timely, high interest readings for Spanish students.

Texas

Población: 20.851.820, de los cuales 6.669.666 son hispanos

Área: 266.807 millas cuadradas. Sólo Alaska es más grande.

Capital: Austin

Ciudades principales: Houston, Dallas, San Antonio, El Paso, Austin, Fort Worth

Clima: templado en el noroeste, subtropical en la costa del sur, desértico en el oeste, con mucha variación en las otras regiones

Economía: petróleo, gas natural, productos petroleros, computadoras, ganado, algodón, leche, frutas

Historia: Poblado originalmente por indígenas norteamericanos. Primeras misiones españolas establecidas en 1682. Independencia de México en 1836. La República de Texas se hizo estado de los Estados Unidos en 1845.

Nuevo México
Oklahoma
Arkansas
Cordillera Guadalupe
Fort Worth
Dallas
Louisiana
El Paso
Cordillera Davis
TEXAS
Cordillera Santiago
Río Grande
Río Bravo del Norte
Austin
Houston
San Antonio
Golfo de México
MÉXICO
N
0 100 200 Kilómetros
0 50 100 Millas

internet

MARCAR: go.hrw.com
PALABRA CLAVE:
WV3 TEXAS

◄ **Estos jóvenes pasan el rato en el Paseo del Río en San Antonio.**

121

MOTIVATING ACTIVITY

With their textbooks closed, have students brainstorm about the ways various ethnic groups influence life in the United States. (music, art, literature, cooking) Look at the photos on pages 120–123 and see if they confirm students' presuppositions.

USING THE PHOTO ESSAY

1 The Fiesta San Antonio tradition began in 1891 with a celebration on April 21, San Jacinto Day, in honor of the day on which Texas won its independence from Mexico in 1836. The Battle of Flowers Parade, which began around 1896, is an important part of the Fiesta tradition. The parade features historic commemorations, art shows, festivals, band concerts, sporting events, fireworks, and coronations.

2 Big Bend National Park combines the natural beauty of the Rio Grande, the Chihuahuan Desert, and the Chisos Mountains. The park has several hundred miles of hiking trails. Many visitors take the opportunity to cross the Rio Grande and spend a few hours in Mexico.

TEXAS

Texas was part of New Spain and Mexico for much longer than it has been a part of the United States. Did you know that Texas was once an independent nation called the Republic of Texas? Its ties with Mexico make it an exciting place to be as the economies of Mexico and the U.S. become more interdependent.

Música y folklor ▶
Mexican-American Texans take great pride in their cultural heritage. These young people are performing one of many colorful Mexican folk dances.

◄ Un parque nacional
Big Bend National Park is 801,163 acres of rugged, spectacular mountain and desert scenery along the Rio Grande in Southwestern Texas. Visitors to the park enjoy camping, hiking, rafting and watching for the hundreds of species of birds and animals that live in the area.

In Chapters 9 and 10, you'll get to know Eva, Lisa, and Gabi. These three friends live in San Antonio, Texas, one of the ten largest cities in the United States. San Antonio is famous for its blend of cultures, with predominantly Texan and Mexican flavors. As you'll see, people who live in Texas have lots of places to go and things to do.

③

Una fiesta en junio ▲
Every June 19th (known as "Juneteenth") Texans commemorate the end of slavery in Texas with parades, parties, and other events.

Un pintor tejano ►
In this painting, *Summer Nights*, the Mexican-American painter Fidencio Durán recalls his childhood on a farm near Lockhart in central Texas. In the evening, the kids in the family would gather on the front porch for games of fantasy and imagination.

④

⑤

◄ El telescopio más grande de Texas
The McDonald Observatory is located 450 miles west of Austin in the isolated Davis Mountains. The Hobby-Eberly telescope, at 360 inches in diameter, is the third-largest in the world. Visitors come to enjoy the views of the night skies.

LOCATION OPENER
CAPÍTULOS 9 Y 10

③ On June 19, 1865, Major General Gordon Granger read the Emancipation Proclamation in Galveston, Texas. Although Lincoln had signed the proclamation two and a half years earlier, it was not recognized in Texas because the Confederate forces there did not surrender until 1865. Juneteenth is a state holiday in Texas and Oklahoma.

CULTURE NOTE
El Cinco de Mayo
began as a commemoration of a battle at **Puebla** between Mexico and France, but in Texas it has grown into a major celebration of Mexican American culture. The celebrations in San Antonio feature art exhibitions by Mexican artists as well as Tejano, **conjunto**, and **mariachi** music. Performances of **baile folklórico** include dances from throughout Mexico, especially the **jarabe tapatío**, often called the national dance of Mexico.

④ Fidencio Durán was born on a tenant farm near Lockhart, Texas. His paintings and murals reflect Mexican-American cultural and historical themes, as well as his personal experiences. His murals may be seen throughout central and south Texas.

⑤ The McDonald Observatory is part of the University of Texas at Austin, which has the largest astronomy department in the world. Construction of its first telescope began in 1933 and was completed in May of 1939. Today the observatory houses more than 11 telescopes.

STANDARDS: 2.1, 3.1   **123**

De antemano pp. 126–129	¿Qué le compramos a Héctor?			
	FUNCTIONS	**GRAMMAR**	**VOCABULARY**	**RE-ENTRY**
Primer paso pp. 130–137	• Talking about giving gifts, p. 131 • Asking for and giving directions downtown, p. 134	• **Gramática:** Indirect object pronouns **le** and **les**, p. 133	• Gift items, p. 132 • Store names, p. 135	• **ir** + **a** + infinitive for discussing plans • Describing family • Talking about locations • Talking about where things are
Segundo paso pp. 138–145	• Commenting on clothes, p. 139 • Making comparisons, p. 144	• **Nota gramatical:** Use of **ser** to tell what something is made of, p. 142 • **Gramática:** Making comparisons: **más...que, menos...que, tan...como,** p. 145	• Clothing, pp. 140, 143	• **ir** + **a** + infinitive for discussing plans • Present tense of **ser** for description
Tercer paso pp. 148–153	• Expressing preferences, p. 149 • Asking about prices and paying for something, p. 150	• **Nota gramatical:** Using the demonstrative adjectives **este** and **ese**, p. 150	• Expressions related to cost, p. 151	• Numbers 0 to 100,000
Letra y sonido	**p. 153**	The letters **s, z,** and **c**	**Dictado:** Textbook Audiocassette 2A/Audio CD 9	
Enlaces	**pp. 154–155**	**Las misiones españolas de California y Texas**		
Vamos a leer	**pp. 156–157**	**San Antonio**	**Reading Strategy:** Scanning for specific information	
Review	**pp. 158–161**	**Repaso,** pp. 158–159	**A ver si puedo...,** p. 160	**Vocabulario,** p. 161

Culture
- **Nota cultural:** Specialty stores in Spanish-speaking countries, p. 136
- **Nota cultural:** Personal care and dress in Spanish-speaking countries, p. 138
- **Panorama cultural:** ¿Estás a la moda?, pp. 146–147
- **Nota cultural:** Currencies in Spanish-speaking countries, p. 153

Lesson Planning

One-Stop Planner
Lesson Planner with Substitute Teacher
Lesson Plans, pp. 16–20

Listening and Speaking

Listening Activities
- Student Response Forms for Listening Activities, pp. 61–63
- Additional Listening Activities 9-1 to 9-6, pp. 13–15
- Additional Listening Activities (song), p. 16
- Scripts and Answers, pp. 39–41

Video Guide
- Teaching Suggestions, pp. 24–25
- Activity Masters, pp. 26–28
- Scripts and Answers, pp. 56–58, 67

Activities for Communication
- Communicative Activities, pp. 19–24
- Realia and Teaching Suggestions, pp. 54–58
- Situation Cards, pp. 80–81

¡Ven conmigo! Level 1
TPR Storytelling Book, pp. 33–36

Reading and Writing

Reading Strategies and Skills, Chapter 9
¡Lee conmigo! 1, Chapter 9
Practice and Activity Book, pp. 37–48

Grammar

Grammar and Vocabulary Workbook, pp. 18–26

¡Ven conmigo! Level 1
Grammar Tutor for Students of Spanish
Chapter 9

Assessment

Testing Program
- Paso Quizzes and Chapter Test, pp. 55–66
- Midterm Exam, pp. 133–138
- Score Sheet, Scripts and Answers, pp. 62–72, 139–142

Grammar and Vocabulary Quizzes
- Quizzes 9-1A, 9-2A, 9-3A
- Alternative Quizzes 9-1A, 9-2A, 9-3A

Alternative Assessment Guide
- Portfolio Assessment, p. 13
- Performance Assessment, p. 21
- CD-ROM Assessment, p. 28

¡Ven conmigo! Level 1
Standardized Assessment Tutor
- Reading, pp. 35–37
- Writing, p. 38

Native Speakers

¡Ven conmigo! Level 1
Cuaderno para hispanohablantes, pp. 41–45

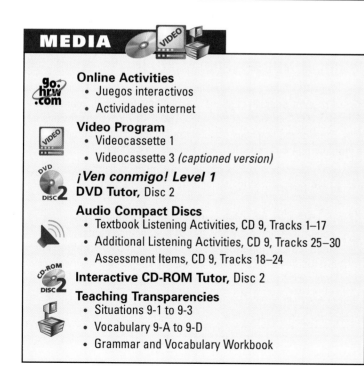

Online Activities
- Juegos interactivos
- Actividades internet

Video Program
- Videocassette 1
- Videocassette 3 *(captioned version)*

¡Ven conmigo! Level 1
DVD Tutor, Disc 2

Audio Compact Discs
- Textbook Listening Activities, CD 9, Tracks 1–17
- Additional Listening Activities, CD 9, Tracks 25–30
- Assessment Items, CD 9, Tracks 18–24

Interactive CD-ROM Tutor, Disc 2

Teaching Transparencies
- Situations 9-1 to 9-3
- Vocabulary 9-A to 9-D
- Grammar and Vocabulary Workbook

One-Stop Planner CD-ROM

Use the **One-Stop Planner CD-ROM with Test Generator** to aid in lesson planning and pacing.

For each chapter, the **One-Stop Planner** includes:
- Editable lesson plans with direct links to teaching resources
- Printable worksheets from resource books
- Direct launches to the HRW Internet activities
- Video and audio segments
- Test Generator
- Clip Art for vocabulary items

¡Vamos de compras!
TECHNOLOGY

Videocassette 1, Videocassette 3 (captioned version)
DVD Tutor, Disc 2 See Video Guide, pages 23–28.

De antemano • ¿Qué le compramos a Héctor?
Eva, Lisa, and Gabi go shopping for graduation presents for Héctor. They take a few moments to look at some clothing for themselves. Finally they decide to split up and shop separately and meet back together in half an hour. Without knowing, each of the girls buys Hector exactly the same poster as a gift.

¿Estás a la moda?
People from Spain, Venezuela, and Costa Rica tell about what they think is in style and what is not. In additional interviews, people from various Spanish-speaking countries tell us their opinions about fashion.

A continuación
When Eva, Lisa, and Gabi get back together, they walk around San Antonio and listen to a **mariachi** band. When they realize that they all have the same gift, Eva and Gabi decide to return theirs for a CD and a different poster.

Videoclips
2x1: advertisement for a department store

INTERACTIVE CD-ROM TUTOR

Activity	Activity Type	Pupil's Edition Page
En contexto	*Interactive conversation*	
1. Vocabulario	¡Super memoria!	p. 132
2. Así se dice	Patas arriba	p. 131
3. Gramática	¡A escoger!	p. 145
4. Vocabulario	Imagen y sonido ¡Exploremos! ¡Identifiquemos!	p. 140
5. Así se dice	¿Cuál es?	pp. 149-150
6. Gramática	¡A escoger!	p. 150
Panorama cultural	¿Estás a la moda? ¡A escoger!	pp. 146-147
¡A hablar!	*Guided recording*	pp. 158-159
¡A escribir!	*Guided writing*	pp. 158-159

Teacher Management System
Launch the program, type "admin" in the password area and press RETURN. Log on to **www.hrw.com/CDROMTUTOR** for a detailed explanation of the Teacher Management System.

DVD-ROM TUTOR ¡VEN CONMIGO! LEVEL 1

The *DVD Tutor* contains all material from the Level 1 *Video Program.* Spanish captions are available for use at your discretion for all sections of the video. The *DVD Tutor* also provides a variety of video-based activities that assess students' understanding of the **De antemano, A continuación,** and **Panorama cultural.**

This part of the *DVD Tutor* may be used on any DVD video player connected to a television or video monitor.

In addition to the video material and the video-based comprehension activities, the *DVD Tutor* also contains the entire Level 1 *Interactive CD-ROM Tutor* in DVD-ROM format. Each DVD disc contains the activities from all 12 chapters of the *Interactive CD-ROM Tutor.*

This part of the *DVD Tutor* may be used on a Macintosh® or Windows® computer with a DVD-ROM drive.

One-Stop Planner CD-ROM

To preview all resources available for this chapter, use the **One-Stop Planner CD-ROM**, Disc 3.

internet

MARCAR: go.hrw.com
PALABRA CLAVE:
WV3 TEXAS-9

INTERNET CONNECTION

*Have students explore the **go.hrw.com** Web site for many online resources covering all chapters. All Chapter 9 resources are available under the keyword **WV3 TEXAS-9**. Interactive games help students practice the material and provide them with immediate feedback. You will also find a printable worksheet that provides Internet activities that lead to a comprehensive online research project.*

JUEGOS INTERACTIVO

You can use the interactive activities in this chapter

- to practice grammar, vocabulary, and chapter functions
- as homework
- as an assessment option
- as a self-test
- to prepare for the Chapter Test

ACTIVIDADES INTERNET

Students use Web sites that sell clothes to choose and then describe various items of clothing they like.

- To prepare students for the **Hoja de actividades,** have them review the vocabulary from the **Segundo paso** by completing the related activities in the Grammar and Vocabulary Workbook.

- After students have completed the **Hoja de actividades,** encourage them to work with a partner and ask that partner about his or her favorite clothes. Why do they like those clothes? Do they choose clothing because of comfort? style? fabric?

Proyecto

High-fashion designers often create ridiculous combinations of style, colors, and fabrics. Have students find a fashion **(moda)** Web site. Ask them to choose two or three articles of clothing pictured on the site. Have them first describe each article of clothing in as much detail as they can, then critique each of them. You might have students download free images and include the images with their descriptions.

For Student Response Forms, see Listening Activities pp. 61–63

PRIMER PASO   pp. 130–137

6 Los regalos   p. 131

1. A mi padre le encanta escuchar la música.
2. A mi madre le gusta mirar películas en casa.
3. A mi hermano Santiago le gustaría tocar un instrumento musical.
4. A mi hermana Eva le gusta practicar deportes.
5. A mi abuelo le encantan los animales.
6. A mi hermana Silvia le encanta decorar su cuarto con carteles.

Answers to Activity 6

1. d	**4.** c
2. f	**5.** b
3. e	**6.** a

13 Las tiendas   p. 135

1. Necesito comprar unas galletas y un pastel para el cumpleaños de mi hermanito.
2. Me gustaría comprar unos aretes para mi amiga.
3. Necesito comprar un juego de mesa para mi primo Luis.
4. Busco sandalias para la playa.
5. Busco una camisa elegante para llevar a la fiesta de Enrique este sábado.
6. Quiero comprar plantas para mi casa.
7. Voy a comprar pan dulce para la fiesta de mi papá.

Answers to Activity 13

1. d	**5.** g
2. c	**6.** f
3. e	**7.** b
4. a	

SEGUNDO PASO   pp. 138–145

20 ¿Qué necesitas llevar?   p. 140

CARLOS Tengo que comprar unos bluejeans, una camiseta y unos zapatos de tenis.

ELENITA Quiero buscar un traje de baño porque hace mucho calor.

SERGIO Necesito unas camisetas, unos pantalones cortos y unos zapatos de tenis.

TERESA Necesito pantalones y una blusa blanca. También necesito zapatos pardos.

LUIS Yo busco una camisa blanca, una corbata, calcetines y zapatos negros.

Answers to Activity 20

Answers will vary. Possible answers:

Carlos—clases

Elenita—ir a la piscina

Sergio—jugar al tenis

Teresa—trabajar en la oficina/un baile

Luis—trabajar en la oficina/un baile

28 ¿Cómo son?   p. 145

1. Es menos gordo que el otro.
2. Es más grande que el otro.
3. Es más elegante que el otro.
4. Es menos largo que el otro.
5. Es más larga que la otra.
6. Es menos larga que la otra.

Answers to Activity 28

1. b	**4.** b
2. a	**5.** b
3. a	**6.** a

37 ¡Qué caro!   p. 151

1. — Perdón, señorita. ¿Cuánto cuesta esta blusa?
   — ¿La roja? El precio es de cincuenta y ocho dólares.
   — ¡Qué cara!

2. — Bueno, me gustaría comprar esta camisa.
   — ¿La blanca?
   — Sí. ¿Cuánto cuesta?
   — Son ocho dólares con cincuenta y cinco centavos.
   — ¡Qué ganga!

3. — Perdón, señor. Necesito unos bluejeans.
   — Usted tiene suerte, señor. Aquí tenemos unos baratos.
   — ¿Sólo diecisiete dólares? ¡Qué baratos!

4. — Señorita, busco un vestido elegante para un baile.
   — Tenemos varios. Este azul, por ejemplo. O si prefiere otro color, lo tenemos también en rojo y en negro.
   — ¿Cuánto cuesta el vestido rojo?
   — Sólo setecientos sesenta dólares.
   — ¡Ay, qué caro!

5. — Busco unos zapatos negros.
   — Aquí tenemos varios estilos. Éstos, por ejemplo, cuestan sólo ciento ochenta y nueve dólares.
   — ¡Ciento ochenta y nueve dólares! ¡Qué caros! Gracias, pero no.

Answers to Activity 37

1. c	**4.** b
2. e	**5.** d
3. a	

LETRA Y SONIDO   p. 153

For the scripts for Parts A and C, see p. 153. The script for Part B is below.

B. Dictado

Para la tía Silvia una blusa de seda.

Para César un suéter azul.

Para Simón unas sandalias.

Y para Celia unos zapatos.

1   p. 158

SARA   Ana, mañana es la fiesta de Lisa. ¿Ya tienes tu ropa?

ANA   Sí, voy de King Kong. ¿De qué vas tú?

SARA   Voy de payaso, pero todavía tengo que comprar mi ropa. ¿Me acompañas?

ANA   ¡Cómo no!

SARA   Necesito una corbata bastante fea.

ANA   Ay, sí. Compra una corbata de los años setenta.

SARA   Ja, ja, ja. Oye, ¿qué te parece si vamos a una tienda ahora?

ANA   Sí, perfecto. ¿Qué más necesitas?

SARA   Bueno, una camisa de cuadros, unos zapatos grandes y unos pantalones grandes.

ANA   ¿Sabes qué? Mi hermano tiene unos pantalones viejos que puedes usar.

SARA   ¡Fantástico!

Answers to Repaso Activity 1

(d) una corbata fea y (b) unos pantalones grandes

CAPÍTULO 9

¡Vamos de compras!
PROJECTS

EL CATÁLOGO DE ROPA DE MODA

This project links clothing vocabulary review with number review.

Introduction

Ask students if they buy clothes from catalogs. What companies are the most popular? What kinds of clothing are offered in different catalogs? Are there catalogs just for teens? What are the prices like? What are the latest styles?

Materials students may need

- ◆ Magazine or advertising circulars
- ◆ Clothing catalogs
- ◆ Colored construction paper and white paper
- ◆ Glue sticks and stapler
- ◆ Scissors
- ◆ Markers

Sequence

1. Have students make a clothing catalog with a partner. Pairs write a list of 15–20 clothing items from this chapter's vocabulary in Spanish. Pairs cut out or draw pictures of the items of clothing on their list. Students may have different categories of clothing such as **ropa para señores, ropa para señoras, ropa para jóvenes, ropa para niños** in their catalog.

2. Pairs glue the clothing pictures onto paper, label each item of clothing and its color in Spanish, and mark its price in Spain's or Mexico's monetary unit. (You may need to look up the current exchange rate.)

3. Pairs decide on a Spanish title for their catalog. They write their title page and make up an address and telephone number for their company.

4. Have two sets of partners get together to shop from each other's catalog. Each set makes a shopping list in Spanish of ten items they would like to purchase from the other pair's catalog.

Grading the project

Suggested point distribution (total = 100 points):

15–20 items	**20**
Vocabulary accuracy	**20**
Neatness, appearance	**20**
Creativity	**20**
Cooperation	**20**

LA ROPA INDÍGENA

Students research an item of traditional clothing of the indigenous people of the Americas. Then they create a poster and present it to the class. You may have students compare styles, materials, dyes, embroidery, weaving techniques, and other aspects of clothing across cultures. Possible countries include Argentina, Guatemala, and Mexico.

Materials students may need

- ◆ Library resources
- ◆ Poster board
- ◆ Glue or tape
- ◆ Scissors
- ◆ Markers or colored pencils
- ◆ Magazines

Sequence

1. Have students conduct library research to select a type of clothing and obtain information on it. Types of clothing might include **huipiles** and **sarapes**.

2. Have students prepare posters representing the clothing using magazine pictures or drawing pictures of the clothing. Some students may bring in authentic costumes or fabrics.

3. Have students prepare a presentation in Spanish telling where the clothes originated, what they are made of, and why they are worn. (climate, natural resources, aesthetic reasons, place of origin, marital status)

4 Students present their information to the class. When all of the presentations have been completed, display the posters around the room.

Grading the project

Suggested point distribution (total = 100 points):

Accuracy of information **40**
Poster **20**
Presentation to class **40**

LA CAJA DE ROPA

Students prepare a hands-on collection of clothing that represents this chapter's vocabulary. Students identify and label articles of clothing, and incorporate the clothing into an oral exercise.

Introduction
Discuss students current fashions. What's "in" and what's not? What was "in" in the 90s? the 80s? the 70s? How important are clothes to them and their friends? Ask them if they like to be individual or follow the crowd. Would they rather be comfortable or in style?

Materials students may need
◆ Index cards   ◆ Tape
◆ Clothes   ◆ Large box
◆ Markers

Sequence
1 Students work in groups of three to brainstorm the category of clothing they wish to collect for their box. Groups decide what clothes to emphasize: children's, girls', boys', 70s, 80s, or 90s clothing. They make a list in Spanish of at least 12 items of clothing from the vocabulary items on pages 140 and 142.

2 Each student brings in clothing items to put in the box. Each student prepares an index card label in Spanish for his or her item of clothing.

3 Students remove labels after practicing the vocabulary with the other members of the group.

4 Groups share their vocabulary items with other groups and teach other groups new clothing words.

Grading the project

Suggested point distribution (total = 100 points):

Correct number of items **20**
Correct labels **20**
Spanish pronunciation **20**
Clarity, presentation **20**
Cooperative effort **20**

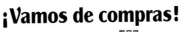

CAPÍTULO 9

¡Vamos de compras!

GAMES

ASÍ SE HACE UNA FRASE

This game provides an opportunity to practice verb conjugation, to review question words and the formation of phrases. It is helpful for verb review before evaluation.

Preparation

1. Give students a list of **-ar**, **-er**, and **-ir** verbs, as well as the irregular verbs they know.

2. Begin with any infinitive, for example, the verb **comprar**. Lead a question-and-answer session. Ask questions with **comprar**, for example, **¿Quién compra?**, **¿Qué compran ustedes?**, **¿Dónde compran ustedes los regalos?**, **¿Para quién compran ustedes los regalos?**, and build a pyramid similar to the one below.

3. Demonstrate the question-and-answer method of building sentences with several students at the chalkboard. Students play this game in pairs at the chalkboard or with five or six teams of four to six students who send a pair forward to represent their team.

> **Comprar**
> **(Nosotros) compramos**
> **Compramos los regalos.**
> **Compramos los regalos en la tienda.**
> **Compramos los regalos en la tienda para Eva y Lisa.**

Procedure

1. Have two students come to the chalkboard. Student #1 begins by giving Student #2 an infinitive in Spanish.

2. Student #2 must ask a question in Spanish using the verb in order to continue.

3. The game continues with questions from Student #2. Student #1 writes the answers on the board. Students alternate asking and answering questions.

4. Student pairs score 50 points for each correct answer on the board up to a total of a possible 250 in each round. Use each infinitive only once.

5. The pair with the most points wins.

¿QUÉ VEO?

This game reviews both the vocabulary presented in the chapter and the vocabulary for classroom objects from Chapter 2.

Procedure

1. One student writes the name of an object in the classroom on a piece of paper and gives it to you. The student tells the class either the color of the object or the material it is made of. For example, **Veo algo rojo** or **Veo algo de algodón**.

2. The class then has one minute to guess what the item is. The student who guesses correctly chooses an object next.

3. If the class doesn't guess the object in the allotted time, the student who wrote the word has another student choose an object.

¿QUÉ ES ESTO?

In this activity, students identify objects by touch. It is good for tactile learners.

Preparation

1. Place various objects representing vocabulary from this or previous chapters into a large bag or pillowcase.

2. For this chapter, items might include a CD case, a toy, a T-shirt, a plastic flower, a greeting card, a sock, and so on. Students may also choose to lend items to put in the bag for this game.

Procedure

1. Hold the bag open as a blindfolded student reaches into it, holds up an object, and tries to identify it in Spanish. (**Ésta es una corbata, ¿no?**)

2. The rest of the class can see what the object is but cannot tell. You may wish to divide the class into smaller groups and put objects in two or three bags.

STANDARDS: 1.2, 5.1

¿QUÉ LLEVAS?

This game reviews clothing items and the colors learned in earlier chapters.

Procedure

1 Divide the class into two teams. Designate a Scorekeeper and a Questioner.

2 Each team lines up along opposite walls of the classroom.

3 The Questioner asks someone from Team A **¿Qué lleva _____?** The person from Team A must name three things that the person is wearing. (3 points total). If the student can name the color of the clothing as well, the team earns 1 point for each color (3 points total) or 6 possible points total for each answer.

4 The Questioner goes to the next member of Team A and asks the same question about another person.

5 The game continues until each member of the team has participated. The team with the most points wins.

UN REGALO

In this game students practice vocabulary for gift items by identifying activities that people like to do.

Preparation

1 Have students help brainstorm to list in Spanish all possible items from Chapter 9 that could be bought as a gift for someone. (For example, clothing, personal items)

2 Have each student make an index card with the Spanish word for a gift on it. (For example, **blusa, dulces, flores,** and so on)

3 Have students brainstorm a list of preferences or likes (**le gusta nadar, le gusta la música, le gusta comer el chocolate, le gusta jugar juegos, le gusta esquiar, le gusta correr, le gusta jugar al tenis, le gusta el jardín, le gusta escribir cartas, le gusta el frío, le gusta el calor, le gusta el azúcar, le gusta llevar ropa de moda**). Have each student prepare a card with one "like" or preference.

4 Collect the cards to play the game.

Procedure

1 Divide the class into teams of four. Give each person one card with a gift on it.

2 Select a preference card and read it aloud to the class. For example, **le gusta nadar.** Each group collaborates and decide if they hold a gift card that would be appropriate to give to that person.

3 A Scorekeeper asks each group to say, in turn, the gifts they have decided on. The Scorekeeper keeps a tally of how many possible gifts each group has for each category.

4 The group with the highest number of possible gift ideas after all categories have been used wins.

¡Vamos de compras!
ANSWERS TO CHAPTER 9 ACTIVITIES

Listening activity answers appear on Scripts pages 123E–123F. Answers to all other activities appear on corresponding pupil pages.

PRIMER PASO   pp. 130–137

8
1. c
2. d
3. b
4. a
5. f
6. e

10 Answers will vary. Possible answers:
1. Le voy a regalar unos libros de aventuras.
2. Les voy a regalar una planta.
3. Le voy a regalar una camiseta morada.
4. Voy a regalarles un disco compacto.
5. Nos va a regalar un béisbol nuevo.
6. Va a regalarme una novela cómica.
7. Me va a regalar unas pinturas y pinceles.
8. Va a regalarnos un disco compacto con música para bailar.

14 —Necesito comprar unas sandalias.
—Tienes que ir a la zapatería.

—Quiero comprar unas flores.
—Tienes que ir a la florería.

—Quiero comprar unos juguetes.
—Tienes que ir a la juguetería.

—Necesito comprar unos zapatos de tenis.
—Tienes que ir a la zapatería.

—Necesito comprar pan.
—Tienes que ir a la panadería.

—Quiero comprar unas galletas.
—Tienes que ir a la tienda de comestibles.

—Necesito comprar una corbata.
—Tienes que ir al almacén.

TERCER PASO   pp. 148–153

31 Answers will vary. Possible answers:
1. —¿Prefieres los pantalones cortos verdes o los bluejeans para pescar en el lago?
—Prefiero los pantalones cortos verdes.
2. —¿Prefieres las sandalias pardas o los zapatos de cuero para ir al trabajo?
—Prefiero los zapatos de cuero.
3. —¿Prefieres la camiseta de rayas o la camisa blanca para ir a la boda de Antonio?
—Me gusta la camisa blanca.
4. —¿Qué calcetines prefieres con los pantalones negros? ¿Los negros o los blancos?
—Prefiero los negros.
5. —¿Prefieres el traje gris o los bluejeans para ir de compras?
—Prefiero los bluejeans.
6. —¿Qué camisa prefieres con el traje gris? ¿La camisa amarilla o la rosada?
—Prefiero la camisa rosada.

32 Answers will vary. Possible answer:
Prefiero el uniforme de Mariano Duncan porque no me gustan las rayas. El uniforme de Mariano Duncan es gris con rojo y blanco y lleva zapatos rojos. Le queda muy bien su uniforme.

33 Answers will vary. Possible answers:
1. Esa camisa es muy cara, ¿no?
2. Estas botas blancas son muy feas.
3. Este suéter de algodón es bonito pero me queda muy pequeño.
4. Esos zapatos pardos son baratos, ¿no?
5. Esa falda te queda muy grande.
6. Ese cinturón es muy bonito pero es muy caro.
7. Esa chaqueta es muy barata.
8. Este vestido de seda es caro.

VAMOS A LEER   pp. 156–157

C
1. Sí, hay restaurantes con picantes platillos mexicanos.
2. Tome un taxi acuático.
3. Se llama El Paseo del Río.
4. Ésta en la Misión San José.
5. La Muestra Ganadera y Rodeo es en febrero.

HOMEWORK SUGGESTIONS

Chapter Section	Presentation	Homework Options
Primer paso	**Así se dice,** p. 131	CD-ROM, Disc 3, Chapter 9, Activity 2
	Vocabulario, p. 132	*Pupil's Edition,* p. 132, Activity 7 *Grammar and Vocabulary,* p. 18, Activities 1–2 CD-ROM, Disc 3, Chapter 9, Activity 1
	Gramática, p. 133	*Pupil's Edition,* p. 133, Activity 9 *Grammar and Vocabulary,* pp. 19–20, Activities 3–5
	Así se dice, p. 134	*Pupil's Edition,* p. 134, Activities 11–12 *Grammar and Vocabulary,* p. 20, Activity 6
	Vocabulario, p. 135	*Grammar and Vocabulary,* p. 21, Activities 7–8 *Practice and Activity Book,* pp. 39–40, Activities 5–6
Segundo paso	**Así se dice,** p. 139	*Pupil's Edition,* p. 139, Activity 19
	Vocabulario, pp. 140, 142	*Pupil's Edition,* p. 141, Activity 21 *Grammar and Vocabulary,* p. 22, Activities 9–10 CD-ROM, Disc 3, Chapter 9, Activity 4
	Nota gramatical, p. 142	*Pupil's Edition,* p. 143, Activity 25 *Grammar and Vocabulary,* p. 23, Activities 11–12
	Así se dice, p. 144	*Pupil's Edition,* pp. 144–145, Activities 27, 29
	Gramática, p. 145	*Grammar and Vocabulary,* p. 24, Activities 13–14 *Practice and Activity Book,* p. 42, Activities 9–10 CD-ROM, Disc 3, Chapter 9, Activity 3
Tercer paso	**Así se dice,** p. 149	*Pupil's Edition,* p. 149, Activity 32 *Practice and Activity Book,* p. 44, Activity 12
	Nota gramatical, p. 150	*Pupil's Edition,* p. 150, Activity 33 *Grammar and Vocabulary,* p. 25, Activities 15–16 CD-ROM, Disc 3, Chapter 9, Activity 6
	Así se dice, p. 150	*Pupil's Edition,* p. 151, Activity 36 *Practice and Activity Book,* p. 105, Activity 14
	Vocabulario, p. 151	*Grammar and Vocabulary,* p. 26, Activity 19

¡Vamos de compras!

MOTIVATING ACTIVITY
Ask students to think about what they like to shop for and where they like to shop. Do they enjoy looking for clothes, sports equipment, or gifts for other people? Do they prefer shopping with a group of friends, one friend, or alone?

PHOTO FLASH!
① This photo was taken in San Antonio, where the video episode for this chapter was filmed. The actors in the video episodes for Chapters 9 and 10 are from San Antonio.

CULTURE NOTE
Ask students to name occasions on which they give or receive gifts. (Christmas, Hanukkah, Valentine's Day, birthday) In Latin America and Spain, children often receive gifts on both their birthday and their saint's day. In Spain, gifts are customarily exchanged on **el Día de los Reyes Magos** (January 6) rather than on Christmas. This reflects the belief that the Wise Men arrived and presented their gifts on that date. Ask your students about the diversity of gift-giving customs in their community.

CAPÍTULO 9

¡Vamos de compras!

① ¿Qué le compro a Héctor para su graduación?

In this chapter you will learn to

PRIMER PASO

- talk about giving gifts
- ask for and give directions downtown

SEGUNDO PASO

- comment on clothes
- make comparisons

TERCER PASO

- express preferences
- ask about prices and pay for something

📶 internet

MARCAR: go.hrw.com
PALABRA CLAVE:
WV3 TEXAS-9

2 **¿Cuál de estas camisetas prefieres?**

3 **Oye, mira este disco compacto. Es buena esta música, ¿no?**

FOCUSING ON OUTCOMES

- Have your students read the learner outcomes and match them with the photos. (Photo 1: discussing gift suggestions; Photo 2: expressing preferences and making comparisons; Photo 3: commenting on things one can buy.)
- Ask students when they are expected to give a gift. In general do they give more gifts or receive more gifts?
- Have students discuss alternatives to buying gifts. Do they make their own gifts? Do they enjoy giving or receiving personal gifts, such as washing the car, making a special treat, or cooking a meal for someone?

SUGGESTION

2 Have students describe their favorite T-shirt to a partner. Ask them to explain why it is their favorite. Then, have several students describe their own T-shirt to the class.

CRITICAL THINKING

Teach your students the expression **El que más tiene más quiere.** Ask them to work with a partner to understand its meaning (The more you have, the more you want). Have each pair tell whether or not they agree with the sentiment of the proverb, and why. Lead a class discussion to go over students' opinions of the proverb.

125

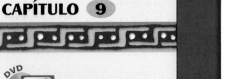

VIDEO INTEGRATION

En camino LEVEL 1B

Video Program

Videocassette 1, 47:26–51:25 OR

Videocassette 3, 1:30:06–1:34:05 (captioned version)

¡Ven conmigo! LEVEL 1

DVD Tutor, Disc 2

TEACHER NOTE

The **fotonovela** is an abridged version of the video episode.

VIDEO SYNOPSIS

Eva, Lisa, and Gabi discuss what gift to buy Héctor. As they shop, they also look at some clothes for themselves. They continue looking for Héctor's gift but cannot decide what to get him. Finally, they agree to separate for half an hour to shop for Héctor on their own—but they end up choosing the same poster as a gift.

BACKGROUND

The girls are shopping at El Mercado, a popular market in San Antonio. They are in the indoor shopping part, which was once the city's Farmers' Market.

MOTIVATING ACTIVITY

Ask students if they ever have problems deciding what to give someone. How do they solve this problem? Do they have any advice for others with the same problem?

DE ANTEMANO

¿Qué le compramos a Héctor?

CD 9 Trs. 1–2

Eva's brother, Héctor, is graduating from high school. Eva, Lisa, and Gabi are downtown shopping for a graduation gift and doing some window shopping as well. Why do you think the girls will be surprised when each sees what the others have bought?

p. 37
Acts. 1–2

Eva

Lisa

Gabi

①

LISA Bueno, ¿qué le van a comprar a Héctor para su graduación?

EVA No sé, tal vez unos discos compactos de Gloria Estefan.

GABI Me gustaría regalarle algo divertido.

LISA Gabi, ¡yo también quiero regalarle algo divertido!

EVA ¿Por qué no le compran regalos divertidos las dos? Pero tenemos que encontrarlos hoy... ¡su fiesta de graduación es el viernes!

LISA ¿Quieren entrar en esta tienda de ropa? Para mirar, nada más. Y después, vamos a la papelería para comprarle a Héctor las tarjetas.

②

EVA ¿Cuál prefieren, la blusa roja o la de rayas?

GABI Yo prefiero la roja. ¿Cuánto cuesta?

EVA Uy, cuarenta dólares. Es cara.

LISA ¿Qué les parecen estos pantalones cortos?

GABI Eh... de verdad, Lisa, no me gustan para nada los cuadros.

GABI ¿Qué tal esta falda?

EVA Es bonita.

LISA Y es de algodón...

EVA Y sólo cuesta 12 dólares. ¡Qué barata!

GABI Sí, ¡es una ganga!

LISA Bueno, ¿qué le compramos a Héctor?

EVA Uf... es difícil. No sé... le interesan los libros, ¿tal vez un libro? Hay una librería al lado de la zapatería.

GABI No, eso no, prefiero regalarle algo divertido.

PRESENTATION
Have students skim the **fotonovela**. Then have them work in pairs to list in Spanish all of the things that Eva, Lisa, and Gabi consider buying for Héctor. Have them discuss which of the items they think Héctor would like most and why. Then pairs compare lists to make sure they haven't missed any items. Do they agree on which gift Héctor would like most?

SUGGESTION
Have students look at the story frame by frame. Ask **¿Cómo se llaman las tres chicas? ¿Dónde están? ¿Cuántos años tienen?** Then have students guess what is happening. Next play the first frame. Play the rest of the video without sound. Have students revise their predictions before watching the video with sound.

CRITICAL THINKING
Ask students to point out expressions in which **le** is used, and to infer what it means from the context of the expressions.

CHALLENGE
Ask students to draw another frame for the **fotonovela** in which they include the conversation between the girls when they meet after buying their gifts.

DE ANTEMANO · *ciento veintisiete* **127**

STANDARDS: 1.1, 1.2, 5.1 · **127**

NATIVE SPEAKERS

As you present clothing, gift giving, and shopping vocabulary in this chapter, you may want to have native speakers list alternate words. You may want to share these regional variations with the class.

A continuación

You may choose to continue with *¿Qué le compramos a Héctor? (a continuación)* at this time or wait until later in the chapter. At this point, Eva, Lisa, and Gabi meet after shopping for Hector's gifts. They discover that they have all purchased the same gift. You may wish to have students discuss what they would do in a situation similar to that described in the second part of the video.

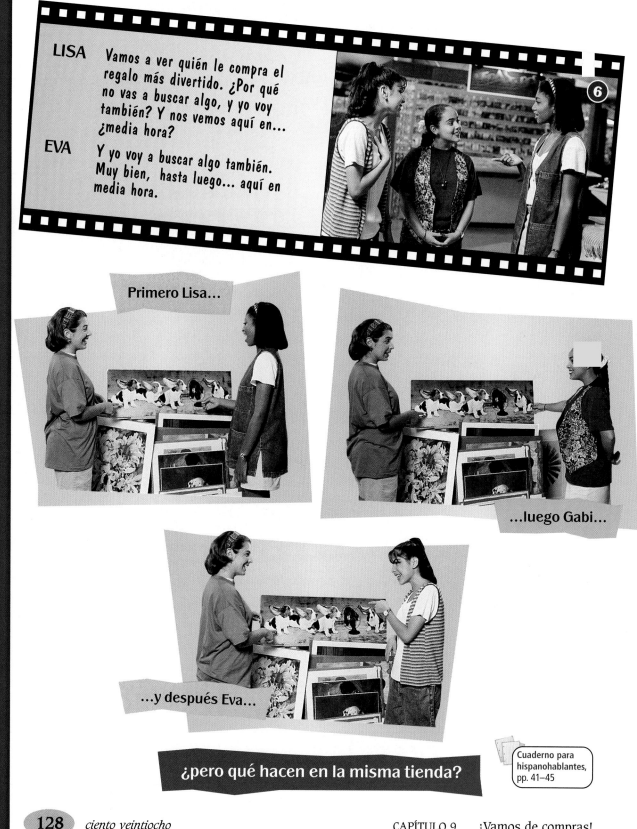

6

LISA Vamos a ver quién le compra el regalo más divertido. ¿Por qué no vas a buscar algo, y yo voy también? Y nos vemos aquí en... ¿media hora?

EVA Y yo voy a buscar algo también. Muy bien, hasta luego... aquí en media hora.

Primero Lisa...

...luego Gabi...

...y después Eva...

¿pero qué hacen en la misma tienda?

Cuaderno para hispanohablantes, pp. 41–45

1 ¿Comprendes?

Contesta las preguntas. Acuérdate *(Remember)*... si no lo sabes, puedes adivinar *(guess)*.

These activities check for global comprehension only. Students should not yet be expected to produce language modeled in **De antemano**.

1. ¿Para quién compran Eva, Lisa y Gabi los regalos? Héctor
2. ¿Por qué le van a comprar los regalos? Es su graduación.
3. ¿Adónde van primero? ¿Qué miran allí? a una tienda de ropa; miran ropa
4. ¿Qué tipo de regalo quieren comprar Lisa y Gabi? algo divertido

2 ¿Cierto o falso?

Indica si las oraciones son ciertas o falsas. Corrige las oraciones falsas.

Answers in side column

1. Las chicas le compran regalos a Héctor.
2. Van a la zapatería para comprar tarjetas.
3. Gabi prefiere la blusa azul.
4. La falda es de algodón.
5. A Héctor no le interesan los libros.
6. Las chicas compran tres regalos diferentes.

3 ¿Cómo se dice?

Imagine that you're a friend of Héctor's. Find the phrases you could use . . .

1. to say you'd like to buy him something fun Me gustaría regalarle algo divertido.
2. to ask how much something costs ¿Cuánto cuesta?
3. to say that something is made out of cotton Es de algodón.
4. to ask "What should we buy for Héctor?" ¿Qué le compramos a Héctor?
5. to say he's interested in books A él le interesan los libros.

4 ¿Quién lo dijo?

Identifica la persona que dijo *(said)* lo siguiente.

Eva

Lisa

Gabi

1. Sólo cuesta 12 dólares. ¡Qué barata! Eva
2. Vamos a la papelería para comprarle a Héctor las tarjetas. Lisa
3. Yo prefiero la roja. ¿Cuánto cuesta? Gabi
4. Hay una librería al lado de la zapatería. Eva

DE ANTEMANO

ciento veintinueve **129**

CAPÍTULO 9

SLOWER PACE

3 Before having students begin this activity, write on a transparency or on the board Spanish question words in one column and their English equivalents in another. Have students match each English meaning with its Spanish counterpart and make up questions in Spanish using the question words. Then have them do the activity in the text.

SUGGESTION

4 After students have answered the questions, have them look again at the **fotonovela** on pages 126–128 and justify their answers based on what each character says.

Answers to Activity 2
1. cierto
2. falso; Van a la papelería para comprar tarjetas.
3. falso; Gabi prefiere la blusa roja.
4. cierto
5. falso; A Héctor le interesan los libros.
6. falso; Las chicas compran el mismo regalo.

STANDARDS: 1.2 **129**

DVD VIDEO

VIDEO INTEGRATION

En camino LEVEL 1B

Video Program

Videocassette 1, 47:43–48:25 OR

Videocassette 3, 1:30:23–1:31:05 *(captioned version)*

¡Ven conmigo! LEVEL 1

DVD Tutor, Disc 2

 Bell work

On the board or on a transparency write the following familiar poem, asking students to fill in the names of the months.

Treinta días tiene s _____, a _____, j _____ y n _____. F _____ tiene veintiocho y los otros treinta y uno. ¿Qué son? Los m _____ del a _____.

Then have students list in Spanish the months of the year and the dates for exchanging gifts they associate with those months. Ask students when children in Latin America and Spain receive gifts. (**El Día de los Reyes Magos**, their birthdays and saints' days)

☀ MOTIVATE

In pairs, have students discuss what makes a good gift. Have they ever received an inappropriate gift? What about a really great gift? What is the best gift they have ever received? Ask volunteers to share some of their answers.

PRIMER PASO

TPR

Storytelling Book pp. 33, 36

WV3 TEXAS-9

Talking about giving gifts; asking for and giving directions downtown

LISA	Bueno, ¿qué le van a comprar a Héctor para su graduación?
EVA	No sé, tal vez unos discos compactos de Gloria Estefan.
GABI	Me gustaría regalarle algo divertido.
LISA	Gabi, ¡yo también quiero regalarle algo divertido!

5 Algo para Héctor

Lee lo que dicen las chicas y contesta las preguntas.

1. ¿Quién va a celebrar una graduación?
2. ¿Qué piensa Eva regalarle a Héctor?
3. ¿Qué quiere regalarle Gabi?
4. ¿Qué dice Lisa sobre *(about)* la idea de Gabi?
5. Para ti, ¿cuál es un regalo divertido? ¿Por qué?

1. Héctor
2. unos discos compactos de Gloria Estefan
3. algo divertido
4. Ella también quiere regalarle algo divertido.
5. Answers will vary.

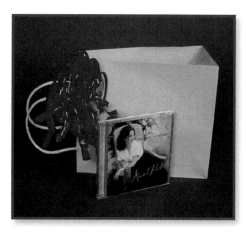

ASÍ SE DICE Talking about giving gifts

pp. 38–39
Acts. 3–4

To find out what gift a friend has in mind for someone, ask:

¿Qué tipo de regalo buscas?
What kind of gift are you looking for?

¿Para quién es el regalo?
Who is the gift for?

¿Qué piensas regalarle a tu hermano?
What are you planning to give (as a gift) to your brother?

Your friend might answer:

Busco unos pantalones para mi primo.
I'm looking for some pants for my cousin.

El regalo **es para** mi amiga.
The gift is for my friend.

Le voy a dar una camiseta.
I'm going to give him a T-shirt.

9-1

6 Los regalos Script and answers on p. 123E

CD 9 Tr. 3

Listen and take notes as Rodolfo tells you what his family members like. Then match what they like to their photos.

1 Mi padre

2 Mi madre

a

b

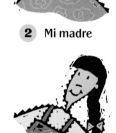
3 Santiago

4 Eva

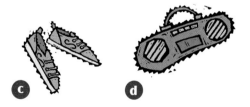
c

d

5 Mi abuelo

6 Silvia

e

f

⁂ **TEACH**

PRESENTATION
ASÍ SE DICE
Ask students to look back at the **fotonovela** and have them find some of the expressions introduced in **Así se dice.** Point out to students that **¿Para quién es...?** is for one item and **¿Para quién son...?** is for more than one item. Then model pronunciation of the words in the **Vocabulario** on page 132 and have students take the role of the friend to practice the expressions and the new vocabulary. You may want to have students work in pairs to practice the expressions and vocabulary.

SUGGESTION
6 Review the vocabulary for each item before playing the audio portion of the activity. Follow up by having students use expressions from **Así se dice** to ask and answer questions about what gifts Rodolfo has in mind for each family member.

LANGUAGE NOTE
The verb **buscar** means *to look for.* Emphasize that *for* is not translated. Remind students that they should use **"a" personal** if they're looking for a person.

The verb **buscar** is also commonly used to mean *to go get.*

STANDARDS: 1.2, 2.3, 5.2 **131**

PRESENTATION

VOCABULARIO

Display Teaching Transparency 9-A. Have students identify each gift while you ask the question **¿Qué piensas regalarle a tu amigo?** Have students answer with **Le voy a regalar** _____ and fill in the blank with the item you point to. Remind them to include **un, una, unos,** or **unas** in their answers.

NATIVE SPEAKERS

Have native speakers say which words they use for these items. For example, some people say **los pendientes** for **los aretes** and **unos caramelos** for **unos dulces.** For some **una planta** is **una mata,** and for some **una billetera** is **una cartera.** For some **una cartera** means *purse*.

SUGGESTION

7 Have students rewrite and personalize these statements. Point out the Additional Vocabulary on pages 294–296.

Answers to Activity 7

Answers will vary. Possible answers:
1. Le voy a comprar un juego de mesa.
2. Voy a comprarle unos aretes.
3. Le voy a comprar un disco compacto.
4. Le voy a comprar una corbata.
5. Voy a comprarles una planta.
6. Voy a comprarle unos dulces.

132 STANDARDS: 1.2, 5.1

GV p. 18 Acts. 1–2

9-A

VOCABULARIO

un disco compacto

unos aretes y un collar

una cartera

unas corbatas

unos dulces

unas flores

un juego de mesa

unos juguetes

una planta

una tarjeta

7 Regalos para todos

Using the gift items in the **Vocabulario,** write sentences telling what you'll buy each of these people. Base your choices on what they like. Use **Le(s) voy a comprar...** or **Voy a comprarle(s)...** Answers in side column

1. A tu hermano le gusta jugar en casa.
2. A tu hermana le encantan las joyas *(jewelry)*.
3. A tu mejor amigo/a le gusta escuchar música.
4. A tu padre le gusta vestirse bien.
5. A tus abuelos les encanta su jardín.
6. A tu profesor/profesora le encanta el chocolate.

8 ¿Para quién es?

Match each gift to a person in Activity 7: **el regalo (d) es para mi hermana porque le gustan las joyas.** Answers on p. 123K

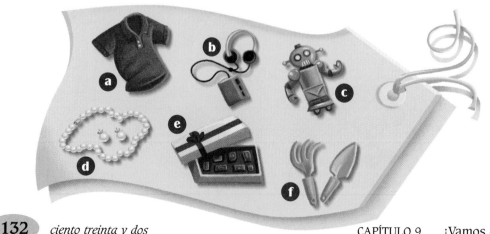

GRAMÁTICA Indirect object pronouns **le** and **les**

GV
pp. 19–20
Acts. 3–5

Indirect objects tell *to whom* or *for whom* something is intended.

1. Indirect object pronouns either go before a conjugated verb or may be attached to an infinitive.

> **Le** quiero regalar algo divertido a Héctor.
>
> Quiero regalar**le** algo divertido a Héctor.
>
> *I want to give Héctor something fun.*
>
> Quiero regalar**le** algo cómico. *I want to get him something funny.*

2. **Le** can mean *to him, to her,* or *to you* (singular). **Les** can mean *to them* or *to you* (plural). To clarify **le** or **les,** you can add the phrase **a** + *pronoun* or **a** + *noun.*

> ¿Qué **le** compramos **a él**? *What do we buy for him?*
>
> **Les** voy a regalar unos juguetes **a mis hermanos**.

9 Ir de compras

Completa el párrafo con **me, te, le, nos** o **les.**

¡Qué divertido es ir de compras! A mi hermana ___1___ voy a regalar un collar y a mi hermano ___2___ doy una camiseta. A mamá y papá ___3___ regalo un video de su película favorita. ___4___ voy a regalar aretes a mi abuelita, y a mi abuelito ___5___ quiero regalar una corbata. ¿Qué crees que ___6___ voy a regalar a ti? ¡Es una sorpresa! ¿Qué crees que Roberto ___7___ va a regalar a mí? Papá ___8___ va a regalar boletos para el concierto a mi hermano y a mí. ¿Qué te parece?

1. le
2. le
3. les
4. Le
5. le
6. te
7. me
8. nos

10 El regalo perfecto

A Work with a partner. Take turns saying what you're going to give the following people, according to what they like. Use **le** or **les** in your sentences. Answers on p. 123K

> MODELO mi amigo—escribir cartas
> —Le voy a regalar un bolígrafo.

1. mi primo—leer
2. mis padres—el jardín
3. mi hermana—la ropa
4. mis amigos—escuchar música

B Now guess what a friend is going to give you and your friends.

> MODELO a Rubén y a mí—el cine
> Va a regalarnos unos boletos para la película nueva.

5. a Berta y a mí—los deportes
6. a mí—los libros
7. a mí—el arte
8. a Juan y a mí—bailar

PRESENTATION
GRAMÁTICA
Write on the board or on a transparency **Le doy unos aretes a mamá. Mamá les regala los carteles a sus hijos. Los chicos quieren regalarles unas flores a las chicas.** Help students recognize the indirect objects in the sentences. Remind them that **le(s)** can have several meanings and that **a** + pronoun or **a** + noun is often added for clarification.

ENGLISH LINK
Have students think about how they know which noun is the indirect object in English in the sentence *He's going to give his mom some flowers.* (the person who receives the direct object is in the indirect object) Emphasize that in Spanish the indirect object must always be preceded by the preposition **a**.

SLOWER PACE
9 Write this paragraph on a transparency and go through it as a class. Break it into smaller parts as needed.

SUGGESTION
10 Number the "likes" in the activity and write them on cards. Pass them out and say **Número uno, levanta tu tarjeta.** Ask another student **¿A** (name of student) **qué le vas a regalar?** The student says **A** (name) **le voy a regalar** (gift appropriate to the "like.")

STANDARDS: 1.1, 4.1, 5.1 133

PA
p. 40
Act. 6

9-1

PRESENTATION

ASÍ SE DICE

Use a puppet to role-play the dialogues, altering them for directions in your area. For example, the puppet asks **Perdón, ¿dónde está el Almacén _____?** and you respond with appropriate directions, using the phrases in the text. Then ask students to answer the puppet's questions.

CHALLENGE

11 Have students make their own map, similar to the one shown. They draw the eight stores presented in **Vocabulario** on page 135. On a separate sheet of paper students write eight sentences like the ones in this activity telling where the stores are located. Collect all maps and directions. Distribute five maps and five sets of directions to groups of students. Each group attempts to match the maps with their corresponding instructions.

Answers to Activity 12

1. falso; El almacén Super está al lado de la Biblioteca Central.
2. cierto
3. falso; El almacén queda lejos de la joyería.
4. cierto
5. cierto

ASÍ SE DICE   Asking for and giving directions downtown

To find out where a shop is located, ask:

Some responses might be:

Perdón, ¿dónde está el almacén?
Excuse me, where's the department store?

Está a dos cuadras de aquí.
It's two blocks from here.

¿Me puede decir dónde queda la joyería?
Can you tell me where the jewelry store is?

Queda al lado de la zapatería.
It's next to the shoe store.

11 El regalo de graduación 🏠

Raúl asked one of his neighbors for directions to places to shop for Héctor's graduation present. He took notes, but now they're all out of order. Help Raúl by putting the dialogue in the correct order and then write what he's going to get for Héctor. c, a, b, e, d; un reloj

a. —Está a tres cuadras de aquí.
b. —También quiero ir al almacén. ¿Me puede decir dónde queda?
c. —Perdón, ¿dónde está la joyería? Quiero comprarle un reloj a mi amigo.
d. —Muchas gracias. ¡Hasta luego!
e. —¿El almacén Estilo? Queda al lado del centro comercial.

12 ¿Cierto o falso? 🏠   Answers in side column

Mira el mapa y escribe **cierto** o **falso** para cada oración. Corrige las oraciones falsas.

1. El almacén Super está al lado de la zapatería Los Pies Dorados.
2. La joyería La Perla está a dos cuadras de la zapatería.
3. El almacén queda cerca de la joyería.
4. La Biblioteca Central está lejos de la zapatería.
5. El almacén está al lado de la biblioteca.

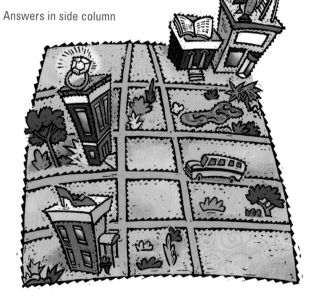

PA
p. 39
Act. 5

GV
p. 21
Acts. 7–8

9-B

PRESENTATION

VOCABULARIO

Write the name of each shop on an index card. Using props or pictures, set up eight stations in the classroom representing the shops, (bread for **panadería,** a flower for **florería,** etc.) Have a student select a card, show it to you, and ask its location, (e.g. **¿Dónde está la panadería?)** The student brings the card to the appropriate station and responds **La panadería está aquí.** When the stations are all identified, ask location questions such as **¿Está la panadería al lado de la zapatería?**

13 Las tiendas Script and answers on p. 123E

CD 9 Tr. 4 Where is Elisa going to shop? First study the following list of gift items and stores. Then listen as Elisa talks about what she's going to buy. Match each item with the correct store.

a. Zapatería Monterrey

b. Panadería La Molina

c. Joyería Central

d. Pastelería Río Grande

e. Juguetería de San Antonio

f. Florería Martínez

g. Almacén Vargas

KINESTHETIC LEARNERS

Arrange several of the students' desks to form a downtown area. Place a sign with the name of a store on each desk. One student then asks directions and a second student answers. The first student then walks to the desired location. You might change the signs around to provide additional practice.

LANGUAGE NOTE

In Spain and Latin America **manzana** is often used instead of **cuadra** for *block*. Also, in direction-giving situations in which English speakers would say "Walk four blocks," many Spanish speakers would say **Camine cuatro calles.**

PHOTO FLASH!
Point out the use of **panadería** and **dulcería** in the photos. Ask students to try to guess the meanings of one of the signs based upon their current knowledge of Spanish.
(**pan caliente** *hot bread*)

ADDITIONAL PRACTICE
15 Ask students to work in groups of three or four to develop a dialogue in which they list a few things they want to buy, talk about the best places to shop for these items, and ask for directions to get to the store.

☀ CLOSE

Use Teaching Transparency 9-1 to review the vocabulary and functions in this **paso.** See suggestions for using the transparency.

🌐 Nota cultural

Although Spanish-speaking people in Texas or elsewhere in the U.S. are more likely to shop in large supermarkets, many shoppers in Spanish-speaking countries still shop at smaller stores that specialize in one thing (i.e., a bakery, a butcher shop, etc.). Shoppers in Madrid or Mexico City might choose to shop at a supermarket, but they could also choose to shop in smaller stores, buying only what is needed for a day or two at a time. That way the food in the kitchen is always fresh, and the shoppers have a chance to meet and chat with friends in the neighborhood. Where does your family shop for groceries?

14 ¿Dónde está?

Imagine that you and your partner are downtown with this shopping list. Take turns saying what kinds of stores you have to visit to get each item. Answers on p. 123K

MODELO   —Quiero comprar un collar.
—Ah, bueno, tienes que ir a la joyería.

collar
sandalias
flores
juguetes
zapatos de tenis
pan
galletas
corbata

15 ¡Vamos de compras!

Get together with two or three classmates and make a list of four things you buy often, such as school supplies, food, compact discs, and books. Then ask each other for the names of stores in your city or town where you can buy the different items you've listed. Say where the stores are located. Be sure to take notes and be ready to report to the class.

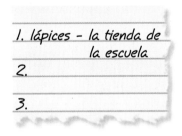

1. lápices – la tienda de la escuela
2.
3.

16 Un regalo para...

Lee el anuncio *(advertisement)* y contesta las preguntas.

1. ¿Qué tipo de regalo es éste? Es un juego de mesa.
2. ¿Cómo se llama este regalo? Se llama Ecojuego.
3. ¿Para qué edades sería *(would it be)* bueno el regalo? Es para personas de doce años o más.
4. ¿Cuánto cuesta? Cuesta cuatro mil setecientas cincuenta pesetas.

• EL JUEGO • Ecológico

Familiarizarse con los grandes y graves problemas del medio ambiente e intentar resolverlos de forma amena y divertida ahora es posible gracias al juego de mesa *Ecojuego*. Está pensado para jóvenes de 12 años en adelante, y consiste en asignar a cada participante — un máximo de seis — el saneamiento ecológico de un tipo de industria contaminante. Su precio es de 4.750 pesetas.

Más información: Grupo Hermes.

Teléfono: 496 14 00 (Barcelona).

17 Amigos y familiares

For each item, write how old the person is, something he or she likes, and a gift idea for this person.

1. your best friend
2. two family members
3. an elderly person you know

Mi mejor amiga Lucila tiene catorce años. Le gustan los videos cómicos. Voy a regalarle un video de Mafalda.

CHALLENGE
Teach students **doble a la derecha** *(turn right)*, **doble a la izquierda** *(turn left)*, and **siga derecho** *(keep going straight ahead)*. Students can then give more elaborate directions for a downtown area, using either a map of your town or the student desks (see Kinesthetic Learners, p. 135).

☀ ASSESS

▸ Testing Program, pp. 55–56
  Quiz 9-1
  Audio CD 9, Tr. 18

▸ Grammar and Vocabulary Quizzes
  Quiz 9-1A or
  Alternative Quiz 9-1A

▸ Alternative Assessment Guide, p. 21

PERFORMANCE ASSESSMENT
Ask students to write a note in Spanish to their parent or guardian saying that they are not going to be home right after school because they have to buy a gift for a friend. They should include what they plan to give the friend and where they are going to buy the gift.

STANDARDS: 1.2, 5.2   **137**

VIDEO INTEGRATION

En camino LEVEL 1B
Video Program
Videocassette 1, 49:18–50:17 OR
Videocassette 3, 1:31:58–1:32:57
(captioned version)

¡Ven conmigo! LEVEL 1
DVD Tutor, Disc 2

 Bell work
On the board or on a transparency write a list of several local stores. Have students identify what type of store each is. (Smith's Bakery—**panadería**) Use the types of stores included in **Vocabulario** on page 135.

☀ MOTIVATE

Ask students whether they prefer to wear new clothes or comfortable old clothes. When do they like to get all dressed up? When do they like to wear what is comfortable?

PREVIEWING

18 Have students use these questions as advance organizers before they watch the video.

SEGUNDO PASO TPR
Storytelling Book
pp. 34, 36

WV3 TEXAS-9

Commenting on clothes; making comparisons

GABI   ¿Qué tal esta falda?
EVA   Es bonita.
LISA   Y es de algodón...
EVA   Y sólo cuesta 12 dólares. ¡Qué barata!
GABI   Sí, ¡es una ganga!

18   ¡No es para Héctor!

Lee lo que dicen las chicas y contesta las preguntas.

1. ¿Qué quiere decir *(what does it mean)* **falda**? ¿Cómo lo sabes?
2. ¿A Eva le gusta la falda? ¿Por qué?
3. Para Eva, ¿doce dólares es mucho o poco dinero?

1. skirt; Gabi is holding up a skirt and asking for an opinion about it
2. Yes, she says it's pretty.
3. It's not very much; she says it's cheap.

PA
Nota cultural
p. 48
Act. 18

In Spanish-speaking countries, looking nice in public is usually considered very important. In general, people never leave their house without clean and well-ironed clothes. This attention to personal care is true even if a household doesn't have indoor plumbing. Clothes may not be new or luxurious, but they're usually immaculately clean. The need to look nice in public also results in rules about what one can and can't do in public. Combing one's hair and putting on makeup are generally done within the privacy of a bedroom or bathroom. Can you think of some "rules" about appearance and grooming in your school or community?

ASÍ SE DICE Commenting on clothes

PA
p. 41
Act. 7

9-2

To find out what someone is wearing, ask:	Your friend might say:

¿Qué ropa lleva hoy Alberto?
What's Alberto wearing today?

¡Lo de siempre! Una **camiseta** con **bluejeans.** *The usual! A T-shirt with bluejeans.*

¿No tiene algo más formal?
Doesn't he have something more formal?

Sí, pero **prefiere llevar ropa cómoda.**
Yes, but he'd rather wear comfortable clothes.

19 ¿Qué dicen?

Read the conversation between Eugenia and Rodolfo. Then figure out the correct order for the illustrations below. Match each illustration to its corresponding sentence or question.

1. ¿Qué ropa vas a llevar a la fiesta? d
2. ¡Lo de siempre! Mi ropa favorita: unos bluejeans con una camiseta. a

3. ¿No tienes algo más formal? c
4. Sí, pero no me gustan los vestidos. Prefiero llevar ropa cómoda. b

TEACH

PRESENTATION
ASÍ SE DICE
Model the expressions in **Así se dice.** Then call on several pairs of students to role-play the first question and answer. After they practice with their books open, have them ask and answer the questions with books closed. Do the same for the second question.

KINESTHETIC LEARNERS
19 Have students role-play the conversation before they put the illustrations in order.

NATIVE SPEAKERS
Ask native speakers for other expressions for talking about clothes they have on and plan to wear. Some other expressions for *to wear* may include **usar** and **tener puesto.** The reflexive verb **ponerse** is quite common for talking about what you plan to wear. (**Voy a ponerme una blusa para ir al baile.**) Encourage native speakers to give other expressions for saying what they're wearing. Have them check spelling of any words they're unsure of.

STANDARDS: 1.1, 1.2, 5.1   **139**

PRESENTATION

VOCABULARIO

Fill a bag with the clothes listed. Name the objects as you hold them up. Then ask **sí/no** questions followed by either/or questions and finally simple questions. Ask students to repeat the vocabulary after you and then have them answer questions such as ¿**De qué color es la blusa de la mujer? ¿Qué tipo de zapatos lleva la mujer? ¿Qué cosas son pardas?**

SLOWER PACE

20 To review expressions students have learned in previous chapters, have students listen and indicate if the speaker is talking about something he or she needs, wants to buy, is looking for, or has to buy.

RE-ENTRY

To review adjective agreement, write the following adjectives on the board and have students match them to the person(s) in **Vocabulario** they describe. (**cómica, alto, morenos, rubias, alta, bajo, simpáticos**)

PRELISTENING

20 As a pre-listening activity have students list the clothes they could possibly wear in each of the situations in Column 2.

PA p. 41 Act. 8

GV p. 22 Act. 9

 9-C

VOCABULARIO

CD-ROM DISC 3

¿Qué ropa vas a llevar tú?

- una camisa blanca
- una blusa amarilla
- una chaqueta gris
- unas botas negras
- una camiseta blanca
- unos bluejeans
- un traje de baño morado
- unos pantalones cortos anaranjados
- una falda parda
- un traje de baño rojo
- unos calcetines azules
- unas sandalias pardas
- unos zapatos de tenis blancos

20 ¿Qué necesitas llevar? Script and answers on p. 123E

Listen as various people talk about the clothing they need for certain occasions. On a separate sheet of paper, write an activity from the word box next to each person's name. Use the cues in the word boxes. And remember, some outfits may be appropriate for more than one kind of event.

CD 9 Tr. 5

Carlos	un baile
Elenita	clases
Sergio	jugar al tenis
Teresa	ir a la piscina
Luis	trabajar en la oficina

 140 *ciento cuarenta* CAPÍTULO 9 ¡Vamos de compras!

21 Mis preferencias

Completa las oraciones con tus preferencias personales.

1. Cuando hace calor, me gusta llevar...
2. En el invierno, cuando hace mucho frío, llevo...
3. Cuando voy al colegio, por lo general llevo...
4. Cuando salgo con mis amigos, llevo...
5. Cuando voy a una fiesta, me gusta llevar...
6. Me gusta practicar deportes. En general llevo...
7. Voy a ir a un picnic. Voy a llevar...
8. En la primavera, me encanta llevar...

22 ¿Cómo es su ropa?

Work with a partner. Describe the clothing someone in your class is wearing. See if your partner can guess the name of the person you're describing.

MODELO —Esta persona lleva una falda azul y una blusa roja.
—¡Es nuestra profesora!

23 El fin de semana

Working in pairs, tell your partner three or four places you'll be going this weekend. Then take turns suggesting what each of you should wear.

MODELO —Voy al cine y al centro comercial.
—Para ir al cine debes llevar bluejeans y una camiseta.

VOCABULARIO EXTRA

la cancha de tenis/fútbol
tennis court/soccer field

el estadio   *stadium*

la iglesia   *church*

el mar   *sea*

las montañas   *mountains*

la pista de correr   *running track*

la sinagoga   *synagogue*

ADDITIONAL PRACTICE

21 After students have finished the written activity, have them talk about their preferences with a partner.

RE-ENTRY

22 Review the names of the colors using square pieces of construction paper. You may want to have students review the colors in the Additional Vocabulary on pages 294–296.

Ask students **¿Qué lleva la señora que escribe en la pizarra?**

SLOWER PACE

23 Before beginning the activity, review vocabulary for the following places with students:

la piscina
el gimnasio
el parque
el lago
el campo
el teatro
el museo
un restaurante
una boda

PRESENTATION

VOCABULARIO

NOTA GRAMATICAL

Hold up photos of people wearing the new articles of clothing. Point out the items to the students and model the vocabulary, having students repeat. Then shuffle the photos and ask **¿Qué lleva _____?** Have them include vocabulary from page 140. Ask them what each is made of, using **ser de** + material.

TACTILE LEARNERS

Bring in pieces of cotton, wool, silk, leather, striped fabric, and plaid fabric. Let students see and feel them as you teach the vocabulary words. Ask students to group the fabrics according to the season they're most often worn in.

LANGUAGE NOTE

Instead of **una camiseta**, some Spanish-speaking countries use **un jersey, una playera, un polo,** or **una remera.** Other words for **los bluejeans** include **los pantalones vaqueros, los mahones, los tejanos,** and **las mezclillas.**

P A p. 43 Act. 10

G V p. 22 Act. 10

9-D

VOCABULARIO

un vestido de algodón

un traje de seda

un cinturón de cuero

de rayas

un suéter de lana

unos zapatos de cuero

de cuadros

---

24 ¿De qué es?

Match the material or pattern to the object it describes.

1. de cuero b
2. de lana d
3. de rayas e
4. de algodón c
5. de seda a

NOTA GRAMATICAL

So far you've used **ser** to describe people and things and to tell where someone is from. The formula **es/son + de** + *material* is used to tell what something is made of.

El suéter **es de lana.**

¿**Son de cuero** tus botas?

G V p. 23 Acts. 11–12

a

b

c

d

e

---

25 ¡Qué ropa tan rara!

What do you think is wrong in each situation pictured? Write a sentence telling what the people are wearing. Then write a sentence telling what you think they should be wearing instead.

MODELO
1. Ella lleva un traje de baño y no lleva zapatos pero está en la nieve. Debe llevar unos pantalones de lana, un suéter, un abrigo,...

VOCABULARIO EXTRA

el abrigo   *coat*
la bolsa   *purse*
la gorra   *cap*
los guantes   *gloves*
el impermeable   *raincoat*
las medias   *stockings*
el paraguas   *umbrella*
el sombrero   *hat*

Modelo

1

2

3

4

26 Una encuesta

Working in groups of three or four, take a survey of what clothing group members wear in the situations listed. Make a chart showing what each person wears and report to the class. Compare your findings with those of other groups.

MODELO —¿Qué ropa llevas para ir al centro comercial con tus amigos?
—Llevo unos pantalones, una camiseta y sandalias.

1. para ir a la escuela
2. para ir de paseo con tu clase
3. en el verano
4. para ir al parque
5. para caminar con el perro
6. para jugar al basquetbol

	Ricky	Monika	Luis
1	una camisa y unos bluejeans		
2			
3			

RE-ENTRY
Clothing Have students cut pictures of clothing from a magazine or construction paper and hang them with tape on a clothesline that you have drawn on the board. As you point to an article of clothing, ask the students **¿Qué es esto?** Then ask individual students to go to the board and point out the article of clothing you ask for. (**Enséñame una camisa.**)

SUGGESTION
26 You may wish to provide each group with a transparency for their chart. Compile the data in the charts on one transparency and make generalizations about class preferences. Have a simple discussion about **la ropa favorita de los jóvenes. (Los jóvenes prefieren los bluejeans, zapatos de tenis, camisas de rayas o de cuadros. Para un baile las chicas prefieren vestidos elegantes, zapatos y medias.)**

CULTURE NOTE
The sizes used for clothes in Spain and Latin America are different from those used in the United States. For example, women's pants that are size 10 in the United States are size 42 in Europe and Latin America, and men's size 32 pants are size 81.

PRESENTATION

ASÍ SE DICE

Bring in a watch, a compact disc, some posters, and a toy. Attach a price tag to each, making sure the compact disc is cheaper than the watch, and the posters and the toy have the same price. Model the conversations in **Así se dice**. Then have students role-play the conversations with each other. After students are comfortable with the exchanges, change the price tags and have students form new conversations.

ADDITIONAL PRACTICE

Bring in pictures of famous people for a photo bank. Compare yourself to one of the people. Have students guess the person to whom you are comparing yourself.

MATH LINK

Ask students to figure out how much money they can save on the following items if they buy them on sale. Then have them calculate their total savings. On the board or on a transparency write the following:

Precios reducidos:	Originalmente	Ahora
Trajes de seda	$225.00	$189.95
Camisas de algodón	25.95	18.00
Zapatos de cuero	63.00	49.98

p. 42
Act. 9

ASÍ SE DICE   Making comparisons

To compare things, you might ask:

¿Cuál es más barato—el reloj o el disco compacto?
Which is cheaper—the watch or the compact disc?

¿Son los carteles tan caros como el juguete?
Are the posters as expensive as the toy?

Some responses might be:

El disco compacto **cuesta menos.**
El reloj es **más caro.**
The compact disc costs less. The watch is more expensive.

Sí. **Son del mismo precio.**
Yes. They're the same price.

27   El periódico de descuentos

Lee el anuncio y contesta las preguntas.

1. ¿Cuál es más caro—los bluejeans o la camiseta tejida *(knit)*? los bluejeans
2. ¿Qué es tan barato como las camisetas de rayón? la camiseta tejida
3. ¿Cuántos colores hay para los jeans? cuatro

Camiseta
de Rayón, Polyester y Algodón IMPORTADA
Unidad
8.450

Camiseta
Tejida Manga Corta Tipo Cachemir
IMPORTADA
Unidad
8.450

Bluejeans
en Variados Colores
Unidad
16.950

144   *ciento cuarenta y cuatro*   CAPÍTULO 9   ¡Vamos de compras!

144   STANDARDS: 1.1, 3.1, 5.1

GRAMÁTICA Making comparisons

1. To make comparisons with adjectives in Spanish, use the following formulas:

más + *adjective* + **que**	*more . . . than*
menos + *adjective* + **que**	*less . . . than*
tan + *adjective* + **como**	*as . . . as*

p. 24
Acts.
13–14

2. The adjective matches the gender and number of the thing it describes.

La camisa blanca es **más bonita que** el vestido azul.

Las sandalias son **menos cómodas que** los zapatos de tenis.

El cinturón es **tan barato como** la corbata.

28 ¿Cómo son? Script and answers on p. 123E

CD 9 Tr. 6

Look at the pairs of drawings. Listen and match what you hear with the item being described.

1. 2. 3. 4. 5. 6.

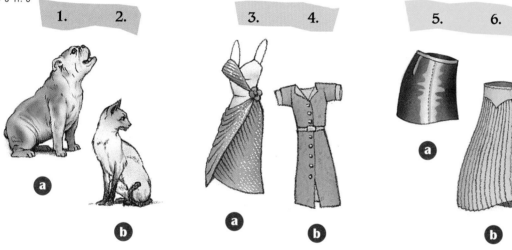

29 Regalos y más regalos

You need to buy gifts for two family members and two friends. Using the gift ideas from this chapter, write two sentences for each person: say what he or she wants or needs, then say what you want to buy him or her. Use a comparison to explain your choice.

MODELO Mi hermana necesita ropa nueva. Quiero comprarle una blusa porque es más barata que un vestido. Los vestidos son caros.

PRESENTATION
GRAMÁTICA
Prepare sentences like those in **Así se dice** on page 144 and cut out each word. Give each group an envelope with a sentence written on slips of paper. Have groups arrange the words to form a sentence.

☀ CLOSE

Ask the class about the material of various students' clothing. (**¿De qué es el suéter de** [name]**?**) Then have pairs tell each other what they are wearing and describe its material and color. How do the seasons affect their clothing choices?

☀ ASSESS

▶ Testing Program, pp. 57–58
Quiz 9-2
Audio CD 9, Tr. 19

▶ Grammar and Vocabulary Quizzes
Quiz 9-2A or
Alternative Quiz 9-2A

▶ Alternative Assessment Guide, p. 21

PERFORMANCE ASSESSMENT
Have students write a letter to a friend describing their favorite outfit in detail. (colors, fabrics, where they wear it, a comparison of this outfit with others)

STANDARDS: 1.1, 1.2, 4.1, 5.1, 5.2 **145**

VIDEO INTEGRATION

En camino **LEVEL 1B**
Video Program
Videocassette 1, 55:35–58:30

¡Ven conmigo! LEVEL 1
DVD Tutor, Disc 2

TEACHER NOTES
• See *Video Guide* for activities related to the **Panorama cultural.**

• Remind students that cultural information may be included in the Quizzes and the Chapter Test.

• The interviewees' language represents informal, unrehearsed speech. Occasionally, text has been edited for clarity.

MOTIVATING ACTIVITY
Ask students to look at the clothing of teenagers in photos throughout this book and to compare it with the clothing they like to wear. Ask them to identify clothing styles that are popular both with them and the Spanish-speaking teenagers. Do they notice any differences?

LANGUAGE NOTE
Bárbara says she's wearing **un vestido de vaquero.** In Spain, **vaquero** *(cowboy)* refers to denim. **Vaqueros** are blue-jeans, for example.

Panorama cultural

CD 9
Trs. 7–10

CD-ROM DISC 3

¿Estás a la moda?

Hispanic teens usually try to look as fashionable as they possibly can. Much of what is popular in the United States is also in style in Spain and Latin America. But what counts is quality, not quantity. Here are some comments from teenagers about what is usually **de moda** and what's definitely not.

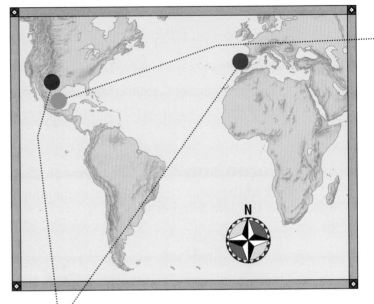

¿Está de moda en tu pueblo la ropa de Bárbara? ¿Por qué sí, o por qué no?

Bárbara
Sevilla,
España
CD 9 Tr. 8

Hoy llevo un vestido vaquero a cuadros, un reloj, una pulsera de tela, una pulsera de cuero, unos pendientes y un collar, que es el elefante de la suerte.

Luis Manuel describe lo que le gusta llevar. ¿A ti te gusta la ropa que le gusta a él?

Luis Manuel
San Antonio,
Texas CD 9 Tr. 9

Pues, me gusta llevar pantalones largos y una camiseta. Me gustan el verde, azul, blanco y negro.

Lo que se pone Héctor depende de la ocasión. ¿Qué lleva para una fiesta de un amigo?

● **Héctor**
México, D.F., México
CD 9 Tr. 10

Camisa, pantalones de jeans, zapatos, ir bien peinado.

¿Y si es una fiesta que organizan tus padres?

Saco, camisa, corbata, también zapatos.

1 ¿Lleva Bárbara un vestido o unos pantalones? un vestido

2 ¿Puedes nombrar una joya *(a piece of jewelry)* que lleva Bárbara? Possible answers: una pulsera de tela, una de cuero, unos pendientes, un collar, un reloj

3 ¿Cuáles son los colores que a Luis Manuel le gusta llevar? el verde, el azul, el blanco y el negro

4 ¿Cuáles le gustan más a Luis Manuel, los pantalones largos o los pantalones cortos? los pantalones largos

5 La ropa que lleva Héctor para ir a una fiesta de sus padres es diferente a la ropa que lleva para una fiesta de un amigo. ¿Cómo es diferente? Lleva ropa más formal para ir a la fiesta de sus padres.

6 Nombra un artículo de ropa que lleva Héctor para ir a una fiesta de sus padres. Possible answers: una corbata, un saco

Para pensar y hablar... Answers will vary.
A. Work with two other classmates. Suggest three reasons why people should be concerned with style, and three reasons why they shouldn't.
B. Describe two articles of clothing that the interviewees talk about that you like or don't like, and say why.

Cuaderno para hispanohablantes, pp. 44–45

147

PRESENTATION
Have students listen to the audio recording or watch the video. Ask for volunteers to read one of the interviews aloud for pronunciation practice. As a challenge ask students to guess the meanings of the following words:
la pulsera *bracelet*
un collar *necklace*
el saco *coat*

PREGUNTAS
1. ¿Quién es de San Antonio? ¿de México? ¿de España? (Luis Manuel, Héctor, Bárbara)
2. ¿Qué lleva Bárbara hoy? (un vestido vaquero de cuadros)
3. ¿Qué tipo de pantalones le gustan a Luis Manuel? (largos)
4. ¿Cuándo lleva Héctor ropa más formal? (cuando sus padres organizan una fiesta)

CRITICAL THINKING
Students learned the word **peine** in Chapter 7. Ask them to guess what Héctor means when he says **ir bien peinado.**

148

VIDEO INTEGRATION

En camino LEVEL 1B

Video Program
Videocassette 1, 48:49–49:17 OR
Videocassette 3, 1:31:29–1:31:57
(captioned version)

¡Ven conmigo! LEVEL 1
DVD Tutor, Disc 2

Bell work

On a transparency write the description in Spanish of a person and the clothes he or she is wearing. Have students use colored pencils, markers, or crayons to draw this person. After a few minutes, students share their drawings and see if they included all the details, such as hair/eye color, height, and clothes.

KINESTHETIC LEARNERS

30 Have students work in groups of three to practice the conversation from the **paso** opener before they correct the false statements. Have them use props if available.

☀ MOTIVATE

Ask students what types of things they talk about before deciding to buy something. Do they ask for opinions from friends and family? What phrases do they use? Do they shop around for a good price? What stores do they go to?

TERCER PASO

(TPR) Storytelling Book pp. 35, 36

Expressing preferences; asking about prices and paying for something

WV3 TEXAS-9

EVA ¿Cuál prefieren, la blusa roja o la de rayas?

GABI Yo prefiero la roja. ¿Cuánto cuesta?

EVA Uy, cuarenta dólares. Es cara.

LISA ¿Qué les parecen estos pantalones cortos?

GABI Eh... de verdad, Lisa, no me gustan para nada los cuadros.

30 La ropa nueva

Lee las oraciones y contesta **cierto** o **falso**.
Después corrige las oraciones falsas.

1. A Gabi le gusta más la blusa de rayas.
2. A Lisa no le gustan los pantalones cortos de cuadros.
3. Eva piensa que la blusa roja es cara.
4. Lisa mira un vestido.

1. falso; Gabi prefiere la blusa roja.
2. falso; A Gabi no le gustan los pantalones cortos de cuadros.
3. cierto
4. falso; Lisa mira unos pantalones cortos.

ASÍ SE DICE Expressing preferences

p. 44
Acts. 11–12

9-3

To find out which thing a friend prefers, ask:

¿Cuál de estos trajes prefieres?
Which of these suits do you prefer?

¿Qué camisa te gusta más? ¿La verde o la amarilla?
Which shirt do you like better? The green one or the yellow one?

Your friend might say:

Prefiero el azul.
I prefer the blue one.

La verde. **Además, te queda muy bien.**
The green one. Besides, it looks good on you.

31 La ropa del tío Pepe

Tío Pepe has no fashion sense at all. Help him figure out what clothes to wear for different activities. With a partner, take turns role-playing tío Pepe and his **sobrino/a** *(nephew/niece).* Answers on p. 123K

MODELO para ir a la iglesia / pantalones negros / pantalones anaranjados

TÍO PEPE ¿Cuál de estos pantalones prefieres para ir a la iglesia? ¿Los negros o los anaranjados?

SOBRINO/A Prefiero los negros.

1. para pescar en el lago / pantalones cortos verdes / bluejeans
2. para ir al trabajo / sandalias pardas / zapatos de cuero
3. para ir a la boda de Antonio / camiseta de rayas / camisa blanca
4. para llevar con unos pantalones negros / calcetines blancos / calcetines negros
5. para ir de compras / traje gris / bluejeans
6. para llevar con el traje gris / camisa amarilla / camisa rosada

BERNIE WILLIAMS
Receptor

PEDRO MARTINEZ
Lanzador

32 Los uniformes

¿Cuál de estos uniformes prefieres? Escribe tres oraciones. Describe el uniforme que más te gusta. También escribe si le queda bien al jugador. Answers on p. 123K

※ **TEACH**

PRESENTATION

ASÍ SE DICE
Bring in magazine pictures of people wearing various types of clothing to introduce expressing preferences. Then ask **¿Cuál de estas camisas prefieres para un partido de fútbol? Yo prefiero la roja.**

LANGUAGE NOTES
• In **Prefiero el azul,** the noun **traje** has been left out. Point out that the article and the adjective always agree with the omitted noun.

• Point out that **te queda bien** is patterned after the expressions students know with **gustar.** Ask students how to say that the shoes look good on someone. (**Le quedan muy bien los zapatos.**)

BACKGROUND
Bernie Williams was born in San Juan, Puerto Rico. He won the American League Gold Glove for outfielders from 1997–99.

Pedro Martinez was born in Manoguayabo, Dominican Republic. As a pitcher for the Boston Red Sox he leads all active starting pitchers in career winning percentage and earned run average.

PRESENTATION

NOTA GRAMATICAL

Model two items of different gender. (**¿Qué te gusta más para ir a la iglesia, esta falda o este vestido?**) Then ask various students to express their preferences.

ASÍ SE DICE

To introduce talking about prices, put price tags on the articles of clothing used for the Presentation on page 149. The tags should be large enough to be easily read by the whole class.

ADDITIONAL PRACTICE

34 Have students work in pairs to create conversations in which they shop for clothes, and comment about what they see. Ask volunteers to perform their conversations in front of the class.

PA
p. 45
Act. 13

GV
p. 25
Acts. 15–16

NOTA GRAMATICAL

Demonstrative adjectives point out people and things. Like other adjectives, they agree in gender and number with the noun they modify.

MASCULINE

este vestido | **estos** vestidos
this dress | *these dresses*

ese vestido | **esos** vestidos
that dress | *those dresses*

FEMININE

esta falda | **estas** faldas

esa falda | **esas** faldas

33 Opiniones

Alicia and her sister Mónica are shopping for clothes. Write a sentence that Alicia might say about each item of clothing they look at. Use demonstrative adjectives. Answers on p. 123K

MODELO   blusa / feo
—Oye, Mónica, esta blusa es fea, ¿no?

1. camisa / caro
2. botas / feo
3. suéter / pequeño
4. zapatos / barato
5. falda / grande
6. cinturón / bonito
7. chaqueta / barato
8. vestido / caro

34 Opiniones diferentes

Now it's Mónica's turn! Work with a partner. Using your sentences from Activity 33, take turns giving Mónica's responses to Alicia's comments.

MODELO   —Oye, Mónica, esta blusa es fea, ¿no?
—No, Alicia, esa blusa no es fea. Es bonita.

35 Preferencias

Work in groups of three. Look at the advertisement on page 144. Take turns asking and answering which things you prefer. Explain why you prefer each thing.

PA
pp. 45–46
Acts. 14–15

GV
p. 26
Acts. 17–18

ASÍ SE DICE   Asking about prices and paying for something

To ask how much one thing costs, say:

¿Cuánto cuesta esta chaqueta?
How much does this jacket cost?

To ask how much two or more things cost, say:

¿Cuánto cuestan los zapatos?
How much do the shoes cost?

Some responses might be:

Cuesta 90 dólares.

Cuestan 175 sucres.

150 STANDARDS: 1.1, 4.1

36 El regreso al colegio

Elena and Verónica are buying new clothes to go back to school. Complete their conversation with **este/estos, esa/esas,** or **cuesta/cuestan.**

ELENA Necesito dos pares de bluejeans. Prefiero comprar uno negro y uno azul. ¿Cuánto ___1___ esos bluejeans? cuestan

VERÓNICA Cuestan veintinueve dólares cada uno. Mira, Elena, ¿qué piensas de ___2___ cinturón de cuero? este/ese

ELENA Me encanta. ¿Cuánto ___3___? cuesta

VERÓNICA Sólo ___4___ tres dólares. ¡Qué barato! cuesta

ELENA Me lo llevo *(I'll take it)*. También quiero unos aretes negros y blancos. Pero no tengo mucho dinero.

VERÓNICA ¿Qué piensas de ___5___ aretes? ___6___ cinco veinticinco. estos/esos, Cuestan

ELENA Son baratos, pero no me gustan para nada. Prefiero comprar ___7___ falda de lana. ¿Cuánto ___8___? esa/esta, cuesta

VERÓNICA ¡Uy! ¡___9___ cuarenta y ocho dólares! Cuesta

GV
p. 26
Act. 19

VOCABULARIO

¡Es un robo!	*It's a rip-off!*
¡Qué barato!	*How cheap!*
¡Qué caro!	*How expensive!*
¡Qué ganga!	*What a bargain!*

LOS MEJORES PRECIOS DE LAS VACACIONES

37 ¡Qué caro!

Script and answers on p. 123F

CD 9 Tr. 11 Listen to the conversations between a clerk and some customers. Based on what you hear, match each item and the price.

1. blusa
2. camisa
3. bluejeans
4. vestido
5. zapatos

a. $17.00
b. $760.00
c. $58.00
d. $189.00
e. $8.55

38 La ropa para el verano

Take turns asking each other the price of six of the items shown in the advertisement. Answer by making up what you consider a fair price for that item.

MODELO —¿Cuánto cuestan los zapatos azules y rojos?
—Cuestan once dólares.
—¡Qué ganga!

Answers will vary.

PRESENTATION

VOCABULARIO

Ask questions one by one about prices of articles of clothing. Include the expressions from the **Vocabulario.** (**¿Cuánto cuesta esta corbata? Cuesta treinta dólares. ¡Es un robo!**) Then hold up objects and ask individual students to answer the question **¿Cuánto cuesta(n) _____?** Each student is to answer by giving a price and an appropriate expression from the **Vocabulario.**

SLOWER PACE

37 Review colors and numbers before having students listen to this activity.

☀ **CLOSE**

Use Teaching Transparency 9-3 to review the material from this **paso** with students. If time permits, use Teaching Transparencies 9-1 and 9-2 for a comprehensive review.

📖 **EN MI CUADERNO**
40 For an additional journal entry suggestion for Chapter 9, see *Practice and Activity Book*, p. 88.

NATIVE SPEAKERS
Ask students to make a shopping list with at least 10 items that contain the letters *s, c,* and *z* other than the examples in **Letra y sonido** on page 153. Have students exchange lists to check spelling.

 **COOPERATIVE LEARNING**
Divide the class into groups of three. Each group member is reponsible for helping the other members practice two language functions from each **Así se dice.** Then have students practice the functions with their group until everyone can do each one. At random select a student from each group and have her or him demonstrate one of the functions by responding to your cues. Give the entire group the grade which that student earned. Select a person from another group for a second function, and so forth.

39 De compras

Imagine that you and your partner are shopping for gifts by catalogue. For each pair of things, take turns asking each other which thing you prefer. Say why you prefer that item, ask how much it is, and then comment on the price. Answers will vary.

MODELO —Para mi mamá, ¿prefieres la blusa de rayas azules y blancas o la blusa amarilla?
—Prefiero la blusa amarilla. ¿Cuánto cuesta la blusa amarilla?
—Cuesta veintidós dólares.
—¡Qué ganga!

40 En mi cuaderno

 Write a conversation in your journal. Pretend to be a clerk who is trying to talk a customer out of buying clothes that don't look good on him or her. Tell the customer that the colors don't look good or that the clothes are too big or too small. Tell the customer about some clothes that do look good instead.

152 *ciento cincuenta y dos* CAPÍTULO 9 ¡Vamos de compras!

152 STANDARDS: 1.1, 1.2, 5.1

Nota cultural PA p. 48 Act. 17

Have you ever wondered what kind of money is used in other countries? In some Latin American countries, currency is named after a person: Colón, Balboa, Bolívar.

Argentina el peso   **Guatemala** el quetzal
Colombia el peso   **México** el nuevo peso
Costa Rica el colón   **Panamá** el balboa
Ecuador el sucre   **Perú** el nuevo sol
España el euro   **Venezuela** el bolívar

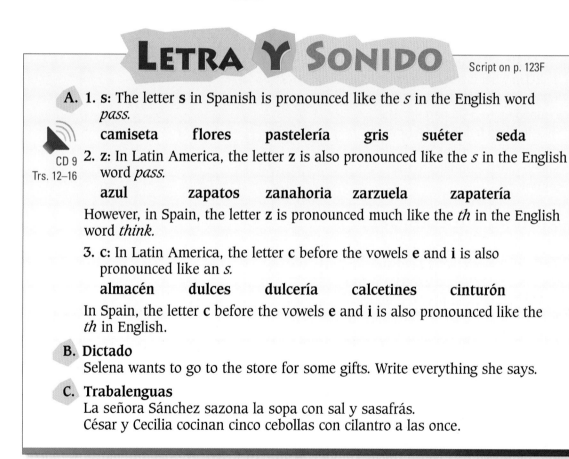

LETRA Y SONIDO

Script on p. 123F

CD 9
Trs. 12–16

A. 1. s: The letter **s** in Spanish is pronounced like the *s* in the English word *pass.*

camiseta   flores   pastelería   gris   suéter   seda

2. z: In Latin America, the letter **z** is also pronounced like the *s* in the English word *pass.*

azul   zapatos   zanahoria   zarzuela   zapatería

However, in Spain, the letter **z** is pronounced much like the *th* in the English word *think.*

3. c: In Latin America, the letter **c** before the vowels **e** and **i** is also pronounced like an *s.*

almacén   dulces   dulcería   calcetines   cinturón

In Spain, the letter **c** before the vowels **e** and **i** is also pronounced like the *th* in English.

B. Dictado
Selena wants to go to the store for some gifts. Write everything she says.

C. Trabalenguas
La señora Sánchez sazona la sopa con sal y sasafrás.
César y Cecilia cocinan cinco cebollas con cilantro a las once.

CULTURE NOTE
Other currencies of Spanish-speaking countries are as follows:
Bolivia *el boliviano*
Chile *el peso*
Cuba *el peso*
El Salvador *el colón*
Honduras *el lempira*
Nicaragua *la córdoba*
Paraguay *el guaraní*
República Dominicana *el peso*
Uruguay *el peso*

☀ ASSESS

▸ Testing Program, pp. 59–60
Quiz 9-3
Audio CD 9, Tr. 20

▸ Grammar and Vocabulary Quizzes
Quiz 9-3A or
Alternative Quiz 9-3A

▸ Alternative Assessment Guide, p. 21

PERFORMANCE ASSESSMENT
Have pairs of students create a dialogue between a customer and the clerk in a clothing store. Have them include expressions of courtesy, express preferences, inquire about prices, and pay for their purchases. The work may be performed or written. Encourage students to try out different selling styles. (hard sell, soft sell)

PRESENTATION

Ask students who the first people to live in North America were. (American Indians) Who were next after the American Indians to move into places like Florida, Texas, and California? (the Spanish) How did they help each other? (They shared food.) What did the American Indians teach the Spanish about? (new vegetables and other local foods) What did the Spanish teach the American Indians? (how to raise pigs, sheep, and cattle) What might cause conflicts between them? (different customs, different religions)

TEACHER NOTES

• The first Spanish missions were in Florida.

• A friar is a monk or a member of a religious order. A friar leads a life of poverty and has no personal property.

• St. Francis of Assisi (1181?–1226) founded an order of monks in 1209. Franciscan friars preach and do charitable and missionary work.

CHALLENGE

Have students research the Alamo to present the historical events that took place there. You might contrast this by showing the movie *The Alamo* starring John Wayne.

LA HISTORIA

Misiones españolas Franciscan friars founded missions in northern New Spain between the 1500s and 1700s in what are today the states of California, Arizona, Texas, New Mexico, and Florida. These missions were founded in order to claim land for Spain and to convert the native people to Catholicism.

Misión San José was built in 1720 in what is now San Antonio, Texas. At one time, the compound housed up to 350 people. The mission had fields and a farm nearby, and a large cattle and sheep ranch 25 miles to the southwest.

1 ¿Producir o comprar?

According to the paragraph above and the drawing, what food and supplies could the people who lived in the mission compound produce for themselves? What other supplies might they have needed to buy? Use the list below.

chicken	vegetables
beef	water
coffee	wool blankets
salt	horseshoes
corn	clothes

mission: corn, vegetables, water, beef, chicken, horseshoes, clothes; **outside supplies:** coffee, salt, wool blankets

1. Church
2. Friar Housing
3. Convent Garden
4. Garden Well
5. Well
6. East Gate
7. Housing
8. Bastion
9. Southeast Gate
10. Southwest Gate
11. Ovens
12. West Gate
13. Granary
14. Carpentry Shop
15. Kilns
16. Mill
17. Vat
18. Aqueduct

2 El trabajo

From the drawing above, what work would most interest you if you had lived in the San José mission? Building furniture? sewing clothes? shearing sheep? Explain your reasons. Answers will vary.

LA GEOGRAFÍA/LAS MATEMÁTICAS

Las misiones de Alta California San Diego de Alcalá Mission was founded in 1769 in what is now San Diego, California. In 1770, San Carlos Borromeo de Carmelo was founded, 650 miles to the north in what is now the town of Carmel. In the beginning, mules were used to deliver food and supplies between San Diego and Carmel. Since the trip was both difficult and dangerous, a chain of missions was founded along **El Camino Real** to provide rest, shelter, and protection for travelers. Each mission was about one day's journey from another by mule.

3 Cincuenta millas en mula

1. Carmel is 650 miles to the north of San Diego. If a mule travels about fifty miles in one day, how many missions should the friars establish between San Diego and Carmel? 13

2. Count the missions between San Diego and Carmel on the map. How many more missions were constructed than you might have guessed? 14, 1 more

4 Las primeras misiones

1. Which missions were built first, the missions in Texas or in California? Texas

2. Why do you think they built missions in that region first?
Possible answer: Texas is closer to Mexico City

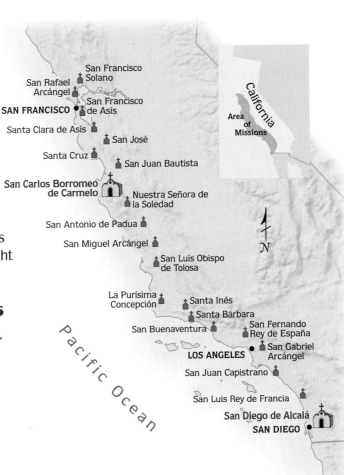

San Francisco Solano
San Rafael Arcángel
San Francisco de Asís
SAN FRANCISCO
Santa Clara de Asís
San José
Santa Cruz
San Juan Bautista
San Carlos Borromeo de Carmelo
Nuestra Señora de la Soledad
San Antonio de Padua
San Miguel Arcángel
San Luis Obispo de Tolosa
La Purísima Concepción
Santa Inés
Santa Bárbara
San Buenaventura
San Fernando Rey de España
LOS ANGELES
San Gabriel Arcángel
San Juan Capistrano
San Luis Rey de Francia
San Diego de Alcalá
SAN DIEGO

California
Area of Missions

Pacific Ocean

N

PRESENTATION
Have students brainstorm names of cities in California before they look at the map on this page. How many have Spanish names?

CHALLENGE
Have students make a time-table for the following missions using the information on these pages. Mission list: San Diego de Alcalá, San Carlos Borromeo de Carmelo, San Antonio de Valero. What other events in Spanish history could they include in this timetable?

HISTORY LINK
California was part of Mexico until 1848 when the Treaty of Guadalupe was signed at the end of the Mexican American War. Mexico lost California, New Mexico (including Arizona), and Texas.

VAMOS A LEER

READING STRATEGY
Scanning for specific
information

TEACHER NOTE
After they have read **Estrategia,**
ask students what additional
strategies they have used in
previous readings that might
be helpful. They might mention
using cognates, using background knowledge, or guessing
words from context.

 PREREADING

MOTIVATING ACTIVITY

Ask students about San
Antonio. Have they ever visited
it, read about it, or seen anything about it on TV? Do they
know anything about San
Antonio's festivals? If so, ask
them to share their knowledge
with the class.

RE-ENTRY
Listening Read aloud
descriptions of the four sections of the reading as a listening comprehension activity.
Students are to respond with
the name of the corresponding
section.

READING

ADDITIONAL PRACTICE

C Students might also develop a telephone conversation
between an employee of the
San Antonio Chamber of
Commerce and a prospective
visitor to the city.

 Estrategia

Scanning for specific
information means looking
for one thing at a time, without concerning yourself with the rest of the text.
Some examples of scanning are looking
up the spelling of a word in a dictionary
or hunting through the TV listing to see
what time a certain show comes on.

¡A comenzar!
Let's look at the pictures and titles in
this brochure about San Antonio.

A Using pictures only, determine
which of these topics are
addressed in the article.

1. sports
2. a zoo
③ eating
④ shopping
⑤ community celebrations
⑥ an old Spanish building
7. holidays

B Suppose you're in a hurry and
don't have time to read every
section. Look only at the titles to
determine where you could read
about the following. Write the
name of the appropriate title for
each.

1. where to shop Compras
2. churches Las misiones
3. where to have dinner Restaurantes
4. some local celebrations Festivales

Al grano
From the photos and subtitles you
get a general overview of this article.
You know what areas are mentioned,
and you should be able to locate
important details quickly.

¿Te acuerdas?

Use pictures, titles, and subtitles first. It will
make understanding easier and it will save you
time. Sometimes you're only interested in one
small part of an article.

C Imagine that you work for the
Chamber of Commerce. Answer
the tourists' questions, using the
information in the brochure. You
already know where to look for
the answers, but you'll have to
read the descriptions thoroughly
to find out the details. Answer the
questions in Spanish. Answers on p. 123K

1. Are there any restaurants that
serve spicy food?
2. How do I get to the riverfront
shopping district?
3. What's the name of the riverfront area that has stores?
4. In which mission does the
Mariachi Mass take place?
5. In what month does the
Muestra Ganadera y Rodeo
festival take place?

D Escribe una lista de lo que te gustaría hacer en San Antonio. Describe por lo menos tres actividades.

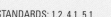

Ofrece generosas porciones de su vida cosmopolita, incluyendo finos restaurantes, vida nocturna, deportes profesionales y bellas artes. Nuestros grupos étnicos añaden su propio sabor.

SAN ANTONIO

Las Misiones

Parte del sistema de Parques Nacionales, es el conjunto más completo de misiones españolas en los Estados Unidos. Cada una de las cuatro misiones hermanas del Álamo tiene una historia fascinante que contar. No deje de asistir a la Misa de los Mariachis los domingos en la Misión San José. Es un recuerdo inolvidable.

Compras

¿Listo para ir de compras? Tome un taxi acuático al refrescante centro comercial al lado del Paseo del Río. Encuentre tesoros deslumbrantes en los centros comerciales de la ciudad. Disfrute de las artesanías de La Villita y El Mercado.

Restaurantes

Nuestra herencia multicultural hace posible que usted pueda escoger entre muchos restaurantes, desde parrilladas de estilo tejano y picantes platillos mexicanos hasta la cocina continental, oriental y "alta americana".

Festivales

En abril hay desfiles y fiestas en la calle. En febrero tenemos la Muestra Ganadera y Rodeo. En agosto, se celebra la herencia multicultural de Texas en el Festival "Texas Folklife".

Cuaderno para hispanohablantes, pp. 41–43

GROUP WORK

Have each student write one question about each section of the reading. Have the students ask these aloud in small groups and see which group member can correctly answer first.

※ POSTREADING

SUGGESTION

Have students do class presentations on some aspect of San Antonio. Information on historical places such as the Alamo is readily available and travel guides discussing restaurants and shopping can be obtained from many libraries. Or you could create a bulletin board about San Antonio, with students bringing in pictures or drawings with Spanish captions.

TEACHER NOTE

For additional readings, see *Practice and Activity Book*, p. 47.

 MULTICULTURAL LINK

Divide the class into two groups to research and write a report on the Battle of the Alamo and the events that led up to it. One group will write their report from the perspective of the Texans, and the other from the Mexican perspective. Follow a presentation of the reports with a discussion of how and why the two reports are different.

The **Repaso** reviews and integrates all four skills and culture in preparation for the Chapter Test.

SUGGESTION

Hold up two magazine or catalog photos of clothing and tell the class which you prefer. Repeat with several pairs of pictures. Then show two pictures of the same item and ask **¿Cuál de estos/as _____ prefieres?** or **¿Qué _____ te gusta más?** Have students answer. Pass out catalogs or photos and have students continue this activity in small groups.

SLOWER PACE

3 Allow students to conduct this activity using notes.

REPASO

MARCAR: go.hrw.com
PALABRA CLAVE:
WV3 TEXAS-9

Script and answers on p. 123F

1 Listen as Sara and Ana talk about what Sara needs for the costume party (**fiesta de disfraces**). Choose the things she mentions. Not all items will be used.

CD 9
Tr. 17

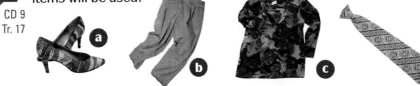

2 Alberto va a ayudar a comprar los regalos para la familia. Él y su mamá van de compras, pero primero tienen que hacer una lista. Lee su conversación y contesta las preguntas.

ALBERTO A papi le quiero regalar un cinturón. Podemos comprarle uno de cuero en el Almacén Borinquen. Es buena idea, ¿no?

MAMÁ Pienso que le va a gustar. ¿Qué le compramos a tu hermanita?

ALBERTO En la Juguetería El Gozo tienen un juego de damas chinas *(Chinese checkers)* muy barato.

MAMÁ Yo prefiero regalarle unos libros. Podemos ir a la Librería Doménico después de comprar el regalo para tu papá. La librería está a una cuadra del almacén.

ALBERTO ¿Qué piensas regalarme a mí?

MAMÁ ¿A ti? ¡Te voy a regalar unos calcetines! Eso es lo que quieres, ¿verdad?

ALBERTO ¡Ay, mamá!

1. ¿Qué le van a regalar al papá de Alberto? un cinturón de cuero
2. ¿Qué le van a regalar a la hermana de Alberto? unos libros
3. ¿Adónde van después de comprar el regalo del papá de Alberto? a la Librería Doménico
4. ¿Qué dice la mamá que le va regalar a Alberto? unos calcetines

3 Read the sentences and write **cierto** or **falso** for each one.
1. Teenagers in Spanish-speaking countries follow many of the same fashions as teens in the United States. cierto
2. Shoppers in Spanish-speaking countries do all their shopping in department stores and large grocery stores. falso
3. The currency in several Spanish-speaking countries is named after important cities. falso

158 *ciento cincuenta y ocho*   CAPÍTULO 9   ¡Vamos de compras!

158 STANDARDS: 1.1, 1.2, 4.2

4 Take turns telling your partner that you're going to give the following things to various relatives for their birthday. *Answers in side column*

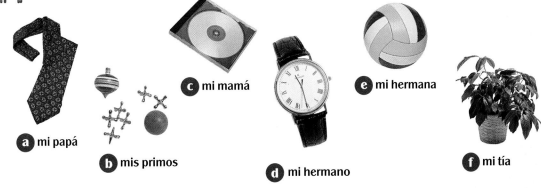

a mi papá

b mis primos

c mi mamá

d mi hermano

e mi hermana

f mi tía

5

Vamos a escribir

Write an advertisement for a newspaper, announcing a big sale on all types of clothing for the next season. Include different colors, materials, and prices. Be sure to stress the bargains. Be creative! And remember, when you're writing for publication it's very important to check your work for accuracy and clear presentation.

Estrategia

Revising After writing your first draft, have a classmate proofread your work. Use the corrections your proofreader suggests to help you revise your advertisement. In addition to spelling and grammar corrections, remember to make any changes that will make your advertisement clearer and more effective. Ask yourself if there's any information missing that would make it a better advertisement. Then rewrite your advertisement with the corrections.

6 ## S I T U A C I Ó N

Work with a partner. One of you will play the role of a customer and the other the role of a salesperson in a gift shop. The customer is looking for a gift. Create a dialogue in which the salesperson tries to help the customer by making some gift suggestions (using the items given in the **Vocabulario** on p. 132). After both the customer and the store clerk have talked about prices, made comparisons, and expressed preferences, the customer finally decides on a gift.

Cuaderno para hispanohablantes, p. 44

📁 **PORTFOLIO**

4 Oral Suggest that students record their dialogue from this activity as an oral Portfolio entry. For Portfolio suggestions, see *Alternative Assessment Guide,* p. 13.

5 Written This activity may be used as a written Portfolio entry. For Portfolio suggestions, see *Assessment Guide,* p. 13.

SUGGESTION

6 You may wish to have students use play money as they buy items, so they can practice making change. Have students create a cashier's booth. Explain that in many stores in Spanish-speaking countries customers pay at the cashier's booth, where they are given a receipt stamped "paid." They then return to the checkout counter, where the clerk delivers the merchandise and gives them another receipt. Have students price the items using one of the currencies in **Nota cultural,** page 153.

Answers to Activity 4

Answers will vary. Possible answers:

a. Le voy a regalar una corbata a mi papá.

b. Les voy a regalar unos juguetes a mis primos.

c. Voy a darle un disco compacto a mi mamá.

d. Voy a regalarle un reloj a mi hermano.

e. Le voy a regalar un voleibol a mi hermana.

f. Le voy a regalar una planta a mi tía.

STANDARDS: 1.3, 5.1, 5.2   **159**

This page is intended to help students prepare independently for the Chapter Test. It is designed for the students to work on their own initiative and consists of a brief checklist of the major points covered in the chapter. The students should be reminded that it is a checklist only and not necessarily everything that will appear on the test. Remind students that cultural information is included in the Chapter Test.

Answers to Activity 1

1. ¿Qué le regalo a Yolanda?
2. Answers will vary. Possible answer:
   Puedes comprarle un reloj.

Answers to Activity 2

Answers will vary. Possible answers:

¿Dónde está la librería? Está a dos cuadras de aquí.

¿Me puede decir dónde queda la panadería? Queda al lado de la zapatería.

Answers to Activity 4

Answers will vary. Possible answers:

a. El collar es más caro que los aretes.
b. La chaqueta de cuadros es más larga que la chaqueta de cuero.
c. El zapato negro es más formal que la sandalia.

¡A VER SI PUEDO...

WV3 TEXAS-9

▼ Can you talk about giving gifts?　p. 131

1 You and a friend are shopping for presents for Yolanda's birthday party on Saturday. How would you . . .? Answers in side column

1. ask your friend what you should give Yolanda as a gift
2. suggest to your friend what present to buy

▼ Can you ask for and give directions downtown? p. 134

2 You're at the spot marked X on this map. Can you ask someone where the bookstore and the bakery are? How would he or she answer?

Answers in side column

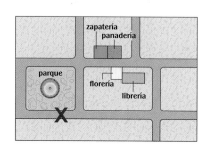

▼ Can you comment on clothes? p. 139

3 How would you describe the clothes you're wearing right now? Are they formal or ordinary? Describe the color, pattern, and material of each item and say whether you like it. Answers will vary.

▼ Can you make comparisons? p. 144

4 How would you compare the two things in each drawing? Answers in side column

▼ Can you express preferences? p. 149

5 Look at the drawings in Activity 4. For each pair of things, tell which one you prefer and why. Answers will vary.

▼ Can you ask about prices and pay for something? p. 150

6 You're at a shopping center in Mexico. How would you ask the prices of the following items? How might the clerk answer?

a. a yellow cotton blouse ¿Cuánto cuesta la blusa amarilla de algodón? Cuesta...
b. a silk tie ¿Cuánto cuesta la corbata de seda? Cuesta...
c. some candy ¿Cuánto cuestan los dulces? Cuestan...
d. a greeting card ¿Cuánto cuesta la tarjeta? Cuesta...

VOCABULARIO

PRIMER PASO

Talking about giving gifts

el arete — *earring*
buscar — *to look for*
la camiseta — *T-shirt*
la cartera — *wallet*
el collar — *necklace*
la corbata — *tie*
dar — *to give*
el disco compacto — *compact disc*
los dulces — *candy*
las flores — *flowers*
el juego de mesa — *(board) game*
los juguetes — *toys*
le — *to/for her, him, you (sing.)*
les — *to/for them, you (pl.)*
me — *to/for me*
nos — *to/for us*
los pantalones — *pants*
¿Para quién...? — *For whom . . .?*
la planta — *plant*
¿Qué tipo de...? — *What kind of . . .?*
regalar — *to give (as a gift)*
el regalo — *gift*
la tarjeta — *greeting card*
te — *to/for you*

Asking for and giving directions downtown

a dos cuadras de aquí — *two blocks from here*
el almacén — *department store*
la cuadra — *city block*
la dulcería — *candy store*

la florería — *flower shop*
la joyería — *jewelry store*
la juguetería — *toy store*
¿Me puede decir...? — *Can you tell me . . .?*
la panadería — *bakery*

la pastelería — *pastry shop; sweet shop*
Perdón. — *Excuse me.*
quedar — *to be (located)*
la tienda de comestibles — *grocery store*
la zapatería — *shoe store*

SEGUNDO PASO

Commenting on clothes

de algodón — *(made of) cotton*
amarillo/a — *yellow*
anaranjado/a — *orange*
blanco/a — *white*
los bluejeans — *bluejeans*
la blusa — *blouse*
las botas — *boots*
los calcetines — *socks*
la camisa — *shirt*
la camiseta — *T-shirt*
la chaqueta — *jacket*
el cinturón — *belt*
cómodo/a — *comfortable*
de cuadros — *plaid, checkered*
de cuero — *(made of) leather*
cuesta — *costs*
la falda — *skirt*
formal — *formal*
gris — *gray*
de lana — *(made of) wool*
llevar — *to wear*
lo de siempre — *the usual*
morado/a — *purple*
los pantalones cortos — *shorts*
pardo/a — *brown*
de rayas — *striped*
rojo/a — *red*
la ropa — *clothes*
las sandalias — *sandals*
de seda — *(made of) silk*
el suéter — *sweater*
el traje — *suit*
el traje de baño — *bathing suit*
el vestido — *dress*
los zapatos — *shoes*
los zapatos de tenis — *tennis shoes*

Making comparisons

barato/a — *cheap*
caro/a — *expensive*
más... que — *more . . . than*
menos... que — *less . . . than*
el precio — *price*
Son del mismo precio. — *They're the same price.*
tan... como — *as . . . as*

TERCER PASO

Expressing preferences

además — *besides*
esa, ese — *that*
esas, esos — *those*
esta, este — *this*
estas, estos — *these*
¿La verde o la amarilla? — *The green one or the yellow one?*
Te queda muy bien. — *It looks good on you.*

Asking about prices and paying for something

¿Cuánto cuesta...? — *How much does . . . cost?*
¿Cuánto cuestan...? — *How much do . . . cost?*
¡Es un robo! — *It's a rip-off!*
¡Qué barato! — *How cheap!*
¡Qué caro! — *How expensive!*
¡Qué ganga! — *What a bargain!*

GAME

Regalos Give each student an index card with a word for a gift on it. Put the following questions on the board: **¿Qué le(s) vas a regalar a _____? ¿Qué me vas a regalar a mí?** Students answer with the item they have on their card.

CHAPTER 9 ASSESSMENT

▸ **Testing Program**
Chapter Test, pp. 61–66
Audio Compact Discs, CD 9, Trs. 21–22
Speaking Test, p. 130

▸ **Alternative Assessment Guide**
Performance Assessment, p. 21
Portfolio Assessment, p. 13
CD-ROM Assessment, p. 28

▸ **Interactive CD-ROM Tutor, Disc 3**
¡A hablar!
¡A escribir!

▸ **Standardized Assessment Tutor**
Chapter 9

▸ **One-Stop Planner, Disc 3**
Test Generator
Chapter 9

▸ **Midterm Exam**
Testing Program, pp. 133–138
Audio CD 9, Trs. 23–24

STANDARDS:1.2, 5.1

161

Celebraciones
CHAPTER OVERVIEW

De antemano pp. 164–167	¡Felicidades, Héctor!			
	FUNCTIONS	**GRAMMAR**	**VOCABULARY**	**RE-ENTRY**
Primer paso pp. 168–175	• Talking about what you're doing right now, p. 171 • Asking for and giving an opinion, p. 174	• **Gramática:** Present progressive, p. 172	• Holidays, p. 169	• **estar** • Months and seasons • Extending, accepting, and turning down invitations
Segundo paso pp. 178–183	• Asking for help and responding to requests, p. 179 • Telling a friend what to do, p. 181	• **Nota gramatical:** Informal commands, p. 181	• Party expressions, p. 180	• **tú** versus **usted** • Household chores
Tercer paso pp. 186–193	• Talking about past events, p. 187	• **Así se dice:** Preterite forms of **hacer: hiciste, hizo,** p. 187 • **Nota gramatical:** Preterite tense of regular **-ar** verbs, p. 187 • **Gramática:** Direct object pronouns **lo** and **la,** p. 191	• Time expressions, p. 188	• Days of the week • Question words **¿quién?** and **¿quiénes?** • Free-time activities • Places • Household chores

Letra y sonido	p. 193	Listening for Spanish syllables	**Dictado:** Textbook Audiocassette 2B/Audio CD 10
Enlaces	pp. 194–195	El día del árbol	
Vamos a leer	pp. 196–197	Festivales del mundo hispanohablante	**Reading Strategy:** Making comparisons
Review	pp. 198–201	Repaso, pp. 198–199	**A ver si puedo...,** p. 200 **Vocabulario,** p. 201

Culture	• **Nota cultural: Día del santo,** p. 170 • **Nota cultural: La quinceañera,** p. 171 • **Encuentro cultural: El Paseo del Río,** pp. 176–177	• **Nota cultural:** Traditional holiday foods, p. 178 • **Panorama cultural: ¿Qué hacen ustedes para celebrar?,** pp. 184–185

Lesson Planning

**One-Stop Planner
Lesson Planner with Substitute Teacher
Lesson Plans,** pp. 21–25

Listening and Speaking

Listening Activities
- Student Response Forms for Listening Activities, pp. 64–66
- Additional Listening Activities 10-1 to 10-6, pp. 17–19
- Additional Listening Activities (song), p. 20
- Scripts and Answers, pp. 42–44

Video Guide
- Teaching Suggestions, pp. 30–31
- Activity Masters, pp. 32–35
- Scripts and Answers, pp. 58–61, 67

Activities for Communication
- Communicative Activities, pp. 25–30
- Realia and Teaching Suggestions, pp. 59–63
- Situation Cards, pp. 82–83

¡Ven conmigo! Level 1
TPR Storytelling Book, pp. 37–40

Reading and Writing

Reading Strategies and Skills, Chapter 10
¡Lee conmigo! 1, Chapter 10
Practice and Activity Book, pp. 49–60

Grammar

Grammar and Vocabulary Workbook, pp. 27–36

¡Ven conmigo! Level 1
Grammar Tutor for Students of Spanish
Chapter 9

Assessment

Testing Program
- Paso Quizzes and Chapter Test, pp. 73–84
- Score Sheet, Scripts and Answers, pp. 85–90

Grammar and Vocabulary Quizzes
- Quizzes 10-1A, 10-2A, 10-3A
- Alternative Quizzes 10-1A, 10-2A, 10-3A

Alternative Assessment Guide
- Portfolio Assessment, p. 14
- Performance Assessment, p. 22
- CD-ROM Assessment, p. 29

¡Ven conmigo! Level 1
Standardized Assessment Tutor
- Reading, pp. 39–41
- Writing, p. 42

Native Speakers

¡Ven conmigo! Level 1
Cuaderno para hispanohablantes, pp. 46–50

MEDIA

Online Activities
- Juegos interactivos
- Actividades internet

Video Program
- Videocassette 2
- Videocassette 3 *(captioned version)*

¡Ven conmigo! Level 1
DVD Tutor, Disc 2

Audio Compact Discs
- Textbook Listening Activities, CD 10, Tracks 1–17
- Additional Listening Activities, CD 10, Tracks 23–28
- Assessment Items, CD 10, Tracks 18–22

Interactive CD-ROM Tutor, Disc 2

Teaching Transparencies
- Situations 10-1 to 10-3
- Vocabulary 10-A to 10-B
- Grammar and Vocabulary Workbook

One-Stop Planner CD-ROM

Use the **One-Stop Planner CD-ROM** with **Test Generator** to aid in lesson planning and pacing.

For each chapter, the **One-Stop Planner** includes:
- Editable lesson plans with direct links to teaching resources
- Printable worksheets from resource books
- Direct launches to the HRW Internet activities
- Video and audio segments
- Test Generator
- Clip Art for vocabulary items

CAPÍTULO 10

Celebraciones
TECHNOLOGY

DVD/VIDEO

Videocassette 2, Videocassette 3 (captioned version)
DVD Tutor, Disc 2 See Video Guide, pages 29–35.

De antemano • ¡Felicidades, Héctor!
The Villarreal family is preparing for Héctor's graduation party. While making **tamales,** Héctor's grandmother tells Lisa, Eva, and Gabi about holidays in Mexico. At the end of the episode, Héctor's father discovers that he has forgotten to send out the invitations to the party, which is set to begin in two hours.

A continuación
Héctor's mother calls all the guests on the telephone and invites them to the party. Eva, Lisa, and Gabi go to the bakery to pick up the cake and mistakenly bring back the wrong one. Fortunately, they have just enough time to exchange the cake and return before Héctor gets home. In the end, the party is a success.

¿Qué hacen ustedes para celebrar?
Spanish-speakers from Texas, Spain, and Venezuela tell about holidays and celebrations where they live. In additional interviews, people from various Spanish-speaking countries tell us about their favorite celebrations and holidays.

 El Paseo del Río

 Videoclips
- **Idea:** public service announcement concerning Christmas holidays

INTERACTIVE CD-ROM TUTOR

Activity	Activity Type	Pupil's Edition Page
En contexto	*Interactive conversation*	
1. Vocabulario	¡Super memoria!	p. 169
2. Gramática	¿Qué falta?	p. 172
3. Gramática	¡A escoger!	p. 181
4. Vocabulario	¿Cuál es?	p. 180
5. Gramática	¿Qué falta?	p. 187
6. Gramática	¡A escoger!	p. 191
Panorama cultural	¿Qué hacen ustedes para celebrar? ¡A escoger!	pp. 184–185
¡A hablar!	*Guided recording*	pp. 198–199
¡A escribir!	*Guided writing*	pp. 198–199

Teacher Management System
Launch the program, type "admin" in the password area and press RETURN. Log on to **www.hrw.com/CDROMTUTOR** for a detailed explanation of the Teacher Management System.

DVD-ROM TUTOR ¡VEN CONMIGO! LEVEL 1

 The *DVD Tutor* contains all material from the Level 1 *Video Program.* Spanish captions are available for use at your discretion for all sections of the video. The *DVD Tutor* also provides a variety of video-based activities that assess students' understanding of the **De antemano, A continuación,** and **Panorama cultural.**

This part of the *DVD Tutor* may be used on any DVD video player connected to a television or video monitor.

 In addition to the video material and the video-based comprehension activities, the *DVD Tutor* also contains the entire Level 1 *Interactive CD-ROM Tutor* in DVD-ROM format. Each DVD disc contains the activities from all 12 chapters of the *Interactive CD-ROM Tutor.*

This part of the *DVD Tutor* may be used on a Macintosh® or Windows® computer with a DVD-ROM drive.

One-Stop Planner CD-ROM

To preview all resources available for this chapter, use the **One-Stop Planner CD-ROM**, Disc 3.

MARCAR: go.hrw.com	
PALABRA CLAVE: WV3 TEXAS-10	

INTERNET CONNECTION

*Have students explore the **go.hrw.com** Web site for many online resources covering all chapters. All Chapter 10 resources are available under the keyword **WV3 Texas-10**. Interactive games help students practice the material and provide them with immediate feedback. You will also find a printable worksheet that provides Internet activities that lead to a comprehensive online research project.*

JUEGOS INTERACTIVO

You can use the interactive activities in this chapter

- to practice grammar, vocabulary, and chapter functions
- as homework
- as an assessment option
- as a self-test
- to prepare for the Chapter Test

ACTIVIDADES INTERNET

Students research holidays in Spanish-speaking countries on the Internet. They choose a holiday to celebrate, describe how to prepare for the celebration, and say how their party turned out.

- In preparation for the **Hoja de actividades,** have students watch the dramatic episode and the **Panorama cultural** on Videocassette 3.
- After students have completed the activity sheet, have them compare their celebration with that of a classmate who chose a different holiday, preferably in a different country. Which customs are similar?

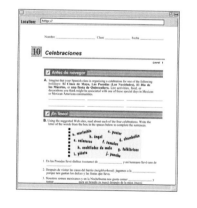

Proyecto

Have students choose a celebration they learned about from their own research or a classmate's in the **Hoja de actividades.** Ask them to use the Internet to research how, if at all, that holiday has been adapted by immigrants from that country whose descendents make their home in the United States.

For Student Response Forms, see Listening Activities pp. 64–66.

PRIMER PASO   pp. 168–175

6 ¡De fiesta!   p. 170

1. Me llamo Rolando. Vivo en Miami. Nosotros celebramos el Día de Acción de Gracias, pero como todas las familias, nuestra cena tiene cosas especiales de nuestra tradición cubana. Servimos pavo, pero también servimos arroz con frijoles negros.

2. Soy Marta. Vivo en San Antonio. Mi día favorito es el Día de los Enamorados que celebramos en febrero. Mando tarjetas a mis amigos y mi novio siempre me regala chocolates, flores o algo especial.

3. Soy Daniela. En mi familia nuestra fiesta favorita es la Navidad. Toda la familia va a la casa de mis abuelos. Vamos a misa a las doce de la noche y luego regresamos a casa para una cena fabulosa.

4. Yo me llamo Bernardo. Tengo seis años. Mi día favorito es mi cumpleaños. Este año mi mamá me va a llevar al zoológico. Luego vamos al cine y después voy a tener una fiesta.

Answers to Activity 6

1. d	**3.** c
2. a	**4.** b

9 Un día especial   p. 172

Esta tarde va a haber una fiesta estupenda en nuestra casa. Es el cumpleaños de mi abuelo y mi familia y yo vamos a hacer una fiesta para él. Pero hay muchas cosas que tenemos que hacer antes de la fiesta. Julia está limpiando la cocina. Mi tía Rosita está preparando una cena muy especial para mi abuelo. Mi hermana Sarita está en el patio. Ella está poniendo la mesa. Mis primos Teresa y Mauricio están lavando los platos. Roberto está decorando la sala. Y yo, ¿qué estoy haciendo yo? Bueno, yo estoy organizando mi cuarto. ¡Es un desastre!

Answers to Activity 9

1. Julia, c
2. Rosita, b
3. Sarita, e
4. Teresa y Mauricio, f
5. Roberto, a
6. Guadalupe, d

SEGUNDO PASO   pp. 178–183

20 ¿Me haces el favor...?   p. 180

1. Roberto, ¿me puedes ayudar a decorar la sala?
2. Elenita, ¿me haces el favor de llamar a Gregorio? Toca muy bien la guitarra.
3. Oye, ¿quién me ayuda con las decoraciones?
4. Jaime, ¿me haces el favor de ir a la pastelería?
5. Laura, ¿quiénes van a traer la música para bailar?
6. Mamá, ¿me ayudas a preparar los sándwiches?
7. ¿Me traes una silla, por favor?

Answers to Activity 20

1. lógico
2. ilógico
3. lógico
4. ilógico
5. lógico
6. ilógico
7. lógico

25 Preparativos p. 182

1. — Buenos días. Habla Nicolás. ¿Qué necesitan para la fiesta?
   — Este... trae unos refrescos, por favor.
2. — Hola, soy Soledad. ¿Qué hago para la fiesta?
   — A ver... eh... ve al supermercado y compra helado, por favor.
3. — ¿Qué tal? Habla Gustavo. ¿Qué puedo traer a la fiesta?
   — Trae unos discos compactos, por favor.
4. — Buenas tardes. Habla Verónica. ¿Ya está todo listo para la fiesta? ¿Puedo preparar algo especial?
   — A ver... prepara una ensalada de frutas, por favor.
5. — ¿Qué tal? Habla Gloria. ¿Qué puedo hacer para la fiesta?
   — Bueno... Tú tienes una cámara, ¿verdad? Saca fotos de todos, por favor.
6. — Hola, soy Cristóbal. ¿Necesitan algo para la fiesta?
   — Sí, Cristóbal. Compra los globos, por favor.

Answers to Activity 25

1. f	**3.** a	**5.** e
2. b	**4.** c	**6.** d

TERCER PASO   pp. 186–193

32 La fiesta de Abby p. 188

1. Raquel y Gloria jugaron a las cartas con Felipe y su hermano Guillermo.
2. Un amigo mío, Shoji, cantó unas canciones en español y Kerry tocó la guitarra.
3. Bárbara bailó con su novio Miguel. Ellos bailaron en la fiesta toda la noche.
4. Pablo miró la televisión. ¡A él no le gustan las fiestas para nada!
5. Patricia preparó un postre muy rico para la fiesta anoche.
6. Gracie y Kim jugaron a los videojuegos.
7. Andrés y Valerie escucharon música.
8. Y Francisco, ¡a él le encanta nadar! Nadó mucho en nuestra piscina.

Answers to Activity 32

1. a	**3.** b	**5.** g	**7.** h
2. c	**4.** d	**6.** e	**8.** f

LETRA Y SONIDO   p. 193

For the scripts for Parts A and C, see page 193. The script for Part B is below.

B. Dictado

Bueno, primero tengo que ayudar a lavar la ropa. Después, a las seis, voy a comprar unas zapatillas nuevas. Y luego, a las ocho, voy a una película con unos amigos.

REPASO   pp. 198–199

1 p. 198

Me llamo Mariana y vivo en San Antonio. En diciembre viajamos a Monterrey para celebrar las fiestas de Navidad con mis abuelos. ¡Qué viaje más fantástico! Mi abuela preparó unas decoraciones bonitas. Todos mis primos llegaron de Guadalajara y preparamos una cena maravillosa de pavo, enchiladas, bacalao y ensalada de Nochebuena. Cenamos a las ocho. Después bailamos, cantamos y hablamos toda la noche. La Navidad es mi día festivo favorito porque siempre la pasamos en México con mis abuelos.

Answers to Repaso Activity 1

1. Monterrey
2. para celebrar la Navidad con sus abuelos
3. diciembre
4. decoraciones bonitas
5. bailaron, cantaron y hablaron toda la noche
6. la pasan en México con sus abuelos

CAPÍTULO 10

Celebraciones

PROJECTS

NUESTRA CAJA DE CULTURA

In this group activity, students will use all four skills to create a permanent culture reference source for the Spanish classroom.

Introduction

Ask students to think of all the different aspects of Hispanic culture they have learned about up to now. Review map names of different Spanish-speaking countries, the names of cities, and other geographic terms.

Materials students may need

- ◆ Index cards
- ◆ Index tabs
- ◆ Shoe box or other container
- ◆ Old magazines
- ◆ Markers
- ◆ Glue or tape
- ◆ Reference materials to use in the classroom including a Spanish-English dictionary

Sequence

1 After explaining the project by giving some suggestions for culture card topics, allow time for library research and set due dates for different parts of the project. Some possible index tabs include

las comidas
los bailes típicos
la historia
la cultura indígena
los deportes
los lugares de interés

las canciones
las costumbres
los hispanos famosos
los mapas
la moneda
las diversiones

2 Divide the students into groups of four or five. Decide on a particular number of culture reference cards each group must produce. Provide a sample card as a pattern for students to follow. Remind them they may be as creative as they like as long as they include basic information such as:

- country/city/Spanish-speaking area of U.S.
- significance of particular cultural card

- correct words in Spanish
- document source such as dictionary, encyclopedia, book, author, title, date of publication and where published

Grading the project

Suggested point distribution (total = 100 points):

Basic information included **25**
Number of words included **25**
Neatness **25**
Correct documentation format **25**

TARJETAS CLÁSICAS

This project reviews the common holidays and special days that we celebrate with family and in our communities. Students will design an invitation or card to accompany a given celebration.

Introduction

Ask students to brainstorm about different special days. Which religious holidays do we celebrate? (Christmas, Hanukkah, Easter, Passover). Which are national holidays? (Thanksgiving Day, Independence Day, Labor Day, Memorial Day). Which are regional or local holidays? (**el Cinco de Mayo**, local festivals). Which are personal celebrations? (birthday, Valentine's Day). What are the common invitations or announcements that accompany these celebrations? Have students imagine that they are forming a greeting card company.

Materials students may need

- ◆ Colored construction paper (8 1/2 × 11)
- ◆ White paper (8 1/2 × 11)
- ◆ Fine-point markers
- ◆ Crayons, rulers, pencils

Sequence

1. In groups of four, students imagine they own a greeting card company and give their company a name in Spanish. The greeting card company needs to promote their product—i.e. invitations or announcements.

2. Each group makes cards for four different holidays or special days. The group designs an assortment of cards or invitations for a presentation. Each student is responsible for the design and message of his or her particular card or invitation.

3. Students present their "Promotion Package" of greeting cards to other groups in the class. Students give feedback to the different "Companies" and vote on which one to buy the cards or invitations from.

Grading the project

Suggested point distribution (total = 100 points):

Creativity 20
Grammatical accuracy 20
Cooperative effort 20
Pronunciation 20
Comprehensibility 20

CELEBRACIONES

In this project students work in groups to create puppet shows about holiday celebrations. Each group researches the history, customs, and cultural significance of a different holiday. Then they produce a five- to ten-minute puppet show that tells how the holiday is celebrated.

Materials students may need

- Small paper bags, socks to make puppets
- Glue
- Marker
- Table large enough for students to sit under
- Cloth to cover the front and sides of the table

Sequence

1. Explain the project to the students and set due dates for their research, a written script, and the show.

2. Divide the students into groups of four or five students of varying abilities. Ask students to decide on a holiday they would like to learn more about.

3. Allow the students time to do research and to write their script. Remind students to use the Spanish they know in writing their scripts. You might suggest they use a dictionary as needed.

4. Make puppets one day in class. Have students bring in the necessary materials. (socks, yarn, string, buttons) You may wish to have them look up the Spanish words for these materials in a dictionary, write them on the board, and speak in Spanish as much as possible.

5. Groups hand in a written copy of their script. You might also ask students to write a short paragraph describing key information about the celebration they researched.

6. Allow the students time to rehearse in class or have them rehearse outside of class before they present their shows.

Grading the project

Suggested point distribution (total = 100 points):

Cultural research 20
Accurate Spanish in script 25
Creativity in script 10
Accurate Spanish in show 25
Creativity in show 10
Cooperative effort 10

NOTE

Ask students to assess their own contribution to the script and to the show on a sheet of paper using a scale of 1 to 5 (5 being the highest).

CAPÍTULO 10 · Celebraciones

GAMES

LA ADIVINANZA

This game reviews typical -ar, -er, and -ir verbs that students have had throughout the year and reinforces the present progressive in Spanish.

Preparation

1. Ask students to submit a list of ten verb infinitives (-**ar**, -**er**, and -**ir**) they have learned.

2. Collate the information and make flash cards with the present progressive of the verbs: **estoy cantando, estoy estudiando, estoy bailando,** etc. Refer to previous chapters for verb infinitives to review. The pack of cards should contain at least 25 conjugated verbs.

Procedure

1. Divide the class into teams. Designate a Scorekeeper, a Timekeeper, and an Emcee.

2. The Emcee takes the first card and give it to the first person on the team. The student reads the card silently and has one minute to act out the action using body language only. Members of his or her team guess the correct action in Spanish using the **tú** form of the present progressive.

3. If the team guesses correctly, that team earns one point.

4. Alternate teams until all cards have been used.

NOTE

If a student doesn't understand the verb on the printed card, the team forfeits its turn, and the card goes to the next team. If the student from that team cannot correctly act out the card, move on to the next card and proceed.

EL JUEGO DEL PRETÉRITO

This game is an enjoyable way for students to practice conjugating verbs in the present and the preterite tenses.

Preparation

1. Ask students to submit a list of ten -**ar** verb infinitives that they have learned. Students then make a similar list of verbs by conjugating the forms in different persons in the present tense, and then in the preterite tense (**hablar, hablo, hablé; bailar, baila, bailó**)

2. Collate the information and make flash cards for each verb in the present tense using various persons: **hablas, bailamos, cantan.** Prepare at least 25 cards.

Procedure

1. The object of the game is for the student to recognize the present tense conjugation, and to change it to the preterite conjugation form.

2. Organize the class into two teams. Designate a Scorekeeper and a Student Leader.

3. The Student Leader shows one card to the first student of Team A. The student tries to correctly change the verb from the present tense to the preterite tense. For each correct answer, the student earns a point for his or her team.

4. If the student from Team A cannot correctly conjugate the verb, a student from Team B has the chance to answer. If successful, Team B earns a point.

5. The team with the most points wins.

Variation

Make a second set of flash cards, each with an infinitive and a personal pronoun. (**hablar, yo**) Have the students on each team conjugate the infinitive in the present and the preterite tense, according to the personal pronoun.

MI REGALO

*This game provides practice with vocabulary, reading, and writing skills. Play this game after the **Tercer paso** to review vocabulary.*

Preparation

Give each student three index cards. On the front of each card, have the students write four sentences describing a gift. Remind students to match the adjectives to the gift they describe. (**Es roja. Es de algodón. No es muy grande pero no es pequeña. La llevo mucho.**) On the back of the card have them write the Spanish word for the gift. (**una camiseta**)

Procedure

1 Divide the class into two teams. Ask the first player on Team A to read his or her clues to a Team B player.

2 The Team B player has four chances to guess the gift. He or she should guess by saying **Creo que es _____.** The team 1 player answers either **Sí, tienes razón** or **No, no tienes razón.**

3 If the Team B player guesses correctly, Team B gets a point. Otherwise, the Team A player reveals the gift and Team A receives a point.

4 Alternate between teams until everyone has had a chance to play. The team with the higher score wins.

UN AÑO DE CELEBRACIONES

This game provides practice with the preterite tense and the names of several holidays. It also tests students' knowledge of various holidays and festivals. Use it as a review at the end of the chapter.

Preparation

On index cards, have students write verbs associated with activities or celebrations, (**acampar, ayudar, bailar, caminar, cenar, comprar, cuidar, decorar, descansar, inflar, mandar, escuchar, llevar, tomar**) Place these in a pile face down so that students may draw from a deck. On the board, write the 12 months of the year in order. Then ask students to name one holiday in each month. These may be holidays discussed in this chapter or other celebrations such as someone's birthday or a special day at school.

Procedure

1 Divide the class into two teams. The object of the game is for each team to proceed through the year and "celebrate" each holiday. Teams celebrate a **día festivo** by having a player from the team use a preterite verb correctly in a sentence about the holiday. A Team A player starts in **enero.** The class has chosen to celebrate **el Día de los Reyes Magos,** for example. The player takes a card (**caminar**). He or she must construct a sentence using that verb in the preterite tense. The sentence must have something to do with the holiday. (**El Día de los Reyes Magos, los reyes caminaron por los pueblos.**)

2 If the student makes a logical sentence and uses the verb correctly, Team A goes on to the next month, and the play switches to Team B. If he or she does not make a logical sentence, Team A does not does not go on to the next month, and the play switches to Team B. When Team A has a turn again, the player makes a sentence with a new verb about the holiday in **febrero.** The first team to celebrate all 12 holidays wins.

Challenge

1 Students play on several small teams. All teams simultaneously construct a sentence for the same holiday. Each team has a different verb, however. Set a time limit and some rules about looking up words in the book or in a dictionary. (Students may not look up verb conjugations.)

2 When time is up, have one representative from each team read the group's sentence. Groups whose sentences are correct advance to the next month to make a new sentence about that month's holiday. Groups whose sentences are not right must draw another verb and make a new sentence about the same holiday. The first team to celebrate all 12 holidays wins.

ANSWERS TO CHAPTER 10 ACTIVITIES

Listening activity answers appear on Scripts pages 161E–161F. Answers to all other activities appear on corresponding pupil pages.

PRIMER PASO   pp. 168–175

11 Answers will vary. Possible answers:
a. ¿Qué está haciendo Roberto? Está decorando la sala.
b. ¿Qué está haciendo Rosita? Está preparando la comida.
c. ¿Qué está haciendo Julia? Está limpiando la cocina.
d. ¿Qué está haciendo Guadalupe? Está organizando su cuarto.
e. ¿Qué está haciendo Sarita? Está poniendo la mesa.
f. ¿Qué están haciendo Teresa y Mauricio? Están lavando los platos.

13 Answers will vary. Possible answers:
1. ¿Qué te parece si le regalamos un libro de arte francés?
   Me parece perfecto.
2. ¿Crees que a Ricardo le gustaría una revista de cocinar?
   Creo que no le gustaría.
3. ¿Qué te parece si le damos unas tarjetas de béisbol?
   Creo que le van a gustar.
4. ¿Crees que a Patricia le gustaría un collar rosado?
   Creo que le gustaría más un collar negro.
5. ¿Qué te parece si le regalamos un libro de aventura?
   Me parece muy buena idea.
6. ¿Crees que a Ángela le gustaría ese disco compacto de música de piano?
   Si es de jazz, le va a gustar.

SEGUNDO PASO   pp. 178–183

19 Answers will vary. Possible answers:
1. ¿Me ayudas a inflar los globos?; ¿Me haces el favor de llamar a los invitados?
2. ¿Me ayudas a colgar las decoraciones? ¿Me ayudas a decorar la casa, por favor?
3. ¿Me haces el favor de mandar las invitaciones?
4. ¿Me ayudas a abrir los regalos?

21 Answers will vary. Possible answers:
1. ¿Me ayudas a limpiar la cocina y lavar los platos, por favor?
   Claro que sí.
2. ¿Me ayudas a comprar la comida para la fiesta?
   Lo siento, pero tengo una cita.
3. ¿Me ayudas a llamar a los invitados?
   Claro que sí. ¿Dónde están los números de teléfono?
4. ¿Me haces el favor de poner la mesa?
   Cómo no. ¿Dónde están los platos y las decoraciones?
5. ¡Tengo mucha prisa! ¿Me haces el favor de colgar las decoraciones?
   Un momentito. Tengo que poner la mesa primero.
6. ¿Me traes las sillas de la cocina, por favor?
   Lo siento, pero no puedo. Estoy ocupado/a.

26 1. María, saca unas fotos del grupo.
2. Guillermo, ven a la sala.
3. Mercedes, baila con Héctor.
4. Gabi, canta unas canciones populares.
5. Eva, toca la guitarra para Gabi.
6. Lisa, pon la música de tu grupo favorito.
7. Héctor, abre los regalos pronto.
8. Rebeca, descansa un poco, por favor.

TERCER PASO   pp. 186–193

35 Answers will vary. Possible answers:
— Gloria limpió la cocina.
— Gloria lavó la ropa.
— Gloria sacó la basura.
— Gloria compró unas flores.
— Gloria organizó la ropa.

40 1. No, no lo invité.
2. Sí, la limpiamos.
3. No, no lo decoré.
4. No, no la preparé.
5. Sí, lo compramos.
6. Sí, la llamé.
7. Sí, lo ayudé.
8. No, no lo compramos.

VAMOS A LEER   pp. 196–197

A Answers will vary. Possible answers:
1. Halloween, Purim
2. Fourth of July, Veteran's Day, Memorial Day, Juneteenth
3. Christmas, Easter, Hanukkah, Passover, Ramadan
4. Thanksgiving, Sukkot
5. drumming, foods such as corn, chocolate, tomato and potato, pow-wows, harvest festivals
6. singing spirituals, blues and jazz music, Gullah language, foods such as sweet potato pie, Juneteenth

B 1. throwing water balloons and with parades and costumes

Answers will vary. Possible answers:
2. parades, costumes, masks
3. to give thanks for a good harvest

C Answers will vary. Possible answers:
1. Mardi Gras: parades, costumes, music
2. Halloween: people wear costumes and masks
3. Thanksgiving: it's a harvest festival

Chapter Section	Presentation	Homework Options
Primer paso	**Vocabulario,** p. 169	*Pupil's Edition,* p. 169, Activity 5 *Grammar and Vocabulary,* p. 27, Activity 1 *CD-ROM,* Disc 3, Chapter 10, Activity 1
	Así se dice, p. 171,	*Pupil's Edition,* p. 171, Activity 8 *Practice and Activity Book,* pp. 50–52, Activities 4, 6, 7
	Gramática, p. 172	*Pupil's Edition,* p. 173, Activity 12 *Grammar and Vocabulary,* pp. 28–29, Activities 2–6 *CD-ROM,* Disc 3, Chapter 10, Activity 2
	Así se dice, p. 174	*Pupil's Edition,* p. 175, Activity 16 *Practice and Activity Book,* p. 52, Activity 8
Segundo paso	**Así se dice,** p. 179	*Pupil's Edition,* p. 179, Activity 18 *Practice and Activity Book,* p. 53, Activity 9
	Vocabulario, p. 180	*Pupil's Edition,* p. 180, Activity 19 *Grammar and Vocabulary,* p. 30, Activities 7–8 *CD-ROM,* Disc 3, Chapter 10, Activity 4
	Así se dice, p. 181	*Pupil's Edition,* p. 181, Activity 22 *Practice and Activity Book,* pp. 54–55, Activities 10–12 *CD-ROM,* Disc 3, Chapter 10, Activity 3
	Nota gramatical, p. 181	*Pupil's Edition,* p. 183, Activity 26 *Grammar and Vocabulary,* pp. 31–32, Activities 9–12
Tercer paso	**Así se dice/Nota gramatical,** p. 187	*Pupil's Edition,* p. 187, Activity 30 *Grammar and Vocabulary,* pp. 33–34, Activities 13–15 *Practice and Activity Book,* pp. 56–57, Activities 13–15 *CD-ROM,* Disc 3, Chapter 10, Activity 5
	Vocabulario, p. 188	*Pupil's Edition,* p. 188–189, Activity 31, Activity 34 *Grammar and Vocabulary,* p. 34, Activities 16–17
	Gramática, p. 191	*Pupil's Edition,* pp. 191–192, Activities 38, 40 *Grammar and Vocabulary,* pp. 35–36, Activities 18–21 *CD-ROM,* Disc 3, Chapter 10, Activity 6

Celebraciones

MOTIVATING ACTIVITY
Ask students what holidays they celebrate. Which is their favorite, and why? Do they celebrate with family, with friends, or both? What do they do?

 CULTURE NOTE
Since Roman Catholicism is the predominant religion the Spanish-speaking world, a nativity scene (**nacimiento, pesebre,** or **belén**) is more common there than a Christmas tree.

 MULTICULTURAL LINK
Ask students to think of traditions from Spanish-speaking countries adopted by people in the United States who are not Hispanic. (**piñatas, luminarias,** and **flor de pascuas**) Ask students to research a holiday in the United States that originated in Europe, Asia, or Africa.

RE-ENTRY
Ask students to think of foods from Spanish-speaking countries they learned about in Chapter 8. What are typical foods from several countries? (Ecuador: **sancocho, ají, empanadas;** Mexico: **tacos, tamales;** Spain: **tortilla española, gazpacho, paella**) Which dishes are often prepared for parties? (**tamales** in Mexico)

CAPÍTULO

10 Celebraciones

1 ¿Decoraste la sala tú sola?

162

In this chapter you will learn to

PRIMER PASO

- talk about what you're doing right now
- ask for and give an opinion

SEGUNDO PASO

- ask for help and respond to requests
- tell a friend what to do

TERCER PASO

- talk about past events

internet

go.hrw.com

MARCAR: go.hrw.com
PALABRA CLAVE:
WV3 MEXICO-10

② Estamos celebrando el Cinco de Mayo.

③ ¿Me ayudas a preparar los tamales?

¡FELIZ AÑO NUEVO!

163

FOCUSING ON OUTCOMES
Ask students which photos correspond to which outcomes. (Photo 1: talking about past events; Photo 2: talking about what you're doing right now; Photo 3: asking for help.) For the first outcome, ask them to talk about things they are doing right now.

CULTURE NOTE
El Cinco de Mayo commemorates the Mexican victory at the Battle of Puebla in 1862 against the invading French army. The French forces later installed Maximilian as emperor of Mexico. While in power, Maximilian restored the **Castillo de Chapultepec** and created the **Paseo de la Reforma,** Mexico City's most elegant boulevard. The Mexicans defeated the invaders in 1867 and Benito Juárez was restored as president. The Battle of Puebla is considered the first and most symbolic Mexican victory of the war.

NATIVE SPEAKERS
Ask students from Spanish-speaking families whether they observe holiday customs that originated in another country.

VIDEO INTEGRATION

En camino LEVEL 1B
Video Program
Videocassette 2, 1:17–5:20 OR
Videocassette 3, 1:38:19–1:42:23
(captioned version)

¡Ven conmigo! LEVEL 1
DVD Tutor, Disc 2

TEACHER NOTE
The **fotonovela** is an abridged version of the video episode.

VIDEO SYNOPSIS
The Villarreal family is busy preparing for Héctor's graduation party. While making the **tamales,** Dolores, the grandmother, tells Lisa, Eva, and Gabi about holidays in Mexico and which is her favorite. Manuel and his brother Tomás are talking in the backyard when Tomás holds up a package. Manuel realizes he has forgotten to send the invitations.

RE-ENTRY
Ask students to write a paragraph about a male and a female in the **fotonovela.** They describe what each is wearing and what each looks like, including height, color of hair and eyes. Ask students what the two people might like to do and where they might like to go.

SUGGESTION
For previewing or prereading, have students read the questions in Activity 1, p. 167.

DE ANTEMANO

¡Felicidades, Héctor!

 CD 10 Trs. 1–2

 Lots of things are going on at once in the Villarreal household. They're getting ready for a really big celebration! Look at the photos to see what they're doing. Have they forgotten something?

P/A p. 49 Acts. 1–2

Abuelo, Abuela, Eva, Héctor, Rebeca y Manuel Villarreal

Tío Tomás, Tía Marcela y Juan

Lisa y Gabi

1

¡Tomás! Mira... ¿qué te parece?

No sé... pregúntale a Juan.

Perfecto. Oye, Marcela. ¿Dónde están los globos?

¡Juan! ¿Tienes los globos?

2

Aquí están.

¿Me ayudas a inflar los globos?

¡Claro que sí, papá! ¿Qué tal si usamos de todos los colores? Hay de violeta, rojo, azul, verde...

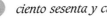

PRESENTATION
- Have students focus on non-linguistic cues by playing the video without sound. Ask them to hypothesize what the story is about. Then play the video again with sound.
- Stop the audio- or video-tape occasionally to ask comprehension questions to build students' confidence. For example, **¿Para quién es la fiesta?**

CRITICAL THINKING
Tell students that a rite of passage is a ceremony or celebration that takes place when a person changes status in life. Some major rites of passage are graduation, marriage, and parenthood. Do students think Héctor's graduation party can be considered a rite of passage? Why or why not?

SUGGESTION
Ask students to list different expressions they use to give an opinion in English, to ask for help, or to respond to a request. Ask them to keep their list until they complete **Segundo paso.** They then check to see how many of the expressions they can say in Spanish.

MOTIVATING ACTIVITY

Ask students to brainstorm things they might do to get ready for a party at their house. How many of these words do they already know in Spanish?

KINESTHETIC LEARNERS

Assign the role of each of the characters in the video to a student in the class. Ask the students to act out the video, beginning with an introduction of themselves as they appear in the first three photos. Continue with the photos that follow, asking each student to read his or her lines.

A continuación

You may choose to continue with *¡Felicidades, Héctor!* *(a continuación)* at this time or wait until later in the chapter. At this point, Héctor's mother begins to call everyone who was supposed to be invited so that they know about the party. Eva has to make two trips to the bakery because the first time they gave her the wrong cake. You may wish to have students compare their celebrations to the celebration depicted in the video.

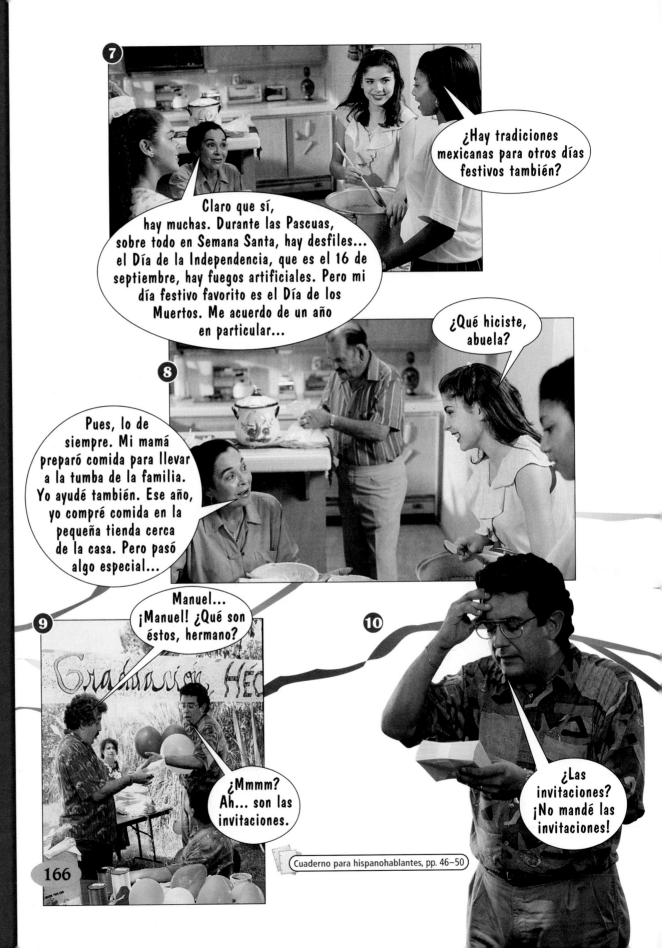

7

¿Hay tradiciones mexicanas para otros días festivos también?

Claro que sí, hay muchas. Durante las Pascuas, sobre todo en Semana Santa, hay desfiles... el Día de la Independencia, que es el 16 de septiembre, hay fuegos artificiales. Pero mi día festivo favorito es el Día de los Muertos. Me acuerdo de un año en particular...

¿Qué hiciste, abuela?

8

Pues, lo de siempre. Mi mamá preparó comida para llevar a la tumba de la familia. Yo ayudé también. Ese año, yo compré comida en la pequeña tienda cerca de la casa. Pero pasó algo especial...

9

Manuel... ¡Manuel! ¿Qué son éstos, hermano?

¿Mmmm? Ah... son las invitaciones.

10

¿Las invitaciones? ¡No mandé las invitaciones!

Cuaderno para hispanohablantes, pp. 46–50

166

1 ¿Comprendes? Answers in side column

¿Comprendes lo que pasa en la fotonovela? Contesta las preguntas. Si no estás seguro/a, adivina.

1. ¿Quiénes son las personas en la fotonovela?
2. ¿Qué tipo de fiesta preparan? ¿Para quién es la fiesta?
3. ¿Qué hacen Eva, Lisa y Gabi? ¿Quién las ayuda?
4. ¿Qué descubre *(discovers)* el señor Villarreal al final?
5. ¿Qué crees que el señor Villarreal debe hacer en esta situación?

These activities check for global comprehension only. Students should not yet be expected to produce language modeled in **De antemano**.

2 Ordena las oraciones

Mira la fotonovela para poner estas oraciones en el orden correcto. b, d, a, c, e

El señor Villarreal llama a la pastelería. **a**

La tía Marcela ayuda con las decoraciones. **b**

La abuela explica unas tradiciones mexicanas. **c**

Juan y su papá inflan los globos. **d**

El tío Tomás pregunta por las invitaciones. **e**

3 ¿Cómo dirías?

If you were having a party, what words and phrases from the **fotonovela** could you use . . .? Answers in side column

1. to ask for help with the balloons
2. to say that you didn't send the invitations
3. to ask for help making the **tamales**
4. to ask someone what they think of the music
5. to say "I'm talking with the bakery."

No mandé las invitaciones

¿Me ayudas a inflar los globos?

¿Qué te parece la música?

Estoy hablando a la pastelería.

¿Me ayudas a preparar los tamales?

La familia Suárez está preparando los tamales.

SUGGESTIONS

1 Have students work in pairs to answer the comprehension questions.

3 Have students identify the frame in the **fotonovela** where each expression is found.

Answers to Activity 1

1. La familia Villarreal, Lisa y Gabi.
2. una fiesta de graduación para Héctor
3. Preparan tamales; la abuela Dolores
4. que no mandó las invitaciones
5. Possible answer: Debe llamar a los invitados.

Answers to Activity 3

1. ¿Me ayudas a inflar los globos?
2. No mandé las invitaciones.
3. ¿Me ayudas a preparar los tamales?
4. ¿Qué te parece la música?
5. Estoy hablando a la pastelería.

VIDEO INTEGRATION

En camino LEVEL 1B
Video Program
Videocassette 4, 2:54–3:08 OR
Videocassette 3, 1:39:56–1:40:10
(captioned version)

¡Ven conmigo! LEVEL 1
DVD Tutor, Disc 2

Bell work
On the board or a transparency write the following sentence:**¿Cómo preparas la casa para una fiesta?** Give students three minutes to make a list of preparations.

MOTIVATING ACTIVITY
4 Before students begin the activity, have a class discussion about celebrations that often include cakes. (birthdays, graduations, weddings) Ask students for examples of what might be written on the cakes for those celebrations.

LANGUAGE NOTE
The Villarreals use **la escuela secundaria** for *high school.* Point out that school systems vary from country to country as do the words used to refer to them. Other words for *school* include **el colegio** and **el liceo.** Ask native speakers what the schools are called in the countries they are from.

PRIMER PASO (TPR)

Storytelling **B**ook
pp. 37, 40

go.
hrw
.com
WV3 MEXICO-10

*Talking about what you're doing right now;
asking for and giving an opinion*

4 La celebración

Lee cada *(each)* oración. En una hoja de papel, escribe **cierto** o **falso.** Si la oración es falsa, escribe una oración correcta.

1. El señor Villarreal está hablando por teléfono con una persona del correo.
2. El señor Villarreal llama para pedir un pastel de fresas.
3. Los señores Villarreal están haciendo una fiesta de graduación para su hijo.
4. El señor Villarreal le pregunta a su esposa qué quiere escribir en el pastel.

1. falso; El señor Villarreal habla con una persona de la pastelería.
2. falso; El señor Villarreal llama para pedir un pastel de chocolate.
3. cierto
4. cierto

VOCABULARIO

p. 50
Act. 3

p. 27
Act. 1

10-A,
10-1

Los días festivos

la Nochevieja y
el Año Nuevo

la Nochebuena y
la Navidad

las Pascuas

el Día de
los Enamorados

el Día de Acción
de Gracias

el Día de las Madres

el Día del Padre

el Día de
la Independencia

---

5 Los días de fiesta

Read the sentences below. Decide which holiday or holidays each sentence describes. You may use some holidays more than once.

1. Es en el mes de junio. el Día del Padre
2. Es en el otoño. el Día de Acción de Gracias
3. Es en el mes de febrero. el Día de los Enamorados
4. Casi siempre comen pavo *(turkey)*. el Día de Acción de Gracias
5. Es en el mes de mayo. el Día de las Madres
6. Es en el invierno. la Nochebuena y la Navidad o la Nochevieja y el Año Nuevo o el Día de los Enamorados
7. Muchas ciudades lo celebran con fuegos artificiales *(fireworks)*. el Día de la Independencia
8. Lo celebran con un árbol *(tree)* decorado y regalos. la Nochebuena y la Navidad
9. Celebramos dos años diferentes en dos días. la Nochevieja y el Año Nuevo
10. Lo celebran en la primavera con huevos pintados y con dulces. las Pascuas

---

☀ MOTIVATE

Ask students to make a list of holidays they celebrate. Are they all included in the vocabulary list? Ask them to write the Spanish equivalent beside each item. If they celebrate a holiday that is not on the list, have them look it up in a dictionary and add it to their list. Be aware that some religions do not celebrate holidays.

☀ TEACH

PRESENTATION

VOCABULARIO

Have students look at the photos as you describe them in Spanish. (**La Nochevieja es el 31 de diciembre. El primero de enero es el Año Nuevo.**) Continue describing the photos in this manner, pausing between each. Then ask several students when each holiday is this year. (**¿En qué mes es el Día de las Madres?**) Have a current calendar available.

TACTILE LEARNERS

5 Show students how to make a simple calendar. Give students paper and ask them to fold it into 12 squares. They should label each square with a month of the year, then fill in the holidays from the **Vocabulario.** They may also add the additional holidays from the **Motivate** activity.

CAPÍTULO 10

SUGGESTION

6 Have students work in pairs or small groups to make holiday greeting cards. They will need paper, pictures from magazines, colored markers, and glue or tape. Allow them to use bilingual dictionaries. Have the class vote on the most colorful and creative cards.

ADDITIONAL PRACTICE

7 Give students several minutes to work alone and write a short description of a holiday without mentioning the name of the day. The description should be full of clues. Then have several students read their descriptions aloud. Other students guess the holiday.

LANGUAGE NOTE

The Spanish word **fiesta** comes from the Latin *festa* meaning *festivals*. Some common words for *holiday* include **día festivo, día de fiesta, día feriado,** and **día holgado.**

CULTURE NOTE

The feast day of Saint John the Baptist (**el Día de San Juan Bautista**), celebrated the night of June 23, is important in many Spanish-speaking countries. Many traditions surrounding it are inspired by the ceremony of baptism (**bautismo, bautizo**). In Puerto Rico the residents of San Juan (**sanjuaneros**) walk backward into the ocean three times at midnight.

6 **¡De fiesta!** Script and answers on p. 161E

You'll hear four conversations, each about a different holiday. Match each conversation with the most appropriate greeting card.

CD 10 Tr. 3

7 **¿Cuál es tu día festivo favorito?**

Ask your partner about his or her favorite holidays. Find out what he or she does to celebrate. In the word box are some questions to get you started.

Answers will vary.

¿Comes algo especial?

¿Con quién(es) pasas el día?

¿Cantas o bailas?

¿Adónde vas?

¿Ves un partido en la televisión?

Nota cultural

In small towns and cities throughout the Spanish-speaking world, there are special celebrations for many occasions. You've already learned that in Spanish-speaking countries many people celebrate not only their birthday but also their **Día del santo.** Many cities and countries have a special "patron" saint, whose days are celebrated as holidays. These are called **fiestas patronales.** Curiepe, in Venezuela, celebrates Saint John the Baptist's Day on June 24 and 25 with a procession and dancing in the **plaza.** Does your town celebrate a special day?

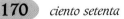

ASÍ SE DICE

Talking about what you're doing right now

pp. 50–51
Acts. 4,
6–7

To find out what someone is doing right now, ask:

Lisa, ¿qué estás haciendo?
Lisa, what are you doing?

¿Y tu hermano?

¿Todos **están decorando** la casa?
Are you all decorating the house?

He or she might say:

Estoy colgando las decoraciones.
I'm hanging the decorations.

Él **está limpiando** la sala.
He's cleaning the living room.

Sí, **estamos decorando** la casa.
Yes, we're decorating the house.

8 ¿Ahora?

Si la oración dice lo que *(what)* la familia Robles está haciendo ahora, contesta con **ahora**. Si la oración dice lo que hace la familia con frecuencia, contesta con **regularmente**.

1. Los sábados siempre limpio mi cuarto. regularmente
2. Estamos limpiando la casa antes de la fiesta de Ricky. ahora
3. Esmeralda decora la sala con plantas y flores. regularmente
4. Manuel y yo estamos decorando la sala. ahora
5. Estoy haciendo mis quehaceres con mucha prisa. ahora
6. Fernando y Milagros están colgando decoraciones en el comedor. ahora

Estamos celebrando la fiesta de quinceañera de mi hermana.

Nota cultural

The fifteenth birthday party for many Hispanic girls is a coming-of-age celebration. This party is called **una fiesta de quinceañera**, and can range from a small, informal gathering to a celebration as elaborate as a wedding. In most cases a local **conjunto** *(group of musicians)* plays. Usually the **padrino** or **madrina** presents the **quinceañera** with a special gift.

PRIMER PASO

ciento setenta y uno **171**

PRESENTATION
ASÍ SE DICE
Model the conversation between Lisa and her friend, using gestures to emphasize meaning. For example, **Lisa, ¿qué estás haciendo?** Then pretend to hang decorations as you answer **Estoy colgando las decoraciones.** Walk around the classroom describing what you are doing, using gestures to reinforce meaning.

COOPERATIVE LEARNING
8 Have students work in groups to practice the difference between the present and present progressive. Each student writes the words **ahora** and **regularmente** on separate pieces of paper. The leader says a sentence, for example, **Estoy lavando los platos.** The rest of the group holds up the paper that says **ahora.** Each student should get a chance to be the leader once.

NATIVE SPEAKERS
If any native Spanish speakers in your class have been to a **quinceañera,** ask them to write a page reporting on it. Ask them to describe the music, the decorations, and anything else that made it a special occasion.

PRESENTATION

GRAMÁTICA

First, have students silently read the explanation. Then model pronunciation and explain the formation of the present progressive. Ask students to write five sentences describing things they are or are not doing. (**Estoy pensando. No estoy nadando.**) Then ask students to read their sentences aloud.

🏰 **GAME**

Estoy conjugando Make index cards of the forms of **estar,** three or four verb infinitives with the endings in parentheses, **com(er)** for example, and the present progressive endings. Have one team make a sentence with the cards. Then the other team must say the phrase aloud and act it out. For example, they say **Estoy comiendo** and pretend to be eating. If they act it out within 30 seconds, they win a point. After two sentences, the teams switch roles.

PRELISTENING

9 Have students describe people's actions in each photo before playing the audio recording.

172   STANDARDS: 1.2, 4.1, 5.1

GRAMÁTICA   Present progressive

The *present progressive* is used to talk about what's happening right now. Use **estar +** the *present participle* of the verb.

- For -**ar** verbs, add -**ando** to the stem:
  Estoy bailando ahora. No **están cantando.**
- For -**er** and -**ir** verbs, add -**iendo** to the stem:
  ¿Qué **están comiendo** ustedes? Enrique **está escribiendo** las invitaciones.
- If the stem ends in a vowel, the -**iendo** changes to -**yendo:**
  ¿**Estás leyendo** el periódico?

GV
pp. 28–29
Acts. 2–6

9 **Un día especial** Script and answers on p. 161E

🔊
CD 10 Tr. 4

What are these people doing right now? Listen to Guadalupe talking about the party her family will have. Match the name or names with the correct photo.

1. Julia c
2. Rosita b
3. Sarita e
4. Teresa y Mauricio f
5. Roberto a
6. Guadalupe d

10 Las actividades

Busca la frase que describe lo que probablemente está haciendo cada persona ahora.

1. El cuarto de Ricardo está sucio. d
2. Nuria y tú tienen hambre. e
3. Mis amigos tienen mucha energía. b
4. Esteban tiene un partido ahora. f
5. Miriam y Raquel tienen mucha sed. c
6. Tú tienes un examen de español. a

a. Estoy estudiando mi libro.
b. Están corriendo en el parque.
c. Están comprando jugo de naranja.
d. Está limpiando su cuarto.
e. Estamos preparando arroz con pollo.
f. Está jugando al béisbol.

11 La familia de Guadalupe

Ask your partner what three of the people in the photos in Activity 9 are doing. Then answer your partner's questions about the other three people. Answers on p. 161K

12 ¿Qué están haciendo? H

Escribe seis oraciones sobre las fotos. Describe lo que *(what)* están haciendo las personas.

Están bailando porque es un día de fiesta.

Está leyendo el periódico.

Están comiendo en un restaurante; Están pidiendo comida.

Están corriendo juntos en el parque.

Está escuchando música. Está escribiendo en su cuaderno.

Están tocando música. Están escuchando música.

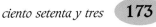

RE-ENTRY Have students work in pairs. One makes a request and the partner explains that he or she is busy doing something else. (**¿Quieres ir al parque? Lo siento, pero no puedo. Estoy estudiando.**) Refer students to Chapters 7 and 8 for some of these expressions.

CHALLENGE
10 Have students cover up sentences a through f and think of possible answers.

SUGGESTION
11 Have students work in pairs to role-play a phone conversation. One student pretends to be cleaning the day before he or she throws a party, and the other asks about the preparations. Each partner should have at least six lines.

ADDITIONAL PRACTICE
12 Have students draw three action scenes or cut out three pictures from magazines and write a description of what is happening in each.

SUGGESTION
Have groups of students choose a holiday to present to the class. They research the holiday and write a short report to read to the class. In addition, students bring costumes, props, food (just enough to have a taste), photographs, or music.

STANDARDS: 1.1, 1.3, 5.1 — 173

PRESENTATION

ASÍ SE DICE

Model the expressions in **Así se dice** for correct pronunciation and intonation. Ask students questions and have them respond with appropriate answers. Then ask some students to give their opinions and have them respond with their books closed. For example, **¿Crees que tenemos bastante tarea? ¿Qué te parece la clase de ciencias?**

SUGGESTIONS

13 Ask students questions to get them thinking about what someone else might like. For example, **¿Qué es un buen regalo para alguien a quien le gusta leer? (un libro)**

14 Allow students a few minutes to discuss their party plans. Tell students it is important for each group member to use phrases from **Así se dice** to express opinions about the people to invite, the food, etc.

ADDITIONAL PRACTICE

14 Have students work with a partner to write a four-question survey about their classmates' party preferences. For example, **¿Qué te parece si servimos comida mexicana?** Each pair asks three other pairs their questions and reports their findings.

PA
p. 52
Act. 8

ASÍ SE DICE   Asking for and giving an opinion

To find out what a friend thinks about something, ask:

Your friend might say:

¿Crees que hay bastante comida para la fiesta?
Do you think that there's enough food for the party?

Creo que sí.
I think so.

Creo que no.
I don't think so.

¿Qué te parece si llamamos a Eva?
How do you feel about calling Eva?

Me parece bien.
That's fine with me.

Perfecto.

Buena idea.

13 Compramos regalos

You and a small group of classmates must decide on gifts for various relatives' birthdays. Read the statements. Take turns giving your opinion on an appropriate gift for each person. Answers on p. 161K

MODELO   A Gustavo le gustan mucho los animales.
—¿Qué te parece si le regalamos el video "El mundo de los animales"?
—Me parece buena idea.

1. A Carolina le gusta mucho el arte.
2. A Ricardo le encanta cocinar.
3. A Marcos le gustan todos los deportes.
4. A Patricia le encantan las joyas.
5. A Malena le gusta leer.
6. A Ángela le encanta el jazz.

14 ¡Vamos a la fiesta!

In your small groups, choose a favorite holiday and plan a celebration for it. Decide who will attend, the food you would like to serve, and what kinds of activities there will be. When your partners say what they want to do, give your opinion. Choose a spokesperson to report your plans to the class.

MODELO   —Nos parece buena idea celebrar el Día...
—Vamos a invitar a...
—Vamos a servir...
—Vamos a... (actividades)

15 Lectura

Read the magazine article from *El Mundo Joven* about the traditional holiday of **las Fallas** in Valencia, Spain. Then answer the following statements with **cierto** or **falso**. Correct the false statements.

1. Celebran la fiesta de las Fallas en diciembre durante el invierno. falso; Se celebra del 12 al 19 de marzo cuando empieza la primavera.
2. Ana María lleva blue jeans y una camiseta para la fiesta. falso; Lleva un vestido típico.
3. Las fallas, que son unos muñecos *(dolls)* muy grandes, se queman *(are burned)* durante la noche del fuego *(fire)*. cierto

La fiesta de las Fallas comienza el día 12 de marzo y termina el 19, el día de San José. Valencia está totalmente transformada durante esta fiesta. Las Fallas celebra el comienzo de la primavera. Esta tradición tiene cuatrocientos años.

Las fallas

Pintando las fallas

Le preguntamos a Ana María Cárdenas Samaniego, una chica de Valencia que tiene catorce años, —¿qué te parece la fiesta de las Fallas?

"Me encanta la música en la calle día y noche. Me gusta llevar un vestido muy lindo y típico. Las fallas con sus muñecos grandes y cómicos son increíbles. Durante la noche del fuego, estos muñecos son quemados. Creo que ésta es mi fiesta favorita."

16 El día festivo [H]

Think up your own holiday. Decide who or what will be honored. Write a paragraph in Spanish explaining the holiday you propose. Explain how it should be celebrated.

MODELO Creo que debemos celebrar el Día del Perro porque los perros son muy buenos amigos. Para celebrar esta fiesta todos los chicos deben llevar sus perros al parque...

PRIMER PASO

ciento setenta y cinco **175**

NATIVE SPEAKERS
15 Have native speakers look in the **Fallas** article for three **palabras agudas con acento** (José, está, tradición) and three **palabras esdrújulas** (Cárdenas, música, típico, cómicos) to write in their accent notebooks.

CLOSE
Write several holidays and their dates on the board or on a transparency. Have a student choose one of the holidays and imagine today is that day. Ask **¿Con quién pasas el día?** The student answers **Paso el Día de las Madres con mi madre**, for example. Vary the questions for each student.

ASSESS
▸ Testing Program, pp. 73–74
Quiz 10-1
Audio CD 10, Tr. 18

▸ Grammar and Vocabulary Quizzes
Quiz 10-1A or
Alternative Quiz 10-1A

▸ Alternative Assessment Guide, p. 22

PERFORMANCE ASSESSMENT
Ask students to imagine that today is a holiday. In pairs, students develop phone conversations in which one describes the celebration preparations and the other asks questions about what everyone is doing. (**¿Con quién estás pasando la Nochebuena? Estoy pasando el día con mi familia.**)

STANDARDS: 1.2, 2.1, 5.1   **175**

VIDEO INTEGRATION

En camino LEVEL 1B
Video Program
Videocassette 2, 11:18–14:00

MOTIVATING ACTIVITY

Have students find San Antonio on the map on page 121 or on the United States map at the beginning of the book. Ask students if anyone has been to San Antonio. Then ask students how they would describe their town to someone from another country. Tell them to be sure to talk about restaurants, parks, museums, malls, and other points of interest.

CRITICAL THINKING

Ask students to think of some cities that have Hispanic influence. (Los Angeles, San Antonio, Santa Fe, Miami, New York) Ask students why they think those cities have this influence (near border with Mexico, immigration, etc.)

PRESENTATION

Show the video, read Alan's description aloud, or ask a volunteer to play the part of Alan talking about San Antonio. Then have students work in pairs to complete the questions in Activity 1. Follow up by talking about the answers as a class. Does San Antonio sound like a place the students would like to visit? Why or why not?

ENCUENTRO CULTURAL

El Paseo del Río

Alan es de San Antonio. Es una ciudad en Texas que está muy cerca de México. A él le encanta el Paseo del Río, una zona muy popular de tiendas y restaurantes. Alan nos va a enseñar el Paseo y describir lo que le gusta más allí.

Voy a enseñarte el famoso Paseo del Río que corre por el centro de la ciudad. Hay mucho que hacer en el Paseo del Río. Vienen muchos turistas al Paseo, pero también viene la gente de San Antonio. Hay muchos restaurantes aquí. Puedes comer comida Tex-Mex buenísima en San Antonio. Ésta es La Villita. Hay tiendas y galerías de arte.

"Vienen muchos turistas al Paseo, pero **también viene la gente de San Antonio.**"

"Puedes comer **comida Tex-Mex buenísima** en San Antonio."

"Ésta es La Villita. Hay **tiendas y galerías de arte.**"

1 ¿Qué dijo?

Alan describes many things to do and see on the **Paseo del Río.** See if you can figure out what he says.

1. Is the **Paseo del Río** only a tourist attraction? How can you tell? no; Alan says the people of San Antonio go there, also.
2. What kind of food does Alan mention as being very good in San Antonio?
   (a.) Tex-Mex food
   b. seafood
   c. Spanish food
3. Which two things can you do in **La Villita**?
   a. go swimming
   (b.) go shopping
   (c.) look at art

2 ¡Piénsalo! Answers in side column

1. Why do you think Tex-Mex food is so popular in San Antonio?

2. Are there any foods on the Tex-Mex menu that you often eat?

3. Which foods on this menu would you like to try? Why?

≋ BOTANAS ≋

Queso Especial
Full Order $ 5.50   Half Order $ 3.00
*White melted cheese with or without chorizo, pico de gallo, and
guacamole. Served with flour or corn tortillas.*

Pellizcaditas $ 4.95
*Corn dough pinched around the edges, topped with beans, beef
or chicken, hot sauce, cheese, and sour cream.*

Quesadillas $ 4.50
*Two homemade flour tortillas filled with melted cheeses and pico
de gallo. Served with guacamole and sour cream.*

≋ ENCHILADAS ≋

Enchiladas Verdes   (3) $ 7.95
*Corn tortillas filled with chicken, covered with green sauce and
melted cheese and topped with sour cream.*

Enchiladas de Mole   (3) $ 7.95
*Corn tortillas filled with chicken, covered with mole sauce and
topped with sour cream. Served with rice and beans.*

Enchiladas del Norte   (3) $ 7.95
*Corn tortillas filled with beef tips and green onions covered with
ranchero sauce and melted cheese. Served with guacamole salad.*

3 ¿Y tú?

How would you tell Alan about your city?   Answers will vary.

1. Un lugar interesante de mi ciudad es ====.

2. Me gusta porque ====.

3. En mi opinión, el mejor restaurante de mi ciudad es ====.

4. Aquí hay mucho que hacer. Por ejemplo, puedes ====.

ENCUENTRO CULTURAL

ciento setenta y siete   **177**

NATIVE SPEAKERS
Ask native speakers to talk about their favorite traditional foods from their family's country of origin, if they feel comfortable doing so.

PAIR WORK
3 Have students work in pairs to create a dialogue. One student pretends to be Alan asking questions about the town where his partner lives, and the other describes an interesting place and his or her favorite restaurant.

CULTURE NOTE
Tex-Mex food is common all across Texas and the Southwestern United States. **Guacamole** is made of avocadoes, onions, and lemon juice. **Pico de gallo** is a **salsa** made of fresh tomatoes, onions, cilantro, and chilies. **Mole** is a rich, traditional sauce made of chocolate, chilies, tomatoes, almonds, and garlic. Ingredients for **mole** vary from recipe to recipe, except for the special ingredient, chocolate.

Answers to Activity 2

1. Possible answers: close to Mexico, many people from Mexico and of Mexican descent live there
2. Answers will vary.
3. Answers will vary.

VIDEO INTEGRATION

En camino LEVEL 1B
Video Program
Videocassette 2, 3:23–4:01 OR
Videocassette 3, 1:40:25–1:41:03
(captioned version)

¡Ven conmigo! LEVEL 1
DVD Tutor, Disc 2

Bell work
On the board or a transparency write **regalo,** with space between each letter. Under the letter *r* write the word **radio.** Tell students to think of five more ideas for gifts using the remaining letters for a friend's upcoming birthday.

CULTURE NOTE
Tamales are a popular party food throughout Mexico, Central America, and parts of the United States. In Honduras, a **nacatamal** is made with meat and a **tamal** is made without meat.

LANGUAGE NOTE
The Spanish word **tamal** (plural **tamales**) comes from the Nahuatl word **tamalli,** a food staple of the Aztec empire.

Answers to Activity 17
1. ¿Me pasas las hojas?
2. Porque es la comida favorita de Héctor.
3. También preparan tamales para la Navidad.
4. La familia es de México.

SEGUNDO PASO

(TPR) Storytelling Book pp. 38, 40

WV3 TEXAS-10

Asking for help and responding to requests; telling a friend what to do

> Eva, ¿me pasas las hojas? Gracias.

> Preparar tamales es mucho trabajo, ¿no?

> Pero es la comida favorita de Héctor. Generalmente, sólo preparamos muchos tamales en diciembre para la Navidad. Es una tradición de la cultura mexicana.

17 Los tamales
Contesta las preguntas.

Answers in side column

1. ¿Qué dice la abuela para pedir ayuda?
2. ¿Por qué preparan tamales para la fiesta de graduación de Héctor?
3. Además de la fiesta de graduación, ¿cuándo preparan tamales en la casa de la familia Villarreal?
4. ¿De dónde es la familia originalmente?

Nota cultural

Tamales are an important Mexican Christmas tradition. The Mexican **tamal** is made of cornmeal, and usually stuffed with meat and spices and wrapped in cornhusks. It is then steamed. In Venezuela, families prepare **hallacas** at Christmas time. These are larger than **tamales** and are cooked in banana leaves. Puerto Rican families prepare **pasteles,** which are also cooked in banana leaves, but use **masa** *(dough)* made from root vegetables. All these traditional foods are prepared by a gathering of family and friends. Does your family prepare holiday foods together?

ASÍ SE DICE

Asking for help and responding to requests

10-2

To ask for help, say:

¿Me haces el favor de llamar a Gabi?
Could you call Gabi for me, please?

¿Me ayudas a decorar la sala?

¿Me traes una silla, por favor?

¿Me pasas el helado?

To agree to help, say:

Claro que sí.

Cómo no.

¡Con mucho gusto! *Sure!*

Un momentito. *Just a second.*

To politely refuse to help, say:

Lo siento, pero en este momento estoy ocupado.
I'm sorry, but right now I'm busy.

Perdóname, pero no puedo.
Sorry, but I can't.

¿Me ayudas con las compras, por favor?

¡Con mucho gusto!

18 ¿Me ayudas?

Read the following requests for help. Match each request with a drawing.

1. ¿Me pasas la regla, por favor? c

2. ¿Me traes mi suéter, por favor? a

3. ¿Me haces el favor de ir a comprar más leche? d

4. ¿Me ayudas a cuidar a mis hermanos, por favor? b

a

b

c

d

☀ MOTIVATE

Ask students to think of three instances when they asked someone for help recently. How did they ask, and how were they answered? Ask them to name different ways to ask for help and agree or refuse to help.

☀ TEACH

PRESENTATION
ASÍ SE DICE
Model pronunciation and question construction. Have students work in pairs to practice asking for help or responding to requests. Remind them to reverse roles so that each person practices both the requests and the responses. Finally, ask each person to make up at least three new requests and have the other person respond appropriately.

NATIVE SPEAKERS
The word **momentito** is an example of a diminutive using the ending **-ito/a**. In many parts of the Caribbean the ending **-ico/a** is preferred. (**momentico**)

ADDITIONAL PRACTICE
18 Have students practice asking each other for favors, using their school supplies as props. (**¿Me pasas el bolígrafo?**)

PRESENTATION

VOCABULARIO

Use Teaching Transparency 10-B as reference for students to answer questions that include the new vocabulary from **Así se dice**. For example **¿Me ayudas a inflar los globos?** Then, call on a student to ask a classmate a question using a vocabulary word.

LANGUAGE NOTE
Point out that the word **globo** can mean *balloon*, *globe*, or *hot air balloon*.

SUGGESTION
20 Preview the sentences with students and ask clarifying questions. For example, ask which sentences refer to music or balloons. In which sentences do people agree to help and in which do they politely refuse?

SLOWER PACE
21 Have students work in pairs to list items they need to get ready for the party. Together, pairs create questions asking for help with each item.

PA
p. 53
Act. 9

GV
p. 30
Acts.
7–8

10-B

VOCABULARIO

CD-ROM
DISC **3**

inflar los globos
llamar a los invitados

colgar las decoraciones
decorar la casa

mandar las invitaciones

recibir regalos
abrir los regalos

19 Las fiestas

Look at the drawings in the **Vocabulario.** How would each person ask you to help with what he or she is doing? Answers on p. 161K

20 ¿Me haces el favor...? Script and answers on p. 161E

Listen as various people help each other get ready for the upcoming party. For each request the speaker makes, answer **lógico** or **ilógico** to say if the response below makes sense or not.

CD 10 Tr. 5

1. Sí. ¿Dónde pongo los globos? lógico
2. Oye, ¿dónde están los regalos? ilógico
3. Todos te ayudamos, Adela. lógico
4. En este momento no puedo ayudar con las decoraciones. ilógico
5. Creo que todos van a traer música. lógico
6. Lo siento, pero no tengo tiempo para inflar los globos. ilógico
7. Claro que sí. ¿Necesitas algo más? lógico

21 ¿Necesitas ayuda?

Pretend that you're getting ready for a party at your house. Work with a partner and take turns asking for help in each of the situations below. Your partner can accept or refuse. Remember to give a polite explanation if you refuse to help. Answers on p. 161K

1. Your kitchen is dirty and has dirty dishes.
2. You don't have any food for the party.
3. You need to invite 50 people to the party.
4. You still need to set the table for the party.
5. The party is in one hour and the house is not decorated.
6. You need the chairs from the kitchen in the living room.

ASÍ SE DICE Telling a friend what to do

To tell a friend what to do, say:

Prepara la ensalada y **limpia** la cocina, **¿quieres?**
Make the salad and clean the kitchen, will you please?

Por favor, **decora** la sala y **llama** a los invitados.
Please decorate the living room and call the guests.

Your friend might respond:

De acuerdo. *All right.*

Está bien.

PA
pp. 54–55
Acts.
10–12

GV
pp. 31–32
Acts. 9–12

22 La lista de Efraín

El papá de Efraín le dejó una lista antes de ir al trabajo. Completa la lista de las cosas que debe o puede hacer Efraín.

1. Llama a tu mamá en su trabajo.
2. ===== tu cuarto.
3. ===== a tu abuela.
4. ===== una ensalada de papas para la cena.
5. ===== la cocina.

Answers in side column

23 ¡Ven!

For each of the following situations, use an informal command.

MODELO   Rosa necesita encontrar un libro.
—Ve a la biblioteca.

1. Evelina está en el jardín, pero tienes que hablar con ella ahora.
2. Rubén está cuidando a sus hermanos, pero tiene que hacer una llamada por teléfono.
3. Ricardo está mirando la televisión, pero su mamá cree que hace muy buen tiempo.
4. Arlinda tiene un examen de inglés muy difícil mañana.
5. Sabrina quiere leer su libro pero su hermano quiere jugar a su lado.

Answers in side column

NOTA GRAMATICAL

CD-ROM DISC 3

Informal commands are used with people you would address as **tú**. To give informal commands, drop the **-s** endings of the verb:

tú hablas → ¡Habla!

tú escribes → ¡Escribe!

Some commands are irregular. A few of these forms are:

haz *do, make!*   **pon** *put!*
ve *go!*   **ven** *come!*
vete *go away!*

¡Vete! ¡Estoy de mal humor!

PRESENTATION

ASÍ SE DICE
NOTA GRAMATICAL

TPR Have several students mime various party preparations as you give them simple commands. (**Pon las decoraciones, por favor. Prepara la ensalada. Decora la sala,** etc.) Then have students give each other commands in pairs with partners miming the response. Follow up with Teaching Transparency 10-2.

ADDITIONAL PRACTICE

22 Ask students to write a list in Spanish using informal commands of four things their parent or guardian might tell them to do today after school.

23 Have students play **Simón dice** using the commands they have learned. For example, **Simón dice—Escribe una jota.**

Answers to Activity 22

2. Limpia or Organiza
3. Llama, Visita or Ayuda
4. Prepara
5. Limpia

Answers to Activity 23

Answers will vary. Possible answers:

1. Ven aquí, por favor.
2. Cuida a mis hermanos por un rato, por favor.
3. Ve al jardín a jugar.
4. Estudia bastante esta noche.
5. ¡Vete! Ve a jugar a tu cuarto.

STANDARDS: 1.2, 4.1, 5.1   **181**

STANDARDS: 1.1, 1.2, 5.1

SLOWER PACE
24 Review home-related vocabulary before students do Activity 24. For example, **la sala, la cocina, limpiar, lavar los platos.**

CHALLENGE
24 Have students act out the parts of Cinderella (**la Cenicienta**) and her bossy stepsisters. The stepsisters tell her what to do for them so they can get ready for a dance.

CHALLENGE
25 Replay the audio recording. After each exchange, press pause and ask students to write a response to each request offering an alternative idea or an explanation. Repeat the recording as many times as necessary. For example, after hearing **Buenos días. Habla Nicolás. ¿Qué necesitan para la fiesta? Este... trae unos refrescos, por favor.** The student might respond **Lo siento, no puedo traer refrescos. ¿Te puedo traer unos discos compactos?**

24 ¿Qué tienen que hacer?

Los señores Contreras se van a la playa este fin de semana. Están celebrando su aniversario de boda. Lee las instrucciones que escribieron *(they wrote)* para sus hijos Ana y Marcos y para Juliana, la niñera *(babysitter)*. Después contesta las preguntas.

Juliana

Prepara macarrones con queso y una ensalada el sábado.

Ayuda a Ana con su tarea.

Lava la ropa de Marcos y Ana.

Prepara sándwiches para los almuerzos.

Los niños pueden jugar con sus amigos. Regresamos a las cinco el domingo. En caso de emergencia, estamos en el Hotel Miramar, teléfono 22-74-66. ¡Gracias!

Ana

Haz tu tarea de matemáticas.

Ve a tu práctica de fútbol el sábado.

Corta el césped.

Ve a visitar a tu abuela el domingo.

Marcos

Cuida al gato el sábado y el domingo.

Ve a visitar a tu abuela el domingo.

Limpia tu cuarto.

Lee el libro para la clase de ciencias sociales.

1. ¿Cuáles son los quehaceres de Marcos? Debe cuidar al gato y limpiar su cuarto.
2. ¿Qué van a hacer juntos Ana y Marcos? Van a visitar a su abuela el domingo.
3. Además de cocinar y lavar, ¿qué debe hacer Juliana? Debe ayudar a Ana con su tarea.
4. Además de sus quehaceres, ¿qué va a hacer Ana? Va a practicar fútbol y visitar a su abuela.

25 Preparativos Script and answers on p. 161F

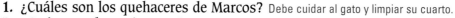

CD 10 Tr. 6

Listen as several people call the Villarreal house to ask how they can help prepare for Héctor's graduation party. Match each person with the correct task.

1. Nicolás f
2. Soledad b
3. Gustavo a
4. Verónica c
5. Gloria e
6. Cristóbal d

a. traer unos discos compactos
b. ir al supermercado
c. preparar la ensalada
d. comprar los globos
e. sacar las fotos
f. traer unos refrescos

26 ¡Qué divertido!

Imagine that you're at Héctor's graduation party and Mr. Villarreal wants everyone to have a good time. How would he tell each person to do the following things? Answers on p. 161K

MODELO   Tomás / tomar más refresco
—Tomás, toma más refresco de naranja.

1. María / sacar unas fotos del grupo
2. Guillermo / venir a la sala
3. Mercedes / bailar con Héctor
4. Gabi / cantar unas canciones populares
5. Eva / tocar la guitarra para Gabi
6. Lisa / poner la música de tu grupo favorito
7. Héctor / abrir los regalos pronto
8. Rebeca / descansar un poco

27 Cosas que hacer

You're having a party and your partner is helping you get ready. You've already made many of the preparations, but you still have some things left to do. Take turns telling each other to do the items left on the list. Don't forget to be polite!

Compra los refrescos, por favor.
Prepara la comida, por favor.
Decora la sala, por favor.
Infla los globos, por favor.
Limpia la sala, por favor.
Llama a nuestros amigos, por favor.
Pon la ropa en el armario, por favor.
Trae los discos compactos, por favor.

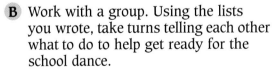

comprar los refrescos
preparar la comida
decorar la sala
inflar los globos

limpiar la sala
llamar a nuestros amigos
poner la ropa en el armario
traer los discos compactos

28 El baile

A Tu colegio va a hacer un baile para el fin de año. Mira la foto del gimnasio donde van a tener el baile. Haz una lista de ocho cosas que deben hacer antes de la fiesta. Debes poner comida y bebida en la lista.

MODELO   1. comprar refrescos

B Work with a group. Using the lists you wrote, take turns telling each other what to do to help get ready for the school dance.

MODELO   Aníbal, trae unos discos compactos de música rock, por favor.

Answers to Activity 28

Answers will vary. Possible answers:
1. comprar refrescos
2. colgar los globos y decoraciones
3. limpiar el gimnasio
4. encontrar música buena

SEGUNDO PASO

ciento ochenta y tres   **183**

SLOWER PACE

27 Allow partners several minutes to make a to-do list using the infinitive of the verb. Students then change the verb to the command form during role-play.

☀ CLOSE

(TPR) Ask individual students to do things that involve moving around the room. For example, **ven acá, escribe en la pizarra, pon el cuaderno en este escritorio.** After you have given several commands, ask students to tell a classmate what to do.

☀ ASSESS

▸ Testing Program, pp. 75–76
  Quiz 10-2
  Audio CD 10, Tr. 19

▸ Grammar and Vocabulary Quizzes
  Quiz 10-2A or
  Alternative Quiz 10-2A

▸ Alternative Assessment Guide, p. 22

PERFORMANCE ASSESSMENT

Tell students they're planning a big party for their grandparents' wedding anniversary. Ask them to write a list, telling family members how to help get ready for the party. They may include any number of people in the family for this activity.

VIDEO INTEGRATION

En camino LEVEL 1B
Video Program
Videocassette 2, 14:01–16:53

¡Ven conmigo! LEVEL 1
DVD Tutor, Disc 2

TEACHER NOTES
• Remind students that cultural information may be included in the Quizzes and the Chapter Test.

• The language of the people interviewed represents informal, unrehearsed speech. Occasionally, text has been edited for clarity.

MOTIVATING ACTIVITY
Have your students list the elements that make a celebration or holiday special to them.

HISTORY LINK
The celebration Ana María describes commemorates the founding of **Villa de San Francisco de Quito** on December 6, 1534 by Spaniard Sebastián de Benalcázar. The place where it was founded had been an Inca city, but the Inca general Rumiñahui destroyed it to avoid surrendering the city to Benalcázar.

Panorama cultural

CD 10
Trs. 7–10

¿Qué hacen ustedes para celebrar?

Festivals are a very important part of life in Spanish-speaking countries. Often the whole community participates. Here is how some people celebrate holidays in their communities.

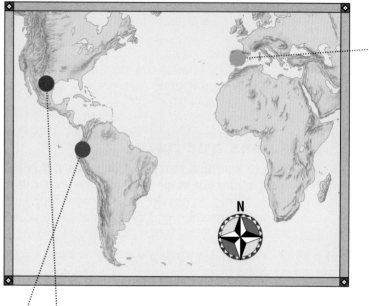

Ana María enjoys celebrating the founding of her city, Quito. Do you know when your city or town was founded?

● **Ana María**
Quito, Ecuador
CD 10 Tr. 8

[Celebramos] la Fundación de Quito el seis de diciembre. [Es mi fiesta favorita] porque hay toros *(bulls)*, sales a las fiestas con tus amigos y *todo el mundo está muy contento.*

Jorge likes spending his favorite holiday with his family. What's your favorite holiday? How do you celebrate it?

● **Jorge**
San Antonio, Texas
CD 10 Tr. 9

Mi día festivo favorito es la Navidad, porque mi familia visita y estamos siempre juntos. Me gustan los regalos y las decoraciones.

In Spain, many people enjoy their city's **feria**, or fair. What are fairs like where you live?

Ana Rosa CD 10 Tr. 10
Sevilla, España

Me gusta mucho la Feria de Abril, porque estás con la familia y amigos. Además, en la feria cantamos, bailamos, vamos a las atracciones, comemos helados y golosinas *(sweets)*. Además, me gustan mucho los coches de caballos *(horse-drawn carriages)* y las niñas... verlas vestidas de gitana *(like Gypsies)*.

1 ¿Cuándo celebra Ana María la Fundación de Quito? el seis de diciembre
¿Por qué le gusta esta fiesta? Hay toros, fiestas y puede salir con sus amigos.

2 ¿Cuál es el día festivo favorito de Jorge? la Navidad
Menciona dos cosas que le gustan en esta fiesta. los regalos y las decoraciones

3 Durante la feria, ¿con quién está Ana Rosa? con sus amigos y su familia

4 ¿Qué hace Ana Rosa para celebrar la Feria de Abril?
Menciona dos cosas. Possible answers: Baila, canta, come helados

Para pensar y hablar...

A. Think of some holidays in the United States that would not be celebrated in the Spanish-speaking world. How would you tell Ana Rosa and Ana María why you like one of these festivals?

B. Choose a holiday that one of the interviewees mentions, or another holiday that you'd like to learn more about. Use an encyclopedia or search the Internet to find out more about it. Then describe to your class what you've learned.

Cuaderno para hispanohablantes, pp. 49–50

PRESENTATION
Before you play the video, have students list words about holidays they might expect to hear. (**comer, bailar, celebrar**) Play or show the **Panorama cultural** and have students see which of these words they hear the interviewee mention. Then play or show the recording or video again. This time have students:
1. Listen for the date of the celebration Ana María mentions.
2. Listen for Jorge's favorite holiday and what he likes about it.
3. Listen for when the **Feria de Abril** is and what Ana Rosa and her family do.

SUGGESTION
Have students research Seville's **Feria de Abril** as an outside assignment.

NATIVE SPEAKERS
Ask native speakers to listen closely to the three distinct accents on the audio or video recording. What similarities and differences can they identify?

STANDARDS: 1.2, 3.2, 4.2   **185**

DVD VIDEO

VIDEO INTEGRATION

En camino LEVEL 1B
Video Program
Videocassette 2, 4:32–4:55 OR
Videocassette 3, 1:41:34–1:41:57
(captioned version)

¡Ven conmigo! LEVEL 1
DVD Tutor, Disc 2

Bell work
Write the following on the board or a transparency: **Hay un gran baile este fin de semana. Todos se visten muy de moda. ¿Qué vas a llevar tú?** Students are to include as many details as possible.

⚛ MOTIVATE

Have each student write at least five things in Spanish that they are doing today. Then ask them to write **Ayer _____ también** next to those they also did yesterday. Have them keep their lists to see how many blanks they can fill in after they have completed this **paso.**

SLOWER PACE

29 Have students look at the photo for visual clues about what the conversation might be about. What is the relationship of the people in the photo? In which room of the house does the conversation take place?

TERCER PASO

(TPR) Storytelling Book pp. 39, 40

WV3 TEXAS-10

Talking about past events

> ¿Qué hiciste, abuela?

> Pues, lo de siempre. Mi mamá preparó comida para llevar a la tumba de la familia. Yo ayudé también. Ese año, yo compré comida en la pequeña tienda cerca de la casa. Pero pasó algo especial...

29 ¿Qué dicen Eva y la abuela?

Look at the photo and then answer the questions.

1. Is Eva asking her grandmother what she is doing or is she asking her what she did? How do you know?
2. What are the two things that her grandmother answers?
3. How is this day special? How do you think Eva will tell her own grandchildren about this day? Choose a sentence she would be likely to use.

1. what she did; possible answer: because Eva can already see what she is doing now.
2. Yo ayudé también. Yo compré comida.
3. Possible answer: The day is special because the family is working together. Yo ayudé también.

ASÍ SE DICE — Talking about past events

To find out what a friend did, ask:

¿Qué hiciste anoche en la fiesta?
What did you do last night at the party?

¿Qué hizo Kathy **ayer?**
What did Kathy do yesterday?

¿Lo pasaron bien la semana pasada?
Did you have a good time last week?

Your friend might answer:

Bailé un poco y **hablé** con Lisa.
I danced a little and I talked with Lisa.

Cantó unas canciones.
She sang some songs.

Sí, **lo pasamos bien.**

10-3

30 La semana de Eva

PA
pp. 56–57
Acts. 13–15

GV
pp. 33–34
Acts. 13–15

Eva has had an exciting week. Look at this page from her journal and figure out if she's writing about herself (**yo**), her parents (**ellos**), Héctor (**él**), or Gabi and herself (**nosotras**).

NOTA GRAMATICAL

Use the preterite tense to talk about events completed in the past. The preterite endings for **trabajar**, a regular **-ar** verb, are:

(yo) trabaj**é**	(nosotros) (nosotras) trabaj**amos**
(tú) trabaj**aste**	(vosotros) (vosotras) trabaj**asteis**
(usted) (él) trabaj**ó** (ella)	(ustedes) (ellos) trabaj**aron** (ellas)

Notice the accent marks and how they affect pronunciation in the **yo** and the **él/ella/usted** forms.

¡Todos en mi familia hicieron mucho la semana
[1]
pasada! El lunes, <u>ayudamos</u> a mis papás a
[2]
limpiar la casa. El miércoles <u>compré</u> un regalo
para Héctor. El jueves mis hermanas pasearon
[3]
en la plaza conmigo. También <u>trabajaron</u> en el
jardín. El viernes celebramos la fiesta de
[4]
Héctor. <u>Bailó</u> mucho en su fiesta. ¡Lo <u>pasé</u>
[5]
bien la semana pasada!

1. nosotras
2. yo
3. ellos
4. él
5. yo

TEACH

PRESENTATION

ASÍ SE DICE
Post a large two-week calendar and highlight the current date. Write the word **fiesta** on yesterday's date. Model the phrases from **Así se dice** using the calendar to indicate that the events took place yesterday. Then have students role-play the conversations, replacing the verbs with verbs of their choice.

NOTA GRAMATICAL
Read the following sentences aloud and have students indicate whether you're talking about something you did last night or not. Explain that without more context, the meaning of 5 is unclear.
1. Hablé con mi padre.
2. Bailo en la fiesta.
3. Canté una canción.
4. Trabajó mucho.
5. Caminamos con el perro.

SUGGESTION
Have auditory learners listen for the sound of the pronounced accent when they are learning the preterite. Have visual learners note the placement of the written accent. Have kinesthetic learners make a gesture as they pronounce the stressed syllable-final vowel.

188   STANDARDS: 1.1, 1.2, 5.1

PRESENTATION

VOCABULARIO

Write the following expressions on the board or a transparency: **bailar el sábado pasado, mirar la televisión anteayer, estudiar mucho el año pasado.** Have students ask their classmates questions, using the **tú** form of these phrases in the preterite tense. The person asked responds using the **yo** form. Ask them to find at least one person who did each of the activities.

ADDITIONAL PRACTICE

32 After doing this activity as a listening comprehension exercise, call on several students and ask questions about the characters on the audio recording. (**¿Qué hicieron Andrés y Valerie?**)

 **COOPERATIVE LEARNING**

Divide students into groups of three. On the board or a transparency write six expressions such as **comprar un regalo** or **mirar la televisión.** Have students practice the preterite tense using the following model:

JUAN	**María, ¿qué compró Pablo?**
MARÍA	**No sé. Pablo, ¿qué compraste?**
PABLO	**Le compré un regalo a mi mamá.**
MARÍA	**Le compró un regalo a su mamá.**

PA p. 58 Act. 17

VOCABULARIO

GV p. 42 Acts. 16–17

anteayer	*the day before yesterday*
el año pasado	*last year*
el sábado pasado	*last Saturday*
el verano pasado	*last summer*

31 ¿Cuándo? Ⓗ

When did these events take place? See if you can figure that out by reading the clues. Use the **Vocabulario.**

1. Es el año 2001. El año 2000 fue *(was)* _____. el año pasado
2. Hoy es miércoles y ayer fue el martes. Pues, _____ fue el lunes. anteayer
3. Este verano voy a ir a la playa, como _____. el verano pasado
4. La fiesta no es este sábado, fue _____. el sábado pasado

32 La fiesta de Abby   Script and answers on p. 161F

Abby's party was great! Listen as she tells her grandmother about what some of her friends did last night. Match the names to the correct drawing.

CD 10 Tr. 11

1. Raquel y Gloria a
2. Kerry y Shoji c
3. Bárbara y Miguel b
4. Pablo d
5. Patricia g
6. Gracie y Kim e
7. Andrés y Valerie h
8. Francisco f

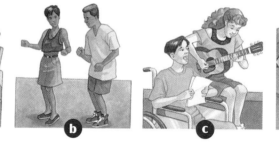

33 En el pasado

Work with a partner and take turns asking each other if and when you did the following activities. Be sure to include where and with whom you did each activity. Answers will vary.

MODELO   bailar
—¿Bailaste el sábado pasado?
—Sí, bailé en la escuela de baile con María Inés.

1. anteayer / hablar por teléfono
2. el verano pasado / nadar
3. anoche / escuchar música
4. ayer / caminar con el perro

5. anteayer / tomar helado
6. el año pasado / estudiar
7. el verano pasado / montar en bicicleta
8. anoche / mirar la televisión

34 ¿Qué hicieron todos?

Imagine that you and your friends had a great time outdoors last week. Write a paragraph about the interesting things everyone did during your trip by answering the following questions. Answers will vary.

1. ¿A qué hora llegaron?
2. ¿Quiénes montaron a caballo?
3. ¿Nadaron todos?

4. ¿Quién pescó?
5. ¿Quiénes jugaron al voleibol?
6. ¿Quién no hizo nada?

35 ¿Qué pasó aquí? Answers on p. 161K

Look at the two drawings. What did Gloria do to the room that makes it look so different? Describe at least five changes that were made. Use the verbs in the word box.

MODELO   —Gloria lavó los platos.

> limpiar   organizar   sacar   lavar   comprar

antes

después

SUGGESTION

33 Have students practice playing detective with a partner. One student gives a present tense clue about his or her past action. For example, **No necesito más lápices.** His or her partner guesses why, **¿Compraste lápices ayer?**

VISUAL LEARNERS

34 Have students make drawings or bring in photos and magazine ads. Have them use these to illustrate what they did on a recent vacation.

CHALLENGE

34 Have students choose a memorable vacation and write about it. Allow them to use a dictionary to look up additional vocabulary as necessary.

ADDITIONAL VOCABULARY

Write the following vacation vocabulary on the board for students to use, **andar por la arena** *to walk in the sand,* **volar una cometa** *to fly a kite,* **construir un castillo de arena** *to build a sandcastle,* and **buscar caracoles** *to look for seashells.*

VISUAL LEARNERS

35 After this activity, ask students to look closely at both pictures and memorize as many details as they can. Then have them close their books and recall the pictures without looking at them. See how many differences between the pictures the class can remember.

SLOWER PACE
36 Have students write out what Héctor did each day before doing this activity orally.

CHALLENGE
36 Have students write their typical weekly agenda like Héctor's. Have students talk about daily schedules in pairs to see which items they have in common.

ART LINK
37 Have students make a poster of their imaginary Web page. They begin by writing three sentences in Spanish about their favorite holiday. Then students draw their Web page so that it looks like it is on a computer screen and attach the sentences to it.

RE-ENTRY
Preterite Make cards and fasten them on the board in vertical columns as follows: (1) subject pronouns and people's names, (2) verb stems of regular **-ar** verbs, (3) preterite endings of **-ar** verbs, (4) direct objects, adverbs, and prepositional phrases. Model a sentence for each verb ending. Then have students make sentences using a card from each column. For further practice, students can also write the sentences.

36 Una semana ocupada

Look at Héctor's agenda. With a partner, take turns asking and answering questions about his activities for the week.

MODELO —¿Qué hizo Héctor el lunes?
—El lunes Héctor tomó un examen a las nueve y media.
—¿Con quién estudió?

> **AGENDA**
>
> lunes: tomar un examen (9:30)
> martes: estudiar con Gabi (4:00)
> miércoles: visitar a mis tíos (7:30)
> jueves: cantar en el coro (8:15)
> viernes: tomar un helado con Eva (9:00)
> sábado: acampar con mis primos (3:00)
> domingo: hablar con los abuelos (2:00)

37 La página web de la familia Esparza...

The Esparza family has put their most recent holiday celebration on their Web page for out-of-town relatives to see. Look at the photo. Then read what it says and answer the questions. What recent family event would you put on a Web page?

1. ¿Qué celebró la familia Esparza? Celebró el Día de los Muertos.
2. ¿Qué hizo Ángel? ¿Con quién? Ángel decoró el altar con Laura.
3. ¿Con qué decoraron el altar? Decoraron el altar con fotos, velas y flores.
4. ¿Qué preparó Tía Linda? Tía Linda preparó los tamales.
5. ¿Para quién hizo esta celebración la familia Esparza? Para su padre y abuelo Juan Antonio Esparza García

Día de los Muertos

Go To: http://www.esparzagarcia/familia.htm

Bienvenidos a nuestra página Web

Juan

mi familia
pasatiempos
cosas divertidas
buzón de correo
enlaces

mis sitios favoritos

Celebramos el Día de los Muertos aquí en San Antonio el noviembre pasado. Laura y Ángel decoraron el altar con fotos, velas° y papel colorado. Miguelito ayudó también con las flores tradicionales del Día de los Muertos. Tía Linda preparó los tamales y todos limpiaron las tumbas° después de ir a la iglesia. Así recordamos a nuestro querido abuelo y padre Juan Antonio Esparza García.

velas *candles*   **tumbas** *graves*

GRAMÁTICA lo and la

pp. 35–36
Acts.
18–21

Just as we use subject pronouns to avoid repetition of names, we can use direct object pronouns to refer to someone or something already mentioned when it is the direct object in a sentence. The singular forms of these pronouns are:

lo him, it, you (formal)   **la** her, it, you (formal)

The pronoun agrees in gender with the noun replaced and comes right before the verb.

Sarita compró **el regalo** ayer.   Daniel, ¿lavaste **la ropa** anoche?

Sarita **lo** compró ayer.   No, no **la** lavé.

38 ¿Lo hiciste?

Rafael's mom is making sure he did all the things she told him to do while she was away yesterday. Help him answer by choosing **lo** or **la** to complete the sentences.

MAMÁ   —Rafael, ¿terminaste *(did you finish)* la tarea?

RAFAEL   —Sí, Mamá. ___1___ terminé ayer. la

MAMÁ   —¿Y compraste el libro para tu papá?

RAFAEL   —Sí, ___2___ compré. lo

MAMÁ   —¿También cortaste el césped?

RAFAEL   —Sí, ___3___ corté. lo

MAMÁ   —¡Qué bien! ¿Y ayudaste a tu papá a preparar
          la comida?

RAFAEL   —Sí, ___4___ ayudé. lo

MAMÁ   —Gracias, mi hijo. ¿Y limpiaste la cocina
          después?

RAFAEL   —Pues, eso no. No ___5___ limpié. la

MAMÁ   —Bueno, está bien. Tu papá puede ayudarte.

39 ¿Qué haces de lunes a viernes?

With a partner, take turns asking each other if you do these activities during the week. Include when and how often you do each activity. Use the correct direct object pronoun.

MODELO   —¿Cuándo practicas la guitarra? Answers will vary.
          —La practico todos los días.

1. hacer la cama
2. leer el periódico
3. preparar el almuerzo
4. mirar la televisión
5. limpiar el cuarto
6. estudiar español
7. lavar la ropa o lavar
   el carro
8. hacer la tarea

¿La guitarra? La practico todos los días.

PRESENTATION
GRAMÁTICA
Demonstrate the usefulness of object pronouns by writing the following sentences on the board: **Sara compró el regalo ayer. Sara llevó el regalo a la fiesta. Sara dejó el regalo en la mesa para Martín. Ahora Martín quiere abrir el regalo.** Point out the repetitiveness that pronouns help avoid. Have students identify the direct objects and replace them with pronouns as appropriate. After they are comfortable with the concept, ask them questions which they answer using a direct object pronoun. **¿Qué haces con la basura? (La saco.)**

PAIR WORK
38 Have students work in pairs to make a dialogue of their own in which a parent asks a teenager about five different household tasks. Students model the dialogue after Activity 38 and use different verbs and activities than **Mamá** and **Rafael** mentioned.

ADDITIONAL PRACTICE
39 As a follow-up ask students these questions in the past tense.

PAIR WORK

40 After students write their answers, have them work in pairs to role-play one of Mr. Villarreal's conversations. One person will be Mr. Villarreal and the other will be one of the people he is calling. The person he is calling will explain why he or she has not done what Mr. Villarreal asked and ask for a different task. Volunteers present their dialogues to the class.

SUGGESTION

Students often have difficulty with negative answers that begin **No, no...** Point out that the second **no** is required to make the verb negative. You might also point out that an affirmative answer can also be introduced by a **no** when the answer is unexpected: **¿Limpiaste la cocina? No, la limpió Abel.**

ADDITIONAL PRACTICE

41 Make index cards with the words and phrases from Activity 41 written on them. Also make **¿quién?, lo,** and **la** cards. Have students practice making questions and substituting **lo** and **la** for the objects.

GAME

¿Qué dibujas? Whisper a vocabulary word or phrase to a student. The students draws a simple representation of it on the board. This can be clarified through mime. The rest of the class must then guess the word or phrase.

40 ¿Todo listo? [H]

Mr. Villarreal wants to make sure that everything is ready for Héctor's graduation party. How would the following people answer his questions? Be sure to use the correct direct object pronoun in your answers. Answers on p. 161K

MODELO —Rebeca, ¿ya compraste el pastel? (no)
—No, no lo compré.

1. Eva, ¿ya invitaste al profesor de Héctor? (no)
2. Gabi y Lisa, ¿ya limpiaron la casa? (sí)
3. Lisa, ¿ya decoraste el patio? (no)
4. Abuela, ¿ya preparaste la comida? (no)
5. Tomás y Juan, ¿ya compraron el regalo? (sí)
6. Marcela, ¿ya llamaste a Victoria? (sí)
7. Aníbal, ¿ya ayudaste a tu papá? (sí)
8. Gabi y Eva, ¿ya compraron el helado? (no)

41 Un sábado ocupado

Last Saturday was a busy day at the Ramírez house. With a partner, take turns telling each other who did the following things. Use direct object pronouns. Answers will vary.

MODELO Susana (limpiar la cocina)
—Susana la limpió.

el señor Ramírez
Diana y Bernardo
Susana
la tía Elena
Carlos y yo
tú
yo

preparar la cena
lavar la ropa
lavar el carro
pasar la aspiradora
cortar el césped
cuidar al hermano
limpiar la cocina

42 ¡Chicos traviesos!

Look at the cartoon and answer the questions.

1. ¿Cree la mamá que sus hijos están mirando la televisión?
2. ¿Adónde mandó la mamá a sus hijos?
3. ¿Quién está mirando la televisión?

1. No, no lo cree.
2. Los mandó a la cama.
3. Los chicos están mirando la televisión.

43 ¿Y qué hizo? Answers will vary.

Find at least one thing your partner and his or her friend did at the following times.

MODELO —¿Qué hiciste ayer?
—Estudié mucho.
—¿Qué hizo tu amiga ayer?
—Maribel compró un reloj.

1. el año pasado
2. el domingo pasado
3. anteayer
4. ayer por la mañana
5. ayer a las doce
6. hoy antes de llegar al colegio

44 En mi cuaderno

Create a journal entry with at least seven sentences telling what you did each day last week. Use the verbs you've learned in the preterite.

Gustavo jugó al ajedrez con su abuelo el sábado pasado.

Script on p. 161F

CD 10
Trs. 12–16

A. You may sometimes feel that Spanish is spoken very fast. This is because in Spanish, syllables are pronounced evenly. Here are some guidelines to help you.

1. Two vowels that come together are joined and are not separated even if each one is part of a different word.
   él va ⌣a ⌣hablar
   lo ⌣encuentro
   entra ⌣en la casa
   hablo ⌣inglés

2. If a word ends in a consonant and the next one begins with a vowel, the preceding consonant begins the new syllable.
   Daniel ⌣es ⌣inteligente.
   Tiene los ⌣ojos ⌣azules.

3. Identical vowels and consonants are reduced to a slightly longer single sound.
   ¿Tienes ⌣soda?
   Sus ⌣hijos ⌣son ⌣nuestros ⌣amigos.
   Quieren ⌣nadar.

B. Dictado
Listen as Ricardo tells you what he's going to do tonight. Write what you hear.

C. Trabalenguas
Abre, cierra, saca afuera.
No tires chicle en la acera.

EN MI CUADERNO

44 For an additional journal entry suggestion, see *Practice and Activity Book,* page 89.

CLOSE

Write the following questions on the board or a transparency. **¿Quién lavó la ropa? ¿Quién limpió la cocina la semana pasada? ¿Quién preparó la cena anoche? ¿Quién lavó el carro ayer? ¿Quién organizó el cuarto?** Call on students to answer one of the questions based on the information in Activity 35 on page 189. Then ask more questions having students answer with their books closed.

ASSESS

▸ Testing Program, pp. 77–78
Quiz 10-3
Audio CD 10, Tr. 20

▸ Grammar and Vocabulary Quizzes
Quiz 10-3 or
Alternative Quiz 10-3A

▸ Alternative Assessment Guide, p. 22

PERFORMANCE ASSESSMENT

Have students work in pairs to role-play a telephone conversation in which they talk about what they did this past weekend.

PRESENTATION
Arbor Day and Earth Day are both spring holidays that promote a healthy environment. Arbor Day, on which people plant trees to landscape cities, began in 1872. Ask students if any area near school would benefit from having trees planted. What kind of trees would they choose to plant there?

 CULTURE NOTE
The **araguaney,** or *tecoma,* is the Venezuelan national tree. It is a flowering tree found mainly in the countryside. The blooms are a bright yellow.

Answers to Activity 1

1. Possible answers: avocado tree; could eat the avocadoes; Trees are important for shade, food, and clean air.
2. Possible answers: If the student is 13; 7'9" at 18 and 31'9" at 50
3. Arbor Day or Earth Day

BIOLOGÍA/MATEMÁTICAS

1 El día del árbol

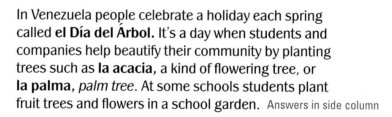

In Venezuela people celebrate a holiday each spring called **el Día del Árbol.** It's a day when students and companies help beautify their community by planting trees such as **la acacia,** a kind of flowering tree, or **la palma,** *palm tree.* At some schools students plant fruit trees and flowers in a school garden. Answers in side column

1. What kind of tree would you prefer to plant and why? How do trees help the environment?

2. If you plant a four-foot-tall palm tree this year that grows nine inches a year, how tall will it be when you're 18? when you are 50?

3. Is there a similar holiday where you live? Explain.

LITERATURA

2 La invitación

Look at the following poem. See if you can guess what the poem is about before you begin reading. Make sure to use reading strategies such as thinking about the topic, looking for cognates, and looking for words you've already learned.

Sube a mi tronco

El árbol gigantesco te invita

El que bebe agua cristalina y canta aire azul

¡Ven! Sube a mis hombros, juega en mis brazos

¡Ven! Conoce el mundo desde un océano lejano

Descansa con la música verde de mis hojas

Baila conmigo el flamenco de mis flores

Y come la fruta rica del bosque

¡VEN!

SUBE

¡VEN!

SUBE

¡VEN!

1. What do you think the poem is about? What is the tree inviting someone to do? It's about climbing trees. It invites someone to climb it.

2. Write your own poem about your favorite park or your favorite holiday celebration. Play with the shape as shown in the poem above, and make your letters ilustrate what you're describing.

MOTIVATING ACTIVITY

2 As a pre-reading activity, ask students what the poem looks like? (a tree) Ask students if they have ever climbed a tree. How did they climb it? How big was the tree? What was it like to be high above the ground? What did they see?

PRESENTATION

2 Lead a class discussion about the poem. What does it talk about? (climbing a tree) Ask volunteers to share an experience they had climbing a tree. Was their experience similar to what the poem described? How was it different?

TEACHER NOTE

The following are possible interpretations of the poem's metaphors (**metáforas**):

Canta aire azul: The tree breathes air high in the blue sky.

juega en mis brazos: Play in my branches.

océano lejano: The leaves or the sky are an ocean far from the ground.

música verde de mis hojas: the sound of the leaves rustling

Baila conmigo el flamenco de mis flores: Enjoy the wind blowing and swaying my branches and flowers.

READING STRATEGY
Making comparisons while reading

☀ PREREADING

MOTIVATING ACTIVITY
A Ask students what words come to mind to describe the pictures on page 197. Ask a volunteer to list them on the board. Have students work in groups on Activity A.

☀ READING

🜲 RE-ENTRY
B and **C** Have students use previously learned reading strategies to understand these passages. For example, finding cognates, skimming for main ideas, and making an outline.

NATIVE SPEAKERS
Ask native speakers to discuss which celebrations or holidays are most important to them and why.

CRITICAL THINKING
Ask students what aspects of holidays around the world make them special. (time with family and friends, special foods, costumes)

VAMOS A LEER

Estrategia
Making comparisons
When you read an article that discusses a topic from more than one point of view, it's natural to make comparisons. You can either make comparisons in your head, or you can write them down. You'll remember more if you write your comparisons as you read.

¡A comenzar!
This reading passage is about festivals in Latin America. As you read, you'll be able to make some comparisons with festivals in the United States.

A Work with two or three other students to complete these statements about festivals where you live. Be sure to write down your answers. Not every item will apply.

In our hometown . . .   Answers on p. 161K

1. people wear masks and costumes during ═══.
2. people have parades during ═══.
3. people celebrate religious holidays such as ═══.
4. people celebrate the harvest during ═══.
5. people celebrate Native American traditions with food, music, and holidays such as ═══.
6. people celebrate African American traditions with foods, music, languages, and holidays such as ═══.

Al grano
B Imagine you found this article in a magazine. As you read it, keep in mind what holidays are like where you live. Answer the questions: Answers on p. 161K

1. What are two different ways that **Carnaval** is celebrated?
2. What are some things you may see at the **Festival de las Máscaras** in Puerto Rico?
3. Why do people bring things to the **árbol de la basura**?

C Now read about festivals in Latin America. Answer the questions to help you figure out if there are any similarities or differences with holidays in your hometown.   Answers on p. 161K

1. Is **Carnaval** celebrated where you live? How? If not, do any of your holidays reflect similar customs or traditions? Explain.
2. Is the **Festival de las Máscaras** similar to a holiday you know about? Which one(s)?
3. What holiday does **Las Turas** remind you of? Why?

D Imagínate que puedes participar en uno de estos festivales. ¿Por qué te parece divertido o interesante? Haz una lista de tus razones *(reasons)*. Después, reúnete con dos compañeros de clase para decidir qué festival quieren celebrar.

Festivales
del mundo hispanohablante

LAS fiestas del mundo hispanohablante tienen sus raíces en las culturas europeas, indígenas y africanas. Con el tiempo, estas celebraciones están cambiando y se van enriqueciendo con los aportes de cada comunidad.

Muchas de las fiestas son de carácter festivo o religioso, mientras que otras combinan la espiritualidad y la sana diversión. La mayoría de las fiestas religiosas son cristianas, pero también se celebran festivales judíos como el Hánukkah, fiestas musulmanas como el Ramadán y varias fiestas de otras religiones.

LA fiesta de Las Turas, de origen indígena, se celebra el 23 y 24 de septiembre en el estado Falcón en Venezuela. El festival da las gracias por una cosecha buena. Los participantes llevan maíz y caña de azúcar y lo dejan al pie del "árbol de la basura". El nombre de la fiesta viene de unos instrumentos llamados turas, hechos de tallos de bambú y cráneo de venado.

UN festival importante de raíces africanas se celebra en Puerto Rico en el pueblo de Hatillo. Es el Festival de las Máscaras. Los puertorriqueños lo celebran el 28 de diciembre en conjunto con la fiesta cristiana del Día de los Inocentes. En el festival hay desfiles de gente con máscaras y disfraces coloridos.

EL Carnaval se celebra por todo el mundo hispanohablante un lunes y martes en febrero o marzo, cuarenta días antes de las Pascuas. En el Ecuador lo celebran con mucho entusiasmo, tirando globos llenos de agua a las personas en las calles. En Argentina las personas se disfrazan y celebran el Carnaval con desfiles en las calles.

ESTOS tres festivales son un pequeño ejemplo de las numerosas fiestas celebradas en el mundo hispano. Representan los aportes indígenas, africanos y europeos a nuestra cultura actual.

Cuaderno para hispanohablantes, pp. 46–48

MULTICULTURAL LINK

Major festivals like **la Feria de Sevilla, el Día de los Muertos, las Fallas de Valencia,** and **Fiesta** in San Antonio unite cities in a spirit of goodwill. What other cultural festivals do students know about? (Chinese New Year, German Oktoberfest)

☀ POSTREADING

SUGGESTIONS

D Have students write sentences describing the festival mentioned here that they would like most to attend and why.

🌑 **CULTURE NOTES**
• **El Día de los Inocentes** in Hatillo, Puerto Rico is celebrated on December 28 with a parade of people wearing masks of African origin and a party in the town square. In many Latin American countries it is celebrated like April Fool's Day.

• **La Fiesta de Las Turas** is a harvest festival much like Thanksgiving. Participants shuck corn and leave it under the **árbol de la basura**, a specially chosen tree. Later they use the corn kernels for future planting, to protect their next harvest.

• **Carnaval** is a major holiday in Brazil.

TEACHER NOTE

For additional readings, see *Practice and Activity Book,* p. 59.

Repaso reviews all five skills and culture in preparation for the Chapter Test.

CHALLENGE

2 Assign students to work in groups so they can pool their information to create a detailed description of what the people are doing. Challenge groups to add as much information as possible. Ask the groups to share their descriptions with the class.

PAIR WORK

3 Assign each student a partner. Have students role-play a dialogue in which one student is the interviewer and the other is Tomás. Partners combine the questions they wrote for this activity, eliminating duplicate questions. Then the interviewer uses the combined list of questions to ask Tomás about the picnic. Tomás uses the information from the reading to answer.

📁 PORTFOLIO

Oral Ask students to role-play a phone conversation with a friend or relative who will be coming home to celebrate a special family holiday. They tell each other what they are doing now to get ready for the occasion and ask the person's opinion about a special gift for someone in the family. For portfolio suggestions, see *Alternative Assessment Guide,* p. 14.

198   STANDARDS: 1.2, 5.1

REPASO

CD-ROM DISC 3

internet
MARCAR: go.hrw.com
PALABRA CLAVE:
WV3 TEXAS-10

1 Listen to Mariana tell about her favorite holiday, then answer the questions.   Script and answers on p. 161F

CD 10 Tr. 17

1. ¿Adónde viajaron Mariana y su familia?   Monterrey
2. ¿Por qué viajaron allí?   Porque celebraron la Navidad con sus abuelos.
3. ¿En qué mes viajaron?   en diciembre
4. ¿Qué preparó la abuela?   decoraciones bonitas
5. Después de la cena, ¿qué hicieron todos?   bailaron, cantaron y hablaron toda la noche
6. ¿Por qué es la Navidad su fiesta favorita?   porque siempre la pasan en México con sus abuelos

2 Imagine that you're at Héctor's house getting ready for his graduation party. What is each person listed doing right now?   Answers will vary.

yo   Héctor   Héctor y yo   sus padres

3 You're going to interview Tomás about the last Spanish Club picnic. First read his report. Then write at least five questions you can ask him.

> ### Las noticias del club de español   Semana no. 3
>
> El sábado lo pasamos bien. Todos llegamos al parque para el picnic del Club de Español a las nueve de la mañana. Cada persona preparó algo para comer. Yo preparé un postre y la profesora preparó unos sándwiches muy ricos.
>
> Celebramos el cumpleaños de la profesora con pastel y helado. Le compramos un reloj. En la fiesta, Alicia tocó la guitarra y Felipe y Sara cantaron canciones en español. Muchas personas bailaron también. Nadamos en el lago y jugamos al béisbol y al tenis. A las nueve de la noche llegamos a casa cansados pero contentos.
>
> Tomás Wilson, secretario

Answers will vary. Possible answers:
1. ¿Qué hizo el club de español el sábado pasado?
2. ¿Qué celebraron?
3. ¿Qué preparó la profesora?
4. ¿Qué hicieron en la fiesta?
5. ¿Qué le regalaron a la profesora?

4 Vamos a escribir

Write a paragraph about what you did last Saturday. It can be about real or imaginary events. Use verbs you know in the preterite. Include some lively and interesting details in your report to make your writing come to life.

Estrategia

Using details A good way to choose the right details to include is to ask yourself: who? what? where? why? when? and how?

Prewriting

1. Make a list of five things you did on Saturday. Choose the most interesting activities. What did you do? With whom?
2. Organize your information in chronological order (in order of *when* the events happened, from first to last).

Writing

1. Write the events in the order they happened, using words like **después, antes, primero,** and **luego.**
2. Use as many details as possible. **Compré una blusa roja para mi abuela** is more interesting than **Compré un regalo.**

Revising

1. Make sure you didn't leave out any important information. Add more details if possible.
2. Does your paragraph make sense? Rewrite if necessary.
3. Check your work for spelling, logic, and use of details, then rewrite your paragraph with the necessary changes.

5 SITUACIÓN

You're on a committee to plan the end-of-year field trip. But your class doesn't have enough money! Work with three or four classmates to discuss a solution. What food, activities, music, and location will fit the budget? You may also suggest ways to earn money for the project.

Cuaderno para hispanohablantes, p. 49

📁 PORTFOLIO

Written Ask each student to create a greeting card to send to a friend or relative using expressions from Chapter 10 and previous chapters. The card could include drawings or magazine photos. Students may include their greeting card in their written Portfolio. For Portfolio suggestions, see *Alternative Assessment Guide,* p. 14.

♖ GAME

Treinta segundos Prepare a list of questions before class to ask what people are doing at a particular moment. (**¿Qué está haciendo el profesor de matemáticas? ¿Qué están haciendo tus amigos? ¿Qué estoy haciendo?**) Divide the class into two teams. Each team receives one point per logical answer given in 30 seconds. An answer might be **El profesor está hablando y está escribiendo en la pizarra.** As a variation, ask students what people did in the past, using -**ar** verbs (**Qué compraste ayer? Compré un regalo para María.**)

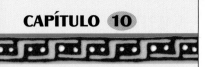

WV3 TEXAS-10

This page is intended to help students prepare independently for the Chapter Test. It is a brief checklist of the major points covered in the chapter. The students should be reminded that it is only a checklist and does not necessarily include everything that will appear on the Chapter Test.

Answers to Activity 1

Answers will vary. Possible answers:

1. Estoy abriendo regalos y jugando con mis hermanos.
2. Estoy en casa de mis abuelos y estamos comiendo y hablando.

Answers to Activity 2

1. Héctor está abriendo regalos.
2. Rebeca está llamando a los invitados.
3. Mario y Juan están decorando la sala.
4. La abuela está preparando los tamales.

Answers to Activity 3

Answers will vary. Possible answers:

1. ¿Qué piensas de la fiesta?
2. ¿Qué piensas de la comida?
3. ¿Qué te parece la música?
4. ¿Te gusta el postre?

Answers to Activity 5

1. Ayuda más en casa.
2. Haz tu tarea.
3. Limpia tu cuarto.
4. Lee tu libro.

Answers to Activity 6

Answers will vary. Possible answers:

a. Los señores Medrano miraron la televisión.
b. La señora Walker habló por teléfono.
c. El señor Juárez cocinó.
d. Larry y Marisa estudiaron anoche.

200

STANDARDS: 1.2

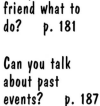 **Can you talk about what you're doing right now?** p. 171

 **Can you ask for and give an opinion?** p. 174

Can you ask for help and respond to requests? p. 179

Can you tell a friend what to do? p. 181

Can you talk about past events? p. 187

1 Imagine that it's one of the following holidays right now. Can you tell your friend on the phone what you are doing right now? Answers in side column

1. la Navidad
2. el Día de Acción de Gracias

2 How would you say that . . .? Answers in side column

1. Héctor is opening gifts
2. Rebeca is calling the guests
3. Mario and Juan are decorating the living room
4. Grandmother is preparing the tamales

3 How would you ask a guest what he or she thinks of . . .?
Answers in side column

1. the party
2. the food
3. the music
4. the dessert

4 The Spanish Club is planning an end-of-the-year party. Can you write notes to five club members asking for their help in completing the preparations? Answers will vary.

5 How would you tell a friend . . .? Answers in side column

1. to help at home
2. to do his or her homework
3. to clean his or her room
4. to read his or her book

6 Can you write a sentence for each drawing saying what these people did last night? Use your imagination and think of a name for each person. Answers in side column

VOCABULARIO

PRIMER PASO

Talking about what you're doing right now

el Año Nuevo *New Year's Day*
colgar (ue) las decoraciones
  to hang decorations
decorar *to decorate*
el Día de Acción de Gracias
  Thanksgiving Day
el Día de la Independencia
  Independence Day
el Día de las Madres
  Mother's Day
el Día de los Enamorados
  Valentine's Day
el Día del Padre *Father's Day*
los días festivos *holidays*
la Navidad *Christmas*
la Nochebuena *Christmas Eve*
la Nochevieja *New Year's Eve*
las Pascuas *Easter*

Asking for and giving an opinion

Buena idea. *Good idea.*
creer *to believe, to think*
Creo que no. *I don't think so.*
Creo que sí. *I think so.*
Me parece bien. *It's fine with me.*
Perfecto. *Perfect.*
¿Qué te parece si...? *How do you feel about . . . ?*

SEGUNDO PASO

Asking for help and responding to requests

abrir los regalos *to open the gifts*
¡Con mucho gusto! *Sure!*

inflar los globos *to blow up balloons*
llamar a los invitados *to call the guests*
mandar las invitaciones *to send invitations*
¿Me ayudas a...? *Can you help me to . . . ?*

¿Me haces el favor de...? *Could you please . . . ?*
¿Me pasas...? *Can you pass me . . . ?*
¿Me traes...? *Can you bring me . . . ?*
Un momentito. *Just a second.*
Perdóname. *Excuse me.*
recibir regalos *to receive gifts*

Telling a friend what to do

De acuerdo. *All right.*
haz *do, make*
pon *put, place*
ve *go*
ven *come*
vete *go away*

¡Vete! ¡Estoy de mal humor!

TERCER PASO

Talking about past events

anoche *last night*
anteayer *the day before yesterday*
el año pasado *last year*
ayer *yesterday*
la *it/her/you (formal)*
lo *it/him/you (formal)*
¿Qué hiciste? *What did you do?*
¿Qué hizo? *What did he/she/you do?*
el sábado pasado *last Saturday*
la semana pasada *last week*
el verano pasado *last summer*

🏰 **GAME**
Palabras prohibidas
Make vocabulary cards. Divide the class into two teams. A reader from one team and a guesser from the other come forward. Give the reader five cards. When you say **¡Empieza!** the reader gives verbal clues without saying the word itself or a derivative of it. The guesser's team gets one point for each word guessed correctly.

CHAPTER 10 ASSESSMENT

▶ **Testing Program**
Chapter Test, pp. 79–84
🔊 Audio Compact Discs, CD 10, Trs. 21–22
Speaking Test, p. 131

▶ **Alternative Assessment Guide**
Performance Assessment, p. 22
Portfolio Assessment, p. 14
CD-ROM Assessment, p. 29

▶ **Interactive CD-ROM Tutor, Disc 3**
💿 ¡A hablar!
¡A escribir!

▶ **Standardized Assessment Tutor**
Chapter 10

▶ **One-Stop Planner, Disc 3**
✎ Test Generator
☞ Chapter 10

¡Ven conmigo a Puerto Rico!
LOCATION OPENER CHAPTERS 11, 12

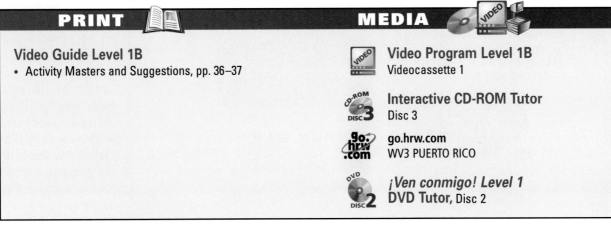

PRINT

Video Guide Level 1B
- Activity Masters and Suggestions, pp. 36–37

MEDIA

Video Program Level 1B
Videocassette 1

Interactive CD-ROM Tutor
Disc 3

go.hrw.com
WV3 PUERTO RICO

¡Ven conmigo! Level 1
DVD Tutor, Disc 2

You may wish to point out the following images as students view the Puerto Rico Location Opener. These images will be seen on both the Video Program and the DVD Program. If you are using the DVD Program they may be freeze-framed for presentation and discussion purposes.

About three fourths of Puerto Rico is mountainous. The **Cordillera Central** extends from the east coast to the west coast. The highest peak, **Cerro de Punta,** just north of Ponce, is about 1,338 m (4,400 ft.) high. Puerto Rico's tropical climate, with an annual mean temperature of 24°C (75°F), allows for a year-round growing season.

San Juan has four main plazas: **Plaza de San José, Plaza del Quincentenial, Plaza de Armas,** and **Plaza de Colón.** Plaza de Armas has four 100-year-old statues representing the four seasons.

El Faro, a neoclassical lighthouse built in 1880 at Cabezas de San Juan near Fajardo, is one of two operating lighthouses on the island. The light, originally a wick fueled by oil and magnified by a Fresnel lens, could be seen 18 miles away. The lighthouse is still used by the U.S. Coast Guard. Its light is now electric, and its beam extends 26 miles.

On the northeastern end of the island, the 28,000 acres of the tropical rain forest preserve **El Yunque** contain over 250 species of trees and many rare species of birds and other animals. Officially called the Caribbean Nations Forest (**Bosque Nacional del Caribe**), El Yunque is the only tropical forest in the U.S. National Forest System. Students will have a chance to see more of **El Yunque** in Chapter 12.

Old San Juan is a seven-square-block walled area originally conceived as a military stronghold. It is the second-oldest settlement in the Americas and has been honored by such designations as National Historic Zone, National Historic Site, and World Heritage Site. The streets in this area are paved with cobblestones made from furnace slag brought over as ballast on Spanish ships.

PROJECT

VISITEMOS PUERTO RICO

This bulletin board project familiarizes students with the indigenous people of Puerto Rico, the geography of the island, and things to do when planning a trip there.

Introduction

Puerto Rico is a beautiful island with many treasures to explore: people, geography, language, culture, foods, industries, and wildlife. Ask students if they have ever been to Puerto Rico or the Caribbean. What is the climate like? What are the people like? What is the pace of life like?

Have your students imagine that they are planning a class trip to Puerto Rico. They will need to gather information about the geography, food, culture, language, money, and places of interest.

From the information gathered, students prepare a class bulletin board to be used as a reference for Chapters 11 and 12.

Materials students may need

- Brochures on Puerto Rico
- Poster board
- Large- and medium-point felt-tipped markers
- Thumbtacks, stapler
- Map and pictures of Puerto Rico
- Scissors, glue, tape

Sequence

1 Divide the class into groups of three or four students and assign each group a topic to research for the bulletin board. Each group will have a Researcher, an Artist (labeler), a Cutter/Paster, and a Presenter. If the group has three students, the Artist and Cutter/Paster can be combined into one job.

2 Each group will produce a collage relevant to the list of topics to be included in the bulletin board. Each collage should have at least 10 items of interest for the bulletin board. The topics of information that will be presented as part of the bulletin include:

- Tropical fruits and vegetables
- El Yunque rain forest
- Map of Puerto Rico, with major cities and geographical features
- Tourist information, places of interest, activities of interest
- Wildlife indigenous to Puerto Rico
- Famous people from Puerto Rico
- Legends about the Taino and Puerto Rican people

3 The Researcher selects the pictures from the travel brochures that will be used for the collage. The Cutter/Paster cuts the pictures, and glues them to the poster board. The Artist labels the necessary items and titles the collage.

4 The map group is responsible for drawing a map of Puerto Rico and labeling the major cities, rivers, mountains, rain forests, and reserves.

5 For the indigenous people component, students will try to find examples of one or two legends in the school library, summarize them, and display the stories on a collage. The stories can be illustrated.

6 Have groups present their collages to the class. Use the collages for the class bulletin board.

Grading the project

Suggested point distribution (total = 100 points):

Information	30
Creativity	25
Oral presentation	20
Neatness	15
Cooperative effort	10

LOCATION
6

¡Ven conmigo a Puerto Rico!
LOCATION OPENER CHAPTERS 11, 12 (cont.)

Using the Map

- You may want to direct students to the map in the *Pupil's Edition,* page xxi.
- Ask students to point out the West Indies archipelago. (Greater Antilles, Lesser Antilles, Bahama Islands)
- Have students locate the islands that make up the Greater Antilles archipelago. (Cuba; Jamaica; Hispaniola, which includes Haiti and the Dominican Republic)
- Ask students to identify the bodies of water that surround Puerto Rico. (Atlantic Ocean and Caribbean Sea) You may want to tell students that it takes only about six hours to drive around the island.

History Link

El Morro *(headland* or *promontory)* is the oldest and most strategic fort in San Juan. Its six levels rise more than 140 feet and dominate the harbor entrance. It was originally named **San Felipe del Morro,** in honor of King Philip III of Spain. A deep moat surrounds its 18-foot-thick walls, and it is equipped with barracks, wells, supply rooms, dungeons, a chapel, and an armory.

Language Note

Puerto Ricans speak differently depending on where they are from on the island. For example, the people from Mayagüez on the west coast pronounce the trilled *r* much like the uvular *r* in French, and the people from Jayuya in the central Cordillera pronounce word-final **e** as an **i** (**leche** would be pronounced *lechi*). You may want to refer to the Native Speaker suggestion on page 210 for more information on Puerto Rican accents.

Culture Note

During the 18th century, horse racing in the streets of San Juan was common. According to legend, in 1753 a horse racer named Baltasar Montáñez failed to make the turn at the south end of **Calle Cristo** and plunged over the cliff—but miraculously survived. **Capilla de Cristo** was built both to commemorate the miracle and to block off the street.

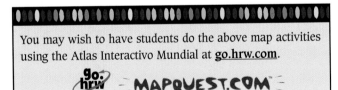

You may wish to have students do the above map activities using the Atlas Interactivo Mundial at **go.hrw.com.**

Culture Note

The Taino, the native people of Puerto Rico, called the island *Borinquen,* or "Island of the Noble Lord." Today, many Puerto Ricans still refer to themselves as **boricuas.**

Language Note

In Puerto Rico, a *dollar* is sometimes called a **peso.** The *half-dollar* is called **medio peso,** a *quarter* is a **peseta,** a *nickel* is a **níquel** or **vellón,** and a *penny* is a **chavo** or **centavo.** As in English, a ten-cent coin is called a *dime.* People sometimes say **chavos** for *money,* and someone without it is **pelado** or **sin chavos.**

Suggestions

- Display a detailed map of Puerto Rico for reference throughout the chapter, if available.
- Post photographs of famous Puerto Rican people including Rosie Perez, Rita Moreno, Jimmy Smits (actors), Chayanne (singer), Juan González and Iván Rodríguez (baseball players), and the late Raúl Julia (actor).

Culture Notes

- The Taino, the indigenous people of Puerto Rico, cultivated corn (**maíz**), peanuts (**maní**), yams (**ñame**), taro (**yautía**), and cassava (**yuca**). Fruits such as guava (**guayaba**), pineapple (**piña**), and sea grapes (**uvas playeras**) grew wild. These foods are all still popular in Puerto Rico today. The Taino also cultivated arrowroot (**arrurruz**), which they called *aru-aru,* meaning "meal of meals."

- Some typical Puerto Rican dishes include deep-fried **tostones,** made from sliced plantains or breadfruit (**pana**). Pork dishes include fried rinds (**chicharrones**), a tripe stew (**mondongo**), and **gandinga,** made from minced liver, heart, and kidney. Bananas are often fried to make a sweet dessert. Another popular food is **pastel,** which is not a dessert, but a **tamal** made with meat, olives, onions, and plantain flour.

- The **plena** is a Puerto Rican folk dance that combines Afro-Caribbean music and dance traditions. It originated in and around Ponce, on the southwestern part of the island. The Spanish **pandero,** a large tambourine-like instrument often associated with the dance, is also of African origin. See pages 202–203 for a photo of people dancing **la plena.**

¡Ven conmigo
a Puerto Rico!

**VIDEO
INTEGRATION**

En camino LEVEL 1B
Video Program
Videocassette 2, 17:44–20:05

¡Ven conmigo! LEVEL 1
DVD Tutor, Disc 2

MOTIVATING ACTIVITY

Ask students if they can name
any Caribbean islands. (Puerto
Rico, U.S. Virgin Islands, Cuba)
Ask students what they know
about Puerto Rico. Do they
think the climate is warm or
cool there? (warm) Tell students that Puerto Rico is a
popular vacation spot because
it has 300 miles of shoreline.

BACKGROUND

Puerto Rico is the smallest of
the Greater Antilles Islands. Its
first known inhabitants were the
Taino, who greeted Columbus
and the Spanish settlers in
1493. Some interesting sights
in Puerto Rico are the Arecibo
Observatory, the world's
largest radio telescope; the
Camuy Caves, dramatic caves
with 170-foot-high ceilings;
El Faro, the lighthouse built in
the 1800s; the Phosphorescent
Bay at La Parguera, where the
plankton glow when disturbed
at night; and the official mas-
cot, the **coquí.** (a frog native
only to Puerto Rico)

¡Ven conmigo
a Puerto Rico!

Puerto Rico

Población: 3.889.501 (el 99,9% habla español, pero la mayoría habla inglés también)

Área: 9.104 kilómetros cuadrados (3.515 millas cuadradas), más grande que Delaware, pero más pequeño que Connecticut

Ubicación: una isla con el océano Atlántico al norte y el mar Caribe al sur

Capital: San Juan, con un millón de habitantes

Gobierno: estado libre asociado de los Estados Unidos

Industrias: la pesca, productos farmacéuticos, maquinarias y metales, turismo

Cosechas principales: azúcar, café, piña, plátanos

Unidad monetaria: el dólar

Idiomas: español, inglés

ESTADOS
UNIDOS

San Juan
★
PUERTO RICO
Ponce   (US)

CUBA

Mar Caribe

REPÚBLICA
DOMINICANA

N

0   500 Kilómetros
0   250 Millas

◀ **La plena es un baile folklórico que viene de Ponce.**

📶 internet

MARCAR: go.hrw.com
PALABRA CLAVE:
WV3 PUERTO RICO

203

go.hrw.com

HRW ATLAS INTERACTIVO MUNDIAL

MAPQUEST.COM

Have students go to the interactive atlas at **go.hrw.com** to find out more about the geography of Puerto Rico.

USING THE ALMANAC

- **Gobierno:** Since 1952 Puerto Rico has been a commonwealth of the United States, or **estado libre asociado.** When living on the island, Puerto Ricans cannot vote in presidential elections and do not pay federal income tax. However, they have full U.S. citizenship. If Puerto Ricans move to the United States mainland, they may vote, and must also pay federal taxes.

- **Unidad monetaria:** Puerto Rico uses United States currency.

- **Idiomas:** On January 28, 1993, Governor Pedro Rosselló of Puerto Rico declared Spanish and English joint official languages of the island. Spanish had been the official language since 1991 when the Puerto Rican Congress declared it so. Before 1991, no official language had been declared for the island.

CNNenEspañol.com

Have students check the CNN en español Web site for news on Puerto Rico. The CNN en español site is also a good source of timely, high interest readings for Spanish students.

USING THE PHOTO ESSAY

1 Since oranges originated in the part of Asia that now includes China, oranges are usually called **chinas** in Puerto Rico.

2 **El Día de los Reyes Magos,** January 6 is a Catholic holiday that celebrates the visit of the three Kings to the newborn Jesus. On January 5, children prepare a box with a combination of fresh-cut grass, flowers, or corn. They put the box under their beds or in the living room and excitedly wait for the next day when the camels (or horses) will have eaten the grass and the three Kings will have left gifts for them. The family celebration continues there with a feast of **lechón asado** (roast pork), **arroz con gandules** (peas and rice), **tembleque** (coconut custard), and **arroz con dulce** (rice pudding); traditional music, and a game of dominoes.

3 Surfing is a popular sport all year round in Puerto Rico. Some good surfing beaches are **La Concha** in San Juan, **Aviones** in Piñones, and **Los Tubos** in Vega Baja.

PUERTO RICO

CD-ROM DISC 3

First seen by Columbus on November 19, 1493, Puerto Rico is one of the most beautiful islands in the Caribbean. This tropical island is mostly mountainous and has many picturesque beaches. Puerto Rican culture has influences from Spain, Africa, and North America.

▲ **Mariscos y frutas**
Throughout Puerto Rico you'll find tantalizing foods, ranging from a wide variety of seafood to delicious tropical fruits.

▲ **Las fiestas**
Almost every holiday is an occasion for a festival in Puerto Rico.

▼ **Una isla tropical**
Puerto Rico is known for its beautiful, sunny beaches. With 300 miles of coastline, it's a great place for all kinds of water sports.

204 *doscientos cuatro*

Chapters 11 and 12 will introduce you to Ben and his sister Carmen, two New Yorkers visiting relatives in Puerto Rico. They, along with their mother and grandfather, visit some of the fascinating and beautiful places on the island of Puerto Rico. How would you like to spend two weeks on a tropical island?

▲ **La música puertorriqueña tradicional**
The traditional music of Puerto Rico has its roots in both Africa and Europe.

La historia colonial ▶
Begun in 1604, the historic Alcaldía (*City Hall*) houses both the local government and small businesses. The adjacent Plaza de Armas served as the training field for Spanish soldiers defending the colonial islands.

❹ **La música jíbara** makes use of many traditional instruments, including the **cuatro,** a guitar-like instrument with twelve strings. Another popular music style in the Caribbean is **salsa. La música salsa** is derived from the **rumba,** a dance music of Afro-Cuban origin. The instruments normally used for **salsa** are the piano, trumpet, saxophone, and percussion instruments like the **güiro,** conga and bongo drums. Vocals are crucial to **salsa.** The lyrics often combine poetry and politics. **Salsa** was introduced in the 1930s in the dance halls of New York City, where it became very popular. Since then, legendary **salseros** Willie Colón, Celia Cruz, Rubén Blades, Ricky Martin, and Tito Puente have made **salsa** a favorite musical style throughout the Spanish-speaking world and beyond.

❺ The City Hall (**la Alcaldía**) was built in stages from 1604 to 1789. It is one of the government buildings that surrounds the **Plaza de Armas,** so named for the drills carried out by the city's residents in preparation for attack by pirates. Planned in the 16th century as San Juan's main square, the **Plaza de Armas** later became a social gathering place.

205

Para vivir bien

CHAPTER OVERVIEW

De antemano pp. 208–211	*Un recorrido por San Juan*			
	FUNCTIONS	**GRAMMAR**	**VOCABULARY**	**RE-ENTRY**
Primer paso pp. 212–217	• Making suggestions and expressing feelings, p. 213	• **¿Te acuerdas?:** The verb **dormir**, p. 213 • **Nota gramatical:** Present tense of **sentirse**, p. 214	• Keeping fit, p. 215	• **e → ie** stem-changing verbs • Food vocabulary • Expressions of frequency
Segundo paso pp. 220–227	• Talking about moods and physical condition, p. 221	• **Nota gramatical:** The verb **doler** with **me, te, le,** p. 224	• Physical conditions, p. 221 • Parts of the body, p. 223	• Definite articles • **estar +** condition • **o → ue** stem-changing verbs
Tercer paso pp. 228–235	• Saying what you did, p. 229 • Talking about where you went and when, p. 231	• **Nota gramatical:** The verb **jugar** in the preterite, p. 229 • **Nota gramatical:** The verb **ir** in the preterite, p. 232	• Different sports fields, p. 232	• Use of preterite tense to discuss past events • Sports

Letra y sonido	**p. 235**	Strong versus weak vowels	**Dictado:** Textbook Audiocassette 3A / Audio CD 11
Enlaces	**pp. 236–237**	**El béisbol**	
Vamos a leer	**pp. 238–239**	**Para estar en forma**	**Reading Strategy:** Background knowledge
Review	**pp. 240–243**	**Repaso,** pp. 240–241	**A ver si puedo...,** p. 242 **Vocabulario,** p. 243

Culture	• **Panorama cultural: ¿Qué deporte practicas?,** pp. 218–219 • **Nota cultural:** Expressions used when someone sneezes, p. 220 • **Nota cultural:** Body parts in common expressions, p. 224	• **Nota cultural:** Athletes from Spanish-speaking backgrounds, p. 227 • **Nota cultural:** Sports in Spanish-speaking countries, p. 231 • **Nota cultural:** Desserts from tropical fruits, p. 234

Lesson Planning

One-Stop Planner
Lesson Planner with Substitute Teacher
Lesson Plans, pp. 26–30

Listening and Speaking

Listening Activities
- Student Response Forms for Listening Activities, pp. 67–69
- Additional Listening Activities 11-1 to 11-6, pp. 21–23
- Additional Listening Activities (song), p. 24
- Scripts and Answers, pp. 45–47

Video Guide
- Teaching Suggestions, pp. 39–40
- Activity Masters, pp. 41–43
- Scripts and Answers, pp. 108–110, 117–118

Activities for Communication
- Communicative Activities, pp. 31–36
- Realia and Teaching Suggestions, pp. 64–68
- Situation Cards, pp. 84–85

¡Ven conmigo! Level 1
TPR Storytelling Book, pp. 41–43

Reading and Writing

Reading Strategies and Skills, Chapter 11
¡Lee conmigo! 1, Chapter 11
Practice and Activity Book, pp. 61–72

Grammar

Grammar and Vocabulary Workbook, pp. 37–44

¡Ven conmigo! Level 1
Grammar Tutor for Students of Spanish
Chapter 11

Assessment

Testing Program
- Paso Quizzes and Chapter Test, pp. 91–102
- Score Sheet, Scripts and Answers, pp. 103–108

Grammar and Vocabulary Quizzes
- Quizzes 11-1A, 11-2A, 11-3A
- Alternative Quizzes 11-1A, 11-2A, 11-3A

Alternative Assessment Guide
- Portfolio Assessment, p. 15
- Performance Assessment, p. 23
- CD-ROM Assessment, p. 30

¡Ven conmigo! Level 1
Standardized Assessment Tutor
- Reading, pp. 43–45
- Writing, pp. 46

Native Speakers

¡Ven conmigo! Level 1
Cuaderno para hispanohablantes, pp. 51–55

MEDIA

Online Activities
go.hrw.com
- Juegos interactivos
- Actividades internet

Video Program
- Videocassette 2
- Videocassette 3 *(captioned version)*

¡Ven conmigo! Level 1
DVD Tutor, Disc 2

Audio Compact Discs
- Textbook Listening Activities, CD 11, Tracks 1–16
- Additional Listening Activities, CD 11, Tracks 22–27
- Assessment Items, CD 11, Tracks 17–21

Interactive CD-ROM Tutor, Disc 2

Teaching Transparencies
- Situations 11-1 to 11-3
- Vocabulary 11-A to 11-D
- Grammar and Vocabulary Workbook

 One-Stop Planner CD-ROM

Use the **One-Stop Planner CD-ROM with Test Generator** to aid in lesson planning and pacing.

For each chapter, the **One-Stop Planner** includes:
- Editable lesson plans with direct links to teaching resources
- Printable worksheets from resource books
- Direct launches to the HRW Internet activities
- Video and audio segments
- Test Generator
- Clip Art for vocabulary items

DVD/VIDEO

Videocassette 2, Videocassette 3 (captioned version)
DVD Tutor, Disc 2 See Video Guide, pages 38–43.

De antemano • Un recorrido por San Juan

Ben, Carmen, and their mother are visiting family in Puerto Rico. Ben and Carmen go sightseeing, but they need to meet their mother at 3:00. In a park they meet Pedro, who takes them on a tour of the city. Later, Ben realizes that it is 2:55, and they must hurry.

¿Qué deporte practicas?

Teens from Mexico, Spain, and Florida tell what sports they like to play and why. In other interviews, people from various countries talk about their favorite sports.

A continuación

Ben, Carmen, and Pedro hurry to la **Plaza de Hostos** and make it in time to meet their mother. Ben and Carmen introduce Pedro to their mother, who realizes that Pedro is actually Ben and Carmen's cousin. Later that day they all go to watch Pedro, Ben, and Carmen's uncle play baseball.

Videoclips

• **Happydent®**: advertisement for sugarless chewing gum

INTERACTIVE CD-ROM TUTOR

Activity	Activity Type	Pupil's Edition Page
En contexto	*Interactive conversation*	
1. Gramática	¿Qué falta?	p. 214
2. Vocabulario	¿Cuál es?	p. 215
3. Vocabulario	¡Super memoria!	p. 222
4. Vocabulario	Imagen y sonido ¡Exploremos! ¡Identifiquemos!	p. 223
5. Así se dice	¡A escoger!	p. 229
6. Gramática	¿Qué falta?	pp. 229, 232
Panorama cultural	¿Qué hacen ustedes para celebrar? ¡A escoger!	pp. 218–219
¡A hablar!	*Guided recording*	pp. 240–241
¡A escribir!	*Guided writing*	pp. 240–241

Teacher Management System

Launch the program, type "admin" in the password area and press RETURN. Log on to **www.hrw.com/CDROMTUTOR** for a detailed explanation of the Teacher Management System.

DVD-ROM TUTOR ¡VEN CONMIGO! LEVEL 1

The *DVD Tutor* contains all material from the Level 1 *Video Program.* Spanish captions are available for use at your discretion for all sections of the video. The *DVD Tutor* also provides a variety of video-based activities that assess students' understanding of the **De antemano, A continuación,** and **Panorama cultural.**

This part of the *DVD Tutor* may be used on any DVD video player connected to a television or video monitor.

In addition to the video material and the video-based comprehension activities, the *DVD Tutor* also contains the entire Level 1 *Interactive CD-ROM Tutor* in DVD-ROM format. Each DVD disc contains the activities from all 12 chapters of the *Interactive CD-ROM Tutor.*

This part of the *DVD Tutor* may be used on a Macintosh® or Windows® computer with a DVD-ROM drive.

One-Stop Planner CD-ROM

To preview all resources available for this chapter, use the **One-Stop Planner CD-ROM,** Disc 3.

MARCAR: go.hrw.com
PALABRA CLAVE:
WV3 PUERTO RICO-11

INTERNET CONNECTION

*Have students explore the **go.hrw.com** Web site for many online resources covering all chapters. All Chapter 11 resources are available under the keyword **WV3 Puerto Rico-11.** Interactive games help students practice the material and provide them with immediate feedback. You will also find a printable worksheet that provides Internet activities that lead to a comprehensive online research project.*

JUEGOS INTERACTIVO

You can use the interactive games in this chapter

- to practice grammar, vocabulary, and chapter functions
- as homework
- as an assessment option
- as a self-test
- to prepare for the Chapter Test

ACTIVIDADES INTERNET

Students research nutrition and healthy living habits on the Internet. They determine which parts of the body benefit most from the various good foods and exercise routines.

- As preparation for the **Hoja de actividades,** have students review the Grammar and Vocabulary Workbook for the **Segundo paso.** You may also want to have them view the dramatic episode on Videocassette 3.

- After students complete the activity sheet, have them compare wellness plans with a partner. Ask pairs to think critically about which foods and exercises may or may not be good for people with special needs or other health issues.

Proyecto

Have students create a Web site devoted to healthy living. Have them give recommendations on their site about what foods to eat and what exercises and activities are best for different types of people. Have them suggest, if they can, activities that are designed to have specific outcomes: giving people more energy, relieving stress, or building strength, for example.

For Student Response Forms, see Listening Activities pp. 67–69.

PRIMER PASO pp. 212–217

5 Régimen de salud p. 213

1. Estudio todo el tiempo. Siempre me siento muy cansada. ¿Qué hago?
2. Tengo ganas de empezar a hacer ejercicios, pero me parece difícil.
3. Me siento mal. Tomé muchos refrescos.
4. Me siento cansado. Trabajo en la oficina día y noche.
5. Me encanta comer pizza, hamburguesas y papas fritas, pero después me siento muy mal.
6. No me siento bien porque casi siempre estoy en casa. Debo salir más.

Answers to Activity 5

1. Natalia
2. Raúl
3. Soledad
4. Fernando
5. Daniel
6. Adriana

SEGUNDO PASO pp. 220–227

17 ¿Cómo te sientes hoy? p. 222

1. ¡Uy! ¡Me siento muy mal! Tengo una fiebre de 102 grados.
2. ¡Hombre! No sé qué hacer. Hoy tengo un examen muy difícil en la clase de álgebra.
3. Esta noche voy a cantar por primera vez en un concierto y no estoy listo.
4. ¡Qué lástima! No puedo pasar las vacaciones con mi tía en Puerto Rico.

5. Ay, mi hermanita es terrible. Siempre quiere llevar mis camisas y mis suéteres.
6. No me siento bien. No puedo asistir a clases hoy.
7. Todo el mundo está enfermo. Yo también.

Answers to Activity 17

1. 6
2. 2, 5
3. 2, 5
4. 4
5. 3
6. 1, 6, 7, 8
7. 1, 6, 7, 8

21 Las quejas p. 224

1. ¿Qué tienes, Rubén?
   Canté cuatro horas ayer. Me la pasé practicando para un concierto.
2. ¿Qué te pasa, Berta?
   Pasé toda la mañana paseando con mis amigas pero mis zapatos son muy pequeños.
3. ¿Cómo estás, Blanca?
   ¡Ay! Pasé tres horas leyendo en la biblioteca. Tengo un libro muy bueno, pero ahora, ¡qué dolor!
4. ¿Qué te pasa, David?
   Tenía mucha prisa esta mañana. No tomé el almuerzo ni el desayuno.
5. ¿Cómo estás, Elena?
   No muy bien. Hace mucho frío y no llevo guantes.

Answers to Activity 21

1. d. Le duele la garganta.
2. a. Le duelen los pies.
3. e. Le duelen los ojos.
4. b. Le duele el estómago.
5. c. Le duelen las manos.

36 ¿Adónde fuiste? p. 233

1. Ricardo y Miguel fueron al estadio a desayunar.
2. Angélica y Marta fueron a la cancha de tenis a bailar con Roberto y Sergio.
3. Gabriel fue a la piscina a nadar.
4. Yo fui a la pista de correr a hacer yoga.
5. María y Pablo fueron a la biblioteca a escuchar un concierto.
6. Mi hermano fue al gimnasio a levantar pesas.
7. Mis padres fueron al estadio a ver un partido de fútbol.
8. Mis hermanos y yo fuimos al cine a jugar al basquetbol con nuestros primos.

Answers to Activity 36

1. ilógico		**5.** ilógico	
2. ilógico		**6.** lógico	
3. lógico		**7.** lógico	
4. ilógico		**8.** ilógico	

LETRA Y SONIDO p. 235

For the scripts for Parts A and C, see page 235. The script for Part B is below.

B. Dictado

Mi horario no es fácil. Estudio geometría, historia y física. Me gusta estudiar por la tarde y ver televisión por la noche.

1 p. 240

ANTONIO Hola, Miriam. ¿Qué tal?

MIRIAM ¡Ay, Antonio! Me siento horrible. Me duele la garganta y la cabeza y tengo mucha fiebre.

ANTONIO ¿Qué te pasa?

MIRIAM Tengo gripe. Descansé todo el día. Esta tarde fui al doctor. Y tú, ¿cómo estás?

ANTONIO Yo me siento muy bien, pero estoy un poco preocupado por ti. Fuiste al colegio ayer, ¿no?

MIRIAM No fui porque estaba enferma. ¿Por qué preguntas?

ANTONIO Participé en el campeonato de natación. Estaba muy nervioso.

MIRIAM ¿Ganaste?

ANTONIO Sí, gané la copa de 100 metros pero Angélica ganó la copa de 250 metros.

Answers to Repaso Activity 1

1. Miriam tiene gripe. Le duele la cabeza y la garganta y tiene fiebre.
2. Descansó todo el día.
3. Antonio se siente bien pero está preocupado por Miriam.
4. Antonio nadó ayer y ganó.

CAPÍTULO 11

Para vivir bien
PROJECTS

This activity allows students to ask meaningful questions concerning lifestyle, moods, general health, and physical condition.

Introduction

Ask students about their favorite talk show. Explain that they will produce a TV talk show in Spanish. If possible, show a video of a Spanish-speaking star being interviewed and encourage students to find out about Hispanic American stars. Provide a checklist of vocabulary words from this lesson for them to include in their questions.

Sequence

1 Divide the class into groups. Have groups decide which members will host the show, which will be prompters, and which will be interviewed.

2 Have the interviewees decide what type of celebrity to be. (sports star, actor or actress, politician, writer, musician, or any other public figure)

3 Allow time in class for groups to prepare their TV talk show and set a date for groups to present their shows.

4 Have groups choose a name for their show, create scripts for the program, and learn their parts. Groups choose a name for their show and design a simple set. They may also use simple props such as microphones and costumes.

5 Each group has a prompter to cue anyone who forgets a line. Tell them it's fine to ad lib.

6 If you have access to the necessary equipment, record or videotape the talk shows to play them for the students later.

Grading the project

Suggested point distribution (total = 100 points):

Vocabulary use **20**

Preparation of script **20**

Creativity **20**

Grammar usage **20**

Oral presentation **20**

This project allows students to review different sports and leisure activities. It also reinforces students' knowledge of nutrition and general health.

Introduction

Have students imagine they are the owner of a health club resort. They design programs and menus for a resort that offers activities and services that appeal to a variety of age groups—young children, teenagers, adults, and senior citizens.

Materials students may need

- Folders with double pockets (one for each group)
- Lined paper
- Glue sticks
- Magazines
- Colored pencils, fine-tipped markers
- Colored construction paper

Sequence

1 Divide the class into groups of four. Each group assigns the following roles:
   - Manager—provides a list of activities to offer at the resort, giving a variety of indoor and outdoor activities, for various age groups
   - Personal Trainer—outlines a daily workout regimen
   - Dietitian—plans a daily menu
   - Public Relations Manager—designs a brochure to describe the resort

2 The Dietitian and Personal Trainer add their information to the folder along with the brochure.

3 Have groups give oral presentations about their resorts to the class in Spanish. The report consists of the activities offered, as well as the services of the Dietitian and Trainer.

Grading the project

Suggested point distribution (total = 100 points):

Manager's list of activities **15**
Brochure **15**
Dietitian's menu **15**
Personal Trainer's schedule **15**
Cooperative effort **20**
Oral presentation **20**

REFRANES

In this activity students will translate a Spanish proverb and make a poster to illustrate it. It is very good for students with verbal/linguistic intelligence.

Introduction

Go over these proverbs with students. Make sure they are familiar with what each one means.

A bird in the hand is worth two in the bush.

Don't count your chickens before they're hatched.

Clothes don't make the man.

Where there's a will, there's a way.

All that glitters is not gold.

You can't judge a book by its cover.

Every cloud has a silver lining.

Birds of a feather flock together.

Materials students may need

- Pens and markers
- Glue
- Magazines
- Bilingual dictionary
- Scissors

Sequence

1 Divide the class into small groups and assign one of the following **refranes** to each:

Más vale pájaro en mano que cien volando.

Hijo no tenemos y nombre le ponemos.

El hábito no hace al monje.

Querer es poder.

No todo lo que brilla es oro.

Cara vemos, corazón no sabemos.

No hay mal que por bien no venga.

Dime con quién andas y te diré quién eres.

2 Have groups look up the words in a bilingual dictionary and write a translation of each word.

3 Have groups try to think of the English proverb with the same meaning and add it to their literal translation.

4 Have students make a poster on which they write and illustrate their **refrán**.

5 Have students present their posters to the class in Spanish, explaining what the **refrán** means and why they illustrated it as they did. Group members participate equally in talking about the poster.

Grading the project

Suggested point distribution (total = 100 points):

Literal translation **30**
Equivalent English proverb **20**
Poster content and design **20**
Oral presentation **30**

FAMILY LINK

Students might ask their parents or grandparents for more English proverbs that have the same meaning as their **refrán**. Native speakers might also ask their parents or grandparents to tell them their favorite proverb.

CAPÍTULO 11

Para vivir bien
GAMES

HAGAMOS UN CUENTO

This game provides students with an opportunity to put together a simple story. Students have fun while practicing various communicative functions.

Preparation
Write vocabulary words or phrases on index cards or slips of paper and place them in a box.

Procedure
1. Have every student draw one slip of paper from the box. Allow time for students to make sure they know what their word or phrase means.
2. Choose one student to begin a story in Spanish using that vocabulary word, verb form, or phrase. Write each sentence on the board or on a transparency for students to follow along.
3. The next person continues the story using his or her word, the story is continued by the next person, and so on. If a student is unable to continue the story, he or she says **paso** and tries again later.
4. You may choose to have students stand to tell the story and sit down if they are unable to continue.

SIMÓN DICE

This game helps reinforce the vocabulary for the body parts. Students have fun practicing the vocabulary while playing a familiar game. It is also good practice for kinesthetic and auditory learners.

Procedure
1. Have volunteers take turns coming forward to be **Simón.** Have the rest of the class stand. **Simón** calls out commands to the class, **Toquen** (body part including appropriate definite article) or **Simón dice—Toquen...**
2. Students carry out the command only when it is preceded by **Simón dice...** Any student who carries out the command when **Simón** doesn't say **Simón dice** sits down. Continue until all or the majority of the class is seated.

3. Continue with a new volunteer being **Simón.** As students become comfortable with the game, try to have **Simón** speak faster.
4. The last person left standing is the winner.

Suggestion
Have students play the game in groups of two to four so more students have a chance to be **Simón.**

VERDUGO

This game gives students an opportunity to practice and review letters of the alphabet in conjunction with vocabulary for body parts. It can be played in pairs, small groups, or two teams.

Procedure
1. This game follows the basic rules of Hangman. Divide the class into two groups. One player from Group A comes to the board, chooses a word from this chapter's or a previous chapter's **Vocabulario,** and on the board draws one blank line for each letter in that word.
2. Players from Group B take turns guessing letters that they think spell out the mystery word.
3. If the word does contain the letter, the player from Group A fills in the all the blanks that correspond to that letter, and the player from Group B has a chance to guess the word. If the player guesses correctly, Group B wins the round and a new round begins.
4. If the word does not contain the letter, the player from Group A begins drawing the figure of a person, one body part at a time (head, right and left arms, body, and right and left legs). As the player from Group A draws each body part, the player from Group B must say it in Spanish. Teach students **derecho** and **izquierdo. (la pierna izquierda, el brazo derecho,** etc.)
5. If the player from Group A completes the figure with all six body parts before Group B guesses the mystery word, Group A wins the round and a new round begins.
6. Play as many rounds as time permits. The group that has guessed more words correctly wins the game.

STANDARDS: 1.2, 5.1

JUGAR AL BÉISBOL

In this game players practice new chapter vocabulary words and expressions and review vocabulary from previous chapters. It may be played at the end of the chapter.

Preparation

Develop a list of questions whose answers require the players to use the chapter vocabulary and vocabulary from previous chapters.

MODELO   ¿Qué haces para evitar el estrés?

Practico _____.

Procedure

1. Divide the class into two teams. Ask one player to be scorekeeper. Draw a baseball diamond with four bases on the board. Set a number of innings or a time limit for playing.

2. The first player on Team A is the batter. You serve as the pitcher and ask the batter a question. If the batter gives a correct answer, he or she moves to first base. The scorekeeper places a mark on first base.

3. You then ask a question of the second batter on Team A. If the second batter answers correctly, she or he goes to first base. If there is a player on first base, he or she advances to second base and the scorekeeper places a mark on second base.

4. A batter who cannot answer is out.

5. A team scores a run by advancing a player around the bases to home plate. Team A continues batting until it has three outs. Then Team B goes to bat. When Team B has three outs, the first inning is over. Teams get one point for each run, and the team with the higher score wins.

¡DIBÚJALO!

This game reviews vocabulary and is good for visual and kinesthetic learners. It may be played after the Primer paso.

Preparation

Write down words or phrases from this or a previous chapter on index cards or slips of paper.

Procedure

1. Divide the class into two teams.

2. Players from each team take turns coming forward. They pick a card and draw a picture that represents the vocabulary word. The drawing does not need to be elaborate or very accurate, it just needs to convey the word or phrase.

3. After one minute the team member stops drawing. His or her team must guess the word from the drawing to earn a point. If the team does not guess the word, the other team gets a chance to guess to earn a point.

¡ANDA A PESCAR!

This game can be used to practice any vocabulary category, the verb tener, and direct object pronouns. It may be played after this chapter's Segundo paso.

Materials you may need

◆ Index cards   ◆ Magazines   ◆ Markers

Preparation

Divide players into groups of three to five. Give each group 48 index cards. Have them make a card deck by writing one body part on four cards, another body part on four other cards, and so on until they have 12 sets of four cards. You might have players draw body parts or paste on pictures instead of write them.

Procedure

1. This game follows the same basic rules as Go Fish. The dealer shuffles the cards and deals five cards to each player. The remaining cards are placed face down in the middle of the table. The object of the game is to form as many matching pairs as possible.

2. The dealer begins by asking a player for a card that matches one he or she has. (¿**Tienes una nariz?**) If the player has the card, he or she answers **Sí, tengo una nariz** and gives it to the dealer.

3. The dealer places the matching pair on the table and asks any of the players for another card. If the player doesn't have the card, he or she says ¡**Anda a pescar!** and the dealer must draw a card from the stack. Then it is the next player's turn. The game ends when one of the players has no more cards. The player with the most pairs is the winner.

ANSWERS TO CHAPTER 11 ACTIVITIES

Listening activity answers appear on Scripts pages 205E–205F. Answers to all other activities appear on corresponding pupil pages.

PRIMER PASO pp. 212–217

7 Answers will vary. Possible answers:
1. En mi opinión se sienten mal.
2. Creo que te sientes bien.
3. Creo que se sienten cansados.
4. En mi opinión se siente bien.
5. Creo que se siente magnífica.
6. Me parece que se sienten cansados.

SEGUNDO PASO pp. 220–227

15
1. Está nerviosa.
2. Está bien.
3. Está nervioso. *or* Está preocupado.
4. Está preocupado. *or* Está triste.
5. Está mal. Tiene gripe.
6. Está triste.

19 Answers will vary. Possible answers:
1. los brazos, las piernas, la espalda
2. la boca, la oreja, el oído, la mano
3. los pies, las piernas, los brazos
4. la cabeza, el pelo, la mano, el brazo
5. las piernas, los brazos, los pies, la espalda
6. los dedos, las manos, los brazos
7. los dedos, las manos
8. las piernas, los brazos, las manos, la espalda
9. las piernas, los brazos, los pies
10. el oído

22 Answers will vary. Possible answers:
1. Me duelen los ojos.
2. Le duelen las piernas.
3. Me duele la cabeza.
4. Me duelen los dientes.
5. Le duelen los brazos y las piernas.
6. Me duele la garganta.

TERCER PASO pp. 228–235

34
1. jugó al basquetbol en el parque
2. fue al cine con su hermana
3. su primo lo visitó en casa
4. fue al colegio
5. fue a la casa de Elena

37
1. Jugaron las Águilas y los Toros.
2. Las Águilas ganaron.
3. Fue en el estadio municipal El Hatillo.
4. Le gustan más las Águilas.
   Answers will vary: Porque habla tres veces de Las Águilas y Los Toros sólo una vez.

39 Answers will vary. Possible answers:
1. Carmen y Ben fueron a la playa para nadar y correr.
2. Carmen y Ben caminaron por las calles.
3. Carmen y Ben hablaron con Pedro.
4. Ben presentó a Carmen a Pedro.
5. Ben, Carmen y Pedro compraron unos batidos.
6. Ben y Carmen presentaron a Pedro a su mamá.

ENLACES pp. 236–237

1 Answers will vary. Possible answers:
batear—to bat
el jonrón—homerun
ranqueado—ranked
pichear—to pitch
un hit—a hit
un récord—a record

2
patio—recreation area next to a house
taco—a folded, crisp-fried, corn tortilla filled with seasoned meat or other fillings
rodeo—a performance with bull riding, roping, bronco riding
salsa—a spicy sauce; a style of music
tornado—a violent destructive wind with a funnel-shaped cloud
corral—a pen for livestock
adobe—a brick of clay and straw or a building material of clay and straw
lasso—a rope used for catching horses and cattle
mosquito—a flying insect (literally *a small fly*)
arroyo—a gully carved by water
poncho—a kind of woolen cloak
mesa—a broad flat-topped hill

3 They are from Puerto Rico, U.S., Dominican Republic, and Venezuela. These countries are near the equator and south of the U.S. They are tropical and the weather is warm all year around.

4 The baseball season in the U.S. starts in March, after the conclusion of the winter season in the Caribbean, and ends in October with the World Series.

VAMOS A LEER pp. 238–239

A
1. exercises
2. strengthen muscles
3. eliminate tension

B Answers will vary. Possible answers:
1. Debes hacer ejercicios con movimientos suaves y lentos. Haz yoga o tal vez te gustaría levantar pesas.
2. Haz unos ejercicios para estirar los hombros, la espalda y el cuello.

A VER SI PUEDO... p. 242

5 Answers will vary. Possible answers:
1. Roberto fue a la piscina. Nadó.
2. Silvia y Sofía fueron a la cancha de tenis. Jugaron al tenis.
3. La familia Pérez fue a la cancha de fútbol. Ellos jugaron al fútbol.
4. Mi hermana y yo fuimos a la tienda de discos. No compramos nada.
5. Tú fuiste al estadio. Miraste un partido.
6. Mónica y Gabi fueron a la biblioteca. Estudiaron.
7. Federico y sus padres fueron al parque. Caminaron con el perro.
8. Fui al gimnasio. Levanté pesas.

HOMEWORK SUGGESTIONS

Chapter Section	Presentation	Homework Options
Primer paso	**Así se dice,** p. 213	*Practice and Activity Book,* p. 61, Activity 1
	Nota gramatical, p. 214	*Pupil's Edition,* p. 214, Activity 7 *Grammar and Vocabulary,* p. 37, Activities 1–2 *Practice and Activity Book,* p. 62, Activities 3–4 *CD-ROM,* Disc 3, Chapter 11, Activity 1
	Vocabulario, p. 215	*Pupil's Edition,* pp. 216–217, Activities 19, 13 *Grammar and Vocabulary,* p. 38, Activities 3–4 *Practice and Activity Book,* pp. 63–64, Activities 5–6 *CD-ROM,* Disc 3, Chapter 11, Activity 2
Segundo paso	**Así se dice,** p. 221	*Pupil's Edition,* p. 221, Activity 15
	Vocabulario, p. 222	*Grammar and Vocabulary,* pp. 39–40, Activities 5–7 *Practice and Activity Book,* pp. 65–66, Activities 7–8 *CD-ROM,* Disc 3, Chapter 11, Activity 3
	Vocabulario, p. 223	*Grammar and Vocabulary,* p. 40, Activities 8–9 *Practice and Activity Book,* p. 66, Activity 9 *CD-ROM,* Disc 3, Chapter 11, Activity 4
	Nota gramatical, p. 224	*Grammar and Vocabulary,* p. 41, Activities 10–11
Tercer paso	**Así se dice,** p. 229	*Pupil's Edition,* p. 229, Activity 30
	Nota gramatical, p. 229	*Grammar and Vocabulary,* p. 42, Activities 12–13 *Practice and Activity Book,* p. 68, Activity 11 *CD-ROM,* Disc 3, Chapter 11, Activity 5
	Así se dice, p. 231	*Pupil's Edition,* p. 231, Activity 34
	Nota gramatical, p. 232	*Grammar and Vocabulary,* p. 43, Activities 14–16 *Practice and Activity Book,* p. 69, Activity 12 *CD-ROM,* Disc 3, Chapter 11, Activity 6
	Vocabulario, p. 232	*Pupil's Edition,* pp. 233–234, Activities 37–38 *Grammar and Vocabulary,* p. 44, Activities 17–18 *Practice and Activity Book,* p. 70, Activity 13

Para vivir bien

MOTIVATING ACTIVITY
Have a discussion with students about physical fitness. What do they like to do for exercise? Do they play sports? What do they like to do outdoors?

 RE-ENTRY
Review the sports vocabulary that the students have learned in previous chapters and the verbs **jugar, mirar, gustar,** and **encantar.** Have students interview each other in Spanish by asking which sports they like to play and which ones they like to watch. They should take notes (**tomar apuntes**) on what their partner says so they can report the conversation to the class.

PHOTO FLASH!
① Roller skating (**patinar sobre ruedas**) is a very popular sport in Puerto Rico. Ice skating (**patinar sobre hielo**) is also popular. San Juan has both ice-skating and roller-skating rinks.

CULTURE NOTE
At midnight on June 23, the eve of **el Día de San Juan Bautista** (*Saint John the Baptist's feast day;* Saint John is the patron saint of San Juan), **sanjuaneros** (*people from San Juan*) traditionally walk into the sea backward three times for good luck in the coming year. In San Juan, as well as on the rest of the island, many festivals celebrate this event.

CAPÍTULO

11 Para vivir bien

① **¿Qué tal si patinamos sobre ruedas?**

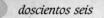

menos
...ida balanceada
al día. La nutrición es
esencial para una buena
salud y proporciona
defensas contra el estrés.

2. Dormir por lo menos 8 horas
cada noche. Un sueño apropiado
puede añadir años de vida. Trate
de acostarse y levantarse a la
misma hora.

3. Hacer ejercicio, por lo menos
3 veces por semana. Busque
una actividad divertida, como la bicicleta, o como caminar o nadar.

Claves
para manejar el...
ESTRÉS

5. Salir y cultivar sus amistades; un buen amigo es un
gran soporte. Tener amigos cercanos es algo valioso; un buen
amigo puede añadir a la moral con
sólo estar presente.

6. Organizar su tiempo. Planee
su uso y empléelo.

7. Sea optimista: las personas
optimistas tienen menos problemas mentales y síquicos.

In this chapter you will learn to

PRIMER PASO

- make suggestions and express feelings

SEGUNDO PASO

- talk about moods and physical condition

TERCER PASO

- say what you did and talk about where you went and when

🖥 internet

go.hrw.com

MARCAR: go.hrw.com
PALABRA CLAVE:
WV3 PUERTO RICO-11

② No puedo correr más.
Me duelen los pies.

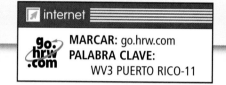

③ En Puerto Rico fuimos a un gran partido de béisbol.

FOCUSING ON OUTCOMES

- Have students look at the photos on these pages and identify which learner outcomes correspond to which photo. (Photo 1: making suggestions; Photo 2: talking about physical condition; Photo 3: saying where you went) Have students suggest other situations in which the outcomes could be used.

- Ask students how they feel about discussing moods and feelings with friends or family. How would they feel if they were unable to express these things?

PHOTO FLASH!
③ Many Puerto Ricans are devoted baseball fans. They follow U.S. baseball and keep up with their favorite professional teams and their favorite Puerto Rican baseball players. Many U.S. teams have training camps in Puerto Rico. During the winter, fans watch the Puerto Rican professional league.

🌐 **CULTURE NOTE**
In addition to the sporting activities pictured, Puerto Rico has all types of water sports, golf, tennis, hiking, horse racing, basketball, and boxing. Due to the island's tropical climate, most sports can be enjoyed year-round.

207

VIDEO INTEGRATION

En camino LEVEL 1B
Video Program
Videocassette 2, 20:06–27:36 OR
Videocassette 3, 1:48:02–1:55:33
(captioned version)

¡Ven conmigo! LEVEL 1
DVD Tutor, Disc 2

TEACHER NOTE
The **fotonovela** is an abridged version of the video episode.

VIDEO SYNOPSIS
Ben, Carmen, and their mother are New Yorkers visiting family in Puerto Rico. Ben and Carmen's mother drops them off for a day of sightseeing in San Juan and tells them she will pick them up at 3:00 at **la Plaza de Hostos.** After some sightseeing they stop to rest and meet Pedro, a boy from San Juan. Pedro decides to go with them to the next site, **el Castillo del Morro.** While the three are exploring **el Castillo,** Pedro asks if they have seen **la Plaza de Hostos.** Ben looks at his watch and sees that it is now 2:55.

MOTIVATING ACTIVITY
Ask students how they and their friends decide what to do as a group. What do they do? Where do they go? Do a few people in their circle of friends always seem to have good ideas?

DE ANTEMANO

Un recorrido por San Juan

CD 11 Trs. 1–2

Ben and Carmen have taken time to do some exploring in San Juan, Puerto Rico. Read the **fotonovela** to find out what they see and who they meet. Why might Ben and Carmen get into trouble at the end of the episode?

p. 61
Acts. 1–2

Benjamín

Carmen

la señora Corredor

Pedro

1 Bueno, hijos... a las tres paso por ustedes por la Plaza de Hostos. Y después, vamos al partido de béisbol de su tío. ¿De acuerdo?

Sí. Te esperamos en la Plaza de Hostos a las tres. ¡Adiós!

2 ¡Vamos! Tenemos todo el día para explorar el Viejo San Juan. ¿Tienes ganas de caminar?

PRESENTATION
Play the video or audio recording. Then have students form groups of four to practice reading the roles of all four characters. You might ask one or two groups to read the dialogue aloud for the class before answering the questions on page 211.

SUGGESTION
Ask students to guess the age of Ben, Carmen, and Pedro by completing the expression **Me parece que...**

PHOTO FLASH!
You'll notice that Ben is wearing braces on his teeth. The Spanish term for braces is **los frenos.**

BACKGROUND
Pablo Casals (1876–1973), one of the world's leading cellists, died in Río Piedras, Puerto Rico. Casals was born in Vendrell, Spain and was an outspoken opponent of fascism. He lived most of his life in exile. He moved to Puerto Rico in 1956, where he continued his personal musical crusade for peace. He revitalized public interest in the works of Bach, especially the six unaccompanied suites for cello. At the **Museo Pablo Casals,** one can see his cello and other memorabilia. Casals is honored by Puerto Ricans at an annual festival in mid-June in San Juan.

DE ANTEMANO

doscientos nueve **209**

NATIVE SPEAKERS

Puerto Rican Spanish has several distinctive characteristics that it shares with other dialects of Spanish. For example, some speakers pronounce the **s** or **z** at the end of a syllable as an aspiration similar to the English *h (graciah, ¿cómo ehtáh tú?)*. The **d** between vowels often becomes silent *(habla'o, pehca'o, mira'a)*. The **r** at the end of a syllable is sometimes pronounced like an **l**, as in *pol favol*. You'll notice that Ben and Pedro say **exploral** and **veldad**.

A continuación

You may choose to continue with *Un recorrido por San Juan (a continuación)* at this time or wait until later in the chapter. At this point, the children rush to meet Ben and Carmen's mother, but they find she has not arrived. When she arrives, they discover that Pedro is Ben and Carmen's cousin. Later, they all attend a baseball game. Have students discuss the importance of sports or sporting events in their vacation plans.

Cuaderno para hispanohablantes, pp. 51–55

1 ¿Comprendes?

Contesta las preguntas para ver si entiendes lo que pasa en la fotonovela.

These activities check for global comprehension only. Students should not yet be expected to produce language modeled in **De antemano**.

1. Where are Ben and Carmen, and why? They're in Puerto Rico to visit family.
2. What are they doing today? Sightseeing in San Juan
3. Who do they meet and where is that person from? Pedro; he's from San Juan.
4. What do Ben and Pedro talk about? Sports
5. Why is Ben upset at the end of the story? Because they're late meeting their mother.
6. What do you think they'll do? What would you do? Answers will vary.

2 ¿Cómo se dice?

Find the phrases in the **fotonovela** that you might use to say the following things.

1. to suggest that you go somewhere with a friend ¿Qué tal si yo te acompaño?
2. to say that your feet hurt Me duelen los pies.
3. to ask if someone feels like walking ¿Tienes ganas de caminar?
4. to say that you've already been to the museum Ya fuimos al museo.
5. to say that you and a friend exercise a lot Mi amigo/a y yo hacemos mucho ejercicio.
6. to say that a friend is waiting for you in the plaza Mi amigo/a me espera en la plaza.

3 ¿Quién lo diría?

Con base en la fotonovela, ¿quién diría lo siguiente?

1. ¡Patinar sobre ruedas es mi deporte favorito! Benjamín
2. Son las tres. ¿Qué están haciendo mis hijos? la señora Corredor
3. A mí me gustaría visitar Nueva York. Pedro
4. ¡No quiero caminar más! Tengo ganas de descansar. Carmen
5. Yo voy con ustedes al Castillo del Morro. Pedro
6. Me encanta hacer ejercicios aeróbicos con mi mamá. Carmen

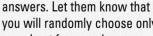
COOPERATIVE LEARNING
1 through **3** Have students do these exercises in groups of two to four. Their answers should be identical; this means they need to agree on their answers. Let them know that you will randomly choose only one sheet from each group. Every member will receive the grade on that sheet.

SUGGESTION
3 Ask students to explain how they decided on their answers. What cues did they identify in the **fotonovela**?

BIOLOGY LINK
In the video, Carmen orders a **batido de guanábana** (custard apple or soursop milkshake) from a vendor in Old San Juan. The **guanábana** is a sweet, acidic fruit from the **guanábano** tree of the *Annona* genus that is native to the Caribbean. Have students look up information about other trees that are native to the Americas. (guava, papaya)

PHOTO FLASH!
Ask students to write a caption for this photo, which señora Corredor put in the family album after they returned to New York from Puerto Rico.

VIDEO INTEGRATION

En camino LEVEL 1B

Video Program

Videocassette 2, 24:15–24:47 OR

Videocassette 3, 1:52:11–1:52:43

(captioned version)

¡Ven conmigo! LEVEL 1

DVD Tutor, Disc 2

Bell work

On the board or on a transparency write the following words and ask students to write their opposites: (**hola, bajo, aquí, campo, nada, debajo de, antes, frío, viejo**)

☀ MOTIVATE

Ask students to think of ways to invite a friend in English to do something. (Would you like to . . .? How about . . .?) Write their suggestions in one column on the board or on a transparency. Ask students if they can think of ways to make similar suggestions in Spanish using vocabulary from previous chapters. (**¿Te gustaría...?** or **¿Quieres...?**)

PRIMER PASO

(TPR) Storytelling Book pp. 41, 44

WV3 PUERTO RICO-11

Making suggestions and expressing feelings

¿Adónde van ahora?

Yo tengo ganas de ver el Castillo del Morro. ¿Podemos?

¿Qué tal si yo los acompaño?

Bueno, ya fuimos a la Puerta de San Juan y al Museo Pablo Casals.

4 ¿Qué tal si...?

Escribe **cierto** o **falso** para cada oración y corrige las oraciones falsas.

1. Carmen quiere ir al Castillo del Morro.
2. Pedro no quiere ir con ellos.
3. Benjamín va a ir al Museo Pablo Casals.
4. Pedro va a acompañarlos al Castillo del Morro.

1. cierto
2. falso; Él quiere ir con ellos.
3. falso; Benjamín ya fue al museo.
4. cierto

El Castillo del Morro

ASÍ SE DICE — Making suggestions and expressing feelings

To suggest something to a friend, say:

¿Qué tal si vamos al gimnasio?
How about if we go to the gym?

¿Por qué no vamos mañana?
Why don't we go tomorrow?

Your friend might answer:

Gracias, pero no quiero.

No, en realidad **no tengo ganas.**
No, I don't really feel like it.

To ask how a friend is feeling, say:

¿Qué tienes? ¿Te sientes mal?
What's the matter? Do you feel bad?

No, **me siento bien.** *No, I feel fine.*

Estoy un poco cansado, **nada más.**
Quiero **dormir.** *I'm a little tired, that's all. I want to sleep.*

p. 63 Act. 5

¿Te acuerdas?

Do you remember the **o → ue** verbs like **poder**? **Dormir** follows the same pattern.

d**ue**rmo	dorm**imos**
d**ue**rmes	dorm**ís**
d**ue**rme	d**ue**rmen

5 Régimen de salud

CD 11 Tr. 3

Look at the drawings of the following people to see what they're doing. Listen while they talk about their daily lives and then choose the correct name, according to what they say.

Script and answers on p. 205E

Adriana

Raúl

Daniel

Fernando

Soledad

Natalia

☀ TEACH

PRESENTATION
ASÍ SE DICE
After introducing the grammar, model both sides of the conversation to present the phrases for making suggestions and expressing feelings. Next, involve students by having them answer your questions. Finally, have students practice the dialogue in pairs.

SLOWER PACE
5 Have students talk about what the people in the drawings may be thinking or feeling before beginning the listening activity.

ADDITIONAL PRACTICE
5 In pairs, students write captions for the drawings. Have them create both true and false statements about them. Then they share their statements with another pair and have that pair decide whether the captions are true or false.

STANDARDS: 1.1, 1.2, 5.1   **213**

PRESENTATION

NOTA GRAMATICAL

Ask a student ¿**Cómo te sientes?** After the student replies, ask another student to report how the first one feels. (**Miguel, ¿cómo se siente Susana?**)

Explain to students that **sentirse (ie)** is a reflexive verb that means *to feel (a certain way)*, while **sentir (ie)** (as in **lo siento**) is not reflexive and means *to regret* or *to be sorry about*.

SLOWER PACE

6 Have students write two sentences about the people in each situation. The sentences should include what each person does during the day and how he or she feels. Have students share their sentences with a partner; their partners try to match the description with the picture.

CHALLENGE

7 Have students explain why each person feels a certain way. For example, for sentence 1, **Ellos se sienten mal porque no comen comida sana.**

NOTA GRAMATICAL

CD-ROM DISC 3

PA p. 62 Act. 3

GV p. 37 Acts. 1–2

In Chapter 7 you used the infinitive of reflexive verbs to talk about getting ready. **Sentirse** *(to feel)* is also a reflexive verb and has an **e→ie** stem change.

¿Cómo **se siente** usted?
How do you feel?

Me siento magnífico.
I feel great.

me	**siento**	nos	sent**imos**
te	s**ientes**	os	sent**ís**
se	s**iente**	se	s**ienten**

Note that when you conjugate a reflexive verb, you must always put the pronoun (**me, te, se, nos**) before the verb.

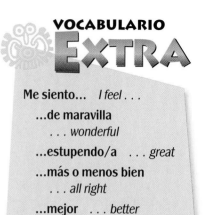

VOCABULARIO EXTRA

Me siento...   *I feel . . .*

...de maravilla
   . . . wonderful

...estupendo/a . . . *great*

...más o menos bien
   . . . all right

...mejor . . . *better*

...peor . . . *worse*

...pésimo/a . . . *awful*

...raro/a . . . *strange*

6 Situaciones

Read each situation. Then match each with the correct reflexive verb form.

1. Danielle y Dylan jugaron al basquetbol por cuatro horas. c
2. Mi hermano y yo descansamos bien, comemos bien y hacemos ejercicio. e
3. Estudié hasta las once de la noche. a
4. Tú no descansaste después de tu partido de fútbol, ¿verdad? d
5. Perry lleva una vida sana. b
6. Tú siempre comes muchas verduras y frutas. f

a. Me siento cansado/a.
b. Se siente bien.
c. Se sienten cansados.
d. Te sientes cansado.
e. Nos sentimos bien.
f. Te sientes bien.

7 ¿Cómo se sienten ellos?

Escribe una frase por cada descripción. Explica cómo se siente cada persona o grupo. Usa las expresiones de abajo.   Answers on p. 205K

MODELO   Yo hago mucho ejercicio.
—Creo que te sientes bien.

1. Paula y Ricardo comen muchos dulces.
2. Yo nado todas las mañanas.
3. Nosotros nunca desayunamos.
4. Mark come muchas verduras.
5. Amy va al gimnasio todos los días.
6. Mis hermanos siempre estudian muy tarde por la noche.

Me parece que...

En mi opinión...

Creo que...

VOCABULARIO

Para llevar una vida sana...

CD-ROM DISC **3**

p. 64
Act. 6

GV
p. 38
Acts. 3–4

11-A, 11-1

hacer yoga

patinar sobre ruedas

levantar pesas

estirarse

8 ¿Qué deben hacer?

Work with a partner. Take turns pretending to be a sports trainer and a person asking for suggestions about fitness activities. Use words from the **Vocabulario** to give a suggestion. Answers will vary. Possible answers:

MODELO —A Cynthia y a mí nos gusta ir al parque para practicar deportes. ¿Qué debemos hacer?
—¿Por qué no patinan sobre ruedas?

1. A mis amigos Patricia y Carlos les gusta descansar y pensar. ¿Por qué no hacen yoga?
2. Me gustan las actividades con mucho movimiento. ¿Qué tal si patinas sobre ruedas?
3. Yo quiero ser fuerte *(strong)*. ¿Por qué no levantas pesas?
4. Quiero saber lo que debo hacer antes de correr. ¿Por qué no te estiras primero?
5. Me gusta estar en casa. ¿Por qué no haces yoga?
6. A mi hermano le encanta el fútbol. ¿Qué más debe hacer? Debe estirarse todos los días.

PRESENTATION

VOCABULARIO

Tell a story about what these people are doing. **Felipe se estira. Mónica y Ricardo hacen yoga. Luisa levanta pesas y María patina sobre ruedas.** As you name the new activities, act out their meanings. Have students repeat your story, pointing to each person in the drawing as they describe him or her. Continue with questions such as **¿Te estiras todas las mañanas? Ana y Luis, ¿patinan sobre ruedas ustedes algunas veces por semana?** Have students ask classmates questions using the new vocabulary.

ADDITIONAL VOCABULARY

practicar el esquí acuático
  to water-ski
ir de vela   *to sail*
practicar tabla de vela   *to wind-surf*
practicar tabla hawaiana
  to surf
jugar al golf   *to play golf*

CHALLENGE

8 Ask two volunteers to play the roles of health expert and talk show host. Have the class ask the health expert questions. Have the host field the questions. Have the health expert answer them.

216

SLOWER PACE

9 Scramble the order as you write the answers on the board or a transparency and ask students to match them with the blanks in the text.

ADDITIONAL PRACTICE

10 Have students explain to their partners why they like or don't like an activity. If they like the activity, have them tell each other when and how often they do it.

MULTICULTURAL LINK

Yoga, meaning *union* or *joining* in Sanskrit, is a Hindu discipline and system of breathing and stretching exercises to promote control of the body and mind. Many non-Hindus in Western countries practice forms of yoga to improve their physical and mental well-being. Athletes in general work to control and discipline mind and body. Have students discuss the sports they play to strengthen both mind and body. Why is this helpful?

Answers to Activity 9

Answers will vary. Possible answers:

1. debes estirarte
2. Cinco minutos
3. debes levantar pesas
4. debes asistir a una clase de ejercicios aeróbicos
5. A las seis de la mañana
6. Sí. ¡Hasta luego!

9 Una nueva rutina

You've asked Jill, your new coach at the recreation center, to help you get into shape. Complete her part of the conversation on your own paper. Answers in side column

Tú

Quiero cambiar mi rutina pero no sé qué hacer. ¿Me ayudas?

¿Estirarme? ¿Por cuántos minutos?

Ay, pero no me gusta levantar pesas sola.

Muy bien. ¿A qué hora empieza la clase?

¡Dios mío! ¿Tan temprano?

Jill

Con mucho gusto. Primero, ___1___

___2___ Entonces, ___3___

Bueno, ___4___

___5___

___6___

10 Y a ti, ¿qué te gusta?

¿Cuáles de las actividades en las fotos te gustan? Pregúntale a un/a compañero/a si le gustan también. Luego compartan *(share)* sus ideas con la clase. Answers will vary.

STANDARDS: 1.1, 3.1, 4.2, 5.1

11 Un cuestionario

Escribe con qué frecuencia haces lo siguiente. Usa oraciones completas. *Answers will vary.*

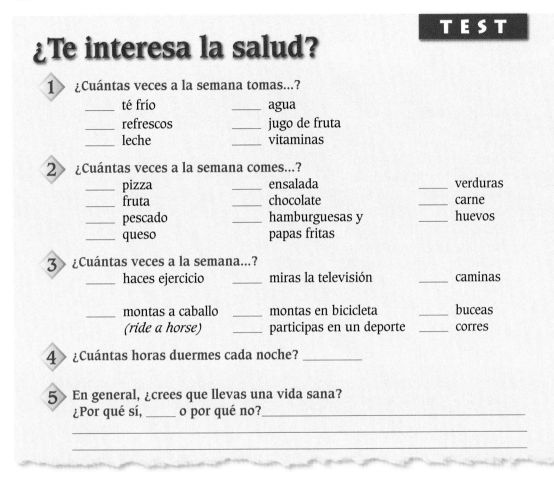

TEST

¿Te interesa la salud?

1 ¿Cuántas veces a la semana tomas...?

____ té frío   ____ agua
____ refrescos   ____ jugo de fruta
____ leche   ____ vitaminas

2 ¿Cuántas veces a la semana comes...?

____ pizza   ____ ensalada   ____ verduras
____ fruta   ____ chocolate   ____ carne
____ pescado   ____ hamburguesas y   ____ huevos
____ queso   papas fritas

3 ¿Cuántas veces a la semana...?

____ haces ejercicio   ____ miras la televisión   ____ caminas

____ montas a caballo   ____ montas en bicicleta   ____ buceas
     (ride a horse)   ____ participas en un deporte   ____ corres

4 ¿Cuántas horas duermes cada noche? _____

5 En general, ¿crees que llevas una vida sana?
¿Por qué sí, ____ o por qué no? _____
_____
_____

12 Una vida diferente

Get together with three classmates and compare your answers from Activity 11. Make suggestions about how each person in your group can improve his or her weekly routine. Be prepared to share your suggestions with the class.

13 La rutina cotidiana

Imagine that you and a friend want to get into shape and feel better. Write a paragraph in your journal suggesting what the two of you might do to improve your daily routine.

MODELO ¿Qué tal si...?

☀ CLOSE

Have student pairs create dialogues. One partner is very energetic and wants to exercise and the other gives many reasons not to. Have them use vocabulary and expressions from this chapter. (—**¿Qué tal si vamos al gimnasio? —No, me duele el pie.**)

☀ ASSESS

▶ Testing Program, pp. 91–92
Quiz 11-1
Audio CD 11, Tr. 17

▶ Grammar and Vocabulary Quizzes
Quiz 11-1 or
Alternative Quiz 11-1A

▶ Alternative Assessment Guide, p. 23

PERFORMANCE ASSESSMENT

Write the following letter on the board or a transparency and have students write replies:

Querido/a _____,

Vas a estar en Puerto Rico en menos de dos semanas. Tengo muchas ganas de verte. Estoy haciendo planes para lo que podemos hacer. ¿Qué tal si todas las mañanas vamos al parque para patinar sobre ruedas? Después podemos hacer otras cosas que te gustan. ¿Qué te gustaría hacer? Hasta pronto. Tu primo, Pedro

VIDEO INTEGRATION

En camino LEVEL 1B
Video Program
Videocassette 2, 34:30–37:08

¡Ven conmigo! LEVEL 1
DVD Tutor, Disc 2

TEACHER NOTES
• See *Video Guide* for activities related to **Panorama cultural.**
• Remind students that cultural information may be included in the Quizzes and the Chapter Test.
• The language of the people interviewed represents informal, unrehearsed speech.

MOTIVATING ACTIVITY
Ask students if they have played or seen any unusual sports (**jai alai, el paracaidismo** *parachuting* or *sky diving,* **el rodeo, el surfing, la ascensión sobre hielo** *ice climbing)* Which ones would they like to try? Which ones seem too dangerous?

PRESENTATION
After watching the video, ask ¿**Qué deporte practica Rodrigo?** ¿**Alejandra?** ¿**Fernando?** After several comprehension questions, ask a student ¿**Qué deportes practicas tú?** Next, have students ask each other what sports they play and why. Then show the video again and have students answer the questions.

Panorama cultural

CD 11
Trs. 4–7

¿Qué deporte practicas?

Although the most popular spectator sports in Spanish-speaking countries are soccer and baseball, there are other sports that many people play. In this chapter, we asked some people what sport they play, and why.

Rodrigo's favorite sport is popular all over the world. What is your favorite sport?

● Rodrigo
San Miguel de Santo Domingo, Costa Rica
CD 11 Tr. 5

El deporte favorito me es el fútbol porque uno... [porque] se fortalecen los músculos y además uno aprende.

Alejandra does various things to stay fit. Do you do any of the things she does?

● Alejandra
San Juan, Puerto Rico
CD 11 Tr. 6

Bueno, no practico un deporte pero bailo con el equipo de baile de la escuela. Hago ejercicio y también como bien y duermo.

Fernando plays two sports to stay fit and have fun. How many do you play?

Fernando

México D.F., México
CD 11 Tr. 7

> [Juego al] soccer y [hago el] patinaje. Me emociona meter un gol. [Jugar deportes] me mantiene en forma.

1 ¿Cuál es el deporte favorito de Rodrigo? el fútbol

2 Según Rodrigo, ¿qué se fortalece *(gets stronger)* jugando el fútbol? Se fortalecen los músculos.

3 ¿Alejandra juega un deporte? ¿Cómo se mantiene en forma?
No, pero baila con el equipo de su escuela.

4 ¿Qué más hace Alejandra para mantener la salud?
Hace ejercicio, come bien y duerme.

5 Según Fernando, ¿qué beneficio hay en jugar deportes?
Le mantiene en forma.

6 ¿Qué le gusta del *soccer?* meter un gol

Para pensar y hablar...

A. Rodrigo and Fernando give reasons why they like to play sports. What are they? Do you agree with them? Why or why not?

B. In Spanish, tell a partner one sport you enjoy and one sport you want to do. Share your ideas with the class, and see how many of your classmates have similar interests.

Cuaderno para hispanohablantes, pp. 54–55

LANGUAGE NOTE
Point out that when Rodrigo says "**El deporte favorito me es el fútbol....**" me is an example of an indirect object pronoun. A more common way to express this is **Mi deporte favorito es...**

NATIVE SPEAKERS
Ask native speakers what kind of words the following from the interview text are examples of: **fútbol (palabras llanas), también, además (palabras agudas), músculos (palabras esdrújulas)**. Have them write these words in their spelling notebooks.

CULTURE NOTE
The Basque words **jai alai** mean *merry festival.* **Jai alai** is a fast and exciting game that resembles handball. Players use a narrow wicker basket to throw a hard ball against the front wall of a court. The basket, called a **cesta,** has a glove on one end that fits the player's hand. The other end is used for throwing and catching the ball, **pelota,** which is slightly smaller than a baseball. **Jai alai** is played in a walled court called a **cancha.** **Jai alai** originated from a game played in the Basque country of Spain and France during the 1600s. Ask students if they have ever seen or played **jai alai**.

VIDEO INTEGRATION

En camino LEVEL 1B
Video Program
Videocassette 2, 23:14–23:45 OR
Videocassette 3, 1:51:10–1:51:41
(captioned version)

¡Ven conmigo! LEVEL 1
DVD Tutor, Disc 2

Bell work
Have students write their answers to these questions: **¿Te gusta patinar sobre ruedas? ¿Levanta pesas en el gimnasio tu hermano o hermana? ¿Cuántas veces a la semana te estiras? ¿Cómo te sientes hoy?**

SUGGESTION
14 Have students read these questions as advance organizers before they watch the video.

☀ MOTIVATE

Ask students how they feel after eating. How do they feel after physical education class? After exercising vigorously? After staying up late to finish homework? After hearing very good news? How many of these feelings can they already express in Spanish?

SEGUNDO PASO

(TPR) Storytelling Book pp. 42, 44

WV3 PUERTO RICO-11

Talking about moods and physical condition

14 El descanso

Answer the questions below.

1. What does Carmen mean when she says **me duelen los pies**?
   a. She's tired.
   b. Her feet hurt.
2. What is Carmen doing that helps you figure out what **me duelen los pies** means?
3. What solution does Ben suggest?

1. b. Her feet hurt.
2. She's holding her foot.
3. He suggests they rest on the bench.

Nota cultural

(PA) p. 72 Act. 16

Bless you! Gesundheit! (German for *Health!*). These are phrases you might hear when you sneeze. Some Spanish-speakers have a series of sayings to use if a person sneezes more than once in a row. The first time someone sneezes they say **¡Salud!** *(Health!)*. They say **¡Amor!** *(Love!)* for the second time, and **¡Dinero!** or **¡Pesetas!** *(referring to money)* for the third time. If someone sneezes a fourth time, they say **¡Y tiempo para gozarlos!** *(And time to enjoy them!)* What do people in your family say when someone sneezes?

ASÍ SE DICE Talking about moods and physical condition

11-2

To find out what kind of mood or condition a friend is in, ask:

> **¿Cómo estás?**

Your friend might say:

> **Estoy nerviosa.** Tengo un examen hoy.

> **¿Cómo te sientes?**

> **Estoy** mal. **Tengo gripe.**
> *I'm sick. I have the flu.*

> **¿Qué le pasa a** Roberto?
> *What's wrong with Roberto?*

> No sé pero me parece que **está preocupado por algo.**
> *I don't know but it seems to me that he's worried about something.*

15 Está muy bien

Lee las siguientes situaciones. Busca la respuesta que describa cómo se siente cada persona. Answers on p. 205K

1. Teresa tiene que tocar el violín en un concierto dentro de quince minutos.
2. Hoy es el cumpleaños de Mariana.
3. Darío tiene un partido de voleibol muy importante esta tarde.
4. Hay problemas en la familia de Javier.
5. Ayer Amara caminó en la nieve *(snow)* sin su chaqueta.
6. Raimundo no tiene nada que hacer, está solo y hace mal tiempo.

Está nervioso/a.

Está triste.

Está bien.

Está contento/a.

Está mal. Tiene gripe.

Está preocupado/a.

16 ¿Cómo estamos?

Completa las siguientes oraciones. Usa el modelo como ejemplo. Answers will vary.

MODELO Estoy de mal humor cuando...
Estoy de mal humor cuando no puedo salir con mis amigos.

1. Mi amigo/a está de buen humor cuando...
2. Mi profesor/a está feliz cuando...
3. Tengo vergüenza a veces si...
4. Mi mamá está de mal humor cuando...
5. Todos tenemos calor durante...
6. Hoy estoy... porque...

VOCABULARIO EXTRA

estar... *to be . . .*
  contento/a *happy*
  de buen/mal humor *in a good/bad mood*
  feliz *happy*
tener... *to be . . .*
  frío *cold*
  calor *hot*
  vergüenza *embarrassed*

☀ TEACH

PRESENTATION
ASÍ SE DICE
Review spelling, pronunciation, and intonation of question words with students. Ask several students **¿Cómo te sientes?** and **¿Cómo estás?** Students answer with **Estoy... Me siento...** and a new vocabulary word.

ADDITIONAL PRACTICE
15 Tell volunteers **Tienes un examen de ciencias hoy por la tarde.** Then ask **¿Cómo te sientes?** Then assign partners and have students make up four new situations. One partner asks the other about how he or she feels in each of the imaginary situations. Partners then switch roles.

PAIR WORK
Have students role-play a conversation in which one partner is having a very bad day and the other is having a great day. One partner asks the other how he or she is doing. The partner not only answers but gives four or five reasons why the day is or is not going well. (—**¿Cómo estás?** —**Estoy mal. Estoy de mal humor porque hace frío. Estoy cansado. No tengo almuerzo hasta la una de la tarde y tengo hambre.**) Ask volunteers to perform their skits for the class.

STANDARDS: 1.1, 3.1, 5.1 **221**

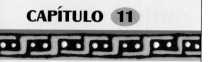

PRESENTATION

VOCABULARIO

Use Teaching Transparency 11-B to present this vocabulary. Have students say the phrases after you and mimic the facial gestures they imply. Then say the phrases and have students express the facial expressions for each, mimicking the art.

KINESTHETIC LEARNERS

17 Use the listening activity to reinforce the new vocabulary. First play the recording for recognition only, having students act out what the sentences describe. Have them answer the questions the second time through.

NATIVE SPEAKERS

Encourage native speakers to list and share with the class regional vocabulary variations for expressions related to how one is feeling: **tener catarro** *(to have a cold);* **tener ansias, estar comiendo ansias** *(to feel anxious);* **tener calambre** *(to have a cramp);* **tener náuseas, estar nauseabundo/a** *(to feel nauseated).*

ADDITIONAL PRACTICE

18 Have students work in pairs to create dialogues. Have them ask how their partners feel and tell why they do not feel well. The dialogues may be exaggerated for humorous effect.

PA pp. 65–66 Acts. 7–8

GV pp. 39–40 Acts. 5–7

11-B

VOCABULARIO

CD-ROM DISC 3

1. estar resfriado/a
2. estar nervioso/a
3. estar enojado/a
4. estar triste

5. estar preocupado/a
6. tener fiebre
7. tener tos
8. tener gripe

17 ¿Cómo te sientes hoy? Script and answers on p. 205E

CD 11 Tr. 8

Listen to these people talk about how they feel today. Use the drawings in the **Vocabulario** above. Write the correct number or numbers that go with each description.

18 ¿Qué les pasa? Answers will vary. Possible answers:

Completa las oraciones con expresiones del **Vocabulario.** Usa la forma correcta de los verbos **estar** o **tener** en las expresiones.

1. Daniel y yo ═══ ═══ porque no estudiamos para el examen de inglés. estamos nerviosos
2. Mis primos ═══ ═══ porque su perro huyó *(ran away).* están tristes
3. Los hijos de la señora Crespo se sienten mal porque ═══ ═══. tienen gripe / tienen fiebre / tienen tos / están resfriados
4. Vas a viajar solo, ¿no? ¿Tú ═══ ═══? estás nervioso
5. Mis padres ═══ ═══ porque mi hermano está en el centro con sus amigos y hace mal tiempo. están preocupados
6. Yo ═══ ═══ porque mi papá no me deja *(doesn't let me)* salir. estoy enojado/a

222 STANDARDS: 1.1, 1.2, 5.1

VOCABULARIO

El cuerpo humano

el ojo
la nariz
la boca
la garganta
el oído/la oreja
el cuello
los dedos
la mano

la pierna
el pie
la espalda
el estómago
el pelo
la cabeza
los dedos
el brazo

PA
p. 66
Act. 9

GV
p. 40
Acts. 8–9

11-C

19 ¿Para qué sirve?

 ¿Qué parte o partes del cuerpo usamos en las siguientes situaciones? Tu compañero/a y tú deben mencionar una parte diferente. Answers on p. 205K

1. para nadar
2. para hablar por teléfono
3. para correr por el parque
4. para peinarse
5. para hacer ejercicios aeróbicos
6. para tocar el piano
7. para escribir una carta
8. para levantar cosas
9. para montar en bicicleta
10. para escuchar música rock

20 Simón dice...

Work in groups to play **Simón dice.** Take turns being the leader, and practice the words in the **Vocabulario.** Here are some words you may need.

> MODELO Simón dice, ¡cierra los ojos!

levanta	*lift*
toca	*touch*
señala	*point to*
cierra	*close*
abre	*open*
mueve	*move*

SEGUNDO PASO

doscientos veintitrés **223**

PRESENTATION

VOCABULARIO

Model the new words by pronouncing them as you point to the correct part of the body. Teach parts of the body by using TPR and playing **Simón dice.** After a few rounds of play in which you call out the words, have a student be **Simón.**

LANGUAGE NOTE

La oreja is the term for the *outer ear,* while **el oído** means *inner ear* and refers to the hearing organ.

VISUAL/AUDITORY LEARNERS

Mnemonic devices may help your students remember the difference between **oreja** and **oído.** Tell your students to visualize the world **oído** with each **o** as an ear and the **i** as the inner ear. Or, have students visualize the **j** in **oreja** as the outer ear. If this technique helps, ask students to make up some more memory devices for other vocabulary.

VISUAL LEARNERS

19 Hold up magazine pictures of people doing different activities. Students tell you in Spanish which parts of the body are being used. You might ask them to express this in a sentence. (**Para hablar por teléfono, uno usa la boca, el oído y la mano.**)

STANDARDS: 1.2, 5.1   223

STANDARDS: 1.2, 2.1, 4.1, 5.1

PRESENTATION

NOTA GRAMATICAL

Review the use of **gustar,** a verb that students are comfortable with. Ask several students **¿Te gusta montar en bicicleta?** and other questions with vocabulary from **Primer paso.** Explain the similar use of **doler (ue).** Have students work in pairs asking each other questions. (**¿Te duele el pie?**) Then have six volunteers come to the front of the class. Hand them each a card with a body part written on it. (**estómago, cabeza**) Have student volunteers use gestures to pretend that the body part hurts.

RE-ENTRY

21 Review the parts of the body in Spanish that will be mentioned. Have students repeat the words after you and point to their feet, stomach, and so on.

TEACHER NOTE

21 This activity contains some language unfamiliar to students. Make sure students focus on what they do understand so they can answer the questions.

PA p. 67 Act. 10

GV p. 41 Acts. 10–11

NOTA GRAMATICAL

Doler *(to hurt, ache)* is an **o** to **ue** stem-changing verb. Like **gustar** (**me gusta, te gustan**), **doler** is used with indirect object pronouns and can be singular or plural. Do the following sentences use definite articles (**el, la,** etc.) or possessive adjectives (**mi, tu,** etc.) with parts of the body?

Me duele el estómago.	**¿Te duele** la garganta?
Le duele la cabeza.	**Me duelen** los pies.
Te duelen las piernas.	**¿Le duelen** los brazos?

21 Las quejas
Script and answers on p. 205E

 CD 11 Tr. 9

Listen as several people tell you about a complaint. Find the item on the list that tells you about that person's physical condition.

1. Rubén	a. Le duelen los pies.
2. Berta	b. Le duele el estómago.
3. Blanca	c. Le duelen las manos.
4. David	d. Le duele la garganta.
5. Elena	e. Le duelen los ojos.

22 ¿Qué te pasa?

Haz una entrevista a tu compañero/a con estas preguntas. Después contesta las preguntas de tu compañero/a. Answers on p. 205K

MODELO —¿Cómo te sientes si comes mucha comida?
—Si como mucha comida me duele el estómago.

1. ¿Cómo te sientes cuando lees demasiado?
2. ¿Cómo se siente tu amigo/a cuando corre demasiado?
3. ¿Cómo te sientes si comes un helado con mucha prisa?
4. ¿Cómo te sientes cuando vas al dentista?
5. ¿Cómo se siente tu amigo/a cuando levanta pesas?
6. ¿Cómo te sientes cuando estás resfriado/a?

Nota cultural

In Spanish, parts of the body are used in many common expressions. People point to their eye and say **¡Ojo!** as a warning or to mean "Pay attention!" Something that is a "pain" is sometimes called **un dolor de cabeza. ¿Me estás tomando el pelo?** is used to mean "Are you teasing me?" To say someone is stingy, people say **Es muy codo** *(elbow),* or they might tap their elbow with the palm of their hand. When something is very expensive, people might say **Cuesta un ojo de la cara.** Can you think of similar sayings in English?

PA p. 72 Act. 17

23 ¿Cómo se siente?

Look at the drawings. With a partner, take turns saying what you think is wrong with each person. Then say what each person should do to feel better.

Answers will vary. Possible answer:

MODELO —A Midori le duele la rodilla. Debe... A Midori le duele la pierna. Debe descansar.

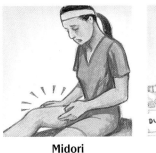
Midori

Joe

Conchita

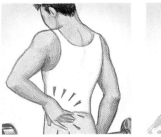
Jeff

Laura

Linda

Donna

Benito

24 ¿Cómo están hoy?

Write a questionnaire to find out how your classmates are doing today. Include at least five questions. First ask how they're feeling. Then ask some more specific questions to find out what kind of mood they're in and why. Also find out if they feel like doing some specific activities today. Answers will vary.

ADDITIONAL PRACTICE

23 Have students, working in pairs, use the preterite tense to talk about what they think happened to the people in the drawings. Have students create a short dialogue for each of the drawings and ask them to present one to the class. (—¿Por qué le duele el estómago? —Porque tomó diez vasos de leche. —Pues, debe descansar, no comer mucho y luego hacer ejercicio.)

PAIR WORK

24 Have students develop skits in pairs. One partner describes his or her horrible day and the other asks questions and gives advice. Ask volunteers to perform their skits for the class.

VISUAL LEARNERS

Ask students to draw a monster using the body parts in **Vocabulario** on page 223 (something with two heads, three arms, etc.) Tell them not to let other students see what they draw. Then have them describe their monster to a partner, holding it so the partner cannot see it. The student draws the monster his or her partner describes. They should then compare the two monsters and evaluate description, comprehension, and creative interpretation. You may wish to display students' artwork.

CHALLENGE

26 Have students list seven ways to manage different aspects of everyday life. For example, **7 claves para aguantar a los hermanitos.**

COOPERATIVE LEARNING

26 Ask students to work with people they do not usually work with to discuss stress management. Afterwards, assign them to small groups. Have them talk about their answers. Then have each group make a poster, or write a song or skit to present to the class five to seven ways to avoid stress. The posters are to reflect what students do for fun, what makes them laugh, and what activities they like to do outside of school. Additional vocabulary: **reír** *to laugh* and **canción** *song* (**1. Reír cada día. 2. Comer un desayuno grande. 3. Cantar con la radio. 4. Tocar la guitarra.**)

AUDITORY LEARNERS

Have students role-play the following situation in pairs. One partner is a television counselor (**consejero/a**) for a local Spanish-speaking television station that has a call-in health program to answer viewers' questions. The other is a caller with a question. After the caller asks several questions, the partners switch roles.

25 Una encuesta

Usa el cuestionario que escribiste en la Actividad 24. Haz las preguntas a cuatro de tus compañeros. Presenta los resultados de tu encuesta *(survey)* a la clase.

26 Consejos para vivir mejor

A Lee estos consejos *(advice)* para llevar una vida con menos estrés. Luego contesta las preguntas de abajo.

1. Comer por lo menos una comida balanceada al día. La nutrición es esencial para una buena salud y proporciona defensas contra el estrés.

2. Dormir por lo menos 8 horas cada noche. Un sueño apropiado puede añadir años de vida. Trate de acostarse y levantarse a la misma hora.

3. Hacer ejercicio, por lo menos 3 veces por semana. Busque una actividad divertida, como la bicicleta, o como caminar o nadar.

4. No debe tomar demasiada cafeína. Puede producir irritabilidad, dolor de cabeza, ansiedad y depresión.

5. Salir y cultivar sus amistades; tener buenos amigos ayuda a mantener en alto el autoestima.

6. Organizar su tiempo. Debe planear el uso de su tiempo y emplearlo bien.

7. Tener una actitud positiva: las personas optimistas tienen menos problemas mentales y físicos.

B Después de leer los consejos, contesta las siguientes preguntas.

1. ¿Comes por lo menos una comida balanceada al día? ¿Qué comes?
2. ¿Cuántas horas duermes cada noche?
3. ¿Cuántas veces por semana haces ejercicio? ¿Qué te gusta hacer?
4. ¿Tomas muchos refrescos? ¿Tienen cafeína?
5. ¿Tienes un buen amigo o una buena amiga con quien puedes hablar?
6. ¿Eres una persona positiva o eres una persona que piensa que todo va a salir mal?
7. ¿Planeas el tiempo para estudiar y el tiempo para pasar el rato con tus amigos?

Nota cultural

p. 72
Act. 18

Athletes from Spanish-speaking backgrounds are important to the success of U.S. teams in many different sports, but nowhere is this more visible than in baseball. Since 1911, more than 500 Spanish-speaking athletes from Puerto Rico, Colombia, Cuba, the Dominican Republic, Mexico, Nicaragua, Panama, and Venezuela have made it into baseball's major leagues. Among the players enshrined in the Baseball Hall of Fame are several of Hispanic origin: Lefty Gómez, Puerto Rico's Roberto Clemente, Cuba's Tony Pérez and Martín DiHigo, the Dominican Republic's Juan Marichal, Venezuela's Luis Aparicio, and Panama's Rod Carew. Women, too, have made a mark: Cuban American Lisa Fernández pitched for the 2000 U.S. Women's Olympic softball team in Sydney. Can you name any other baseball players from Spanish-speaking countries?

27 Una semana sin estrés

¿Puedes reducir *(reduce)* el estrés durante una semana? Escribe un párrafo de seis oraciones en que describas con detalles las cosas que puedes hacer durante la próxima semana para reducir el estrés.

28 El estrés

Imagine that tomorrow there is a major school event, such as a championship basketball game, band concert, or year-end play. You're participating, and you're feeling nervous. With a partner, take turns telling each other how you're feeling and suggesting what to do to relieve stress. Use advice from the reading in Activity 26.

MODELO —Estoy nervioso/a porque mañana es el partido de basquetbol.
—Haz algo divertido esta tarde. Y también debes...

SOCIAL STUDIES LINK
Ask students to name athletes from Spanish-speaking countries who play on major league sports teams. Have the class write the names down as an informal dictation exercise. Students then choose Hispanic athletes, actors, scientists, or politicians and research their childhoods, choice of professions, where they grew up, and other details of their lives.

CLOSE

Review the material from this **paso** by using Teaching Transparency 11-2. Then have students play **Simón dice** using both the adjectives and body part vocabulary.

ASSESS

▸ Testing Program, pp. 93–94
Quiz 11-2
Audio CD 11, Tr. 18

▸ Grammar and Vocabulary Quizzes
Quiz 11-2A or
Alternative Quiz 11-2A

▸ Alternative Assessment Guide, p. 23

PERFORMANCE ASSESSMENT
Ask students to write dialogues between a doctor and a patient using as much **paso** vocabulary as possible. When they have completed their dialogues, have students present them to the class. You might grade both the written dialogues and oral presentations.

VIDEO INTEGRATION

En camino LEVEL 1B
Video Program
Videocassette 2, 26:57–27:38 OR
Videocassette 3, 1:54:53–1:55:34
(captioned version)

¡Ven conmigo! LEVEL 1
DVD Tutor, Disc 1

Bell work
On the board or on a transparency, write the following expressions: **estar resfriado/a, estar enojado/a, estar triste, estar preocupado/a, estar bien.** Have students illustrate each with their books closed.

PRE-VIEWING
29 Before students watch the video or re-read the **fotonovela,** have them use the questions and answers from this activity as advance organizers.

☼ MOTIVATE

Take a poll of the class to find out some of the things they did yesterday. (**¿Cuántas personas estudiaron ayer? ¿Cuántos ayudaron en casa ayer? ¿Cuántos desayunaron ayer? ¿Cuántos llevaron bluejeans ayer? ¿Cuántos compraron ropa ayer?**) Write the number of students who did each thing on the board.

TERCER PASO (TPR)

Storytelling Book
pp. 43, 44

WV3 PUERTO RICO-11

Saying what you did; talking about where you went and when

> Bueno, ¿tienen ganas de ir a otra parte? ¿Ya fueron a la Plaza de Hostos?

> No... ¡La Plaza de Hostos! ¡Ay, no! ¡Carmen, si son las tres menos cinco! ¡Mamá nos espera en la Plaza de Hostos a las tres!

29 ¿Qué pregunta Pedro?

Read the questions that Pedro asks Benjamín and Carmen. Choose the sentence that best describes what he is asking them. Be prepared to explain why you chose the answer you did.

1. ¿Tienen ganas de ir a otra parte?
   a. He wants to know if they feel like going somewhere else.
   b. He invites them to a party.

2. ¿Ya fueron a la Plaza de Hostos?
   a. He wants to know if they went to the plaza.
   b. He wants to know if they like the plaza.

La Plaza de Hostos, con la estatua de Eugenio María de Hostos

ASÍ SE DICE   Saying what you did

To find out what a friend did last night, ask:

¿Qué hiciste anoche?
What did you do last night?

¿Ganaste?
Did you win?

Your friend might say:

Jugué al tenis.
I played tennis.

No. Mi prima **ganó. Jugó** muy bien.
No. My cousin won. She played very well.

PA
p. 68
Act. 11

11-3

NOTA GRAMATICAL

In the preterite, **jugar** *(to play)* has **u** in the ending for the **yo** form.

(yo)	jug**ué**	(nosotros) (nosotras)	jug**amos**
(tú)	jug**aste**	(vosotros) (vosotras)	jug**asteis**
(usted) (él) (ella)	jug**ó**	(ustedes) (ellos) (ellas)	jug**aron**

PA
p. 68
Act. 12

GV
p. 42
Acts. 12–13

30 Una semana divertida

Completa el párrafo con la forma correcta del verbo **jugar**. Answers in side column·

El lunes pasado Marcos y yo ___1___ al tenis en el parque. Más tarde, yo ___2___ al basquetbol con unos amigos. El viernes por la noche mis hermanos y yo ___3___ al dominó. Y finalmente, el domingo mi amigo Pepe ___4___ a las cartas con María Eugenia. ¿Y tú? ¿___5___ un deporte la semana pasada?

Mi abuela jugó en un torneo de golf el sábado pasado.

31 ¿Qué jugaste?

 Interview your group members about when they last played a specific sport or game. Then answer your group members' questions. Be sure to use **jugar** in the preterite. Be prepared to report your answers to the class.

☀ TEACH

PRESENTATION
ASÍ SE DICE
NOTA GRAMATICAL

Model the forms of verbs in the preterite tense by asking students personalized questions such as **¿Qué hiciste ayer?** Then practice the dialogue with a number of students. (**¿Qué hizo _____ anoche?**) Encourage students to answer with an activity that is not mentioned in **Así se dice.** When students seem comfortable with the verb **hacer,** have them read the **Nota gramatical** silently while you put several sentences using **jugar** on the board or on a transparency. (**Ayer, yo jugué al voleibol** or **Alicia jugó al fútbol.**) Have students practice asking each other questions with **hacer** and answering them with **jugar.** You might wish to introduce the Additional Vocabulary on pages 294–296.

Answers to Activity 30

1. jugamos
2. jugué
3. jugamos
4. jugó
5. Jugaste

ADDITIONAL PRACTICE

32 Have students work in pairs to write a conversation about what they did last weekend. Remind students that they may talk about imaginary activities, if they prefer. Then have volunteers present their conversations to the class.

ADDITIONAL VOCABULARY

las cartas *playing cards*

el dominó *dominoes*

el crucigrama *crossword puzzle*

el rompecabezas *jigsaw puzzle*

el ajedrez *chess*

las damas *checkers*

32 Un día en el parque

El domingo pasado la familia de Marcela y Joaquín pasó un día fabuloso en el parque. Imagínate que tú eres Marcela o Joaquín. Descríbele a tu compañero/a lo que hicieron los miembros de tu familia.

33 Una semana llena

En un grupo, describe lo que tú hiciste y lo que hizo otro miembro de tu familia durante la semana pasada. Incluye los días de la semana y adónde fueron. Menciona un mínimo de cuatro actividades por cada persona. Un miembro del grupo debe tomar apuntes *(take notes)*. Mira el modelo.

MODELO

	lunes	martes	miércoles	jueves	viernes	sábado	domingo
Susana			visitó a su amiga María		jugó al voleibol	compró una blusa	miró televisión
la hermana de Susana	jugó a los video-juegos		jugó al béisbol	tomó un refresco con amigas		escuchó música en casa	limpió la cocina
Jim							

Nota cultural

The majority of sports played in the United States are also popular in Spanish-speaking countries. One exception is American football, which is only played on an informal basis. Soccer, known as **el fútbol**, is highly organized, and Spanish-speaking countries have World Cup-caliber teams. Some games are more common in Spanish-speaking countries than in the U.S. **Bolas criollas** is very popular in Venezuela. This game is similar to the game of bocce, a European lawn game.

Bolas criollas

ASÍ SE DICE   Talking about where you went and when

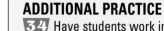
p. 70
Act. 13

To ask where someone went, say:

¿Adónde **fuiste** anoche?
Where did you go last night?

Your friend might answer:

Anoche **fui** al parque con mi familia.

To talk about different times in the past, you might say:

¿Adónde fuiste **anteayer?**
Where did you go the day before yesterday?

Anteayer **fui** a la piscina y **anteanoche fui** al cine.
The day before yesterday I went to the swimming pool and the night before last I went to the movies.

34 Los acontecimientos de la semana

En el siguiente párrafo Eduardo describe las cinco cosas que hizo *(he did)* durante el fin de semana. Pon las cinco actividades de Eduardo en orden.   Answers on p. 205K

—Jorge, déjame contarte. Estoy muy cansado. Hoy fui al colegio. Antes de regresar a casa, fui a la casa de Elena. Anteayer fui al parque con mi amigo Jaime. Le gané en basquetbol. Anoche mi primo nos visitó en casa y pasó la noche con nosotros. Hicimos mucho ruido *(we made a lot of noise)* hasta las doce. Mi mamá estaba *(was)* muy enojada con nosotros. Y anteanoche fui al cine con mi hermana.

PRESENTATION
ASÍ SE DICE
Read the examples from **Así se dice** aloud. Have individual students repeat the sentences. Ask several students **¿Adónde fuiste anoche?** and elicit answers with **Fui.** Explain that **adónde** is used with **ir,** while **dónde** is used with **estar.**

ADDITIONAL PRACTICE
34 Have students work in pairs to write a paragraph-long story that includes five sentences with five different activities using the phrases from **Así se dice.** The partners write about what someone did during the last few days using **ayer, anteayer, primero, luego,** and so on. Then they write the sentences on five strips of paper, mix them up, and have another pair put them in order.

SLOWER PACE
34 Have students find the key words that show when something happened. (**ayer, anoche,** and so on) Then have them draw a timeline and write the key words on it in the correct order. They then fill in the timeline with the correct events.

STANDARDS: 2.2, 4.2, 5.1   **231**

PRESENTATION

NOTA GRAMATICAL

¿Adónde fueron ustedes el verano pasado? ¿Adónde fuimos en el Capítulo 9 de *En camino?* After you have modeled questions and answers, ask students to practice in small groups. You might also review **¿cuándo?** and have students ask people in their group: When did you go to the movies? to a game? to a party? to a restaurant? You might ask several students to tell the class what their group members said about what they did and when.

VOCABULARIO

Display Teaching Transparency 11-D. Point out to students that they already know much of this new vocabulary (**tenis, correr, fútbol**), but in order to describe these sports completely, they need to know how to say where they are played. Model pronunciation and then ask several students **¿Dónde jugaste al tenis?**

NATIVE SPEAKERS

Point out that many Spanish speakers add an **-s** to the **tú** form in the preterite (**fuistes, jugastes**) in informal speech. Ask students to use **fuiste** (without the **-s**) for oral and written testing purposes in class.

GV p. 43 Acts. 14–16

NOTA GRAMATICAL

The verb **ir** is irregular in the preterite. Use it to talk about where people went.

(yo)	**fui**	(nosotros) (nosotras)	**fuimos**
(tú)	**fuiste**	(vosotros) (vosotras)	**fuisteis**
(usted)		(ustedes)	
(él) (ella)	**fue**	(ellos) (ellas)	**fueron**

La familia Arroyo fue al cine anteayer.

Fuiste a jugar con Esmeralda, ¿no?

35 La semana pasada

Pregunta lo que tu compañero/a hizo durante la semana pasada. Después dile lo que tú hiciste. Deben estar listos para dar un informe a la clase.

MODELO —¿Adónde fuiste ayer?
—Ayer mis amigos y yo fuimos a la biblioteca para estudiar.

GV p. 44 Acts. 17–18

11-D

VOCABULARIO

la cancha de fútbol

la cancha de tenis

el estadio

la pista de correr

36 ¿Adónde fuiste? Script and answers on p. 205F

CD 11 Tr. 10 Listen while various people say what they did last week. They will mention a place and say what they did there. If it's something that is normally done in that place, write **lógico**. If not, write **ilógico**.

37 La página deportiva

Lee el artículo del periódico. Después busca las palabras indicadas en las páginas 297–314. Por último, contesta las preguntas. Answers on p. 205K

TERMINAN A TODO VAPOR

Las Águilas les ganaron a los Toros en su casa, donde terminaron con un impresionante récord de 23-4.

Betancourt permitió un solo hit

Las Águilas vencieron ayer a los Toros dos carreras a una en el estadio municipal El Hatillo. Ricardo Betancourt, pícher de las Águilas, jugó su mejor partido del año, permitiendo un solo hit.

Por las Águilas, Alejandro García dio un jonrón y un sencillo, Freddie Martínez conectó un doble y un sencillo y Antonio González un hit.

Los Toros tomaron ventaja del juego en la tercera entrada cuando Jorge Féliz dio un hit.

El juego fue demorado media hora y comenzó a las cuatro y media debido a que estaba lloviendo antes de su inicio. Con su victoria ayer, las Águilas terminaron la serie regular con 23 victorias y 4 derrotas.

1. ¿Cuáles equipos jugaron ayer, según el artículo?
2. ¿Quiénes ganaron el partido?
3. ¿Dónde fue el partido entre las Águilas y los Toros?
4. Al escritor del artículo, ¿le gustan más las Águilas o los Toros? ¿Por qué crees eso?

> derrota
> carrera
> demorado (demorar)
> inicio
> vencieron (vencer)

RE-ENTRY
To review the names of stores (Chapter 9) and to practice **ir** in the preterite, write the following on the board or a transparency: **tus hermanos/ zapato de tenis, tu hermana/ aretes, tu abuela/pastel, tu papá/arroz con pollo, nosotros/ flores.** Ask students to write where the various people went to buy each thing. (**Mis hermanos fueron a la zapatería.**)

NATIVE SPEAKERS
Have native speakers report about articles in Spanish from a Spanish-language community newsletter or newspaper.

Have native speakers scan the reading for **palabras agudas con acento—jonrón, jugó, comenzó; palabras llanas con acento—récord, Martínez, González; palabras esdrújulas—Águilas**. Ask them to cite the rule that explains why these **palabras llanas** and **agudas** are spelled with a written accent mark.

PRELISTENING
36 As a prelistening activity, ask students questions (**¿Es lógico ir al gimnasio para hacer la tarea?**) Have the class answer with **lógico** or **ilógico**. After asking them several questions, have volunteers ask questions of their own.

derrota *loss*
carrera *run*
demorado *delayed*
inicio *beginning*
vencieron *defeated*

GROUP WORK

38 In large groups or with the entire class, create a story using the vocabulary and expressions from this chapter. One student begins by saying a sentence in the preterite. Another student adds to the story by saying another sentence. Other classmates continue. Once students are comfortable with this format, designate a theme to the story and ask the students to use words that go with it.

 **PORTFOLIO**

38 **Written** This activity may be used as a written portfolio entry. For portfolio suggestions, see *Alternative Assessment Guide,* p. 15.

39 **Oral** This activity may be used as an oral portfolio entry. For portfolio suggestions, see *Alternative Assessment Guide,* p. 15.

COOPERATIVE LEARNING

39 Assign groups of three. Have each member write a description of two pictures. After they complete their descriptions, have them read them to their group members. The group tries to guess which picture is being described.

SUGGESTION

39 Supply students with a list of verbs to complete this activity. (**ir, caminar, hablar, presentar, comprar, tomar**)

---

38 Un día libre en San Juan

Answers will vary.

Imagine that you spent the day with Ben and his family in San Juan. Using items in each box, create a story describing the day. Include where each person went and what each person did there. Be creative!

Carmen
Pedro y tío Juan
Benjamín
Abuelo
Yo

fui
fuiste
fue
fuimos
fueron

al estadio municipal
a la cancha de fútbol
a la cancha de tenis
a la piscina
a la pista de correr
al centro

Nota cultural

Tropical fruits are used in a wide variety of ways in Puerto Rico. In addition to juices and **batidas,** a wide variety of sweets and desserts are made out of fruit. **Arroz con dulce,** a rice pudding made with grated fresh coconut, coconut milk, rice, raisins, and, of course, sugar, is popular all the time, but is a special treat during the Christmas season. **Dulce de coco** is a very sweet coconut candy and **besitos de coco** are cookies made from grated coconut. Fruits such as the **guayaba** are made into **pasta** (a solid jelly dessert), or are served as **cascos de guayaba** (preserved, sweetened guayaba halves) together with **queso del país** (locally made white cheese). What locally made foods are popular where you live?

39 Una excursión de los amigos

Mira las fotos de Ben, Carmen y Pedro. Escribe lo que pasó durante su día en San Juan. Compara tu descripción con la descripción de tu compañero/a. Answers on p. 205K

40 En mi cuaderno

Escribe un párrafo que incluya cinco cosas que hiciste durante los últimos tres días. Incluye cuándo, con quién y adónde fuiste para hacer cada actividad. También incluye dos cosas que no hiciste. Acuérdate de *(Remember)* usar **anteayer, ayer** y **anoche** en tu párrafo. Aquí tienes unas sugerencias.

cuidar a mis hermanos

dibujar

jugar al...

limpiar el...

ir al...

patinar

escuchar música

estudiar para mis clases

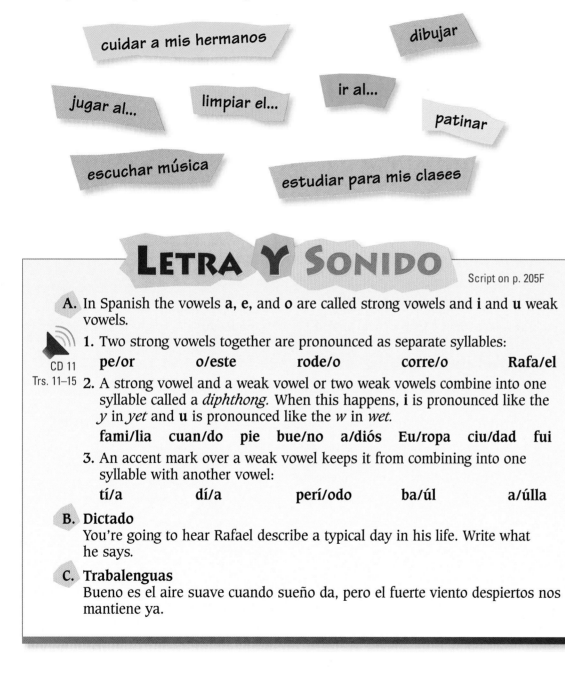

LETRA Y SONIDO

Script on p. 205F

A. In Spanish the vowels **a**, **e**, and **o** are called strong vowels and **i** and **u** weak vowels.

CD 11
Trs. 11–15

1. Two strong vowels together are pronounced as separate syllables:

pe/or	o/este	rode/o	corre/o	Rafa/el

2. A strong vowel and a weak vowel or two weak vowels combine into one syllable called a *diphthong.* When this happens, **i** is pronounced like the *y* in *yet* and **u** is pronounced like the *w* in *wet.*

fami/lia cuan/do pie bue/no a/diós Eu/ropa ciu/dad fui

3. An accent mark over a weak vowel keeps it from combining into one syllable with another vowel:

tí/a	dí/a	perí/odo	ba/úl	a/úlla

B. Dictado

You're going to hear Rafael describe a typical day in his life. Write what he says.

C. Trabalenguas

Bueno es el aire suave cuando sueño da, pero el fuerte viento despiertos nos mantiene ya.

☀ CLOSE

Tell students to imagine that they took a Caribbean cruise (**un crucero por el mar Caribe**) together as a class. They were on a huge ship (**barco**) with lots of recreational facilities and activities. (**pista para correr, cancha de tenis, pista de baile, restaurantes, piscina**) They also spent several days in Puerto Rico, sightseeing and visiting friends. You want to know what they did, where they went, and when. Ask students **¿Qué pasó el primer día? ¿Adónde fueron ustedes la primera noche?**

☀ ASSESS

▸ Testing Program, pp. 95–96
Quiz 11-3
Audio CD 11, Tr. 19

▸ Grammar and Vocabulary Quizzes
Quiz 11-3A or
Alternative Quiz 11-3A

▸ Alternative Assessment Guide, p. 23

PERFORMANCE ASSESSMENT

Ask students to write a summary of the Caribbean cruise from the CLOSE suggestion or of a recent memorable trip or weekend. Have them write five sentences saying what they did, where they went, and when. You might have them present their sentences to the class. Remind them that they may include imaginary information.

PRESENTATION

Ask students what their favorite baseball teams are. What leagues are the teams in? What positions do their favorite baseball players play? Have students list common baseball terms and list them on the board. (home run, first base, second base, third base, home, batter, outfielder, pitcher, and so on)

ENGLISH LINK

2 English has borrowed words from many different languages. Some examples of words borrowed from French are **ballet, hors d'oeuvre, déjà vu, croquet,** and **chic.** Words borrowed from German include **frankfurter, hamburger, bratwurst, kaput(t),** and **kindergarten.**

HISTORY LINK

Explain that, although baseball originated in the United States, it is very popular in Latin America as well. Three examples of Latin American athletes who play for baseball teams in the United States are Dominican designated hitter Manny Ramirez; Cuban pitcher Liván Hernández; and Venezuelan shortstop Omar Vizquel.

IDIOMAS

El béisbol   Baseball is very popular in Latin America, especially in the Caribbean. Many players from Caribbean countries have gone on to play in the major leagues in the United States. Because baseball originated in the U.S., many of the Spanish words for the sport come from the English words. Words borrowed directly from one language to another are called loanwords.

1 El lenguaje del béisbol   Answers on p. 205K

Work with a group to identify which of the baseball terms below are borrowed from English. Decide which English word each comes from.

el pelotero/la pelotera	batear	el récord
el jardinero/ la jardinera	el hit	pichear
el lanzador/la lanzadora	la pelota	el jardín izquierdo
vueltas remolcadas	el jonrón	ranqueado

2 Palabras del español   Answers on p. 205K

English has also borrowed words from Spanish. Below are some Spanish loanwords in English. What does each word mean? Use a dictionary if you're not sure.

patio	mesa	adobe	tornado
rodeo	taco	lasso	poncho
salsa	corral	arroyo	mosquito

236   STANDARDS: 3.1, 4.1, 5.1

CIENCIAS SOCIALES

Los peloteros latinoamericanos   Approximately one out of every six players in the major leagues in the United States is from Latin America.

Livan Hernandez es de Villa Clara, Cuba. Es un lanzador.

Receptor

Manny Ramirez es de Santo Domingo, República Dominicana. Es un receptor.

Lanzador

3 El clima y el béisbol   Answers on p. 205K

What three countries are the players shown in the baseball cards from? Look at the map on pages xviii–xix and find the countries. Where are these countries in relation to the equator? Where are they in relation to the U.S.? Based on what you know about weather and seasons, what do you think the climate is like in these countries?

4 Las temporadas   Answers on p. 205K

Mexico, Puerto Rico, Venezuela, and the Dominican Republic play in the Caribbean Series every February. This event ends the winter baseball season for those countries. How does this compare with the baseball season in the U.S.?

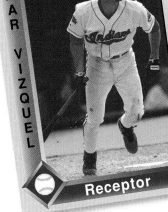

Omar Vizquel es de Caracas, Venezuela. Es un receptor.

Receptor

ENLACES

doscientos treinta y siete   **237**

PRESENTATION
Ask students if they know the names of some athletes from Spanish-speaking countries who play or played baseball. (Puerto Rico's Roberto Clemente, Cuba's Martín Dihigo, the Dominican Republic's Juan Marichal, Venezuela's Luis Aparicio, and Panama's Rod Carew)

GEOGRAPHY LINK
Explain that the tropics are between the Tropic of Cancer and the Tropic of Capricorn. Have students look at the maps of Central and South America in their books and find the tropics. (**trópico de Cáncer, trópico de Capricornio**) In tropical areas there is an almost constant temperature year round. The weather alternates between rainy and dry seasons.

 CULTURE NOTE
Mexico, Puerto Rico, the Dominican Republic, and Venezuela play in the Caribbean Series, a Latin American winter baseball championship.

STANDARDS: 3.1, 4.2, 5.1   **237**

VAMOS A LEER

238 STANDARDS: 1.2, 3.1, 5.2

READING STRATEGY
Using background knowledge.

☀ PREREADING

A Have students talk about the benefits of exercise. What parts of the body does swimming strengthen? running? aerobics?

MOTIVATING ACTIVITY
Ask students about their exercise habits. Where do they go to exercise indoors? outdoors? Which activities do they prefer?

SUGGESTION
• Before doing the Prereading activities, review the parts of the body with students.

• Have students look at the reading to identify words that are similar to English expressions used to describe exercises.

• Have students compare and discuss their answers to **¡A comenzar!** before you go over the correct answers. Once students have completed this section, remind them of how using background knowledge helped them.

☀ READING

VISUAL LEARNERS
B Have students act out the exercises as you read. Or ask for volunteers to read and act out the movements in front of the class.

Estrategia
Background knowledge Before you read something, take a minute to remember what you already know about that topic. Doing this will make it easier to guess the meanings of difficult words or phrases.

¡A comenzar!

A Look at pictures, the title, and subtitles first. Then, complete the following statements: Answers on page 205K

1. Both of these readings are about _____.
2. In Reading A, the goal of doing these activities is to _____.
3. In Reading B, the goal of doing the activity is to _____.

Compare your answers with a classmate's.

Al grano Answers on page 205K

B Imagine that you work as a personal trainer at a gym. Your clients often ask for your advice about their exercise programs. To answer their questions, use your background knowledge about exercise, as well as information from the article. Follow the steps outlined below.

Client 1: "High-impact aerobics are not for me! Those classes hurt my legs and back. What other sorts of exercises can I do instead?"

Using background knowledge: What do you know about low-impact exercises, calisthenics, and stretching?

Using the article: Where in the article can you find more information about this sort of exercise? Use reading strategies such as scanning and looking at pictures.

Client 2: "I spend all day at my computer, and get very stiff and tense. What can I do to feel better?"

Using background knowledge: What parts of your body become tired or tense from sitting and working at the computer?

Using the article: Where in the article can you find information about this topic? Remember that reading strategies such as using context and cognates can help you understand more and guess the meaning of unknown vocabulary.

C Now you're ready to answer your clients' questions from Activity B. Combine what you already know about these topics with what you've learned from the article and write some advice for each client. Use informal commands and **(No) debes...** + *infinitive*.

D Trabaja en un grupo. Escoge uno de los ejercicios. Lee la descripción mientras tus compañeros siguen tus instrucciones y hacen el ejercicio. Después escucha mientras uno de tus compañeros lee las instrucciones de otro ejercicio. Haz lo que te dice. Repitan hasta hacer todos los ejercicios.

A MÚSCULOS EN FORMA PARA UNA FIGURA SENSACIONAL

Hacer ejercicio al aire libre es ideal cuando tomamos vacaciones en la playa o en el bosque. Lo importante es comenzar con los ejercicios simples, semejantes a los que hacemos día a día, pero de una manera constante. No se trata de saltar° de un lado para otro, sino de hacer movimientos suaves, continuos y lentos, especialmente diseñados para ejercitar todos los músculos del cuerpo.

saltar *to jump*

1 Con los antebrazos y las rodillas en el suelo, levante una pierna, flexionándola con el pie en punta. Repite diez veces con cada pierna y fortalece los músculos.

2 Recostado, flexione una pierna hasta que pueda sujetar el pie con la mano; luego estire la pierna. Repite diez veces con cada pierna.

3 Acostada pero con los hombros° levantados, flexione las piernas. Repite diez veces para endurecer los abdominales y las piernas.

los hombros *shoulders*

B DILE ADIÓS A LAS TENSIONES ¡CON EJERCICIOS!

Aprende a eliminar la tensión muscular sin moverte de tu asiento. Las personas que pasan mucho tiempo en sillas —en la escuela o en la oficina— frecuentemente sufren de dolores de cabeza, en el cuello, en la barbilla°, en los hombros y en la espalda. Para eliminar esas desagradables tensiones, aquí tiene un ejercicio sencillo y fácil de realizar, que te ayudará muchísimo.

la barbilla *chin*

4 Para los hombros y la espalda: Cruza los brazos poniendo las palmas° encima de los hombros (como si te estuvieras abrazando). Respira profundamente y ve girando tu cuerpo (de la cintura° hacia arriba) todo lo que puedas de izquierda a derecha y en dirección contraria. Suelta el aire cuando estés en el centro. De tu cintura hacia abajo nada debe moverse.

las palmas *palms (of the hands)*
la cintura *waist*

Cuaderno para hispanohablantes, pp. 51–53

VAMOS A LEER

doscientos treinta y nueve **239**

CRITICAL THINKING

Ask students which body parts will be toned or relaxed in each of the exercises.

VISUAL/AUDITORY LEARNERS

D Hold up pictures of three different exercises. Give oral directions for one of the three exercises. The class is to guess which one you described.

NATIVE SPEAKERS

Have native speakers look for examples of **palabras esdrújulas (músculos, muchísimo), llanas (fácil)** and **agudas (tensión, dirección)** to write in their spelling notebooks. Have them cite the rule that explains why the written accents are necessary.

☀ POSTREADING

PAIR WORK

D Ask students to imagine that they didn't understand the directions for an exercise. Have them write an additional question about how to do each exercise. Then have students exchange questions with a partner and see if they can answer their partner's questions.

TEACHER NOTE

For additional readings, see *Practice and Activity Book*, p. 71, and *Cuaderno para hispanohablantes*, pp. 51–53.

STANDARDS: 1.2, 5.2 **239**

CAPÍTULO 11

Repaso reviews and integrates all four skills and culture in preparation for the Chapter Test.

SLOWER PACE
Use pictures clipped from magazines to review the various expressions and vocabulary in this chapter.

PREREADING
2 As a prereading activity, have students draw on their background knowledge of Puerto Rico to guess what activities might be mentioned in the letter. Brainstorm as a class before students begin reading.

📁 PORTFOLIO
Oral Ask students to work in pairs. One partner is to take the role of a doctor and the other partner is to be a patient. Instruct pairs to develop a conversation between doctor and patient in which (1) the patient complains of an ailment, (2) the doctor inquires about how, when, and where it occurred or began, (3) the patient answers, and (4) the doctor recommends a cure. You might recommend that students include their conversation in the Oral Portfolio. For Portfolio suggestions, see *Alternative Assessment Guide,* p. 15.

MARCAR: go.hrw.com
PALABRA CLAVE:
 WV3 PUERTO RICO-11

1 Listen as Miriam and Antonio talk on the telephone. Answer the questions in Spanish. Script and answers on p. 205F

CD 11 Tr. 16

1. ¿Cómo se siente Miriam?
2. ¿Qué hizo ayer?
3. ¿Cómo se siente Antonio?
4. ¿Qué hizo ayer?

2 Read the letter that Sara and Rafi's mother sent from Puerto Rico to her sister in the United States. Then read the sentences below. Write **cierto** or **falso** for each. Correct each false sentence.

> Querida Marisela,
> Llegamos bien y hemos tenido unas vacaciones maravillosas. Papá está bien y está disfrutando mucho de tener los nietos° a su lado. Anteayer fuimos de paseo al Yunque. No vas a creer lo bonito que es ese bosque°. Caminamos hasta El Salto° La Mina. Vimos un loro° puertorriqueño. Es verde con alas azules y es un pájaro° muy raro. Llovió muchísimo por la tarde después de un día de bastante calor. Fue una tremenda aventura. Ayer fuimos a la playa en Fajardo. Sara y Rafi nadaron todo el día y yo descansé y leí un buen libro. Esta semana se ha terminado muy rápidamente. Te veo pronto.
> Cariño,
> *Lourdes*

1. Lourdes fue al bosque del Yunque y a la playa durante sus vacaciones en Puerto Rico.
2. No hizo calor en el Yunque.
3. Lourdes buceó en la playa.
4. A Rafi y Sara les gusta nadar.

1. cierto
2. falso
3. falso
4. cierto

nietos	*grandchildren*
bosque	*forest*
salto	*waterfall*
vimos un loro	*we saw a parrot*
pájaro	*bird*

3 Vamos a escribir

Imagine you're a reporter. Write an interview you conducted with Benjamín and his mother about their recent vacation in Puerto Rico. Introduce your interviewees. Then write some dialogue, including what you asked them and what they answered.

Estrategia

Using dialogue is a good way to make your writing more lively and vivid. When writing a dialogue, consider who your characters are and make their style of speaking appropriate for their personalities and ages.

MODELO —Ben, ¿qué lugares visitaron ustedes el primer día?
—Fuimos al Morro y al Museo Pablo Casals.

Prewriting

Think of three questions you want to ask each person about their recent vacation. Put them in logical order.

Writing

1. Write a short, 2–3 sentence introduction, telling your readers what the interview is about.
2. Write a question for either Ben or his mother.
3. Give the answer. Remember to write the answer from either Ben's or his mother's point of view.
4. Repeat items 2 and 3 with the rest of the interview questions. Be sure to include as many details as you can.

Revising

1. Working with a partner, look over your dialogue. Think of the following elements: Are the questions and answers clear? Are the ideas well organized? Check your spelling.
2. Make all necessary changes to your article.

4 SITUACIÓN

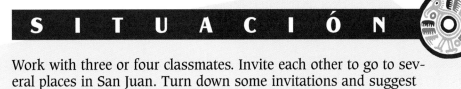

Work with three or four classmates. Invite each other to go to several places in San Juan. Turn down some invitations and suggest other places to go. In the end, your group must decide on one activity. Prepare the scene for presentation to the class.

Cuaderno para hispanohablantes, pp. 53–54

SUGGESTION

3 To begin the prewriting activity, have students write down things they remember about Puerto Rico. What parks, historic places, and beaches did Benjamín and his mother visit? What questions would students like to ask them about their activities there?

ADDITIONAL PRACTICE

3 Have students work in pairs to act out the interviews they wrote.

SUGGESTION

Have students look back to the Location Opener on pages 202–205 or to the Chapter Opener on pages 206–207 for ideas to support the **Situación**.

GAME

MÍMICA Before class, write activities similar to the following on small sheets of paper: **montar en bicicleta, nadar, caminar, correr, esquiar, jugar al voleibol, al basquetbol, al béisbol.** Fold the papers and place them in a container. Divide the class into two teams. The first player on Team A selects a paper and acts out the activity. Team A players try to guess their teammate's activity. Once they guess correctly, Team B has a turn.

This page is intended to help students prepare independently for the Chapter Test. It is designed for the students to work on their own initiative and consists of a brief checklist of the major points covered in the chapter. The students should be reminded that this is only a checklist and does not necessarily include everything that will appear on the Chapter Test.

Answers to Activity 1

Answers will vary. Possible answers:
1. Deben hacer más ejercicio.
2. Debes dormir ocho horas todas las noches.
3. Debes hacer yoga.
4. Deben estirarse y levantar pesas tres veces por semana.

Answers to Activity 2

1. Me siento mal.
2. Me siento bien.
3. Estoy cansado.

Answers to Activity 3

Answers will vary. Possible answers:
1. Me duelen los ojos y la cabeza.
2. Me duele la garganta.
3. Me siento preocupado/a y triste.
4. Me siento preocupado/a.
5. Me duelen las piernas y estoy cansado/a.
6. Me duele el estómago.

Answers to Activity 4

1. los pies
2. las manos
3. las piernas, los pies
4. las manos
5. la boca
6. los brazos, los pies
7. la boca, el oído
8. las piernas, los brazos
9. los ojos

WV3 PUERTO RICO-11

▼ **Can you make suggestions and express feelings?** p. 213

1 What would you suggest to the following people who want to live a healthy life? Be sure to give them all different advice! *Answers in side column*

1. tus padres
2. tu mejor amigo/a
3. tu hermano/a
4. tus primos

2 Look at the drawings. What would each person probably say about how they feel? *Answers in side column*

❶ ❷ ❸

▼ **Can you talk about moods and physical condition?** p. 221

3 Write a sentence telling how you feel in these situations. *Answers in side column*

1. cuando lees mucho
2. cuando tienes tos
3. cuando recibes una mala nota
4. cuando no estudias para un examen
5. cuando corres mucho
6. cuando comes muy rápido

4 What parts of the body do you use most in these activities? *Answers in side column*

1. patinar
2. preparar la cena
3. bailar
4. dibujar
5. hablar por teléfono
6. nadar
7. cantar
8. esquiar
9. leer

▼ **Can you say what you did and talk about where you went and when?** pp. 229, 231

5 For each combination below, write a sentence telling where and when the person or people went, and what they did there.

1. Roberto / la piscina
2. Silvia y Sofía / la cancha de tenis
3. La familia Pérez / la cancha de fútbol
4. Mi hermana y yo / la tienda de discos
5. Tú / el estadio
6. Mónica y Gabi / la biblioteca
7. Federico y sus padres / el parque
8. Yo / el gimnasio

Answers on p. 205K

VOCABULARIO

PRIMER PASO

Making suggestions and expressing feelings

estirarse   *to stretch*
hacer yoga   *to do yoga*
levantar pesas   *to lift weights*
llevar una vida sana   *to lead a healthy life*
magnífico/a   *great*
nada más   *that's all*
patinar sobre ruedas   *to roller skate*
¿Por qué no...?   *Why don't . . .?*
¿Qué tal si...?   *What if . . .?*
¿Qué tienes?   *What's the matter?*
sano/a   *healthy*
sentirse (ie)   *to feel*
tener ganas   *to feel like*
la vida   *life*

SEGUNDO PASO

Talking about moods and physical condition

la boca   *mouth*
el brazo   *arm*
la cabeza   *head*
el cuello   *neck*
el cuerpo   *body*
el dedo   *finger, toe*
doler (ue)   *to hurt, to ache*
enojado/a   *angry*
la espalda   *back*
el estómago   *stomach*
la garganta   *throat*
la mano   *hand*
la nariz   *nose*
nervioso/a   *nervous*
el oído   *(inner) ear*
el ojo   *eye*
la oreja   *(outer) ear*
el pelo   *hair*
el pie   *foot*

la pierna   *leg*
preocupado/a por algo   *worried about something*
¿Qué le pasa a...?   *What's wrong with . . .?*
estar resfriado/a   *to have a cold*
tener fiebre   *to have a fever*
tener gripe   *to have the flu*
tener tos   *to have a cough*
triste   *sad*

TERCER PASO

Saying what you did and talking about where you went and when

anteanoche   *the night before last*
la cancha de fútbol   *soccer field*
la cancha de tenis   *tennis court*
el estadio   *stadium*
ganar   *to win, to earn*
la pista de correr   *running track*

TEACHER NOTE

This active vocabulary list is intentionally light to allow your class more time for end-of-the-year wrap-up activities, such as oral interviews or completion of long-term projects. The next chapter integrates and reviews Chapters 1–11 and contains no new grammar.

CHAPTER 11 ASSESSMENT

▶ **Testing Program**
Chapter Test, pp. 97–102
    Audio Compact Discs, CD 11, Trs. 20–21
Speaking Test, p. 132

▶ **Alternative Assessment Guide**
Performance Assessment, p. 23
Portfolio Assessment, p. 15
CD-ROM Assessment, p. 30

▶ **Interactive CD-ROM Tutor, Disc 3**
    ¡A hablar!
    ¡A escribir!

▶ **Standardized Assessment Tutor**
Chapter 11

▶ **One-Stop Planner, Disc 3**
    Test Generator
    Chapter 11

Las vacaciones ideales
CHAPTER OVERVIEW

De antemano pp. 246–249	*Unas vacaciones ideales*			
	FUNCTIONS	**GRAMMAR**	**VOCABULARY**	**RE-ENTRY**
Primer paso pp. 250–257	• Talking about what you do and like to do every day, p. 251 • Making future plans, p. 253	• **Gramática:** Stem-changing verbs, p. 252 • **Gramática:** Verbs + infinitives, p. 254	• Vacation items, p. 254	• Chapter 12 is a global review of Chapters 1–11.
Segundo paso pp. 260–265	• Talking about what you would like to do on vacation, p. 262	• **¿Te acuerdas?:** Present progressive, p. 262 • **Gramática:** The verbs **ser** and **estar,** p. 264	• Vacation activities, p. 261	
Tercer paso pp. 268–273	• Saying where you went and what you did on vacation, p. 269	• **Gramática:** Preterite tense, p. 269	• Countries, p. 272	

Letra y sonido	**p. 273**	The letters *p, t, k*	**Dictado:** Textbook Audiocassette 3B/ Audio CD 12
Enlaces	**pp. 274–275**	**Las ciencias y la astronomía**	
Vamos a leer	**pp. 276–277**	**¿Cuáles son las vacaciones ideales para ti?**	**Reading Strategy:** Recognizing text organization
Review	**pp. 278–281**	**Repaso, pp. 278–279**	**A ver si puedo...,** p. 280 **Vocabulario,** p. 281

Culture
- **Nota cultural:** The Amazon River, p. 250
- **Encuentro cultural: Las vacaciones por el mundo hispano,** pp. 258–259
- **Nota cultural:** Los Roques, p. 260
- **Panorama cultural: ¿Adónde vas y qué haces en**

las vacaciones?, pp. 266–267
- **Nota cultural:** Travel between Puerto Rico and the mainland, p. 268
- **Nota cultural:** Spain's **paradores,** p. 272

Lesson Planning

One-Stop Planner
Lesson Planner with Substitute Teacher
Lesson Plans, pp. 31–35

Listening and Speaking

Listening Activities
- Student Response Forms for Listening Activities, pp. 70–72
- Additional Listening Activities 12-1 to 12-6, pp. 25–27
- Additional Listening Activities (song), p. 28
- Scripts and Answers, pp. 48–50

Video Guide
- Teaching Suggestions, pp. 45–46
- Activity Masters, pp. 47–50
- Scripts and Answers, pp. 63–65, 68

Activities for Communication
- Communicative Activities, pp. 37–42
- Realia and Teaching Suggestions, pp. 69–73
- Situation Cards, pp. 86–87

¡Ven conmigo! Level 1
TPR Storytelling Book, pp. 45–48

Reading and Writing

Reading Strategies and Skills, Chapter 12
¡Lee conmigo! 1, Chapter 12
Practice and Activity Book, pp. 73–84

Grammar

Grammar and Vocabulary Workbook, pp. 45–55

¡Ven conmigo! Level 1
Grammar Tutor for Students of Spanish
Chapter 12

Assessment

Testing Program
- Paso Quizzes and Chapter Test, pp. 109–120
- Final Exam, pp. 143–150
- Score Sheet, Scripts and Answers, pp. 121–126, 151–156

Grammar and Vocabulary Quizzes
- Quizzes 12-1A, 12-2A, 12-3A
- Alternative Quizzes 12-1A, 12-2A, 12-3A

Alternative Assessment Guide
- Portfolio Assessment, p. 16
- Performance Assessment, p. 24
- CD-ROM Assessment, p. 31

¡Ven conmigo! Level 1
Standardized Assessment Tutor
- Reading, pp. 47–49
- Writing, p. 50
- Math, pp. 51–52

Native Speakers

¡Ven conmigo! Level 1
Cuaderno para hispanohablantes, pp. 56–60

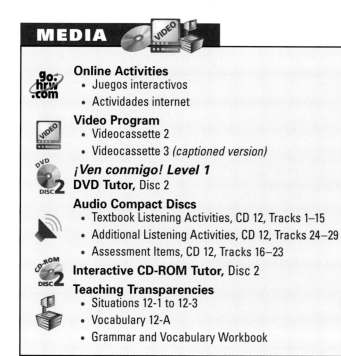

MEDIA

Online Activities
- Juegos interactivos
- Actividades internet

Video Program
- Videocassette 2
- Videocassette 3 *(captioned version)*

¡Ven conmigo! Level 1
DVD Tutor, Disc 2

Audio Compact Discs
- Textbook Listening Activities, CD 12, Tracks 1–15
- Additional Listening Activities, CD 12, Tracks 24–29
- Assessment Items, CD 12, Tracks 16–23

Interactive CD-ROM Tutor, Disc 2

Teaching Transparencies
- Situations 12-1 to 12-3
- Vocabulary 12-A
- Grammar and Vocabulary Workbook

One-Stop Planner CD-ROM

Use the **One-Stop Planner CD-ROM with Test Generator** to aid in lesson planning and pacing.

For each chapter, the **One-Stop Planner** includes:
- Editable lesson plans with direct links to teaching resources
- Printable worksheets from resource books
- Direct launches to the HRW Internet activities
- Video and audio segments
- Test Generator
- Clip Art for vocabulary items

DVD/VIDEO

De antemano • Unas vacaciones ideales

Ben and Carmen's grandfather asks them what they would do on their ideal vacation. Ben says that he would travel down the Amazon and explore the jungle. Carmen says that she would sail the Pacific and find a deserted island. Then Ben and Carmen's mother comes in and tells them that they are going to take a short trip, but she won't tell them where.

¿Adónde vas y qué haces en las vacaciones?

Teenagers from Argentina, Puerto Rico, and Venezuela talk about what they do and where they go during their vacations. In additional interviews, people from various Spanish-speaking countries tell us about their vacations.

A continuación

Ben and Carmen's mother surprises them by taking them to El Yunque National Park, where Ben finds an orchid and they hear a coquí. The next day they go to the beach for a picnic. With these two trips, Ben and Carmen feel they have experienced their ideal vacation.

Las vacaciones por el mundo hispano

Videoclips
• Los parques acuáticos: informational report about water parks in Spain

INTERACTIVE CD-ROM TUTOR

Activity	Activity Type	Pupil's Edition Page
En contexto	*Interactive conversation*	
1. Vocabulario	¡Super memoria!	p. 254
2. Gramática	¿Qué falta?	p. 252
3. Vocabulario	¿Cuál es?	p. 261
4. Gramática	¡A escoger!	p. 264
5. Así se dice	Patas arriba	p. 269
6. Gramática	¿Qué falta?	p. 269
Panorama cultural	¿Adónde vas y qué haces en las vacaciones? ¡A escoger!	pp. 266–267
¡A hablar!	*Guided recording*	pp. 278–279
¡A escribir!	*Guided writing*	pp. 278–279

Teacher Management System

Launch the program, type "admin" in the password area and press RETURN. Log on to **www.hrw.com/CDROMTUTOR** for a detailed explanation of the Teacher Management System.

DVD-ROM TUTOR ¡VEN CONMIGO! LEVEL 1

The *DVD Tutor* contains all material from the Level 1 *Video Program*. Spanish captions are available for use at your discretion for all sections of the video. The *DVD Tutor* also provides a variety of video-based activities that assess students' understanding of the **De antemano, A continuación,** and **Panorama cultural.**

This part of the *DVD Tutor* may be used on any DVD video player connected to a television or video monitor.

In addition to the video material and the video-based comprehension activities, the *DVD Tutor* also contains the entire Level 1 *Interactive CD-ROM Tutor* in DVD-ROM format. Each DVD disc contains the activities from all 12 chapters of the *Interactive CD-ROM Tutor.*

This part of the *DVD Tutor* may be used on a Macintosh® or Windows® computer with a DVD-ROM drive.

One-Stop Planner CD-ROM

To preview all resources available for this chapter, use the **One-Stop Planner CD-ROM,** Disc 3.

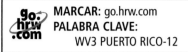

MARCAR: go.hrw.com
PALABRA CLAVE:
WV3 PUERTO RICO-12

INTERNET CONNECTION

*Have students explore the **go.hrw.com** Web site for many online resources covering all chapters. All Chapter 12 resources are available under the keyword **WV3 Puerto Rico-12.** Interactive games help students practice the material and provide them with immediate feedback. You will also find a printable worksheet that provides Internet activities that lead to a comprehensive online research project..*

JUEGOS INTERACTIVO

You can use the interactive activities in this chapter

- to practice grammar, vocabulary, and chapter functions
- as homework
- as an assessment option
- as a self-test
- to prepare for the Chapter Test

ACTIVIDADES INTERNET

Students choose a place they would like to visit on a fantasy vacation. They then research the destination on the Internet and write about what activities they would do there.

- To prepare students for the **Hoja de actividades,** encourage them to list their criteria for a perfect vacation. If they do not know how to express an idea in Spanish, have them look it up in a dictionary before searching the Internet.

- After completing the activity sheet, have students review the **Panorama cultural** on page 266. Do any of those teenagers do the things they like to do on vacation? Ask them to choose one person and research the place he or she mentions.

Proyecto

Travel writing is a popular genre. Good travel writers not only describe facts, but they include how a place makes them feel and what beauty and humor they find there. Ask students to describe a recent vacation, either a real trip or the "perfect" one they took in the **Hoja de actividades.** Encourage them to describe their experience in as much detail as possible.

TEXTBOOK LISTENING ACTIVITIES SCRIPTS

For Student Response Forms, see Listening Activities pp. 70–72.

PRIMER PASO   pp. 250–257

11 De vacaciones   p. 254

1. — ¡Ay, las montañas de Colorado! Me encanta esquiar.
   — Sí, pero debes tener cuidado.

2. — Es el viaje de mis sueños—una semana en la playa.
   — ¡Qué maravilla! Voy a pasar todos los días nadando y descansando.

3. — ¡Dos semanas en el Caribe! Pensamos acampar, estar lejos de todo, sin trabajar, ni estudiar.
   — Y espero dar muchos paseos. Va a ser fantástico.
   — A propósito, ¿tienes la cámara?

Answers to Activity 11

1. a
2. c
3. b

SEGUNDO PASO   pp. 260–265

25 Me gustaría   p. 263

SARA   Me llamo Sara Mercado y vivo en San Juan, Puerto Rico. A mí me gustaría viajar a España porque quiero ver el país de mis abuelos. Quiero visitar las montañas y los castillos. Pienso viajar con mis primos que viven en Nueva York.

DAVID   Soy David Álvarez Medellín y vivo en Guadalajara. A mí me gustaría ver las Islas Galápagos. Quiero ir de excursión a las Islas Galápagos porque tengo muchas ganas de ver los animales que viven allí.

MARTÍN   Me llamo Martín Valerio y vivo en Los Ángeles. Tengo muchas ganas de viajar a la Argentina. Me gustaría esquiar y escalar una montaña en los Andes. Argentina es un país muy interesante. Ahora, ¡vamos a ver si mi familia quiere ir!

Answers to Activity 25

SARA — España; ver las montañas y los castillos
DAVID — las Islas Galápagos; ver los animales de allí
MARTÍN — la Argentina; esquiar y escalar una montaña

TERCER PASO   pp. 268–273

33 ¡Qué divertido!   p. 269

1. CARLOS   ¡Qué divertido el viaje!
   YOLANDA   Sí, tienes razón. Me gustó mucho el día en que fuimos a la playa con la prima Mari y preparamos una comida.
   CARLOS   Sí, tomamos el sol, hablamos con Mari y luego jugamos al voleibol. ¿Te gustó el partido?
   YOLANDA   Sí, muchísimo.

2. CARLOS   Y a mí me gustó mucho ver El Yunque. Cuando pienso en Puerto Rico, voy a pensar en las flores y la selva.
   YOLANDA   Sí, es muy bonito. Caminamos mucho ese día, ¿no?
   CARLOS   Sí, y sacamos muchas fotos.

3. YOLANDA   ¿Te acuerdas de la fiesta con los amigos de Miguel?
   CARLOS   ¡Claro que sí! Lo pasé muy bien. Voy a escribirles cartas a todos ellos.

4. YOLANDA   La visita a los abuelos también fue muy bonita. Su vida es muy diferente de nuestra vida en Nueva York, pero me encantó.
   CARLOS   Sí, a mí también.

Answers to Activity 33

1. b
2. a
3. d
4. c

For the scripts for Parts A and C, see p. 273. The script for Part B is below.

B. Dictado

Hola, Pablo, habla Pedro. Hoy tenemos que preparar la cena para papá. Voy a comprar la comida en la tienda. Tú necesitas poner las papas en el horno a las cinco. Hasta entonces.

1 Repaso Activity 1   p. 278

1. **MARTA** Espero ir de vacaciones en julio. Este verano pienso ir con mi mejor amiga al norte de California para saltar en paracaídas.

2. **FRANCISCO** Voy a pasar mis vacaciones en Colorado, en las montañas. Ahí pienso acampar, pescar y dar caminatas por el bosque. Por eso necesito comprar una tienda de camping.

3. **JUAN** Yo no voy a ningún lugar. Pienso quedarme en casa y pasar el verano con mi mejor amigo.

4. **ROSARIO** A mí me gusta mucho el océano. Por eso me gustaría ir de vela este verano con mi perro. A él también le gusta.

5. **SILVIO** Para mí no hay nada mejor que tomar el sol con unos buenos libros. Por eso me gustaría pasar una semana en la playa.

6. **LETICIA** Espero ir a México este verano. Quiero escalar unas montañas con mi padre.

Answers to Repaso Activity 1

1. c
2. b
3. f
4. e
5. d
6. a

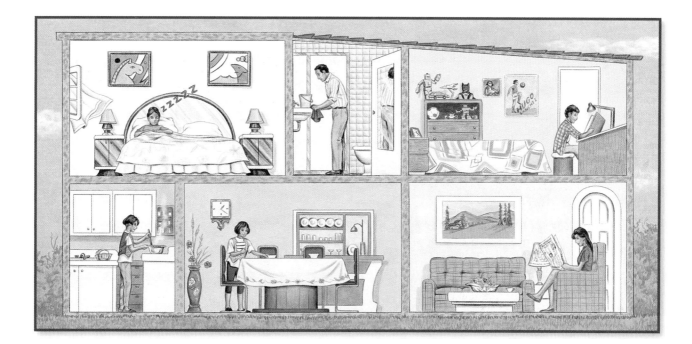

CAPÍTULO 12 — Las vacaciones ideales
PROJECTS

LA FAMILIA VA DE VACACIONES

This project incorporates a variety of skills and vocabulary that students have learned throughout the entire year to put together a family trip. Students plan the trip, the wardrobe, meals, and also make a list of souvenirs to buy.

Introduction

Ask students if they have had experience planning a family trip or vacation. What are the decisions to be made within the family? Who makes the decisions? Explain that in "families" of four (two adults, two children) students will decide in what Spanish-speaking location they would like to take their vacation. Each family member is responsible for one aspect of the vacation.

Materials students may need

- ◆ 1 suitcase
- ◆ 1 box for souvenirs
- ◆ Collection of clothing
- ◆ Collection of gifts or souvenirs
- ◆ Colored construction paper
- ◆ Notebook paper
- ◆ Markers
- ◆ Magazines
- ◆ Glue sticks
- ◆ Scissors

Sequence

1 Group students into families of four: Adult 1, Adult 2, Child 1, Child 2. Responsibilities of the family members include:

- • **Adult 1**—prepare a list of clothing needed based on the time of year and the location of the vacation
- • **Adult 2**—prepare a list of 10 activities to do or places to visit
- • **Child 1**—prepare a list of foods the family would like to try while on vacation
- • **Child 2**—prepare a list of gifts or souvenirs to buy for family and friends while on vacation

2 After the family has planned the details of the trip, each member prepares a hands-on presentation for the project:

- • **Adult 1**—a suitcase containing 10 clothing items that the family will need, all labeled in Spanish

- • **Adult 2**—a page of illustrations of the activities and places, all labeled in Spanish
- • **Child 1**—a page of illustrations of foods the family would like to eat on the trip, all labeled in Spanish
- • **Child 2**—a box of gifts and souvenirs that the family will buy for themselves and for family and friends, all labeled in Spanish

3 The family will prepare a scrapbook of their vacation to present orally to the other members of the class.

Grading the project

Suggested point distribution (total = 100 points):

Each member receives the same grade, based on the following:

Each member's list.	**10 (4 members=40)**
Each member's props	**10 (4 members=40)**
Oral presentation	**10**
Cooperative effort.	**10**

LAS VACACIONES PERFECTAS

In this activity students describe their ideal vacation spot to the class. They create collages to enhance their presentation.

Introduction

Ask students what their ideal vacation spot would be: the beach? a ski resort? a theme park? a camping ground? What kinds of things would they like to do there? Explain that in this project, they prepare a presentation on their ideal vacation spot.

Materials students may need

- ◆ Poster board
- ◆ Magazines
- ◆ Crayons or markers
- ◆ Index cards
- ◆ Scissors
- ◆ Glue
- ◆ Tape

Sequence

1. Depending on class size and time available, assign this activity as individual or group work.

2. Have students decide which vacation spot to illustrate and research by consulting almanacs, world reference books, or travel magazines. Local travel agencies often have world travel information available.

3. Have students gather materials for their collages, such as drawings, photographs, magazine pictures, or small objects such as ribbons. All text should be in Spanish.

4. Students lay out their collages on a large sheet of paper using paper clips or removable tape. When they decide on a final design, they glue or tape materials to poster board.

5. Have students make a brief written outline of how they plan to present their vacation spot. Provide general feedback and suggestions. You may also have them exchange outlines with classmates for peer-review.

6. Students practice their presentation with a partner. As a challenge, have them try to present it without reading it. After all students have made their presentations, display the posters in class.

Grading the project
Suggested point distribution (total = 100 points):

Creativity **20**
Labels and explanations **20**
Neatness **10**
Presentation content **20**
Vocabulary and grammar **20**
Oral presentation **10**

 MI PROYECTO

Another good idea for a final project is to allow students to choose an area of interest and create a presentation for the class about it. This could be an individual or group activity depending on time and class size.

Introduction

Ask students what school subject they enjoy the most. Suggest that they explain a project they have already completed for another class, such as a science or social studies project in Spanish. Ask what they enjoy doing in their spare time. They could describe something they enjoy collecting,

or create an original poem, short story, or other creative work to share with the class. Allow for a variety of possible hobbies and interests.

Sequence

1. Since this a dictionary-intense activity, you will need to provide enough resources for students to use. Remind students of the pitfalls of literal translation.

2. Suggest they begin with vocabulary they already know, and especially to stay within the grammar structures they have learned.

3. Set a specific time limit for the oral presentation such as 5 minutes for individual, or 10 to 20 minutes for groups.

4. Written copy could be included in the portfolio for individual work, or a poster or display for groups.

Grading the project
Suggested point distribution (total = 100 points):

Written material or poster in Spanish **25**
Organization **25**
Fluency **25**
Grammar **25**

Las vacaciones ideales
GAMES

MEMORIA

This game is an enjoyable way to review the vocabulary this chapter, and to review the numbers from 1–20.

Materials you may need

◆ 25 or more index cards ◆ Double-sided removable tape
◆ Markers

Procedure

1. Choose 10 vocabulary words from this chapter and randomly write one word per card in Spanish. Make a corresponding card in English to match each Spanish card.

2. Shuffle and randomly number each on the opposite side from 1 to 20.

3. Tape the cards to the blackboard (or pin them to a bulletin board) with the numbers facing out, in numerical sequence. The ideal configuration is four rows of five cards.

4. Divide the class into two teams. Designate two Card Turners and a Scorekeeper.

5. The Scorekeeper will ask the first person on Team A to begin. The first student must say in Spanish, **"Quiero el número _____"**. The Card Turner reveals the card. Then the student asks for another card to be revealed. **"Quiero el número _____"**. If the Spanish and English words correspond, the team earns a point. The Card Turner removes the two cards from the board.

6. Play then goes to Team B and the sequence is repeated until all cards have been revealed. The team with the higher score wins.

LA PERSONA MISTERIOSA

The following game is fun to play towards the end of the school year when students know each other fairly well. It provides both written and oral practice of language using higher-order thinking skills.

Materials you may need

◆ Index cards

Procedure

1. Divide the class into two or more teams and give each student an index card. Students write five sentences about themselves on the card. Remind them that they are trying to stump the other team, so encourage them to choose information that, while true, may be surprising or unknown to the other students.

2. Provide the following or other examples, but allow students to be as original as possible:

   No me gusta / Me gusta <u>la sal</u>.
   Soy <u>extrovertido</u>.
   Mi clase favorita es <u>el español</u>.
   Mi pasatiempo favorito es <u>cantar</u>.
   Tengo <u>un perro</u>.

3. Have teams turn in their stack of index cards separately. Explain the object of the game is to guess the mystery person using as few of the clues provided as possible.

4. One student from each team may be chosen as team reader. Announce a specific time limit, or use an egg timer or other device. The team reader chooses a card from the stack and reads a clue to the group. Team members may discuss who they think is being described, but should try to keep the discussion in Spanish. If the team fails to guess the person, or does not respond in the time allotted, points go to the other team or teams.

5. Score a specific number of points for the number of clues necessary to guess the person. For example, 15 points for one clue, 10 points for two clues, five points for three clues.

LAS VACACIONES PERFECTAS

In this game, students learn the location and pronunciation of various cities. It can be used at any time.

Materials you may need

◆ Index cards

Preparation

Write the names of two Spanish-speaking cities on an index card, one for each student. Tape a large world map (or a map of Latin America) on the chalkboard. Cut a piece of string long enough to reach across the map.

Procedure

1 Divide the class into two teams.

2 Give the first player on Team A a card. The player is to say **Vivo en** (first city on card) **y voy a** (second city on card) **para las vacaciones.** If the player can locate and connect the two cities with the string, his or her team earns one point.

3 The string and a new card then go to the first player on Team B. Follow the same procedure as with Team A. When all cards have been used, the team with the higher score wins.

Variation

Instead of Spanish-speaking cities, write the names in Spanish of any two countries in the world and ask students to connect them. Refer students to the world map on pages xviii–xix and tell them that the names of most places in Spanish will be similar to the English forms.

TEACHER NOTE

At this point your students have probably had an opportunity to play several kinds of games. You might offer them an opportunity to make up their own game. Give them a definite goal, such as practicing "telling what happened" or reviewing descriptive adjectives, and set limits on the kind of play that is allowed and the amount of time they can use. Then ask them to write the rules for the game and try playing it. You may want to have your students teach successful games to other Spanish classes.

¿QUÉ VOY A NECESITAR PARA MIS VACACIONES?

In this game students will use many of the vocabulary words related to vacations.

Procedure

1 Before beginning, remind students that **llevar** means both *to wear* and *to take along*.

2 Ask one student to leave the room. The class decides on a place where the absent student is to take a vacation.

3 When the student returns, he or she tries to guess the vacation spot by asking questions such as **¿Qué voy a llevar?** Class members are to provide clues with answers such as **Vas a llevar un traje de baño.** Each student should have a three-minute time limit to try to guess the vacation spot.

4 As a variation have students name activities they did as clues to where they went on their vacations.

CAPÍTULO **12**

Las vacaciones ideales

ANSWERS TO CHAPTER 12 ACTIVITIES

Listening activity answers appear on Scripts pages 243E–243F. Answers to all other activities appear on corresponding pupil pages.

DE ANTEMANO   pp. 246–249

1
1. Están en la casa de su abuelo en Puerto Rico, porque están de vacaciones.
2. Porque no hay nada interesante que hacer.
3. ¿Qué les gustaría hacer? ¿Cómo son unas vacaciones ideales?
4. Benjamín sueña con unas vacaciones en la selva amazónica. Carmen sueña con navegar por el océano Pacífico en un barco de vela antiguo.
5. Les dice que van a hacer un viaje.

2
1. cierto
2. falso; Están aburridos porque no hay nada interesante que hacer.
3. falso; A Benjamín le gustaría bajar el río Amazonas en canoa, acampar en la selva y explorar.
4. cierto
5. falso; Van a hacer un viaje.

PRIMER PASO   pp. 250–257

6 Answers will vary. Possible answers:
Marcos está en su cuarto. Estudia todos los días de lunes a viernes.
Claudia está en la cocina. Ella prepara la comida a veces.
María está en la sala. Lee el periódico después del colegio.
Papá limpia el baño todos los sábados.
Mamá duerme en su cuarto. Descansa antes de la cena cuando está cansada.
Marcia pone la mesa. Ayuda en casa todos los fines de semana.

8 Answers will vary. Possible answers:
1. Prefiero tomar clases por la tarde porque tengo sueño por la mañana.
2. Mis amigos y yo almorzamos en la cafetería.
3. Mi amiga Wendy puede hablar muy bien el español.
4. Los lunes empiezo las clases a las ocho y cuarto.

ENCUENTRO CULTURAL   pp. 258–259

1
1. when you speak Spanish well
2. Possible answers: visit historical monuments and go to restaurants
3. c

2 Answers will vary. Possible answers:
1. El Salto Ángel está en Venezuela y La Plaza de Cibeles está en España. El Salto Ángel está en el campo y La Plaza de Cibeles está en la ciudad. Son iguales en que los dos tienen agua.
2. Un turista en el Salto Ángel probablemente va a explorar la selva, acampar y escalar montañas. Un turista en La Plaza de Cibeles probablemente puede hacer turismo, sacar fotos y estudiar historia.
3. Answers will vary.

SEGUNDO PASO   pp. 260–265

29 Answers will vary. Possible answer:
Querido amigo,
Aquí estoy en Toledo, España. Estoy bien pero cansado. Esta ciudad es muy bonita y vieja. Estoy caminando mucho, sacando fotos y visitando iglesias y castillos. Toledo es bastante grande. ¡Me duelen mucho los pies! Hasta luego.

ENLACES   pp. 274–275

3 Radar waves are used in the navigation of ships and planes, radar guns used by the police, air traffic control, military uses and meteorologists use it to track storms.

4 No, radio telescopes can be used day or night and in bad weather. Light telescopes are used at night to receive distant light that is not visible during the day with the intense light of the sun. Radio telescopes receive longer radio waves, that can penetrate clouds and be received during the day.

VAMOS A LEER   pp. 276–277

C
1. un campamento
2. quedarse en casa y leer un buen libro
3. visitar las pirámides de México

REPASO   pp. 278–279

2 Answers will vary. Possible answers:
1. Porque hace mucho calor y sol.
2. Porque hay muchos ríos y no es fácil viajar en coche.
3. No. Es difícil porque es muy grande.

A VER SI PUEDO...   p. 280

7
1. Mis padres visitaron a su familia en Chicago.
2. Mi hermana y yo no fuimos a ningún lugar.
3. Cuidé a mis hermanos.

Chapter Section	Presentation	Homework Options
Primer paso	**Así se dice,** p. 251	*Pupil's Edition,* p. 251, Activity 6
	Gramática, p. 252	*Pupil's Edition,* p. 252, Activities 7–8 *Grammar and Vocabulary,* pp. 45–46, Activities 1–3 *CD-ROM,* Disc 3, Chapter 12, Activity 2
	Así se dice, p. 253	*Pupil's Edition,* p. 253, Activity 10 *Practice and Activity Book,* pp. 75–76, Activities 4–5
	Vocabulario, p. 254	*Grammar and Vocabulary,* pp. 47–48, Activities 4–7 *CD-ROM,* Disc 3, Chapter 12, Activity 1
	Gramática, p. 254	*Pupil's Edition,* p. 255, Activities 13–14 *Grammar and Vocabulary,* pp. 49–50, Activities 8–11 *Practice and Activity Book,* p. 74, Activity 3
Segundo paso	**Vocabulario,** p. 261	*Pupil's Edition,* p. 262, Activity 22 *Grammar and Vocabulary,* p. 51, Activity 12 *Practice and Activity Book,* p. 77, Activity 7 *CD-ROM,* Disc 3, Chapter 12, Activity 3
	Así se dice, p. 262	*Pupil's Edition,* p. 263, Activity 26 *Practice and Activity Book,* p. 77, Activity 8
	Gramática, p. 264	*Pupil's Edition,* pp. 264–265, Activities 28–29 *Grammar and Vocabulary,* pp. 52–53, Activities 13–16 *CD-ROM,* Disc 3, Chapter 12, Activity 4
Tercer paso	**Así se dice,** p. 269	*Pupil's Edition,* pp. 270–271, Activities 34–36 *CD-ROM,* Disc 3, Chapter 12, Activity 6
	Gramática, p. 269	*Practice and Activity Book,* pp. 140–141, Activities 13–15 *Grammar and Vocabulary,* p. 54, Activities 17–18 *CD-ROM,* Disc 3, Chapter 12, Activity 5
	Vocabulario, p. 272	*Pupil's Edition,* p. 273, Activity 40 *Grammar and Vocabulary,* p. 55, Activities 19–20

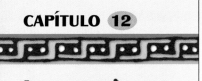

Las vacaciones ideales

MOTIVATING ACTIVITY

Hang a large world map on the wall and give each student a self-stick note. Ask students to write their names on a note and stick it next to their ideal vacation spot. They then explain in Spanish to a partner why they chose their location.

RE-ENTRY

Review vocabulary for free-time activities. Have students interview a partner in Spanish asking what he or she likes to do on vacation. They take notes on what their partner says, and report to the class.

GEOGRAPHY LINK

A popular vacation spot is Puerto Rico's El Yunque rain forest. It comprises 17 square miles of the Caribbean National Forest. It can receive more than 200 inches of rain per year, while the rest of the island averages 70 inches. Have students locate El Yunque on a map.

BIOLOGY LINK

The **coquí** is a tiny tree-frog often referred to as **"la mascota nacional"** of Puerto Rico. It is not found anywhere else in the world. It croaks very loudly, changes its color from a light beige to black or brown, and has suction cups on its toes that enable it to walk upside-down on smooth surfaces.

CAPÍTULO

12 Las vacaciones ideales

Parador Villa Antonio
Rincón, Puerto Rico

- Los Almendros y Black Eagle (playas/surfing)
- Balneario de Añasco
- Playa Crash-Boat-Aguadilla
- Balneario Pico de Piedra-Aguada
- Playa de Surfing "Wilderness-Ag...
- Playa de Surfing "S...

En excelentes playas, ideales para el deporte de "surfing", se encuentra este tranquilo Parador tropical. Todo el esplendor natural del Caribe en un ambiente de completo relajamiento.

1 ¡Vamos a salir de vacaciones!

El Rincón

244

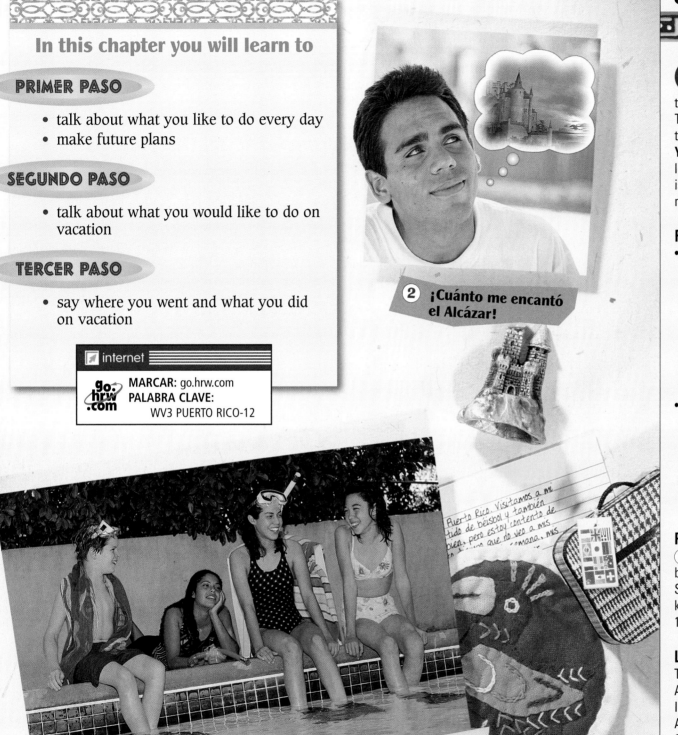

In this chapter you will learn to

PRIMER PASO

- talk about what you like to do every day
- make future plans

SEGUNDO PASO

- talk about what you would like to do on vacation

TERCER PASO

- say where you went and what you did on vacation

internet

MARCAR: go.hrw.com
PALABRA CLAVE:
WV3 PUERTO RICO-12

② **¡Cuánto me encantó el Alcázar!**

③ **Me gustaría ir a la Isla Culebra. Dicen que es muy bonita para bucear.**

doscientos cuarenta y cinco **245**

 CULTURE NOTE
El Yunque is located in the Luquillo mountain range. The name Luquillo comes from the name of the good spirit **Yuquiyú**. According to **Taíno** legend, **Yuquiyú** protected the island and its people from his mountain-top home.

FOCUSING ON OUTCOMES
- Have students identify which learner outcome corresponds to which photo on these pages. (Photo 1: making future plans; Photo 2: saying where you went and what you did on vacation; Photo 3: talking about what you would like to do on vacation.)
- Ask students what an ideal vacation day during each season would be for them. Ask them to compare their ideas about ideal vacations with those of the **fotonovela** characters.

PHOTO FLASH!
② The castle in the thought bubble is the **Alcázar** in Segovia, Spain, home of the kings of Castile during the 12th and 13th centuries.

LANGUAGE NOTE
The word **alcázar** is an Arabic word meaning *castle*. In Spanish it means *fortress*. Ask students if they know why Spanish has many words from Arabic. (Parts of Spain were controlled by Arabic-speaking people for over 700 years.)

VIDEO INTEGRATION

En camino LEVEL 1B
Video Program
Videocassette 2, 38:21–42:34 OR
Videocassette 3, 2:02:32–2:06:45
(captioned version)

¡Ven conmigo! LEVEL 1
DVD Tutor, Disc 2

TEACHER NOTE

The **fotonovela** is an abridged version of the video episode.

VIDEO SYNOPSIS

Ben and Carmen, two New York residents, are visiting their grandfather in Puerto Rico. He is surprised that they are bored and asks what they would like to do on an ideal vacation. Ben would like to go to a tropical forest in South America and travel down the Amazon in a canoe. Carmen would like to cruise around the Pacific in an old-fashioned ship and find a desert island. While they are talking, their mother comes in and announces that they are going to take a short mystery trip.

DE ANTEMANO

Unas vacaciones ideales

CD 12 Trs. 1–2

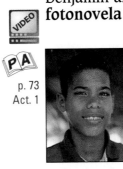

Can you imagine being bored on a trip to a tropical island? Benjamín and Carmen were, at least for a while! Read the **fotonovela** to find what their ideal vacations are.

p. 73
Act. 1

Benjamín **Carmen** **Abuelo** **la señora Corredor**

1

Aquí las playas son muy bonitas. Carmen está jugando con el abuelo en la arena, y mamá está leyendo una novela. Pasamos un día maravilloso el sábado — fuimos a un bosque tropical, El Yunque. Todo comenzó por la mañana...

246

MOTIVATING ACTIVITY
Ask students to discuss where they would have to go to visit their relatives. Would they have to go to another country or state, or would they be able to visit them near their home?

PRESENTATION
Play the video or audio recording. After students have watched the video or listened to the audio recording, have them form groups of three or four to practice reading the roles of **Abuelo, la señora Corredor**, Ben, and Carmen. Then have groups prepare written answers to the questions in Activity 1, page 249.

PAIR WORK
Ask students to tell a partner in Spanish whether they would prefer Ben's ideal vacation or Carmen's, and why. Ask students who like neither to explain their opinion and tell what kind of vacation they would like. Have students work in pairs to describe their ideal vacation to a partner.

BACKGROUND

In the second act of the video, the characters visit El Yunque, a tropical rain forest that supports many different trees, vines, and tropical flowers. More than 200 species of birds live there. It is the only tropical rain forest managed by the U.S. Forest Service. For other information, see the notes on page 244.

A continuación

You may choose to continue with *Unas vacaciones ideales (a continuación)* at this time or wait until later in the chapter. At this point, Sra. Corredor tells Ben and Carmen what they will need for their trip. They visit **El Yunque** and end the day having a picnic supper on the beach. You may wish to have students write an alternative script for the second half of the video that includes their ideas about what makes an ideal vacation.

Cuaderno para hispanohablantes, pp. 56–60

1 ¿Comprendes?

¿Comprendes lo que pasa en la fotonovela? Contesta las preguntas. Si es necesario, adivina *(guess)*. Answers on p. 243K

1. ¿Dónde están Benjamín y su familia, y por qué?
2. ¿Por qué están tristes Carmen y Benjamín en la segunda foto?
3. ¿Qué les pregunta su abuelo en la tercera foto?
4. ¿Con qué sueñan *(dream)* Benjamín y Carmen?
5. ¿Qué les menciona su mamá que los hace sentirse mejor?

These activities check for global comprehension only. Students should not yet be expected to produce language modeled in **De antemano.**

2 ¿Cierto o falso?

Decide si las oraciones son **ciertas** o **falsas.** Si son falsas, corrígelas *(correct them)*. Answers on p. 243K

1. Benjamín escribe en su diario sobre sus vacaciones en Puerto Rico.
2. Benjamín y Carmen están aburridos porque hace mal tiempo.
3. Las vacaciones ideales de Benjamín consisten en ir a la playa y nadar.
4. Las vacaciones ideales de Carmen consisten en navegar en barco de vela.
5. Benjamín y Carmen no van a hacer nada interesante hoy.

3 ¿Cómo se dice?

Find the words and phrases in the **fotonovela** that you could use to . . .

1. ask what people are doing in the house
2. say that the weather is great
3. say that you'd like to go camping in the jungle
4. say that you plan to discover a desert island

1. ¿Qué hacen aquí en la casa?
2. Hace un tiempo maravilloso.
3. Me gustaría acampar en la selva.
4. Pienso descubrir una isla desierta.

4 ¿Quién lo dijo?

Según la fotonovela, ¿quién dijo lo siguiente?

1. No hay nada interesante que hacer, abuelo. Benjamín
2. Vamos a hacer un pequeño viaje. la señora Corredor
3. A mí me gustaría navegar por el océano Pacífico en un barco de vela. Carmen
4. Hace un tiempo maravilloso. Abuelo
5. Me gustaría viajar a una selva. Benjamín

SUGGESTIONS

3 Once students have located the Spanish expressions, have them practice saying them with a partner. If they have difficulty identifying the phrases, play the segment of the audio recording or video-cassette or videodisc where these expressions are used.

RE-ENTRY
After students have watched the video and completed Activities 1–4, ask them to make two packing lists in Spanish: one for the things Ben would need to pack for his ideal vacation, and another for Carmen. When students have finished, ask them to compare their list with a partner's to see if they have forgotten anything.

NATIVE SPEAKERS
Ask native speakers to write a journal entry about a trip, real or imaginary, that they have made to visit a friend or relative. Review any spelling and writing skills you have targeted with your native speakers over the course of the school year, and ask them to incorporate all of these skills globally in their reports.

VIDEO INTEGRATION

En camino LEVEL 1B
Video Program
Videocassette 2, 41:17–41:41 OR
Videocassette 3, 2:05:28–2:05:52
(captioned version)

¡Ven conmigo! LEVEL 1
DVD Tutor, Disc 2

Bell work

On the board or on a transparency, write the following verbs with their letters scrambled: **jugar, visitar, viajar, acampar, navegar,** and **descubrir.** Ask students to unscramble them and write their answers.

CULTURE NOTE
The Amazon River is the world's second-longest river. Only the Nile is longer. In volume the Amazon is the world's largest river. Roughly 20% of all water that runs off the surface of the Earth is drained by the Amazon. With more than 1,000 tributaries, the Amazon is the centerpiece of the world's richest and most biologically varied ecosystem. The rain forest that lines its banks stretches from the Atlantic Ocean to the eastern foothills of the Andes Mountains. This ecosystem is home to millions of species of plants, birds, insects and other animals.

PRIMER PASO (TPR)
Storytelling Book pp. 45, 48

go.hrw.com
WV3 PUERTO RICO-12

Talking about what you do and like to do every day; making future plans

5 ¿Qué va a hacer Benjamín?

Según lo que dice Benjamín, indica si son **probables** o **improbables** las siguientes actividades.

1. En su viaje, piensa ir al correo.
2. Piensa sacar muchas fotos.
3. Piensa hacer la tarea.
4. Quiere ver muchos animales.

1. improbable
2. probable
3. improbable
4. probable

Nota cultural
p. 84 Act. 18

The Amazon River, about 4,000 miles long, is the second longest river in the world. It begins in the high Andes mountains of Peru. The Amazon and its tributaries flow to the Atlantic Ocean through Venezuela, Ecuador, Colombia, and Bolivia, but the longest part is in Brazil. **El río Amazonas** was named by the Spanish explorer, Francisco de Orellana, after the women warriors of Greek mythology. The Amazon region's rich plant and animal life is a resource important to the whole world. Can you name plants and animals that are found in the Amazon basin?

ASÍ SE DICE

Talking about what you do and like to do every day

p. 74
Act. 2

12-1

To find out what someone does on a regular basis, ask:

> Bueno, ¿qué haces tú **todos los días**?

Your friend might answer:

> **Primero** voy al colegio, y **después** regreso a casa y hago mi tarea. Ceno con mi familia a las seis y **luego** miro la televisión.

To ask about someone's routine, say:

> ¿**Con qué frecuencia** sales con tus amigos?

Your friend might answer:

> Pues, salgo **todos los viernes**.

> ¿Qué te gusta hacer **después de** clases?

> Me gusta escuchar música en casa. También me gusta jugar al basquetbol.

6 ¿Qué hacen los demás? [H]

Describe las rutinas de las personas en el dibujo. Explica dónde están, qué hacen y con qué frecuencia hacen estas actividades.

MODELO Marcia pone la mesa en el comedor *(dining room)* todos los días antes de la cena. Answers on p. 243K

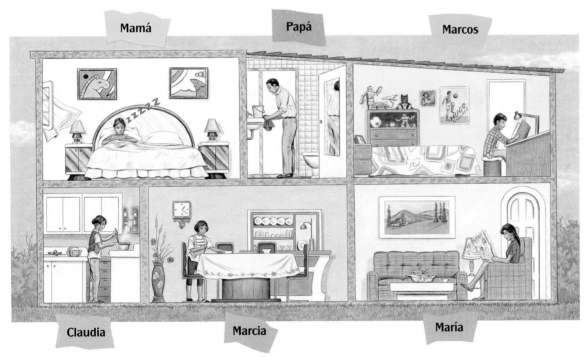

Mamá · Papá · Marcos · Claudia · Marcia · María

☀ MOTIVATE

Have students list in Spanish things that they have to do every day and things that they like to do every day.

☀ TEACH

PRESENTATION
ASÍ SE DICE

Tell your students a story in Spanish about what you do every day, using the expressions presented in **Así se dice.** Model the questions and answers, then ask students to work with a partner and practice the expressions in this section. After they have done so, ask them to practice answering **¿Qué haces todos los días?**, using the verbs in the lists they made for Motivate. They should include **primero, después,** and **luego** in their responses.

ADDITIONAL PRACTICE

6 Ask students to tell you how often they or other members of their family do the various activities illustrated in the drawing. (**¿Con qué frecuencia...?**)

STANDARDS: 5.1 **251**

PRESENTATION
GRAMÁTICA

Put several sentences on the board or on a transparency that include the stem-changing verbs from **Gramática.** Ask how the **yo** and **ellos** forms of the verb **tener** are different. (The **yo** form ends in **-go** and the **ellos** form has stem-changes.) Have students write a note to a friend asking three questions with **querer, empezar,** and **preferir.** They also ask two questions concerning their friend and another person using **venir** and **tener.** Then have students exchange notes with a partner and answer each other's questions.

LANGUAGE NOTE
7 The slang word **panas** is used in Venezuela; it means *friends.*

SUGGESTION
To practice **preferir,** ask students where they prefer to swim. **¿Prefieres nadar en un lago? ¿en una piscina? ¿en...?**

GRAMÁTICA Stem-changing verbs

pp. 45–46
Acts. 1–3

1. Many verbs have a stem change in the present tense. In verbs such as **querer, empezar,** and **preferir, -e** changes to **-ie** in all forms except **nosotros** and **vosotros.** The yo form of the verbs **venir** and **tener** ends in **-go** and e doesn't change to **ie.** (Vengo, tengo...) To review these forms, see page 52.

2. Other verbs, including **poder, almorzar,** and **dormir** have **-o** to **-ue** stem changes. To review these forms, see page 92.

7 Diferentes rutinas

Santos y su hermano Jesús son muy diferentes. Completa el párrafo con la forma correcta de los verbos.

1. empiezan
2. prefiero
3. duerme
4. tiene
5. almuerza
6. prefiere
7. prefiero
8. prefiere

Las clases en mi colegio ___1___ a las ocho y cuarto. Siempre voy al colegio a las siete y media porque ___2___ pasar el rato con mis amigos. Mi hermano ___3___ hasta las ocho menos cuarto y tiene que ducharse y vestirse con mucha prisa para no estar atrasado para las clases. Cuando va al colegio, mi hermano ___4___ mucha hambre porque no desayuna. A las doce, siempre ___5___ bien; come un poco de todo. Mi hermano y yo somos muy diferentes. Él ___6___ dormir lo más posible y yo ___7___ no tener prisa y poder pasar el rato con mis panas. Cuando empiezan las vacaciones, yo estoy muy cansado pero mi hermano ___8___ ir a jugar.

dormir

empezar

preferir

almorzar

tener

8 ¿Qué hacen tus amigos?

Contesta las siguientes preguntas sobre lo que hacen tú y tus amigos en el colegio. Answers on page 243K

1. ¿Prefieres tomar clases por la mañana o por la tarde? ¿Por qué?

2. ¿Quiénes almuerzan en la cafetería?

3. ¿Cuáles de tus amigos pueden hablar español?

4. ¿A qué hora empiezas las clases los lunes?

9 ¿Por qué no vamos a...?

Work in groups of three. Imagine that you have some time after school and that all three of you would like to get together. Find out what everyone in your group likes so you can decide where to go and what to do. Make a list of your first, second, and third choices. Be prepared to share your decisions with the class.

ASÍ SE DICE   Making future plans

pp. 75–76
Acts. 4–5

To ask what a friend is planning to do, say:

Your friend might answer:

¿Adónde **piensas** viajar algún día?

A Europa, si *(if)* puedo.

¿**Quieres** viajar a México?

No, pero **espero** hacer un viaje a Guatemala.
No, but I hope to go on a trip to Guatemala.

¿Qué **vas a hacer** este verano?

Voy al Perú.

Mi hermano espera viajar a Honduras para explorar las ruinas de Copán.

10 Los amigos

Ernesto likes to know what his friends are planning. Match their answers to his questions.

1. ¿Qué vamos a hacer hoy después de clases? Hace mucho calor. b
2. ¿Esperas hacer un viaje este verano? d
3. ¿Qué piensa hacer tu hermano esta tarde? c
4. ¿Adónde piensas ir mañana? a

a. Voy a ir al acuario nuevo, si puedo.
b. Vamos a la piscina, ¿no crees?
c. Va a la casa de Raimundo.
d. Pienso visitar a mis abuelos en Lima.

PRESENTATION
ASÍ SE DICE
After modeling the expressions, replay the audio recording of the **fotonovela** on pages 246–248. Ask students to listen carefully to the phrases Ben and Carmen use to describe their dream vacations and future plans. Then walk around the room and ask the questions of several students. For further practice, modify the questions by using other future time expressions. (**mañana, la semana que viene, el domingo por la tarde**)

CULTURE NOTE

The ruins of **Copán** lie on the west bank of the **Copán** River, about 35 miles west of **Santa Rosa de Copán, Honduras.** The city was built by the Mayans around 300 A.D. and was a major center of culture, art, and science. The city reached its peak during the 8th century A.D. but began to decline shortly thereafter. By 1200 A.D. it had been completely abandoned. Today the ruins consist of various temples, pyramids, staircases, and plazas.

VISUAL LEARNERS
10 Find magazine pictures of the indicated places, post them, and use them to enhance this activity or to elicit answers from the entire class.

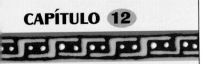

STANDARDS: 1.1, 1.2, 4.1

PRESENTATION

VOCABULARIO

Bring the objects listed in the vocabulary to class in a suitcase. Role-play a vacationer unpacking. Say the name of each thing as you unpack it and ask students to repeat after you. Later, the suitcase and its contents can be used to review vocabulary.

TPR As a continuation of the **Vocabulario** presentation, adapt the game **Hacer la maleta** on page 278 to practice informal command forms.

GRAMÁTICA

Say the infinitives aloud, modeling the correct pronunciation of each. Read the example sentences in the **Gramática.** You may want to add some of your own. (**Ella espera nadar en el mar Caribe. Usted me puede llamar por teléfono.**) Call on individual students to change the subjects in each of the example sentences to the plural. (**Ellas esperan nadar en el mar Caribe.**)

LANGUAGE NOTE

Point out to students some words that vary regionally (**espejuelos, anteojos,** or **gafas** for **lentes; sandalias** for **chancletas;** and **bronceador** for **bloqueador**).

VOCABULARIO

p. 76
Act. 6

pp. 47–48
Acts. 4–7

12-A **a**

- la chaqueta
- la bufanda
- los esquís
- hacer la maleta
- la cámara
- el boleto **b**
- los lentes de sol
- el traje de baño
- la toalla
- el bloqueador
- las chancletas **c**

---

11 De vacaciones Script and answers on p. 243E

Look at the drawings and listen to the conversations. Decide which conversation matches each drawing in the **Vocabulario** above.

CD 12 Tr. 3

12 Las maletas

 Work with a partner. Choose a place you would like to travel to. Make a list of eight things you plan to take. Guess where your partner is planning to travel by asking questions about what he or she plans to take along. Then answer your partner's questions so that he or she can guess where you plan to go.

MODELO —¿Traes un traje de baño?
          —¿Vas a llevar un abrigo?

---

p. 74
Act. 3

pp. 49–50
Acts. 8–10

GRAMÁTICA Verbs + infinitives

1. You've learned a number of verbs that may be followed by an infinitive and others that require **a** or **que** before the infinitive

querer	deber	
necesitar	esperar	} + infinitive
pensar	poder	

ir a	
tener que	} + infinitive

2. Remember to conjugate only the first verb.

Pienso pasear en bicicleta.   **¿Quieres** venir conmigo?

---

13 Hacen de todo

Gabriel habla de sus planes para el verano y también de los planes de su amigo Rafael. Completa las oraciones con la forma correcta del verbo que va con el infinitivo. Usa los siguientes verbos.

Rafael ___1___ que hacer la maleta esta noche porque sale de viaje a las cinco de la mañana. Él ___2___ a acampar cerca del lago Agua Fría. Él ___3___ poner su traje de baño en la maleta. Este verano no voy de viaje. ___4___ que cuidar a mis hermanitos. Por las tardes, cuando viene mi mamá del trabajo, ___5___ a nadar en la piscina con mis amigos. El año que viene ___6___ viajar durante las vacaciones.

1. tiene
2. va
3. necesita, debe
4. Tengo
5. voy
6. espero, pienso, quiero

poder   tener   pensar   deber
necesitar   esperar   ir   querer

14 ¿Qué piensan hacer?

Mira los dibujos en el **Vocabulario** en la página 254. Menciona tres cosas que cada persona piensa hacer durante sus vacaciones. ¡Usa tu imaginación! Answers in side column

15 ¡A viajar!

Planea unas vacaciones ideales con tu compañero/a.

1. ¿Adónde quieren ir?
2. ¿Cuándo piensan salir?
3. ¿Cómo quieren viajar (en coche, por avión, por tren, en autobús)?
4. ¿Qué necesitan llevar?
5. ¿Cuánto tiempo piensan quedarse *(to stay)*?
6. ¿Qué quieren hacer?
7. ¿Qué quieren comer?
8. ¿Cuánto dinero piensan que van a necesitar?

CHALLENGE
14 After students have listed the activities of each person in the drawings, have them write a paragraph on one of them, detailing what the person is planning to do, and why.

SUGGESTION
15 Have students use the maps on pages xvii–xxiii to choose their destination and plan their trip before getting together with their partners.

ADDITIONAL PRACTICE
15 After students plan their trips with their partner, have them create a dialogue in which they talk about their vacation plans using the information they decided on in the activity. Then have students look in magazines for pictures of the types of things they want to do on their vacation and label them in Spanish. Then have each pair perform their dialogues for the class using the magazine pictures as props.

Answers to Activity 14

Answers will vary. Possible answers:
a. Ellos van a esquiar todo el día. Después de esquiar piensan comer una cena rica. Luego quieren ver una película.
b. Ellas piensan sacar muchas fotos de iglesias y museos. Esperan caminar por toda la isla.
c. Ellas piensan nadar en la playa. Quieren descansar mucho. Pueden leer sus libros en la playa.

MATH LINK

17 The temperature in drawing **a.** is in degrees Fahrenheit, although Celsius is the standard in most Spanish-speaking countries. Ask students to convert the current temperature from Fahrenheit to Celsius. (subtract 32 degrees, multiply by 5, and divide by 9)

CHALLENGE

18 Have students develop a follow-up conversation in which the assistant and the customer discuss the date and time the customer could leave, the cost, and what the customer needs to take.

Answers to Activity 17

Answers will vary. Possible answers:

a. Es el invierno. Hace mucho frío. Necesito llevar una chaqueta y una bufanda.

b. Es el otoño. Hace viento. Necesito llevar una chaqueta y unos bluejeans. Quiero dar un paseo.

c. Es el verano. Hace sol. Voy a llevar un traje de baño porque quiero nadar.

d. Es la primavera. Hace buen tiempo. Voy a llevar una camiseta y unos pantalones cortos. Quiero ir al parque.

e. Es la primavera. Llueve a cántaros. Voy a llevar una chaqueta y usar un paraguas.

f. Es el invierno. Nieva mucho. Voy a llevar unos pantalones, un abrigo, una bufanda y unas botas. Quiero esquiar.

16 Te invito...

Haz una lista de cinco cosas divertidas que puedes hacer durante las vacaciones donde tú vives. Imagínate que estás hablando con tu primo/a que vive en otra ciudad. Invita a tu primo/a a visitarte y dile las cosas divertidas que piensas hacer.

MODELO —¿Quieres venir a San Diego este verano? Podemos ir al parque de diversiones y...

17 ¿Qué tiempo hace?

¿Qué estación del año representan los siguientes dibujos? ¿Qué tiempo hace? ¿Qué necesitas llevar o qué quieres hacer si vas de vacaciones a estos lugares? Usa el **Vocabulario** de la página 254 y otras palabras que conoces. Answers in side column

18 Agente de viajes

Imagine that you're a travel agent. One of your jobs is to give advice to customers. How would you respond to the following questions and comments? Role-play the activity with a partner and take turns playing the travel agent and the customer. Use the maps on pages xvii–xxiii as a reference. Answers will vary. Possible answers:

1. Tengo vacaciones en julio y quiero esquiar. ¿Adónde puedo viajar? Nueva Zelandia o Argentina
2. Quiero pasar dos semanas en una playa tropical. ¿Adónde puedo ir? Puerto Rico, México, Hawaii
3. Me gustan las ciudades grandes, el teatro, los museos y los conciertos. Nueva York, la ciudad de México, Londres, París, Madrid
4. Nos gusta mucho la aventura. ¿Adónde podemos ir? África, China, Australia

19 Lectura

Lee el artículo de la revista. Luego contesta las preguntas. Answers in side column

De viaje por Latinoamérica

Si hablas español y te gusta viajar tienes que ir a Latinoamérica. Hay diecinueve países para visitar, desde México en el norte hasta Chile y Argentina en el sur. Hay mucho que ver: paisajes° increíbles y variados, animales y plantas, historia y cultura y mucho más. Aquí vemos cómo puedes ir en tu viaje.

En tren

En Perú puedes tomar el tren más alto del mundo y viajar por los Andes. El tren va desde Lima al centro del país, subiendo° del nivel del mar hasta 4.829 metros en las montañas.

En avión

Viajar en avión es más rápido pero también es más caro. Cada país tiene su propia compañía aérea nacional para vuelos nacionales e internacionales.

En autobús

Tomar un autobús es fácil y barato. Puedes ir en bus a todas partes. En Costa Rica y en otros países de Centroamérica es una tradición decorar los autobuses con colores y diseños alegres.

En taxi

La ciudad de México es una de las ciudades más grandes del mundo y tiene mucho tráfico pero no es difícil viajar en la capital. Tiene un metro moderno, barato y rápido. También hay muchos autobuses y taxis. Pero hay también taxis colectivos. Se llaman peseros. Son taxis que compartes° con otras personas y el viaje sale más económico.

From "De viaje por Latinoamérica" from ¿Qué tal?, vol. 30, no. 2, November/December 1996. Copyright © 1996 by *Mary Glasgow Magazines, London.* Reprinted by permission of the publisher.

1. ¿Qué tipo de transporte debe usar una persona que quiere viajar en un día desde El Salvador hasta Chile?
2. ¿Qué tipo de transporte puede usar una persona que quiere viajar hasta los altos *(highlands)* de los Andes en el Perú?
3. ¿Por qué son baratos los peseros en México?

paisajes *landscapes*
subiendo *going up*
compartes *you share*

☀ CLOSE

Tell students to imagine they are in San Juan on an exchange program and their host family is making suggestions of what to do and see around town. Using the expressions that they have learned in **Primer paso,** they should respond by telling their host family what they would and would not like to do. (**Quiero ver El Morro. Pienso visitar el Viejo San Juan. Puedo ir de compras a Isla Verde.**)

☀ ASSESS

▸ Testing Program, pp. 109–110
 Quiz 12-1
 Audio CD 12, Tr. 16

▸ Grammar and Vocabulary Quizzes
 Quiz 12-1A or
 Alternative Quiz 12-1A

▸ Alternative Assessment Guide, p. 24

PERFORMANCE ASSESSMENT

Have students write a letter to a travel agent requesting information on a place they plan to visit. Each student should ask the cost of the ticket, when the plane will leave, and what he or she will need to take.

Answers to Activity 19

1. Debe viajar en avión.
2. Puede viajar en tren.
3. Porque compartes un pesero con otras personas.

VIDEO INTEGRATION

En camino **LEVEL 1B**

Video Program
Videocassette 2, 49:15–52:00

MOTIVATING ACTIVITY

Ask students what places they would recommend to a visitor to the United States. What places would be fun to visit during the summer? the fall? the winter? the spring? What are some of the interesting sights to see? What historical places would they recommend? What foods should the visitor try?

PRESENTATION

Show the video or read Mariano's speech bubble and have students answer the questions in **¿Qué dijo?** As a follow-up, ask students to talk about places in Latin America and Spain that interest them.

PAIR WORK

In pairs, have students look at the maps on pages xvii–xxii and talk about where they would like to visit in the Spanish-speaking world. Have them think about places that were mentioned in the location openers and talk about why they would like to visit a particular Spanish-speaking country.

ENCUENTRO CULTURAL

Las vacaciones por el mundo hispano

Aunque es de México, a Mariano le interesan muchas otras partes del mundo. Le gusta viajar y conocer otras regiones, sobre todo el mundo hispano. Nos cuenta de las muchas actividades que se pueden hacer cuando uno viaja "en plan de turista".

1 ¿Qué dijo?

Mariano tells what it's like to travel in the Spanish-speaking world. Use the adjectives he uses to help you understand his main ideas.

Answers on p. 243K

▶ **Cuando hablas bien el español,** puedes visitar muchos lugares interesantes en el mundo hispano.

▶ En todo el mundo hispano, hay **lugares bonitos, monumentos históricos** y **muchísimos museos** y **restaurantes…**

▶ Si te gusta el **frío o el calor, las ciudades o el campo,** puedes tomar tus vacaciones en un país del mundo hispano.

Uno de mis lugares favoritos es aquí, en México. Bonito, ¿no? Cuando hablas bien el español, puedes visitar muchos lugares interesantes en el mundo hispano. En todo el mundo hispano, hay lugares bonitos, monumentos históricos y muchísimos museos y restaurantes… Si te gusta el frío o el calor, las ciudades o el campo, puedes tomar tus vacaciones en un país del mundo hispano.

1. When does Mariano think it's best to visit Spanish-speaking countries?

2. Name two things you can do and see in the Spanish-speaking world.

3. Visiting Spanish-speaking countries is fun for people who like _____.
   a. warm weather and cities
   b. cold weather and the countryside
   c. all of the above

2 ¡Piénsalo! Answers on page 243K

1. Compara los dos lugares que se ven en las fotos. ¿Cómo son diferentes? ¿En qué son iguales?

2. ¿Qué actividades piensas que un turista en el Salto Ángel puede hacer? ¿Y un turista en La Plaza de Cibeles? Piensa en tres ideas para cada lugar.

3. ¿Cuál de los dos lugares te gustaría más a ti? ¿Por qué?

El Salto Ángel en Venezuela, la cascada más alta del mundo

La Fuente de Cibeles en España, en la plaza del mismo nombre en el centro de Madrid

3 ¿Y tú? Answers will vary.

Tell Mariano a little bit about your dreams for future vacations.

1. A mí me gustaría visitar _____.

2. Este lugar me interesa porque _____.

3. Allí quiero hacer muchas cosas como (such as) _____.

BACKGROUND

• The water of **el Salto Ángel** *(Angel Falls)* in Venezuela drops 3,212 feet, making it the highest waterfall in the world. It is 15 times higher than Niagara Falls.

• The 18th-century **Fuente de Cibeles** is in the center of a roundabout at the intersection of **Paseo del Prado, Gran Vía,** and **Calle de Alcalá.** It is one of the most beloved and familiar landmarks of Madrid. Enthusiastic fans of the **Real Madrid** soccer team come to splash around in the fountain to celebrate every important win for their team.

NATIVE SPEAKERS

Review accents with native speakers. Remind them that **palabras llanas** are words with the main stress on the next-to-the-last syllable (**lápiz**), **palabras agudas** have the main stress on the last syllable (**sartén**), and **palabras esdrújulas** are words with the main stress two syllables from the last (**cámara**).

Have native speakers scan the **Encuentro cultural** for **palabras agudas con acento** (**aquí**), and **palabras esdrújulas** (**México, históricos, muchísimos**) and include them in their notebooks.

STANDARDS: 1.2, 3.1, 3.2, 5.1   **259**

VIDEO INTEGRATION

En camino LEVEL 1B
Video Program
Videocassette 2, 41:41–42:00 OR
Videocassette 3, 2:05:52–2:06:11
(captioned version)

¡Ven conmigo! LEVEL 1
DVD Tutor, Disc 1

Bell work
On the board or on a transparency write the following words: **playa, ciudad, campo.** Students write as many associated words as they can for each word.

SUGGESTION
20 Have students use the questions as a prelistening or prereading activity before they watch the video or read what Carmen says.

CULTURE NOTE
The archipelago of Los Roques, Venezuela has been a national park since 1972. It is a popular place to swim and snorkle. You can also see lizards, birds, and marine turtles.

SEGUNDO PASO (TPR)

Storytelling Book
pp. 46, 48

WV3 PUERTO RICO-12

Talking about what you would like to do on vacation

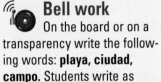

> A mí me gustaría ir de vela, navegar por el océano Pacífico en un barco de vela antiguo... ¡Pienso descubrir una isla desierta!

20 La isla desierta

Imagínate que Carmen está explorando una isla desierta. ¿Qué crees que Carmen va a hacer allí? Contesta **sí** o **no** para cada actividad.

1. Va a nadar y pescar. sí
2. Va a patinar. no
3. Va a visitar a sus amigas. no
4. Va a caminar por toda la isla. sí

Nota cultural

There are many desert islands to explore in Latin America. Los Roques is an archipelago of 364 islands, about 80 miles from the coast of Venezuela. The islands are extremely arid. Few plants live on the islands except **manglares,** or mangroves, plants which grow with their root system in the ocean water. A great variety of water birds, fish, shellfish, and especially the giant pink conch bring life to these desert islands. An explorer on one of these islands might find ten-foot-high mountains of conch shells, or **caracoles,** deposited by the waves and tides. Have you ever explored an uninhabited area?

La Isla del Paraíso

saltar en paracaídas

escalar montañas

hacer turismo

explorar la selva

dar una caminata por el bosque

bajar el río en canoa

tienda de camping

acampar

tomar el sol

ir de vela

PA p. 77 Act. 7

GV p. 51 Act. 12

12-2

21 Adivina, adivinador

Haz una lista de dos cosas que necesitas para hacer cada una de las actividades en la Isla del Paraíso. Después, toma turnos diciéndole a tu compañero/a lo que necesitas. Tu compañero/a debe adivinar *(guess)* cuál de la actividades vas a hacer.

MODELO —Pienso llevar un traje de bano.
—¿Vas a tomar el sol en la playa?

☀ MOTIVATE

Ask students to look at the drawing and discuss the things they would or would not like to do, and why or why not.

☀ TEACH

PRESENTATION

VOCABULARIO

Give a "tour" of **La Isla del Paraíso.** Talk about the activities illustrated and give details as students point to each activity you mention. Then have students repeat the words after you, using backward build-up for accurate pronunciation. (**-mo, -rismo, turismo**)

ADDITIONAL PRACTICE

Ask each student to make up five true or false statements about what the people in the drawing are doing, ending each with ¿**...verdad?** Students are then to respond to a partner's statements, correcting false statements and repeating true ones.

LANGUAGE NOTES

• Some expressions used for *surfing* are **montar en tabla de vela** or **tabla hawaiana** and **el surfing.**

• Another way to say *to go sailing* is **ir en barco de vela.**

• **Adivina, adivinador** is a common expression used to ask someone to guess the answer to a riddle.

SLOWER PACE
22 If students are having difficulty, ask them to focus first on the topography of the places. (**las playas del Golfo de México, las montañas de Chile**) Then, have them complete the sentences with the new vocabulary.

PORTFOLIO
23 **Written** This activity may be used as a written portfolio entry. For portfolio information, see *Alternative Assessment Guide*, pages 9 and 16.

PRESENTATION
ASÍ SE DICE
Write the vocabulary words from **Vocabulario** on page 261 on index cards. Then call on individual students to take a card and, without telling the others what is on the card, act out the activity. When a student knows what activity is being mimed, he or she responds with a phrase from **Así se dice** (affirmative or negative) plus the activity.

Answers to Activity 22

1. tomar el sol
2. escalar montañas
3. hacer turismo
4. tomar el sol, hacer turismo, dar una caminata en el bosque, acampar
5. hacer turismo, ir de vela, tomar el sol
6. acampar; tienda de camping

---

22 ¿Qué pueden hacer?

¿Qué pueden hacer estas personas en sus vacaciones? Completa cada oración con una o más frases del **Vocabulario** de la página 261.

1. Benjamín y Carmen van a pasar sus vacaciones en Texas, en las playas del Golfo de México. Allí pueden ═══.
2. Margarita y sus padres piensan ir a los Andes de Chile. Ellos pueden ═══.
3. Elizabeth va a pasar una semana en Madrid. Ella quiere ═══.
4. Roberto y Carlos esperan ir a Puerto Rico en verano. Ellos van a ═══.
5. Voy a Miami, Florida, porque quiero ═══.
6. Luz María y su familia piensan ir a las montañas en agosto para ═══. Por eso necesitan comprar una nueva ═══. Answers in side column

¿Te acuerdas?

To talk about what is happening right now, use **estar** + the present participle of the verb.

- for **-ar** verbs, add **-ando** to the stem
  Evita está visitando el Salto Ángel.

- for **-er** and **-ir** verbs, add **-iendo** to the stem
  La familia Santiago está haciendo turismo en Barcelona.

- if the stem ends in a vowel, the **-iendo** changes to **-yendo**
  Manuel está leyendo en la playa.

---

23 ¿Qué están haciendo?

Mira el dibujo de la Isla del Paraíso en la página 261. Escribe lo que está haciendo cada persona en este momento.

MODELO

La chica está tomando el sol en la playa y está leyendo un libro.

PA
p. 77
Act. 8

ASÍ SE DICE
Talking about what you would like to do on vacation

To find out what a friend would like to do, ask:

¿Qué te gustaría hacer este verano?

¿Adónde te gustaría ir este verano?

¡Qué aburrido estoy! Y tú, **¿qué tienes ganas de hacer?**

Your friend might answer:

Pues, a mí **me gustaría** ir a las playas en México. Dicen que son fantásticas.

A mí **me gustaría** escalar montañas en Colorado porque son muy bonitas.

Tengo ganas de dar una caminata por el bosque. ¿Vamos?

---

24 Destinos

Work with a partner. Look at the list below and choose two places where you'd like to go. Don't tell each other which places you've chosen. Then take turns asking each other what you'd like to do in each of the places. Can you guess where your partner is going?

1. el río Amazonas
2. Madrid, España
3. San Juan, Puerto Rico
4. San Antonio, Texas
5. el Parque Nacional de Yellowstone
6. México, D. F.
7. El Yunque, Puerto Rico
8. Los Ángeles, California

25 Me gustaría   Script and answers on p. 243E

CD 12 Tr. 4

Sara, David and Martín are saying how they want to spend their vacation. As you listen to what they say, write down where each one would like to go, and what he or she wants to do there.

Le gustaría ir a...

Quiere...

26 En Puerto Rico

Lee este anuncio *(advertisement)* de un parador *(hotel)* puertorriqueño. Después contesta las preguntas.   Answers in side column

1. ¿Dónde está el Parador Villa Antonio?
2. ¿Cómo es este parador?
3. ¿Para qué deporte son ideales las playas del Parador Villa Antonio?
4. ¿Qué te gustaría hacer en ese lugar?

Parador **Villa Antonio** Rincón, Puerto Rico

- **Los Almendros y Black Eagle (playas/surfing)**
- **Balneario de Añasco**
- **Playa Crash-Boat-Aguadilla**
- **Balneario Pico de Piedra-Aguada**
- **Playa de Surfing "Wilderness-Aguadilla"**
- **Playa de Surfing "Surfer Beach"-Aguadilla**

En excelentes playas, ideales para el deporte de "surfing", se encuentra este tranquilo Parador tropical. Todo el esplendor natural del Caribe en un ambiente de completo relajamiento.

55 habitaciones
Atractivos Cercanos

27 ¡Ven a la Isla del Paraíso!

Work with a group of students to write a short ad. Try to convince people to spend their vacation on **la Isla del Paraíso** on page 261. First describe the place with three adjectives. Then mention three things people can do on the islands.

SEGUNDO PASO   *doscientos sesenta y tres*   **263**

SLOWER PACE
24 Have students prepare by looking up three of the locations on a map and listing two activities they might enjoy in each location.

SUGGESTION
25 Have students write the names Sara, David, and Martin on their papers with a few lines between each. Play the tape twice. The first time through, have students listen for where each person would like to go and write the place next to their name. The second time through have them listen for what each would like to do and write it underneath the place the person would like to go. As a follow-up activity, ask students questions about where Sara, David, and Martin would like to go and what they would like to do there.

ADDITIONAL PRACTICE
27 Have students expand their written ad into a television commercial. Each person in the group has two or three lines talking about **la Isla del Paraíso**, trying to convince people that it is a fun place to visit. Have students perform their commercials for the class. Videotape their presentations if the necessary equipment is available.

Answers for Activity 26
1. Está en Rincón, Puerto Rico
2. Es tranquilo.
3. Son ideales para el surfing.
4. Answers will vary.

RE-ENTRY
Suggest acronyms to help students remember the uses of **ser** and **estar.** MOPEDTOT for **ser** (Material, Origin, Possession, Equivalence, Definition, Time, Occupation, and Traits) CLEP for **estar** (Condition, Location, Emotions, and Present progressive) Encourage students to create their own.

PRESENTATION
GRAMÁTICA
Read the examples given in **Gramática** and then model the use of both verbs. Ask students questions to elicit answers with the correct usage of **ser** and **estar.** (¿De dónde es Juana? ¿Dónde está Juana?)

SUGGESTION
28 Have students explain which rule from **Gramática** they used to get their answer.

ADDITIONAL PRACTICE
28 Have students write a paragraph about a friend including appearance, type of clothing preferred, place of birth, birthday, personality, and where he or she is right now.

GRAMÁTICA   ser and estar

You've learned to use **ser** and **estar,** the two Spanish verbs for *to be.*

Use **ser . . .**

1. to say what someone or something is like:
   ¿Cómo **es** Juanita?   **Es** simpática y muy lista.
2. to say where someone or something is from:
   ¿De dónde **son** ustedes?   **Somos** de Guadalajara.
3. to define something or someone:
   ¿Quién **es** la chica?   **Es** mi amiga Marta. **Es** estudiante.
4. to say what something is made of:
   ¿De qué **son** tus calcetines?   **Son** de algodón.
5. to give the date or the time:
   ¿Qué hora **es**?   **Son** las dos menos cuarto.

Use **estar...**

1. to talk about states and conditions:
   ¿Cómo **está** Rogelio hoy?   ¡Uy! **Está** de mal humor.
2. to talk about location:
   ¿Dónde **está** mi libro de matemáticas? **Está** debajo de tu cama.
3. with the present participle, to talk about what's happening right now:
   ¿Qué **están haciendo** Ana Clara y Meme?   **Están jugando** al voleibol en la playa.

28 ¡Apúrate!

Rubén y su hermano Marcos tienen que salir inmediatamente para el aeropuerto. Completa su diálogo con la forma apropiada de **ser** o **estar.**

RUBÉN   ¡Marcos! ¿Por qué no ___1___ listo? estás

MARCOS   Es que todavía ___2___ haciendo la maleta. estoy

RUBÉN   ¡Ay, Marcos! ¡(Tú) ___3___ muy desorganizado! eres

MARCOS   Ayúdame a encontrar mi camiseta favorita. ___4___ roja y ___5___ de algodón. Es, es

RUBÉN   ¿Por qué no sabes dónde ___6___? está

MARCOS   ¿Por qué ___7___ (tú) de mal humor? Hombre, en tres horas vamos a ___8___ en las playas de Puerto Rico. ¡Qué bien! estás, estar

RUBÉN   Ya sé, pero el avión sale a las tres. Ya ___9___ las dos. son

MARCOS   Mira, ¡aquí tengo la camiseta! Ahora, ¿dónde ___10___ mis zapatos de tenis? están

PA
pp. 78–79
Acts. 9–11

GV
pp. 52–53
Acts. 13–16

29 Estoy aquí en...

Imagínate que estás de vacaciones en uno de estos lugares. Escribe una tarjeta postal a tu mejor amigo/a. Dile dónde estás y cómo es el lugar. Menciona también cómo estás y lo que estás haciendo. Usa un mínimo de tres adjetivos para describir el lugar y menciona tres actividades en que estás participando. Answers on p. 243K

México, D. F.

Ponce, Puerto Rico

Los Andes

Toledo, España

30 Cada cual a su gusto

Entrevista a un/a compañero/a. Pregúntale qué le gustaría hacer en sus vacaciones. Luego sugiere *(suggest)* adónde debe ir de vacaciones. Usa las frases **¿Por qué no vas a...?** y **Debes ir a...**

31 Quedarse en casa

Muchas personas pasan las vacaciones en casa. Escribe un párrafo *(paragraph)* que explica qué vas a hacer en casa este verano. Escribe por lo menos cuatro oraciones.

MODELO   Este verano voy a nadar y jugar en la piscina todos los días. Mis amigos...

SEGUNDO PASO

doscientos sesenta y cinco **265**

CAPÍTULO 12

SUGGESTION
29 Have students do this activity as a journal entry. For additional journal entry suggestions, see *Practice and Activity Book*, p. 91.

SLOWER PACE
31 Before they write the paragraph, ask students to tell a partner what they do during the summer that they don't do during the school year. Partners report one or two things about each other's summer activities to the class.

☀ CLOSE
Use Teaching Transparency 12-2 to review material from this **paso.**

☀ ASSESS
▸ Testing Program, pp. 111–112
  Quiz 12-2
  Audio CD 12, Tr. 17

▸ Grammar and Vocabulary Quizzes
  Quiz 12-2A or
  Alternative Quiz 12-2A

▸ Alternative Assessment Guide, p. 24

PERFORMANCE ASSESSMENT
Students in pairs create a dialogue between a travel agent and a client using as much of the vocabulary as possible from this **paso.** When they have completed their dialogues, students present them to the class. If possible, have props available, such as used airline tickets, a passport, or an itinerary.

STANDARDS: 1.1, 1.3, 5.1

DVD VIDEO
VIDEO INTEGRATION

En camino LEVEL 1B
Video Program
Videocassette 2, 52:01–54:44

¡Ven conmigo! LEVEL 1
DVD Tutor, Disc 2

TEACHER NOTES
• See *Video Guide* for activities related to the **Panorama cultural.**

• Remind students that cultural information may be included in the Quizzes and Chapter Test.

• The language of the people interviewed represents informal, unrehearsed speech. Occasionally, text has been edited for clarity.

MOTIVATING ACTIVITY
Ask students what they consider the top tourist attractions in the United States. If a group of students from a Spanish-speaking country came to the United States for the first time, which attractions would they suggest that the group see? Ask students to list their top five recommendations in order.

LANGUAGE NOTE
Point out that **y** becomes **e** before another [i] sound as in ...**e hice...**

Panorama cultural

CD 12
Trs. 5–8

¿Adónde vas y qué haces en las vacaciones?

If you lived in a Spanish-speaking country, what would you look forward to doing on your vacation? The answer would depend on which country you lived in. We asked these teenagers in Spanish-speaking countries what they do and where they go during their vacations.

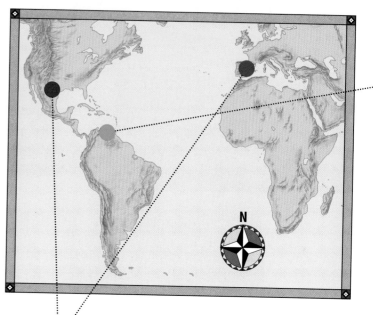

Daniel, like many Europeans, travels to other countries in Europe on vacation.

● **Daniel**
Sevilla,
España
CD 12 Tr. 6

El año pasado
fuimos a Inglaterra y
visitamos a mis primos
y a mis tíos. En Inglaterra
practiqué el inglés e hice
muchas actividades.

Verónica and her family went to Los Angeles on their last vacation. What U.S. city would you like to visit?

● **Verónica**
San Antonio,
Texas CD 12 Tr. 7

El verano
pasado fuimos a Los
Ángeles. Fui con mi familia.
Fuimos a la playa y caminamos
por la calle de Rodeo. Entonces
fuimos a todas las tiendas
y los restaurantes
famosos.

266

During his December school vacation, Davie enjoys his time off at home. What do you do on your winter break?

Davie
*Caracas,
Venezuela*
CD 12 Tr. 8

En diciembre nos dan aproximadamente unos quince días. Juego, celebro... celebro el cumpleaños, estudio y hago deportes.

1 ¿Con quién fue Daniel a Inglaterra? Fue con su familia.

2 ¿Qué hizo Daniel en Inglaterra? Visitó a su familia, practicó el inglés y también hizo muchas actividades.

3 ¿Cuándo fue Verónica a Los Ángeles? Fue el verano pasado.

4 Nombra dos cosas que hizo Verónica en Los Ángeles. Possible answer: Fue a la playa y a la calle de Rodeo.

5 ¿Cuántas semanas de vacaciones tiene Davie en diciembre? Tiene dos semanas, más o menos.

6 ¿Cómo pasa Davie sus vacaciones del colegio? Juega deportes, celebra su cumpleaños y estudia.

Para pensar y hablar... Answers will vary.
A. Do you enjoy any of the same vacation activities as the interviewees? If so, name two of them. If not, name in Spanish two things you do or two places you go on vacation.
B. With a partner, talk in Spanish about which place or country you want to visit. Say what you need to bring and what you want to do when you're there.

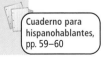
Cuaderno para hispanohablantes, pp. 59–60

PRESENTATION
Have students watch the video or read the speech bubbles. Ask **¿Adónde fue Daniel? ¿Verónica? ¿Davie?** After you have asked and received answers for several comprehension questions, ask a student **¿Adónde vas tú?** Then have students ask each other where they go and what they do on vacation. Then play the video again and have students answer the questions.

FAMILY LINK
Have students interview a family member about where he or she would like to travel. Ask volunteers to report their findings to the class in Spanish.

STANDARDS: 1.2, 3.2, 5.1   **267**

VIDEO INTEGRATION

En camino LEVEL 1B
Video Program
Videocassette 2, 40:46–41:16 OR
Videocassette 3, 2:04:57–2:05:27
(captioned version)

¡Ven conmigo! LEVEL 1
DVD Tutor, Disc 1

Bell work

Have students copy the following columns and draw lines connecting the verb in column 1 with an appropriate ending in column 2. (column 1. **Viajé, Trabajamos, Estudiaron, Hiciste, Preparó**; column 2. **en casa el sábado, a San Juan, las matemáticas, la maleta para tu viaje, un pastel para el cumpleaños de mi hermana**)

HISTORY LINK

Spain ceded Guam, Puerto Rico, and the Philippines to the United States in the peace treaty signed after the Spanish-American War in 1898. The United States Congress passed the Jones Act in 1917, giving Puerto Ricans United States citizenship. Since 1952, as a commonwealth, Puerto Rico has been self-governing with an elected governor as the head of the country. In 1993, Puerto Ricans voted to continue as a commonwealth rather than to become the 51st state of the United States or to become an independent country.

TERCER PASO   (TPR) Storytelling Book pp. 47, 48

WV3 PUERTO RICO-12

Saying where you went and what you did on vacation

Yo visité a los vecinos ayer. No hay nada interesante que hacer, abuelo.

¿Por qué no visitan a los vecinos?

¿Cómo que no hay nada interesante que hacer? Están en una isla, hace un tiempo maravilloso y están de vacaciones. Díganme, entonces... ¿qué les gustaría hacer? En su opinión, ¿qué son las vacaciones ideales?

32 En el pasado

Ayer, Benjamín visitó a los vecinos. Vamos a imaginar otras cosas que hicieron Benjamín y Carmen durante sus vacaciones. Conjuga cada verbo en el pretérito.

1. Anteayer Carmen (jugar) con el abuelo en la playa. jugó
2. El sábado pasado Benjamín (caminar) por el parque. caminó
3. Anoche Carmen (tomar) un jugo de frutas tropicales. tomó
4. La semana pasada Benjamín (pescar) con su abuelo. pescó
5. Benjamín (visitar) a los vecinos ayer. visitó

Nota cultural p. 84 Act. 19

It's common for Puerto Ricans to travel back and forth between the island and the mainland United States. Puerto Ricans are U.S. citizens, and as such don't need a passport or other documents to travel back and forth. Because many Puerto Ricans living on the mainland U.S. have relatives in Puerto Rico, they visit often. At times, children will live with grandparents in Puerto Rico for a period of time while their parents are working on the mainland. Some people move back and forth because of jobs or other family circumstances. The children in those families are generally fully bilingual. What are the advantages and disadvantages of living in different places?

ASÍ SE DICE

Saying where you went and what you did on vacation

pp. 80–81
Acts. 13–15

To find out about a friend's vacation, ask:

Your friend might answer:

¿Adónde viajaste el verano pasado?

Yo **no fui a ningún lugar.**
I didn't go anywhere.

¿Adónde fueron tú y tu familia durante las vacaciones?

Fuimos a Puerto Rico.

¿Qué hiciste cuando fuiste a Buenos Aires?

En Buenos Aires, **visité** la Plaza de Mayo.

12-3

33 ¡Qué divertido! Script and answers on p. 243E

CD 12 Tr. 9

Carlos and Yolanda have just returned from their trip to Puerto Rico. Listen to them describe their trip, and then put the drawings in order.

a **b** **c** **d**

GRAMÁTICA Preterite tense

p. 54
Acts.
17–18

12-3

To talk about what happened in the past, use the preterite tense. All regular **-ar** verbs follow the same pattern as **trabajar.** The verb **ir** is irregular in the preterite.

trabaj**é**	trabaj**amos**		**fui**	**fuimos**
trabaj**aste**	trabaj**asteis**		**fuiste**	**fuisteis**
trabaj**ó**	trabaj**aron**		**fue**	**fueron**

☀ MOTIVATE

Ask students **¿Cuántos estudiantes viajaron a otra ciudad el verano pasado? ¿Cuántos visitaron a sus parientes?**

☀ TEACH

PRESENTATION
ASÍ SE DICE

Using a wall map of the world or Map Transparency 2, point to the locations as you model questions and answers. Have students practice the phrases in pairs. Then ask them to develop some original statements using the expressions and another location. Have students report their partner's answers to the class.

GRAMÁTICA

After reviewing the preterite forms of **trabajar** and **ir,** write those forms on the board. Ask a student to give an original sentence using one of the forms of **trabajar.** After the student has done so, erase that form. Continue until students have given an original sentence for each form of both verbs.

PRELISTENING

33 As a prelistening activity, have students work in pairs to name and list the activities in each picture in Spanish.

ADDITIONAL PRACTICE

34 Have students write five sentences in the preterite in pairs. As in the activity, they do not include names or pronouns in the sentences. They put the names and pronouns in rectangles to the side of the sentences, mixing up their order. Then they exchange their sentences with another pair and decide who is speaking in each sentence.

PREREADING

35 As a prereading activity, have students read the questions to focus their attention on the information they are looking for in the diary entry.

Answers to Activity 35

Answers will vary. Possible answers:
1. Vive en la ciudad. Camina a las tiendas y al lugar donde toma un refresco.
2. Fueron a visitar a los abuelos de Elsa. Viven en el campo. Elsa ayuda a cuidar los animales.
3. Answers will vary.
4. Answers will vary.

34 ¿Adónde fueron?

Lee las oraciones. Decide de quién habla cada oración.

1. Fue al cine a ver una película en francés.
2. Fuimos a la casa porque hizo mucho frío ayer.
3. Fui a Río Chico el fin de semana pasado.
4. Fueron a la Argentina y montaron a caballo.

4 **Melinda y Edwin**

1 **Clara**   3 **yo**

2 **Joaquín y yo**

35 El diario de Elsa

Lee esta página del diario de Elsa y después contesta las preguntas. Answers in side column

martes, 15 de agosto

Hoy dormí hasta las once. Me encantan las vacaciones. Preparé un desayuno rico y después fui a caminar a ver qué había de nuevo en las tiendas. Me encontré con Magdalena. Compré unos pantalones cortos de color morado para el viaje. Después fuimos a tomar un refresco porque hacía muchísimo calor. Tengo que dormirme ya. Salimos de viaje a las cuatro de la mañana.

miércoles, 16 de agosto

No puedo escribir mucho porque estoy muy cansada. ¡Todo el día sentada en el carro con mi hermano antipático! Por fin llegamos a la casa de mi abuela a las ocho y media de la noche.

jueves, 17 de agosto

Llovió toda la mañana. Mi mamá y yo ayudamos a mi tío a cuidar los animales. Por la tarde hizo sol y fuimos a nadar en el río. Mi hermano cree que sabe nadar mejor pero yo le gané tres carreras. Mi abuela hizo un pastel de manzana para el postre de la cena. Quiero aprender a hacerlo porque es la cosa más rica del mundo.

1. ¿Dónde crees que vive Elsa? En el campo o en la ciudad? ¿Cómo lo sabes?
2. ¿Adónde fueron de vacaciones Elsa y su familia? ¿Fueron al campo o a la ciudad? ¿Cómo lo sabes?
3. ¿Cuál de los tres días que describe Elsa te parece el más divertido? ¿Por qué?
4. ¿Cuál de los tres días te parece el menos divertido? ¿Por qué?

36 Ya regresaron

Carmen y Benjamín están mirando las fotos de su viaje a Puerto Rico. Ayúdalos a organizar sus fotos. Escribe dos oraciones para cada foto. Di lo que hicieron y adónde fueron.

37 Destino desconocido

First make a list of ten things that you packed for a recent trip. Then your partner tries to guess if you traveled to a city, the mountains, a beach, a forest, or a jungle. Switch roles and ask yes or no questions until you know where your partner went.

MODELO —¿Llevaste un traje de baño?
—No, no llevé traje de baño.
—¿Llevaste unas botas?
—Sí, llevé unas botas.
—¿Fuiste a una montaña?

FAMILY LINK
36 Ask students to bring photos from home of a recent family activity and write captions for them. You may want to preview the photos to be sure they are appropriate for class.

PREWRITING
36 As a prewriting activity, have students brainstorm the vocabulary they need for the activities shown in the photos.

VISUAL LEARNERS
37 As a variation, have students guess the activities their partners did on vacation as clues to where they went. (**¿Caminaste en la playa?**)

BIOLOGY LINK
Ask students if they know the location of tropical forests other than El Yunque. (Central America, Amazon River Basin of South America, Congo River Basin of Africa, Southeast Asia) Discuss the environmental consequences of destruction of the world's rain forests. (disruption of weather patterns, permanent loss of plant and animal species, land erosion)

PRESENTATION

VOCABULARIO

After students have practiced the pronunciation of the countries, have them consult a world map. Ask students to list five countries that are near and five that are far from where they live. You might also have them list the six countries they would most like to visit and why.

 CULTURE NOTES
• **Parador de Zafra** is a castle with many beautiful decorative details. **Parador Reyes Católicos** was founded by Ferdinand and Isabella in 1499 to provide lodging for pilgrims traveling to Santiago de Compostela. It is considered the oldest hotel in the world. **Parador Alarcón** is a castle in Cuenca, Spain, between Madrid and Valencia. **Parador Conde de Orgaz** has a beautiful view of the Tajo River and the **Alcázar** of Toledo.

• Puerto Rico has a number of **paradores** patterned after the **paradores nacionales** in Spain. Some are guest houses; others are tourist villas and small hotels.

 PORTFOLIO
39 **Oral** Students may include a recording of this activity as an oral portfolio entry. Also see *Alternative Assessment Guide,* p. 16.

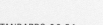
 p. 82 Act. 16

 p. 55 Acts. 19–20

VOCABULARIO

Alemania
Germany

Francia
France

China
China

Inglaterra
England

Egipto
Egypt

Italia
Italy

Vista de Toledo, España, desde el Parador Conde de Orgaz

38 Al extranjero

Usa el mapa mundial en las páginas xviii–xix. Escoge *(choose)* dos países. Adivina en qué países está pensando tu compañero/a.

MODELO
—¿Está cerca de Rusia?
—Sí.
—¿Está al lado de Mongolia?
—Sí.
—¿Está lejos de Kazajstán?
—No.
—Estás pensando en China.
—Sí.

 Nota cultural p. 84 Act. 20

Several Spanish-speaking countries offer fascinating **paradores,** or inns, for travelers to stay overnight. In Spain, numerous **paradores** are in old castles, palaces, convents, or monasteries. In the **Parador de Zafra,** for example, you can sleep in the same castle where Hernán Cortés stayed before setting out for the New World. You can stay in a room at the **Parador Reyes Católicos** in Santiago de Compostela founded by King Ferdinand and Queen Isabella. And if you get a room at the **Parador Alarcón,** you'll sleep in a castle built in the eighth century by Moors from North Africa. What's the oldest building you've ever seen? What was it originally used for, and what is it used for now?

39 Una entrevista

Interview a classmate who has taken a trip. Find out where he or she went and what he or she did. Ask as many questions as you can. Take notes and report your findings to the class.

> MODELO —¿Adónde fuiste?
> —Fui a Colorado.
> —¿Qué hiciste allá?
> —Acampé con mi familia.

Típicamente hace sol y calor en las playas de Puerto Rico.

40 En mi cuaderno

Escribe un párrafo de cinco oraciones para explicar a qué lugar esperas viajar algún día y por qué. Incluye qué quieres hacer allí y qué tiempo hace típicamente.

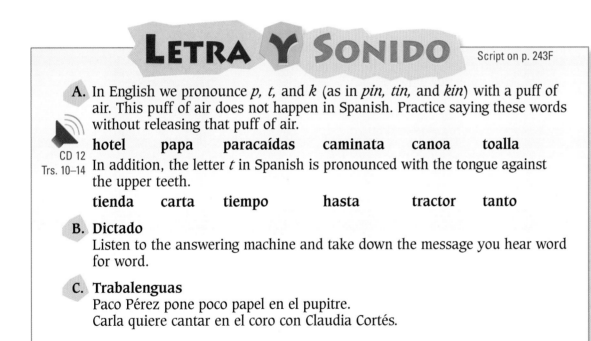

LETRA Y SONIDO

Script on p. 243F

CD 12
Trs. 10–14

A. In English we pronounce *p, t,* and *k* (as in *pin, tin,* and *kin*) with a puff of air. This puff of air does not happen in Spanish. Practice saying these words without releasing that puff of air.

| hotel | papa | paracaídas | caminata | canoa | toalla |

In addition, the letter *t* in Spanish is pronounced with the tongue against the upper teeth.

| tienda | carta | tiempo | hasta | tractor | tanto |

B. Dictado
Listen to the answering machine and take down the message you hear word for word.

C. Trabalenguas
Paco Pérez pone poco papel en el pupitre.
Carla quiere cantar en el coro con Claudia Cortés.

📖 **EN MI CUADERNO**
40 Ask students to write about what each member of their family likes to do and where they like to go on vacation. For an additional journal entry suggestion, see *Practice and Activity Book,* p. 91.

☀ **CLOSE**

Give each student a small piece of paper with the name of a country on it and tell them to imagine that they have just returned from a trip there. Students tell a partner where they went, who they went with, what they took with them, what they did there, and if they had a good time.

☀ **ASSESS**

▸ Testing Program, pp. 113–114
Quiz 12-3
Audio CD 12, Tr. 18

▸ Grammar and Vocabulary Quizzes
Quiz 12-3A or
Alternative Quiz 12-3A

▸ Alternative Assessment Guide, p. 24

PERFORMANCE ASSESSMENT
Ask students to imagine they have just returned from a vacation. They are to create a photo album with pictures clipped from magazines and write a brief description under each picture explaining where they went and what they did.

CAPÍTULO 12

PRESENTATION

Have students name several things that give off light. (lightbulb, candle, flashlight, lantern, sun, stars, and so on) Ask students what marine organisms give off light. (lantern fish and some other fishes, some shrimp, some squid, some jellyfish, and many plantlike organisms)

BIOLOGY LINK

Although phytoplanktons are found at the sea surface, many species of bioluminescent marine life live deep underwater. Biologists have found that 90% of fish and marine organisms that live from 300 to 3,000 feet underwater glow. Some sea creatures use bioluminescence to camouflage themselves from predators. Their glow makes them invisible from below because they blend in with the background of sunlight.

Answer to Activity 1

a. A visitor is most likely to see the phosphorescent glow on a moonless night with lots of waves. The glow cannot be seen in daylight and it is hard to see in moonlight. The glow occurs as a reaction to the movement from breaking waves or other movement such as a paddle stroke.

Answer to Activity 2

c. A firefly is luminescent. The others give off both heat and light.

Enlaces

LAS CIENCIAS

1 De vacaciones en Puerto Rico

Many people in San Juan take vacations in La Parguera, a fishing village along **la Bahía Fosforescente,** or Phosphorescent Bay, on the southwest coast. Millions of tiny organisms (known as algae or dinoflagellates) glow in the water of this bay. It takes mechanical energy, such as the breaking of a wave, to trigger the reaction that releases green light. Under which of the following circumstances would a visitor be most likely to see the phosphorescent glow? Why? Answers in side column

a. on a moonless night with lots of big waves

b. in the middle of a stormy day

c. on a full moon night with calm water

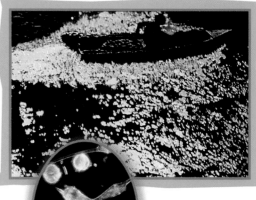

2 La luminescencia

These glowing sea algae are *luminescent,* which means they give off light but not heat. All of the following generate light. Which are luminescent?

a. a star   b. a lightbulb   c. a firefly   d. a candle Answers in side column

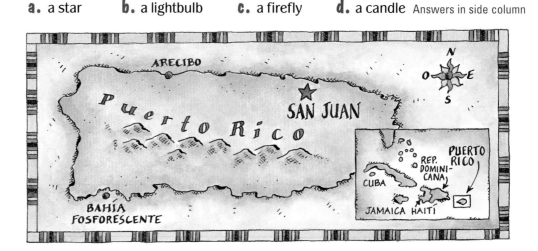

 274 *doscientos setenta y cuatro*   CAPÍTULO 12   Las vacaciones ideales

274 STANDARDS: 3.1, 5.1

LA ASTRONOMÍA

Many Puerto Ricans and tourists enjoy visiting the Arecibo Observatory, the largest and most sensitive single-dish radio telescope in the world. It is located ten miles south of the city of Arecibo. Galaxies, erupting stars, clouds of gas, pulsars, and quasars give off radio waves that are invisible to the naked eye, but that can be seen using radio telescopes. The Arecibo Observatory also uses planetary radar to study planets, moons, asteroids, and comets in our solar system. This is done by sending a powerful beam of radio energy at the object and analyzing the information about the radio echo that is reflected back to the Arecibo telescope.

3 El radar   Answers on p. 243K

Radio waves are used to study distant objects in our solar system because they can be used to "see" objects through clouds, darkness, and at a great distance. Radio waves were used by the Arecibo Observatory to map Venus. This use of radio waves is also known as radar. What other uses for radar do you know about?

4 Los telescopios   Answers on p. 243K

Traditional telescopes must be used at night and in good weather. Do you think this is true of radio telescopes? Why or why not?

5 ¡Qué grande!   Answer: 1000.4 feet in diameter

The spherical reflector of the Arecibo radio telescope is 305 meters in diameter (measurement across). Calculate the diameter in feet. (Hint: 1 meter = 3.28 feet)

MOTIVATING ACTIVITY
Ask students what sources of light can be seen with the naked eye on a cloudy night. (light bulb, candle, flashlight, and so on) Which can be seen with the naked eye on a clear night from 500 miles or farther away? (city lights, stars, planets, the moon)

BACKGROUND
- In radio astronomy scientists use a large spherical reflector dish to collect natural radio energy that is emitted from pulsars, quasars, galaxies, erupting stars, and clouds of gas. Computers turn the radio waves into images that are displayed on a video monitor. Scientists study the radio waves to measure distances and study rotating stars (pulsars).

- In planetary radar, a radar beam is sent to bounce off planets, moons, asteroids, comets, or other celestial bodies. After faint echoes of the radio waves are received by the reflector, computers turn them into images that are displayed on a video monitor. Scientists analyze the echo data to determine information about the size, shape, composition, rotation, and path of the target object.

CHALLENGE
Have students calculate the circumference of the telescope. The formula is $2\pi r$ (957.7 meters / 3141.3 feet).

READING STRATEGY

Recognizing text organization

MOTIVATING ACTIVITY

Ask students to list five things they would like to do on an ideal vacation. Where could they do all five things?

☀ PREREADING

A After students have read the hints, have them make a list of the activities talked about in the reading and list all the countries mentioned.

SUGGESTION

Since this is the last chapter, briefly review the reading strategies presented throughout the *Pupil's Edition* by asking students to name as many strategies as they can remember. (looking for cognates, looking at titles and subtitles, using background information, scanning for specific information, using pictures, and so on)

☀ READING

CRITICAL THINKING

B and **C** To help them understand as they read, ask students to name as many things in the illustration as they can.

CHALLENGE

Ask students to invent a country complete with climate, economy, population, and perhaps even history. Their goal is to convince their classmates that it is a good place to visit.

Estrategia

Recognizing text organization Before reading a passage in detail, you should try to recognize how it's organized. This helps you follow along more easily, and can save you time if you need to look only for a certain piece of information.

¡A comenzar!

A The reading on these pages is about how to choose the vacation that's best for you. How is the reading organized? Be sure to look at the following hints.

1. **¿Te gusta mucho el sol?** is the beginning.
2. Notice the footprints, and think about their purpose. Write your answer and then discuss it with two classmates. Make sure you all agree about how this text is organized.

Al grano

B Suppose there are two Costa Rican students in your school, Matías and Berta. You can find out a little about them by seeing what choices they made on the flow chart. Matías's path is blue, and Berta's is red. Read through all their choices. Then answer *true* or *false*.

Berta . . .

1. doesn't like the beach falso
2. thinks dancing is fun cierto

sí ¿Sabes nadar? sí

¿Te gustan los deportes acuáticos, por ejemplo el windsurf, el esquí acuático o la vela?

no

no sí

¿Te gusta aprender cosas nuevas?

Hay sitios ideales para practicar deportes acuáticos en España, en las Canarias, y en el Caribe.

no sí

¿Te gusta charlar con los amigos, tomar el sol e ir a bailar por la tarde?

no

sí

Para ti son ideales unas vacaciones en Acapulco, en México, o el Caribe, en Puerto Rico o en la República Dominicana.

Busca un campamento de verano donde puedes practicar deportes, tocar un instrumento musical o aprender a pintar.

Visita México. Es un país tan rico en cultura antigua como Egipto. Visita las pirámides. Son fascinantes.

3. likes the sun *cierto*
4. is a great swimmer *falso*

Matías . . .

1. loves wintertime *falso*
2. really likes sports *falso*
3. is interested in history *cierto*
4. likes the sun *falso*

C Imagine that you're a travel agent and several people come to you for advice about where to spend their vacation. According to the map, which of the seven destinations would you recommend for a person who . . .? Answers on p. 243K

1. likes the sun, the beach, and learning new things, but can't swim
2. likes being indoors and likes art and culture
3. doesn't like to play sports but does like history

D Mira el mapa una vez más. Decide dónde quieres pasar tus vacaciones. Sigue las instrucciones y contesta cada pregunta con cuidado *(with care)*. Piensa en los lugares que recomienda el mapa y decide qué lugares prefieres para tus vacaciones ideales. Escribe un párrafo corto y explica adónde quieres ir y por qué. Puedes usar la siguiente frase: **Quiero ir a... porque...**

Answers will vary.

Cuaderno para hispanohablantes, pp. 56–58

☀ **POSTREADING**

D To extend Activity D, have students make oral presentations. Ask them to choose one place they would like to visit and to prepare a brief oral description of that location. Suggest that they make a visual to facilitate listening comprehension.

• Ask students whether they would be able to do all the things they listed for the Motivating Activity on page 276 in any of the ideal vacation spots in the reading. Would they need to take more than one vacation to accomplish this?

• Have students check the cost of their ideal vacation in the travel section of their local paper or in a magazine. How expensive is their ideal trip compared to others listed?

NATIVE SPEAKERS
Ask native speakers if they have any photographs at home of a memorable vacation. If so, ask them to bring the photos in and give a short oral report about it.

TEACHER NOTE
For additional readings, see *Practice and Activity Book,* p. 83.

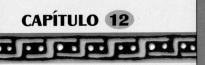

The **Repaso** reviews and integrates all four skills and culture in preparation for the Chapter Test.

SLOWER PACE
1 Before they listen to the tape, ask students to identify a specific word or phrase for each picture. By listening for that phrase, they can identify the drawing more easily.

CHALLENGE
2 Ask students to write their opinion about taking a trip down the Amazon. Students write whether they would or would not like to go there and why using information from the article. (**Me gustaría porque...** or **No me gustaría porque...**)

♜ GAME
Hacer la maleta For this game you will need a suitcase and things to put in it. You might use the items you used to teach the vocabulary or objects in the classroom. The first student begins by saying **Voy a poner un/a _____ en la maleta,** and puts the item in the suitcase. You then call a second student. The second student repeats what the first student said, adds a new item at the end of the sentence, and puts the new item in the suitcase. (**Voy a poner una camisa y un traje de baño en la maleta.**) The game continues following this pattern.

MARCAR: go.hrw.com
PALABRA CLAVE:
WV3 PUERTO RICO-12

1 Las siguientes personas describen sus planes para las vacaciones. Para cada descripción que oyes, indica el dibujo que corresponde.

CD 12 Tr. 15

Script and answers on p. 243F

2 Lee el artículo. También revisa *(review)* la **Nota cultural** de la página 250. Luego contesta las preguntas. Answers on p. 243K

1. ¿Por qué deben llevar ropa liviana de algodón los turistas?
2. ¿Por qué crees que es común viajar en barco o canoa en el Amazonas?
3. ¿Crees que es fácil pescar un pirarucu?

EN EL AMAZONAS es muy común viajar en lancha, barco o canoa. El paseo en canoa les da a los turistas una gran oportunidad de ver los animales y pájaros coloridos y raros. La variedad de animales incluye el pirarucu, un pez° muy grande que puede ser de 325 libras°, las pirañas, la iguana, la anaconda y los tucanes. Si viajan al río Amazonas lleven sus cámaras, ropa liviana de algodón, sombreros para protegerse del sol tropical y ¡no olviden repelente contra los mosquitos!

pez *fish*   **libras** *pounds*

3 Vamos a escribir

Write an article for your school yearbook about your Spanish class. Describe some events you participated in this year, such as games, concerts, or trips. Conclude by summarizing the year.

Estrategia

Writing good conclusions will help tie your ideas together. You might review the highlights of the school year. A conclusion is also a good place to consider the positive and negative aspects of your topic.

> La clase de español
>
> Fue un año estupendo porque hicimos muchas cosas. Pero no me gustó...

Prewriting

1. List several highlights of the year. Include what happened and when, what you did, and where you went.
2. Organize the events with a cluster diagram or an outline.

Writing

For your first draft, use some writing strategies you've practiced.

- Think about grammar and vocabulary you'll need. Review preterite forms and words for school and free-time activities.
- Don't forget that connectors such as **y**, **también**, and **pero** will make your sentences flow more smoothly.

Revising

1. Switch papers with a classmate, and check each other's paper to see if you've followed all the instructions given above.
2. Write a final draft of your article, making any changes and corrections.

4 SITUACIÓN

Imagine that you're on a bus traveling from San Juan to Ponce. With a partner, role-play a scene where you find out a fellow passenger's name and age, and where he or she is from. Then ask where your new friend is going and what he or she plans to do there. Also find out where your new friend already went in Puerto Rico and what he or she did there.

(Cuaderno para hispanohablantes, pp. 58–59)

PORTFOLIO

3 Written Your students may want to consider including their finished articles in their portfolio. For portfolio suggestions, see *Assessment Guide*, p. 16.

SUGGESTION

4 Have each pair develop its discussion into a skit. Then have them present it to the class.

COOPERATIVE LEARNING

On the board or a transparency write the following: **Quiero... Necesitan... ¿Piensas...? Debemos... Mi amigo/a espera... Ustedes pueden... Vamos a... Tengo que...** Divide the class into groups of three. Ask each group to complete the sentences with an infinitive and any other words necessary. All sentences are to relate to a class trip the students are planning. Group members assume the roles of Discussion Leader, Writer, and Reporter. The Discussion Leader guides the discussion as members create the sentences. The Writer records the sentences. The Reporter reads the completed sentences to the class. Call on different groups until you have two or three completed sentences for each verb. To assist visual learners, you could have a student write the completed sentences on the board or on a transparency as they are read out.

 A VER SI PUEDO...

WV3 PUERTO RICO-12

This page is intended to help prepare students for the Chapter Test. It is a brief checklist of the major points covered in the chapter. The students should be reminded that this is only a checklist and does not necessarily include everything that will appear on the Chapter Test.

Answers to Activity 1

Answers will vary. Possible answers:

1. ¿Qué haces todos los días? Voy al colegio y después escucho música con mis amigos y hago la tarea.
2. ¿Qué haces todos los días? Practico al fútbol americano y leo mucho.
3. ¿Qué hacen todos los días? Trabajamos, preparamos la cena y miramos la televisión.
4. ¿Qué hacen todos los días? Estudiamos, pasamos el rato en la casa de un amigo y jugamos videojuegos.

Answers to Activity 2

a. ¿Te gustaría saltar en paracaídas?
b. ¿Te gustaría bajar el río en canoa?
c. ¿Te gustaría hacer una caminata en la montaña?
d. ¿Te gustaría tomar el sol en la playa?

Answers to Activity 3

1. ¿Qué vas a hacer mañana?
2. ¿Qué piensas hacer este verano?

Answers to Activity 6

1. Fui a Egipto el verano pasado.
2. Mi familia y yo fuimos a la Ciudad de México.
3. Mis amigos y yo fuimos a Nueva York.

▼ **Can you talk about what you do and like to do every day?** p. 251

1 How would you ask the following people what they do every day? How would they answer? Answers in side column

1. your best friend
2. a new student in your class
3. your aunt and uncle
4. a group of friends

2 How would you ask someone if he or she would like to do the following? Answers in side column

a   b   c   d

▼ **Can you make future plans?** p. 253

3 How do you ask someone . . .? Answers in side column

1. what he or she is going to do tomorrow
2. what he or she plans to do this summer

4 Tell a friend about a future trip to Mexico. Say what you plan and hope to do. Use these cues: Answers will vary.

1. ir a México, D. F. este verano
2. hacer turismo
3. practicar el español

▼ **Can you talk about what you would like to do on vacation?** p. 262

5 How would you answer if someone asked you the following questions? Answers will vary.

1. ¿Qué te gustaría hacer hoy?
2. ¿Adónde te gustaría viajar?

▼ **Can you say where you went and what you did on vacation?** p. 269

6 How would you tell your friend that . . .? Answers in side column

1. you went to Egypt last summer
2. you and your family took a trip to Mexico City
3. you and your friends went to New York

7 How would you tell someone that . . .? Answers on p. 243K

1. your parents visited relatives in Chicago
2. you and your sister didn't go anywhere
3. you took care of your brothers

VOCABULARIO

PRIMER PASO

Making future plans

el bloqueador   *sunscreen*
el boleto   *ticket*
la bufanda   *scarf*
la cámara   *camera*
las chancletas   *sandals, slippers*
la chaqueta   *jacket*
los esquís   *skis*
esperar   *to hope*
hacer la maleta   *to pack the suitcase*
los lentes de sol   *sunglasses*
quedarse   *to stay, to remain*
la toalla   *towel*
el traje de baño   *bathing suit*

SEGUNDO PASO

Talking about what you would like to do on vacation

acampar   *to camp*
bajar el río en canoa   *to go canoeing*
el bosque   *forest*
dar una caminata   *to go hiking*
la isla   *island*
escalar montañas   *to go mountain climbing*
explorar   *to explore*
hacer turismo   *to go sightseeing*
ir de vela   *to go sailing*
el paraíso   *paradise*

saltar en paracaídas   *to go skydiving*
la selva   *jungle*
la tienda de camping   *camping tent*
tomar el sol   *to sunbathe*

TERCER PASO

Saying where you went and what you did on vacation

Alemania *(f.)*   *Germany*
China *(f.)*   *China*
Egipto *(m.)*   *Egypt*
Francia *(f.)*   *France*
Inglaterra *(f.)*   *England*
Italia *(f.)*   *Italy*
ningún lugar   *nowhere, not anywhere*

VISUAL LEARNERS

Scramble the letters of vocabulary to be reviewed. (**rache mosritu** for **hacer turismo**) Make a list of scrambled words for vacation activities, distribute it to students, and have them try to unscramble the words.

CHAPTER 12 ASSESSMENT

▶ **Testing Program**
Chapter Test, pp. 115–122
🔊 Audio Compact Discs, CD 12, Trs. 19–20
Speaking Test, p. 132

▶ **Alternative Assessment Guide**
Performance Assessment, p. 24
Portfolio Assessment, p. 16
CD-ROM Assessment, p. 31

▶ **Interactive CD-ROM Tutor, Disc 3**
CD-ROM DISC 3   ¡A hablar!
¡A escribir!

▶ **Standardized Assessment Tutor**
Chapter 12

▶ **One-Stop Planner, Disc 3**
☀ Test Generator
✍ Chapter 12

▶ **Final Exam**
Testing Program, pp. 143–150
Audio CD 12, Trs. 21–23

SUMMARY OF FUNCTIONS

Functions are probably best defined as the ways in which you use a language for specific purposes. When you find yourself in specific situations, such as in a restaurant, in a grocery store, or at a school, you'll want to communicate with those around you. In order to do that, you have to "function" in Spanish: you place an order, buy something, or talk about your class schedule.

Such language functions form the core of this book. They are easily identified by the boxes in each chapter that are labeled **Así se dice.** The functional phrases in these boxes are the building blocks you need to become a speaker of Spanish. All the other features in the chapter—the grammar, the vocabulary, even the culture notes—are there to support the functions you're learning.

Here is a list of the functions presented in this book and the Spanish expressions you'll need in order to communicate in a wide range of situations. Following each function is the chapter and page number where it was introduced.

SOCIALIZING

Saying hello Ch. 1, p. 27

Buenos días.	Buenas noches.
Buenas tardes.	Hola.

Saying goodbye Ch. 1, p. 27

Adiós.	Hasta luego.
Bueno, tengo clase.	Hasta mañana.
	Tengo que irme.
Chao.	

Introducing people and responding to an introduction Ch. 1, p. 29

Me llamo...	Ésta es mi amiga...
Soy...	Se llama...
¿Cómo te llamas?	¡Mucho gusto!
Éste es mi amigo...	Encantado/a.
	Igualmente.

Asking how someone is and saying how you are Ch. 1, p. 31

¿Cómo estás?	Estupendo.
¿Y tú?	Excelente.
¿Qué tal?	Regular.
Estoy (bastante) bien, gracias.	Más o menos.
	(Muy) mal.
Yo también.	¡Horrible!

Talking on the telephone Ch. 7, p. 49

Aló.	La línea está ocupada.
Diga.	¿Puedo dejar un recado?
¿Quién habla?	
¿Está ..., por favor?	Un momento...
	Llamo más tarde.
¿De parte de quién?	

Extending and accepting invitations Ch. 7, p. 51

¿Te gustaría...?	¿Quieres...?
Sí, me gustaría...	Te invito.
Nos gustan...	¡Claro que sí!

Making plans Ch. 7, p. 59

¿Qué piensas hacer hoy?	Pienso...
	¿Piensas...?

Talking about getting ready Ch. 7, p. 63

¿Estás listo/a?	No, porque necesito...
No, todavía necesito...	

Turning down an invitation and explaining why Ch. 7, p. 67

¡Qué lástima!	Tengo que...
Ya tengo planes.	Me gustaría, pero no puedo.
Tal vez otro día.	
Lo siento, pero no.	Estoy cansado/a y un poco enfermo/a.
Estoy ocupado/a.	
Tengo una cita.	

EXCHANGING INFORMATION

Asking and saying how old someone is Ch. 1, p. 35

¿Cuántos años tienes?	¿Cuántos años tiene?
	Tiene ... años
Tengo ... años	

Asking where someone is from and saying where you're from Ch. 1, p. 38

¿De dónde eres?	¿De dónde es...?
Soy de...	Es de...

Talking about what you want and need Ch 2, p. 66

¿Qué quieres?	Necesito...
Quiero...	¿Qué necesita?
Quiere...	Ya tengo...
¿Qué necesitas?	Necesita...
¿Necesitas...?	

Saying what's in your room Ch. 2, p. 76

¿Qué hay en tu cuarto?	Hay ... en su cuarto.
	¿Tienes...?
Tengo ... en mi cuarto.	¿Qué tiene ... en su cuarto?
¿Qué hay en el cuarto de...?	Tiene ... en su cuarto.

Talking about what you need and want to do Ch. 2, p. 85

¿Qué necesitas hacer?	¿Qué quieres hacer?
Necesito...	Quiero hacer...
¿Qué necesita hacer...?	¿Qué quiere hacer...?
Necesita...	No sé, pero no quiero...
	Quiere...

Talking about classes and sequencing events Ch. 3, p. 110

¿Qué clases tienes este semestre?	Primero tengo..., después... y luego...
Tengo...	Por fin...
¿Qué clases tienes hoy?	¿Y mañana?

Telling time Ch. 3, p. 112

¿Qué hora es?	Son las...
Es la una.	Son las ... y cuarto.
Es la una y cuarto.	Son las ... y media.
	¿Ya son las...?
Es la una y media.	Es tarde.

Telling at what time something happens Ch. 3, p. 119

¿A qué hora es...?	¡Es ahora!
(Es) a las ... de la tarde.	En punto.

Talking about being late or in a hurry Ch. 3, p. 122

Estoy atrasado/a.	Tengo prisa.
Está atrasado/a.	¡Date prisa!

Describing people and things Ch. 3, p. 125

¿Cómo es...?	¿Cómo son...?
Es...	Son...
No es...	No son...

Talking about what you and others do during free time Ch. 4, p. 152

¿Qué haces después de clases?
Antes de regresar a casa...
En el tiempo libre...

Telling where people and things are Ch. 4, p. 161

¿Dónde estás?	No, no está aquí.
Estoy en...	Está en...
¿No está en...?	

Talking about where you and others go during free time Ch. 4, p. 171

¿Adónde vas?	Va a...
Voy a...	Va al...
¿Adónde va...?	Va a la...

Discussing how often you do things Ch. 5, p. 195

¿Con qué frecuencia...?	¿Todavía...?
	Durante la semana
Todos los días	A veces
Siempre	Muchas veces
Nunca	Sólo cuando...

Talking about what you do during a typical week Ch. 5, p. 209

¿Qué haces típicamente durante el día?
¿Qué hace ... por la mañana?
¿Qué hacen ... por la tarde?
¿Qué hacen ... por la noche?

Giving today's date Ch. 5, p. 213

¿Cuál es la fecha?
¿Qué fecha es hoy?
Hoy es el primero de...
Hoy es el ... de...

Talking about the weather Ch. 5, p. 216

¿Qué tiempo hace?
Hace buen tiempo.
Hace muy mal tiempo hoy.

Describing a family Ch. 6, p. 236

¿Cuántas personas hay en tu familia?	Somos...
	¿Cómo es tu familia?
Hay ... en mi familia.	Tenemos...

Describing people Ch. 6, p. 245

¿Cómo es...?	¿De qué color es...?
Tiene...	¿De qué color son...?

Discussing things a family does together Ch. 6, p. 248

¿Qué hacen ustedes los fines de semana?
¿Hacen ustedes algo durante el verano?

Talking about meals and food Ch. 8, p. 87

¿Qué tomas para
el desayuno?

¿Qué tomas para
el almuerzo?

A veces tomo...

No me gusta ... para
nada.

Tengo sed. ¿Qué hay
para tomar?

¿Qué prefieres?

Ordering dinner in a restaurant
Ch. 8, p. 108

¿Qué vas a pedir?

Voy a pedir...

¿Qué le puedo traer?

Yo quisiera...

**Asking for and paying the bill in a
restaurant** Ch. 8, p. 109

¿Nos puede traer
la cuenta?

La cuenta, por favor.

¿Desean algo más?

¿Cuánto es?

¿Está incluida la
propina?

No, no está incluida.

Es aparte.

Talking about giving gifts Ch. 9, p. 131

¿Qué piensas
regalarle a...?

Le voy a dar...

¿Para quién es
el regalo?

El regalo es para...

¿Qué tipo de regalo
buscas?

Busco...

Asking for and giving directions downtown
Ch. 9, p. 134

Perdón, ¿dónde está...?

Está a ... cuadras de aquí.

¿Me puede decir dónde queda...?

Queda al lado de...

Making comparisons Ch. 9, p. 144

¿Cuál es más barato?

El ... es menos caro que el...

¿Son los ... tan caros como el...?

Son del mismo precio.

**Asking about prices and paying for
something** Ch. 9, p. 150

¿Cuánto cuesta...?

Cuesta...

¿Cuánto cuestan...?

Cuestan...

Talking about what you're doing right now
Ch. 10, p. 171

¿Qué estás haciendo?

Estoy colgando las decoraciones.

Él está limpiando la sala.

¿Todos están decorando la casa?

Sí, estamos decorando la casa.

Talking about past events Ch. 10, p. 187

¿Qué hiciste
anoche?

Bailé y hablé con...

¿Qué hizo ... ayer?

¿Lo pasaron bien la
semana pasada?

Sí, lo pasamos bien.

Saying what you did Ch. 11, p. 229

¿Qué hiciste
anoche?

¿Ganaste?

Jugué...

Jugó...

Talking about where you went and when
Ch. 11, p. 231

¿Adónde fuiste anteayer?

¿Adónde fuiste anteanoche?

Anoche fui...

**Talking about what you do and like to do
every day** Ch. 12, p. 251

¿Qué haces todos
los días?

Primero...

Después...

Y luego...

¿Con qué frecuencia...?

¿Qué te gusta hacer
después de clases?

Me gusta...

Making future plans Ch. 12, p. 253

¿Adónde piensas viajar algún día?

¿Quieres viajar a...?

No, pero espero hacer un viaje a...

¿Qué vas a hacer este verano?

**Saying where you went and what you did
on vacation** Ch. 12, p. 269

¿Adónde viajaste el verano pasado?

No fui a ningún lugar.

¿Adónde fueron durante las vacaciones?

Fuimos a...

¿Qué hiciste cuando fuiste a...?

EXPRESSING ATTITUDES AND OPINIONS

Talking about what you like and don't like
Ch. 1, p. 43

¿Qué te gusta?

¿Te gusta...?

Me gusta (más)...

No me gusta...

**Talking about things you like and explaining
why** Ch. 3, p. 129

¿Te gustan...?

Sí, me gustan.

¿Cuál es...?

¿A ella le gustan...?

Sí, a ella le gustan
mucho.

¿Por qué?

Porque...

Talking about what you and others like to do Ch. 4, p. 149

¿Qué te gusta hacer?	¿A él le gusta...?
Me gusta...	¿A quién le gusta...?
No, no le gusta..., pero le gusta...	A mí me gusta...
	Por eso, me gustan...

Talking about what you and your friends like to do together Ch. 5, p. 203

¿Qué les gusta hacer?	Nos gusta...
	¿Les gusta ... juntos?

Discussing problems and giving advice Ch. 6, p. 255

Tengo un problema.	Debes ... menos.
¿Qué debo hacer?	Debes ... más.

Commenting on food Ch. 8, p. 97

¿Cómo está...?	¿Cómo están...?
Está...	Están...

Commenting on clothes Ch. 9, p. 139

¿Qué ropa vas a llevar?	¿No tienes algo más formal?
¡Lo de siempre!	Sí, pero prefiero llevar...

Expressing preferences Ch. 9, p. 149

¿Cuál de estos ... prefieres?
Prefiero el azul.
¿Qué camisa te gusta más? ¿La verde o la amarilla?
La verde. Además, te queda muy bien.

Asking for and giving an opinion Ch. 10, p. 174

¿Crees que...?	Me parece bien.
Creo que sí.	Perfecto.
¿Qué te parece si...?	Buena idea.

Talking about what you would like to do on vacation Ch. 12, p. 262

¿Qué te gustaría hacer este verano?
A mí me gustaría...
¿Adónde te gustaría ir este verano?
¿Qué tienes ganas de hacer?
Tengo ganas de...

Making suggestions and expressing feelings Ch. 11, p. 213

¿Qué tal si...?	No me siento bien.
Gracias, pero no quiero.	Estoy un poco cansado/a, nada más.
En realidad no tengo ganas.	Entonces, ¿por qué no...?
¿Qué tienes?	
¿Te sientes mal?	

Talking about moods and physical condition Ch. 11, p. 221

¿Cómo estás?	¿Qué le pasa a...?
Estoy...	Está preocupado/a por algo.
¿Cómo te sientes?	
Tengo gripe.	

PERSUADING

Making polite requests Ch. 8, p. 105

Camarero/a, ¿nos puede traer..., por favor?
¿Me puede traer..., por favor?

Asking for help and responding to requests Ch. 10, p. 179

¿Me haces el favor de...?	Un momentito.
Claro que sí.	Me pasas...
¿Me ayudas a...?	Lo siento, pero en este momento estoy ocupado/a.
Cómo no.	
¿Me traes...?	Perdóname, pero...
¡Con mucho gusto!	

Telling a friend what to do Ch. 10, p. 181

Prepara ... y limpia ..., ¿quieres?
De acuerdo.
Por favor, decora ... y llama...
Está bien.

The **Grammar and Vocabulary Workbook** re-presents all major grammar points and offers additional focused practice with the structures, words, and phrases targeted in each **Paso**.

GRAMMAR SUMMARY

NOUNS AND ARTICLES

GENDER OF NOUNS

In Spanish, nouns (words that name a person, place, or thing) are grouped into two classes or genders: masculine and feminine. All nouns, both persons and objects, fall into one of these groups. Most nouns that end in -**o** are masculine, and most nouns that end in -**a**, -**ción**, -**tad**, and -**dad** are feminine.

MASCULINE NOUNS	FEMININE NOUNS
libro	casa
chico	universidad
cuaderno	situación
bolígrafo	mesa
vestido	libertad

FORMATION OF PLURAL NOUNS

Add -**s** to nouns that end in a vowel.		Add -**es** to nouns that end in a consonant.		With nouns that end in -**z**, the -**z** changes to -**c**.	
SINGULAR	PLURAL	SINGULAR	PLURAL	SINGULAR	PLURAL
libro	libro**s**	profesor	profesor**es**	vez	ve**ces**
casa	casa**s**	papel	pape**les**	lápiz	lápi**ces**

DEFINITE ARTICLES

There are words that signal the class of the noun. One of these is the definite article. In English there is one definite article: *the.* In Spanish, there are four: **el, la, los, las.**

SUMMARY OF DEFINITE ARTICLES

	MASCULINE	FEMININE
Singular	**el** chico	**la** chica
Plural	**los** chicos	**las** chicas

CONTRACTIONS

a	+	el	→	**al**
de	+	el	→	**del**

INDEFINITE ARTICLES

Another group of words that are used with nouns is the *indefinite article:* **un, una,** *(a or an)* and **unos, unas** *(some or a few).*

SUMMARY OF INDEFINITE ARTICLES

	MASCULINE	FEMININE
Singular	**un** chico	**una** chica
Plural	**unos** chicos	**unas** chicas

PRONOUNS

SUBJECT PRONOUNS	DIRECT OBJECT PRONOUNS	INDIRECT OBJECT PRONOUNS	OBJECTS OF PREPOSITIONS
yo	me	me	mí (conmigo)
tú	te	te	ti (contigo)
él, ella, usted	lo, la	le	él, ella, usted
nosotros, nosotras	nos	nos	nosotros, nosotras
vosotros, vosotras	os	os	vosotros, vosotras
ellos, ellas, ustedes	los, las	les	ellos, ellas, ustedes

ADJECTIVES

Adjectives are words that describe nouns. The adjective must agree in gender (masculine or feminine) and number (singular or plural) with the noun it modifies. Adjectives that end in -**e** or a consonant only agree in number.

		MASCULINE	FEMININE
Adjectives that end in -**o**	Singular	chico alt**o**	chica alt**a**
	Plural	chicos alt**os**	chicas alt**as**
Adjectives that end in -**e**	Singular	chico inteligent**e**	chica inteligent**e**
	Plural	chicos inteligent**es**	chicas inteligent**es**
Adjectives that end in a consonant	Singular	examen difícil	clase difícil
	Plural	exámenes difícil**es**	clases difícil**es**

DEMONSTRATIVE ADJECTIVES

	MASCULINE	FEMININE
Singular	**este** chico	**esta** chica
Plural	**estos** chicos	**estas** chicas

	MASCULINE	FEMININE
Singular	**ese** chico	**esa** chica
Plural	**esos** chicos	**esas** chicas

When demonstratives are used as pronouns, they match the gender and number of the noun they replace and are written with an accent mark.

POSSESSIVE ADJECTIVES

These words also modify nouns and tell you *whose* object or person is being referred to (*my* car, *his* book, *her* mother).

SINGULAR		PLURAL	
MASCULINE	FEMININE	MASCULINE	FEMININE
mi libro	**mi** casa	**mis** libros	**mis** casas
tu libro	**tu** casa	**tus** libros	**tus** casas
su libro	**su** casa	**sus** libros	**sus** casas
nuestro libro	**nuestra** casa	**nuestros** libros	**nuestras** casas
vuestro libro	**vuestra** casa	**vuestros** libros	**vuestras** casas

AFFIRMATIVE AND NEGATIVE EXPRESSIONS

AFFIRMATIVE	NEGATIVE
algo	nada
alguien	nadie
alguno (algún), -a	ninguno (ningún), -a
o ... o	ni ... ni
siempre	nunca

INTERROGATIVE WORDS

¿Adónde?	¿Cuánto(a)?	¿Por qué?
¿Cómo?	¿Cuántos(as)?	¿Qué?
¿Cuál(es)?	¿De dónde?	¿Quién(es)?
¿Cuándo?	¿Dónde?	

COMPARATIVES

Comparatives are used to compare people or things. With comparisons of inequality, the same structure is used with adjectives, adverbs or nouns. With comparisons of equality, **tan** is used with adjectives and adverbs, and **tanto/a/os/as** with nouns.

COMPARATIVE OF INEQUALITY

más	+	adjective adverb noun	**más**	+ **de** + number
menos			**menos**	

COMPARATIVE OF EQUALITY

tan + adjective or adverb + **como**
tanto/a/os/as + noun + **como**

VERBS

REGULAR VERBS

In Spanish we use a formula to conjugate regular verbs. The endings change for each person, but the stem of the verb remains the same.

PRESENT TENSE OF REGULAR VERBS

INFINITIVE	PRESENT			
hablar	(yo) hablo		(nosotros/as)	hablamos
	(tú) hablas		(vosotros/as)	habláis
	(él/ella/usted) habla		(ellos/ellas/ustedes)	hablan
comer	(yo) como		(nosotros/as)	comemos
	(tú) comes		(vosotros/as)	coméis
	(él/ella/usted) come		(ellos/ellas/ustedes)	comen
escribir	(yo) escribo		(nosotros/as)	escribimos
	(tú) escribes		(vosotros/as)	escribís
	(él/ella/usted) escribe		(ellos/ellas/ustedes)	escriben

VERBS WITH IRREGULAR YO FORMS

hacer		poner		saber		salir		traer	
hago	hacemos	**pongo**	ponemos	**sé**	sabemos	**salgo**	salimos	**traigo**	traemos
haces	hacéis	pones	ponéis	sabes	sabéis	sales	salís	traes	traéis
hace	hacen	pone	ponen	sabe	saben	sale	salen	trae	traen

VERBS WITH IRREGULAR FORMS

ser		estar		ir	
soy	somos	estoy	estamos	voy	vamos
eres	sois	estás	estáis	vas	vais
es	son	está	están	va	van

PRESENT PROGRESSIVE

The present progressive in English is formed by using the verb *to be* plus the *-ing* form of another verb. In Spanish, the present progressive is formed by using the verb **estar** plus the -**ndo** form of another verb.

-**ar** verbs	-**er** and -**ir** verbs	For -**er** and -**ir** verbs with a stem that ends in a vowel, the -**iendo** changes to -**yendo**:
hablar → estoy habl**ando** trabajar → trabaj**ando**	comer → com**iendo** escribir → escrib**iendo**	leer → le**yendo**

STEM-CHANGING VERBS

In Spanish, some verbs have an irregular stem in the present tense. The final vowel of the stem changes from **e** → **ie** and **o** → **ue** in all forms except **nosotros** and **vosotros.**

e → ie		o → ue		u → ue	
preferir		**poder**		**jugar**	
pref**ie**ro	preferimos	p**ue**do	podemos	j**ue**go	jugamos
pref**ie**res	preferís	p**ue**des	podéis	j**ue**gas	jugáis
pref**ie**re	pref**ie**ren	p**ue**de	p**ue**den	j**ue**ga	j**ue**gan

The following is a list of some **e** → **ie** stem-changing verbs:	The following is a list of some **o** → **ue** stem-changing verbs:
empezar **pensar** **querer** **preferir**	**almorzar** **doler** **encontrar** **poder**

THE VERBS GUSTAR AND ENCANTAR

To express likes and dislikes, the verb **gustar** is used in Spanish. The verb **encantar** is used to talk about things you really like or love. The verb endings for **gustar** and **encantar** always agree with what is liked or loved. The indirect object pronouns always precede the verb forms.

gustar		encantar	
If one thing is liked:	If more than one thing is liked:	If one thing is really liked:	If more than one thing is really liked:
me te le nos les } gusta	me te le nos les } gustan	me te le nos les } encanta	me te le nos les } encantan

PRETERITE OF REGULAR VERBS

INFINITIVE	PRETERITE OF REGULAR VERBS			
hablar	(yo) hablé	hablaste (tú)	(nosotros/as) hablamos	(vosotros/as) hablasteis
	(él/ella) habló		(ellos/ellas) hablaron	
comer	(yo) comí	(tú) comiste	(nosotros/as) comimos	(vosotros/as) comisteis
	(él/ella) comió		(ellos/ellas) comieron	
escribir	(yo) escribí	(tú) escribiste	(nosotros/as) escribimos	(vosotros/as) escribisteis
	(él/ella) escribió		(ellos/ellas) escribieron	

PRETERITE OF HACER, IR, SER, AND VER

hacer	ir	ser	ver
hice	fui	fui	vi
hiciste	fuiste	fuiste	viste
hizo	fue	fue	vio
hicimos	fuimos	fuimos	vimos
hicisteis	fuisteis	fuisteis	visteis
hicieron	fueron	fueron	vieron

REVIEW VOCABULARY

This list includes vocabulary that you may use for activities in the review chapter ¡**En camino!** and to help you recall words that you learned in **Adelante.** If you can't find a word here, try the Spanish-English vocabulary and English-Spanish vocabulary sections beginning on page 297.

ACTIVIDADES *(ACTIVITES)*

acampar *to go camping*
asistir a una clase de ejercicios
  aeróbicos *to attend an aerobics class*
ayudar en casa *to help at home*
beber *to drink*
bucear *to scuba dive*
comer *to eat*
comprar ropa *to buy clothes*
correr *to run*
cuidar a tu hermano/a *to take care of*
  your brother/sister
desayuno *breakfast*
descansar en el parque
  to rest in the park
esquiar *to ski*
escribir tarjetas postales
  to write postcards

escuchar música
  to listen to music
hacer ejercicio *to exercise*
lavar el carro *to wash the car*
lavar la ropa *to wash the clothes*
leer las tiras cómicas en el periódico
  to read the comic strips in the newspaper
mirar la televisión *to watch TV*
nadar *to swim*
pescar *to fish*
recibir cartas *to receive letters*
sacar la basura *to take out the trash*
ver la película *watch a movie*

LAS COSAS QUE TIENES EN TU CUARTO *(THINGS IN YOUR ROOM)*

el armario *closet*
la cama *bed*
el cartel *poster*
el cuarto *room*
el escritorio *desk*
la lámpara *lamp*
la mesa *table*
la puerta *door*
la radio *radio*
el reloj *clock*

la revista *magazine*
la ropa *clothes*
la silla *chair*
el televisor *TV set*
la ventana *window*
los zapatos de tenis *tennis shoes*

DESCRIBIENDO *(DESCRIBING)*

aburrido/a *boring*
alto/a *tall*
antipático/a *unpleasant*
atractivo/a *attractive*
bajo/a *short*
bonito/a *pretty*
bueno/a *good*
cariñoso/a *loving, affectionate*
cómico/a *comical, funny*
difícil *difficult*
divertido/a *fun, amusing*
estricto/a *strict*
fácil *easy*
feo/a *ugly*
gordo/a *fat*
grande *big*
guapo/a *good-looking*
inteligente *intelligent*
interesante *interesting*
listo/a *clever*
malo/a *bad*
mayor *older*
menor *younger*
moreno/a *dark-haired, dark-skinned*
nuevo/a *new*
pelirrojo/a *red-headed*
pequeño/a *small*
rubio/a *blond*
simpático/a *nice*
travieso/a *mischievous*
viejo/a *old*

LA FAMILIA *(FAMILY)*

la abuela *grandmother*
el abuelo *grandfather*
los abuelos *grandparents*

la **esposa**   *wife*
el **esposo**   *husband*
la **gata**   *cat* (f.)
el **gato**   *cat* (m.)
la **hermanastra**   *stepsister*
el **hermanastro**   *stepbrother*
los **hermanos**
        brothers and sisters
la **hija**   *daughter*
el **hijo**   *son*
los **hijos**   *children*
la **madrastra**   *stepmother*
la **madre**   *mother*
la **media hermana**   *half sister*
el **medio hermano**   *half brother*
el **padrastro**   *stepfather*
el **padre**   *father*
la **perra**   *dog* (f.)
el **perro**   *dog* (m.)
la **tía**   *aunt*
el **tío**   *uncle*

LA COMIDA   *(FOOD)*

el **agua**   *water*
el **chocolate**   *chocolate*
la **comida mexicana/italiana/china**
        Mexican/Italian/Chinese food
la **fruta**   *fruit*
la **hamburguesa**   *hamburger*
el **jugo**   *juice*
las **papas fritas**   *french fries*
la **pizza**   *pizza*
el **sándwich**   *sandwich*

NÚMEROS 0–199   *(NUMBERS 0–199)*

cero   *zero*
uno   *one*
dos   *two*
tres   *three*
cuatro   *four*
cinco   *five*
seis   *six*
siete   *seven*
ocho   *eight*
nueve   *nine*
diez   *ten*
once   *eleven*
doce   *twelve*
trece   *thirteen*
catorce   *fourteen*
quince   *fifteen*

dieciséis   *sixteen*
diecisiete   *seventeen*
dieciocho   *eighteen*
diecinueve   *nineteen*
veinte   *twenty*
veintiuno   *twenty-one*
veintidós   *twenty-two*
veintitrés   *twenty-three*
veinticuatro   *twenty-four*
veinticinco   *twenty-five*
veintiséis   *twenty-six*
veintisiete   *twenty-seven*
veintiocho   *twenty-eight*
veintinueve   *twenty-nine*
treinta   *thirty*
treinta y uno   *thirty-one*
treinta y dos   *thirty-two*
...
cuarenta   *forty*
cincuenta   *fifty*
sesenta   *sixty*
setenta   *seventy*
ochenta   *eighty*
noventa   *ninety*
cien   *one hundred*
ciento uno   *one hundred and one*
ciento dos   *one hundred and two*
ciento dieciséis   *one hundred and sixteen*
ciento veintiocho   *one hundred and twenty-eight*
ciento treinta y cinco   *one hundred and thirty-five*
ciento cuarenta y tres   *one hundred and forty-three*
ciento cincuenta   *one hundred and fifty*
ciento sesenta y ocho   *one hundred and sixty-eight*
ciento setenta y siete   *one hundred and seventy-seven*
ciento ochenta y cuatro   *one hundred and eighty-four*
ciento noventa y nueve   *one hundred and ninety-nine*

LAS MATERIAS   *(SCHOOL SUBJECTS)*

el **almuerzo**   *lunch*
el **arte**   *art*
las **ciencias**   *science*
las **ciencias sociales**
        social studies

la **computación** *computer class*
el **descanso** *recess, break*
la **educación física** *physical education, gym class*
el **francés** *French class*
la **geografía** *geography class*
el **inglés** *English*
las **matemáticas** *mathematics*

COSAS PARA EL COLEGIO
(SCHOOL SUPPLIES)

el **bolígrafo** *ballpoint pen*
la **calculadora** *calculator*
la **carpeta** *folder*
el **cuaderno** *notebook*
el **diccionario** *dictionary*
la **goma de borrar** *eraser*
el **lápiz** *pencil*
el **libro** *book*
la **mochila** *bookbag, backpack*
el **papel** *paper*
la **regla** *ruler*

LAS ESTACIONES *(SEASONS)*

el **invierno** *winter*
el **otoño** *fall*
la **primavera** *spring*
el **verano** *summer*

EL TIEMPO *(WEATHER)*

Está lloviendo. / Llueve. *It's raining.*
Está nevando. / Nieva. *It's snowing.*
Está nublado. *It's cloudy.*
Hace (mucho) calor. *It's (very) hot.*
Hace fresco. *It's cool.*
Hace (mucho) frío. *It's (very) cold.*
Hace sol. *It's sunny.*
Hace (mucho) viento. *It's (very) windy.*
el **pronóstico del tiempo** *weather report*

¿DÓNDE ESTÁ? *(WHERE IS IT?)*

al lado de *next to*
allá *there*
aquí *here*
cerca de *near*
debajo de *under, beneath*
encima de *on top of*
lejos de *far from*

ADDITIONAL VOCABULARY

This list includes additional vocabulary that you may want to use to personalize activities. If you can't find a word you need here, try the Spanish-English and English-Spanish vocabulary sections beginning on page 297.

ANIMALES

las aves *birds*
el caballo *horse*
el canario *canary*
el canguro *kangaroo*
la cebra *zebra*
el cocodrilo *crocodile*
el conejillo de Indias *hamster*
el conejo *rabbit*
la culebra *snake*
el delfín *dolphin*
el elefante *elephant*
la foca *seal*
el gorila *gorilla*
el hipopótamo *hippopotamus*
la jirafa *giraffe*
la lagartija *lizard*
el león *lion*
la mascota *pet*
el mono *monkey*
el oso *bear*
el oso blanco *polar bear*
el pájaro *bird*
el pez de colores *goldfish*
el pingüino *penguin*
el ratón *mouse*
la serpiente *snake*
el tigre *tiger*

COMIDA *(FOOD)*

el aguacate *avocado*
las arvejas *peas*
el bróculi *broccoli*
la carne asada *roast beef*
la cereza *cherry*
la chuleta de cerdo *pork chop*
el champiñón *mushroom*
la coliflor *cauliflower*
los espaguetis *spaghetti*
las espinacas *spinach*
los fideos *noodles*
el filete de pescado *fish fillet*
los macarrones con queso *macaroni and cheese*

los mariscos *shellfish*
la mayonesa *mayonnaise*
el melón *cantaloupe*
la mostaza *mustard*
la pasta *spaghetti / pasta*
el pavo *turkey*
la pimienta *pepper*
el puré de papas *mashed potatoes*
la sal *salt*
la salsa *sauce*
el tomate *tomato*
el yogur *yogurt*

COMPRAS *(SHOPPING)*

el abrigo *coat*
el álbum *album*
la billetera *wallet*
la bolsa *purse*
con botones *with buttons*
con cierre *with a zipper*
de moda *in fashion*
el estéreo *stereo*
la gorra *cap*
los guantes *gloves*
hace juego con... *it matches with . . .*
el impermeable *raincoat*
las llaves *keys*
las medias *stockings*
no hace juego con... *it doesn't match with . . .*
el oro *gold*
un par *a pair*
el paraguas *umbrella*
la plata *silver*
el regalo *present, gift*
el sombrero *hat*

CUIDO PERSONAL

bañarse *to bathe*
el cepillo *brush*
el cepillo de dientes *toothbrush*
el jabón *soap*
el maquillaje *makeup*
la navaja de afeitar *razor*

la pasta de dientes *toothpaste*
el peine *comb*
vestirse *to get dressed*

DEPORTES

las artes marciales *martial arts*
el atletismo *track and field*
el boxeo *boxing*
el ciclismo *cycling*
la gimnasia *gymnastics*
la lucha libre *wrestling*
patinar sobre hielo *ice skating*

DIRECCIONES (GIVING DIRECTIONS)

a la derecha de *to the right of*
a la izquierda de *to the left of*
en frente de *in front of*
Dobla a la derecha. *Turn right.*
Sigue derecho. *Go straight.*

EN LA CASA

la alcoba *(bed)room*
la alfombra *rug, carpet*
el balcón *balcony*
las cortinas *curtains*
el cuarto de baño *bathroom*
el despertador *alarm clock*
el disco compacto *compact disc*
las escaleras *stairs*
el espejo *mirror*
el estante *bookshelf*
el garaje *garage*
la lavadora *washing machine*
los muebles *furniture*
el patio *patio*
la pecera *fishbowl*
la planta *plant*
el refrigerador *refrigerator*
la secadora *(clothes) dryer*
el sillón *easy chair*
el sofá *couch*
el sótano *basement*
el timbre *doorbell*

EN LA CIUDAD (IN THE CITY)

el aeropuerto *airport*
la alcaldía *town hall, mayor's office*
la aldea *small village*
la autopista *highway*
la avenida *avenue*

la calle *street*
el banco *bank*
la barbería *barber shop*
la corte *court (of law)*
el cuartel *police station*
la esquina *corner*
la fábrica *factory*
la farmacia *pharmacy*
el hospital *hospital*
la iglesia *church*
la mezquita *mosque*
la oficina *office*
el palacio municipal
    *town hall, mayor's
    office* (Mexico)
la parada de autobuses *bus stop*
el pueblo *town*
el puente *bridge*
el rascacielos *skyscraper*
el salón de belleza *beauty salon*
el semáforo *traffic light*
el templo *temple*

MÚSICA

el acordeón *accordion*
el bajo *bass*
la batería *drum set*
el clarinete *clarinet*
la flauta *flute*
la guitarra eléctrica *electric guitar*
el oboe *oboe*
el saxofón *saxophone*
el sintetizador *synthesizer*
el tambor *drum*
el trombón *trombone*
la trompeta *trumpet*
la tuba *tuba*
la viola *viola*
el violín *violin*

NÚMEROS ORDINALES

primero/a *first*
segundo/a *second*
tercero/a *third*
cuarto/a *fourth*
quinto/a *fifth*
sexto/a *sixth*
séptimo/a *seventh*
octavo/a *eighth*
noveno/a *ninth*
décimo/a *tenth*

PASATIEMPOS *(PASTIMES)*

el anuario   *yearbook*
la banda   *band*
la canción   *song*
coleccionar... *to collect . . .*
el coro   *choir*
coser   *to sew*
el cuento de aventuras   *adventure story*
el debate   *debate*
el drama   *drama*
la fotografía   *photography*
jugar a las cartas
      to play cards
jugar a las damas
      to play checkers
jugar al ajedrez
      to play chess
la orquesta   *orchestra*
el poema   *poem*
el taller   *shop*

PROFESIONES

la abogada, el abogado   *lawyer*
la agricultora, el agricultor   *farmer*
la arquitecta, el arquitecto   *architect*
la bombera, el bombero   *firefighter*
la carpintera, el carpintero   *carpenter*
la cartera, el cartero   *mail carrier*
la doctora, el doctor   *doctor*
la enfermera, el enfermero   *nurse*
el hombre de negocios   *businessman*
la ingeniera, el ingeniero   *engineer*
la mujer de negocios   *businesswoman*

la plomera, el plomero   *plumber*
el policía   *police officer*
la policía   *police officer* (fem.)
la secretaria, el secretario   *secretary*
la trabajadora, el trabajador   *worker*

LA SALUD Y LAS EMOCIONES

contento/a   *happy*
de buen/ mal humor   *in a good/bad mood*
feliz   *happy*
Me corté el/la...   *I cut my . . .*
Me lastimé.   *I hurt myself.*
Me rompí el/la...   *I broke my . . .*
Me siento...   *I feel . . .*
      estupendo.   *great.*
      de maravilla.   *wonderful.*
      pésimo.   *awful.*
      mejor.   *better.*
      peor.   *worse.*
tener frío   *to be cold*
tener calor   *to be hot*
tener vergüenza   *to be embarrassed*

TRANSPORTACIÓN

el autobús   *bus*
el avión   *airplane*
el barco   *boat*
la bicicleta, la bici   *bicycle, bike*
la canoa   *canoe*
el coche, el carro   *car*
el metro   *subway*
la moto   *moped, motorcycle*

SPANISH-ENGLISH VOCABULARY

This vocabulary includes almost all words in the textbook, both active (for production) and passive (for recognition only). Active words and phrases are practiced in the chapter and are listed on the **Vocabulario** page at the end of each chapter. You are expected to know and be able to use active vocabulary. An entry in **boldface** type indicates that the word or phrase is active.

All other words are for recognition only. You will not be tested on these words unless your teacher chooses to add them to the active list. These are found in **De antemano**, in the **Pasos**, in realia (authentic Spanish-language documents), in **Enlaces, Panorama cultural, Encuentro cultural, Vamos a leer,** and in the **Location Openers** (travelogue sections). Many words have more than one definition; the definitions given here correspond to the way the words are used in the book. Other meanings can be looked up in a dictionary.

Nouns are listed with definite article and plural form, when applicable. The numbers after each entry refer to the chapter where the word or phrase first appears or where it becomes an active vocabulary word. Vocabulary from the preliminary chapter is followed by the letters "PREL." Vocabulary from the bridge chapter is followed by the word "PUENTE."

Although the **Real Academia** has deleted the letters **ch** and **ll** from the alphabet, many dictionaries still have separate entries for these letters. This end-of-book vocabulary follows the new rules, with **ch** and **ll** in the same sequence as in English.

Stem changes are indicated in parentheses after the verb: **poder (ue).**

a *to,* 4; *at,* 3
a comenzar *let's begin,* 1
a dos cuadras de aquí *two blocks from here,* 9
a ellas *to them,* 5
a ellos *to them,* 5
a menudo *often,* 5
A mí me gusta + infinitive *I* (emphatic) *like (to) . . . ,* 4
¿A qué hora...? *At what time. . .?,* PUENTE
¿A qué hora es...? *At what time is . . .?,* 3
¿A quién le gusta...? *Who likes (to) . . .?,* 4
¿A ti qué te gusta hacer? *What do you* (emphatic) *like to do?,* 4
a todo color *in full color,* 2
a ustedes *to you,* 5
a veces *sometimes,* 5, PUENTE
a ver si puedo *let's see if I can,* 1
el abrazo *hug,* 1
el abrigo *coat,* 9
abril (m.) *April,* 5
abrir *to open;* **abrir los regalos** *to open the gifts,* 10
la abuela *grandmother,* 6

el abuelo *grandfather,* 6
los abuelos *grandparents,* 6
abundar *to abound,* 6
aburrido/a *boring,* 3; **No es aburrido/a.** *It's not boring.,* 3
acabemos *let's finish,* 5
acampar *to camp,* 5
el acceso *access,* 4
el aceite *oil,* 7
la aceituna *olive,* 8
el acento *accent mark,* PREL
acercarse *to approach,* 7
acompañar *to accompany,* 4
acordarse *to remember,* 10
acostado/a *lying down,* 11
la actitud *attitude,* 3
la actividad *activity,* 4
el actor *actor* (male); mi actor favorito es *my favorite actor is,* PREL
la actriz *actress;* mi actriz favorita es *my favorite actress is,* PREL
el acuario *aquarium,* 7
acuático/a *aquatic, water* (adj.)
el acuerdo *agreement,* 11
adelante *let's get started,* PREL
además *besides,* 9
adiós *goodbye,* 1, PUENTE
adivinar *to guess,* 6;

¡Adivina, adivinador! *Guess!,* 6
¿adónde? *where (to)?,* 4; **¿Adónde vas?** Where are you going?, 4
adoptivo/a *adopted,* PUENTE
aeróbico *aerobic,* 5; **una clase de ejercicios aeróbicos** *aerobics class,* 5
afeitarse *to shave,* 7
afuera *outside,* 12
agitar *to agitate, to stir up,* 3
agosto (m.) *August,* 5
agotar *to use up; to exhaust,* 3
agresivo/a *aggressive,* 6
la agricultura *agriculture,* 3
el agua (f.) *water,* 5; **el agua mineral** *mineral water,* 8
el águila *eagle,* PREL
la ahijada *godchild,* 6
el ahijado *godchild,* 6
ahora *now,* 1
el ajedrez *chess,* 5
el ají *chile pepper,* 3
al (a + el) *to the,* 4; al contrario *on the contrary,* 3; al grano *to the point,* 1; **al lado de** *next to, to one side of, beside,* 4; el cafetín de al lado *the coffee shop around the corner,* 6
la alberca *swimming pool,* 4
el álbum *album,* 6

alcanzar *to reach*, 7
alegre *happy*, 6
Alemania (f.) *Germany*, 12
el alfabeto *alphabet*, PREL
algo *something*, 6, PUENTE
el **algodón** *cotton*; **de algodón**
   (made of) cotton, 9
algún día *someday*, 12
alguno/a (masc. sing. algún)
   some, any; alguna parte
   someplace; alguna vez
   sometime, 6
alimentar *to feed*, PUENTE
allá *there*, 4
allí *there*, 4
el almacén *department store*, 9
el almendro *almond tree*, 12
el almíbar *syrup*, 8
almorzar (ue) *to eat lunch*, 8
el **almuerzo** *lunch*, 8
   Aló *Hello*, 7
alquilar *to rent*, 5
alrededor de *around*, 6
alta mar: en alta mar *on the
   high seas, deep water*, 6
alto/a *tall*, 3
la altura *height*, 7
la alumna *student (female)*, 3
el alumno *student (male)*, 3
   amarillo/a *yellow*, 9
el ambiente *environment*, 12;
   el medio ambiente
   environment, 9
ameno/a *pleasing*, 9
americano/a *American*, 1
la **amiga** *friend (female)*, 1, 4;
   Ésta es mi amiga. *This is
   my (female) friend.*, 1
el **amigo** *friend (male)*, 1, 4;
   amigo/a por correspondencia
   pen pal, PREL; **Éste es mi
   amigo.** *This is my (male)
   friend.*, 1; **nuevos amigos**
   new friends, 2; **pasar el rato
   con amigos** *to spend time
   with friends*, 4
la amistad *friendship*, 1
amplio/a *large*, 4
añadir *to add*, 8
   anaranjado/a *orange*, 9
   ¡Ándale! *Hurry up!*, 3
los anfibios *amphibians*, 2
el ángulo *angle*, 3
el animal *animal*, 2
el **Año Nuevo** *New Year's
   Day*, 10
el **año pasado** *last year*, 10
el **año** *year*, 5; ¿Cuántos
   años tiene? *How old is
   (he/she)?*, 1; ¿Cuántos

años tienes? *How old are
   you?*, 1, PUENTE; **Tengo ...
   años.** *I'm . . . years old.*,
   1; **Tiene ... años.** *He/She
   is . . . years old.*, 1
anoche *last night*, 10
anteanoche *the night before
   last*, 11
anteayer *day before yesterday*, 10
el antebrazo *forearm*, 11
antes de *before*, 4, PUENTE
antipático/a *disagreeable*, 3
el anuncio *advertisement*, 9
el apartado postal *post office
   box*, 4
el apellido *last name*, 1
apenas *hardly*, PUENTE
apetecer *to appeal, to
   appetize*, 7
los aportes *contributions*, 10
aproximadamente *approxi-
   mately*, 7
aquí *here*, 4
el árbol *tree*, 4; el árbol
   genealógico *family tree*, 6
la arboleda *grove (of trees)*, 4
el arco *bow*; Andean stringed
   musical instrument, 4
el área *area*, 7
el arete *earring*, 9
el armario *closet*, 2
la arquitecta *architect*, 3
el arquitecto *architect*, 3
arreglar *to arrange, to pick
   up (one's room)*, 6
el arroz *rice*, 8
el arte *art*, 3 (pl. las artes)
las artesanías *hand-made
   crafts*, 9
artístico/a *artistic*, 6
las arvejas *peas*, 1
asado/a *roasted*, 6
así *in this way, so, thus*, 6;
   así se dice *here's how you
   say it*, 1
el asiento *seat*, 7
la asistencia *attendance*, 3
asistir a *to attend*, 5
la **aspiradora** *vacuum cleaner*;
   pasar la aspiradora *to
   vacuum*, 6
asqueroso/a *disgusting*, 8
atlético/a *athletic*, 6
el atletismo *track and field*, 4
atractivo/a *attractive*, 2
atrasado/a *late*; **Está
   atrasado/a.** *He/She is
   late.*, 3; **Estoy atrasado/a.
   I'm late., 3

el atún *tuna*, 8
el auditorio *auditorium*, 4
aunque *although*, 12
el **autobús** *bus*, 5; **tomar el
   autobús** *to take the bus*, 5
la avenida *avenue*, 4
las aventuras *adventures*, 1
las aves *birds*, 2
el avión *airplane* (pl. los
   aviones), 4
ayer *yesterday*, 10
ayudar *to help*; **ayudar en
   casa** *to help at home*, 5
el **azúcar** *sugar*, 8
   azul *blue*, 6

bailar *to dance*, 4
el **baile** *dance*, 3
   bajar *to go down*; **bajar
   el río en canoa** *to go
   canoeing*, 12
   bajo/a *short*, 3; *under*, 4
el balneario *beach resort*, 12
el **baloncesto** *basketball*, 1
   bañarse *to take a bath*, 5
la banca *bench*, 11
el banco *bank*, 2
los banquetes *banquets*, 4
las barajas *card games; decks
   of cards*, 3
   barato/a *cheap*, 9
la barbacoa *barbecue*, 6
la barbilla *chin*, 11
el barco *boat, ship*, 5
el basquetbol *basketball*, 1
   bastante *quite; pretty* (adv.),
   1; **Estoy (bastante) bien,
   gracias.** *I'm (pretty) well,
   thanks.*, 1
la **basura** *garbage, trash*;
   sacar la basura *to take
   out the trash*, 4
el **batido** *milkshake*, 8
   batir *to beat*, 8
el bautizo *baptism*, 1
   beber *to drink*, 5
la **bebida** *beverage*, 8
el **béisbol** *baseball*, 1
las bellas artes *fine arts*, 9
la bendición *blessing*, 7
el beso *kiss*, 2
la **biblioteca** *library*, 4, PUENTE
la bici *bike*, 7
la **bicicleta** *bicycle*; **montar en
   bicicleta** *to ride a bike*, 4;
   pasear en bicicleta *to ride a
   bicycle*, 3

bien *good; well,* 1; Está
bien. *All right.,* 2;
**Estoy (bastante) bien,
gracias.** *I'm (pretty) well,
thanks.,* 1
bienvenido/a *welcome,* PREL
la biología *biology,* 3
el bistec *steak,* 8
blanco/a *white,* 9
el bloqueador *sunscreen,* 12
los bluejeans *bluejeans,* 9
la blusa *blouse,* 9
la boca *mouth,* 11
la boda *wedding,* 7
el boleto *ticket,* 12
el bolígrafo *ballpoint pen,* 2
el bolívar *unit of currency in
Venezuela,* 2
la bolsa *purse,* 9
bonito/a *pretty,* 3
borrar *to erase;* **goma de
borrar** *eraser,* 2
el bosque *forest,* 12
botar *to throw (out),* 4
las botas *boots,* 9
el boxeo *boxing,* 4
el brazo *arm,* 11
Bs. *abbreviation for bolí-
vares, unit of Venezuelan
currency,* 2
bucear *to scuba dive,* 5
Buena idea. *Good idea.,* 10
Bueno... *Well . . .,* 1;
Bueno, tengo clase. *Well,
I have class (now).,* 1
bueno/a *good,* 3; **Buenos
días.** *Good morning.,* 1,
PUENTE; **Buenas noches.**
Good night., 1; **Buenas
tardes.** *Good afternoon.,* 1
la bufanda *scarf,* 12
el burro *donkey,* PREL
buscar *to look for,* 5; busco
I'm looking for, PREL
buscar *to look for,* 9
el buzón *mail box,* 10

C

el caballo *horse,* 6
el cabello *hair,* 7
la cabeza *head,* 11
el cachorro *cub,* PUENTE
cada *each,* 2
el café *coffee;* **de color café**
brown, 6
el cafecito *little cup of coffee,* 5
la cafetería *cafeteria,* 1
el cafetín *coffee shop,* 6

el caimán *alligator* (pl. los
caimanes), 5
la caja *box,* 3
el calamar *squid,* 8
los calcetines *socks,* 9
la calculadora *calculator,* 2; la
calculadora gráfica *graph-
ing calculator,* 2
el calendario *calendar,* PREL
caliente *hot,* 8
la calificación *grade,* 3
la calle *street,* 12
el calor *heat;* **Hace calor.** *It's
hot.,* 5; Hace un calor espan-
toso. *It's terribly hot.,* 5
la cama *bed,* 2; **hacer la cama**
to make the bed, 6, PUENTE
la cámara *camera,* 12
la camarera *waitress,* 8
el camarero *waiter,* 8
los camarones *shrimp,* 8
el cambio *change,* 4
caminar *to walk;* **caminar
con el perro** *to walk the
dog,* 4
el camino *way;* en camino
on the way, 8
la camisa *shirt,* 9
la camiseta *T-shirt,* 9
el campamento de verano
summer camp, 12
la campana *bell,* 3
el campeón *champion* (f. la
campeona), 4
el campo *country,* 7
el canario *canary,* 7
las canas *gray hair,* 6; **Tiene
canas.** *He/She has gray
hair.,* 6
la cancha de fútbol *soccer
field,* 11
la cancha de tenis *tennis
court,* 11
cansado/a *tired,* 7
cantar *to sing,* 4
el cántaro *pitcher;* llover a cántaros *to rain cats and
dogs,* 5
la capital *capital city,* 3
el capítulo *chapter,* 1
la cara *face,* 6
el Caribe *Caribbean Sea,* 1
el cariño *affection,* 2
cariñoso/a *affectionate,* 6
la carne colorada *red meat, an
Andean dish,* 8
la carne *meat,* 8; la carne
asada *roast beef,* 1; **la
carne de res** *beef,* 8
caro/a *expensive,* 9

la carpeta *folder,* 2
la carrera *run; career,* 11
el carro *car,* 7; **lavar el carro**
to wash the car, 4
la carta *letter,* 5; la carta de
amor *love letter,* 5
el cartel *poster,* 2
la cartera *wallet,* 9
la casa *house, home,* 4,
PUENTE
la cascada *waterfall,* 12
casero/a *home-made,* 4
casi *almost,* 6; **casi siempre**
almost always, 6
la casilla *post office box,* 4
caso: en caso de *in case of,* 1
castaño/a *brown, chestnut-
colored,* 6
las castañuelas *castanets,* PREL
el castellano *Spanish language,* 2
el castillo *castle,* 1
la cátedra bolivariana *teachings
about Bolívar,* 3
la categoría *category,* 1; categoría liviano *lightweight*
(adj.), 4; categoría mediano
middleweight (adj.), 4
catorce *fourteen,* 1
cazar *to hunt,* PUENTE
el cazón *dogfish,* 8
la cebolla *onion,* 8
celebrar *to celebrate,* 10
la cena *dinner,* 4; **preparar la
cena** *to prepare dinner,* 4
cenar *to eat dinner,* 6
el centro *downtown,* 4
Centroamérica *Central
America,* 1
el centro comercial *shopping
mall,* 2
el cepillo *brush;* el cepillo de
dientes *toothbrush,* 7
cerca de *near,* 4
el cerdo *pig,* 2
el cereal *cereal,* 8
cero *zero,* 1
el césped *grass,* 6; **cortar el
césped** *to cut the grass,* 6
el ceviche *marinated raw fish,* 8
el chaleco *vest,* PREL
la chamaca *girl,* 4
el chamaco *guy,* 4
el champú *shampoo,* 7
las chancletas *sandals,
slippers,* 12
Chao. *'Bye.,* 1, PUENTE
la chaqueta *jacket,* 9
el charango *Andean stringed
musical instrument,* 4
la charla *chat,* 1

charlar *to chat*, 12

la charrería *rodeo-like exhibition of horseback riding skills*, 3

la chava *girl*, 4

el chavo *guy*, 4

la **chica** *girl*, 5

el **chico** *boy*, 5

China (f.) *China*, 12

chino/a *Chinese*, 6

el **chocolate** *chocolate*, 1

la chuleta de cerdo *pork chop*, 8

el ciclismo *cycling*, PREL

cien, ciento *one hundred*, 2

cien mil *one hundred thousand*, 8

las **ciencias** *science*, 3; ciencia ficción *science fiction*, 5; ciencias naturales *natural sciences*, 3; **ciencias sociales** *social studies*, 3

cierto *true*, 6; **No es cierto.** *It isn't true.*, 6

la cima *summit, top*, 4

cinco *five*, 1

cincuenta *fifty*, 2

el **cine** *movie theater*, 4, PUENTE

la cintura *waist*, 11

el **cinturón** *belt*, 9

el **circo** *circus*, 7

la **cita** *a date, an appointment*, 7

la **ciudad** *city*, 7

el civismo *civics*, 3

el clarinete *clarinet*, 4

¡Claro que sí! *Of course!*, 7

claro/a *light color*, PREL

la **clase** *class, classroom*, 1, PUENTE; **Bueno, tengo clase.** *Well, I have class (now).*, 1; **la clase de baile** *dance class*, 5; **la clase de inglés** *English class*, 1; **una clase de ejercicios aeróbicos** *aerobics class*, 5; **¿Qué clases tienes?** *What classes do you have?*, 3; **¿Qué haces después de clases?** *What do you do after school?*, 4, PUENTE

clásico/a *classical*, 1

el clima *climate*, 9

el club campeón *champion (first-rank) club*, 4; club deportivo *sports club, gym*, 5

el cobre *copper*, 7

el coche *car*, 7

la **cocina** *kitchen*, 6; **limpiar la cocina** *to clean the kitchen*, 6, PUENTE

la cocinera *cook* (female), 6

el cocinero *cook* (male), 6

el coco *coconut*, 6; *head (slang)*, 7

el cognado *cognate*, 1

el **colegio** *school, high school*, 2, PUENTE

colgar (ue) *to hang;* **colgar las decoraciones** *to hang decorations*, 10

la coliflor *cauliflower*, 1

el **collar** *necklace*, 9

el **color** *color*, 6; a todo color *in full color*, 2; **de color café** *brown*, 6; **¿De qué color es/son...?** *What color is/are . . .?*, 6; lápiz de color *colored pencil*, 2

colorido *coloring*, 7

la comadre *term used to express the relationship between mother and godmother*, 6

la comedia *comedy*, 3

comer *to eat*, 5, PUENTE

comercial: centro comercial *shopping mall*, 2

la cometa *kite*, 5

cómico/a *comical, funny*, 3

la **comida** *food; meal* (Mex.); *lunch;* **la comida mexicana/italiana/china** *Mexican/Italian/Chinese food*, 1

el comienzo *beginning*, 1

el comité *committee*, PUENTE

como *like; as*, 9

¡Cómo no! *Of course!*, 7

¿Cómo? *How?*, 1; **¿Cómo es...?** *What's . . . like?*, 3; **¿Cómo está usted?** *How are you* (formal), PUENTE; **¿Cómo es tu familia?** *What's your family like?*, 6, PUENTE; **¿Cómo estás?** *How are you?*, 1; **¿Cómo se escribe?** *How do you write (spell) it?*, PREL; **¿Cómo son?** *What are . . . like?*, 3; **¿Cómo te llamas?** *What's your name?*, 1

cómodo/a *comfortable*, 9

el compadrazgo *relationship between parents and godparents of a child*, 6

el compadre *friend* (male), 4; *term used to express the relationship between father and godfather*, 6

la **compañera** *friend, pal, companion* (female), 3

el **compañero** *friend, pal, companion* (male), 3; compañero/a de clase *classmate*, 3

la compañía *company*, 8

la comparación *comparison*, 2

compartir *to share*, 12

la competencia *competition*, 3

completamente *completely*, 6

la compra *purchase;* las compras *shopping*, 2

comprar *to buy*, 2, PUENTE; comprarse *to buy (for) oneself*, 6

comprender *to understand*, 1

compuesto/a *composed*, 2

la **computación** *computer science*, 3

la computadora *computer*, 2

común *common* (pl. comunes), PREL

¡Con mucho gusto! *Sure!*, 10

con base en *based on*, 6

con *with*, 4; **con frecuencia** *often;* **conmigo** *with me*, 4; **contigo** *with you*, 4; **¿con qué frecuencia?** *how often?*, 5, PUENTE

el **concierto** *concert*, 3

el concurso *game; competition, contest*, 3

el condimento *condiment*, 8

el conejo *rabbit*, 6

confirmar *to confirm*, 4

el conflicto *conflict*, 6

el conjunto *group, collection; band*, 9

conmigo *with me*, 4

conocer a *to get to know (someone)*, 2; **conocer** *to be familiar or acquainted with*

los conocimientos *information; knowledge*, 2

el consejo *advice*, 6

la constitución *constitution*, 4

la construcción *construction*, 1

construido/a *built*, 4

contar *to tell*, 9

contento/a *happy*, 11

contestar *to answer*, 1

contigo *with you*, 4

continuo/a *continuous*, 11

convertir *to convert*, 3

la **corbata** *tie*, 9

la cordillera *mountain range*, 1

el córdoba *unit of currency in Nicaragua*, 2

el coro *choir*, 3

corregir *to correct*, 3

el correo *post office*, 4, PUENTE

correr *to run*, 5, PUENTE

la correspondencia *mail*, 1

cortar *to cut*, 6; **cortar el césped** *to cut the grass*, 6, PUENTE

la cortesía *courtesy*, 1

corto/a *short* (to describe things), 6; pelo corto *short hair*, 6

la cosa *thing*, 2

la cosecha *harvest*, 10

cosmopolita *cosmopolitan*, 9

la costa *coast*, 9

el cráneo *skull*, 10

creativo/a *creative*, 6

crecer *to grow*, PUENTE

creer *to believe, to think*, 10; **Creo que no.** *I don't think so.*, 10; **Creo que sí.** *I think so.*, 10

la crema de maní *peanut butter*, 8

Creo que no. *I don't think so.*, 10

Creo que sí. *I think so.*, 10

criar *to raise*, PUENTE

la cruz *cross* (pl. las cruces), 2

el cuaderno *notebook*, 2; en mi cuaderno *in my journal*, 1; cuaderno de rayas *lined notebook*, 2; cuaderno de cuadros *graph paper notebook*, 6

la cuadra *city block*, 9

cuadrado/a *square*, 7

el cuadro *square*; **de cuadros** *plaid*, 9

cual, cuales *which* (relative pronoun)

¿cuál? *which?*, 3; **¿Cuál es la fecha?** *What is today's date?*, 5; **¿Cuál es tu clase favorita?** *Which is your favorite class?*, 3

cuando *when*, 5; **sólo cuando** *only when*, 5, PUENTE

¿cuándo? *when?*, 3

¿cuánto/a? *how much?*, 2; **¿cuántos/ as?** *how many?*, 2; **¿Cuántos/as...hay?** *How many . . . are there?*, PUENTE; **¿Cuántas personas hay?** *How many people are there?*, PUENTE; **¿Cuántas personas hay en tu familia?** *How many people*

are there in your family?, 6; **¿Cuánto cuesta...?** *How much does . . . cost?*, 9; **¿Cuánto cuestan...?** *How much do . . . cost?*, 9; **¿Cuánto es?** *How much is it?*, 8; **¿Cuántos años tiene?** *How old is (he/she)?*, 1; **¿Cuántos años tienes?** *How old are you?*, 1, PUENTE; ¿Cuántos son en tu familia? *How many (people) are in your family?*, 6

cuarenta *forty*, 2

cuarenta y cinco mil *forty-five thousand*, 8

cuarto *quarter, fourth*; **menos cuarto** *quarter to (the hour)*, 3; **y cuarto** *quarter past (the hour)*, 3

el cuarto *room*, 2

el cuate *friend*, 4

cuatro *four*, 1

cuatrocientos/as *four hundred*, 8

cubano/a *Cuban*, 6

cubierto/a *covered*, 4

la cuchara *spoon*, 8

la cucharada *tablespoon of an ingredient*, 8

el cuchillo *knife*, 8

el cuello *neck*, 11

la cuenta *bill*, 8

cuenta *he/she tells*, 6; cuéntame *tell me*, 1

el cuento *story*, 3; los cuentos de aventuras *adventure stories*, 5

el cuero *leather*; **de cuero** *(made of) leather*, 9

el cuerpo *body*, 11

la cuestión *question*, 1

el cuestionario *questionnaire*, 6

cuidar *to take care of*; **cuidar al gato** *to take care of the cat*, 6, PUENTE; **cuidar a tu hermano/a** *to take care of your brother/sister*, 4, PUENTE

la culebra *snake*, 7

el cumpleaños *birthday*, 3

curioso/a *curious, strange*, 6

da *he/she gives*, 2; dale un click a... *click on . . .*, 4

los dados *dice*, 2

la danza *dance*, 3

dar *to give*, 9

dar una caminata *to go hiking*, 12

¡Date prisa! *Hurry up!*, 3

los datos *facts, data*, PREL; datos personales *personal information*, 6

de *from*, 1; *of*, 2; el cafetín de al lado *the coffee shop around the corner*, 6; de antemano *beforehand*; **de color café** *brown*, 6; **¿De dónde eres?** *Where are you from?*, 1, PUENTE; **¿De dónde es?** *Where is he/she from?*, 1; **de la mañana** *in the morning* (A.M.), 3; **de la noche** *in the evening* (P.M.), 3; **de la tarde** *in the afternoon* (P.M.), 3; **¿De qué color es/son?** *What color is it /are they?*, 6; ¿De qué se hace? *What is it made of?*, 4; de todo *all kinds of things*, 4; de vacaciones *on vacation*, 5; de vez en cuando *once in a while*, 5; de visita *visiting*, 3; de vuelta *returning*, 2; **del (de + el)** *of the, from the*, 3

De acuerdo. *All right.*, 10

de algodón *(made of) cotton*, 9

de antemano *beforehand*, 1

de cuadros *plaid*, 9

de cuero *(made of) leather*, 9

de lana *(made of) wool*, 9

¿De parte de quién? *Who's calling?*, 7

de rayas *striped*, 9

de seda *(made of) silk*, 9

debajo de *under, beneath*, 4

el debate *debate*, 1

deber *should, ought to*, 6; **Debes...** *You should . . .*, 6, PUENTE; **Qué debo hacer?** *What should I do?*, 6

decir *to say*, PREL; para decir *for speaking*, PREL

las decoraciones *decorations*; **colgar (ue) las decoraciones** *to hang decorations*, 10

decorar *to decorate*, 10

el dedo *finger, toe*, 11

dejar de *to stop*, 9

del (de + el) *of the, from the*, 3

delgado/a *thin*, 6

delicioso/a *delicious*, 8
demasiado *too much*, 6, PUENTE
demorar *to delay*, 11
los **deportes** *sports*, 1, PUENTE
el derecho *right*, 1
la derrota *defeat, loss* 11
desagradable *unpleasant*, 11
el desastre *disaster*, 2
desayunar *to eat breakfast*, 5
el **desayuno** *breakfast*, 8
descansar *to rest*, 4; **descansar en el parque** *to rest in the park*, 4
el **descanso** *recess, break*, 3
la descripción *description*, 3
el descubrimiento *discovery*, 2
desde *since*, 3
¿Desean algo más? *Do you want anything else?*. 8
el desfile *parade*, 9
el desierto *desert*, 12
deslumbrante *dazzling*, 9
desorganizado/a *disorganized*, 6
la despedida *farewell, goodbye, leave-taking*, 1
después *after*, 3; **después de** *after*, 4, PUENTE; **¿Qué haces después de clases?** *What do you do after school?*, 4, PUENTE
el destino *destination*, 3
determinar: sin determinar *undetermined*, 4
el **Día de Acción de Gracias** *Thanksgiving Day*, 10
el **Día de la Independencia** *Independence Day*, 10
el **Día de las Madres** *Mother's Day*, 10
el **Día de los Enamorados** *Valentine's Day*, 10
el **Día del Padre** *Father's Day*, 10
el **día** *day*, 4; **Buenos días.** *Good morning.*; día de santo *saint's day*, 1; cada... días *every . . . days*, 5; día escolar *school day*, 3; **día libre** *day off*, 3; los días de semana *weekdays*, 4; los días de la semana *the days of the week*, 5; **los días festivos** *holidays*, 10; **todos los días** *every day*, 5, PUENTE
diariamente *daily*, 6
diario/a *daily*, 8
dibujar *to draw*, 4, PUENTE
el dibujo *drawing*; dibujos ani-

mados *animated cartoons*, 2
el **diccionario** *dictionary*, 2
dice *he/she says*, 1
dice que *he/she says that*, 6
diciembre (m.) *December*, 5
el dictado *dictation*, 1
diecinueve *nineteen*, 1
dieciocho *eighteen*, 1
dieciséis *sixteen*, 1
diecisiete *seventeen*, 1
el diente *tooth*, PUENTE
diez *ten*, 1
diez mil *ten thousand*, 8
difícil *difficult*, 3
Diga. *Hello.*, 7
dijo *he/she said*, 2
el dineral *large sum of money*, 2
el **dinero** *money*, 2
el dinosaurio *dinosaur*, 2
la dirección *address*, 4; en dirección contraria *in the opposite direction*, 11
directo/a *direct*, 4
el director *principal (of a school)* (male), 3
la directora *principal (of a school)* (female), 3
el **disco compacto** *compact disc*, 9; el tocador de discos compactos *CD player*, 2
diseñado/a *designed*, 11
el disfraz *costume*, 10
disfrutar *to enjoy*, 8
el disgusto *distaste*, 1
la diversión *entertainment*, 5
divertido/a *fun, amusing*, 3
divorciado/a *divorced*, 6
doblado/a *dubbed* (film), 2
doce *twelve*, 1
el doctor *doctor* (male), 3
la doctora *doctor* (female), 3
documental *documentary*, 2
el **dólar** *dollar*, 2
doler (ue) *to hurt, to ache*, 11
el dolor *pain*; el dolor de cabeza *headache*, 11
doméstico/a *household*; **los quehaceres domésticos** *household chores*, 6, PUENTE
el domicilio *residence*, 1
el **domingo** *Sunday*, 4
el dominó *dominoes*, 6
don (title of respect for men), 1
donde *where*; **¿Adónde?** *Where (to)?*, 4; **¿De dónde eres?** *Where are you from?*, 1; **¿De dónde es?** *Where is he/she from?*, 1;

¿Dónde? *Where?*, 4; **¿Dónde te gustaría estudiar?** *Where would you like to study?*, 3
dos *two*, 1
doscientos/as *two hundred*, 8
ducharse *to take a shower*, 7
dulce *sweet*, 8
la **dulcería** *candy store*, 9
los **dulces** *candy*, 9
la duración *length, duration*, 2
durante *during*, 5, PUENTE

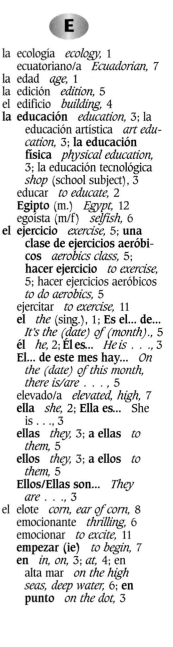

la ecología *ecology*, 1
ecuatoriano/a *Ecuadorian*, 7
la edad *age*, 1
la edición *edition*, 5
el edificio *building*, 4
la **educación** *education*, 3; la educación artística *art education*, 3; **la educación física** *physical education*, 3; la educación tecnológica *shop* (school subject), 3
educar *to educate*, 2
Egipto (m.) *Egypt*, 12
egoísta (m/f) *selfish*, 6
el **ejercicio** *exercise*, 5; **una clase de ejercicios aeróbicos** *aerobics class*, 5; **hacer ejercicio** *to exercise*, 5; hacer ejercicios aeróbicos *to do aerobics*, 5
ejercitar *to exercise*, 11
el *the* (sing.), 1; **Es el... de...** *It's the (date) of (month).*, 5
él *he*, 2; **Él es...** *He is . . .*, 3
El... de este mes hay... *On the (date) of this month, there is/are . . .*, 5
elevado/a *elevated, high*, 7
ella *she*, 2; **Ella es...** *She is . . .*, 3
ellas *they*, 3; **a ellas** *to them*, 5
ellos *they*, 3; **a ellos** *to them*, 5
Ellos/Ellas son... *They are . . .*, 3
el elote *corn, ear of corn*, 8
emocionante *thrilling*, 6
emocionar *to excite*, 11
empezar (ie) *to begin*, 7
en *in, on*, 3; *at*, 4; en alta mar *on the high seas, deep water*, 6; **en punto** *on the dot*, 3

Encantado/a. *Delighted to meet you.*, 1
encantar *to really like, to love*, 8
la **enciclopedia** *encyclopedia*, 2
encima de *on top of*, 4
encontrar (ue) *to find*, 2
el **encuentro** *encounter, meeting*, 2
la **encuesta** *survey*, 1
endurecer *to harden*, 11
enero (m.) *January*, 5
enfermo/a *sick*, 7
los **enlaces** *links, connections, ties*, 1
enojado/a *angry*, 11
enrojecer *to turn red; to blush*, 6
la **ensalada** *salad*, 1
entonces *then*, 3
entrar *to go in, to enter*, 3
entre *among*, 6; entre clases *between classes*, 1
la **entrevista** *interview*, 1
Epa, 'mano! *What's up, brother?*, 1
eres *you are*, 1
Es aparte. *It's separate.*, 8
¡Es un robo! *It's a rip-off!*, 9
es *he/she/it is*, 1; **es de...** *he/she/it is from . . .*, 1; **Es el ... de ...** *It's the (date) of (month).*, 5; **Es la una.** *It's one o'clock.*, 3, PUENTE
esa, ese *that* (adj.), 9
esas, esos *those* (adj.), 9
escalar montañas *to go mountain climbing*, 12
el **esclavo** *slave* (f. la esclava), 6
escoger *to choose*, 9
escolar *school* (adj.), 3; día escolar *school day*, 3
escondido/a *hidden*, 4
escribamos *let's write*, 3
escribir *to write*, 5
el **escritorio** *desk*, 2
escuchar *to listen*, 4; escuchar la radio *listen to the radio*, 4; **escuchar música** *to listen to music*, 4, PUENTE; para escuchar *for listening*, PREL
la **escuela** *school*, 3
eso *that* (pron.), 5; **por eso** *that's why, for that reason*, 4
los **espaguetis** *spaghetti*, 1
la **espalda** *back*, 11
España (f.) *Spain*, 1
el **español** *Spanish (language)*, 1

espantoso/a *terrible*, 5; Hace un calor espantoso. *It's terribly hot.*, 5
especial *special*, 3
especialmente *especially*, 5
la **especie** *species, kind;* una especie de *a kind of*, 8
el **espectáculo** *show; spectacle*, 6
esperar *to hope*, 12
espeso/a *thick*, 8
la **esposa** *wife*, 6
el **esposo** *husband*, 6
esquiar *to ski*, 5
los **esquís** *skis*, 12
esta *this* (adj.), 1; **estas** *these* (adj.), 6
Está bien. *All right.*, 7
¿Está incluida? *Is it included?*, 8
ésta *this* (pron.); **Ésta es mi amiga.** *This is my friend (female).*, 1
esta, este *this* (adj.), 9
el **estacionamiento** *parking*, 4
las **estaciones** *seasons*, 5
el **estadio** *stadium*, 11
la **estadística** *statistic*, 2
el **estado** *state*, 4
estamos *we are*, PREL
las **estampillas** *stamps*, 4
el **estante** *bookcase*, 2
estar *to be*, 4, PUENTE; **¿Cómo estás?** *How are you?*, 1; **Está atrasado/a.** *He/She is late.*, 3; **Está bien.** *It's all right.*, 7; **Está lloviendo.** *It's raining.*, 5, PUENTE; Está lloviendo a cántaros. *It's raining cats and dogs.*, 5; **Está nevando.** *It's snowing.*, 5, PUENTE; **Está nublado.** *It's cloudy.*, 5; **Estoy atrasado/a.** *I'm late.*, 3; **Estoy (bastante) bien, gracias.** *I'm (pretty) well, thanks.*, 1
estar listo/a *to be ready*, 7
estar resfriado/a *to have a cold*, 11
éstas *these* (pron.), 6
estas, estos *these* (adj.), 9
el **este** *east*, 1
este *this* (adj.), 1; **El ... de este mes hay...** *On the (date) of this month, there is/are . . .*, 5
éste *this* (pron.); **Éste es mi amigo.** *This is my friend (male).*, 1
el **estéreo** *stereo*, 2

el **estilo** *style*, 1; el estilo personal *personal style*, 1
estirarse *to stretch*, 11
el **estómago** *stomach*, 11
estos *these* (adj.), 6
éstos *these* (pron.), 6
estoy *I am*, 1; **Estoy atrasado/a.** *I'm late.*, 3; **Estoy (bastante) bien, gracias.** *I'm (pretty) well, thanks.*, 1, PUENTE
la **estrategia** *strategy*, 1
la **estrella** *star*, 1
estricto/a *strict*, 3
el/la **estudiante de intercambio** *exchange student*, 7
el **estudiante** *student* (male), 3
la **estudiante** *student* (female), 3
estudiar *to study*, 4
Estupendo/a. *Great./Marvelous.*, 1; Me siento estupendo. *I feel great.*, 11
estuvieras: *como si estuvieras... as if you were...*, 11
la **etiqueta** *label*, 1
étnico/a *ethnic*, 9
Europa *Europe*, 1
la **evaluación** *grade; grading period*, 3
el **evento** *event*, 7
el **examen** *exam* (pl. **los exámenes**), 3
Excelente. *Great./Excellent.*, 1
la **experiencia** *experience*, 5
explorar *to explore*, 12
exquisito/a *exquisite, delicious*, 7
extranjero/a *foreign;* al extranjero: *abroad, in another country*, 12

F

fabuloso/a *fabulous*, 6
fácil *easy*, 3
la **falda** *skirt*, 9
falso/a *false*, 1
la **falta de asistencia** *absence (from class)*, 3
la **familia** *family*, 6, PUENTE; familia extendida *extended family*, 6; familia extensa *extended family*, 6; familia nuclear *nuclear family, immediate family*, 6; familiar *family* (adj.), 6
los **farmacéuticos** *pharmaceuticals*, 11

fascinante *fascinating*, 9
favorito/a *favorite*, 3; ¿Cuál es tu clase favorita? *What's your favorite class?*, 3
febrero (m.) *February*, 5
la fecha *date*, 5; ¿Cuál es la fecha? *What is today's date?*, 5; ¿Qué fecha es hoy? *What's today's date?*, 5
feliz *happy*, 5
femenil *women's* (adj.), 4
fenomenal *phenomenal*, 6
feo/a *ugly*, 3
la fiebre *fever*; **tener fiebre** *to have a fever*, 11
la fiesta *party*, 3
la fiesta de aniversario *anniversary party*, 7
la fiesta de cumpleaños *birthday party*, 7
la fiesta de graduación *graduation party*, 7
la fiesta de sorpresa *surprise party*, 7
la fila *row*, 7
filmado/a *filmed*, 2
la filosofía *philosophy*, 2
el fin *end*, 4; **el fin de semana** *weekend*, 4, PUENTE; **los fines de semana** *weekends*, PUENTE
la firma *signature*, 1
la física *physics*, 3
flamenco *flamenco* (music, singing, dancing), 6
el flan *custard*, 8
la flauta *flute*, 4
flexionar *to flex*, 11
la florería *flower shop*, 9
las flores *flowers*, 9
flotante *floating*, 7
la forma *shape*, 6; en forma *in shape*, 11
formal *formal*, 9
fortalecer *to strengthen*, 11
la foto *photo*, 6
la fotonovela *illustrated story*, 1
la frambuesa *raspberry*, 8
el francés *French*, 3
Francia (f.) *France*, 12
la frase *sentence, phrase*, PREL
la frecuencia *frequency*, 5; ¿con qué frecuencia? *how often?*, 5, PUENTE
freír *to fry*, 8
la fresa *strawberry*, 8
fresco/a: **Hace fresco.** *It's cool (weather).*, 5

los frijoles *beans*, 8
frío *cold*, 8; **Hace frío.** *It's cold.*, 5; Hace un frío tremendo. *It's incredibly cold.*, 5
la frontera *border*, 7
la fruta *fruit*, 1
la frutería *fruit store*, 2
fue *was*, 4; fue construido/a *was built*, 4
el fuego *fire*, 10; los fuegos artificiales *fireworks*, 10
la fuente *fountain*, 12
fuerte *strong, heavy*, 8
fundado/a *founded*, 2
el fútbol *soccer*, 1; **el fútbol norteamericano** *football*, 1
el futuro *future*, 2

la gaita *bagpipes*, 4
la galería *gallery*, 10
gallego/a *Galician*, 3
la galleta *cookie*, 8
ganadero/a *having to do with livestock*, 9
el ganado *livestock*, 9
ganar *to win, to earn*, 11
ganas: tener ganas (de) *to feel like doing something*, 3
la garganta *throat*, 11
el gato *cat*, 6; **cuidar al gato** *to take care of the cat*, 6
general *general*; por lo general *in general*, 4
generoso/a *generous*, 6
¡Genial! *Great!*, 2
la gente *people*, 3
la geografía *geography*, 3
gigantesco/a *gigantic*, 10
el gimnasio *gym*, 4, PUENTE
girar *to turn around, to rotate*, 11
el globo *balloon*, 10
el gobierno *government*, 6
la goma de borrar *eraser*, 2
gordo/a *fat, overweight*, 6; **un poco gordo/a** *a little overweight*, 6
la gorra *cap*, 9
Gracias. *Thanks.*, 1; Estoy (bastante) bien, gracias. *I'm (pretty) well, thanks.*, 1
la gráfica *graphic*, 2
la gramática *grammar*, 1
grande *big*, 3
el grano *grain*, 8
gratis *free*, 8

la gripe *flu*; **tener gripe** *to have the flu*, 11
gris *gray*, 9
el grupo *group*, 1
¡guácala! *yuck!*, 8
los guantes *gloves*, 9
guapo/a *good-looking*, 3
la guerra *war*, 3
la guía *guide*, 2
el güiro *Andean percussive musical instrument*, 4
la guitarra *guitar*, 4
gustar *to like someone/something*, 1, PUENTE; **A mí me gusta +** infinitive *I* (emphatic) *like to . . .*, 4; ¿A quién le gusta...? *Who likes . . .?*, 4; **le gustan** *he/she likes*, 3; **les gusta** *they like*, 5; **Me gusta...** *I like . . .*, 1; **Me gusta más...** *I prefer . . .*, 1; **me gustan** *I like*, 3; **No me gusta...** *I don't like . . .*, 1; **nos gusta** *we like*, 5; **Nos gustan...** *We like . . .*, 5; ¿Qué te gusta? *What do you like?*, 1; ¿Qué te gusta hacer? *What do you like to do?*, 4; **Sí, me gusta.** *Yes, I like it.*, 1; ¿Te gusta...? *Do you like . . .?*, 1; **Te gustan...** *You like . . .*, 3
el gusto *pleasure, taste*, 8; **Mucho gusto.** *Nice to meet you.*, 1; gustos personales *personal likes*, 1

haber *to have* (auxiliary verb), 4
la habitación *room*, 12
hablando *speaking*, 2
hablar *to speak, to talk*, PUENTE; **hablar por teléfono** *to talk on the phone*, 4
hacer *to do, to make*, 2; **Hace buen tiempo.** *The weather is nice.*, 5; **Hace calor.** *It's hot.*, 5, PUENTE; **Hace fresco.** *It's cool.*, 5; **Hace frío.** *It's cold.*, 5, PUENTE; **Hace mal tiempo.** *The weather is bad.*, 5; **Hace (mucho) frío.** *It's (very) cold.*, 5; **Hace sol.** *It's sunny.*, 5, PUENTE; Hace

un calor espantoso. *It's terribly hot.*, 5; Hace un frío tremendo. *It's incredibly cold.*, 5; Hace un tiempo precioso. *It's a beautiful day.*, 5; Hace viento. *It's windy.*, 5, PUENTE; **hacer ejercicio** *to exercise*, 5; **hacer la cama** *to make the bed*, 6, PUENTE; **hacer la maleta** *to pack the suitcase*, 12; **hacer la tarea** *to do homework*, PUENTE; **hacer turismo** *to go sightseeing*, 12; **hacer un viaje** *to take a trip*, 6; **haga** *do (command)*, 3; **hacer yoga** *to do yoga*, 11; ¿**Qué debo hacer?** *What should I do?*, 6; ¿Qué hacemos? *What shall we do?*, 4; ¿**Qué hacen ustedes los fines de semana?** *What do you do on weekends?*, 6; ¿**Qué tiempo hace?** *What's the weather like?*, 5, PUENTE
hacia *toward;* hacia abajo *downward*, 11; hacia arriba *upward*, 11
el hado *destiny, fate*, 2
haga *do (command)*, 3
la hamaca *hammock*, 7
la hamburguesa *hamburger*, 5
haría *he/she would do/make*, PREL
hasta *until;* **Hasta luego.** *See you later.*, 1, PUENTE; **Hasta mañana.** *See you tomorrow.*, 1
hay *there is, there are*, 2
haz *do, make (command)*, 10
hecho/a *made of*, 10
el **helado** *ice cream*, 4; **tomar un helado** *to eat ice cream*, 4
el helicóptero *helicopter*, PREL
la herencia *heritage*, PREL
la **hermana** *sister*, 6; **la media hermana** *half sister*, 6
la **hermanastra** *stepsister*, 6
el **hermanastro** *stepbrother*, 6
el **hermano** *brother*, 6; **el medio hermano** *half brother*, 6
los **hermanos** *brothers, brothers and sisters*, 6
el **héroe** *hero*, 3
el hielo *ice*, 8
el hierro *iron*, 7
la **hija** *daughter*, 6

el **hijo** *son*, 6
los **hijos** *children*, 6
hispano/a *Hispanic*, PREL
hispanohablante *Spanish speaking*, PREL
la historia *history*, 3
la hoja *leaf*, 10
¡**Hola!** *Hello!*, 1, PUENTE
el **hombre** *man*, 6
el **hombro** *shoulder*, 11
la **hora** *hour, time;* ¿**A qué hora es...?** *At what time is . . .?*, 3; es hora de... *it's time to . . .*, 5; hora latina *Latin time*, 3; hora local *local time*, 3; ¿**Qué hora es?** *What time is it?*, 3, PUENTE
el horario escolar *school schedule*, 3
Horrible. *Horrible.*, 1; ¡Qué horrible! *How terrible!*, 2
el **hospital** *hospital*, 3
hoy *today*, 3; ¿**Cuál es la fecha hoy?** *What is today's date?*, 5; **Hoy es el ... de ...** *Today is the (date) of (month).*, 5; ¿**Qué fecha es hoy?** *What's today's date?*, 5
los **huevos** *eggs*, 8
el **humor** *humor, mood;* de mal humor *in a bad mood*, 7
el huracán *hurricane*, 5

I

el **idioma** *language*, 4
la **iglesia** *church*, 6
igual *equal*, 6
Igualmente. *Same here.*, 1
ilustrada *illustrated*, 2
la imagen *image (pl. las imágenes)*, 4
el **impermeable** *raincoat*, 9
impresionante *impressive*, 11
¡**Increíble!** *Incredible!*, 2
independiente *independent*, 6
indígena *(adj.) indigenous, native*, 7
la industria extractiva *mining industry*, 3
infantil *for children*, 3
inflar *to inflate, to blow up;* **inflar los globos** *to blow up balloons*, 10
el **ingeniero** *engineer (male)*, 3
la **ingeniera** *engineer (female)*, 3
Inglaterra *(f.) England*, 12
el **inglés** *English (language)*, 1;

la **clase de inglés** *English class*, 1
ingresar *to enter*, 1
el **inicio** *start*, 11
inolvidable *unforgettable*, 9
la **instalación** *installation, facility*, 1
instantáneo/a *instant*, 8
el **instituto** *institute*, 3
el **instrumento** *(musical) instrument*, 4; **tocar un instrumento** *to play a musical instrument*, 4, PUENTE
inteligente *intelligent*, 3
intentar *to try*, 9
interesante *interesting*, 3
interrumpirse *to be interrupted*, 6; interrumpe *interrupts*, 6
intocable *untouchable*, 3
la intriga *intrigue*, 3
el **invierno** *winter*, 5
ir + a + infinitive *to be going to (do something)*, 7
ir de vela *to go sailing*, 12
ir *to go*, 2; **ir al centro comercial** *to go to the mall*, 2; ir de compras *to go shopping*, 4
la **isla** *island*, 12
Italia *(f.) Italy*, 12
italiano/a *Italian*, 1; **la comida italiana** *Italian food*, 1

J

el **jabón** *soap*, PREL
la **jalea** *jelly*, 8
el **jamón** *ham*, 8
el **jardín** *garden*, 6; **trabajar en el jardín** *to work in the garden*, 6
el **jazz** *jazz*, 1
el **jefe** *boss*, 3
joven *(pl. jóvenes) young*, 6; **Se ve joven.** *He/She looks young.*, 6
la **joyería** *jewelry store*, 9
judío/a *Jewish*, 10
el **juego** *game;* el juego de ingenio *guessing game*, 1; **el juego de mesa** *board game*, 9; **el videojuego** *videogame*, 3
el **jueves** *Thursday*, 4
jugar (ue) *to play*, 4; jugar al tenis *to play tennis*, 4;

jugar a los videojuegos *to play videogames*, PUENTE

el jugo *juice*, 5; **el jugo de naranja** *orange juice*, 8

la juguetería *toy store*, 9

los juguetes *toys*, 9

juguetón *playful* (f. juguetona), 6

julio (m.) *July*, 5

junio (m.) *June*, 5

juntamos: nos juntamos *we get together*, 4

juntos/as *together*, 5

la juventud *youth*, 3

el kilómetro *kilometer*, PREL

la *the* (sing.), 1; *it/her/you* (formal), 10

el lado *side;* **al lado de** *next to*, 4; el cafetín de al lado *the coffee shop around the corner*, 6

la lagartija *lizard*, 7

el lago *lake*, 7

la lámpara *lamp*, 2

la lana *wool;* **de lana** *(made of) wool*, 9

la lancha *boat*, 5

el lanzador *baseball pitcher*, 11

el lápiz *pencil*, 2; lápiz de color *colored pencil*, 2

largo/a *long*, 5

las *the* (pl.), 3

el latín *Latin (language)*, 3

lavar *to wash;* **lavar el carro** *to wash the car*, 4; **lavar la ropa** *to wash clothes*, 4

lavarse los dientes *to brush one's teeth*, 7

le *to/for her, him, you* (sing.), 9

las lecciones *lessons*, 5; tomar lecciones *to take lessons*, 5

la leche *milk*, 8

la lechuga *lettuce*, 8

leer *to read*, 5; **leer revistas** *to read magazines*, PUENTE

las legumbres *vegetables*, 8

lejano/a *distant*, 10

lejos *far;* **lejos de** *far from*, 4

el lempira *unit of currency in Honduras*, 2

los lentes de sol *sunglasses*, 12

lento/a *slow*, 11

Les gusta + infinitive *They/ You (plural) like to . . .*, 5

les *to/for them, you* (pl.), 9

la letra *(alphabet) letter*, 1

levantado/a *lifted, raised*, 11

levantar *to lift;* **levantar pesas** *to lift weights*, 11; el levantamiento de pesas *weightlifting*, 4

el libertador *liberator*, PREL

libre *free*, 3; **un día libre** *a day off*, 3; **el tiempo libre** *free time*, 4, PUENTE

la librería *bookstore*, 2

el libro *book*, 2

el licenciado *man with academic degree comparable to Bachelor of Arts*, 3

la licenciada *woman with academic degree comparable to Bachelor of Arts*, 3

la licuadora *blender*, 8

ligero *light*, 8

la limonada *lemonade*, 8

limpiar *to clean*, 6; **limpiar la cocina** *to clean the kitchen*, 6, PUENTE

limpio/a *clean*, 8

lindo/a *pretty*, 7

la línea *line*, 4

el lío *mess;* ¡Qué lío! *What a mess!*, 3

liso/a *straight;* pelo liso *straight hair*, 6

la lista *list*, 2

listo/a *clever, smart* (with **ser**), 6; *ready* (with **estar**), 2

la literatura *literature*, 3

la llama *llama, Andean pack animal*, 7

la llamada *telephone call*, 3

llamar a los invitados *to call the guests*, 10

llamarse *to be named;* ¿Cómo te llamas? *What's your name?*, 1; **Me llamo...** *My name is . . .*, 1; **Se llama...** *His/Her name is . . .*, 1; **Llamo más tarde.** *I'll call later.*, 7

la llanta *tire*, PREL

el llapingacho *potato cake with cheese*, 8

llegué *I arrived*, 3

llevar *to wear*, 9

llevar *to carry, to lead;* **llevar una vida sana** *to lead a healthy life*, 11

llover (ue) *to rain;* 5; **Está lloviendo.** *It's raining.*, 5, PUENTE; Está lloviendo a cántaros. *It's raining cats and dogs.*, 5; **Llueve.** *It's raining.*, 5

lo *it/him/you* (formal), 10

lo de siempre *the usual*, 9

lo más rápido posible *as quickly as possible*, 5; lo que pasó *what happened*, 4; lo bueno *what's good; the good thing*, 5

Lo siento, pero no puedo. *I'm sorry, but I can't.*, 7

el lobo *wolf*, 4

localizar *to locate*, 7

lograr *to achieve*, 4

el lomo al carbón *pork loin broiled over charcoal*, 8

el loro *parrot*, 11

¿los conoces? *do you know them?*, PREL

los *the* (pl.), 3

las luces *lights*, 2

la lucha libre *wrestling*, 1

luego *then, later*, 3, PUENTE; **Hasta luego.** *See you later.*, 1

el lugar *place*, 7; **ningún lugar** *nowhere, not anywhere*, 12

el lunes *Monday*, 4

la lupa *magnifying glass*, 2

la luz *light*, 2

los macarrones con queso *macaroni and cheese*, 8

la madera *wood, lumber*, 7

la madrastra *stepmother*, 6

la madre *mother*, 6

el madrileño *resident of Madrid* (male), 1

la madrileña *resident of Madrid* (female), 1

la madrina *godmother*, 6

maduro/a *mature*, 6

los maduros *ripe plantains*, 6

el maestro *teacher* (male), 3

la maestra *teacher* (female), 3

magnífico/a *great*, 11

el maíz *corn*, 8

mal *poorly; bad*, 1; No está mal. *It's not bad.*, 2

la maleta *suitcase;* **hacer la maleta** *to pack the suitcase*, 12 malo/a *bad*, 3; **Hace mal tiempo.** *The weather is bad.*, 5

la **mamá** *mom*, 6

el mamey *mamey* (fruit), 6

el mamífero *mammal*, 2

la **mañana** *morning*, 3, PUENTE; **de la mañana** *in the morning* (A.M.), 3; **por la mañana** *in the morning*, 5, PUENTE

mañana *tomorrow*, 3; **Hasta mañana.** *See you tomorrow.*, 1;

mandar *to send*; **mandar las invitaciones** *to send invitations*, 10

la manga *sleeve*, 9

el **mango** *mango* (fruit), 8

la **mano** *hand*, 11

'mano *friend* (short for 'hermano'), 4

mantener (ie) *to maintain*, 6; mantener correspondencia *to write letters back and forth*, 4

mantuvieron *they maintained*, 6

la **manzana** *apple*, 8

el mapa *map*, 1

el maquillaje *makeup*, 7

maquillarse *to put on makeup*, 7

la máquina del tiempo *time machine*, 2

las maquinarias *machinery*, 11

el mar *sea*, 6; el Mar Mediterráneo *Mediterranean Sea*, 1

la maravilla *marvel*; de maravilla *marvelous*, 11

el marcador *marker*, 2

marino/a *marine*, 7

marrón *brown*, PREL

el **martes** *Tuesday*, 4

marzo (m.) *March*, 5

más *more*, 1; **Más o menos.** *So-so.*, 1, PUENTE; **Me gusta más...** *I prefer . . .*, 1

más... que *more . . . than*, 9

la masa *dough*, 8

la máscara *mask*, PREL

la mascota *pet*, 6

las **matemáticas** *mathematics*, 3

la materia *subject*, 3

la matrícula *enrollment*, 3

mayo (m.) *May*, 5

mayor *older*, 6

la mayoría *majority*, 7

me *(to, for) me*, 1; me

to/for me, 9; me acuesto *I go to bed*, 3; **¿Me ayudas a...?** *Can you help me to . . .?*, 10; **Me gusta... I** *like . . .*, 1, PUENTE; **Me gusta más...** *I prefer . . .*, 1; **Me gustan...** *I like . . .*, 3; **Me gustaría...** *I would like . . .*, 7; **¿Me haces el favor de...?** *Could you please. . .?*, 10; **Me llamo...** *My name is . . .*, 1; me meto, *I go in*, 6; **Me parece bien.** *It's fine with me.*, 10; **¿Me pasas...?** *Can you pass me . . .?*, 10; **Me pongo a estudiar.** *I start studying.*, 3; me quedo con *I stay with*, 6; **¿Me puede decir...?** *Can you tell me . . .?*, 9; **¿Me puede traer...?** *Can you bring me . . .?*, 8; **¿Me traes...?** *Can you bring me . . .?*, 10

las medias *stockings*, 9

el medio ambiente *environment*, 9

medio/a *half*; **media hermana** *half sister*, 6; **medio hermano** *half brother*, 6; **y media** *half past (the hour)*, 3

el mediodía *noon, midday*, 3

mejor *best; better*, 5

menor *younger, youngest*, 6

menos *less*, 6; **Más o menos.** *So-so.*, 1; **menos cuarto** *quarter to (the hour)*, 3, PUENTE

menos... que *less . . . than*, 9

el **menú** *menu*, 8

menudo/a *minute, small*; a menudo *often*, 5

el mercado *market*, 3

el **mes** *month*, 5; **El... de este mes hay...** *On the (date) of this month, there is/are . . .*, 5

la **mesa** *table*, 2; **poner la mesa** *to set the table*, 6, PUENTE

mestizo/a *of mixed Indian and European descent*, 6

meter *to put in*, 6; me meto *I go in*, 6

el metro *subway*, 7

mezclar *to mix*, 8

mi *my*, 2; **mis** *my*, 6

mí *me* (emphatic); **A mí me gusta + infinitive** *I*

(emphatic) *like to . . .*, 4

el microscopio *microscope*, 2

el miedo *fear*, 6

mientras *while*, 10

el **miércoles** *Wednesday*, 4

mil *one thousand*, 8

la **milla** *mile*, 5; las millas por hora *miles per hour*, 5

mimoso/a *affectionate*, 6

mínimo/a *minimum*, 12

el minuto *minute*, 2

mirar *to watch, to look at*, 4; mira *look*, 1; **mirar la televisión** *to watch television*, 4, PUENTE

la misa *mass*, 9

mismo/a *same*, 3

el misterio *mystery*, 1

la **mochila** *book bag; backpack*, 2

el modelo *example, model*, 1

el modo *way, mode*, 2

molido/a *exhausted (coll.)*, 7

un momento *one moment*, 7; **Un momentito.** *Just a second.*, 10

el mono *monkey*, 7

la montaña *mountain*, 5; **escalar montañas** *to go mountain climbing*, 12

montar *to ride*; **montar en bicicleta** *to ride a bike*, 4

la mora *blackberry*, 8

morado/a *purple*, 9

moreno/a *dark-haired, dark-skinned*, 3

la moto *moped, motorbike*, 7

el motoesquí *jet-ski*, 5

el movimiento *movement*, 6

la muchacha *girl*, 3

el muchacho *boy*, 3

mucho *a lot*, 1

mucho/a *a lot (of)*, 2, PUENTE; **Mucho gusto.** *Nice to meet you.*, 1

muchos/as *many, a lot of*, 2; **muchas veces** *often*, 5, PUENTE

muerde *bites*, 6

la muestra *display; sample*, 9

la mujer *woman*, 6

el mundo *world*, PREL

municipal *municipal, city* (adj.), 4

el mural *mural*, 5

el museo *museum*, 3; **el museo de antropología** *anthropology museum*, 7

la **música** *music*, 1; **escuchar música** *to listen to music*,

4; **la música clásica/**
pop/rock *classical/pop/*
rock music, 1; **la música**
de... *music by . . .,* 1
musulmán *Muslim,* 10
muy *very,* 1; **(muy) bien**
(very) well, 1; **(muy) mal**
(very) bad, 1

nada *nothing,* 5, PUENTE;
nada más *that's all,* 11
nadar *to swim,* 4
nadie *nobody,* 5
el **náhuatl** *Nahuatl* (language), 4
la **naranja** *orange,* 6
la **nariz** *nose,* 11
la **natación** *swimming,* 1
la **navaja de afeitar** *razor,* 7
la **Navidad** *Christmas,* 10
necesitar *to need,* 2,
PUENTE; **necesita** *he/she*
needs, 2; **necesitas** *you*
need, 2; **necesito** *I need,* 2
negro/a *black,* 6
nervioso/a *nervous,* 11
nevado/a *snowy, snow-*
capped, 7
nevar (ie) *to snow;* **Está**
nevando. *It's snowing.,* 5,
PUENTE; **Nieva.** *It's snow-*
ing., 5
ni *nor,* 6; **ni... ni...** *neither*
. . . nor . . ., 6
los **nietos** *grandchildren,* 11
la **niña** *child* (female), 2
ningún lugar *nowhere, not*
anywhere, 12
el **niño** *child* (male), 2
los **niños** *children,* 2
el **nivel** *level,* 4
no *no,* 1; **¿no?** *isn't it?,* 3;
No es aburrido/a. *It's not*
boring., 3; **No es cierto.**
It isn't true., 6, PUENTE;
No me gusta... *I don't*
like . . ., 1; **No sé.** *I don't*
know., 2; **No te preocupes.**
Don't worry., 3
la **noche** *night,* PUENTE;
Buenas noches. *Good*
night., 1; **de la noche** *in*
the evening (P.M.), 3; **por la**
noche *at night,* 5
la **Nochebuena** *Christmas*
Eve, 10
la **Nochevieja** *New Year's Eve,* 10

el **nombre** *name,* PREL; **nom-**
bre completo *full name,* 6;
nombres comunes *common*
names, PREL
normal *normal,* 5
normalmente *normally,* 2
el **noroeste** *northwest,* 7
el **norte** *north,* 1
norteamericano/a *of or from*
the U.S., 1
nos *to/for us,* 9; **Nos gus-**
tan... *We like . . .,* 7;
Nos gusta + infinitive
We like to . . ., 5; **nos**
juntamos *we get together,*
¿Nos puede traer la
cuenta? *Can you bring*
us the bill?, 8
nosotros/as *we,* 4; *us* (after
preposition), 5
las **noticias** *news,* 5
notificar *to notify,* 1
novecientos/as *nine*
hundred, 8
la **novela** *novel,* 3
noventa *ninety,* 2
noviembre (m.) *November,* 5
nublado/a *cloudy,* 5;
Está nublado. *It's*
cloudy., 5
nuestro/a *our,* 6
nueve *nine,* 1
nuevo/a *new,* 3; **nuevos**
amigos *new friends,* 2
el **número** *number,* 1; **el**
número secreto *secret*
number, 1
numeroso *numerous,* 6
nunca *never, not ever,* 5,
PUENTE

o *or;* **Más o menos.** *So-so.,* 1
o ... o *either . . . or,* 7
el **oceanario** *oceanography*
institute, 2
el **océano** *ocean,* 5; **Océano**
Atlántico *Atlantic Ocean,*
PREL; **Océano Índico**
Indian Ocean, PREL; **Océano**
Pacífico *Pacific Ocean,*
PREL
ochenta *eighty,* 2
ochenta mil *eighty*
thousand, 8
ocho *eight,* 1
ochocientos/as *eight*
hundred, 8

octubre (m.) *October,* 5
ocupado/a *busy,* 7
el **oeste** *west,* 1
la **oficina** *office,* 4
el **oído** *(inner) ear,* 11
oír *to hear, to listen to,* 4;
¡Oye! *Listen!, Hey!,* 3
los **ojos** *eyes,* 6; **Tiene ojos**
verdes/azules. *He/She has*
green/blue eyes., 6
la **ola** *wave,* 5
olímpico/a *Olympic,* 5
olvidarse *to forget;* **¿Se te ha**
olvidado?: *Have you for-*
gotten?, PUENTE
once *eleven,* 1
operar *to operate,* 5
la **oportunidad** *opportunity,* 7
la **oración** *sentence,* 6
el **orden** *order* (sequence), 6
las **órdenes** *orders;* **a sus**
órdenes *at your service,* 5
la **oreja** *(outer) ear,* 11
organizado/a *organized,* 6
organizar *to organize,* 2;
organizar tu cuarto *to*
clean your room, PUENTE
el **orgullo** *pride,* 3
el **origen** *origin,* 8
el **oro** *gold,* 4
oscuro/a *dark,* PREL
el **oso** *bear,* PREL
el **otoño** *fall,* 5
otro/a *other, another,* 8
¡Oye! *Listen!, Hey!,* 3

el **padrastro** *stepfather,* 6
el **padre** *father,* 6
los **padres** *parents,* 6
el **padrino** *godfather,* 6; **los**
padrinos *godparents,* 1
la **página** *page,* 4
el **país** *country,* 4
el **paisaje** *landscape,* 12
el **pájaro** *bird,* 7
el **palacio de gobierno** *town hall,* 4
la **palma** *palm (of hand),* 11
el **pan** *bread;* **el pan dulce**
sweet roll, 8; **el pan tostado**
toast, 8
la **panadería** *bakery,* 9
los **pantalones** *pants,* 9
los **pantalones cortos** *shorts,* 9
la **papa** *potato,* 5; **las papas**
fritas *french fries,* 5
el **papá** *dad,* 6

la **papaya** *papaya* (fruit), 8
el **papel** *paper*, 2
las **papitas** *potato chips*, 8
el **par** *pair*, 5
para *for, to*, 4; **para** + infinitive *in order to*, 4; **para nada** *at all*, 8; **¿Para quién...?** *For whom . . .?*, 9
el **parador** *roadside stand*, 6
el **paraguas** *umbrella*, 9
el **paraíso** *paradise*, 12
pardo/a *brown*, 9
parecer *to seem, to appear;* **Me parece bien.** *It's fine with me.*, 10
los **paréntesis** *parentheses*, 12
el **pariente** *relative*, 6
el **parking** *parking lot; parking garage* (Spain), 4
el **parque** *park*, 4, PUENTE; **descansar en el parque** *to rest in the park*, 4; **el parque de atracciones** *amusement park*, 7
el **párrafo** *paragraph*, 9
la **parrillada** *barbecue*, 9
participar *to participate*, 5
el **partido de...** *game of . . .* (sport), 3
el **pasado** *past*, 6
el **pasaje** *fare; passage*, 3; *passageway*, 4
pasar *to pass; to spend (time)*, 4; **pasar el rato con amigos** *to spend time with friends*, 4; **pasar la aspiradora** *to vacuum*, 6, PUENTE
el **pasatiempo** *hobby, pastime*, 1
las **Pascuas** *Easter*, 10
el **paseo** *walk, stroll*, 4
el **pasillo** *hallway*, PUENTE
el **paso** *step*, 1
pasó *happened;* **lo que pasó** *what happened*, 4
la **pasta** *spaghetti, pasta*, 8
la **pasta de dientes** *toothpaste*, 7
el **pastel** *cake*, 8
la **pastelería** *pastry shop; sweet shop*, 9
pata: **¡Hola, pata!** *Hey, man!* (slang: Peru), 4
la **patata** *potato* (Spain), 8
paterno/a *paternal*, PUENTE
patinar *to skate;* **patinar en línea** *to in-line skate*, 6; **patinar sobre ruedas** *to roller skate*, 11
el **pavo** *turkey*, 8
la **pecera** *fishbowl*, 2

los **peces** *fish* (sing. el pez), 2
pedir (i) *to order, to ask for*, 8
peinarse *to comb one's hair*, 7
el **peine** *comb*, 7
la **película** *movie, film*, 4; **ver una película** *to see a film*, 4
pelirrojo/a *redheaded*, 6
el **pelo** *hair*, 6
la **pelota** *ball*, 6
el **pendiente** *earring*, 9
pensar (ie) + infinitive *to plan, to intend*, 7
peor *worse*, 11
el **pepino** *cucumber*, 8
pequeño/a *small*, 3
la **pérdida** *loss*, 1
Perdón. *Excuse me.*, 9
Perdóname. *Excuse me.*, 10
perezoso/a *lazy*, 6
Perfecto. *Perfect.*, 10
el **periódico** *newspaper*, 5
el **permiso** *permission, permit*, PREL
pero *but*, 1, PUENTE
el **perro** *dog*, 4; **el perro caliente** *hot dog*, 8
personal *personal*, 2; **anuncios personales** *personal ads*, 4; **estilo personal** *personal style*, 2
la **personalidad** *personality*, 1
pesado/a *heavy*, 2; **¡Qué pesado/a!** *How annoying!*, 2
la **pesca** *fishing*, 11
el **pescado** *fish (for eating)*, 8
pescar *to fish*, 5
la **peseta** *unit of currency in Spain*, 2
¡Pésimo! *Terrible!*, 2
pésimo/a *abominable, very bad*, 11
el **peso** *unit of currency in Mexico (and other countries)*, 2
el **petróleo** *petroleum*, 7
el **pez** (pl. peces) *fish*, 2; **el pez de colores** *goldfish*, 6
el **piano** *piano*, 4, PUENTE
picado/a *ground up*, 8
picante *spicy*, 8
el **pico** *peak*, 7
el **pie** *foot*, 11; **a pie** *on foot*, 7
¡Piénsalo! *Think about it!*, 2
la **pierna** *leg*, 11
la **piña** *pineapple*, 8
el **pincel** *paintbrush*, 2
el **pingüino** *penguin*, 7
pintar *to paint*, 4
la **pintura** *paint*, 2; *painting*, 4
la **pirámide** *pyramid*, 12

los **Pirineos** *Pyrenees (Mountains)*, 1
la **piscina** *swimming pool*, 4, PUENTE
el **piso** *apartment*, 2
la **pista de correr** *running track*, 11
la **pizza** *pizza*, 1
la **pizzería** *pizzeria*, 2
la **placa** *license plate*, PREL
el **plan** *plan;* **en plan de turista** *as a tourist*, 12
planchar *to iron*, 6, PUENTE
el **planeta** *planet*, 5
la **planta** *plant*, 9
la **plata** *silver*, 4
el **plátano** *banana*, 8
el **platero** *silversmith* (f. la platera), 4
el **platillo** *little dish*, 9
el **plato** *plate*, 8; **lavar los platos** *to wash the dishes*, 6
el **plato hondo** *bowl*, 8
la **playa** *beach*, 5; **por la playa** *along the beach*, 5
la **plaza** *town square*, 4
la **pluma** *ballpoint pen*, 2
la **población** *population*, 7
poblado/a *populated*, 9
poco *a little*, 6; **un poco de todo** *a little bit of everything*, 4; **un poco gordo/a** *a little overweight*, 6; **pocas veces** *not very often*, 5
poder (ue) *to be able; can*, 8; **¿Puedo dejar un recado?** *May I leave a message?*, 7
el **poema** *poem*, 5
policíaco/a *police* (adj.), *detective* (adj.), 3
el **pollo** *chicken*, 8
el **pollo asado** *roasted chicken*, 6
pon *put, place*, 10
poner *to put, to place*, 2; **Me pongo a estudiar.** *I start studying.*, 3; **poner la mesa** *to set the table*, 6, PUENTE
ponerse los lentes *to put on one's glasses*, 7
por *at*, 3; *by*, 5; *in; around*, 4; **por eso** *that's why, for that reason*, 4; **por favor** *please*, 8; **por fin** *at last*, 3; **por la mañana** *in the morning*, 5, PUENTE; **por la noche** *at night, in the evening*, 5; **por la playa** *along the beach*, 5; **por la tarde** *in the afternoon*, 5,

PUENTE; **por lo general** *in general*, 8; **por teléfono** *on the phone*, 4, PUENTE
porque *because*, 3
¿Por qué? *Why?*, 3; **¿Por qué no...?** *Why don't . . .?*, 11
la **portada** *cover* (of a book or magazine), 2
posible *possible*, 5
el **postre** *dessert*, 8
practicar *to practice*, 4; **practicar deportes** *to play sports*, 4, PUENTE
el **precio** *price*, 9
precioso/a *beautiful; really nice*, 5; *Hace un tiempo precioso.* *It's a beautiful day.*, 5
preferir (ie) *to prefer*, 7
la **pregunta** *question*, 3
preliminar *preliminary*, PREL
el **Premio Nóbel** *Nobel Prize*, 3
preocupado/a por algo *worried about something*, 11
preocuparse *to worry*; **No te preocupes.** *Don't worry.*, 3
preparar *to prepare*, 4
preparatorio/a *preparatory*, 3
presentable *presentable, well dressed*, 6
presentar *to introduce*, 1
la **prima** *cousin* (female), 6
la **primavera** *spring*, 5
primero/a *first*, 3, PUENTE; **el primero** *the first* (of the month), 5
el **primo** *cousin* (male), 6
los **primos** *cousins*, 6
la **princesa** *princess*, 4
la **prisa** *haste*; **¡Date prisa!** *Hurry up!*, 3; **Tengo prisa.** *I'm in a hurry.*, 3
el **prisionero** *prisoner* (f. la prisionera), 3
probar (ue) *to try, to taste*, 6
el **problema** *problem*, 6
el **profesor** *teacher* (male), 3
la **profesora** *teacher* (female), 3
profundamente *deeply*, 11
el **programa** *program*, 3; *el programa de televisión* *television program*, 3
el **pronóstico del tiempo** *weather report*, 5
pronto *soon*, 8
la **propina** *the tip*, 8
propio/a *own*, 9
el **protagonista** *protagonist, main character*, 2
próximo/a *next*, 5
la **prueba contra reloj** *time trial*, 4

la **psicopedagogía** *educational psychology*, 3
ptas. *abbreviation of* **pesetas,** *currency of Spain*, 2
el **pueblo** *town*, 10
pueden *(they) can*, 2
puedo *I can*, 2
¿Puedo dejar un recado? *May I leave a message?*, 7
el **puente** *bridge*, PUENTE
la **puerta** *door*, 2
pues *well . . .*, 2
la **pulpa** *pulp*, 8
la **pulsera** *bracelet*, 9
la **punta** *point*; *con el pie en punta* *with the foot extended*, 11
punto: en punto *on the dot*, 3
el **pupitre** *student desk*, 2
el **puré de papas** *mashed potatoes*, 8

Q

que *that, which, who*, 4; **Dice que...** *He/She says that . . .*, 6
¿Qué? *What?*; **¡Qué barato!** *How cheap!*, 9; **¡Qué caro!** *How expensive!*, 9; **¿Qué clases tienes?** *What classes do you have?*, 3; **¿Qué fecha es hoy?** *What's today's date?*, 5; **¡Qué ganga!** *What a bargain!*, 9; **¿Qué hacemos?** *What shall we do?*, 4; **¿Qué hacen?** *What are they doing?*, 4; **¿Qué haces después de clases?** *What do you do after school?*, 4, PUENTE; **¿Qué hay?** *What's up?*, 1; **¿Qué hay en...?** *What's in . . .?*, 2; **¿Qué hay para tomar?** *What's there to drink?*, 8; **¿Qué hiciste?** *What did you do?*, 10; **¿Qué hizo?** *What did he/she/you do?*, 10; **¿Qué hora es?** *What time is it?*, 3, PUENTE; **¡Qué horrible!** *How terrible!*, 2; **¿Qué hubo?** *What's up?*, 1; **¡Qué lástima!** *What a shame!*, 7; **¿Qué le pasa a...?** *What's wrong with . . .?*, 11; **¡Qué lío!** *What a mess!*, 3; **¿Qué onda?** *What's up?*, 1; **¡Qué padre!** *How cool!*,

2; **¿Qué pasa?** *What's happening?*, 1; **¡Qué pesado/a!** *How annoying!*, 2; **¿Qué prefieres?** *What do you prefer?*, 8; **¿Qué tal?** *How's it going?*, 1, PUENTE; **¿Qué tal si ...?** *What if . . .?*, 11; **¿Qué te gusta hacer?** *What do you like to do?*, 4; **¿Qué te gusta?** *What do you like?*, 1; **¿Qué te parece si...?** *How do you feel about . . .?*, 10; **¿Qué tiempo hace?** *What's the weather like?*, 5, PUENTE; **¿Qué tienes?** *What's the matter?*, 11; **¿Qué tipo de...?** *What kind of. . .?*, 9
quedar *to be (located)*, 9
quedarse *to stay, to remain*, 12
los **quehaceres domésticos** *household chores*, 6, PUENTE
querer (ie) *to want*, 2
querido/a *dear*, 6
el **queso** *cheese*, 8
el **quetzal** *Guatemalan bird, Guatemalan currency*, PREL
¿quién? *who?*, 4; **¿quiénes?** *who?* (plural), 5
Quiere... *He/She wants . . .*, 2; *quiere decir* *means*, 4; **Quieres...** *You want . . .*, 2; **Quiero...** *I want . . .*, 2, PUENTE; **¿Quieres...?** *Do you want to. . .?*, 7
la **química** *chemistry*, 3
quince *fifteen*, 1
la **quinceañera** *girl celebrating her fifteenth birthday*, 10
quinientos/as *five hundred*, 8
quisiera *I would like*, 8

R

la **ración** *portion*, 8
la **radio** *radio*, 2
las **raíces** *roots*, 10
rallado/a *grated*, 8
rápido/a *quick, fast, quickly*, 5
raro/a *rare*, 7
el **raspado** *snowcone*, 4
la **raya** *stripe*; **de rayas** *striped*, 9
la **razón** *reason*, PUENTE

real *royal,* 1
la realidad *reality,* 7
realizar *to make real, to make happen,* 7
el recado *message;* ¿**Puedo dejar un recado?** *May I leave a message?,* 7
la receta *recipe,* 8
recibir *to receive,* 5
recibir regalos *to receive gifts,* 10
el recorrido *tour,* 4
recostado/a *reclined,* 11
el recreo *recess,* 7
el recuerdo *souvenir, remembrance,* 1
refrescante *refreshing,* 8
el **refresco** *soft drink,* 4; **tomar un refresco** *to drink a soft drink,* 4
refrito/a *refried,* 8
regalar *to give (as a gift),* 9
el **regalo** *gift,* 9
la región *region,* 8
la **regla** *ruler,* 2
regresar *to return, to go back, to come back,* 4
Regular. *Okay.,* 1
la reina *queen,* PREL
el reino *kingdom,* PUENTE
el relajamiento *relaxation,* 12
la religión *religion,* 3
rellenar *to fill,* 8
el **reloj** *clock, watch,* 2
remar *to row,* 4
el remo *paddle, oar,* 5
remolcar *to tow,* 11
el repaso *review,* 1
el reportaje *report,* 5
los reptiles *reptiles,* 2
el **resfriado** *cold;* **estar resfriado/a** *to be congested,* 11
resolver *to solve,* 9
respirar *to breathe,* 11
respondes *you answer,* 1
responsable *responsible,* 6
la respuesta *answer, response,* 2
el **restaurante** *restaurant,* 4, PUENTE
el retrato *portrait,* 6
la reunión *meeting, reunion,* 6
reunirse *to gather, to meet,* 6
la **revista** *magazine,* 2
el rey *king,* 6
rico/a *rich, delicious,* 8
el **río** *river,* 5; **bajar el río en canoa** *to go canoeing on a river,* 12
las riquezas *riches,* 7

el ritmo *rhythm,* 5
la rodilla *knee,* 11
roer *to gnaw,* 6
rojo/a *red,* 9
romántico/a *romantic,* 4
la **ropa** *clothing,* 9; **lavar la ropa** *to wash the clothes,* 4
rosado/a *pink,* PREL
rubio/a *blond(e),* 3
la **rueda** *wheel;* **patinar sobre ruedas** *to roller skate,* 11

S

el **sábado** *Saturday,* 4, PUENTE
el **sábado pasado** *last Saturday,* 10
saber *to know (information);* **No sé.** *I don't know.,* 2; **Sé.** *I know.,* 2; No saben. *They don't know.,* 6
¿sabías? *did you know?,* PREL
el sabor *taste,* 4
el sacapuntas *pencil sharpener,* 2
sacar *to take out,* 4; **sacar la basura** *to take out the trash,* 4, PUENTE; sacar buenas/malas notas *to get good/bad grades;* sacar fotos *to take photographs,* 7
el saco *sportscoat,* 9
la **sala** *living room,* 6; la sala de clase *classroom,* 4
salado/a *salty,* 8
salgo *I go out,* 5
salir *to go out, to leave,* 6
el salón *hall,* 4
la salsa *sauce,* 8
saltar *to jump;* **saltar en paracaídas** *to go skydiving,* 12
el salto *waterfall,* 11
saludar *to greet,* 3
el saludo *greeting,* 1
salvar *to save,* 2
el salvavidas *life jacket,* PREL
el sancocho *soup made of green plantains and corn,* 8
las **sandalias** *sandals,* 9
la sandía *watermelon,* 2
el **sándwich** *sandwich,* 5
sano/a *healthy,* 11
santo/a *saint,* 1
Se llama... *His/Her/Your name is . . .,* 1
Se ve joven. *He/She looks young.,* 6

sé *I know,* 2; **No sé.** *I don't know.,* 2
el secreto *secret,* 1
la **seda** *silk;* **de seda** *(made of) silk,* 9
sedoso/a *silky,* 7
seguidamente *immediately afterward,* 5
segundo/a *second,* 1
seis *six,* 1
seiscientos/as *six hundred,* 8
la **selva** *jungle,* 12
el semáforo *traffic signal,* 5
la **semana** *week,* 4; los días de semana *weekdays;* 4; los días de la semana *the days of the week,* 5; **fin de semana** *weekend,* 4
la **semana pasada** *last week,* 10
semejante *similar,* 11
el **semestre** *semester,* 3
sencillo/a *simple,* 11
señor *sir, Mister,* 1; el señor *the (gentle) man*
señora *ma'am, Mrs.,* 1; la señora *the woman, the lady*
señorita *miss,* 1; la señorita *the young girl; the lady*
el sentido *sense, faculty of sensation,* 5
sentirse (ie) *to feel,* 11
septiembre (m.) *September,* 5
ser *to be,* 1; ¿**Cómo es?** *What's he/she/it like?,* 3, PUENTE; ¿**Cómo son?** *What are they like?,* 3; ¿**De dónde eres?** *Where are you from?,* 1, PUENTE; **Es de...** *He/She is from . . .,* 1, PUENTE; **Es la una.** *It's one o'clock,* 3; **No es cierto.** *It isn't true.,* 6; ser unido(s) *to be close-knit,* 6; **somos** *we are,* 3; **Son las...** *It's . . . o'clock.,* 3, PUENTE; **soy** *I am,* 1; **Soy de...** *I'm from . . .,* 1, PUENTE
serio/a *serious,* 5
el servicio *service,* 1
la **servilleta** *napkin,* 8
sesenta *sixty,* 2
la sesión *session,* 4
setecientos/as *seven hundred,* 8
setenta *seventy,* 2
si *if,* 4
sí *yes,* 1
la sicología *psychology,* 1
siempre *always,* 5, PUENTE;

SPANISH-ENGLISH VOCABULARY

311

Hace buen tiempo. *The weather is nice.*, 5; **Hace mal tiempo.** *The weather is bad.*, 5; Hace un tiempo precioso. *It's a beautiful day.*, 5; pronóstico del tiempo *weather report*, 5; **¿Qué tiempo hace?** *What's the weather like?*, 5, PUENTE

la **tienda** *store*, 4, PUENTE; **la tienda de comestibles** *grocery store*, 9

la **tienda** *tent;* la tienda de campaña *camping tent*, 7; **la tienda de camping** *camping tent*, 12

tiene *he/she has*, 2, PUENTE; **Tiene... años.** *He/She is . . . years old.*, 1; **Tiene canas.** *He/She has gray hair.*, 6

tienes *you have*, 2, PUENTE

la **tierra** *Earth*, 2

las **tijeras** *scissors*, 2

la **tilde** *tilde,* (diacritical mark over the letter ñ), 1

tímido/a *shy*, 6

el **tío** *uncle*, 6

típicamente *typically*, 5, PUENTE

típico/a *typical, characteristic*, PREL

el **tipo** *type, kind*

tirar *to throw*, 10

las **tiras cómicas** *comics*, 5

la **toalla** *towel*, 12

el **tocador de discos compactos** *CD player*, 2

tocar *to touch, to play;* **tocar un instrumento** *to play an instrument*, 4, PUENTE

el **tocino** *bacon*, 8

todavía *still, yet*, 5

todo/a *all, every*, 5; todo el mundo *everyone, everybody*, 4; todo el tiempo *all the time*, 5; **todos los días** *every day*, 5, PUENTE

tomar *to drink, to take*, 4, PUENTE; **tomar el autobús** *to take the bus*, 5; **tomar el sol** *to sunbathe*, 12

el **tomate** *tomato*, 8

el **tomatillo** *fruit resembling a tomato and that grows on trees instead of vines*, 8

el **tomo** *volume, tome*, 2

la **toronja** *grapefruit*, 8

la **tortilla** *omelet* (Spain), 1; *corn cake* (Mexico)

la **tortuga** *tortoise*, PUENTE

la **tos** *cough;* **tener tos** *to have a cough*, 11

los **tostones** *fried green plantains*, 6

trabajador/a *hard-working*, 6

trabajar *to work*, 4; **trabajar en el jardín** *to work in the garden*, 6, PUENTE

el **trabajo** *work, job*, 4

el **trabalenguas** *tongue twister*, 2

tradicional *traditional*, 6

las **tradiciones** *traditions*, 6

traer *to bring*, 8

el **traje** *suit*, 9; **el traje de baño** *bathing suit*, 9

transportado/a *transported*, 2

el **transporte** *transportation*, 1

travieso/a *mischievous*, 6

trece *thirteen*, 1

treinta *thirty*, 1

tremendo/a *tremendous, incredible*, 5; ¡Hace un frío tremendo! *It's incredibly cold!*, 5

tres *three*, 1

trescientos/as *three hundred*, 8

triste *sad*, 11

la **trivia** *trivia*, 1

el **tronco** *trunk (of a tree)*, 10

tu(s) *your* (familiar), 2

tú *you* (familiar), 1

el **tubo** *tube*, 4

la **tumba** *tomb*, 10

el **turismo** *sightseeing, tourism;* **hacer turismo** *to go sightseeing*, 12

tuvo *he/she had*, 4

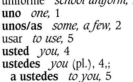

U

la **ubicación** *location*, 7

un *a, an*, 2; **un poco gordo/a** *a little overweight*, 6

una *a, an*, 2; **Es la una.** *It's one o'clock.*, 3

único/a *only, unique*, 1

la **unidad** *unit*, 9

unido/a *close-knit*, 6

el **uniforme** *school uniform*, 2

uno *one*, 1

unos/as *some, a few*, 2

usar *to use*, 5

usted *you*, 4

ustedes *you* (pl.), 4,; **a ustedes** *to you*, 5

útil *useful*, PREL

la **utilización** *use*, 1

las **uvas** *grapes*, 8

V

va *he/she goes*, 5

las **vacaciones** *vacation*, 5, PUENTE

el **vals** *waltz*, 4

vamos a... *let's . . .;* vamos a escribir *let's write*, 3; vamos a leer *let's read*, 1; **¡Vamos!** *Let's go!, we go*, 3

variar *to vary*, 7

la **variedad** *variety*, 7; las variedades *varieties, variety section* (of a magazine or newspaper), 6

varios/varias *various, several*, 3

varonil *men's* (adj.), 4

vas *you go;* **¿Adónde vas?** *Where are you going?*, 4

un vaso de leche *a glass of milk*, 8

ve *go*, 10

las **veces** *times* (sing. **vez**)**;** **a veces** *sometimes*, 5, PUENTE; **muchas veces** *often*, 5

veinte *twenty*, 1

la **vela** *candle*, 10; *sail, sailing*, 10; **ir de vela** *to go sailing*, 12

el **velero** *sailboat*, 5

la **velocidad** *velocity, speed*, 5

ven *come*, 10

el **venado** *deer*, 10

vencer *to defeat*, 11

venezolano/a *of or from Venezuela*, 2

vengo de *I come from*, 1

venir (ie) *to come*, 7

la **ventaja** *advantage*, 11

la **ventana** *window*, 2

ver *to see*, 4; **ver una película** *to see a movie*, 4

verán: ya verán *you'll/they'll (soon) see*, 12

el **verano** *summer*, 5, PUENTE

el **verano pasado** *last summer*, 10

¿verdad? *don't you?, right?*, 3

verde *green*, 6

la **vereda** *trail*, 12

la **vergüenza** *shame,*

embarrassment; **tener vergüenza** *to be embarrassed,* 11

el vertebrado *vertebrate,* 2

el vestido *dress,* 9

vestirse *to get dressed,* 7

vete *go away,* 10

la vez *time, turn, occasion, occurrence;* **de vez en cuando** *once in a while,* 5; **a veces** *sometimes,* 5, PUENTE; **muchas veces** *often,* 5; **tres veces por semana** *three times a week,* 5; **una vez** *once,* 5

el viaje *trip,* 6, PUENTE; **hacer un viaje** *to take a trip,* 6

la vicuña *vicuña, Andean pack animal,* 7

la vida *life,* 11

el video *video,* 1

la videocasetera *VCR,* 2

el videojuego *videogame,* 3, PUENTE

viejo/a *old,* 6

viene de *comes from,* 4

el viento *wind,* 5; **Hace (mucho) viento.** *It's (very) windy.,* 5, PUENTE

el viernes *Friday,* 4

el vinagre *vinegar,* 8

el violín *violin,* 4

visitar *to visit,* 6

las visitas *visitors,* 6

vivir *to live,* 6

vivo *I live,* 1

vivo/a *alive,* 6

el vocabulario *vocabulary; glossary,* 1

volar cometas *to fly kites,* 5

el volcán *volcano,* 7

el voleibol *volleyball,* 1

vosotros/as *you* (familiar plural), 4

votar *to vote,* 4

voy *I go* (from **ir**), 3

el vuelo *flight,* 3

la vuelta *turn,* 11

vuestro/a *your* (pl., Spain), 6

y *and,* 1; **y cuarto** *quarter past (the hour),* 3, PUENTE; **y media** *half past (the hour),* 3, PUENTE; **¿Y tú?** *And you?,* 1

ya *already,* 2

Ya tengo planes. *I already have plans.,* 7

el yahuarlocro *Andean dish,* 8

el yate *yacht,* PREL

la yema *yolk,* 7

el yerno *son-in-law,* 7

yo *I,* 1; **Yo también.** *Me too.,* 1

el yugo *yoke,* 7

la zanahoria *carrot,* 8

la zapatería *shoe store,* 9

las zapatillas de tenis *tennis shoes* (Spain), 2

los zapatos *shoe,* 9; los zapatos de tenis *tennis shoes,* 9

el zócalo *main square* (Mexico), 4

la zona *zone,* 7

el zoológico *zoo,* 7

ENGLISH-SPANISH VOCABULARY

This vocabulary includes all of the words presented in the **Vocabulario** sections of the chapters. These words are considered active—you are expected to know them and be able to use them. Expressions are listed under the English word you would be most likely to look up.

Spanish nouns are listed with the definite article and plural forms, when applicable. If a Spanish verb stem-changing, the change is indicated in parentheses after the verb: **querer (ie)**. The number after each entry refers to the chapter in which the word or phrase is introduced.

To be sure you are using Spanish words and phrases in their correct context, refer to the chapters listed. You may also want to look up Spanish phrases in the Summary of Functions, pp. 282–285.

A

a/an *un, una,* 2
ache, to *doler (ue),* 11
aerobics *los ejercicios aérobicos,* 5
a few *unos, unas,* 2
affectionate *cariñoso/a,* 6
after *después,* 3; *después de,* 4
afternoon *la tarde,* 3; **in the afternoon** *de la tarde,* 3; *por la tarde,* 5
afterward *después,* 3
agreed *de acuerdo,* 10
a little *un poco,* 6
all *todo/a, todos/as,* 5
a lot *mucho,* 1
a lot of; a lot *mucho/a, muchos/as,* 2
all right *está bien,* 7, *De acuerdo.,* 10
almost *casi,* 6; **almost always** *casi siempre,* 6
along *por,* 5; **along the beach** *por la playa,* 5
already *ya,* 2
also *también,* 2
always *siempre,* 5
American *americano/a,* 1; *norteamericano,* 1; **American football** *el fútbol norteamericano,* 1
amusement park *el parque de atracciones,* 7
amusing *divertido/a,* 3
and *y,* 1; **And you?** *¿Y tú?,* 1
angry *enojado/a,* 11
anniversary *el aniversario,* 7; **anniversary party** *la fiesta de aniversario,* 7
another *otro/a, otros/as,* 8
anthropology *la antropología,* 7
apple *la manzana,* 8
appointment *la cita,* 7
April *abril,* 5
aquarium *el acuario,* 7

arm *el brazo,* 11
art *el arte,* 3; *las artes* (pl.)
as . . . as . . . *tan... como... ,* 9
ask for, to *pedir (i),* 8
at *a, por,* 3; **at all** *para nada,* 8; **at last** *por fin,* 3; **at night** *por la noche, en la noche,* 5; **At what time . . .?** *¿A qué hora...?,* 3
attend, to *asistir a,* 5
attraction *la atracción,* 7
August *agosto,* 5
aunt *la tía,* 6
autumn *el otoño,* 5

B

back *la espalda,* 11
backpack *la mochila,* 2
bacon *el tocino,* 8
bad *mal,* 1; **to feel bad** *(estar) mal,* 1; *sentirse mal,* 11; *malo/a,* 3
bakery *la panadería,* 9
balloons *los globos,* 10
ballpoint pen *el bolígrafo,* 2
banana *el plátano,* 8
bargain *la ganga,* 9; **What a bargain!** *¡Qué ganga!,* 9
baseball *el béisbol,* 1
basketball *el baloncesto,* 1; *el basquetbol,* 3
bathing suit *el traje de baño,* 9
be, to *ser,* 1; *estar,* 4; **to be able** *poder (ue),* 8; **to be hungry** *tener hambre,* 8; **to be in a hurry** *tener prisa,* 3; **to be located** *quedar,* 9; **to be ready** *estar listo/a,* 7; **to be sleepy** *tener sueño,* 7; **to be thirsty** *tener sed,* 8; **to be . . . years old** *tener... años,* 1
beach *la playa,* 5
beans *los frijoles,* 8
because *porque,* 3
bed *la cama,* 2
beef *la carne de res,* 8

before *antes de,* 4
begin, to *empezar (ie),* 7
believe, to *creer,* 10
belt *el cinturón,* 9
beneath *debajo de,* 4
besides *además,* 9
beverage *la bebida,* 8
bicycle *la bicicleta,* 4
big *grande,* 3
bill *la cuenta,* 8
birthday *el cumpleaños,* 7; **birthday party** *la fiesta de cumpleaños,* 7
black *negro/a,* 6
block, city *la cuadra,* 9
blond *rubio/a,* 3
blouse *la blusa,* 9
blow up balloons, to *inflar los globos,* 10
blue *azul,* 6
bluejeans *los bluejeans,* 9
board game *el juego de mesa,* 9
body *el cuerpo,* 11
book *el libro,* 2
book bag *la mochila,* 2
bookstore *la librería,* 2
boots *las botas,* 9
boring *aburrido/a,* 3
bowl *el plato hondo, el tazón,* 8
boy *el chico,* 5
bread *el pan,* 8
break *el descanso,* 3
breakfast *el desayuno,* 8
bring, to *traer,* 8
brother *el hermano,* 6; **brothers and sisters** *los hermanos,* 6
brown *de color café,* 6; *pardo,* 9
brunette *moreno/a,* 3
brush one's teeth, to *lavarse los dientes,* 7
bus *el autobús,* 5
busy *ocupado/a,* 7; **The line is busy.** *La línea está ocupada.,* 7
but *pero,* 1
buy, to *comprar,* 2
by *por,* 5
'bye *chao,* 1

C

cafeteria *la cafetería,* 1
cake *el pastel,* 8
calculator *la calculadora,* 2
call, to *llamar,* 7; **to call the guests** *llamar a los invitados,* 10
camera *la cámara,* 12
camp, to *acampar,* 5
Can you bring me . . .? *¿Me puede (formal) traer...?,* 8; *¿Me traes (familiar)...?,* 10; **Can you do me the favor of . . .?** *¿Me haces el favor de...?,* 10; **Can you give me . . .?** *¿Me das...?,* 10; **Can you help me . . .?** *¿Me ayudas a...?,* 10; **Can you pass me . . .?** *¿Me pasas...?,* 10; **Can you tell me . . .?** *¿Me puede decir...?,* 9
candy *los dulces,* 9; **candy store** *la dulcería,* 9
canoe *la canoa,* 12
car *el carro,* 4
card *la tarjeta,* 9
carrot *la zanahoria,* 8
cat *el gato,* 6; **to take care of the cat** *cuidar al gato,* 6
cereal *el cereal,* 8
chair *la silla,* 2
cheap *barato/a,* 9
cheese *el queso,* 8
chicken *el pollo,* 8
children *los hijos,* 6
China *(la) China,* 12
Chinese food *la comida china,* 1
chocolate *el chocolate,* 1
chores *los quehaceres domésticos,* 6
Christmas *la Navidad,* 10; **Christmas Eve** *la Nochebuena,* 10
circus *el circo,* 7
city *la ciudad,* 7
city block *la cuadra,* 9
class *la clase,* 1
classical music *la música clásica,* 1
classmate *el compañero* (male)/ *la compañera* (female) *de clase,* 3
clean *limpio/a,* 8
clean, to *limpiar,* 6; **clean the kitchen, to** *limpiar la cocina,* 6
clever *listo/a,* 6
climb, to *escalar,* 12
clock *el reloj,* 2
close-knit *unido/a,* 6
closet *el armario,* 2
clothes/clothing *la ropa,* 2
cloudy *nublado,* 5; **It's cloudy.** *Está nublado.,* 5
coffee *el café,* 8; **coffee with milk** *el café con leche,* 8
cold *frío,* 8; **It's cold.** *Hace frío.,* 5; **to have a cold** *estar resfriado/a,* 11
color *el color,* 6
comb one's hair, to *peinarse,* 7
come, to *venir (ie),* 7; **Come!** *¡Ven!,* 10; **Come along!** *¡Ven conmigo!,* PREL
comfortable *cómodo/a,* 9
comical *cómico/a,* 3
comics *las tiras cómicas,* 5
compact disc *el disco compacto,* 9
companion *el compañero* (male), *la compañera* (female), 3
computer science *la computación,* 3
concert *el concierto,* 3
cookie *la galleta,* 8
corn *el maíz,* 8
cost, to *costar(ue),* 9
cotton *el algodón,* 9; **made of cotton** *de algodón* 9
cough *la tos,* 11
country *el campo,* 7
cousin *el primo* (male), *la prima* (female), 6
custard *el flan,* 8
cut, to *cortar,* 6; **to cut the grass** *cortar el césped,* 6

D

dad *el papá,* 6
dance *el baile,* 3
dance, to *bailar,* 4
dark-haired *moreno/a,* 3
dark-skinned *moreno/a,* 3
date *la fecha,* 5; *la cita,* 7
daughter *la hija,* 6
day *el día,* 4; **day before yesterday** *anteayer,* 10; **every day** *todos los días,* 5; **a day off** *un día libre,* 3
December *diciembre,* 5
decorate, to *decorar,* 10
decorations *las decoraciones,* 10
delicious *delicioso/a,* 8; *rico/a,* 8
delighted *encantado/a,* 1
department store *el almacén,* 9
desk *el escritorio,* 2
dessert *el postre,* 8
dictionary *el diccionario,* 2
diet *la dieta,* 8
difficult *difícil,* 3
dining room *el comedor,* 12
dinner *la cena,* 4
dirty *sucio/a,* 8
disagreeable *antipático/a,* 3
do, to *hacer,* 2; **Do!** *¡Haz!,* 10;

to do yoga *hacer yoga,* 11; **Do you like . . .?** *¿Te gusta...?,* 1; **Don't worry!** *¡No te preocupes!,* 3
dog *el perro,* 4; **to walk the dog** *caminar con el perro,* 4
dollar *el dólar,* 2
door *la puerta,* 2
downtown *el centro,* 4
draw, to *dibujar,* 4
dress *el vestido,* 9
drink, to *tomar,* 4; *beber,* 5
during *durante,* 5

E

ear (inner) *el oído,* 11; (outer) **ear** *la oreja,* 11
earn, to *ganar,* 11
earring *el arete,* 9
Easter *las Pascuas,* 10
easy *fácil,* 3
eat, to *comer,* 5; **to eat breakfast** *desayunar,* 5; **to eat dinner** *cenar,* 6; **to eat lunch** *almorzar (ue),* 8
education *la educación,* 3; **physical education** *la educación física,* 3
eggs *los huevos,* 8
Egypt *(el) Egipto,* 12
eight *ocho,* 1
eighteen *dieciocho,* 1
eight hundred *ochocientos/as,* 8
eighty *ochenta,* 2
eleven *once,* 1
end *el fin,* 4
England *Inglaterra,* 12
English class *la clase de inglés,* 1
enough *bastante,* 6
erase, to *borrar,* 2
eraser *la goma de borrar,* 2
especially *especialmente,* 5
evening *la noche,* 5; **in the evening** (P.M.) *de la noche,* 3
event *el evento,* 7
every *todo/a, todos/as;* **every day** *todos los días,* 5
exam *el examen,* (pl. *los exámenes),* 3
excellent *excelente,* 1
Excuse me. *Perdón.,* 9; *Perdóname.,* 10
exercise *el ejercicio,* 5; **to exercise** *hacer ejercicio,* 5
expensive *caro/a,* 9
explore, to *explorar,* 12
eyes *los ojos,* 6

F

fall *el otoño,* 5

family   *la familia,* 6
fantastic   *fantástico/a,* 3
far   *lejos,* 4; **far from**   *lejos de,* 4
father   *el padre, el papá,* 6;
   Father's Day   *el Día del Padre,* 10
favorite   *favorito/a,* 3
February   *febrero,* 5
feel, to   *sentirse (ie),* 11; **to feel like (doing something)**   *tener ganas de* + infinitive, 7
fever   *la fiebre,* 11; **to have a fever**   *tener fiebre,* 11
few, a   *unos/as,* 2
fifteen   *quince,* 1
fifty   *cincuenta,* 2
find, to   *encontrar (ue),* 2
finger   *el dedo,* 11
first   *primero/a,* 2
fish   *el pescado,* 8
fish, to   *pescar,* 5
fit, to   *quedar,* 9; **It fits you very well.**   *Te queda muy bien.,* 9
five   *cinco,* 1
five hundred   *quinientos/as,* 8
flowers   *las flores,* 9
flower shop   *la florería,* 9
flu   *la gripe,* 11
folder   *la carpeta,* 2
food   *la comida,* 6; **Chinese food**   *la comida china,* 1; **Italian food**   *la comida italiana,* 1; **Mexican food**   *la comida mexicana,* 1
foot   *el pie,* 11
football   *el fútbol norteamericano,* 1
for   *para,* 9; **For whom?**   *¿Para quién?,* 9
forest   *el bosque,* 12
fork   *el tenedor,* 8
formal   *formal,* 9
forty   *cuarenta,* 2
four   *cuatro,* 1
four hundred   *cuatrocientos/as,* 8
fourteen   *catorce,* 1
France   *Francia,* 12
free day   *el día libre,* 3
free time   *el tiempo libre,* 4
French   *el francés,* 3
french fries   *las papas fritas,* 5
Friday   *el viernes,* 4
friend   *el amigo* (male), *la amiga* (female), 1; *el compañero,* (male), 1; *la compañera,* (female), 3
from   *de,* 1
fruit   *la fruta,* 1
fun   *divertido/a,* 3
funny   *cómico/a,* 3

G

game   *el juego,* 9; **game of . . . (sport)**   *el partido de...,* 3
garbage   *la basura,* 4
garden   *el jardín,* 6
geography   *la geografía,* 3
Germany   *Alemania,* 12
get to know someone, to   *conocer a,* 2
gift   *el regalo,* 9; **to open gifts**   *abrir los regalos,* 10; **to receive gifts**   *recibir regalos,* 10
girl   *la chica,* 5
give, to   *dar,* 9; **to give a gift**   *regalar,* 9
Gladly!   *¡Con mucho gusto!,* 10
glass   *el vaso,* 8
go, to   *ir,* 2; **Go!**   *¡Ve!,* 10; **Go away!**   *¡Vete!,* 10; **to go canoeing**   *bajar el río en canoa,* 12; **to go down**   *bajar,* 12; **to go hiking**   *dar una caminata,* 12; **to go mountain climbing**   *escalar montañas,* 12; **to go out**   *salir,* 6; **to go sailing**   *ir de vela,* 12; **to go sightseeing**   *hacer turismo,* 12; **to go skydiving**   *saltar en paracaídas,* 12; **to go to the mall**   *ir al centro comercial,* 2; **going to (do something)**   *ir + a* + infinitive, 7
good   *bueno/a,* 3; **Good afternoon.**   *Buenas tardes.,* 1; **Good evening.**   *Buenas noches.,* 1; **Good morning.**   *Buenos días.,* 1; **Good night.**   *Buenas noches.,* 1
Goodbye.   *Adiós.,* 1
good-looking   *guapo/a,* 3
graduation   *la graduación,* 7; **graduation party**   *la fiesta de graduación,* 7
grandfather   *el abuelo,* 6
grandmother   *la abuela,* 6
grandparents   *los abuelos,* 6
grapefruit   *la toronja,* 8
grapes   *las uvas,* 8
grass   *el césped,* 6
gray   *gris,* 9; **gray hair**   *las canas,* 6
great   *excelente,* 1; *estupendo,* 1; *magnífico,* 11
green   *verde,* 6
greeting card   *la tarjeta,* 9
grocery store   *la tienda de comestibles,* 9
guests   *los invitados,* 10
guitar   *la guitarra,* 4
gym   *el gimnasio,* 4

H

hair   *el pelo,* 6; **He/She has gray hair.**   *Tiene canas.,* 6
half brother   *el medio hermano,* 6
half past (the hour)   *y media,* 3
half sister   *la media hermana,* 6
ham   *el jamón,* 8
hamburger   *la hamburguesa,* 5
hand   *la mano,* 11
hang up, to   *colgar (ue),* 10
have, to   *tener (ie),* 2; **to have a cold**   *estar resfriado/a,* 11; **to have a cough**   *tener tos,* 11; **to have a fever**   *tener fiebre,* 11; **to have breakfast**   *desayunar,* 5; **to have the flu**   *tener gripe,* 11; **to have to (do something)**   *tener que* + infinitive, 7; **to have to go**   *tener que irse,* 1
he   *él,* 2
head   *la cabeza,* 11
healthy   *sano/a,* 11
heat   *el calor,* 5
heavy   *fuerte,* 8
Hello.   *Aló,* 7; *Diga.,* 7; *¡Hola!,* 1 (telephone greetings)
help   *ayudar,* 5
help at home, to   *ayudar en casa,* 5
her   *su(s),* 2; *la,* 10; **to/for her**   *le,* 9
here   *aquí,* 4
high school   *el colegio,* 2
him   *lo,* 10; **to/for him**   *le,* 9
his   *su(s),* 2
holidays   *los días festivos,* 10
home   *la casa,* 4; **at home**   *en casa,* 4
homework   *la tarea,* 1
hope for, to   *esperar,* 12
horrible   *horrible,* 1
hot   *caliente,* 8; **to be hot**   *hacer calor,* 4
hot dog   *el perro caliente,* 8
hour   *la hora,* 3
house   *la casa,* 4
How?   *¿Cómo?,* 1; **How are you?**   *¿Cómo estás?,* 1
How cheap!   *¡Qué barato!,* 9
How do you feel about . . .?   *¿Qué te parece si...?,* 10
How expensive!   *¡Qué caro!,* 9
How many?   *¿cuántos?, ¿cuántas?,* 2
How much?   *¿cuánto/a?,* 2; **How much do . . . cost?**   *¿Cuánto cuestan...?,* 9; **How much does . . . cost?**   *¿Cuánto cuesta...?,* 9; **How much is it?**   *¿Cuánto es?,* 8

How often? *¿Con qué frecuencia?*, 5
How old are you? *¿Cuántos años tienes?*, 1; **How old is she/he?** *¿Cuántos años tiene?*, 1
How's it going? *¿Qué tal?*, 1
hundred *cien, ciento*, 2
hungry, to be *tener hambre*, 8
hurry *la prisa*; **Hurry up!** *¡Date prisa!*, 3; **I'm in a hurry.** *Tengo prisa.*, 3
hurt, to *doler (ue)*, 11
husband *el esposo*, 6

I

I *yo*, 1
ice cream *el helado*, 4; **to eat ice cream** *tomar un helado*, 4
I would like *quisiera*, 8
iced tea *el té frío*, 8
idea *la idea*, 10
if *si*, 11
I'm sorry. *Lo siento.*
in *en, por*, 4; **in order to** *para + infinitive*, 4; **in the afternoon (P.M.)** *de la tarde*, 3, *por la tarde*, 5; **in the evening (P.M.)** *de la noche*, 3, *por la noche*, 5; **in the morning (A.M.)** *de la mañana*, 3, *por la mañana*, 5
included *incluido/a*, 8
Independence Day *el Día de la Independencia*, 10
inflate, to *inflar*, 10
intelligent *inteligente*, 3
intend, to *pensar + infinitive*, 7
interesting *interesante*, 3
invitation *la invitación*, 10
invite, to *invitar*, 7; **It's my treat.** *Te invito.*, 7
iron, to *planchar*, 6
island *la isla*, 12
isn't it? *¿no?*, 3
it *la, lo*, 10
Italian food *la comida italiana*, 1
Italy *Italia*, 12
It's a rip-off! *¡Es un robo!*, 9
It's cloudy. *Está nublado.*, 5
It's (very) cold. *Hace (mucho) frío.*, 5
It's cool. *Hace fresco.*, 5
It's hot. *Hace calor.*, 5
It's raining. *Está lloviendo.*, 5; *Llueve.*, 5
It's snowing. *Está nevando.*, 5; *Nieva.*, 5
It's sunny. *Hace sol.*, 5
It's (very) windy. *Hace (mucho) viento.*, 5

J

jacket *la chaqueta*, 9
January *enero*, 5
jazz *el jazz*, 1
jewelry store *la joyería*, 9
job *el trabajo*, 4
juice *el jugo*, 5; **orange juice** *el jugo de naranja*, 8
July *julio*, 5
June *junio*, 5
jungle *la selva*, 12

K

kitchen *la cocina*, 6
knife *el cuchillo*, 8
know, to *saber*, 2; *conocer*, 2

L

lake *el lago*, 7
lamp *la lámpara*, 2
last *pasado/a*, 10; **last night** *anoche*, 10; **last Saturday** *el sábado pasado*, 10; **last summer** *el verano pasado*, 10; **last week** *la semana pasada*, 10; **last year** *el año pasado* 10
late *atrasado/a, tarde*, 3; **It is late.** *Es tarde.*; **to be late** *estar atrasado/a*, 3
later *más tarde*, 7
lead, to *llevar*, 11; **to lead a healthy life** *llevar una vida sana*, 11
leather (made of) *de cuero*, 9
leave, to *salir*, 6; **to leave a message** *dejar un recado*, 7
leg *la pierna*, 11
lemonade *la limonada*, 8
less *menos*, 6
less . . . than *menos ... que*, 9
letter *la carta*, 5
lettuce *la lechuga*, 8
library *la biblioteca*, 4
life *la vida*, 11
lift, to *levantar*, 11; **to lift weights** *levantar pesas*, 11
light *ligero/a*, 8
like, to *gustar*, 1; **to really like** *encantar*, 8; **I'd like . . .** *Me gustaría...*, 7
likewise *igualmente*, 1
line *la línea*, 7; **The line is busy.** *La línea está ocupada.*, 7
listen, to *escuchar*, 4; **to listen to music** *escuchar música*, 4
little, a *un poco*, 6
live, to *vivir*, 6
living room *la sala*, 6

M

look at, to *mirar*, 4; **Look!** *¡Mira!*, 4
look for, to *buscar*, 9
lot, a *mucho*, 1
love, to *encantar*, 8
lunch *el almuerzo*, 3

ma'am *señora*, 1
magazine *la revista*, 2
make, to *hacer*, 2
make the bed, to *hacer la cama*, 6
makeup, to put on *maquillarse*, 7
mall *el centro comercial*, 2
mango *el mango*, 8
many *muchos/as*, 2
March *marzo*, 5
mathematics *las matemáticas*, 3
May *mayo*, 5
maybe *tal vez*, 7
meat *la carne*, 8
menu *el menú*, 8
message *el recado*, 7; **May I leave a message?** *¿Puedo dejar un recado?*, 7
me too *yo también*, 1
Mexican food *la comida mexicana*, 1
mile *la milla*, 5
milk *la leche*, 8
milkshake *el batido*, 8
mineral water *el agua mineral*, 8
mischievous *travieso/a*, 6
miss *señorita*, 1
mister *señor*, 1
moment *el momento*, 7
Monday *el lunes*, 4
money *el dinero*, 2
month *el mes*, 5
more *más*, 1
more . . . than *más ... que*, 9
morning *la mañana*, 5; **in the morning (A.M.)** *de la mañana*, 3; *por la mañana*, 5
mother/mom *la madre/mamá*, 6; **Mother's Day** *el Día de las Madres*, 10
mountain *la montaña*, 12; **to go mountain climbing** *escalar montañas*, 12
mouth *la boca*, 11
movie *la película*, 4
movie theater *el cine*, 4
Mr. *señor*, 1
Mrs. *Señora*, 1
museum *el museo*, 7
music *la música*, 1; **classical music** *la música clásica*, 1; **music by . . .** *la música de...*, 1; **pop music** *la música pop*, 1;

rock music   *la música rock,* 1
my   *mi,* 2; *mis,* 6

N

named, to be   *llamarse,* 1; My
   name is . . .   *Me llamo...,* 1
napkin   *la servilleta,* 8
near   *cerca de,* 4
neck   *el cuello,* 11
necklace   *el collar,* 9
need, to   *necesitar,* 2
nervous   *nervioso/a,* 11
never   *nunca,* 5
new   *nuevo/a,* 3; new
   friends   *nuevos amigos,* 2;
   New Year's Day   *el Año
   Nuevo,* 10; New Year's
   Eve   *la Nochevieja,* 10
newspaper   *el periódico,* 5
next to   *al lado de,* 4
nice   *simpático/a,* 3
Nice to meet you.   *Mucho
   gusto.,* 1
night   *la noche,* 1; at night
   por la noche, 5; Good night.
   Buenas noches., 1; last night
   anoche, 10; the night before
   last   *anteanoche,* 11
nine   *nueve,* 1
nine hundred   *novecientos/as,* 8
nineteen   *diecinueve,* 1
ninety   *noventa,* 2
no   *no,* 1
nobody   *nadie,* 5
nor   *ni,* 6
nose   *la nariz,* 11
not   *no,* 1
notebook   *el cuaderno,* 2
nothing   *nada,* 5
novel   *la novela,* 3
November   *noviembre,* 5
now   *ahora,* 3
nowhere   *ningún lugar,* 12
number   *el número,* 1

O

October   *octubre,* 5
of   *de,* 2
Of course!   *¡Claro que sí!,* 7;
   ¡Cómo no!, 7
often   *muchas veces,* 5
okay   *regular,* 1
old   *viejo/a,* 6; older   *mayor,* 6
on   *en,* 3; on the dot   *en punto,*
   3; on top of   *encima de,* 4
one   *uno,* 1; one moment   *un
   momento,* 7
one hundred   *cien, ciento/a,* 2
one thousand   *mil,* 8
onion   *la cebolla,* 8

only   *sólo,* 5
open, to   *abrir,* 10; to open
   gifts   *abrir regalos,* 10
orange   *anaranjado/a,* 9
orange   *la naranja,* 8; orange
   juice   *el jugo de naranja,* 8
order, to   *pedir (i),* 8
organize, to   *organizar,* 2
other   *otro/a,* 8
ought to, should   *deber,* 6
our   *nuestro/a,* 6
overweight   *gordo/a;* (a little)
   overweight   *un poco gordo/a,* 6

P

pack the suitcase, to   *hacer la
   maleta,* 12
paint, to   *pintar,* 4
pal   *el compañero* (male), *la
   compañera* (female), 3
pants   *los pantalones,* 9
papaya   *la papaya,* 8
paper   *el papel,* 2
paradise   *el paraíso,* 12
parents   *los padres,* 6
park   *el parque,* 4; amusement
   park   *el parque de atracciones,* 7
party   *la fiesta,* 3
pastry shop   *la pastelería,* 9
peanut butter   *la crema de maní,* 8
pencil   *el lápiz,* 2, (pl. *los lápices*)
perfect   *perfecto,* 10
perhaps   *tal vez,* 7; perhaps
   another day   *tal vez otro día,* 7
physical education   *la educación física,* 3
piano   *el piano,* 4
pineapple   *la piña,* 8
pizza   *la pizza,* 1
pizzeria   *la pizzería,* 2
place   *el lugar,* 7
plaid   *de cuadros,* 9
plan   *el plan,* 7; I already have
   plans.   *Ya tengo planes.,* 7
plan to, to   *pensar* + infinitive, 7
plant   *la planta,* 9
plate   *el plato,* 8
play an instrument, to   *tocar
   un instrumento,* 4
playing court   *la cancha,* 11
please   *por favor,* 8
pop music   *la música pop,* 1
postcards   *las tarjetas postales,* 5
poster   *el cartel,* 2
post office   *el correo,* 4
potato   *la papa,* 5
potato chips   *las papitas,* 8
practice, to   *practicar,* 4
prefer, to   *preferir (ie),* 7
prepare, to   *preparar,* 4
pretty   *bonito/a,* 3

price   *el precio,* 9; They're the
   same price.   *Son el mismo
   precio.,* 9
problem   *el problema,* 6
purple   *morado/a,* 9
put on makeup, to   *maquillarse,* 7
put, to   *poner,* 2; Put!   *¡Pon!,* 10

Q

quarter to (the hour)   *menos
   cuarto,* 3
quite   *bastante,* 6

R

radio   *la radio,* 2
rain, to   *llover,* 5
read, to   *leer,* 5
ready   *listo/a,* 7
receive, to   *recibir,* 5; to receive
   gifts   *recibir regalos,* 10; to
   receive letters   *recibir cartas,* 5
recess   *el descanso,* 3
red   *rojo/a,* 9
redheaded   *pelirrojo/a,* 6
rest, to   *descansar,* 4; to rest
   in the park   *descansar en el
   parque,* 4
restaurant   *el restaurante,* 4
return, to   *regresar,* 4
rice   *el arroz,* 8
rich   *rico,* 8
ride, to   *montar,* 4; to ride a bike
   montar en bicicleta, 4; to ride a
   horse   *montar a caballo,* 11
right?   *¿verdad?,* 3
rip-off   *el robo,* 9; It's a rip-off!
   ¡Es un robo!, 9
river   *el río,* 12
rock music   *la música rock,* 1
roller skate, to   *patinar sobre
   ruedas,* 11
room   *el cuarto,* 2
ruler   *la regla,* 2
run, to   *correr,* 5
running track   *la pista de
   correr,* 11

S

sad   *triste,* 11
salad   *la ensalada,* 1
salty   *salado/a,* 8
same   *mismo/a,* 9
Same here.   *Igualmente.,* 1
sandals   *las sandalias,* 9; *las
   chancletas,* 12
sandwich   *el sándwich,* 5
Saturday   *el sábado,* 4
say, to   *decir,* 6; he/she says
   that   *dice que,* 6

scarf *la bufanda,* 12
science *las ciencias,* 3
scuba dive, to *bucear,* 5
seasons *las estaciones,* 5
see, to *ver,* 4; **to see a movie**
ver una película, 4
See you later. *Hasta luego.,* 1
See you tomorrow. *Hasta
mañana.,* 1
seem, to *parecer,* 10; **It seems
fine to me.** *Me parece bien.,* 10
semester *el semestre,* 3
send, to *mandar,* 10; **to send
invitations** *mandar las
invitaciones,* 10
separate *aparte,* 8
September *septiembre,* 5
set the table, to *poner la
mesa,* 6
seven *siete,* 1
seven hundred *setecientos/as,* 8
seventeen *diecisiete,* 1
seventy *setenta,* 2
shave, to *afeitarse,* 7
she *ella,* 2
shirt *la camisa,* 9
shoe *el zapato,* 9
shoe store *la zapatería,* 9
shopping mall *el centro
comercial,* 2
short *bajo/a,* 3; (to describe
length) *corto/a,* 9
shorts *los pantalones cortos,* 9
should *deber,* 6
shrimp *los camarones,* 8
sick *enfermo/a,* 7
silk (made of) *de seda,* 9
sing, to *cantar,* 4
sir *señor,* 1
sister *la hermana,* 6
six *seis,* 1
six hundred *seiscientos/as,* 8
sixteen *dieciséis,* 1
sixty *sesenta,* 2
skate, to *patinar,* 11
ski, to *esquiar,* 5
skirt *la falda,* 9
skis *los esquís,* 12
sleepy, to be *tener sueño,* 7
slippers *las chancletas,* 12
small *pequeño/a,* 3
smart *listo/a,* 6
snow *la nieve,* 5; **It's
snowing.** *Nieva.,* 5
soccer *el fútbol,* 1; **soccer
field** *la cancha de fútbol,* 11
social studies *las ciencias
sociales,* 3
socks *los calcetines,* 9
soft drink *el refresco,* 4
some *unos/as,* 2
something *algo,* 6

sometimes *a veces,* 5
son *el hijo,* 6
so-so *más o menos,* 1
sorry, I'm *Lo siento,* 7
soup *la sopa,* 8
Spanish *el español,* 1
speak, to *hablar,* 4
spend time with friends, to
pasar el rato con amigos, 4
spicy *picante,* 8
spoon *la cuchara,* 8
sports *los deportes,* 1
spring *la primavera,* 5
stadium *el estadio,* 11
stay, to *quedarse,* 12
steak *el bistec,* 8
stepbrother *el hermanastro,* 6
stepfather *el padrastro,* 6
stepmother *la madrastra,* 6
stepsister *la hermanastra,* 6
still *todavía,* 5
stomach *el estómago,* 11
store *la tienda,* 4
strawberry *la fresa,* 8
stretch, to *estirarse,* 11
strict *estricto/a,* 3
striped *de rayas,* 9
stroll *el paseo,* 4; **to go
hiking** *dar una caminata,* 12
strong *fuerte,* 8
student *el/la estudiante,* 3
study, to *estudiar,* 4
subject *la materia,* 3
sugar *el azúcar,* 8
suit *el traje,* 9; **bathing
suit** *el traje de baño,* 9
suitcase *la maleta,* 12; **to pack
the suitcase** *hacer la
maleta,* 12
summer *el verano,* 5
sunbathe, to *tomar el sol,* 12
Sunday *el domingo,* 4
sunglasses *los lentes de sol,* 12
sunscreen *el bloqueador,* 12
supermarket *el supermercado,* 4
Sure! *¡Con mucho gusto!,* 10
surprise *la sorpresa,* 7; **surprise party** *la fiesta de sorpresa,* 7
sweater *el suéter,* 9
sweet *dulce,* 8
sweet roll *el pan dulce,* 8
sweet shop *la pastelería,* 9
swim, to *nadar,* 4
swimming *la natación,* 1
swimming pool *la piscina,* 4

T

T-shirt *la camiseta,* 9
table *la mesa,* 2
take, to *tomar,* 4

take a shower, to *ducharse,* 7
take a trip, to *hacer un viaje,* 6
take care of, to *cuidar,* 4; **to
take care of your brother/
sister** *cuidar a tu hermano/a,* 4
take out the trash, to *sacar la
basura,* 4
take the bus, to *tomar el autobús,* 5
talk, to *hablar,* 4; **to talk on the
phone** *hablar por teléfono,* 4
tall *alto/a,* 3
tea *el té,* 8; **iced tea** *el té frío,* 8
teacher *el profesor* (male), *la
profesora* (female), 3
teeth *los dientes,* 7; **to brush
one's teeth** *lavarse los
dientes,* 7
telephone *el teléfono,* 4
television *la televisión,* 4
television set *el televisor,* 2
tell, to *decir,* 6
ten *diez,* 1
tennis *el tenis,* 1; **tennis
court** *la cancha de tenis,* 11;
tennis shoes (Spain) *las
zapatillas de tenis,* 2; *los
zapatos de tenis,* 9
tent *la tienda de camping,* 12
Thanks. *Gracias.,* 1
Thanksgiving *el Día de Acción
de Gracias,* 10
that *esa, ese,* 9
that *que,* 4
that's all *nada más,* 11
that's why *por eso,* 4
the *el, la,* 1; *los, las,* 3
theater *el teatro,* 7
their *su(s),* 6
them *ellas/ellos,* 4; **to/for
them** *les,* 9
then *luego,* 3
there *allá,* 4
there is, there are *hay,* 2
these *estas, estos,* 9
these *éstas, éstos,* 6
they *ellas, ellos,* 3
thin *delgado/a,* 6
thing *la cosa,* 2
think, to *creer,* 10; *pensar (ie),* 7
thirsty, to be *tener sed,* 8
thirteen *trece,* 1
thirty *treinta,* 1
this *esta, este,* 9; *ésta, éste,* 1
those *esas, esos,* 9
thousand *mil,* 8
three *tres,* 1
three hundred *trescientos/as,* 8
throat *la garganta,* 11
Thursday *el jueves,* 4
ticket *el boleto,* 12
tie *la corbata,* 9

time *la hora,* 3; **to spend time with friends** *pasar el rato con amigos,* 4

tip *la propina,* 8; **It (the tip) is separate.** *Es aparte.,* 8; **Is it (the tip) included?** *¿Está incluida?,* 8

tired *cansado/a,* 7

to *a,* 4; **to the** *al (a + el), a la,* 4

to *para,* 9

to/for her, him, you *le,* 9; **to/for me** *me,* 9; **to/for them, you** (pl) *les,* 9; **to/for us** *nos,* 9; **to/for you** *te,* 9

toast *el pan tostado,* 8

today *hoy,* 3

toe *el dedo,* 11

together *juntos/as,* 5

tomato *el tomate,* 8

tomorrow *mañana,* 3

too *también,* 1

too much *demasiado/a,* 6

towel *la toalla,* 12

toys *los juguetes,* 9

toy store *la juguetería,* 9

trash *la basura,* 4

trip *el viaje,* 6; **to take a trip** *hacer un viaje,* 6

true *cierto,* 6; *verdad,* 3

Tuesday *el martes,* 4

tuna *el atún,* 8

twelve *doce,* 1

twenty *veinte,* 1

two *dos,* 1

two hundred *doscientos/as,* 8

typically *típicamente,* 5

U

ugly *feo/a,* 3

uncle *el tío,* 6

under *debajo de,* 4

usual *lo de siempre,* 9

usually *por lo general,* 8

V

vacation *las vacaciones,* 5; **on vacation** *de vacaciones,* 12

vacuum cleaner *la aspiradora,* 6

vacuum, to *pasar la aspiradora,* 6

Valentine's Day *el Día de los Enamorados,* 10

vegetables *las legumbres,* 8

very *muy,* 1; **very bad** *muy mal,* 1; **very well** *muy bien,* 1

videogame *el videojuego,* 3

visit, to *visitar,* 6

volleyball *el voleibol,* 1

W

waiter *el camarero,* 8

waitress *la camarera,* 8

walk *la caminata,* 12

walk, to *caminar,* 4; **to walk the dog** *caminar con el perro,* 4

wallet *la cartera,* 9

want, to *querer (ie),* 2

wash, to *lavar,* 4; **to wash the car** *lavar el coche,* 4; **to wash oneself** *lavarse,* 7

watch *el reloj,* 2

watch, to *mirar,* 4; **to watch TV** *mirar la televisión,* 4

water *el agua,* 5; **mineral water** *el agua mineral,* 8

we *nosotros/as,* 4

wear, to *llevar,* 9

weather *el tiempo,* 5; **The weather is bad.** *Hace mal tiempo.,* 5; **The weather is nice.** *Hace buen tiempo.,* 5

wedding *la boda,* 7

Wednesday *el miércoles,* 4

week *la semana,* 4

weekend *el fin de semana,* 4

weights *las pesas,* 11

well *bien,* 1; **I'm (pretty) well.** *Estoy (bastante) bien.,* 1

Well, . . . *Bueno,...,* 2

what? *¿cuál?,* 3; *¿qué?,* 3

What a bargain! *¡Qué ganga!,* 9

What are . . . like? *¿Cómo son...?,* 3

What a shame! *¡Qué lástima!,* 7

What color is . . .? *¿De qué color es...?,* 6

What did you do? *¿Qué hiciste?,* 10

What do you like? *¿Qué te gusta?,* 1

What do you like to do? *¿Qué te gusta hacer?,* 4

What if . . .? *¿Qué tal si...?,* 11

What is today's date? *¿Cuál es la fecha?,* 5; *¿Qué fecha es hoy?,* 5

What's . . . like? *¿Cómo es . . .,* 3

What's the matter? *¿Qué tienes?,* 11

What's the weather like? *¿Qué tiempo hace?,* 5

What's wrong with . . .? *¿Qué le pasa a...?,* 11

What's your name? *¿Cómo te llamas?,* 1

What time is it? *¿Qué hora es?,* 3

when *cuando,* 5

when? *¿cuándo?,* 3

where *donde,* 1

where? *¿dónde?* 4; **Where are you from?** *¿De dónde eres?,* 1

where (to)? *¿adónde?,* 4

which *que,* 4

which? *¿cuál?,* 3; *¿qué?,* 1

white *blanco/a,* 9

who *que,* 4

who? *¿quién?,* 4; *¿quiénes?,* 5; **Who likes . . .?** *¿A quién le gusta...?,* 4; **Who's calling?** *¿De parte de quién?,* 7

why? *¿por qué?,* 3; **Why don't you . . .?** *¿Por qué no...?,* 11

wife *la esposa,* 6

win, to *ganar,* 11

window *la ventana,* 2

winter *el invierno,* 5

wish, to *querer (ie),* 2

with *con,* 4; **with me** *conmigo,* 4; **with you** *contigo,* 4

wool (made of) *de lana,* 9

work *el trabajo,* 4

work, to *trabajar,* 4; **to work in the garden** *trabajar en el jardín,* 6

worried about something *preocupado/a por algo,* 11

worry, to *preocuparse,* 3; **Don't worry!** *¡No te preocupes!,* 3

Would you like . . .? *¿Te gustaría...?,* 7; **I would like . . .** *Me gustaría...,* 7, *Quisiera...,* 8

write, to *escribir,* 5

Y

year *el año,* 5; **last year** *el año pasado,* 10

yellow *amarillo/a,* 9

yes *sí,* 1

yesterday *ayer,* 10

yet *todavía,* 5; **not yet** *todavía no,* 5

yoga *la yoga,* 11; **to do yoga** *hacer yoga,* 11

you (familiar) *tú, vosotros/as,* 4

you (formal) *usted, ustedes,* 4

young *joven,* 6; **He/She looks young.** *Se ve joven.,* 6

younger *menor,* 6

your (familiar) *tu,* 2; *tus,* 6; *vuestro/a(s),* 6; (formal) *su,* 2; *sus,* 6

Z

zero *cero,* 1

zoo *el zoológico,* 7

GRAMMAR INDEX

Page numbers in boldface type refer to **Gramática** and **Nota gramatical** presentations. Other page numbers refer to grammar structures presented in the **Así se dice, Nota cultural, Vocabulario,** and **¿Te acuerdas?** sections. The terms (1A) and (1B) refer to **Adelante** (Holt Spanish Level 1A) and **En camino** (Holt Spanish Level 1B).

A

a: see prepositions
accent marks: 7 (IA), **30** (IA)
adjectives: agreement—masculine and feminine **78, 127** (IA); agreement—singular and plural **78** (IA), **127** (IA), **287** (IB); demonstrative adjectives all forms **150** (IB), **287** (IB); possessive adjectives 76; all forms **237** (IA), **287** (IB)
adónde: see question words
adverbs: adverbs of frequency—**siempre, sólo cuando, nunca, todavía, todos los días, muchas veces 195** (IA); **una vez, de vez en cuando, todo el tiempo, cada día, a menudo** 209 (IA); adverbs of sequence—**primero, después, luego** 110 (IA), 251 (IB); adverbs of time—**por la mañana, por la tarde, por la noche** 209 (IA); **anoche, ayer, la semana pasada** 187 (IB)
affirmative expressions: **algo, alguien, alguno (algún), alguna, o ... o, siempre 288** (IB)
al: contraction of **a + el 163** (IA), 51 (IB), **286** (IB)
algo: 248 (IA), 109 (IB), 139 (IB), **288** (IB)
almorzar: 92 (IB), **252** (IB)
-ando: see present participle
-ar verbs: see verbs
articles: see definite articles, indefinite articles

C

commands: 122 (IA), 125 (IA); introduction to informal commands **181** (IB)
cómo: see question words
comparisons: with adjectives using **más ... que, menos ... que, tan ... como 145** (IB), **288** (IB); all comparatives, including **tanto/a/os/as ... como 288** (IB)
con: see prepositions
conjunctions: **pero** 43 (IA), 152 (IA), 255 (IA) 67 (IB); **y** 29 (IA), 76 (IA), 85 (IA), 149 (IA) 67 (IB); **o** 31 (IA), 203 (IA), 144 (IB), 149 (IB), **porque** 129 (IA); subordinating conjunction: see **que**
conmigo: 155 (IA)
contigo: 155 (IA)
contractions: see **al** and **del**
cuál: see question words
cuándo: see question words
cuánto: agreement with nouns **78** (IA), **236** (IA); see also question words

D

dates (calendar): **213** (IA)
days of the week: **174** (IA)
de: used in showing possession 121 (IA); used with color 245 (IA); used with material or pattern **142** (IB); see also prepositions
de vez en cuando: see adverbs of frequency
deber: all present tense forms **255** (IA)
definite articles: **el, la 46** (IA), **286** (IB); **los, las 109** (IA), **286** (IB)
del: contraction of **de + el 121** (IA), **286** (IB)
demonstrative adjectives: all forms **150** (IB), **287** (IB)
demonstrative pronouns: see pronouns
diminutives: 247 (IA)
direct object pronouns: see pronouns
doler: with parts of the body **224** (IB); all present tense forms **289** (IB)
dónde: see question words
durante: see prepositions

E

e→ie stem-changing verbs: **52** (IB), **252** (IB), **289** (IB)
el: see definite articles
empezar: 52 (IB), **252** (IB), **289** (IB)
en: see prepositions
encantar: 89 (IB), **290** (IB)
-er verbs: see verbs
estar: all forms **162** (IA), **289** (IB); to ask how someone is and say how you are 31 (IA); to tell where people and things are located 161 (IA); to talk about how things taste, look, or feel **98** (IB); contrasted with **ser 98** (IB), **264** (IB); **estar + present participle 172** (IB), **262** (IB)

F

frequency: adverbs of—**siempre, sólo cuando, nunca, todavía, todos los días, muchas veces 195** (IA); **una vez, de vez en cuando, todo el tiempo, cada día, a menudo** 209 (IA)
future plans: expressions in the present tense 253 (IB)

G

gender of nouns: 286 (IB)

giving the date: **213** (IA)

gustar: to express likes and dislikes 43 (IA), 129 (IA), 149 (IA), 203 (IA); telling what one would like 262 (IB); all present tense forms 290 (IB)

H

hacer: 85 (IA), 248 (IA); all present tense forms **249** (IA), 289 (IB); **hacer** with weather 216 (IA), 217 (IA); preterite 290 (IB)

hay: 76 (IA), 236 (IA), 87 (IB)

I

-iendo: see present participle

imperatives: see commands

indefinite articles: **un, una 66** (IA), **68** (IA), 286 (IB); **unos, unas 68** (IA), 286 (IB)

indirect object pronouns: see pronouns

infinitives: **86** (IA), **254** (IB)

informal commands: see commands

interrogatives: see question words

-ir verbs: see verbs

ir: all present tense forms **172** (IA), 60 (IB), 289 (IB); **ir + a + infinitive 60** (IB), **254** (IB); preterite **232** (IB), **269** (IB), 290 (IB)

irregular verbs: see verbs

J

jugar: all present tense forms 289 (IB); preterite **229** (IB)

L

la: see definite articles, see pronouns

las, los: see definite articles

le, les: see pronouns, indirect object

lo, la: see pronouns, direct object

M

más ... que: see comparisons

me: see pronouns, indirect object

menos ... que: see comparisons

muchas veces: see adverbs of frequency

mucho: agreement with nouns **78** (IA)

N

nada: 196 (IA), 288 (IB)

nadie: 196 (IA), 288 (IB)

necesitar: to express needs 66 (IA), 85 (IA)

negative expressions: **nada, nadie, no, nunca 196**

(IA), 288 (IB); **ninguno/a (ningún), ni ... ni** 288 (IB)

negation: with **nada, nunca, no** and **nadie 196** (IA), 288 (IB)

nouns: definition of, masculine and feminine forms, singular forms **46** (IA), 286 (IB); plural forms **67** (IA), 286 (IB)

numbers: **0–30** 14 (IA), 15 (IA), 36 (IA); **31–199** 88 (IA); **200–100,000** 110 (IB)

nunca: 196 (IA), 288 (IB); see also negative expressions or negation

O

o: see conjunctions

o→ue stem-changing verbs: **92** (IB), 213 (IB), **252** (IB)

object pronouns: see pronouns

objects of prepositions: see pronouns

otro: all forms **106** (IB)

P

para: see prepositons

past tense: see preterite tense

pensar + infinitive: **60** (IB)

pero: see conjunctions

personal **a: 250** (IA), 61 (IB)

plural nouns: **67** (IA), 286 (IB)

poder: 92 (IB), **252** (IB)

poner: all present tense forms **257** (IA), 289 (IB)

por: see prepositions

porque: see conjunctions

por qué: see question words

possessive adjectives: **237** (IA), 287 (IB)

preferir: 52 (IB), **252** (IB), 289 (IB)

prepositions: **antes de, después de** 152 (IA); **al lado de, cerca de, debajo de, encima de, lejos de** 163 (IA); **a 206** (IA), 131 (IB), 221 (IB); **con 155** (IA); **durante** 195 (IA); **en** as "on" 119 (IA), as "at" 195 (IA); **para** as "in order to" 171 (IA), as "for" 131 (IB); **por** as "at" 209 (IA), as "on" 203 (IA), as "in" 209 (IA); with pronouns 287 (IB)

present participle: **172** (IB)

present progressive: **172** (IB), 289 (IB)

present tense: see verbs

preterite tense: regular **-ar** verbs all forms **187** (IB), **269** (IB), 290 (IB); regular **-er** and **-ir** verbs 290 (IB); **jugar 229** (IB); **ir 232** (IB), **269** (IB), 290 (IB); **hacer, ser,** and **ver** 290 (IB)

pronouns: demonstrative pronouns **ésta** and **éste** 29 (IA); direct object pronouns **lo, la 191** (IB), 287 (IB); indirect object pronouns **me, te, le** 129 (IA), **133** (IB), **les 206** (IA), 133 (IB); clarification **206** (IA); all forms 203 (IA), 89 (IB), 287 (IB); relative pronouns: see **que;** subject pronouns **tú** and **yo** 32 (IA), 287 (IB); **él, ella** 70 (IA), 287 (IB); all forms 166 (IA), 287 (IB); as objects of prepositions **mí, ti, él, ella, usted, nosotros/as, ellos, ellas, ustedes** 287 (IB)

punctuation marks: 30 (IA)

GRAMMAR INDEX

323

Q

que: as a relative pronoun **157** (IA); see also: comparisons **que** as "than"; **que** as a subordinating conjunction, **...dice que...** 255 (IA)

qué: see question words

querer: to express wants and needs **66** (IA), **85** (IA); all forms **52** (IB)

quién: see question words

question words (interrogatives): adónde 171 (IA), **172** (IA), **288** (IB); **cómo 39** (IA), 125 (IA), 236 (IA), 245 (IA); **cuál** 129 (IA), 213 (IA), 144 (IB), 149 (IB), 288 (IB); **cuánto 39** (IA), 150 (IB), 288 (IB); **dónde** 38 (IA), **39** (IA), 161 (IA), 134 (IB), 288 (IB); **de dónde 39** (IA), 288 (IB); **de qué** 245 (IA); **qué** 43 (IA), 213 (IA), 248 (IA), 288 (IB); **quién(es) 198** (IA), 288 (IB); **cuándo** 288 (IB); **por qué** 129 (IA), 288 (IB)

R

regular verbs: see verbs

reflexive verbs: **64** (IB), **214** (IB)

S

saber: all present tense forms 289 (IB)

salir: all present tense forms **249** (IA), 289 (IB)

sentirse: 214 (IB)

sequence: adverbs of—**primero, después, luego** 110 (IA), 251 (IB)

ser: soy, eres, es 38 (IA), all present tense forms **126** (IA), 289 (IB); for telling time 112 (IA), **113** (IA); to talk about what something is like or the nature of things **98** (IB); used with **de** + material or pattern **142** (IB); contrasted with **estar 98** (IB), **264** (IB); preterite 290 (IB)

siempre: see adverbs of frequency and affirmative expressions

sólo cuando: see adverbs of frequency

stem-changing verbs: **e→ie: 52** (IB), **252** (IB), 289 (IB); **o→ue: 92** (IB), 213 (IB), **252** (IB); **u→ue: 289** (1B)

subject pronouns: see pronouns

T

tag questions: **¿no?, ¿verdad? 131** (IA)

tan ... como: see comparisons

tanto/a ... como, tantos/as ... como: see comparisons

te: see pronouns, indirect object

telling time: see time

tener: all present tense forms 52 (IB), 68 (IB); with age 35 (IA), **68** (IB); idioms—**tener ganas de, tener prisa, tener sueño 68** (IB); **tener hambre 100** (IB); **tener sed** 87 (IB); **100** (IB); **tener que** + infinitive **68** (IB), 254 (IB)

tilde: 30 (IA)

time: adverbs—**por la mañana, por la tarde, por la noche** 209 (IA); **anoche, ayer, la semana pasada** 187 (IB); at what time 119 (IA), telling time 112 (IA), **113** (IA)

todavía: see adverbs of frequency

todos los días: see adverbs of frequency

traer: all present tense forms 289 (IB)

U

u→ue stem-changing verbs: 289 (IB)

una vez: see adverbs of frequency

un, una, unos, unas: see indefinite articles

V

venir: 52 (IB), **252** (IB)

ver: preterite 290 (IB)

verbs: definition of a verb infinitive **86** (IA); present tense verbs **150** (IA); regular **-ar** all forms **150** (IA), **288** (IB); regular **-er** and **-ir** all forms **207** (IA), **288** (IB); **e→ie** stem-changing verbs: **querer, empezar, preferir, tener, venir 52** (IB), **252** (IB), **289** (IB); **pensar 60** (IB), 289 (IB); reflexives **64** (IB), **214** (IB); **o→ue** stem-changing verbs: **almorzar, poder 92** (IB), **252** (IB); **dormir** 213 (IB), **252** (IB); clarification **252** (IB), 289 (IB); **doler** 224 (IB), **289** (IB); present progressive: **172** (IB), **289** (IB); used with infinitives **254** (IB); preterite tense of regular **-ar** verbs—all forms **187** (IB), **269** (IB), **290** (IB); preterite tense of **jugar** 229 (IB); preterite tense of **ir** 232 (IB), **269** (IB); verbs with irregular **yo** forms—**hacer** 249 (IA), **poner** 257 (IA), **salir** 249 (IA), **289** (IB); irregular verbs 289 (IB); present tense of **jugar** 289 (IB); the verbs **gustar** and **encantar** 290 (IB); preterite of **hacer, ir, ser, and ver** 290 (IB)

W

weather: 216 (1A), 217 (1A)

Y

y: see conjunctions

CREDITS

PHOTOGRAPHY

Abbreviations used: (t) top, (b) bottom, (c) center, (l) left, (r) right, (i) inset, (bkgd) background. All other locations are noted with descriptor.

CHAPTER OPENERS, PANORAMA CULTURAL AND ENCUENTRO CULTURAL PAGES: Scott Van Osdol/HRW Photo.

ENCUENTRO CULTURAL PAGE TITLE PEOPLE: Michelle Bridwell/Frontera Fotos.

All PRE-COLUMBIAN SYMBOLS by EclectiCollections/HRW.

¿TE ACUERDAS? PARROT icon by Image Copyright © 1996 Photodisc, Inc.

All other photos by Marty Granger/Edge Video Productions/HRW except:

FRONT COVER: (bkgd), Suzanne Murphy-Larronde; teens, Steve Ewert/HRW Photo; kite, Julio E. Flores.

TABLE OF CONTENTS: Page vii (cr), Lawrence Migdale; viii (tl), John Langford/HRW Photo; viii (br), Miriam Austerman/Animals Animals; ix (tl), x, Sam Dudgeon/HRW Photo; ix (br), Christine Galida/HRW Photo; x (tl), Michelle Bridwell/Frontera Fotos; xi (tl), Christine Galida/HRW Photo; xi (tr), Bob Daemmrich/Tony Stone Images; xi (br), Sam Dudgeon/HRW Photo; xii (tl), John Langford/HRW Photo; xiv (br), Michelle Bridwell/HRW Photo; xv (tr), John Neubauer/PhotoEdit.

PRELIMINARY CHAPTER: Page 1 (tr), Michelle Bridwell/Frontera Fotos; 1 (cl), John Langford/HRW Photo; 3 (tc), Image Copyright © 1996 Photodisc, Inc.; 3 (cl), © 1997 Radlund & Associates for Artville; 3 (cl), Roy Morsch/The Stock Market; 5 (cr), Denver Bryan/Comstock; 6 (bl), (br), 7 (cl), Christine Galida/HRW Photo; 9 (bc), John Langford/HRW Photo; 10 (tl), FPG International; 18 (bl), Christine Galida/HRW Photo; 18 (bc), (cr), John Langford/HRW Photo; 18 (bc), Sam Dudgeon/HRW Photo; 18 (br), Leon Duque/Duque Múnera y Cia; 25 (tl), M. L. Miller/Edge Video Productions/HRW; 27 (1), John Langford/HRW Photo; 27 (2), (3), (4), Michelle Bridwell/Frontera Fotos; 29 (bl), (br), John Langford/HRW Photo; 34 (cl), Gérard Lacz/Animals Animals.

LOCATION OPENER—ECUADOR: Page 38–39 (bkgd), Mireille Vautier/Woodfin Camp & Associates, Inc.; 40 (tr), J. Sunak/Leo de Wys; 40 (c), Sylvia Stevens/Zephyr Pictures; 40 (br), Suzanne L. Murphy/FPG International; 41 (tl), Bill Holden/Leo de Wys; 41 (bl), Robert Fried; 41 (cr), Image Copyright © 1996 Photodisc, Inc.

CHAPTER 7: Page 42 (bc), David Phillips/HRW Photo; 43 (bl), John Langford/HRW Photo; 49 (c), Comstock; 49 (br), Stuart Cohen/Comstock; 52 (tl), (1), Image Copyright © 1996 Photodisc, Inc.; 52 (2), (3), (4), Sam Dudgeon/HRW Photo; 52 (6), Russel Dian/HRW Photo; 52 (7), Mary J. Andrade/Latin Focus; 59 (tr), Miriam Austerman/Animals Animals; 60 (cl), Sam Dudgeon/HRW Photo; 62 (bc), David Phillips/HRW Photo; 62 (br), Chip & Rosa María de la Cueva Peterson; 63 (all), 64 (tr), 65 (br), Sam Dudgeon/HRW Photo; 67 (tl), John Langford/HRW Photo; 67 (br), Reprinted by permission of Bayard Revistas from *Súper Júnior,* October 1996, p. J5.; 72 (br), Superstock; 73 (br),

DeWys/Japack/Leo de Wys; 73 (t), Howard Hall/Oxford Scientific Films/Animals Animals; 75 (tl), Boyd Norton/Comstock; 75 (bl), Jeff Greenberg/David R. Frazier Photolibrary; 75 (cr), Robert Fried.

CHAPTER 8: Page 81 (cl), Michelle Bridwell/HRW Photo; 85 (br), Christine Galida/HRW Photo; 88 (all), 90 (all), 91 (all), Sam Dudgeon/HRW Photo; 98 (tr), Michelle Bridwell/HRW Photo; 105 (all), Sam Dudgeon/HRW Photo; 108 (a), (b), (c), Michelle Bridwell/HRW Photo; 108 (d), (e), Sam Dudgeon/HRW Photo; 111 (tl), Michelle Bridwell/HRW Photo; 115 (tr), (cl), 118 (all), 119 (cl), (bc), Sam Dudgeon/HRW Photo.

LOCATION OPENER—TEXAS: Page 120–121, John Langford/HRW Photo; 122 (tr), Robert E. Daemmrich/Tony Stone Images; 122 (bl), Laurence Parent Photography, Inc.; 123 (tl), Sung Park/*Austin American-Statesman*; 123 (bl), HRW, Courtesy *Texas Highways Magazine*; 123 (cr), Photo by Paul Bardagjy, *Summer Nights* by Fidencio Durán; acrylic on canvas, 4' × 4'.

CHAPTER 9: Page 125 (c), Christine Galida/HRW Photo; 125 (t), Michelle Bridwell/Frontera Fotos; 126–127, (ribbon), (sweater), (CD), (radio) Sam Dudgeon/HRW Photo; 130 (br), Christine Galida/HRW Photo; 130, (CD), (ribbon), 132 (all), Sam Dudgeon/ HRW Photo; 138 (tc), (ribbon), 139 (bl), (br), 141 (cr), 142-top (all), Sam Dudgeon/HRW Photo; 142-bottom (b), (c) Bob Pizaro/Comstock; 142-bottom (a), (d), (e) Sam Dudgeon/HRW Photo; 143 (br), Victoria Smith/ HRW Photo; 144 (all), 148 (bc), 148 (br), Sam Dudgeon/HRW Photo; 149 (cr), AP/Wide World Photos; (bc), CORBIS/Reuters NewMedia Inc.; 150 (cr), Michelle Bridwell/Frontera Fotos; 153 (tr), Sam Dudgeon/HRW Photo; 157 (all), Courtesy of Atkins Agency, San Antonio, Tx.; 158 (all), 159 (all), 161 (all), Sam Dudgeon/HRW Photo.

CHAPTER 10: Page 162 (c), Christine Galida/HRW Photo; 163 (tr), David Ryan/DDB Stock; 167 (b), Sam Dudgeon/HRW Photo; 169, (Año Nuevo), (Enamorados), Christine Galida/HRW Photo; (Pascuas), John Neubauer/PhotoEdit; (Independencia), Bob Daemmrich Photo, Inc.; (Navidad), Steven D. Elmore/The Stock Market; (Gracias), Bob Daemmrich/Tony Stone Images; (Madres), (Padre), Michelle Bridwell/Frontera Fotos; 172 (all), David Phillips; 173 (tc), M. L. Miller/Edge Video Productions/HRW; 173 (bl), Michelle Bridwell/Frontera Fotos; 173 (bc), Christine Galida/HRW Photo; 175 (l), (c), Addison Geary/Stock Boston, Inc.; 175 (r), Marcelo Brodsky/Latin Stock/The Stock Market; 179 (cl), Daniel J. Schaefer; 183 (br), Christine Galida/HRW Photo; 190 (bc), 191 (r), Sam Dudgeon/HRW Photo; 192 (br), *Billiken,* September 30, 1991, p. 34. Reprinted by permission of Editorial Atlántida S.A.; 193 (tr), David R. Frazier Photolibrary; 194–195 (c), Richard Hutchings/HRW Photo; 194 (tl), Bob Daemmrich/Stock Boston, Inc.; 197 (tr), Héctor Méndez Caratini; 197 (c), Fundación de Etnomusicología y Folklore; 197 (bl), Joe Viesti/Viesti Associates, Inc.; 201 (cl), John Neubauer/PhotoEdit; 201 (br), Sam Dudgeon/HRW Photo.

LOCATION OPENER—PUERTO RICO: Page 202–203, Mari Biasco; 204 (tr), David R. Frazier Photolibrary; 204 (cl), Suzanne Murphy Larronde/DDB Stock; 204 (bc), Steve Fitzpatrick/Latin Focus; 205 (tl), Suzanne Murphy- Larronde; 205 (br), Wolfgang Kaehler Photography.

CHAPTER 11: Page 206 (b), Michelle Bridwell/Frontera Fotos; 207 (tr), John Langford/HRW Photo; 212 (br), Comstock; 216 (tl), Martha Cooper/Viesti Associates, Inc.; 216 (tc), Christine Galida/HRW Photo; 216 (tr), Bob Daemmrich/Stock Boston, Inc.; 216 (cl), (c), 223 (tl), (tr), John Langford/HRW Photo; 224 (br), Sam Dudgeon/ HRW Photo; 228 (br), Steve Fitzpatrick/Latin Focus; 229 (cr), Superstock; 231 (tr), Alexandra Dobrin/Latin Focus; 232 (cl), (bl), Peter Van Steen/ HRW Photo; 232 (br), (cr), Michelle Bridwell/Frontera Fotos; 233 (cr), Bob Daemmrich Photo, Inc.; 236–237 (c), 236 (br), (b), © 1997 Radlund & Associates for Artville; 237 (tl), (br), AP/Wide World Photos; (tr), CORBIS/Reuters NewMedia Inc.; 239 (tl), (tc), (tr), Michelle Bridwell/Frontera Fotos; 239 (bl), 243 (bl), Christine Galida/HRW Photo; 243 (br), Superstock.

CHAPTER 12: Page 245 (tr), James Martin/Allstock; 245 (b), Sam Dudgeon/HRW Photo; 247 (cl), Dan Morrison; 247 (cr), William W. Bacon, III/Allstock; 250 (tl), Dan Morrison; 253 (c), Joe Viesti/Viesti Associates, Inc.; 253 (inset), Bob Daemmrich Photo, Inc.; 257 (tl), Robert Fried Photography; 257 (c), Bob Torrez/Tony Stone Images; 259 (cl), Arnold Newman/Peter Arnold, Inc.; 259 (bl), Robert Fried Photography; 260 (tr), William W. Bacon, III/Allstock; 263 (b), David R. Frazier Photolibrary; 265 (cl), John Heaton/Westlight; 265 (cr), Art Wolfe/Allstock; 273 (tr), David R. Frazier Photolibrary; 274 (tr), Richard Rowan/Photo Researchers, Inc. 274 (inset), Dr. Paul A. Zahl/Photo Researchers, Inc.; 275 (tr), Stephanie Maze/Woodfin Camp & Associates, Inc.

BACK COVER: Robert Frerck/Tony Stone Images; frame, © 1998 Image Farm Inc.

ILLUSTRATIONS AND CARTOGRAPHY

Abbreviated as follows: (t) top, (b) bottom, (l) left, (r) right, (c) center.
All art, unless otherwise noted, by Holt, Rinehart & Winston.

FRONT MATTER: Page ix, Elizabeth Brandt; x, Lori Osiecki; xvi, Elizabeth Brandt; xvii, MapQuest.com; xviii-xix, MapQuest.com; xx, MapQuest.com; xxi, MapQuest.com; xxii, MapQuest.com; xxiii, MapQuest.com.

BRIDGE CHAPTER: Page 8, Edson Campos; 14, Michael Morrow; 17, Edson Campos; 19, Dan Vasconcellos; 20, Lori Osiecki; 22, MapQuest.com; 28, Fian Arroyo/Dick Washington; 30, Edson Campos; 33, Dan Vasconcellos; 34, Fian Arroyo/Dick Washington; 36, Elizabeth Brandt.

CHAPTER SEVEN: Page 39, MapQuest.com; 50, Nishi Kumar; 53, Fian Arroyo/Dick Washington; 54, Edson Campos; 56, MapQuest.com; 61 (tc) Boston Graphics; 61 (br), Lori Osiecki; 63, Meryl Henderson; 65 (tc), Meryl Henderson; 68, Bob McMahon; 69, Edson Campos;

70, Ignacio Gomez/Carol Chislovsky Design, Inc.; 72, Jennifer Thermes/Leighton & Co.; 73, Jennifer Thermes/Leighton & Co.; 75, Annette Cable/Clare Jett & Assoc.; 76, Eva Vagretti Cockrille; 79 (tc, bl, br), Edson Campos; 79 (bc), Meryl Henderson.

CHAPTER EIGHT: Page 93, Edson Campos; 97, Fian Arroyo/Dick Washington; 99, Dan McGowan; 100, Elizabeth Brandt; 102, MapQuest.com; 105, Brian White; 107, Elizabeth Brandt; 112, Annette Cable/Clare Jett & Assoc.; 113, Annette Cable/Clare Jett & Assoc.; 115, John Parks; 119 (c), Fian Arroyo/Dick Washington; 119 (tr, cr), Elizabeth Brandt; 119 (br), Brian White.

CHAPTER NINE: Page 121, MapQuest.com; 131, Lori Osiecki; 132, Brian White; 134, Lori Osiecki; 135, Eva Vagretti Cockrille; 139, Elizabeth Brandt; 140, Edson Campos; 143, Fian Arroyo/Dick Washington; 145, Mauro Mistiano; 146, MapQuest.com; 152, Elizabeth Brandt; 154, Ortelius Design; 155, Ortelius Design; 160 (tr), Precision Graphics; 160 (c), Mauro Mistiano; 161 (bl), Brian White; 161 (bc), Elizabeth Brandt.

CHAPTER TEN: Page 170, Holly Copper; 179, Edson Campos; 181, Dan Vasconcellos; 182, Elizabeth Brandt; 184, MapQuest.com; 188, Meryl Henderson; 189, Deborah Haley Melmon/Sharon Morris Associates; 200, Meryl Henderson; 201 (tr), Deborah Haley Melmon/Sharon Morris Associates; 201 (tc), Edson Campos; 201 (c), Ignacio Gomez/Carol Chislovsky Design, Inc.; 201 (bc), Dan Vasconcellos.

CHAPTER ELEVEN: Page 203, MapQuest.com; 213, Fian Arroyo/Dick Washington; 215, Edson Campos; 218, MapQuest.com; 222, Fian Arroyo/Dick Washington; 225, Edson Campos; 230 (t), Edson Campos; 232, Ignacio Gomez/Carol Chislovsky Design, Inc.; 242, Brian White.

CHAPTER TWELVE: Page 251, José Luis Briseño; 254, Ignacio Gomez/ Carol Chislovsky Design, Inc.; 256, Ignacio Gomez/ Carol Chislovsky Design, Inc.; 257, Leslie Kell; 261, Holly Cooper; 269, Ignacio Gomez/ Carol Chislovsky Design, Inc.; 270, Boston Graphics; 274, Jennifer Thermes/Leighton & Co.; 276-277, Holly Cooper; 278 (t), Bob McMahon; 278 (b), Linda Williams; 280, Meryl Henderson; 281, Holly Cooper.

BACK MATTER: Page 291 (cl), Edson Campos; 291 (bl), Eva Vagretti Cockrille; 291 (tr), Lori Osiecki; 291 (br), Edson Campos; 292 (tl), Lori Osiecki; 292 (cl), Edson Campos; 292 (bl), Elizabeth Brandt; 292 (br), Deborah Haley Melmon/Sharon Morris Associates; 293 (tl) Elizabeth Brandt; 293 (tr), Fian Arroyo/Dick Washington; 293 (b), Bethann Thornburgh; 294 (tl), Fian Arroyo/Dick Washington; 294 (cl), Fian Arroyo/ Dick Washington; 294 (bl), Elizabeth Brandt; 294 (tr), Elizabeth Brandt; 294 (cr), Lori Osiecki; 294 (br), Mauro Mistiano; 295 (tl), Holly Copper; 295 (cl), Brian White; 295 (tr), Lori Osiecki; 295 (br), Lori Osiecki; 296 (cl), Meryl Henderson; 296 (cr), Precision Graphics.

ACKNOWLEDGMENTS

For permission to reprint copyrighted material, grateful acknowledgment is made to the following sources:

A. de S. Alimentos de Saja, S.A.: Advertisement for "Ades®" orange juice.

Alimentos Margarita, C.A.: Label from can of "Margarita" tuna.

Balneario y Manantiales de Lourdes, S.A.: "Aguas Minerales de Lourdes" mineral water.

Bayard Revistas-Súper Júnior: Illustration from "¿Os gusta el deporte?" from *Súper Júnior,* no. 25, October 1996. Copyright © 1996 by Súper Júnior, Bayard Revistas, Hispano Francesa de Ediciones, S.A.

Café El Marino, S.A. de C.V.: "Café Marino®" coffee.

Colsanitas: Adapted from "17 Claves para manejar el Estrés" (Retitled: "7 Claves para manejar el Estrés) from *Bienestar,* no. 9. Copyright © by Colsanitas.

Compañía Nacional de Chocolates, S.A.: Label from package of "Choco Listo."

Compañía de Turismo, Estado Libre Asociado de Puerto Rico: Excerpts and symbols from brochure, "Descubre los Paradores de Puerto Rico."

Editorial Televisa: From "Dile adiós a las tensiones... ¡Con ejercicios!" from *Tú internacional,* año 11, no. 5, May 1990. Copyright © 1990 by Editorial América, S.A.

Editorial Atlántida, S.A.: Adapted from "Madres muy especiales" from *Billiken,* no. 4012, December 2, 1996. Copyright © 1996 by Editorial Atlántida, S.A.

El Corte Inglés: Advertisement "Verano para todos" from brochure for El Corte Inglés.

G y J España Ediciones: From "El juego ecológico" from *Muy interesante,* February 1997. Copyright © by G y J España Ediciones.

Guía Cultura y Diversión al Día: From "Guía de Actividades Culturales-III" from *Guía Cultura y Diversión al Día,* December 1996. Reprinted by permission of the publisher.

San Antonio Convention Center and Visitors Bureau: Text and photograph from "Restaurantes," text and photograph from "Compras," text and photograph from "Las Misiones" and text and photograph from "Festivales" from *San Antonio...Guía de visitantes y mapa* by the Oficina de Convenciones y Visitantes de San Antonio. From Fiesta San Antonio 1994 news release by San Antonio Convention and Visitors Bureau.

Scholastic, Inc.: Adapted text, photographs, and illustrations from "¿Cuáles son las vacaciones ideales para ti?" from *¿Qué tal?,* vol. 24, no. 6, April–May 1990. Copyright © 1990 by Scholastic, Inc.

Tec-Lac: "Chen" yogurt.

Additional credit: *Rebecca Cuningham*: "La invitación."

327